Modern Buildings in Britain

A GAZETTEER

Modern Buildings in Britain

A GAZETTEER

Owen Hatherley

Photographs by Chris Matthews

PARTICULAR BOOKS

CONTENTS

MODERNISM:
AN EVERYDAY REVOLUTION   6

  Hell as Heritage, 1800–60   12

  Back to Nowhere, 1860–1910   16

  From Edwardian Baroque   21
    to Modernismus, 1910–45

  Modernism Takes Command,   28
    1945–79

  Decline, Fall and Rise,   33
    1980–2020

  The View from 2021   38

  How to Use This Book   40

  A Note on Names   42

  A Note on Geography   43

1. GREATER LONDON   **44**

  Central London   47

  SE London   79

  SW London   108

  East London   119

  North London   137

  West London   157

2. EAST OF ENGLAND   **172**

  Commuter Belt North   175

  East Anglia   195

  Cambridge   203

3. SOUTH-EAST   **212**

  Commuter Belt South   215

  Milton Keynes   222

  Oxford   227

  South Coast   234

  Solent   243

4. SOUTH-WEST   **252**

  West Country   255

  Bristol   266

  Plymouth   273

  Cornwall   275

5. WALES   **282**

  South Wales   285

  Cardiff   295

  North Wales   300

6. WEST MIDLANDS — 306
Birmingham — 309
Black Country — 319
Coventry — 324
Commuter Belt Midlands — 332
Potteries — 338

7. EAST MIDLANDS — 342
SE Midlands — 345
City of Nottingham — 352
NE Midlands — 356

8. METROPOLITAN YORKSHIRE — 364
Sheffield — 367
South Yorkshire — 377
Leeds — 380
West Yorkshire — 384
York & Environs — 393

9. GREATER MANCHESTER — 396
City of Manchester — 399
City of Salford — 412
SE Lancashire & NE Cheshire — 415

10. NORTH-WEST — 420
Liverpool — 423
Merseyside — 434
Central Lancashire — 442
North Lancashire & Cumbria — 447

11. NORTH-EAST — 456
Humberside — 459
Teesside — 466
Wearside — 470
Tyneside & Northumberland — 474
Newcastle upon Tyne — 479

12. EDINBURGH & EAST COAST — 490
Borders & Lothians — 493
Edinburgh — 496
Fife & Stirling — 507

13. GREATER GLASGOW — 512
City of Glasgow — 515
Cumbernauld — 535
Strathclyde — 537

14. NORTHERN SCOTLAND — 540
Dundee — 543
Aberdeen — 546
Highlands & Islands — 549

A General Glossary — 560
A Modernist Reading List — 564
Acknowledgements — 568
Index of Buildings — 570
Index of Architects — 584
General Index — 592

Dawson Heights, East Dulwich, London (p. 93)

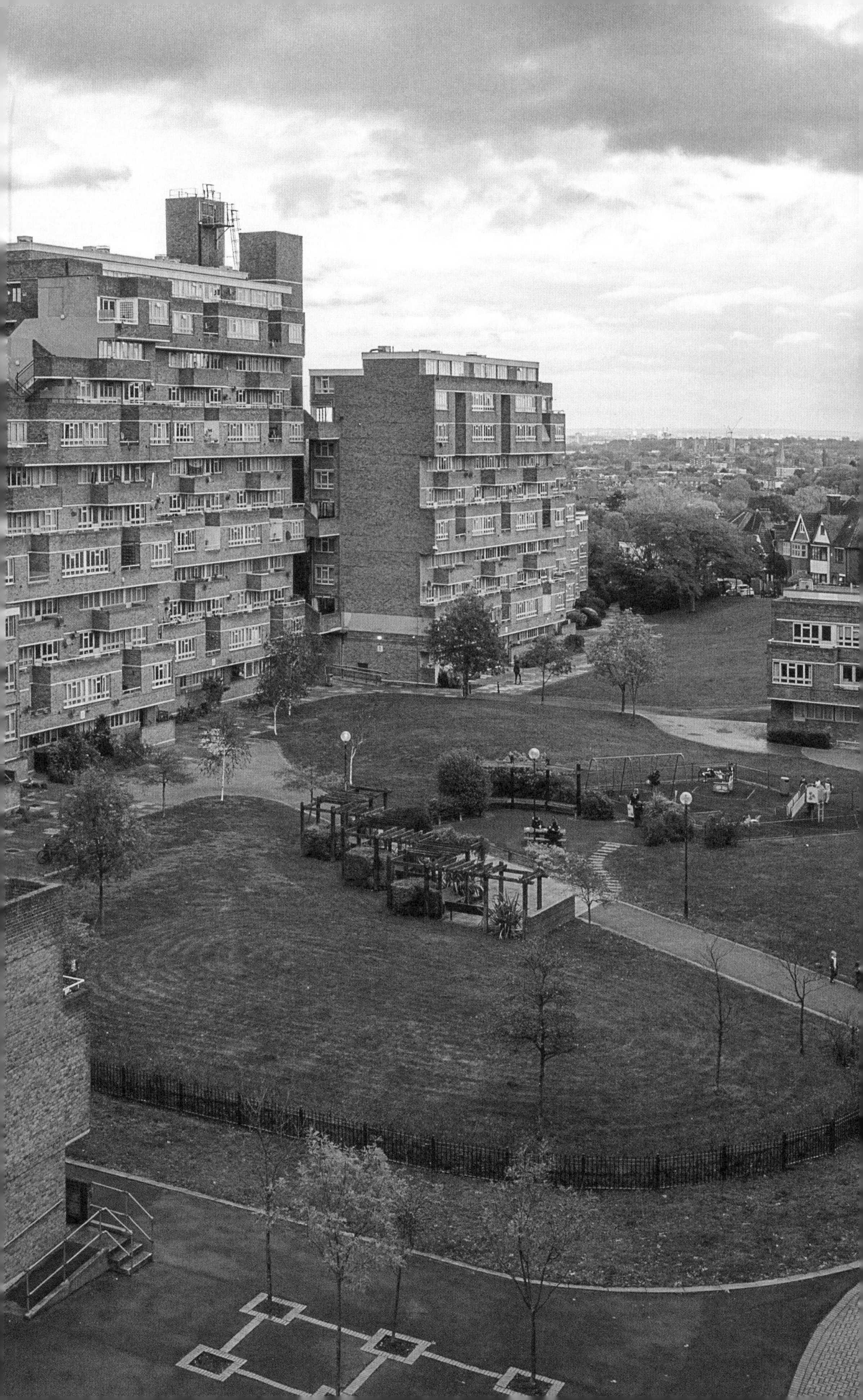

MODERNISM: AN EVERYDAY REVOLUTION

I have written this book in places that would broadly be called 'modernist'. I started in a flat built by the London Borough of Woolwich – as it then was – in 1951, at the centre of what they called, in the sort of technocratic language that shot chills up the spines of my parents' generation, the St Mary's Comprehensive Development Area. This district was then an industrial area that had suffered heavy bomb damage, receiving several visits from the Luftwaffe during the Second World War. Ironically enough, one of its major employers was Siemens, who had a large factory on the Thames here – square, tall and red brick, much of it is now used as artists' studios, next to a drive-thru McDonald's. The other main employer was once the largest mechanized industrial concern on the planet, the Royal Arsenal, the place where the weaponry was built that made it possible for an island in-between the North Sea and the Atlantic to subjugate over a quarter of the globe.

Very little of the housing that would have been lived in by those making guns and cannons and mortars and mines and other instruments to kill and maim in the eighteenth and nineteenth centuries has actually survived (this lack of period property is one reason why the place has taken longer than most riverside districts of London to be 'gentrified'). The slums really were cleared here, by social reformers before and after the war – this was one of the Labour Party and the trade unions' London strongholds – and of course by the air force of Nazi Germany. A few Regency terraces survive, if you know where to find them – elegant enough examples of the genre, nicer looking at any rate than the visibly noxious houses whose photographs are in the local history nostalgia books. A Victorian fire station of terracotta and turrets survives, as does St Mary's Church, a stubby Georgian design without a steeple. The rest has been in the hands of the planners, and of the modern architects.

What happened after 1945 was to gradually reshape the place completely, into a new and 'modern' environment, with spatial and architectural concepts that owe little or nothing to tradition. In the St Mary's Comprehensive Redevelopment Area, this has happened in phases. The earliest 'housing' – not houses, built by developers to make money, but 'housing', built by public bodies, outside the free market – in the area wasn't built by the local authority at all, but by the Church Commissioners in the 1930s. They built some terraced houses and tenements in a style which could very, very vaguely be described as

Post-war housing at its simplest: pitched-roofed blocks and green space at St Mary's, Woolwich, 1951.

'art deco' (more definitions later). The walls are of London stock brick and the roofs are pitched, but the windows are large and curved and there are no traditional decorations. After this scattering of slum replacement, the really big project came in the last couple of years of the 1940s, when the Borough Council embarked on its 'comprehensive redevelopment'. The first phase of St Mary's – which was built, almost without contact with the free market at all, by the council's direct-labour organization – broke completely with the way that housing was laid out in the nineteenth century, when everything was designed to maximize profit, and the early twentieth century, when profit plus the need for private gardens were the driving forces.

Here, everything is laid out towards the sun, which large windows bring right into your living room even in the grimmest months. The buildings are deliberately mixed in shape and size – two- to four-storey blocks of flats, one of them with a shopping parade and a pub, with a collection of squat 'point blocks' (stand-alone towers) and a few short terraces of houses, spread out between wide green spaces which were carefully planted. Seventy years later, the results are verdant, especially in spring and summer, with 'desire lines', i.e. unofficial pathways, winding between them. The buildings are made of concrete, but they've been faced in brick, partly because local labourers didn't have confidence in the quality of their concrete work, and partly because the councillors – in a garrison town – wanted to avoid the buildings looking like 'barracks'. This estate wasn't modernist in the purist sense, which then meant Le Corbusier's 'Five Points of Modern Architecture': open ground floors lifted up on thin piers called 'pilotis', roof gardens on flat roofs, freely designed facades outside and free plans inside the flats made possible by the lack of load-bearing walls, and horizontal windows.

What makes this *modernism* specifically is its deployment of a new conception of space. Rather than the market dictating where your window is, it is dictated by the sun. Rather than private gardens separated by fences, there are gardens for everyone (and, for their critics, also for no one), which have no fences. There is an openness which has been created by people deciding that precedent doesn't matter, tradition doesn't matter, landlords don't matter – and, at least until we get on to the vexed subject of build quality and municipal budgets, capital doesn't matter.

It's also modern in that it's part of a churn of constant reaction and counter-reaction, an almost neurotic series of sudden shifts in fashion and – to use a word architects dislike – style. So after 'my' part of the estate, with its brown bricks, pitched roofs and picturesque paths – a compromised, homely modernism that was derisively called 'People's Detailing' in reference to the Communist politics of many of its designers – there was a second, third, fourth and fifth part, across the 1960s, '70s and '80s. For phase two, in the early 1960s, the council dropped its direct-labour organization, which was considered technologically backward, and hired private architects (the firm of Norman & Dawbarn) and private builders to construct a series of tower blocks, which step down the steep hill of Frances Street. These are 'high' architecture in a way that phase one is not. The towers are on an x-shaped plan to give each balcony as much of a view and the flats inside as much air as possible; the bricks are a pinkish-purple, set into a clear, grid-like concrete frame, which, unlike in my flat, can be *seen* to be a concrete frame. The lower-rise blocks around them are in a tough, unpretentious style of heavy concrete lintels and severe grids, which was being called at the time the 'New Brutalism'. Phase three – which has its own name, Morris Walk – was more technologically ambitious. A long way from

Industrialized housing reaches Britain: system-built concrete panel towers at Morris Walk Estate, Charlton.

the desire of Woolwich Council to avoid 'barracks' and from picturesque planning, it was literally built on a production line, with large concrete panels – a Danish system, recommended to the London County Council by the famed engineer Ove Arup – hauled into place by gantries, using the tracks of the Woolwich–London railway, a linear approach that is still palpable when you walk around it. It has all the same basic components as the earlier parts – large public spaces, large flats, lots of light, minimal involvement of the free market – but it is much more stark and blunt; 'architecture' resides only in the rigours of the grid and the glinting surfaces of the pebbly concrete panels. As I write it is mostly derelict, awaiting demolition.

Phase four, built in the late 1960s, doesn't exist any more. A series of Brutalist blocks linked by walkways, along the ridge of the hill, it was influenced by **Park Hill**, a widely praised housing estate in Sheffield.

A great deal of modern housing built in the sixties got demolished as early as the 1980s and '90s, usually due to structural problems: demolitions for reasons of ideology have largely had to wait until recent years. The next two phases of the estate were based on a reaction against what were already considered to be modern architecture's failures: poor use of experimental technology; monolithic planning; a lack of engagement with the local 'context' – or, in a misused linguistic metaphor, 'vernacular' of the area (i.e., what was there before, which had hitherto been of little interest to many, if not all, modern architects).

The docks closed in the 1970s, and at the end of that decade there were erected around their quiet waters the fifth phase – a set of brick-clad, tall, long blocks, mixed with low-rise terraces around the preserved Custom House, with its evocative old clock tower. But up on the hill, near the since-demolished Brutalist 'streets in the sky', was an area that showed a total change of heart, which we'll call phase six, completed in the early 1980s. It is still modern in a sense – the monopitch roofs and warm brickwork were influenced by the Finnish architect Alvar Aalto. By the mid-1970s, volume housebuilders had started building little neo-Victorian suburban houses, but local authority architects' departments disdained such crass gestures. But there had been a major change in planning ideologies. Rather than open space, light, air and a feeling of privacy in your unit within a greater whole, these little houses – entered through the giant classical gateway of the early-Victorian Cambridge Barracks – are tightly packed around pedestrian pathways, so as to create a sense of 'community', where everyone knows each other and can always see each other – 'eyes on the street', as the American urbanist Jane Jacobs called it; yet of all the parts of the estate, it's the only one I ever felt uncomfortable walking through. And then, when this place was finished in the 1980s,

Historical continuity and humanized housing at Cambridge Barracks Estate, Woolwich, late 1970s.

that was the end of the project. Since then, one new speculative tower, cheap and nasty, was built on the river ten years ago, and the streets in the sky were replaced with very, very mild modernist blocks with stock bricks, gardens and glazed stairwells, back to the 1950s but without the space and the optimism.

This book is a guide to modern buildings in Britain – where you can find them, what they're like to walk around and live in, why they are as they are. That's why I'm beginning this book by describing this estate that I lived in for six years – because, to paraphrase Raymond Williams, modernism is ordinary. Modern architecture in Britain is all about areas like the St Mary's Estate, places that, no matter how mundane they might be, are expressions of a revolutionary approach to who builds in the city, how they build and in whose interest. Modernism was inherently a way of building and planning that rejected continuity. You could see this in the intense three decades in which this estate was built, a near-constant churn of change, of thesis and antithesis and synthesis, which ended only when the government turned off the taps of funding, and which could subsequently have gone in all sorts of directions – as, outside my estate, it has. I'm using it as a stand-in for the particular place in the town or city where you live that might have made you want to read a guide to modern architecture in Britain. At this distance, with modernism being around a century old, it makes no sense to begin with the pure image, the unsullied blueprint, the clear-eyed visionary proposal, because thousands of us live in the results. The consequences – what happens to a building after it has been lived in, and what happens to an idea after its time has passed – are every bit as interesting and worthy of attention.

I want this to be a book that doesn't offer modern architecture as an escape, as a pretty pipe dream, but as an experience, one both ordinary and extraordinary, and that's why it's rooted in empirical descriptions of real places with all their flaws and quirks. For most people modern architecture starts with their experience of it, negative or positive, rather than as something encountered through meeting masterpieces by famous names accredited by the architectural history books. However, these ordinary spaces are conditioned by an extraordinary history, and if we really want to understand them, we have to understand why architects began to design in this way. In Britain, this history runs deeper than perhaps anywhere else. So we can start at the beginning, not in the 1920s, but with the industrial revolution that happened here first.

HELL AS HERITAGE, 1800–60

The United Kingdom of Great Britain and Northern Ireland, to give it its current name, is the place where 'modernity' as we know it was first experienced. One of the great paradoxes of British architecture since the end of the eighteenth century is that a country which likes to think of itself as traditional, insular and conservative in its tastes (and its politics) was also the creator of global capitalism, and the first country to set in motion the industrial revolution that continues to convulse the planet, to the point where it plausibly threatens the future of human life on earth. Like the slums that were built for the people who built this new industrial world to live in, the factories of this era are much easier to contemplate now that they no longer serve that original purpose: now that they no longer stink and pollute, and now that men, women and children no longer have to work in them for twelve hours a day as their lungs are rapidly eaten away; now that they no longer appear, as they did to contemporary observers, like the realization of hell.

In the sixties, the architectural writer J. M. Richards rechristened the buildings where such experiences first happened as the 'functional tradition', and many modern architects – especially of the Brutalist sort – used these often no longer functioning functional structures as inspiration for their own forms. The most stark and powerful of them remain the nineteenth-century cotton mills of Manchester districts like Castlefield and Ancoats – multistorey, metal-framed, almost unornamented, and arranged alongside canals and railways. In terms of technology and in terms of aesthetics (not a category that would have interested their designers) these were unprecedented, and much more so than a Corbusian villa in the 1920s, a Brutalist university in the 1960s or a Zaha Hadid arts centre in the 2000s. Most of these structures have been dulled

The new industrial world: Murray's Mills, Ancoats, Manchester, designed by Thomas Lowe in the 1790s.

by heritage culture and long familiarity, but back then they blasted open what architecture and engineering were capable of. The railway stations built between the 1840s and 1870s at Newcastle, York, Liverpool Lime Street, Darlington, London Paddington, King's Cross and St Pancras, Glasgow Central, Hull, with their vast spans fashioned out of iron and glass and nothing else, are still the most spectacular examples of this proto-modernist architecture. Going up into the Hammersmith and City Line walkway at Paddington and surveying the length of its repeated vaults, with their tensile, looping shape – pure invention on the part of its designers, Isambard Kingdom Brunel and Matthew Digby Wyatt – is still one of the most breathtaking experiences of modern space to be found on this island. Unlike at St Pancras, sanitized with bright blue paint and awful sculpture, you can still 'hear the grinding of gears' (as Hugh Pearman puts it) in the architecture here.

The modernity of nineteenth-century architecture can be startling. There are some mid-Victorian commercial buildings – Peter Ellis's **Oriel Chambers** (1864) and **16 Cook Street** (1866) in Liverpool, Gardners' Warehouse (1856) or the 'Ca' d'Oro' (1872) in Glasgow – that have a true steampunk quality, as if all of the ingredients of the mid-twentieth-century inner-urban landscape had already been discovered, but assembled in an antiquated way, with residual shapes of historic architecture visible in their repetitious, mass-produced lines. The most rationalist strains of modernism – the ruthlessly clear steel-and-glass style that skips from Mies van der Rohe to Norman Foster – are anticipated more by the clean lines, new technologies and inorganic curves of Chatham Dockyard (1838–53), the Palm House at Kew Gardens (1847) or the Kibble Palace in Glasgow (1873) than they are by those sources conventionally found in architectural history such as Art Nouveau,

The new architecture of iron and glass: the block-like Ca' d'Oro, designed by John Honeyman in 1872...

...and the inorganic curves of the Kibble Palace, designed by John Kibble in 1873, both in Glasgow.

the Arts and Crafts movement or abstract painting. There is as much Constructivism to be found in the High Level Bridge across the Tyne (1849), the metal-on-metal clangour of the Forth Rail Bridge (1882–90) from Edinburgh to Fife, or – with their extreme height and their moving parts – the spindly Transporter Bridges of **Newport** (1906) and **Middlesbrough** (1911), as there is in the Mondrian- and Rodchenko-influenced painting of interwar Hampstead and St Ives.

So if, as the architect and historian Alan Colquhoun has defined it, modern architecture is 'the machine aesthetic, combined with a new conception of space', then modern architecture was invented in Britain in the early nineteenth century. But there are significant differences between this Victorian modernity and modernism, not all of them questions of style and ideology. Some of what was built in that century – the brick and stone viaducts, the unornamented mills, the grandly scaled warehouses – has roots in a functional tradition that can go back as far as the Roman Empire, if you want it to. Some of the most thrilling industrial buildings, like the Welsh Back Granary in Bristol (1869), fuse their outrageous scale seamlessly with ornamental patterns borrowed from Florence or Istanbul.

Nonetheless, the most notorious difference from twentieth-century modern*ism* is the maintenance even in many of the most radical Victorian engineering structures of *decorum*, which here meant a corresponding divide between structural innovation at the backside, and decorative continuity at the front. The importance of overcoming this difference was once an article of faith for modernists, and like many such articles of faith it has been kicked at by revisionist historians, but the fact remains that there was an extreme separation between architecture (the traditional masonry facade) and engineering (the iron-and-glass hall behind it) in the great railway stations, particularly after the first,

The 'Bristol Byzantine' of the Welsh Back Granary, by Archibald Penton and William Venn Gough, 1869.

more functionalist crop such as Paddington and King's Cross.

St Pancras exemplifies this split – to hide the iron-and-glass experimentation from view, we have a grand hotel on a swaggering, metropolitan scale, based on a scrupulously researched historical precedent, which in this case happened to be northern-Italian Gothic. In railway station hotels around Britain the source could be Siena, Athens, Bruges, Palmyra, and architectural history developed as a serious discipline in tandem with this search for interesting ways of hiding technology. In Manchester, warehouses with iron frames and plate-glass back ends – specifications that made the Bauhaus director Walter Gropius realize that all their ideas had been anticipated by anonymous Lancastrian engineers – were clad to the street in a lively terracotta baroque, now rather delightful but, in the literal meaning of the words, wholly superficial and facile.

The facades on the street were meant to look familiar and reassuring and antiquarian; the preserve of the fine art of architecture; behind that was the space of engineers, who were at liberty to create new forms and unprecedented spaces out of newly invented materials, just so long as they did it out of public sight. It is something a little like the Victorian attitude to sex, as Michel Foucault described it: greater study of, regulation of and anxiety over the subject than ever before, combined with a new set of prohibitions aimed at expelling its visible signs from public space.

It's a mistake to say this Victorian approach – visible, scholarly, historical front and 'invisible' (but of course frequently seen and used, especially by the working class) back side – is not a modern thing to do. In fact, it was only possible in a modern age, one in which Western Europe embarked upon the subjugation and enslavement of much of the world, then followed that by cataloguing, studying and collecting its art and architecture and inserting it all into an overarching progressive narrative. Rather than an atavistic reproduction of the museums of the Hellenistic world, institutions like the British Museum or the various Natural History museums were unlike anything that had been embarked upon before, and were completely inconceivable in the ancient or medieval worlds, however much they casually resemble Romanesque cathedrals or Attic temples.

There were heated debates throughout the nineteenth century and into the twentieth as to which out of Doric, Ionic, Corinthian, Romanesque, Byzantine, French Gothic, Palladian, Italianate, Dutch, or novel concoctions like 'Queen Anne', 'Jacobethan' and 'Wrenaissance' were most appropriate for the monuments of the new global capitalism centred on Britain. Such matters are now of parochial significance, but being able to collect all of these past styles and assemble them in a narrative, putting them

in their alloted places as if in the glass vitrines of Oxford's bizarre Gothic-futurist Pitt Rivers Museum, is deeply modern. As the Italian historian Manfredo Tafuri suggested, it may well be that this eclectic pile-up of data torn out of its original context is the true aesthetic of capitalism, not the objective display of technology and structure attempted by the modern architects of the twentieth century. Whether they opted in their politics for social democracy, liberalism, fascism or communism, the modern architects of the next century all believed that they were creating the only architecture truly appropriate for their time. This helps explain what the difference is, in architecture, between modernity – which can encompass both halves of St Pancras – and modernism, which sees one part as an escape into copying and idle dreaming, and the other part as a true expression of human and technological possibility. But, before modernism, there was another attempt at solving the same problem – the Arts and Crafts movement.

BACK TO NOWHERE, 1860–1910

The above is intended to explain why there isn't much Victorian architecture in this book (there are a couple of exceptions, which you're welcome to look for in your turn), and to pre-emptively outline the difference as I see it between things that are modern and a modern movement, which sees itself – or, rather, once saw itself – as an avant-garde attempt to change life. But there was, in Victorian Britain, a movement which did anticipate the idea of an 'avant-garde': a conscious group of people trying to use aesthetics and architecture as a means of changing, or at the very least as a way of interpreting the problems of, industrial and capitalist society. Despite their cutesy reputation, this was, quite explicitly, what the Arts and Crafts movement considered themselves to have been up to. Yet unlike the European 'avant-gardes' that would follow it – more of which later – the fact is that this English and Scottish avant-garde was born out of extreme hostility to industrial modernity, not as an embrace of it. The Arts and Crafts is conventionally dated to a revulsion against the products of the Great Exhibition held in London in 1851. Today, the Great Exhibition is celebrated by both imperial nostalgics and modernist architects as a showcase of global reach, universal plunder and technological flamboyance – under an iron-and-glass structure of such a scale and of such High-Tech confidence that it wouldn't be matched for a century after. But, at the time, the likes of John Ruskin and William Morris saw the Crystal Palace as an affront to their notions of what architecture and art should be. The reaction really began in 1859 with Philip Webb's blunt Red House, designed with William Morris for his use in the south-east London suburbs – a building which used local materials and was roughly, bluntly made, but refused to use any of the 'styles' available to the Victorian architect, with no copying, no 'scholarship'. The result was a kind of traditionalist functionalism.

It is almost impossible to extricate the Arts and Crafts' moral objections to industrial production from their aesthetic objections. This is their legacy to architectural debate. The denunciation of these ideas as the 'ethical fallacy' – the belief that the design of an inanimate object such as a building holds within it enduring moral lessons – by the Edwardian classicist Geoffrey Scott has had little effect on an enduring tendency to read ethics from facades.

Understanding Ruskin and Morris's issues with the Crystal Palace is useful both to explain why this 'ethical fallacy' recurs and recurs throughout the architecture of the next 150 years, and why it's not actually all that fallacious. In his attempt to elucidate 'the nature of Gothic' in his architectural-historical tour of the *Stones of Venice*, Ruskin argued

that medieval Gothic architecture was more moral than classical for both religious and workerist reasons. On the one hand, the 'pestilent' architecture of the Renaissance was based upon symmetry and perfection, which was blasphemous, because perfection can only be achieved in nature, that is, by God. This particular criticism need not detain us. The other assertion is that the Gothic masons – there was no specialized profession of 'architect' in the Middle Ages – preferred, aside from an asymmetry that wouldn't offend the Lord, flowing forms, polychromatic stone, flamboyant and untamed organic ornamentation, and contorted, etiolated sculpture. Gothic architecture looked as it did because its workers were able to express themselves in their work, rather than working from a blueprint set by an architect, as was the case with the architecture of the Renaissance. And whereas Renaissance architecture rejected an interest in the expression of structure, preferring an interest in mathematical proportion, Gothic was all about structure – towering vaults, flying buttresses, meaning that you can always see what is holding the building up (and when these buildings came back into fashion in the Victorian era, this was useful as a way of reinforcing Gothic cathedrals, so that they stopped falling down, which they had a tendency of doing). Morality is ornament, and morality is structure.

Needless to say, this was locking the stable door after the horse had long since bolted – reproducing Gothic in a modern age meant modern Gothic, not a true return to this imagined Middle Ages. So while Ruskin's favoured Italian Gothic became the definitive style of high-Victorian Britain – especially England and Wales, as Scotland's classical tradition was stronger – there isn't much evidence that a Victorian mason had any more room for self-expression when the architect was a Goth like William Butterfield rather than a Roman like Charles Robert

The neoclassical Bank of England, Liverpool, designed by Charles Robert Cockerell in 1845...

...and the neo-Gothic Keble College in Oxford, designed by William Butterfield in 1868.

Cockerell, to name two especially talented Victorians who stamped their own personal identity and obsessions on everything they designed. Even so, the deskilling of labour and the alienation of workers from the product of their work reached an extreme degree with the iron-and-glass architecture of the nineteenth century. It was impossible to have even the most minimal engagement with the end result of your labour when all you were doing was sliding together and then welding into place prefabricated pieces of glass and iron.

The reaction to this alienation is too often seen as a form of escapism, as a clique of London-based sensitive plants retreating into a world of smocks, stubby chimneys, cold if tasteful rooms and half-timbering, which was only really accessible to an elite. It's undeniable, for instance, that the reason why William Morris's products were so expensive is that they were not made by alienated

labour – and that realization made Morris a Marxist. Morris's Communism, as revealed in his *News From Nowhere* (1890), broke with Marx in one important respect. While Marx saw capitalism's massive increase in the productive powers of human society as the thing that made Communism possible – because, for the first time, there really was enough to go around for everyone – Morris's imagined future saw the destruction of iron bridges because their alienated work made them ugly, and all London's bridges rebuilt in stone.

Without ever being theorized as such, the emphasis of the Arts and Crafts shifted at the turn of the twentieth century from labour, Ruskin's main preoccupation, to society in a broader sense. Yes, the Arts and Crafts involved a lot of expensive curtains and tables, and it meant a lot of villas and churches. But it would soon also spread to the architectural output of the London

County Council. Its fire stations all over the city, each of them different from the other, are one of the Arts and Crafts' major legacies. More important socially were its early council estates – tall flats in Shoreditch and Millbank (1890–1900), low-slung houses in Tottenham (1904–13) and Tooting (1901–11), all with the sort of bluff yet warm attention to modelling and detail the Arts and Crafts specialized in. These projects showed that even if they couldn't actually bring back the medieval ateliers and their refusal of the division of labour, vaguely socialist Fabian councillors and architects could still create far better housing for the working class than had been imagined to be possible under capitalism. In the first Garden Cities and garden suburbs – Letchworth, New Earswick outside York, Hampstead Garden Suburb, the Well Hall estate in Eltham – such housing was rolled out on a massive scale, suggesting that, in some ways, Morris's 'Nowhere' really was within reach.

The route from the Arts and Crafts to modern architecture is convoluted, although it has been a fixture in all of the histories since Nikolaus Pevsner's *Pioneers of the Modern Movement* in 1936. It entails passing through a linked, later development. This was Art Nouveau, a mechanized sub-species of the Arts and Crafts, with more flamboyant ornament and an amoral welcoming of all the things that a medievalist like Ruskin abhorred: organic curves of reinforced concrete, a whipcrack of fluid iron across the facades, and open, spacious interiors, in the buildings of the likes of Victor Horta in Brussels, Louis Sullivan in Chicago, Antoni Gaudí in Barcelona, Fyodor Shekhtel in Moscow. Art Nouveau, like early modernism after it, would be a fairly minor trend in British architecture, with only a handful of major monuments, many of them pretty but derivative, like the **Royal Arcade** in Norwich or the Black Friar pub in London. The exception here was in Scotland, and

Fabian never-never-land: workers' cottages in Letchworth Garden City, planned by Raymond Unwin in 1903.

MODERNISM: AN EVERYDAY REVOLUTION

A new commercial aesthetic: steel, glass and faïence at George Skipper's Royal Arcade in Norwich, 1899.

especially Glasgow, then the 'second city of the Empire'. Among a clutch of exceptional designers including James Salmon and John James Burnet was the remarkable figure of Charles Rennie Mackintosh. This exceptionally talented designer – who didn't even have his own practice, but was merely an employee of the large firm of Honeyman & Keppie – would later be seen as the missing link, the architect who really straddled Arts and Crafts, Art Nouveau and Modernism.

You can see – in the Hegelian, 'progressive' sense that was so popular among modernists – a totally new conception of space emerge slowly out of Charles Rennie Mackintosh's buildings: from St Cross Church, in a bulging, personal Arts and Crafts; to **Scotland Street School**, where turrets that derive from Scottish Baronial architecture are filled with curved glass windows that evoke 1935 more than 1905, when it was actually built; to the **Glasgow School of Art**, whose first phase is still a kind of experimental historicism,

but which takes off into space in the Library wing, built in 1909 (now, tragically and appallingly, destroyed twice by fire and facing likely total reconstruction). These, aside from a clutch of industrial buildings and eccentricities, are the earliest buildings that are profiled in this gazetteer, and it may be useful here to explain exactly why I think they can be considered 'modernist' rather than just 'modern'.

On a superficial level, the ornamentation of Scotland Street School and especially the School of Art's library wing resembles the abstract art of the 1900s and 1910s or even much later – rectilinear, elongated, a little cubic, somewhat Japanese in appearance, rather than the whipping lines of earlier Art Nouveau. You could, wrote the critic Ian Nairn, have exhibited a section of the gates of Scotland Street School in a contemporary art exhibition in 1965 and people would have asked who the promising young sculptor was. But it runs much deeper than that. Upon entering the Library, you are in a totally new kind of space. There are many double-height libraries built in the Victorian and Edwardian eras with upper-level galleries, but none reduce their structure as this does to bare essentials, thin wooden supports that can be seen to be supporting, with delicate cubic chandeliers descending from the roof in the same abstracted, mechanistic style as the Scotland Street railings. To describe the components of the space is one thing, but it's the effect they create that is so extraordinary. Inside, the huge plate glass windows and the bared structure create an openness and limpidity of space that makes it feel as though you're suspended in air, like time has suddenly stopped. All the weight of precedent and masonry that the architects of Edwardian Britain so revelled in has melted into air: the experience is one of profound freedom and clarity.

FROM EDWARDIAN BAROQUE TO MODERNISMUS, 1910–45

Given his massive posthumous fame, you might expect that a modern movement in architecture would have emerged out of Mackintosh's precepts and precedents in Britain, or at least in Scotland – just as it emerged out of the work of easily comparable designers like Auguste Perret, H. P. Berlage, Michel de Klerk, Josef Hoffmann, Adolf Loos and Peter Behrens, in Paris, Amsterdam, Vienna and Berlin in the 1910s and '20s. Yet, instead, it came as an import to London or Glasgow from the continental cities, at the start of the 1930s. This led to a certain amount of soul-searching. As the émigré historian Nikolaus Pevsner was at pains to argue in the 1930s, when he wanted to convince a British audience that this new architecture was not inherently alien to them, the sources of continental modernism in the 1920s were frequently British. Not just the drama of Victorian engineering; not just

the freedom of planning and social optimism of the Arts and Crafts; but also the Garden Cities and their creation of new residential spaces outside the built-up city in the Edwardian era. Pevsner could have added that many prominent continental modern architects, particularly through institutions like the Deutsche Werkbund, a government-sponsored designers' association, had made extensive study of these British innovations. Another possible source of inspiration for a modern architecture in 1920s Britain was the work of the Vorticists, a group of Londoners and Northerners who had developed around 1914 an abstract art of sinister power and originality. And there were, in the 1910s, architects like Mackintosh, and lesser-known figures such as J. J. Burnet and Charles Holden, who were open and experimental enough in their manipulation of a classical or Gothic tradition, in buildings like the Central Library in Bristol (1906) or **Kodak House** in London (1911). It could have been expected they would develop the genuinely new style that Victorian architects had been arguing for since the era of Ruskin, yet Holden and Burnet would move to modernism much later through encountering it in Germany and the Netherlands. After 1918, meanwhile, our 'missing link', Mackintosh, gave architecture up altogether and became a modernist painter.

So while Britain did have things that fed into modernism – the Garden City, the free planning of the Arts and Crafts, Mackintosh's abstract Art Nouveau – it is genuinely no exaggeration to say that modernist architecture came to Britain at the turn of the 1930s as an importation. The major architects were nearly all from abroad – even the 'British' architects were usually colonials such as the Canadian-Japanese Wells Coates and the New Zealanders Amyas Connell and Basil Ward. Most importantly, there was the hugely influential emigration from continental Europe as it was subsumed by Fascism: Ernő Goldfinger and Marcel Breuer from Hungary, Berthold Lubetkin from the USSR, Erich Mendelsohn and Walter Gropius from Germany, Ernst Freud from Austria, to name only the most famous. Others are less familiar but were more enduring in their influence, such as the Slovak Eugene Rosenberg, the Finn Cyril Mardall, the German Arthur Korn, the Austrian Felix Samuely, the Dane Ove Arup. They brought with them an already existing architecture that had been developed intensively between around 1918 and 1928 to the point where it had become an instantly recognizable 'International Style'.

When this architecture came to Britain, you can see how abrupt the change was in the work of some of the British architects who came to adopt it. Compare Maxwell Fry's Margate Railway Station to his **Sun House** in Hampstead less than ten years later, and you can see not the gradual development from earlier ideas which *could* have led to modernism – the free classicism of Burnet,

the limpid space of Mackintosh, the abstract painting of Wyndham Lewis, to name three – but a flash of lightning, a road-to-Damascus conversion to a pre-prepared new architecture from elsewhere. A richly modelled neo-baroque, well-mannered, scholarly and decorous, has suddenly become an abstract language of white planes of concrete and glass, suspended in space. Sun House shows the 'uniform' of interwar modern architecture at its most complete. It is asymmetrical, a play of volumes set back and thrust forward; it is raised from the ground on thin pillars, pilotis; it has an elegant abstract roof garden, implying sunbathing; windows are in long horizontal strips, made possible by the lack of load-bearing walls; and the walls themselves are gleaming white, as if this were the south of France, not the north of London. Sun House is so generic, so mediocre, an example that it is hard now to imagine how shocking it would have

State of the art: the neo-baroque of Margate Railway Station, designed by Edwin Maxwell Fry in 1926...

...and ten years later, the International Style modernism of the same architect's Sun House in Hampstead.

been in the 1930s – unless you compare it with what the same designer was doing in Margate a decade earlier.

The architecture of late-imperial Britain (a small part of the British Empire's building activity, which then entailed the creation of entire new cities such as New Delhi and Tel Aviv) is now rather indulgently enjoyed, and since the 1970s has been widely rehabilitated. Architects such as Edwin Lutyens, John Belcher or E. Vincent Harris, who were unquestionably masters in their field, and, more questionably, the alternately fey, pompous and whimsical work of Beresford Pite, Edward Maufe, Edwin Cooper, Reginald Blomfield and the atrocious Herbert Baker: all have their defenders. But the dominance of this architecture in the 1920s must have been absolutely crushing for any British architect who wanted to experiment, or who wanted to connect with contemporary developments in technology and society – or, really, to anyone who wanted to do anything other than play clever and learned games with architectural history and express the grandeur of the Empire upon which the sun never set – an Empire which was, in the interwar years, to reach its greatest territorial extent.

Take a look at the government and bank buildings of interwar London, the shipping offices of Liverpool, the public buildings and textile warehouses of Manchester, and at this distance we can admit that they're in many cases attractive, strong, vigorous designs that fit well into their historic context; the same can be said of the continuation of the Garden City ideas into new council suburbs such as Wythenshawe in Manchester or Norris Green in Liverpool. But view them against directly comparable work from the same time in Paris, Berlin, Frankfurt, Stockholm, Rotterdam, Moscow, Milan, and they seem desperately conservative and stifling in their alternation between imperialist hauteur (for public buildings)

George's Dock Building, Liverpool, a combined ventilation shaft and office block by Herbert J. Rowse, 1927–32.

and A. A. Milne tweeness (for housing). Because this imperial baroque/nostalgic cottage style had become so dominant, a younger generation didn't get to 'grow' into modernism organically, but had to discover it anew. It provided no route into, and no room for, modernist design – so modernist design became a weapon against it.

Of course, not everyone had a semi-religious conversion towards a new ideal, as Maxwell Fry did. Very many British buildings in the few years immediately before the Second World War fall between the cracks, most of it in the category variously called 'art deco', 'streamline moderne' or, as it was called at the time, 'Modernistic' or 'jazz modern'. This was another import, although one adopted much more widely than Modernism with a capital M. The retrospective term 'art deco', coined by Bevis Hillier in the 1960s, derives from the 1925 Paris Exhibition of Decorative Arts. In one corner of this World Expo, Le Corbusier

and Konstantin Melnikov pioneered both International Style and Constructivist modern architecture; in another, architects from all over the global north enjoyed putting Egyptian, Assyrian, Mesoamerican, Moorish and neoclassical motifs alongside a bastardized form of Cubism on to flat facades. This, again, is an architecture which is much easier to enjoy now than it was in the 1920s and '30s. Whereas Corbusier and Melnikov, as with all the serious modernist experimenters of the 1920s, were bent upon finding new conceptions of space, new ways to make buildings in a society where technological change was transforming everyday life at a hurtling rate, the art deco designers were interested in inventing novel facades, a new form of surface ornamentation. Nonetheless, there is a lot of this in Britain, especially outside London. Sometimes, this 'art deco' is wholly a stage set architecture, appliqué, enjoyable but also cheap and nasty – think of the cinema,

The rich brickwork and complex geometries of Willem Marinus Dudok's Hilversum Town Hall, 1928–31.

now probably a bingo hall or an evangelical church, on your local high street, where a facade made of faïence tiles in the image of a pharaoh's temple or a sultan's palace is placed over a grim brick box, the seedy sides of which you can clearly see running down the other end of the street. But, on other occasions, it's just a less puritanical version of modernism, where architects have decided to combine their steel or concrete with a continued use of ornament or symmetry.

There is far more of this in Britain than there is of the full-scale International Style. Every town has its Odeon Cinema, probably designed by Harry Weedon in an idiom shamelessly filched from Erich Mendelsohn's Universum Cinema (now the Schaubühne theatre) in Berlin. Many civic buildings, such as **Hornsey Town Hall** (1935) or **Salford Civic Centre** (1938) take their cue not from the fearless glare into the future of Berlin or Moscow circa 1927, but from the milder climate of Scandinavia and the Low Countries, with a richer style developed from the town halls of Stockholm and Hilversum being considerably more popular as a source than the Bauhaus. The massive, angular brick edifices being built in the early 1920s in north Germany – a trend that took its inspiration from the Expressionist movement in art, more than from Cubism or Constructivism – were another important source for middle-of-the-road architecture of the interwar years, especially in the work of Giles Gilbert Scott, who fused it with Georgian and Tudor traditions in giant edifices like **Battersea Power Station** (1929–55) or **Cambridge University Library** (1934). It would be boring to leave these compromised buildings out, especially as their tawdry glamour or icy civic grandeur is more powerful than the strict Corbusian villas that you'll find largely only in north London and as weekend retreats in the Home Counties.

Modern architecture in the 1930s was foreign – indisputably – but it was also considered by its opponents to be dangerously left-wing. The innovative office blocks and private houses of turn-of-the-century Chicago were epically capitalist, and German industrial concerns like AEG and Siemens were an even more important source of early modernism; notoriously, Le Corbusier went round cap in hand to get work from industrialists, especially motor manufacturers, throughout the 1920s. The argument that Germany was advancing beyond Britain industrially in this period has been so comprehensively dismantled by historians over the last few decades that it can no longer be seriously considered as a reason for German industry's relative openness to experimental design; if anything, its relative backwardness was more likely to be the reason for the embrace of what became modernist architecture, as a modern look was more important to countries that

still had in places a pre-modern reality – a principle that applies even more with the USSR and other centres of modernism like Czechoslovakia, Poland and Hungary. The difference was, however, quite real. Compare, for instance, the factories of two of the major innovators of the period, AEG in suburban Berlin and Marconi in Chelmsford, and you'll see an angst-ridden and exciting search for expression and power alongside an image of complacency, comfort and continuity, executed in the 'Wrenaissance' manner.

In terms of social provision, there wasn't actually a vast difference between the housing programmes of interwar Britain and interwar Germany. Both countries built large quantities of low-income housing, courtesy of local councils in the former, trade union building societies in the latter (interwar Vienna, Stockholm and Moscow went much further, in their own very different ways). Berlin, Frankfurt, Cologne, Hamburg's extensive new working-class suburbs,

A modernist garden city: social housing in Britz, Berlin, by Bruno Taut, 1925–30.

swimming baths, schools, lidos, sports centres, cinemas, theatres and apartment blocks parallel those in London, Liverpool, Manchester, Birmingham, Glasgow. The difference is that on the Continent modern designers truly took control, especially in Germany but similarly in the Netherlands, Czechoslovakia and the USSR. There is a widespread idea, based largely on the example of Le Corbusier, that modernist architects mainly spent their time designing villas for the sort of intelligentsia clients who would be expected to show an interest in 'advanced' and 'progressive' design. This is partly true – but by the end of the 1920s many more working-class people were living in modernist buildings on the Continent than were middle-class people. In Germany, especially, modernism of the 'Sun House' sort – zero ornament, clear planes defining airy public space, flat roofs, geometric arrangements – was, because it was the style used in the building programmes of socialist local authorities, so associated with the political left that a demand for 'German' pitched roofs was part of the Nazi Party's early cultural programme. This wouldn't be the case to the same degree in Britain, where the equally large council housing programmes of the (briefly) Labour and (mostly) Tory governments of the interwar period were built in an increasingly vacuous pebbledash version of the Arts and Crafts. Given subsequent developments, it is worth mentioning that, in both countries, houses dominated the programme rather than flats.

Nonetheless, modernism was progressive, and so was socialism (and there was nowhere more progressive than the new Soviet Union, which between 1927 and 1933 was an extremely important international patron of modernist architecture). Modernists organized themselves along the lines of a vanguard Party, via a mock Comintern called the Congrès International d'Architecture Moderne (CIAM). Formed much later than the others, its British branch,

the Modern Architecture Research Group (shortened, with an eye to the 'alien invasion' metaphor, to MARS), announced itself to the world through a plan for the radical socialist replanning of London into a machine-made Garden City, in 1938. The day jobs of the great modernists in Britain at this time – who were overwhelmingly concentrated in London – really did entail the building of blocks of luxury flats, and villas in Hampstead for entrepreneurs and psychoanalysts. Among other things, this makes the subsequent idea that this was a middle-class movement foisting buildings middle-class people would never live in upon a guinea pig-like proletariat deeply puzzling – the London intelligentsia were the MARS group's lab rats. It is no accident that the only British building in the Museum of Modern Art's epochal exhibition *The International Style* was the **Royal Corinthian Yacht Club** in Burnham-on-Crouch. But the social architecture of the day stayed traditional.

Given that it was perceived as foreign, it is unsurprising that many attacks on modernism were openly reactionary and racist. For Reginald Blomfield, the architect of Regent Street (a late-Georgian parade destroyed completely and rebuilt in the imperial baroque in the 1920s), this was *Modernismus*, an ideology which he attacked as Germanic, socialistic and Jewish. Perhaps because of this criticism, you can see the scattered modernist buildings of the 1930s shifting gradually away from the scandalous nudity and wild-eyed purity of, say, Wells Coates's **Isokon Building** or Lubetkin's **Highpoint**, into an engagement with local materials such as Portland stone and stock brick, and more picturesque arrangements, and even decoration in Lubetkin's **Highpoint 2** or the Bauhaus director Walter Gropius's **Impington Village College** in Cambridgeshire. Nonetheless, it is only after the war that a distinctive modern architecture beyond a local variant on the International Style would emerge in Britain.

MODERNISM TAKES COMMAND, 1945–79

The overwhelming majority of modernist architecture in the United Kingdom was built between 1945 and 1979. It was a period in which modernism had a genuine institutional dominance, completely marginalizing the neoclassicism that was prevalent as late as the end of the 1930s, when the Ministry of Defence was being built to epically stodgy designs by E. Vincent Harris. While education in architecture schools has remained broadly modernist since 1979, it was only in those thirty-five years that what was taught in them came to inform what was built at almost every level, right down to previously strongly modernism-resistant preserves such as small towns, private houses and volume housebuilding. Although neoclassicism of various kinds did continue, a new library, office block or town hall built in the 1950s and '60s along traditionalist lines would be liable to be picketed by Anti-Ugly Action, a semi-serious campaign group based around the Royal College of Art, whose glowering Brutalist headquarters in South Kensington had just been completed, lurking gruffly opposite the Royal Albert Hall and the Albert Memorial. For those on the neoclassical side, like the historian Gavin Stamp, this (totally atypical, brief) era was 'a terror', although it is worth pointing out it never actually resulted in the public trial and execution of unrepentant classicists like Raymond Erith or Quinlan Terry: more that they generally had to content themselves with designing country houses for Tory millionaires, rather than the gigantic public commissions their forebears had enjoyed.

The reasons behind this dramatic shift can be found in the very different ways in which both the public and the governing elites dealt with the aftermath of the First and Second World Wars. After the first war, there was some reformist energy – a chaotic period of strikes, culminating in tanks being sent into the centre of Glasgow in 1919, the General Strike in 1926, the rise of the Labour Party and the Liberals' partially fulfilled promise of 'homes fit for heroes' that led to a wave of new garden suburbs. In many cases, though, the response of architects and the people who commissioned them was to retreat into certainties: a grandiose imperial neverland, which can be conceived as a response to the sheer shock of total war. The end of the second war, though, coincided with a wave of disgust at the politics that had preceded it: policies such as the cuts in already meagre benefits to the unemployed and the appeasement of the Third Reich, both of which had been highly electorally popular, were by 1945 synonymous with treason and cruelty. The books widely read by soldiers in the second war were notoriously influential, from Robert Tressell's *Ragged Trousered Philanthropists*, on the corruption of the building industry and the self-defeating conservatism of building workers, to the collectively written *Guilty Men*, an attack on the politicians who ran the country in the 1930s. Propaganda films by the likes of Humphrey Jennings and Paul Rotha, and posters by designers like Abram Games, interpreted the war not just as a fight against Fascism, but as a fight for the chance of a better, democratic, socialist future after it. There's no way to understand the modernist decades without understanding that the ideas circulating among liberal and socialist intellectuals in the 1930s about the construction of a Welfare State and a planned economy had the promotion of modern architecture at their centre.

Many of the famous names that were so influential in the 1930s – genuinely internationally significant Bauhaus teachers like Gropius, Breuer and László Moholy-Nagy, or first-rank architects like Erich Mendelsohn – made their way to the USA at the end of the thirties. Although many less storied interwar exiles would remain in Britain, they were joined for the first time by a group of important designers who had learned their trade in Britain in the 1930s. The projects of the first decade after the war – the **Royal Festival Hall** and the new estates of the London County Council, and the new towns planned around Britain's two densest and largest cities (at that point) London and Glasgow – were designed in a way that broke in numerous ways with the white-wall uniform of the International Style. This came through the work of architects like Leslie Martin and Frederick Gibberd, who abandoned the purist style for something more decorative. While the RFH, or the **Lansbury Estate** in Poplar, east London, displayed many of Le Corbusier's Five Points – free planning, free-flowing circulation around buildings, open ground floors – these pure modernist features were combined with ornamentation, patterns, colours other than white, off-white and black, and, in the case of the Lansbury, little bow windows that had more than a hint of the Regency about them. At around this point, the former Dresden art historian Nikolaus Pevsner spoke on behalf of the 'Englishness of English Art', with particular reference to the Picturesque tradition of apparently casual, informal relationships between buildings and nature. This became a way of explaining the landscapes of the London County Council's new estates, such as Ackroyden in Wimbledon and, especially, the **Alton Estate** in Roehampton, which was one part Le Corbusier's *ville radieuse* and one part Capability Brown's ideal stately home garden.

This change can't be ascribed entirely to a populist desire on the part of architects to ingratiate themselves with a general public who were assumed, not entirely without reason, to be hostile to the abstract rigours of the International Style; nor, although some hostile observers attempted to argue this at the time, can it be the result of the Communist Party affiliations of many of the leading designers in this manner, such as the now veteran Berthold Lubetkin and his partner Francis Skinner, Frederick Gibberd, Oliver Cox and a large part of the LCC Architects' Department. Rather than being an analogue of the 'Socialist Realist' architecture of the Eastern Bloc – whose slogan was 'national in form, socialist in content', albeit realized usually via appliqué local colour on heavy neoclassical structures – the main inspiration was actually the architecture of neutral Sweden, which embarked in the 1940s on a light, relaxed modernism which included the sort of delicate porches, gardens, decorated hallways, picturesque arrangements and pitched roofs which led harder-line modernists to jeer at this as 'People's Detailing'.

The result was more generally called the New Empiricism by its defenders in the architectural press. Whatever we call it, it was in this style that the first new towns, such as Harlow or East Kilbride, or the reconstructed Coventry, were built. There were other ideas around – Plymouth and Hull, for instance, replanned themselves in a manner that was one part interwar neo-Georgian and one part a sobered-up art deco – but these projects were generally ignored by the press and by the architectural taste-makers, who were more likely to praise the combination of tradition and modernity in Coventry, where multilevel precincts were integrated with cathedral spires and decorated with slightly nostalgic public art. Much as with the new NHS, these projects were the envy of much of the rest of Europe, and were widely published and emulated in the countries from which the modernist diaspora had fled in the first place.

What made this possible was also what made a more aggressive counter-reaction possible. That is, a loss of faith in the remarkably homogeneous architecture of the International Style. This architecture, which was based so much on a moral appeal to honesty and the zeitgeist, and which claimed truth to materials, was evidently telling fibs.

Many of the villas and workers' housing estates were not, as they appeared to be, made out of smooth concrete poured into moulds and sculpted into smooth forms as if it were icing sugar. In many cases, it was just brick construction rendered to look like an idea of what concrete looked like – and that idea, derived from the 1920s work of Le Corbusier, Mies van der Rohe and J. J. P. Oud, was often just that, an idea. Concrete didn't really look like this, and the owner of a modernist house or the local-authority owners of a modernist housing block would have to spend lots of money on regular repaintings to keep it looking sparkling and new – especially if it happened to be situated under unforgiving British skies. One reaction against this was just to ignore all of the ideological baggage altogether and develop a folksier, looser modernism that drew from local traditions, and this would happen not just in Britain but in Finland, Italy and Japan, and across Latin America. It could also lead to a reassertion of fundamentals. If the architecture of the interwar period was unsuccessful or compromised, it was because modernist tenets like structural expression, novelty, collectivism, weren't applied properly or were ignored. A new modernism would emerge that stressed these three things to an extremely dogmatic extent. This would become in many respects the most important, most fascinating and by far the most controversial form of architecture in British history. Moreover, in very marked contrast with the white-wall style of the 1930s, it had emerged primarily in Britain, and it was in Britain that it got its name: *Brutalism*.

This has become by far the most fashionable of modern architectures in the last ten years, and you can if you so wish go to the shops of the **Barbican** or the **South Bank Centre** and buy yourself a trolleyfull of Brutalist tat, from tea towels to models and cut-outs. It is one of those peculiar movements where the name predates the emergence of a clear notion of what it actually entails in visual terms. The first Brutalists – a London clique around the wife-and-husband team Alison and Peter Smithson – were very clear about what they were against: a list that included the picturesque, decoration, tweeness and homeliness, structural dishonesty and little Englandism, all of which were expressed in one way or another by 'People's detailing'. What they were *for* was harder to say. The first public building by the Smithsons, **Smithdon School** in Hunstanton, a windy seaside resort in Norfolk, was based on the American work of the Weimar modernist Mies van der Rohe. In his Illinois Institute of Technology (1950–56) and Lakeshore Drive Apartments (1949–51), both in Chicago, Mies had actually taken the 'purity' of the International Style all the way to a new classicism based on obsessive proportion and material fundamentalism, in an expensively detailed steel and glass.

It was only slightly later that Brutalism became more associated with a rough, aggressive and increasingly monumental architecture of heavy bare concrete, raw and tactile surfaces and strange minatory silhouettes. Like the purism of the 1930s, it was derived from a handful of buildings by Le Corbusier. While the likes of Sun House came straight from, say, the Villa Cook outside Paris (1926), Brutalism derived from the Unité d'Habitation in Marseille (1947–52), the La Tourette monastery (1953–60) and the Maisons Jaoul houses outside Paris (1954–6). This post-war shift by the Swiss designer into the rough, raw and fearsome was paralleled by a general move towards more irrational means of expression in painting and sculpture. 'Fuck Henry Moore' was one of the Brutalists' slogans. The results are much more evenly spread, geographically, than the London and Home Counties world of 1930s British modernism. The finest of these buildings included council estates in Sheffield, Catholic churches in Clydeside,

Birth of the new Brutalism: the roof garden of
Le Corbusier's Unité d'Habitation, Marseille, 1947–52.

car parks in Gateshead and shopping centres in Portsmouth.

Given that one of Brutalism's early advocates, the historian and journalist Reyner Banham, called the style a 'brickbat thrown in the public's face', it isn't altogether surprising that it became such a swearword from the 1970s onwards. But what was probably more fateful in generating opposition was its alignment with two shifts in urban-planning policy. One was an increasing numbers game in housing, with Labour and the Conservatives fighting elections on how much they could build; the other was the carve-up of city centres into packages for developers and road engineers, something summed up in the technocratic phrase 'comprehensive redevelopment'. These two pragmatic factors, much more than any ideas dreamed up in the think-tanks of the 1940s or the architecture schools of the 1950s, would be decisive in transforming a majority of the towns and cities where people actually live. The massive house-building programme of the 1950s and '60s isn't solely a story about system-building and cost-cutting. Flat sizes were large, and central heating and sanitation were far above the level of pre-1960s housing; a lot of estates had district heating. Most eyewitness accounts of even 'failed' estates will begin with 'Well, at first, it was like paradise' or 'We hadn't seen anything like it', before the problems started. The more conscientious councils built a wide range of housing, employing large teams of architects to provide specific solutions to specific sites.

The most creative local authorities included the London County Council and many of its boroughs, especially Lambeth and Camden, which favoured low-rise, high-density schemes on dramatic sites; Sheffield, where an exchange scheme allowed people to move easily between the arcadian suburbia of **Gleadless Valley** and the inner-city Brutalism of Park Hill; Norwich, which built a succession of warm and individualistic estates on the outskirts of the old town; Southampton, with dense and monumental housing right in the centre and spacey estates on the hills and on the seashore; and of course the New Towns, especially Stevenage, Harlow, Milton Keynes and Cumbernauld. Yet the seductive promises that system-building could rehouse entire waiting lists almost in an instant steamrollered many councils into letting building firms offload identikit developments, regardless of site, across their jurisdiction. The worst offenders for this – Portsmouth, Sunderland, Glasgow, Birmingham, the London Borough of Newham – had been left enormous housing problems by the nineteenth century, to which systems seemed like a straightforward solution. It wasn't, especially given that the British building industry frequently botched the execution. As with the nineteenth-century housing it replaced, the worst examples

The system-built and recently demolished Lenton Flats, built by Nottingham Council in 1965.

no longer exist, after demolitions in the 1980s and '90s. There were a handful of genuine structural disasters, which included most drastically the partial collapse of Newham's Ronan Point tower in May 1968, and the incredibly short-lived hilltop estate of Portsdown Park just outside Portsmouth, begun in 1964 and demolished as early as 1987. However, maintenance has usually been the biggest problem. Many architecturally drab estates work just fine, while some that are spatially dramatic and unique can be grim and dilapidated concentrations of poverty; aesthetics, intention and care are all mixed up, and don't often align where they seemingly ought to.

The 'comprehensive redevelopment' programmes in the city centres, which transformed Victorian streets into massive concrete malls, lack the genuinely tragic aspect of the housing programme. Second World War bombing, combined with the

(still widespread) belief that nineteenth-century industrial cities were architecturally worthless, running alongside the need for councils to raise capital for their social programmes, led to councils collecting town centre sites into huge package deals for developers, who built throughout the 1950s, 1960s and early 1970s office/shopping/parking complexes on a gigantic scale. These usually came in tandem with road 'improvements' that helped create the cordon sanitaire of dual carriageways that now separates most large city centres outside London from their inner suburbs. This is something unusual in continental cities, which may constitute some sort of sign that Britain had not only caught up but surpassed the rest of Europe in modernity – although it's hard to imagine anyone being particularly proud of the fact that, say, it's easier to drive from the centre of Bradford to its inner suburbs than it is to walk the half-mile distance.

Many of these road systems are along the lines that 1930s modernist planners had lobbied for, and they now appear as by some way the most indefensible aspect of the modernist legacy in Britain. As for the redevelopment schemes themselves, most were of little architectural note, particularly the many built by the Arndale company, which built dozens of megastructures in the 1960s and 1970s. Even these can vary wildly in quality. Manchester's Arndale, the only one that still bears the company's name, is a good measure of the blandness that usually resulted, but the earlier **Piccadilly Plaza** offers a glimpse of the exciting visual possibilities of juxtaposing disparate functions in one giant structure. Among the few really interesting examples of this trend are the skyscraping **Victoria Centre** in Nottingham, with its ascending series of towers above a mall, or south London's **Catford Centre**, notable for its expressive concrete brutality, one of several shopping centres designed by the Owen

The end of utopian modernism: the Arndale Centre in Manchester, Hugh Wilson and J. L. Womersley, 1972–7.

Luder Partnership, of which the best – in Gateshead and Portsmouth – have long been demolished. Because of their commercial nature, these places are especially prone to poor-quality redevelopment to make them look cheerier, so as to not put people off their shopping: once-interesting town centre redevelopments in Blackburn and Preston have been comprehensively cleansed of anything worth looking at.

DECLINE, FALL AND RISE, 1980–2020

By the start of the 1970s, modernism was extremely heavily criticized in the press, in the media, by political movements of both right and left, by the very architects who had designed much of it and the councillors who had been its most crucial sponsors. A series of corruption scandals –

particularly affecting projects in Newcastle and Birmingham, and on British Rail – created an association between concrete, destruction of 'heritage' (the Victorian era was rapidly being positively revalued) and dodgy politicians with their hands in the till. Today, when there's a wave of nostalgia towards modernism – even, and especially, to its most controversial moment, Brutalism – many of these critiques are hard to read, their often salient arguments about undemocratic planning, technocratic power and the destructive effects on historic cities swamped by a caricaturing of opponents, rhetorical exaggeration and prophetic hysteria as severe as that of the MARS group in the 1930s. The 1970s rash of books with grossly emotive titles like *Goodbye London*, *The Sack of Bath* and *The Rape of Britain* now seem wildly overstated. If anything, the rhetorical violence of these books is less forgivable than that of the 1930s modernists. Their excessive condemnation of the nineteenth century's legacy as a pure embodiment of poverty and slum landlordism seems morally more sympathetic today than the notion that the refusal to be 'in keeping' was a harbinger of the destruction of civilization.

Modernist architecture's leap in scale and drama in the sixties could easily be found domineering and bullying; and that the mainstream modernist repertoire was stylistically limited and restrictive is difficult to deny. Most of what was built in Britain between roughly 1955 and 1970, aside from the residual neoclassicism (mostly a matter of country houses, City office blocks and church restorations, excepting a few public buildings by the unusually talented firm of McMorran & Whitby), fits into one of three categories. There's the International Style, which had settled in its British variant into Portland stone and glass curtain walls, seen from Aberdeen to Plymouth, with a few richer clients in London, Manchester and Birmingham commissioning more successful imitations of the all-glass skyscrapers of 1950s New York and Chicago. There was Brutalism, which offered rather more room for individual expression, albeit using a palette of concrete, concrete, concrete and sometimes brick; it certainly had a lot of space for engagement with topographic and regional specificity, particularly in the work of more enlightened councils such as Sheffield and Lambeth and in the New Universities like York, Essex and East Anglia (though almost everywhere, it seemed, could become an 'Italian hill town'). There was also a smaller thread of 'organic' architecture deriving from the work of Alvar Aalto and other Scandinavian designers, which opted for locality and 'warmth' of material and intimacy of scale. But the Postmodernist complaint that this was a limited way of treating architecture's possibilities was not altogether unfair.

The architecture of the 1970s involved much residual Brutalism and Scandomodernism, but this was now alongside several new trends. There was a slightly dour social architecture based upon study of local buildings that called itself, in an inappropriate linguistic analogy, 'vernacular' – Odhams Walk in Covent Garden (1979) being one of the better examples. There was a wave of neo-1930s modernism which has only recently been noticed as a clear trend, where the interwar white-wall style became an object for historical pastiche of varying quality – the flats of **6–10 Gaisford Street** in Kentish Town (1978) being a particularly elegant tribute to the twenties. But much more importantly there was High-Tech, a technocratic version of Modernism based equally upon the lightweight, clip-together American architecture of Charles and Ray Eames or Buckminster Fuller, on the Crystal Palace and Victorian engineering, and on the unbuilt projects of Soviet Constructivism. High-Tech would be the most enduring of all these trends from this era of doubt,

largely because it ignored angst and anxiety in favour of a better, cleaner, less political modernity. These styles can all be found in the 1970s New Town of Milton Keynes, where a car-centred plan is supplemented by housing schemes in each of the available styles around the limpid glass pavilions of the city centre.

Postmodernism was not a continuation of modern architecture or a total rejection of it, so much as a complex game with architectural styles, which made modernism one of many fragments to play with. It began as an architectural term before it was extended into a wider description of society and culture since the decline of a belief in progress, socialism or the future. As architecture, it was distinguished by a peculiar combination of literalism and irony. It is easy to prove that its interest in 'history' was shared by many modernists, particularly of the Brutalist and Aalto-esque sort: as early as the early 1960s, buildings like the **Lillington Gardens** council estate in Pimlico, London, showed an engagement with the local scale and the materials and colours of the local brick Gothic churches that would have been totally inconceivable in the International Style of the 1930s. Housing schemes by Basil Spence in 1950s Edinburgh, by Wheeler & Sproson in 1960s Fife, and by Tayler & Green over several decades in Norfolk were fairly obviously engaged in a dialogue with their historical neighbours, rather than ignoring them or arguing with them. But Postmodernists found this all a little too coy. If designing in an area defined by Gothic churches, why stop at using a rough stone or brick? Why not throw in some pointed arches or a gargoyle or two? If engaging with classical architecture, why pretend that classicism is just about mathematical proportion – why not add a cornice or even a pediment with sculptures in? There was a generation of real Postmodern classicists – Robert Adam, Quinlan Terry, John Simpson – but their

Prince Charles's time machine: one of Quinlan Terry's Regent's Park Villas, built between 1988 and 2002.

work usually displayed the impossibility of time travel, the poverty of construction materials and the poor quality of detailing making clear that the discipline and the craftsmanship which distinguished classical architecture in the first instance were not coming back. This was straightforwardly retro work, totally anti-modern.

But most of the first generation of Postmodernists were too much the jaded sophisticates just to replicate historical architecture. They preferred – in a way anticipated by the Edwardian baroque – to fuse the Renaissance or the Gothic or neoclassicism together with American commercial modernism, with skyscraper proportions, with art deco and even avant-garde movements like Dada and Constructivism, and with motifs and typologies developed by modernism itself, in frequently domineering compositions which exploited the freedoms (for developers) of a deregulated market. The rejection of

'progress' in design went alongside the political rejection of socialism and social democracy under Margaret Thatcher's rule. Architecture between 1976 and 1997 is conspicuous by its abandonment of the social projects to which modernism was devoted. There are exceptions – the continued imaginative design of Milton Keynes, the self-built, clip-together housing schemes that Lewisham Council and the architect Walter Segal devised in the 1980s, and, especially, the **Byker Estate** in Newcastle, the last great heroic housing scheme, where Ralph Erskine combined Brutalism's love of scale and collectivist melodrama with an intimacy of detail and a democracy in planning that had not at all been part of the modernist repertoire up to that point. But, mostly, this is the developers' era.

British Postmodernism can be seen at its best, and worst, in the work of the prolific Terry Farrell, who tried on Brutalism (in his air vents for the Blackwall Tunnel) and then

High-Tech (in a clip-together apartment block in Regent's Park) in the late 1960s before opting for a bumptious, muscular version of American Postmodernism. The results include the atrocious Alban Gate (1990), an 'air rights' building (i.e. the rights to build on the space above a road, a railway station, a railway track) atop the 1960s roadway of London Wall, which before then was lined with International Style glass towers. Here, the architect totally loses control of the proliferation of motifs, from the pink stone ziggurat of the central building to the neo-Tudor brick of its lower parts, in a composition that is both straggling and domineering. But there is much of value in something like Farrell's earlier TV-am building in Camden (1981, recently rebuilt beyond recognition by its current tenants, MTV), or Comyn Ching Triangle in Covent Garden (1978–85). These two are impressive not so much for their jokes (egg cups on the corners) as for their complex splicing together of new additions and existing fragments of warehouses and offices. Similarly, there is a thuggish terror about his late buildings, such as the MI6 Headquarters in Vauxhall (1992) or **Embankment Place**, the evil air rights superstructure above the platforms of Charing Cross Station (1985–90), which speaks of the restatement of the naked power of state and capital in this allegedly more populist era.

On the whole, this era was responsible for the worst examples of planning and architecture in Britain since the nineteenth century. These are the gross retail parks and executive closes made possible by the Conservatives' tearing up of the planning laws, and speculative office blocks and shopping malls which discarded the staid limits of Miesian discipline in favour of a sprawling mass of misunderstood forms, which for all their insistence on 'language' and 'dialogue' speak solely of a chastened architectural profession's fear that it will

The complex warehouse aesthetic of Comyn Ching Triangle in Covent Garden, by Terry Farrell, 1978.

offend the public or the Prince of Wales. This poses the question of whether much of what happened in the 1980s and '90s can be considered 'modernist' at all. By the early 1980s, the 'modern movement' as the social reform movement it had imagined itself to be between the 1920s and 1970s was severely chastened and marginalized. The only built examples in this era that genuinely continue the programme of, say, the MARS group of modern architects in the 1930s – the social efficacy of design, the possibility of human betterment, the necessity of human beings living together socially, and the ability of ordinary people to understand complex or unusual design ideas – are the works of Walter Segal and Ralph Erskine. Even the political left, when it built – in the 1980s Coin Street Community Builders scheme in Lambeth, or the new Liverpool housing estates under the auspices of the Militant Tendency – opted for traditionalism and against modernity. But on every other level it is senseless not to describe the best work of 1980s corporate High-Tech – such as Richard Rogers's dizzying, endlessly fascinating masterpiece, **Lloyd's of London** – as modernist. While the building forecloses all the social optimism of the modern movement, however much the architect himself would elsewhere try to revive it, this thrilling statement of amoral futurism, this utterly dynamic, totally confident revelling in technocratic form, cannot be construed as anything other than modernist. Although not an architecture that the MARS group would recognize as their progeny, it is as aggressive in its fervour about the possibilities enabled by the present as they were about the potentials of the future. The same can be said about some of the work inspired by one of the more outré trends of the 1980s–90s: what was called 'Deconstructivism' (recently rebranded as 'Parametricism' by one of its practitioners, Patrik Schumacher), which was based initially on an engagement with the paper architecture of the interwar avant-garde, with computer technology applied to make the unbuildable buildable. There is little of this in Britain of real quality, and what there is was realized after 1997; these scattered examples, like Zaha Hadid's Kirkcaldy **Maggie's Fife** cancer care centre (2006) or Daniel Libeskind's Trafford **Imperial War Museum North** (1999–2002) show its potentials and pitfalls.

Ironically, Rogers himself would be influential in the attempt, at the end of the 1990s and across the 2000s, to put the genie of neoliberalism and Postmodernism back in the box. Through his work as a Labour peer, chair of Labour's Urban Task Force and compositor of various urban and architectural manifestos, Rogers became the leader of a new version of the optimistic side of modernist architecture, for public clients. This New Labour era concentrated on large public buildings, funded sometimes by dubious means (the National Lottery,

The Millennium Dome in North Greenwich, designed by the Richard Rogers Partnership, 1997–9.

the corrupt Private Finance Initiative) for art galleries, museums, concert halls, libraries and indistinct 'centres' for this and that. They would usually be neighboured by new speculative housing to cater for a middle class that – defying the predictions of modernist and Postmodernist planners and non-planners – was returning to city centres.

Some of these public buildings can now be seen relatively objectively as an interesting combination of techno-flash and public purpose. The quayside ensemble at Gateshead, with the **Baltic Centre for Contemporary Art**, Norman Foster's billowing **Sage Music Centre** and Wilkinson Eyre's **Millennium Bridge**, is of real quality, however much it is let down by poor public spaces and the awful speculative housing around its perimeter. The **Jubilee Line** extension of the London Underground is as good as anything built anywhere in the twentieth century, with all the architects involved – Norman Foster, Michael Hopkins, Richard MacCormac and others – working at the very top of their game. Some of the towers, such as Ian Simpson's **Beetham Tower** in Manchester or, in London, Foster's **30 St Mary Axe** – aka the 'Gherkin' – are now integral and sometimes beloved parts of their respective cities' skylines. Yet the speculative housing of the New Labour era, with its tiny single-aspect flats and bet-hedging pot pourri of cladding materials, seldom matches the generic council building of the 1960s, let alone the best of that period. The very worst comes in hotels, student housing, and the public–private new schools and hospitals of the New Labour era. A golden age for galleries, museums and skyscrapers, and a dark age for homes, hospitals and schools: so runs the epitaph for the self-described 'aspiration' of the recent past.

THE VIEW FROM 2021

Today, the glitzy architecture of 'Regeneration' and its associated 'icons', as seen at places like the Quaysides of Tyneside, Salford or Greenwich, is often as widely rejected as the architecture of the mid-1960s was ten years later – artefacts of the boom, marooned by the financial crisis of 2008 and its ongoing ramifications. Looking around London – which the financial crisis has made even more the overwhelming home of most architectural activity than it was before – the architectural prospect is encouraging, the social prospect disastrous. A housing crisis grips the capital the like of which it hasn't seen for a century, and developers dictate terms to cowed, cash-strapped local authorities. Homelessness and overcrowding are grossly high, and rents are an obscenity. Yet rather than expressing this angst and chaos, contemporary architecture speaks of order, robustness, calm, rectitude, civic virtue. Contemporary housing, insanely unaffordable

though it is, tends to be better built and more spacious than that of the New Labour era recent past. The art galleries of David Chipperfield or Caruso St John, the housing of Maccreanor Lavington, Alison Brooks, Karakusevic Carson, or the office blocks of Patrick Lynch or Eric Parry all show a reconciliation between modern architecture and the traditional city, favouring identifiable 'streets' and squares, fronts and backs and local scale, while refusing the twee, ingratiating and overbearing gestures of Postmodernism. Yet even before looking at the dubious finance behind most of this architecture, its social consequences are not always admirable. Much of it is based on 'densifying' the communal open spaces between council housing, as a way of maximizing value for local authorities in serious need of money – and it is overwhelmingly concentrated in London and Cambridge, which never lost its role as a centre for sensible modern architecture, established in the 1960s.

But looking at the work of Peter Barber, who has designed around a dozen social-housing schemes in London in the last two decades, you can see the values of the modern movement alive and well. In Bow's **Donnybrook Quarter** (2006), there is the white-wall confidence of the 1930s; in Colindale's **Pegasus Court**, in Grahame Park (2015), the monumental scale of the sixties; in a small terrace at **Worland Gardens** in Stratford (2016), the grandeur of the LCC's 1930s courtyards; and at the just-completed Moray Mews in Finsbury Park, there's the cubic geometry and street-focused coherence of the Camden council housing of the 1970s. In each of these, the public spaces – the colonnades, the public squares, and the streets – are imagined as the animating principle, the thing that makes the buildings work, that makes them enjoyable to live in. All these buildings show that modernism now has a history, and a formal repertoire that it can draw on that is as rich as that of traditional architectural styles. Perhaps that makes them retrograde, and the denizens of High-Tech and Parametricism would likely argue so. What makes Barber's work special is that it shows that the ethics and aesthetics of modernism can still run together. Intelligent and humane design, the belief that human beings can live in something better than what 'trickles down' to them from the elite, the unifying and enriching possibilities of urbanism and urban life – they're all there. They could be everywhere.

Travelling around Britain in the 2020s is not always a particularly delightful experience. This is an extremely unequal country, with a public transport system to match – the experiential difference between taking a train between Manchester and Leeds and one between London and Stevenage is akin to that between taking a train in Romania and taking one in Switzerland. This is a tense, polarized country, and events in the last decade have made it much more so, with entire swathes of the island facing a crisis on the scale of the Great Depression, while a handful of cities like London, Cambridge, Oxford, Manchester and Edinburgh face an equally alarming boom. There is also much to be uneasy about in the modernist project itself. It was the product, always, of the industrial revolution, and an economy based on fossil fuels and instant disposability. Modernism is without doubt an epiphenomenon of the process which is already leading to melting ice caps, rising sea levels, scrambles for resources and August temperatures in April afternoons in Basingstoke, as I found out when getting unexpectedly and horribly sunburnt compiling one of the entries in this book. Yet the architecture and planning that can help us adapt are likely to be modernist rather than traditional. The modernist openness to new ideas, new techniques and new ways of living means that we should expect the next architectural vanguard to be Ecomodernist, not Parametricist or

Postmodernist. You can see that already, in places like the **LILAC** housing co-operative in Leeds (2013), whose flats of straw and wood are zero carbon, low energy and modular, and owe little to the architecture of the past. Classicism can't help us much with the wind turbines, the tram networks, the high-speed railways, the solar panels, the buses, the dense and warm housing that we're going to need to build and to retrofit. Modernism helped get us into this mess, and it can help get us out of it.

HOW TO USE THIS BOOK

This book isn't meant to be read from start to finish. It's a gazetteer, meant to be a guide to the place you live, or a place you're visiting, or a place you want to visit. The judgements are mine and mine alone, and you're welcome to find them preposterous – although a bibliography at the end is intended both as historical background and an attempt to back up my opinions. I'll avoid architectural jargon as much as possible, and I've provided a short glossary of styles below, as this is usually one of the more intractable and intimidating sides of modern architecture to those of us many architects still insist upon calling 'laymen'. Architects like to pretend style doesn't enter their heads, but we are free to ignore this affectation: it is impossible to understand the architecture of the last hundred years without taking these sudden shifts in fashion into account.

Each subsection is chronological, and buildings mentioned in passing in the text in **bold** have their own entries. I have also emphasized in the text through a ✪ symbol when a building is one I think it absolutely essential for anyone interested in the area to go and see; and when I know that a building is under threat, I've added a ❶ symbol to warn readers to check before they travel.

Modern Classicism, Chicago School

I use 'Modern Classicism' to describe buildings by architects who bent neoclassical values of solidity, permanence and tradition towards modernist ones of abstraction, reproducibility and contemporaneity, and which therefore fit, just about, in this book. I often draw the line across the oeuvre of particular designers, so that, say, **Senate House**, Charles Holden's abstracted 1930s tower for the University of London, is in here, and his slightly earlier, more rigidly Georgian 1920s tower for London Transport is not. That latter was part

of a different story, about the persistence of neoclassicism into the modern age. 'Chicago School', meanwhile, I've used to describe this form of Classicism when it is modelled on the architecture of the United States, where display of industrial structure and classical discipline often went together.

Constructivism

First-wave modernism, mainly in the USSR, Czechoslovakia and the Netherlands, favouring complex plans, technological display, geometric experiment and a flamboyant use of space – the classic work in Britain being Wells Coates's **Isokon Building** in north London, of 1934.

International Style

This term was coined by New York's Museum of Modern Art in 1932. The 'International Style' generally denotes a generic modernism, roughly in two distinct modes: pre-1939, with white stucco walls, strip windows and roof gardens; and post-war, when it was developed by the German modernist Mies van der Rohe into a corporate glass skyscraper style, deliberately anonymous, precise, sleek and mathematical; the **Western Bank Library** and **Arts Tower** in Sheffield (1956–65) are its great monuments on this side of the Atlantic. Those who shudder at the term 'Style' should mentally substitute the words 'Mainstream Modernism' whenever it is used.

Expressionism

Derived from interwar architecture in the Netherlands and northern Germany, a strange and often tortured attempt to fuse modernity with the Gothic, favouring Hanseatic brickwork, distorted forms, a continuation of craft tradition and a certain gutsy, angsty sense of weight, which appealed to those disturbed by modernism's upsetting of traditional architectural values, but who found neo-Georgian fey and uninteresting. In the hands of Giles Gilbert

Scott, this became an almost ubiquitous commercial and institutional architecture of the interwar years.

Classical Modernism

I use this to talk about fusions between modernism and classicism, which were particularly popular in interwar Italy, but which recur here and there throughout the twentieth century, particularly in the 1970s, right until the present day, as in, for instance, Patrick Lynch's **Zig Zag Building** in Victoria, completed in 2017. Colonnades, long flat roofs, 'discipline' – rational not in the sense of structure or technology but in an obvious inspiration from the rationalism of the eighteenth century.

Moderne

The commercial, bastardized versions of modernism, which in Britain usually outnumber actual International Style buildings by about ten to one. Odeon cinemas, Co-ops, light industry, mansion blocks and the odd suburban villa are the main places to see this tawdry and exciting architecture of fine facades and backsides you're not meant to look at.

Viennese

Grand courtyard buildings, usually symmetrical, always for interwar council housing, modelled on 'Red Vienna', with heroic imagery and axial drama, but without the retro gestures of Modern Classicism or the sexy commercialism of streamline moderne – the sturdy and thumping **Ossulston Estate** in London is the largest remaining example. Originally an explicit socialist architecture, in Britain it is usually a little more mainstream in its politics.

People's Detailing, Googie

'People's Detailing' was a waspish term used for the Communist-aligned, Swedish-influenced, picturesque modern architecture of the first decade after 1945: think of the **Royal Festival Hall**, with its combination of English eccentricities and thrilling space. Other terms meaning much the same thing include the dour 'New Empiricism' (which doesn't register the often decorative and populist nature of these buildings) and the self-explanatory 'Festival Style'. Googie, meanwhile, is a term originally devised to describe similarly populist, but more space-age fifties design in the US – diners in the shape of spaceships and the like, dramatic engineering, designed to be seen when driving past at speed. Anything with a fancy, oyster-like hyperbolic paraboloid roof is in this category, such as Sam Scorer's **Markham Moor Service Station**, of 1961.

Brutalism

Beginning in the London County Council of the 1950s with unpretentious, square and stubby concrete-framed flats, Brutalism developed by the sixties into an aggressive and monumental concrete expressionism that is responsible for most of the genuine masterpieces of twentieth-century architecture in Britain. Enduringly controversial for size, prominence, material (streaky, grey, harsh) and social use.

High-Tech

Glossy, steely architecture, largely for office blocks, developed by partly American-trained designers such as Richard Rogers, Norman Foster, Michael and Patricia Hopkins, and Nicholas Grimshaw, seen in the 1980s, not entirely stupidly, as a revival of the Great British Engineering Tradition of Brunel, Stephenson, Barlow and co. Responsible for some astonishing feats like **Lloyd's of London** and **Stansted Airport**, but gradually tending to become just another branch of mainstream corporate modernism.

Ecomodernism

From the humble **Solar Campus** built in the fifties in Wallasey in the Wirral, various kinds of ecological modernism have thrived at the fringes of British architecture, coming into their own in the 1970s with the lightweight timber-frame houses of Walter Segal. 'Sustainable architecture' today is often a gimmicky world of turfed wonky roofs and inept rain-screens, but there are several examples here of buildings whose architectural integrity matches their energy-saving credentials.

Postmodernism

Largely commercial, unashamedly kitsch, unafraid of all the things modernism supposedly ignores such as ornament, history and populism, but frequently cheap, nasty and unfunny in the way that only men in late middle age trying to be jolly and irreverent can be, Postmodernism is the 'funny tie' in the Brooks Brothers corporate cityscape. Responsible, as with the art deco it sometimes parodies, for some moments of naff grandeur, particularly in the work of CZWG (the **Cascades** flats in London's Docklands, 1987) and John Outram (the astonishing **Judge Institute**, Cambridge, of 1993). 'Pomo' for short.

Deconstructivism, Parametricism

Developed at the elite architecture schools initially as an impossible paper architecture of clashing volumes and non-orthogonal geometries, the work of such as Zaha Hadid, Daniel Libeskind, Frank Gehry and Peter Eisenman was made possible by the digitization of structural engineering. Usually the results are a matter of 'icons' on riversides, such as the Aquatics Centre in Stratford (2008–11) or the **Imperial War Museum North** in Trafford (1999–2002). These can tend to be facile, if occasionally thrilling. Closely linked to ...

Supermodernism, Pseudomodernism

Terms deployed to describe the various forms of modern architecture which emerged in those countries which didn't 'go Postmodernist' in the same way Britain did – Spain and the Netherlands most of all. Office blocks by Rem Koolhaas's Office for Metropolitan Architecture (**Rothschild's** in the City), bridges by Santiago Calatrava (connecting Manchester and Salford), libraries by Will Alsop (**Peckham Library**, 2000) – montages of colour, display and 'humour' but with none of Postmodernism's nods to the architectural past.

Modernist Eclectic

A term to describe the London mainstream of today, which could be applied to the brick-clad Expressionist tower blocks of **'King's Cross Central'**, the mannered, non-retro classicism of Caruso St John, the sense of repose and decorum in the work of David Chipperfield, or the rougher, 'as found' aesthetic of Haworth Tompkins. 'Rules' of modernism and classicism are seldom followed, but there is usually a rigour derived from intensive engagement with the urban environment around.

A NOTE ON NAMES

Architecture is always teamwork; but frequently the name of a firm of architects does not indicate who took the lead in designing the building, which can sometimes be the relatively personal project of particular talented individuals. When I know, I have credited that individual, as it makes no sense not to credit, say, Kate Macintosh with **Dawson Heights**, or Keith Ingham with **Preston Bus Station**, rather than the departments or firms they were working for; similarly, 'Basil Spence' certainly did not always design every Basil Spence building, the best work of 'Gillespie Kidd & Coia' was designed by Andy MacMillan and Isi Metzstein, and so on. Even so, there are many buildings where I will have failed to credit the actual rather than nominal designers, simply because the information is deep in some architect's archive.

A NOTE ON GEOGRAPHY

Britain is a hugely uneven country – the most unequal in Europe outside of the former Soviet Union – and now devolved, with significant centres of power in Cardiff and especially Edinburgh. A book on nineteenth-century architecture would exhibit a more level geographical spread, due to the industrial power of the English North and Midlands, South Wales, and Central Scotland, but in the twentieth century London has been overwhelmingly dominant. There are times when that dominance has faced some attempts at redress – the 1945–79 period, and to a more tokenistic degree in the 1997–2010 New Labour era – but in the 1920s and '30s, the 1980s and '90s, and in the 2010s, it is very hard to find significant modern buildings outside London and its commuter hinterland. The over-representation of London and the South-East in this book compared with, say, Wales or south-west England is not an endorsement of that inequality so much as a reluctant statement of fact. I have, however, aimed for as even a geographical spread as possible.

Public accessibility has been a criterion in the choice of buildings. Many of the private houses by important architects that might appear in a guide to listed buildings have no public access, and are up long and usually heavily guarded pathways and driveways or behind rows of high hedges. There are houses by, for instance, Marcel Breuer, Jørn Utzon and Walter Gropius that are not in this book, because there's no chance you'll get to actually see them unless you've somehow managed to make personal arrangements with their owners to do so. I have no interest in sending people up private driveways to catch a glimpse from a distance of a modernist house in the outer Home Counties before the dogs get set on them. However, several houses in rural or outer suburban areas do feature here if they're properly visible from publicly accessible paths. I've also tried to indicate where possible whether you can explore a building's interior and whether you can't. Readers should also note when preparing to visit places mentioned in this book that Google Streetview is often deceptive – its cameras are carried on cars, so tend not to cover the pedestrianized spaces of precincts, council estates and new towns.

The meanings of 'Britain' and 'the United Kingdom' as used in this book are a little loose, and so need explanation. The whole of the island of Great Britain is here, which is not controversial – English, Welsh and Scottish architecture can be radically different, but have influenced each other in productive and important ways. On the subject of debatable lands, I have *mostly* included those peripheral parts of the country that are in the United Kingdom and send representatives to Westminster, and not those which are self-governing Crown Possessions or Overseas Territories. So Shetland, Orkney and the Isle of Wight are all in here, but the Isle of Man and the Channel Islands are not. I have, however, left out the two parts of the UK (broadly conceived) which are geographically part of other countries – Gibraltar and Northern Ireland. The latter was a particularly tough decision, as Belfast in particular is a remarkable city, a combination of the virtues and vices of Manchester, Glasgow and Dublin, and it has participated in all the major movements in British architecture over the last century in some way – occasionally in the vanguard. Taken as a whole, though, Northern Ireland's architecture belongs to Ireland. I hope someone includes it at some point in *Modern Buildings in Ireland*.

1. GREATER LONDON

National Theatre, South Bank (p. 84)

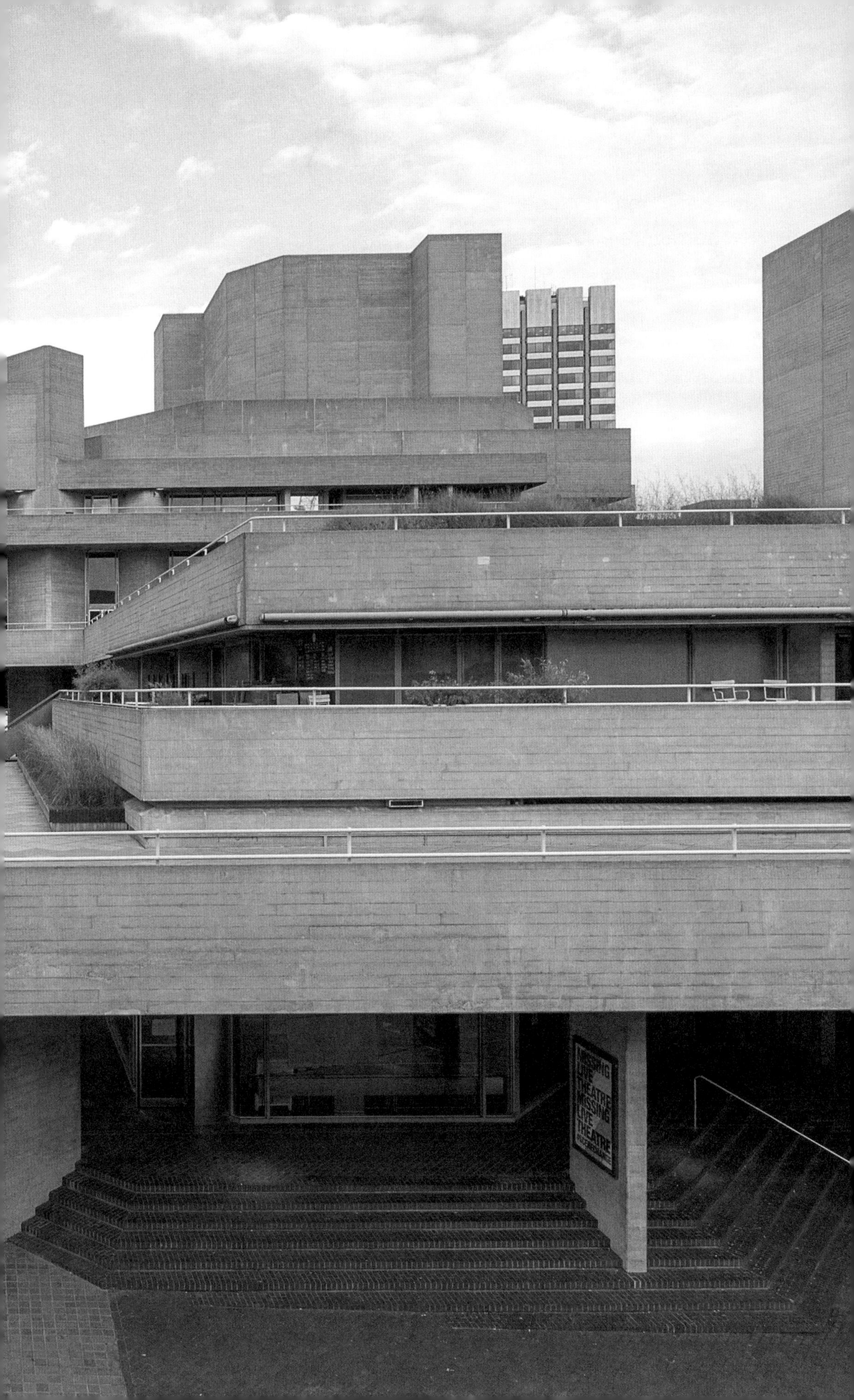
MISSING
LIVE
THEATRE
MISSING
LIVE
THEATRE

London was a late starter in modern architecture – you'll find many more proto-modernist buildings in Liverpool or Glasgow, and even the early International Style is better represented in Essex and Hertfordshire – but from the second half of the 1930s until the present day the capital has not ceased to be a global centre for modernism. It is in London that the generation of exiles who brought modernism to this island created their best buildings, from **Spa Green** to **Trellick Tower**. However, it has always been the case that most of the better work can be found outside the obvious places. The City's many tall office blocks range from the sublime to the ridiculous, and only the remarkable **Lloyd's of London building** is of the very first rank; the West End's better modern edifices tend to be small in scale. No major public or government institution has ever built a great modern building here, with the notable exceptions of the **British Library** and the **National Theatre**.

Outside the centre, however, the capital has an embarrassment of modernist architectural riches. The best of Charles Holden's modernist Tube stations are found in the outskirts, at **Arnos Grove**, **Gants Hill** or **Osterley**. Many boroughs have more great buildings of the twentieth century than cities four or five times their size, and it's worth noting that these derive more from local governments and elected councils than 'starchitects' – the extensive public works of the London County Council, the schools and libraries of 1930s Middlesex, the warm brick housing of 1960s Lambeth and the high-modernist estates of 1970s Camden. It is in these apparently humble places that you will find the best London has to offer.

CENTRAL LONDON

KODAK HOUSE, HOLBORN
Burnet & Tait, 1910–11
Chicago School

Kingsway was a London County Council slum clearance project, carving a wide boulevard through the rookeries around Holborn and Covent Garden, and then lining it with offices for the colonies, the BBC and various industries – architecturally, it is in a bombastic late-imperial style that even classicists tend to find rather stale and overbearing. There is one block which at the time stood out as relatively contemporary – the offices of the Kodak company, pioneers of a 'modern' technology. It looks conventional now, but at the time it was notable for the way its Scottish architects followed American skyscraper designers in refusing to pretend the building was made purely of stone. Instead, these four storeys of offices with a high-ceilinged showroom on the ground floor were clad in a grid of glass-and-bronze panels, fringed in the Portland stone that is sloppily applied across its neighbours. You can see this is cladding, and the steel frame underneath is implied by the regularity of the grid. But the values of the building are still faintly classical – rectitude, order, poise. If it points forward to any modernist architecture, it's to the kind of serene machine rationalism that gave us, say, Sheffield's **Arts Tower (p. 369)**, or, as Christopher Woodward and Edward Jones suggest, the stone-clad classical-brutalist hybrid of the Smithsons' **Economist Plaza (p. 58);** ironically, since the 1960s it has been neighbour to a much kitschier modernism, in the form of Richard Seifert's pop art **Space House (p. 59)**.

HOLLAND HOUSE, CITY ✪
Hendrik Petrus Berlage, 1916
Expressionist

This small building for a Dutch shipping line, now round the back of Norman Foster's 'Gherkin' **(30 St Mary Axe, p. 73)**, is the only evidence in Britain – after the decline of Charles Rennie Mackintosh at any rate – of the early development of the European Modern Movement, which otherwise arrived here almost fully formed fifteen years later. Berlage, from his Amsterdam Stock Exchange (1896–1903) onwards, favoured a pared-down Gothic whose minimalism increasingly emphasized structure and repetition rather than craft and irregularity. Holland House shows his work at a dreamlike stage close to the Expressionists of the 'Amsterdam School'. A steel frame mirrored by a grey-green tile grid, and a geometric wipe-clean interior like Frank Lloyd Wright designing a Victorian public toilet. Industrial and intense, and with a stylized relief of a ship at the corner, it seems to have been almost completely ignored at the time, and is easily missed today. **[A.2]**

———

ADELAIDE HOUSE, CITY
Burnet & Tait, 1921–5
Chicago School

Strict height limits were introduced on London's buildings in the 1890s, explicitly to stop the building of skyscrapers – that's why the only real pre-war skyscraper on this island is the **Royal Liver Building (p. 424)**. However, this remarkable office block in the City is nearly an exception, so clearly does it follow American precedent in its design, its technology and its dramatic scale. It is also perhaps the clearest tribute in Britain to the great American early modernist

Louis Sullivan, both to his essay 'The Tall Building, Artistically Considered' and to his skyscrapers in Chicago, St Louis and Buffalo. As Sullivan had recommended, the building follows the logic of being divided, like a classical column, into a 'base' of granite, facing the river, a 'capital', in the form of the Egyptian-style top storey, and a shaft, in the form of the repetitive seven storeys of offices in-between. But, moreover, the architects – as at **Kodak House (p. 47)**, the Scottish designers J. J. Burnet and Thomas Tait – have also taken care to express the steel frame that lies beneath, by treating most of the block's eleven storeys as a grid, albeit one then encased by giant Portland stone pylons at the corners. Yet what is really exciting about the building is its interaction with London Bridge. The main entrance, with its looming figures, and neo-Egyptian dressings, is entered directly from the Bridge's north-east corner; and it is on the ground level by the river that you can most feel the building's vast bulk. A road not taken, perhaps, where modernism could have been derived from America rather than France and Germany, it has a few Egyptian-Modern cousins, such as **Ideal House (p. 49)** in Soho.

PICCADILLY CIRCUS UNDERGROUND STATION
Charles Holden, 1925–8
Modern Classicism

The start of the great adventure in design that was the London Underground under Frank Pick and Charles Holden – which at this distance seems like the most significant modernist experiment in the interwar capital – never quite going all the way into continental avant-gardism, but with similar ambitions to unite art, architecture and everyday life into a well-functioning, quietly delightful whole. At Piccadilly Circus, Holden and the Underground's engineers took a typically messy old Tube station and

re-created it into a mirroring of the circular public space above. The use of travertine, and the circularity, make Piccadilly Circus Station rather restful for a place so constantly packed – a sort of heavenly anteroom in a perpetual rotating motion. Stop at the map showing the time in all the world's cities, though, and the movement slows, as you concentrate on the dated graphic. You stand still and watch time shift, as the tourists zip around you.

GROSVENOR ESTATE, PIMLICO
Edwin Lutyens, 1928
Modern Classicism

The great neoclassical imperial architect – planner and designer of New Delhi – Edwin Lutyens only once designed social housing, which is a shame, as he proved to be very good at it. The Grosvenor Estate takes up two blocks between the Houses of Parliament and the Tate Gallery, with a series of cubic tenements dressed in a chequerboard pattern to the street, and accessed by the sort of long decks that Alison and Peter Smithson were later to re-imagine as 'streets in the sky'. At ground level, the estate has a Lewis Carroll quality, a giant puzzle. The monumental repetition is offset by little baroque doorways and gateposts, which push the scheme away from any conventional definition of 'modernism', just as the abstraction, repetition, spaciousness and egalitarianism push closer to it than anything else in Lutyens's career. Owned and built by the Duke of Westminster, this remains social housing due to a 1980s court case in which the Conservative Westminster Council tried unsuccessfully to prove that its original purpose as 'housing for the working class' was obsolete because the working class no longer existed.

IDEAL HOUSE, SOHO
Raymond Hood with Gordon Jeeves, 1928
Moderne

Few major American architects have designed really first-rate buildings in Britain, and some of them have graced us with the worst work of their career, as with Eero Saarinen's foul, fascistic US Embassy in Grosvenor Square. That makes this building all the more delightful, a piquant deco office block at the corner where Soho meets Regent Street, designed by the architect of such megalopolitan masterworks as the Rockefeller Center and the Daily News Building. Originally built for the American Radiator Company, Ideal House consists of six storeys of dark, shiny, Gotham-style black granite-clad offices, its minimalism seeming deeply radical and alien from a distance. But, up close, you'll find that starkness and abstraction have been offset with glazed tiles arranged in faintly Egyptian patterns along the entrances, across the ground floor and decorating the rooftop cornice. Most strikingly of all, the building's placing opposite the Mock Tudor of Liberty's department store is the two faces of mainstream interwar British architecture – tawdry Transatlantic glamour, facing off against a retrogressive dreamworld, but both in thrall to commerce and consumerism.

———

CRAWFORD'S, HIGH HOLBORN
Frederick Etchells, 1929
International Style

The most architecturally convincing of the several candidates for 'first modernist building in London', this corner block just off Kingsway was designed by a former Vorticist painter, who would later become a more traditionalist architect. Here, the sharp edges and machine-made materials show a hard-line conception of modernism rooted in the fragmented aggression of the 'men of 1914'.

The chrome strips of the faceted windows have a particular machine-Gothic elegance. Little survives of the original interior, the building is dilapidated by central London standards and there is an inferior, slightly later copy of it next door.

———

SHELL-MEX HOUSE, EMBANKMENT
Joseph's, 1930–31
EMBANKMENT PLACE
Terry Farrell & Partners, 1985–90
Art Deco, Modern Classicism, Postmodernist

Two obnoxious buildings – self-important, unwieldy, slightly silly – which have enough interesting ideas and strength of character to make them perversely enjoyable. Shell Mex House forms part of a mini-Park Avenue on Embankment Gardens of near-skyscraper sized neoclassical buildings – along with the Adelphi and the Savoy – that have a real big-city grandeur about them; Shell-Mex is the best of the three largely just because of the ziggurat clock tower on top, with its fez-wearing clock-bearing figures on either side, easily missed until you notice them for the first time. Embankment Place is on the same scale, an ultra-exploitative 'air rights' superstructure built on top of Charing Cross station, casting its platforms at Charing Cross into permanent darkness; what makes it exciting is, first, the overwhelming scale. It was clearly intended as the fourth of a group of pyramids of power on the north bank of the Thames, which Farrell manages with megalomaniac mastery. What you don't notice from a distance is that this giant hulk encloses one of the strangest pedestrian routes in London. Paths run below, in Victorian archways, and above, in the new walkway, with oblique views into the complex below. It also gives views of a Victorian precursor, of the amazing glazed pedway that shoots off from the Charing Cross Hotel. It's one of Central London's most unusual examples of the *promenade architecturale*.

The sleek 1930s modernism of Ellis & Clarke's building for the *Daily Express*, engineered by Owen Williams.

DAILY EXPRESS BUILDING, FLEET STREET ✪
Ellis & Clarke with Owen Williams, 1933
International Style, Moderne

An attention-grabbing, sinister and sexy integrated office and printing house for the right-wing populist newspaper (which moved from here some decades ago). It is real modern architecture – devoid of the sort of piquant attempts to continue the classical language in jazzed-up form that you can see a few doors up at the *Daily Telegraph's* contemporaneous HQ – but without using any of the clichés of modernism, no white walls, no strip windows, no Bauhaus or Corbusier cribs. Though the building is credited to Ellis & Clarke, the structure is the work of Owen Williams, a notoriously bluff engineer and nobody's acolyte. To the street, it's a symmetrical, curved ziggurat of black glass, vitrolite and chrome, their sheen giving off plenty of the sex appeal of the inorganic; appropriately, it is advertising architecture. It was designed as an image of modernity, one which the *Express* would frequently exploit in its own publicity, right up until the 1980s when the press exodus from Fleet Street happened to coincide with its middle-England readership becoming newly hostile to modernist buildings. However, Williams's elegant and undecorated modernist structure is a little deceptive. Step inside – if you can, the building is only seldom opened to the public – and the timelessness of the exterior is replaced by the designer Robert Atkinson with a hilariously opulent art deco fantasia, crass and fun; it captures as much of the spirit of the thirties as the sweeping lines of the facade. There are more complex and slightly later versions of the same design at Glasgow **(p. 518)** and Manchester **(p. 400)**.

SIMPSON'S, PICCADILLY
Joseph Emberton, 1934–6
International Style

In Prague, Paris, Stuttgart or Bucharest there
are about ten of these each, but we have just
the one in London, so we must cherish it.
The former Simpson's department store is an
impeccable European commercial building of
its period. Tall, occupying a narrow frontage,
its elevations are reduced to strips of glass
and Portland stone, on a steel frame – chic,
minimal, luxurious, and ascending to another
level entirely in its gorgeous five-storey
stairwell, with glass, chrome, red vitrolite and
a full height Bauhaus chromium light fitting,
fully worthy of the buildings it is referencing.
Very well restored as a Waterstones – enjoy
the preserved lift signage in particular.

IBEX HOUSE, CITY
Fuller Hall & Foulsham, 1933–7
Moderne

A great cruiser of streamlined, strip-
windowed, glazed-stairwelled offices at
the south-eastern edge of the City, before it
starts to crumble into the East End. Its curves
of yellow and black faïence and Crittall
windows are all retrofuturist period charm,
but the industrial scale of the building takes
it somewhere other than seaside pavilions
and Odeon cinemas, into an H. G. Wells
world of perfectly functioning machinery
and lacquered hairstyles. There are some
obvious cribs from the tile-clad ripples
of Berlin's pre-Hitler Shell-Haus, but what
it really resembles is the big, mechanized
warehouses along the Hudson River in
Manhattan; as early as this, modernism
in London's financial centre was about
American dreams, not European realities.

SENATE HOUSE, BLOOMSBURY ⊙
Charles Holden, 1932–7
Modern Classicism

An endlessly fascinating building. Designed
as a headquarters for the University of
London at the behest of its then chair
William Beveridge, Senate House was the
closest thing interwar London had to any
kind of skyscraper, at eighteen storeys
of Portland stone, with narrow, high
Georgian windows, a flat roof and a stepped,
buttressed profile creating the pyramidal
effect that the New York Zoning Code had
imposed as a measure to avoid its densely
packed skyscrapers throwing shadow
on to the street, but here it is all done for
a more functional reason. Those buttresses
are actually structural; almost uniquely
for a building of this kind, Senate House
is not a steel or concrete frame building
with the stone applied – it's a tower of pure
stone, going up about as high as a masonry
building will before it becomes dangerous.
At the same time it was being built, Holden
was designing real modernist buildings,
in the terrific series of stations on the outer
reaches of the **Piccadilly Line (p. 137)**; but
an architecture of red brick and plate glass
was evidently considered inappropriate
for a Great University. This was to be
a showpiece, and was initially intended
to be one part of a much wider Portland
stone complex of towers for the University
of London, one which you can see in the
original model on display in the ceremonial
hall. The dull, low-rise brick buildings
around Malet Street were Holden's post-war
austerity attempt to finish the task off.

It was also meant to be eternal, to stand
aside from fashion, whether it was modernism
or Lutyens's fey games with the classical
tradition. But as soon as you're in Senate
House, either approaching it from Russell
Square or from Store Street (where it is
almost, but not quite, on a monumental axis),
the building screams 1930s like nothing else,

caught somewhere between an English rationalist bureaucracy and something more sinister – in its crystalline purity and deathly pallor there is more than a little of Mussolini's Rome, and in its ziggurat profile more than a hint of Stalin's unbuilt Palace of the Soviets. Inside, it is the fittings that really establish the atmosphere – the beautiful woodwork, the chilling travertine public foyer that is also a public right of way under the building, and the serifs urging 'SILENCE'. You can smell the Spam and the Woodbines. Eternal it may be, but it reflects the values and ideas of its era with unparalleled intensity, much more than the pure modernist buildings of that decade. **[D.9]**

———

FINSBURY HEALTH CENTRE
Lubetkin and Tecton, 1938
Constructivist, International Style,
People's Detailing

This is a building of enormous significance, being both one of the great propaganda coups of modern architecture – a well-publicized, attractive showcase of both modernist and socialist social planning, that would even feature on a Second World War poster – and one of the founding buildings of the NHS, free at the point of use a decade before Aneurin Bevan introduced a similar system across the country. But visiting Finsbury Health Centre is an uncomfortable experience. It is tiny, far more monumental in photographs; its facade is almost hidden by the trees that were planted to import some healthy air into noxious Finsbury; it is dilapidated, having nearly been sold off a few years ago and with the local NHS trust not having the funds to restore it properly; and, to add insult to injury, it faces a hideous street of Postmodernist suburban houses covered in 'Beware of the Dog' signs and St George's flags. They seem to have been built opposite the Health Centre as some sort of Thatcherite hex on this emblem

of modernist optimism, but they're actually the product of a 1980s local authority, which is even worse somehow, a baby boomer New Left poking its tongue out at its Welfare State elders. So it's a hard building to enjoy, but it does still manage to communicate, particularly through its casual levity: the little roof terrace, the neo-Victorian typography and the light, elegant tiling, all of which avoid the heaviness and pomposity of 1930s bureaucracy. It promises that health and equality are about being carefree.

———

SPA GREEN, FINSBURY ✪
Lubetkin and Tecton, 1938–49
Constructivist, People's Detailing

Tecton planned an estate on this site before the war, intended to be of a piece with the nearby **Finsbury Health Centre (above)**. When redesigned after the war, Spa Green was transformed by Lubetkin into a mini-manifesto of what the modernist city would be like. International Style severity and the white-walled purity of **Highpoint (p. 139)** were by now completely rejected, in favour of an architecture of generous spaces, individual touches, decorative flourishes and, most of all, entrances. You never feel anywhere in this small estate like you're at the mercy of an impersonal bureaucracy; the small details are all there to create warmth, specificity, identification. It's no wonder that Bevan selected this place as the location for a speech in which he asserted that post-war governments would be judged not by how many houses they build, but how well they build them. These three blocks – huge flats, in two slabs, arranged into a 'Caucasian carpet' pattern of brick and tile, and with one sinuous low-rise block snaking between them, all among tall trees – could never be standardized or universalized. They were for this place, at this time.

The sinuous low-rise blocks of Lubetkin and Tecton's Spa Green Estate, opened by Nye Bevan in 1949.

INSTITUT FRANÇAIS, SOUTH KENSINGTON

Patrice Bonnet, 1939
Moderne, Expressionist

The cultural centre, cinema and library of the Institut Français stand in the stuccoed Italianate streets of upper-class French diaspora South Ken, the area of bistros and boulangeries where Roman Polanski shot *Repulsion*. Architecturally, it's a big break with all those white-plastered facades – red brick, and in an extraordinary Expressionistic variant of art deco. A small block dominated by the high, faceted windows of the library, with the brick shaped into a Grand Guignol version of Gothic tracery, conceals an opulent marble interior and artworks by major French modernists. The finest of these is the abstract Sonia Delaunay tapestry that adorns the stairwell. The effect is both classy and eccentric.

CHURCHILL GARDENS, PIMLICO

Powell & Moya, 1946–62
International Style

One of the first estates built after the war and executed with remarkably little deviation from the original ideas over a decade and a half, this is the post-war new world at its purest, a logical, modular, unpretentious blueprint for rebuilding cities without sentimentality, profit, hierarchy or history. It has always been popular with both residents and critics, which is strange on the face of it, given that this is the basic blueprint for the ordinary, workaday council estate of the 1950s and '60s – serried slabs on the Weimar German *Zeilenbau* ('line-building') principle, tall and wide, but with their giant scale 'humanized' through stock brick, and given a certain dash through fully glazed stairwells. Lower blocks, maisonettes, trees and playgrounds are placed around the slabs, giving them some pedestrian activity. The only unique things about it are the accumulator tower, which once brought energy from **Battersea Power Station (p. 108)** over the river directly into the new homes, and of course the Thameside location. Perversely, the slabs turn their sides to the river, so that views are only oblique. It's average, but a very good average, and one which the new plutocratic blocks opposite could never hope to 'aspire' to. The late low-rise block on Lupus Street that leads you into the estate from Italianate Pimlico is particularly clever, marking a border between the two kinds of city, a rupture as much as a link, but one where it isn't painful to travel between the two sides. The estate is also very easily seen as a totality – any train coming into Victoria Station has a complete view of them in enfilade, to the right.

The complex patterns of Skinner Bailey & Lubetkin's Bevin Court – which was nearly named after Lenin.

BEVIN COURT, FINSBURY ⊙
Skinner Bailey & Lubetkin, 1948–52
Constructivist, People's Detailing

Berthold Lubetkin emigrated from the Soviet Union in the early 1920s, and worked as an architectural attaché for the Soviet government in Paris before moving to London at the start of the 1930s; he was a rare pro-Soviet Russian émigré in London. Bevin Court is where he tried to make that explicit. This Y-plan block of flats on a bombsite surrounded by Georgian fragments is a ready-made architectural-historical myth, frontloaded with so much politics and tragedy it can be hard to appraise just as a building in and of itself. It is just off the neoclassical Percy Circus, where Lenin lived for a time in the 1900s. To commemorate this fact, in 1942, during the period of Soviet–British–American alliance, Finsbury Borough Council commissioned Lubetkin and Tecton to design a memorial. With a

nice recognition of the interchangeability of Soviet iconography, Lubetkin made it a frame for a standardized bust of Vladimir Ilyich, which could be replaced when the memorial would be vandalized by the local branch of the British Union of Fascists.

After the area was bombed, Tecton planned Lenin Court to be the centrepiece of the district. As it started to be constructed after 1946, austerity measures saw balconies and materials pared down, although the decorative treatment, a rhythm of concrete, brick and tile, remained. Lubetkin then put everything into the design of the central staircase – an almost superfluous gesture, given that most people in this multistorey building would be using the lifts. The staircase is the most stunning piece of Constructivist sculpture ever created outside the USSR, an assemblage of intersecting cylinders, constantly moving and shifting as you circle up or down it, with open viewing platforms to let in air and panoramas of

London. On the ground floor is a surrealist mural by Peter Yates – later of the important Newcastle-based firm Ryder & Yates – and a bust of Lenin's replacement, Ernest Bevin. As the Cold War heated up, having a new building named after Lenin was no longer quite so politic. As Lubetkin's partner Francis Skinner pointed out, they only had to change two letters to rename it after Bevin, a former trade union leader and anti-Communist Foreign Secretary, who died in 1951. The memorial was removed from Percy Circus, and the story – too good not to be true – is that Lubetkin buried one of the busts beneath the staircase, where its energy charges the kinetic geometry above. [C.5 & C.6]

CONGRESS HOUSE, BLOOMSBURY
David Du Roi Aberdeen, 1948–56
International Style

The major building of the British labour movement is, no doubt appropriately, a compromise and, similarly justly, a product of the Attlee-era peak of the Trade Union Congress's power and influence. The building sits between the 1930s and the 1950s; its classically proportioned, severe stone-clad street frontage is the official modernist building we never actually had before the war. A little staid, for sure, but very elegantly made. The sculptural representation of solidarity above the entrance canopy by Bernard Meadows is basically Socialist Realism – a burly figure lifting up one who has been thrown to the floor by his employer. What makes it is the side elevation, where the strait-laced front whips round into a complex, Lubetkin-style composition of floating, tilted balconies and blue tile-clad curves. This is also the only place that pedestrians (even subs-paying ones) can catch a glimpse of the building's famous courtyard, where a black granite dais and a shimmering honeycomb of glass bricks frame Jacob Epstein's awesome *Pietà*

– one of the sculptor's harshest and most cubistic works, a vehement statement of injustice and mourning. The rage is kept in an alleyway at the TUC, but it's there.

219 OXFORD STREET
Ronald Ward & Partners, 1951–2
International Style, People's Detailing

This tiny office and retail building in the heart of tourist London is one of the most vivid of the many remnants of the Festival of Britain, hidden in plain sight from the millions that pass it daily. Four storeys, grey stone panels and a sharp curved corner, this is a typical late-thirties retail building realized over a decade too late, but a very elegant one, with lovely detailing to its delicately rounded metal windows, and it was recently well restored as a flagship Zara store. Yet what makes it worth risking stopping in the middle of Oxford Street for is the sculptural low-relief panels celebrating the Festival. Many plaques with the Festival's Britannia logo still exist, but there is only this that combines it with images of the Festival's buildings – abstracted reliefs of the **Royal Festival Hall (p. 84)**, and the demolished Dome of Discovery and Skylon. This example of chic interwar modernism carries on its facade images of the cute and decorative Anglicized modernism that would replace it.

GOLDEN LANE ESTATE, CLERKENWELL ✪
Chamberlin Powell & Bon, 1952–61
International Style, Brutalism

A small estate that is one of the most interesting in Britain, not so much for its buildings – which are decent enough, primary-coloured, clipped International Style blocks around a tall tower, tallest in London, very briefly – but for the approach to public space. This was the first work of Chamberlin

Modernist social housing in the City: one of the blocks of Chamberlin Powell & Bon's Golden Lane Estate.

Powell & Bon, who actually formed as a response to the open competition run by the City of London for the site. This became famous for Alison and Peter Smithson's 'streets in the sky' entry, which was placed second. Chamberlin Powell & Bon, like the runners-up, made three-dimensional public space the most important element of their design, but did so in a way that is – especially compared with the Smithsons' own **Robin Hood Gardens (p. 130)** – easy, intuitive and relaxed.

Perhaps that's because there's no overriding principle, no overarching system of circulation, just a series of little squares and greens, which are, throughout, at multiple levels, creating a constant sense of discovery as you walk through them. This three-dimensionality is extended to the public buildings in the estate, like the swimming pool that lies below, but is visible from, one of the public paths; it can even be found in the sculptural relief maps attached to walls in corners of the estate, a unique feature that was bafflingly seldom emulated by subsequent housing schemes. The last part of the estate, Crescent House, continues the wonderfully crisp, colourful fenestration of the earlier blocks but, in everything else, moves in a very different Brutalist direction, from machine-tooled precision and clarity into rough surfaces in bush-hammered concrete, deep galleries and colonnades, and a baroque approach to form, with a great sweeping curve to the street, with shops on the ground floor. In location and in approach it is both an architectural and practical connection between Golden Lane and the same architects' later **Barbican (p. 66)** just next door. The similarity of finish between this place, an ordinary (though thoroughly Right-to-Buyed) estate, and that always-bourgeois project speaks very well of the architects. [A.12]

WOOD STREET POLICE STATION, CITY ❶
McMorran & Whitby, 1963
Modern Classicism

Classical more than modernist, but so clever in its fusion of the two styles that it would be churlish to keep it out. Here, one of the most imaginative neoclassical firms of their day – which sounds like faint praise, but isn't – respond to the modernist typology of the high-rise tower elevated on a podium that keeps the same scale as the rest of the street around it. Here, the podium is a Mannerist palazzo, an artful and rich little structure, that is in no way modernist; the fabulous tower, on the other hand, could have taught a lot of modern architects a few lessons about minimalism and proportion. It's a de Chirico dream of the Italian ideal city scaled up into an unpretentious high-rise, functional and haunting. At the time of writing there are proposals by the Met's useless inhouse architects to ruin the clarity of the tower so that Babylon can have a little more office space.

HIDE TOWER, PIMLICO
Stillman & Eastwick-Field, 1962
Brutalism, International Style

Imagine this one being built today. Twenty-three storeys of council flats in-between Parliament and the Tate, overlooking a dozen or so government office blocks, all in unfussy, functional concrete, without a decorative hat on top or any aspiration to 'landmark' status – just simple, plain, straight-up housing. It's more than just a matter of negative virtues, though, this one – the concrete is smooth and has aged well despite little maintenance, and the double-height entrance, past the pilotis, creates a feeling of importance, of arrival and repose, that was sadly rare in council towers.

LILLINGTON GARDENS, PIMLICO ❂
Darbourne & Darke, 1961–80
Brutalism

As widely praised as the nearby **Churchill Gardens (p. 53)**, while being seen as a pivot away from everything that place represented – a singular, one-shot redevelopment of a specific area in a specific way, deliberately unrepeatable and unique, one singular but complex, multilevel but low-rise, megastructure in warm brick, enclosing small gardens and squares. Locality, not internationalism; intimacy, not epic space. It is often described as 'vernacular' modernism, although the use of this dubious term – which implies picking up on the common, low 'speech' of an area in what you, the professional, build in it – is, as always, obfuscatory. What Darbourne & Darke took as the key to the area wasn't the stuccoed Italianate terraces that actually dominate Pimlico, but one single building – G. E. Street's tremendous Hanseatic Gothic church of St James the Less, of 1858. The rich black and red brickwork, the asymmetry, and the care to create an interesting and complicated skyline are all taken directly from here; the flats of the new estate are staggered and cantilevered to frame it to maximum effect, through a series of alleys and pocket-sized squares. It's as artificial and modern a project as the heroic slabs on the river, and has almost as little to do with the historic area and the historic architecture, and that's fine. What it is, like many 'alternative' projects of the sixties, is an argument within modernism.

A side-effect, incidentally, of the naming of each block after a thespian is that this estate has the campest council blocks in London. Noël Coward House? [C.16]

UNIVERSITY OF WESTMINSTER, CAVENDISH CAMPUS, FITZROVIA ✪

Lyons Israel Ellis, 1962–70
Brutalist

Lyons Israel Ellis was one of several prolific and creative post-war firms – also including Yorke Rosenberg & Mardall, Robert Matthew Johnson-Marshall, Building Design Partnership, Chamberlin Powell & Bon – who managed to become the architects tasked with designing the Welfare State. Unlike these others, Lyons Israel Ellis did not outlast the 1970s, so have an unblemished record, seemingly only having built to the highest grade, largely for worthy clients, with no gold-tinted glass City offices or pink Timmy Mallett palazzos at the back end of their archives. This is one of their biggest projects, originally designed as a College of Engineering for what was then Regent Street Polytechnic. It makes an interesting contrast with the University of Leicester's **Engineering Building (p. 348)**, by their former employees James Stirling and James Gowan. Whereas that modernist icon in the Midlands is cerebral and intriguing, the London building uses what, on the page, could seem like a similar assemblage of cantilevered lecture theatres, neo-medieval service towers and glazed workshops to far more visceral effect, all heaviness, raw concrete surfaces, squat and bulky forms, and a much greater feeling of compressed, energetic action. You feel it in the gut. If I had to choose between the two, it'd be this one. [B.5]

ECONOMIST PLAZA, ST JAMES'S ✪

Alison and Peter Smithson, 1964
Brutalist, International Style

Located in an old-money part of central London, this was an experiment where the Smithsons tried to apply their theories about modernist planning to a dense and historic site. Rather than just starting anew and creating a fragment of utopia, or creating a nobly isolated tower on a plinth, they took a montage approach. The dominants from a distance are the two towers; but the real fun is on ground level. A low-rise block faces the eighteenth-century Boodles Club; between the towers, the low-rise block and the Georgian club is a raised plaza with steps down to the street. It's surely one of the best places in London for a fag break. It's this planning that makes this the most convincing of all the Smithsons' buildings, and the one where the gap between their flair as theorists and their abilities as architects is least glaring. As form, it's memorable not so much for the chamfered modular grid used on all the buildings as the fossil-filled facing stone used throughout: pale, gentle and fascinating – you could have a great time looking at all those little fossilized crustaceans for the duration of

The Smithsons' Economist Plaza, where the pioneer Brutalists reveal themselves as closet Classicists.

your cigarette before going back into the building to produce some more neoliberal propaganda. Or not – the *Economist* recently moved out of the building, presumably to move into something cheap and nasty. After all, if your job is to demand that everyone else race to the bottom, why not practise what you preach? [A.3 & A.4]

POST OFFICE TOWER, FITZROVIA
Eric Bedford, 1961–4
International Style

Daft and gawky, but also original and appropriately beacon-like, this space-age *Stadtkrone* is ungainly compared with the telecommunications towers of Central Europe or North America, but it also does something they don't. There is a cylindrical office block in the shaft that leads up to the satellites, with the obligatory revolving restaurant on top of that – a realized vision

Eric Bedford's Post Office Tower, montaged rudely but elegantly into the Georgian squares of Fitrovia.

of the utopian architecture of *Thunderbirds*. The Piccadilly Circus neon displays at the top are an appropriate *Blade Runner* touch. When one approaches the city, it says 'LONDON!!!!' louder and prouder than any other building of its time.

SPACE HOUSE, HOLBORN
George Marsh for R. Seifert & Partners, 1964–6
International Style

Space House forms part of Kingsway, a planned Edwardian boulevard along Parisian lines, with strict lines of trees and mandatory Portland stone, either an impressive effort in architectural co-ordination or a prefiguring of the dullest aspects of middle-of-the-road twentieth-century urbanism. Within the building's planning, you can detect a 'developer's architect' working out how to grab as much lettable space as possible from within the confines of the plan. The rectangular Kingsway facade is clad in seven smooth storeys of granite, but, behind, a two-storey overhead walkway connects it to a tall tower, of sixteen storeys – originally intended to be double that height. In the process, Seifert helped Harry Hyams to get around three times the profit that the developers of the adjacent classical schemes could expect. But Seifert – or rather, here, his partner George Marsh – managed to service more than just the client. Space House is full of street details, things to catch and excite the pedestrian eye, from the splayed legs of the pilotis to the abstract relief on the granite side of the mid-rise block, to the prefabricated op art surface of the cylindrical tower, creating an illusion of constant motion. In Marsh's hands, it's flashy, classless, dated and hugely enjoyable; in lesser ones, the results of such land-grabbing could be distinctly less attractive.

CENTRE POINT, HOLBORN
George Marsh for R. Seifert & Partners, 1963–6
EUSTON TOWER
Sidney Kaye, 1965–70
International Style

Two very different towers at either end of Tottenham Court Road, one always visible from the other. Centre Point, the better known of the two, is one of George Marsh's works for Richard Seifert, and another essay in gaming the planning system; the product of commercial graft and cynicism, and another architectural triumph. The story is well known. The developer Harry Hyams couldn't charge as much as he thought the offices were worth, so it sat empty for over a decade until, rather appropriately, the CBI moved in; in the interim it had become a symbol of warped priorities, especially to the homelessness charity which took its name from the scandal. Meanwhile, the usual Seifert maximum profit, minimum public approach led to the bizarre ground floor space, where an attractive, Brazilian-style sculpture garden and fountain practically pushed pedestrians into the path of buses careering down Charing Cross Road. The slender profile and the sculptural, pre-cast pieces create a constantly warping, rippling visual effect.

At the other end of the same road, another corporate tower with a dodgy past, as its developer gamed the system by agreeing to pay for adjacent highway improvements in exchange for planning permission. The two are a study in architectural contrasts, as much as they share the same commercial values. Centre Point's inspiration is Brazil, and Oscar Niemeyer's warping of the International Style into something decorative, flashy and sexy; Euston Tower is 1960s New York, modelled like one of Gordon Bunshaft's clean and hard glass prisms, a skin to wrap around, rather than a dense clothing to enclose. It is the best of

its kind in London, still a vision of machine-made clarity. Neither tower should have been built, and certainly not in this way; but this part of London would miss them if they were gone. Centre Point was recently renovated as flats, which suitably, given its history, are mostly unlet. The beautiful and appallingly placed pool was removed for a Crossrail station.

———

PEDWAYS, CITY
Corporation of London Architects/William Holford/Terry Farrell & Partners/Chamberlin Powell & Bon/Powell & Moya/Basil Spence, Bonnington & Collins/Make, 1960–2019
International Style

Nothing so prosaic as a collection of buildings: these pedestrian walkways are fragments of a different arrangement of the City entirely, a leftover from London as re-imagined by post-war planners, and particularly in the Abercrombie Plan that the 1945–51 Labour government fully expected would be carried out. The byword is the separation of people and traffic. Often, that separation can be rather grim for the pedestrian, as enormous freedoms are allotted to cars to speed along in the knowledge that they aren't going to run anybody over, and nothing comparable given to those on foot. Pissy underpasses are the usual concession, which for some reason were, in Britain, especially unpleasant, seldom with the facilities, shops and other activities they usually have on the Continent (the rule-proving exception: the **Underpasses, p. 222**, at Milton Keynes). What is fun about the overhead, multilevel pedestrian walkways ('Pedways') built over two decades, and revived recently by the Corporation of London, is that they gave the pedestrian a little freedom back, by creating elevated routes across the City that offered views, panoramas, and picturesque juxtapositions. These take advantage of the

Make Architects' latest addition to the City's network of streets in the sky, now growing again after years of decline.

irregularity of the City, now compounded by its crowding with disjointed modern buildings. Many walkways were removed from the 1980s onwards, something which I suspect has more to do with hostility to any notion of co-operation between developers in the manic gold rush that is the post-Big Bang City, than to an attempt at creating a better pedestrian experience. Nonetheless: if you want a real modernist experience of three-dimensional space, these fragments are a rare thrill.

There are three parts to what is left of the Pedway network. One, on Wormwood Street, is so truncated as to be the faintest ghost of an idea, and may not even still be there by the time this book is published (at the time of writing in 2020 with a dilapidated Chinese house placed on it, as part of an art project). It's a remnant of what was once a wider network from the **NatWest Tower (p. 66)** threading through to Bishopsgate, and links two fairly nondescript late-modernist/early-

Postmodernist blocks on either side of the street. The views are nice, though, and the design is a now endangered example of the standard City Pedway – a simple conduit with railings and concrete panels with a lot of shiny grey granite in the aggregate. Much more fun can be had in the elaborate system that connects parts of Upper Thames Street, a bleak canyon carved through the City in the sixties. You can join these walkways just off Blackfriars Station, where mostly you clamber over the workmanlike Brutalism of Bayard House, designed by William Holford; there's a little public sculpture here, and enough working-day pedestrian use to make it a pleasant place to walk in daylight – despite the various dead ends and parts that don't properly link up. As you look down Upper Thames Street, you'll see several more walkways criss-crossing it; some are new or have been recently dressed up in eco or Calatrava clothes, but they're not new walkways, just replacements. There are also entire upper-level pedestrian streets, somewhat like the famous seventeenth-century Rows in Chester, with shops, canopies and entrances to offices along them. The panoramic view of the highway here is close to the dystopian version of the sixties future, a desolate but thrilling multilevel metropolis that has gone to seed. There is a lot of rough sleeping here, and it's startling to find such poverty in the City – even now, the place has its forgotten lanes and forgotten people. Eventually, these walkways peter out. Near the north side of London Bridge is one more on Lower Thames Street, similar to the Wormwood Street Pedway. Cross the Thames and you'll find that, on the other side of London Bridge, there's another walkway fragment, under and then across a drab modernist building, which in turn links to the multilevel railway station (a 'value-engineered', i.e. cheapened, but spatially very impressive redesign by Grimshaw, 2018). When you walk across you'll see there's an enclosed, glazed 1980s twin walkway doing the same job, though this is open during rush-hour only.

The big one – the area where you can walk around unmolested by anything so prosaic as a 'street' or a 'pavement' – is the walkway system around the **Barbican (p. 66)**. Around London Wall, though, the Barbican's 'Highwalks' are supplemented by something that is clearly separate from it. There was once a complex made up of Mini-Mies towers here (visible in Antonioni's *Blowup*); only two are left, but the Postmodernist replacement – Terry Farrell's sprawling Alban Gate – actually built new walkways to continue the system. Farrell's building mounts London Wall and ruins the view from the Barbican Library with its gormlessly heavy profile and pink stone excrescences; but credit where it's due, its remaking and reimagining of the walkway system is very successful, and manages to sustain several commercial spaces at the upper level while remaining permanently open to pedestrians. In fact, with the entrances to office blocks, atria and restaurants all unfussily on the upper level, it's a Postmodernist making clear that the modernist city is still viable, if there's money there to sustain it. Another fragment, around Basil Spence's quirkily Brutalist Salters Hall (1976), was first marooned by walkway demolition, but was re-linked recently by the aggressive commercial architects Make, through the rust-red Corten steel walkways of London Wall Place. Finally, a walkway connects Powell & Moya's Museum of London – an unpretentious and, inside, exceptionally clever multilevel building, slated for demolition – to the Barbican, and provides views of the Roman London Wall itself. In these walks, the essence of modernist London is revealed; never a *tabula rasa* or a new order, but a complex process of montage, where a walk on a concrete pedway can lead you above a townscape in pieces that don't add up, little shards of the Roman, medieval, Victorian and Brutalist city, challenging you to make sense of it all. A similarly ambitious, part-dismantled, part-walkable system can be found in the **Newcastle City Centre Walkway System (p. 483)**.

───

COMMERCIAL UNION TOWER, CITY ❶
Gollins Melvin Ward, 1968
International Style

Mies van der Rohe designed a small high-rise office block for the centre of the City in 1968; after an intellectually offensive decades-long battle it was never constructed. If you want to see whether the Mies values of precision and sobriety were appropriate to the City, you can go and look at this, built for Commercial Union and currently used by Aviva. It works, as the *haut-bourgeois* fixation with quality, order and rectitude in Mies's version of modernism fits rather nicely with how the City used to want to present itself, as the hub of gentlemanly capitalism in the modern age. So too did the opacity of the black-tinted glass, used as if to make clear that you'll never really get to know what goes on in here. Gollins Melvin Ward designed a few other buildings with these glass curtain walls in London, most of them less successful than this; the former Castrol House in Marylebone is the most famous. None of them, the Commercial Union Tower included, compare with their sublime **Arts Tower (p. 369)** for the University of Sheffield – a rare example of the provinces getting a better deal than the capital. For all that, they're worth seeing, particularly as the rapid change in the City sees this generation of towers wiped out. Still standing and in use at the time of writing in 2020, the tower is meant to make way for something called 'the Trellis'.

———

BRUNSWICK CENTRE, BLOOMSBURY ○
Patrick Hodgkinson, 1967–72
Brutalist

A just about still great futurist building and grandiose public space, neutered by grasping developers and an unimaginative local authority. The story is reasonably familiar – two concrete ziggurats, low-rise high-density, a typology responsible for the most interesting British architecture of the 1970s – but here, initially the project of a developer, whose scheme was taken over by Camden Council. It's so close in ethos, if not in finish, to Camden's in-house work that it seems more a product of the hot-house that produced **Alexandra Road (p. 148)**, the **Branch Hill Estate (p. 151)**, **Fleet Road (p. 147)** and **Highgate New Town (p. 150)** than the independent private project it originally was. Hodgkinson's modelling of the stepped apartments is audacious. On Marchmont Street, it's a ferocious, brilliant

battleship, straight out of the Italian Futurist fantasies of Antonio Sant'Elia; inside the square, the pyramid is more regular in appearance, and the dull shops dominate, but then the drama suddenly comes back in the wild triple-height suspension of flats on monumental concrete columns above the subterranean world of the Renoir Cinema. If you can get inside the housing blocks, meanwhile, Piranesian spaces comparable in London only to **Westminster Underground Station (p. 72)** lead through walkways to the – mostly still council – flats. The sad part is the bland clone-town that the shopping centre's owners created in the refurbishment in the early 2000s, which simply swept away a shabby but lively bit of Bloomsbury for an open-air Westfield, with only Skoob second-hand bookshop managing to cling on. An intelligent council should have been able to build on and expand what was here. **[B.6]**

———

DANISH EMBASSY, BELGRAVIA
Arne Jacobsen, 1969–77
International Style

A tricky and personal building from the great Danish designer, and for that reason perhaps more enjoyable than his classicist International Style **St Catherine's College (p. 228)** buildings in Oxford. At ground level, an abstract concrete engineering diagram-like frieze of circles and grids, with, above, cantilevered, curved green-metal offices, gorgeously finished. The ambassador's residence is set back behind these, in a glass block close aesthetically to the machine-made chic of the young High-Tech architects. The street frontage is serene, but at the back the cantilevers become irregular and a glass cylinder of escape stairs creates a more Constructivist, asymmetrical composition.

80 CANNON STREET, CITY
Arup Associates, 1972–6
High-Tech

An extremely early High-Tech building, showing the movement's principles already in place – slick detailing, the ostentatious display of technology and the celebration of structure. Occupying a block of the dense streetscape near Cannon Street railway station, it consists of a thin, mid-rise, all-glass office complex, held up by tubular steel cross-bracing, arranged into a lattice cantilevered by angular steel supports above a fully glazed shop. It originally stood next to a very dour station frontage by the notoriously corrupt Leeds architect John Poulson, but in the 2010s a duller, squarer version of the 80 Cannon Street building was erected as its new neighbour, to the designs of Foggo Associates – the firm founded by Peter Foggo, who designed the original building when he was at Arup Associates.

Decent enough – but the difference between the two shows how an architectural idea can grow stale through overuse.

———

SCHOOL OF ORIENTAL & AFRICAN STUDIES LIBRARY, BLOOMSBURY
Denys Lasdun & Partners, 1973
INSTITUTE OF EDUCATION, BLOOMSBURY
Denys Lasdun & Partners, 1975
Brutalist

Enormous violence was done by these to the historic structure of Bloomsbury, with its regular stock-brick squares. Given that many of those squares – such as the one in front of the long-term home of the Architectural Association in Bedford Square – are still gated and open only to residents, it is unclear exactly why we should give a toss; and given that the immediate post-war neoclassical alternative, represented

Barging into Bloomsbury, the monumental drama of Denys Lasdun's Institute of Education.

by Charles Holden's blocks for ULU, SOAS and Birkbeck, was to avoid architectural disjunction while ruining many of the existing squares, Lasdun's rip-it-up-and-start-again approach at least proposes something of its own. The earlier of the two buildings is a relatively compact block for SOAS, clad in 'fair-faced' concrete with a similar finish to Portland stone, with the top four storeys cantilevered outwards, and rougher concrete used for the ceremonial, hieratic treatment of the service ducts. It sits somewhere between one of Lasdun's ziggurats and the four-square scale of Holden's buildings for the same college (an internal passage leads between them). The same proportional module is used with the concrete outside and the multilevel library inside, which is an appropriately intense, concentrated scholarly space.

The Institute of Education, on the other hand, is strictly for the hardcore. On the SOAS side, it is a black-glass half-pyramid connected with brown-concrete stairwells, aggressive enough; but with the long facade to Bedford Way, it's a thrilling enfilade of glass, hauled up on concrete pillars, with T-shaped piers at the top and upturned Melnikovian lecture theatres at the bottom. It's not friendly – and access from the street is tortuously complex – but I'd exchange a fair few good decent London streets for this ferocious blast. [B.22]

QUEEN ANNE'S GATE, WESTMINSTER
Fitzroy Robinson with Basil Spence, Bonnington & Collins, 1976
Brutalist

Due to its closeness to St James's Park, this is one of the two towers by which Basil Spence 'ruined' two of the great London parks. This one lacks the relative clarity of **Hyde Park Barracks (p. 165)**; it's sprawling, ungainly and wilfully ugly, which seems fairly appropriate to its long-standing role as the home of the Home Office (though the blocks were speculatively built). So why recommend looking at it? Partly because it forms an intriguing contrast in bureaucratic power with Charles Holden's adjacent 55 Broadway, a classicist high-rise on a cruciform plan. Both structures try to offset their enormous bulk via rhythm and visual attraction, and both are clad in Portland stone; Queen Anne's Gate lacks the public arcade that runs through 55 Broadway, but makes up for that with its neurotic, defensive series of fins and its top-heavy, helmet-like form. It's a monument to a very strange architectural moment, when essentially conservative architects tried reintroducing a certain civic monumentality to 'humanize' their designs, but ended up doing the opposite – fusing Brutalist and baroque images of power into almost dementedly domineering form. Here, the result is a giant stone robot permanently glowering over St James's Park. Unlike later fusions of modernism and governmental classicism, like Hopkins's unfortunate Porticullis House, the tension created makes the building more, not less, strange.

---

30 CANNON STREET, CITY
Whinney, Son & Austen Hall, 1974–7
Expressionist

A little-known office block from an unfashionable period, and one of the better modern buildings in the square mile. Like a thirties department store, it uses a corner site to create a whipcrack curve, and then compounds this by having the plan expand outwards slightly on every floor, so that the building appears to rise upwards in profile; this movement is accentuated by a series of down-tapering fins to dress the windows. It has the sort of smooth and expensive finish that bankers like, but for the purposes of a highly imaginative bit of street architecture. A much needed pep in a dull part of the City.

NATWEST TOWER, CITY
R. Seifert & Partners, 1971–80
International Style

Yet another irritatingly good piece of Seifert corporate arse-kissing, this one going so far as modelling its ground plan on the NatWest logo – a gesture that became pointless when the bank sold it off and it became 'Tower 42'. As Barnabas Calder tells the story in his book *Raw Concrete*, Seifert deliberately proposed an ugly, squat tower and an elegant, slim skyscraper for the site in the gamble that this would help the latter get approval, as the City's first 'true' skyscraper, of a then-unprecedented forty-seven storeys. Along with its height, it also had mid-way-up 'sky lobbies', an overhead walkway connection to the City's Highwalk system, and a quality of finish that was way beyond the relatively gimcrack precast panels of Seifert's earlier towers, or of fun but naff kitsch like the **Post Office Tower (p. 59)**. This is a prestigious overlook tower, a display of corporate wealth and reach that would, later, become normal in the City but which at the time must have seemed like a quantum leap from leaky Brutalist towers and neo-Georgian multistorey palazzos. Its rush of thin stainless-steel uprights is more appropriate to the stone and concrete of the City than the supposedly opaque glass that is now ubiquitous. It's the right material for a medieval city, recognizing, like Foggo's **60 Queen Victoria Street (p. 72)**, that the City is a place of mystery and intrigue, not of transparency and democracy; the staggering of the roofline, illuminated sickly green at night, makes for an appropriately darkling steeple. Finished six years before the City's 'Big Bang', its trading floors were too small and so it hasn't really functioned as well as intended – like many skyscrapers, it is more about prestigiousness than usefulness. To the east, a huge cantilever elevates it over an early-Victorian banking hall below, but a bland recent refurbishment has placed a tacky glass entrance on the west side of the building, presumably the reason why this impressive tower was recently refused listing.

——

BARBICAN, CITY ✪
Chamberlin Powell & Bon, 1965–82
Brutalist

When this immense redevelopment of an enormous swathe of the north-eastern fringes of the City of London was finally completed, in the early 1980s, nobody had anything good to say about it. A well-appointed flat in a central location, not much more – dated, monolithic, separated from the existing city, soulless. 'Well-serviced anonymity' is about the best that Christopher Woodward and Edward Jones could say about it. I'm always a little bit haunted by this when writing about new buildings; if the received opinion on a place could have been *this* blind, then best be careful what you base your judgements on. Because the Barbican is one of the most convincing visions of the alternate city built anywhere in the world during the twentieth century, breaking with everything about how urban space was laid out in previous centuries in a thrillingly complete and comprehensive way. At the same time it is a useful thought experiment. Due to it always being intended for the wealthy, or at least comfortable (it was built as council housing of a sort, but the council in question is the Corporation of London, so rents are exceptionally high, and originally rose with the social scale of City workers), we can see here how a typical 1960s project might have looked if it was always, from day one, properly built, properly maintained, and properly funded.

There is no ground level for almost the entire estate. There are around a dozen different entrances, most of them up stairs or along the scattered remnants of the City of London's **Pedways (p. 60)** network.

Brutalist baroque: the extravagant planning and rich, rough surfaces of Chamberlin Powell & Bon's Barbican.

When you're up on the podium, you can walk on elevated walkways for around half a mile – sometimes narrow, sometimes covered, sometimes offering sublime views of the City and the Barbican itself. There are three very tall towers, angular and articulated, never the same when looked at from even slightly different angles, and several mid-rise blocks, hauled up on hulking tree-trunks of bush-hammered concrete; some of them frame lakes, and the covered Gilbert Bridge across them is one of the truly great set pieces of London, both serene and incredibly exciting. When walking across it, you are above a lake, and under a cliff of housing; fountains bubble below you, and in decent weather people are relaxing with an overpriced cup of coffee (or, sometimes, bringing their own). From there you can admire the preserved church, a minor little melange of Gothic and classical that has been turned into a decontextualized art object. Its spire now aligns with the Barbican's concrete towers in views to the north, and in views to the south the lightweight towers of Richard Rogers's **88 Wood Street (p. 72)**. On the ground, vegetation spills over the bull-horn profiles of the cantilevers and balconies of the low-rise blocks, and the immense columns of Gilbert Bridge have a nobility that often leads to classical comparisons, or to a Renaissance ideal city. Architectural form is seldom this elemental, this confident, this guiltless. Unlike in so many council projects of its period there's no moment when you look up close and the tawdriness and low budgets are revealed. There's nothing tragic about the Barbican, no element of heroic dreams dashed against harsh reality – it's a triumphal march, a parade of magnificence.

The Arts Centre is quite simple and undemonstrative from the outside, compared with all this drama, but, inside, the same effect that is created with such mastery in the estate – a constant movement of above and below, a labyrinthine, three-dimensional city – is replicated. Again, wealth has preserved the smaller details that are usually lost in the cheap refurbishments common in public buildings – a personal favourite is the outline of a brogue indicating where to put your foot to pump the taps in the toilets. The second level of the Arts Centre leads to a lush, Ballardian botanical garden, with creepers and tropical plants sprawling across the concrete, and to Frobisher Crescent, a sombre, baroque set-piece. And on ground level, where the 'proper' street is meant to be (?), there's Beech Street, a thrilling dystopian ride, lit by a grid of lights which gives, in Will Wiles's words, 'the overall effect [of] a Renaissance study in perspective with the guide lines left in'. One aspect of the plan that was accurately criticized by the dullards of the 1980s is that it does work like a fortress. You can enter by a variety of routes, of course – you'll get lost the first time, but it's all part of the fun – it is alongside the existing city, not part of it. The imagery of enclosure and completeness reinforces that. That's fine on a formal level, and the pseudo-scientific hocus pocus that people go funny in the head if they walk around at first-storey level is roundly disproved here, but being as it is a citadel of the very wealthy, the imagery is a little unfortunate. You used to be able to walk from one end of the estate to the other without being bothered, but the massive recent rise in homelessness, in a place which has several twenty-four-hour sheltered spots, has seen several reminders put up to let you know that you're not really meant to be here unless you're on your way to art or a flat. That doesn't stop people from occasionally sleeping on the big, comfortable chairs of the foyers. They must recognize that, signs notwithstanding, this remains one of the freest spaces in London, where you can walk wherever you like – above, below, across, inside, outside – as long as you don't expect to arrive where you're going on time. [D.12]

PIMLICO VENTILATION SHAFT
Eduardo Paolozzi, 1982
TOTTENHAM COURT ROAD UNDERGROUND STATION
Eduardo Paolozzi, 1986
High-Tech

The Victoria Line is one of London's most reliable and least architecturally interesting Tube lines, although the graphics on the platforms are cute. The only exception to its street-level blandness is this ventilation shaft adjacent to Pimlico tube, which was actually paid for by the unlovely Postmodernist blocks around the station, in the process known as 'planning gain'. What you can see – twisting, tentacular pipes as 'arms', with a stark steel 'head' and a trunk of relief sculptures – is anthropomorphic, and also of a related family to **Lloyd's of London (p. 69)**, an architecture of machine-tooled entrails, a display of function far too elaborate and fascinating to be seriously functional. It's actually a sculpture, by the pop artist Paolozzi, and so most of it doesn't actually need to 'do' anything. The reliefs below, a sort of town plan made up of tools and cogs, give the game away – this is from a place where futurism and nostalgia are inextricable, and Heath Robinson and Iakov Chernikhov playing happily together. A quick journey and a change at Oxford Circus, meanwhile, will bring you to Paolozzi's epic mural project at the 1890s deep-level Tube of Tottenham Court Road, a chaotic assemblage of machinery, advertising and robotics, sprawled across the poky Victorian dungeons, and *mostly* unaffected by the partial redesign of the station as part of Crossrail. In these two structures, you can see how Eduardo Paolozzi was the *architecte manqué* of post-war Britain, a muralist-sculptor-*bricoleur* with real urban ambitions; his largest scale work in this vein is at the **Kingfisher Centre (p. 336)** in Redditch.

TARGET HOUSE, ST JAMES'S
Tripos, 1979–84
High-Tech

Just opposite the Smithsons' **Economist Plaza (p. 58)**, Target House is a late project by Rodney Gordon, who had designed **Eros House (p. 90)**, the Tricorn Centre and the '*Get Carter* car park'. Abandoning concrete Brutalism, it is nonetheless a strikingly rude presence, especially when placed opposite the buttoned-up good manners of the *Economist* building. Who's the real Brutalist, it seems to ask, with its Gothic assemblage of bunched-together bronze pipes and aluminium cylinders. Unlike the Smithsons' buildings, it follows the original street lines almost perfectly, but rather than deferring in its expression, it opts for distortion and exaggeration, especially with its sliced towers, which seemed to have been lopped off at the last minute. Gordon's game is crass excitement and perspectival bafflement, and he plays it here just on the edge of kitsch. It's a wonderful little balancing act that could only be played by someone supremely arrogant.

LLOYD'S OF LONDON, CITY ✪
Richard Rogers Partnership, 1979–86
High-Tech, Constructivist

Non-Londoners – if you have time in the capital to see one building, make it this one. This outrageous, paranoid, disturbing building is one of the single most thrilling architectural experiences in Europe, an unforgettable, violent work. If that's not enough, it is one of the places to see exactly how self-proclaimed progressives have worked for extremely old institutions to give them new faces. Lloyd's of London – not to be confused with Lloyds Bank – are a venerable firm of underwriters, who have had offices in this spot behind Leadenhall Market since the seventeenth century.

Cyberpunk in the City: Richard Rogers's astonishing futurist Gothic towers for Lloyd's of London.

When Lloyd's got hold of Rogers (or he got hold of them), they were housed in a minor interwar classical building. In Rogers's project, part of it is held up as an abstract fragment, which should give you an idea of his approach to history at the time – not erasing it, but reducing it to shards of the past, spliced into a terrifying and ruthless present (not that Lloyd's, founded as underwriters of slave ships, needed much education in ruthlessness). The original facade is one of the very last things you will notice on visiting the building.

What you see is the assemblage of stacked, curved steel escape staircases, cubic offices like designer shopping containers and intestinal, overlapping bared pipes (an early term for this High-Tech architecture was 'Bowellism'), shoved into a tiny little corner of the City's tangled streets. What it most resembles in architectural history is a combination of the unbuilt projects of the Russian Constructivists – specifically, the Architectural Fantasies of Iakov Chernikhov – and the ingenious planning of the Gothic Revival, such as the making virtue of necessity in the churches of William Butterfield, where mean little alleyways became the venue for experiments in eldritch form. And there is something uncanny, almost a little bit mystical, about the Lloyd's building. It comes as close to animation as an inanimate object like an office block possibly can. That's not just in the supposedly functional, in reality ornamental, cranes at the top, which are meant to extend and replace those pods and containers plugged into the steel framework – they keep still. It's the lifts, which aren't glazed, but are outside the building, shunting up and down in a manner which is dazzling, but which must contribute massively to the building's famously enormous maintenance bill. Both of these point to the contradiction in the building that could never possibly have been resolved. Because Rogers had learned at the shoulder of utopians like Cedric Price and Archigram that the components and services of a building should be (and would be) constantly replaced, Lloyd's have all this machinery to make those replacements. But as an obsessive and highly scrupulous architect, Rogers and his partners have made all these components so beautiful that they surely knew they could never be replaced without raising a furore (and rightly so). The building is now listed, at Grade 1, the same level as St Paul's, which is as it should be. But the fact remains that the rhetoric of the building is at odds with its beauty.

Rogers and his partners (at this point including Laurie Abbott, an old Brutalist who worked for Owen Luder, and designed the techno-Brutalist **Apex Drive, p. 217**) knew they were making something beautiful – why else use such breathtaking metallic finishes, why else create such a gleaming, gorgeous object? But they didn't seem to know much else about it. There was no obvious plan. There are no particularly informative working drawings. The entire beast seems to have been conjured up by the designers and engineers constantly daring each other to go further and further out, to find out without knowing in advance how much they could reduce a building as a solid, finished object into a building as a collection of visually fascinating, technologically complex services. The old functionalist idea, so influential in modernism, was that the display of services and construction could show you how the thing works; but Lloyd's reveals nothing, and remains baffling and unnerving – to the pedestrian, there is no obvious logic to the design; it is there for the thrill of it. It is not wholly without visual precedent, and the usual comparisons made are oil rigs and oil refineries (this being the era of the North Sea oil boom), but there is no good reason why an office block should look like a petroleum extractor. But then what it 'looks like' is perhaps a sore point. As the true extremism of the building became apparent, Rogers was asked by the client: 'Why didn't you tell us it would look like this?' and he replied: 'Because I didn't know.' It is a statement of the importance of process over building-as-image-and-artwork, but it also suggests that dark, uncanny forces took the architects over, and they decided to follow them to their conclusion.

It's on the inside that there is some logic, in the ludicrously lofty atrium, which is designed, through its generous and vertiginous escalators, to encourage the underwriters and clerks to interact between offices that might otherwise be compartmentalized. What that can't explain is The Room, an entire transplanted Robert Adam room that Lloyd's had carried with it through various different buildings; its florid neoclassical space is enclosed in a concrete bunker, suspended in the intestinal frame, as if some monstrous creature has retained the head of its enemy. Except, that would reverse the order – who is bossing who here? Who has won out: is the Establishment at its most Established using the most radical and then-unbuildable ideas of the 1920s and '60s for its own entertainment? What does this building by a supposedly 'civic' architect that meets the street with a moat give to the city around it, other than a mindboggling monument? What does the total disconnect between intention and actuality in the building say about modernism's aspirations to embodying the zeitgeist, to being uniquely functional and logical? None of these questions are answerable, but you can think about them as you gaze at Lloyd's of London in stupefied awe. **[B.28]**

EXCHANGE HOUSE, BROADGATE, CITY
Skidmore Owings & Merrill, 1990
International Style

Outside of **One Canada Square (p. 131)**, Broadgate was the most large-scale attempt at 'planning' in London during the laissez-faire 1980s; a corporate version of the Barbican, less spatially ambitious but similarly coherent and enclosed. The most celebrated part came from Arup Associates – a gently Postmodernist circus around a Richard Serra sculpture, with a sleek, black High-Tech extension down to Finsbury Avenue, very similar to **Gateway House (p. 220)** in Basingstoke – and the least celebrated, the tawdry Tim Burton Gotham of Skidmore Owings & Merrill's 135 Bishopsgate. The cohesiveness and scale of the ensemble have been ruined by a giant 2010s office block by Make, but the most architecturally impressive part is still unscathed. SOM's Exchange House was built, like the rest of Broadgate, above a tangle of railway lines and roads, but, unlike the rest of the complex, it expresses this tension, its ten storeys of offices raised on giant steel pulleys above the infrastructure below.

And while the other buildings in Broadgate now look various kinds of dated, Exchange House combines the stark, dark, hard grids of post-war Chicago modernism with the structural fetishism of High-Tech, with a giant steel arch capping the visible steel frame.

CHANNEL 4, WESTMINSTER
Richard Rogers Partnership, 1990–94
High-Tech, Constructivist

Rogers's firm in its post-**Lloyd's of London (p. 69)** pomp, a Constructivist building on a corner site in a relatively ordinary bit of Westminster, near a street market and Peabody flats, and a convincing contrast with the compromised, classicized approach his old High-Tech confreres Michael and Patricia Hopkins would opt for in Porticullis House on the other side of Parliament Square. On either side of a once-innovative fancy atrium – behind the glass screen of

Channel 4: the dreams of the Russian Constructivists, realized in the backstreets of Westminster.

'London's first hanging curved curtain wall', as the architects' own description points out – are spikily techno-Gothic towers, one with pod lifts shunting up and down, the other enclosing steel boxes of offices. Unlike at Lloyd's, it attempts a public space – the semi-circular plaza made possible by the curve of the building. This suits the relatively small scale of the building, the manic, minutely tooled junglist blare of Lloyd's toned down a little, settling into a more domestic, humane kind of excitement.

---

88 WOOD STREET, CITY
Richard Rogers Partnership, 1994–9
High-Tech

The last Rogers building in London that really thrills, before worthiness and Rave Dad colour schemes start to ruin everything. 88 Wood Street squeezes all the drama it can out of its tightly drawn plot, two stretched and skinny glass towers, cross-braced, with vertiginous stairwells and the then-trademark fully glazed lifts. A tiny firework – at this point in Rogers's career, something this action-packed was just another commission. Next to **Wood Street Police Station, p. 57** (but perhaps best viewed from the library at the **Barbican, p. 66**).

---

60 QUEEN VICTORIA STREET, CITY
Foggo Associates, 1999
High-Tech, Postmodernist

A speculative office block next to James Stirling's Number 1 Poultry (a building which, for all its undoubted mastery of form, is too smug and bumptious to find a place in this book). Like a lot of City office blocks of the 1980s and '90s, Peter Foggo's work here continues the proportions and scale of the Victorian and Edwardian buildings that survive in the City in fragments, after the ministrations of the Luftwaffe

and 'planning' (this was a response not just to homogeneous modernism, but to huge neo-Georgian blocks like the hideous Faraday House). While most buildings of this sort try to recapture Victorian architecture with a kitschy melange of grilles, pediments, reconstituted stone cladding and gew-gaws, 60 Queen Victoria Street opts for a more original fusion of retro and High-Tech. The facade treatment is defined by the washed-out, blue-grey bronze cladding, metal screens like prison windows, and an exposed structural steel frame. There is nothing else from this era in London that approaches its sinister elegance, or risks its practically fetishistic, S&M approach to materials, more H. R. Giger than Edwin Lutyens. **[D.26]**

WESTMINSTER UNDERGROUND STATION ⊙
Hopkins Architects, 1999
High-Tech

An astonishing architectural experience, wrenched out of one of the dullest and most prosaic structures. Both station and building above were designed in the late 1990s by Michael and Patricia Hopkins's firm. The latter, Porticullis House, is an attempt by High-Tech architects to adapt that group's ideas about repetition, interchangeability and the display of machine-made components to the commission, a huge office building directly opposite the most photographed corner of the Houses of Parliament, where Westminster Bridge meets Big Ben. It's not much cop – both fussy in its detailing and lumbering in its massing, an expensive fudge, pleasing neither modernists nor traditionalists. Beneath, Hopkins weren't under duress to please anyone, and created one of the most exhilarating spaces in London. Pass through the ticket gates, and you're in one of Piranesi's dream-prisons, except you can escape from it by catching a District, Circle or Jubilee Line train. Hammered concrete walls enclose a cage of concrete tubes; escalators are piled up on top of each other within it. It's a playground of pure space, gratuitous and functional. After getting to the bottom, you want to get the escalators right back up to the top, like a rationalist helter-skelter. **[B.27]**

SCHOOL OF SLAVONIC & EAST EUROPEAN STUDIES, BLOOMSBURY
Short Associates, 1999
Postmodernist

One of the last Postmodernist buildings in London and also one of the best, by Alan Short, who designed some wonderful Arts and Crafts-influenced educational buildings in the 1990s in Manchester **(Contact Theatre, p. 410)**, for Coventry University **(Lanchester Library, p. 330)** and at De Montfort University, Leicester **(Queen's Building, p. 351)**, made up of strange and perverse skylines of chimneys and funnels, with lush diapered brickwork everywhere. This is a miniaturized essay in the same, built into a dense Bloomsbury street block, with a beautiful wood-panelled interior and a vertiginous library which, appropriately, most resembles the more outré architecture of interwar Eastern Europe – the Czech Cubist movement or the School of Economics in Warsaw.

30 ST MARY AXE, CITY
Foster & Partners, 2001–3
LEADENHALL BUILDING, CITY
Rogers Stirk Harbour, 2013
High-Tech

That's the Gherkin and the Cheesegrater to you. The prehistory of these two skyscrapers lies in that era, not so long ago, when John Major was Britain's representative leader,

and when the disapproval of the Prince of Wales struck terror into the architects of international finance – not necessarily a better age, but a different one.

The bombing of the Baltic Exchange by the Provisional IRA saw Foster propose a hugely ambitious Millennium Tower, which was (as was then routine) refused on the objections of conservationists. His second project for the site won the commission because a change in the City's aesthetic tastes and London's planning regime saw a return to the building of skyscrapers. But unlike scowling, black-suit architecture such as the **NatWest Tower (p. 66)**, these would be fun skyscrapers! Hence 30 St Mary Axe quickly acquiring a nickname, originally the more picturesque 'Erotic Gherkin'. When Foster's old partner in High-Tech and anti-Charles polemics got round to his neighbouring skyscraper a decade later, the nickname was there from the start, coined by the developer. Both towers are about as pretty as they are vacuous; the wraparound, diamond-like crossbracing of the Gherkin is fascinating to run your eyes across, especially from below, where, like CGI, it never quite looks real. It was initially heralded as a 'sustainable' eco-skyscraper; Foster's partner Ken Shuttleworth claimed that it was meant to resemble a pine cone, with the bankers and insurers opening their windows to create a spiky silhouette. Obviously, as the building's enduring nickname suggests, this hasn't happened.

The Cheesegrater is more prosaic, and attempts (this being Rogers) a civic gesture, with the open ground floor escalators, but is visually convincing as a right-angled complement to the curves of the earlier building. It now forms part of a skyline of elementary forms, a metropolis that has been transformed into a skyscraping exhibition of household goods. Probably the most interesting architecture on this site happened when the Cheesegrater's precursor – the P&O building, a Mies-imitating tower

The City of London's 'cluster' of skyscrapers: an unregulated tangle of competing shapes, thrilling and tawdry.

by Gollins Melvin Ward – was dismantled from the ground up, accidentally creating mid-way through a Suprematist sculpture worthy of El Lissitzky.

___

HERON TOWER, CITY
Kohn Pedersen Fox, 2007–11
High-Tech

The first major skyscraper to be built in the City after the Gherkin (**30 St Mary Axe, above**), and notably un-nicknamable; instead, it's named after the developer, which is perhaps not preferable. It's also a tall building of considerable strength and vim, and high enough to come across as stylish and slender – one can easily compare its elegance with the truncated, and consequently rather stubby, skyscraper designed by SOM up the road in Bishopsgate. Facing the City, the Heron Tower is a simple grid; to Shoreditch, heavy

cross-bracing gives the tower a rougher, industrial presence, rhetorically appropriate. The staggered roofline – with glazed lifts going all the way to top-floor sky restaurants – is as dramatic and spire-like as it needs to be. If that doesn't seem like much, compare it with the dozen or so duller towers in Canary Wharf; the City's insistence on 'character' has had some welcome visual effects, and when this emerges into view at the end of one of the square mile's courts and alleyways, there's a real and undeniable thrill, no matter how bleak the City's dominance is in social and economic terms.

___

CITY LIT, HOLBORN
Allies & Morrison, 2005
Modernist Eclectic

A relaxed, low-budget home for a long-standing adult education college. Allies & Morrison's cookie-cutter approach to design

– usually, a prefabricated structure with a skin of pale brick, in a regular grid – can have grim results, as the fussy and ungainly offices and flats near their Southwark headquarters makes clear; but this scheme has just the right tension between regularity and specificity. Crammed into a tight site between some Victorian model dwellings and Seifert's **Space House (p. 59)**, to the street an ever-so-slightly irregular rhythm of deeply inset windows leads to a bulky, curved brick corner leading through to Covent Garden. The fit-out is fairly basic – a double-height café is reasonably pleasant, and that's your lot – but, outside, this is decent, clever street architecture which doesn't try to hide its simplicity.

CINEMA, SCHOOL OF ARTS, BIRKBECK COLLEGE, BLOOMSBURY ✪
Surface Architects, 2007
Deconstructivist

A large chunk of the east side of Gordon Square in Bloomsbury is given over to Birkbeck's School of Arts. As an alumnus, I know very well the internal complexities caused when you take a load of Georgian houses and gut them, turning their shells into university office blocks and classrooms, and preserving the odd original room, of course, if someone famous once used it. This makes them maddeningly maze-like, and at the end of one of those mazes you'll find this explosive piece of theatrics. Just as you walk down one of the interminable staircases, you abruptly come to a Day-Glo digital German Expressionist film set, with sloping walls and ramps in blazing, tasteless colours – the brightest, most lurid purples, yellows and blues. The colours deliberately clash, and the spaces appear to crash across each other. The waxy, artificial sheen applied to the surfaces is already rapidly becoming retro-futurist, making this into some

combination of *The Cabinet of Dr Caligari* and *The Matrix*. This is a wild piece of architecture, and promised an enormous amount from Surface Architects. Soon after it was complete, this kind of computer-aided melodrama went out of fashion, and the firm's full-scale buildings at Queen Mary College are much less exciting. In any case, this is the most brilliant and, appropriately, cinematic cinema space built in Britain since the 1960s. It's sad it isn't better known, and hopefully it'll be rediscovered before Birkbeck put brick slips all over it. One day, it'll make a great set for the eventual period drama set at the end of the 2000s boom, or the start of the financial crisis. This is fearless architecture, welcoming the onrush of a science-fiction future rather than hiding it away.

SAW SWEE HOCK STUDENT CENTRE, LONDON SCHOOL OF ECONOMICS, HOLBORN
O'Donnell & Tuomey, 2014
Expressionist

One architectural consequence of the marketization of higher education has been the 'Gateway Building', a photogenic and dramatic central feature with a big atrium and/or non-orthogonal form to impress parents and students when they're deciding what institution to throw large sums of money at. A practical purpose tends to be somewhat secondary – form *is* the function. Accordingly, many are students' unions, where the function is already opaque and changeable, and such is the case with the best of them, this enormous and wilfully complicated Expressionist complex for LSE. Despite its huge size, the building takes some finding – it's in a back alley in the south of Holborn, not in view of any of the pompous Edwardian classical original buildings, hemmed in by a pub, the tower of some brick Brutalist offices, a second-hand bookshop, and the original Old Curiosity Shop.

Two colossal brick fragments with a 'chimney' at the corner (originally mirroring a Brutalist block opposite, which is being demolished at the time of writing – ah, context) are gruff, rude and monumental, but they feel of a piece with the messy townscape around. Finishes – from the twisted concrete stairwells to the wooden window frames – are superb. It feels a long way from the boring imperial Victory parade of Kingsway – which is, in fact, just next door.

ROTHSCHILD'S, CITY
OMA (Office for Metropolitan Architecture), 2005–11
Modernist Eclectic

I can never decide if this building is admirable or abominably smug. That combination – they'd call it 'ambiguity' – is a common one in OMA's buildings, and the fact that it's deliberate somehow makes it all worse. So what we have here is four 'cubes', one of them high-rise, in drizzly glass, kept up by ostentatiously arbitrary cross-bracing, forced into an alleyway, and with various little gestures referring to the venerable clients – a full-scale painting of the family looks out at you from behind two layers of glass as you walk past. From St Swithin's Lane, a square canopy is opened up, framing Wren's St Stephen Walbrook, itself a balancing act of formal ideas crammed into a tiny space, and hence a precursor of sorts. It looks like you can, as a pedestrian, walk from here to the church's courtyard, but that's employees only. This tricksy, clever-clever ensemble won't let anything be simple, and its favouring of the montage rather than the big clear idea is far better suited to the City's morphology than the big, bland groundscrapers that have been built nearby, such as Foster's twin low-rise behemoths facing Cannon Street. A final perverse gesture can only be enjoyed by you and me from an elevated but close distance (the viewing platforms of **Tate Modern, p. 102**, for instance). One of the 'cubes' is part superimposed above the other, a private, multistorey viewing platform suspended above the London skyline.

ZIG ZAG BUILDING & KING'S GATE, VICTORIA
Lynch Architects, 2017
Classical Modernism

The unfortunate name given to the larger part of this extensive redevelopment of a 1960s office canyon into a 'mixed use scheme' of offices, retail and 'residential' reveals the difficulty that the developers must have had in selling this clear-headed, sober, unfussy piece of city as something 'Iconic' – the sort of vacuous designation that its lead designer, Patrick Lynch, desperately wanted to avoid. This is serious architecture, with a vigour, strength and suaveness that can only provide a rather heartbreaking contrast with the other parts of the same Land Securities scheme all around, most of them in meaningless glass polygons to the designs of the Americans Pelli Clarke Pelli. Lynch's work is in two parts. A high-rise block of flats, King's Gate, is clad in an even, deep, Portland stone grid that looks simple at first glance, but reveals itself to be perverse and witty in its contrapuntal rhythms. Opposite, facing a pedestrianized nook, is the uptight, well-made 1960s middling-modernist Westminster City Hall, which is treated with the same sort of seriousness as a determining factor for the new buildings as Darbourne & Darke used for St James the Less at **Lillington Gardens (p. 57)** – *this* was the place to start, the marker, not, as with the other new Victoria buildings, an unfashionable presence best ignored. On the City Hall's ground floor, Lynch have added a murky photographic mural of a forest by Rut Blees Luxemburg, which is quite the thing to find in Victoria,

15 Clerkenwell Close, a load-bearing stone block full of remnants and salvage from previous buildings on this site.

especially at night. The offices – ignore the chains below if you can – are pulled into a tight mesh of copper fins, which give a really rather dashing presence to the street – an expressionist sense of movement achieved with neoclassical means. To have managed all of this in the grim world of twenty-first-century London commercial architecture is some sort of achievement, but these buildings would be worth seeing anywhere.

15 CLERKENWELL CLOSE, CLERKENWELL ✪ ❶
Amin Taha & Groupwork, 2017
Modernist Eclectic

Context is a strange thing. On either side of this block of flats with an architectural studio on its ground floor are fake eighteenth-century buildings. One of them is just a copy, an imitation bit of rough Georgian vernacular, and the other is more broad-brush, where

the 'masonry' is in the style made famous by Asda in the 1980s. Clerkenwell Close is a quintessential London conservation area, in that nothing truly awful has been allowed to happen, but, aside from the baroque church at the centre of it, nothing particularly interesting either. It has been maintained, nothing more. It's not so surprising that Amin Taha's building has been so controversial – threatened, in 2019, with demolition for allegedly breaking planning rules – as it really is a challenge to how conservation areas are meant to work. With fake load-bearing brick on either side, it's held up with a giant grid of limestone, some of which is chiselled to a clean finish, and much of it left as rough as possible. Taha was asked at one point in the planning process whether he couldn't have treated the limestone just as a facade, a smooth skin wrapped around a steel frame, so that it wouldn't have this effect of giant mass. Well he didn't, and we should be grateful.

The controversy was partly about the caprices of the planning system. Partly, it seems likely, it was about a personal vendetta, but also about something the British planning system usually does reasonably well – conservation. After the battles of the 1960s and '70s, most eighteenth- and much nineteenth-century townscape is reasonably secure from having a giant concrete slab or a fluorescent piloti'd blob inserted into it. The problem is that this version of conservation is based on a philosophy that sees townscape as a sort of landscape painting, to be carefully restored to look as much like an imagined original as possible. That's a long way from how Townscape was envisaged when the term was coined by Ian Nairn and Gordon Cullen, to mean montage more than continuity. A lot of the things that make 15 Clerkenwell Close so much fun are actually made possible by conservation's constraints, from the Mediterranean, Greek-ruin roof garden to the grid that follows the line of the neighbouring buildings. Rather than seeing the past as a picture, it incorporates it as archaeology, with its basement office full of traces of the buildings that were there before. There is an aspect of wind-up about it all, no doubt, but the result is generous and rich before it is jokey. New ideas about how to build in historic areas of London could start from here. At the time of writing, the building has been reprieved from demolition in the courts, though the local authority plans to appeal against the decision.

up new forms and destroys ways of life with nihilistic abandon. 22 Bishopsgate is the tallest building in the City of London, but what makes it so incredibly intimidating is not its height, but its breadth. The shape of the City's skyscrapers in the 2000s was motivated by a mixture of whimsy and planning law – the Corporation of London's then-planner Peter Rees's liking for faintly perverse architectural form intersecting with the Mayor's guidance on 'viewing corridors', which means the towers slope, bulge and slide, so as not to block views of St Paul's from Greenwich Park or Parliament Hill. On this site, no views would be interrupted, so the developers and their architects have simply extruded a curved site as far as it can legally go, and then stepped the profile – and that's it. Far more than the Shard, this is just a monolith, a mass; in views on foot in the City, it has escaped from the 1988 Anime classic *Akira*, a giant leap in scale above the rest of the City's skyscrapers that seems to presage a frightening and exciting future neo-London. Viewed from a distance, it provides less of a punch to the solar plexus, with its tapering profile more visible. In early 2020, all the building's lights were put on at once every night, as a test; this was the most terrifying architectural sight in London, a beacon of pure capital, blaring out for dozens of miles. But, unlike the Shard, even in daylight this is a work of breathtaking, if possibly accidental, power.

22 BISHOPSGATE, CITY
PLP Architecture, 2020
High-Tech, International Style

Like **The Shard (p. 105)**, this is dystopian architecture, encapsulating in one edifice a science fiction vision of a megalopolis where any controls on capital have collapsed and money almost single-handedly throws

SE LONDON

HORNIMAN MUSEUM, FOREST HILL

Charles Harrison Townsend, 1898–1911
Extensions by Architype, 1995/
Allies & Morrison, 2002
Art Nouveau, Ecomodernism,
Classical Modernism

Authentic Art Nouveau architecture, as opposed to fashionable appliqué on otherwise ordinary Victoriana, is hard to find in England; there was no Mackintosh south of the border. The nearest equivalent is C. H. Townsend, and two galleries he designed at the height of the 'progressive era' in late-nineteenth-century London – the Horniman Museum and the **Whitechapel Gallery (p. 119)**. This is the larger and better, and shows his organic originality to the greatest extent. The Horniman stands on a hill, secluded by trees, in one of the most pleasant and airy of south-east London suburbs, with extensive gardens behind, and houses an inexplicable collection of curios, from stuffed walruses to insects, which were arranged into something like a scientific order when it was redesigned by its then-owners, the London County Council, in the thirties. The building is a sprawl of asymmetric pavilions, bulging with odd protrusions and abstract expanses of stone, crowned by a lovely Art Nouveau mosaic, flanked by a curvaceous clock tower. It has the Victorian qualities of weight and mass, it has cornices and swags and arches, but there is no historical borrowing – this is a personal vision, a response to the site, vital and fresh; and while the interiors are less unusual, the main, double-height vaulted exhibition hall is wonderfully spacious.

There are two extensions – the more recent, by Allies & Morrison, which houses the café, is a quiet but decent extension of the pavilions, in modern materials, similarly massed and slightly antiseptic. The earlier Centre for Understanding the Environment, by the local firm Architype, is much more interesting. Some of Architype's designers had been involved in the self-build houses at **Walter's Way & Segal Close (p. 100)**, in nearby Honor Oak Park, and there is a similar feel here. A single storey of modular wood beams, with a roof of turf, and a set of cowls to regulate the air, it has both a rather Japanese structural logic – you can see how it's made at a glance – and a bohemian hippiness that suits this rangy corner of south London. Sometimes it's best to ask the locals.

———

WILLIAM BOOTH TRAINING COLLEGE, CAMBERWELL

Giles Gilbert Scott, 1928–32
Modern Classicism, Expressionist

One could pinpoint the tower of this HQ for the Salvation Army as the point where Giles Gilbert Scott moved beyond the straightforward, if megalomaniacally scaled, neo-Gothic of his Liverpool Cathedral and the mass-production Soane of his phone boxes, into a thicker, reduced, form of Gothic, in which the stuck-on tracery, which seems especially superfluous here, would be discarded in favour of realizing a Gothic 'form' – huge, dramatic, a little scary in a theatrical way – by means of gigantic masses of stock brick. The residual gob-ons would be eliminated altogether in the slightly later and slightly more abstract **University Library (p. 203)** in Cambridge; the tower in Camberwell, though, is the more massive.

In front of the edifice are almost Disneyesque statues of the Booths, who are described as having been 'promoted to glory' on death. Also of note just behind the Training College is the contrast between the 1930s moderne Ruskin Park House, a streamlined private housing block, and two yellow-brick London County Council towers, both working beautifully with the slopes.

___

ST SAVIOUR'S CHURCH, ELTHAM ○
Cachemaille-Day Welch & Lander, 1933
Expressionist

An incredible brick eruption in a bland bit of suburban Eltham, one of a group of interwar churches by Nugent Francis Cachemaille-Day that are small in size, enormous in presence, with others in Gipton **(Church of the Epiphany, p. 380)** and Wythenshawe **(St Michael & All Angels, p. 399)**. Thin, dark-brown bricks, selected with an obsessive eye, piled up into a mountain of brute form, a Gothic tower reduced to the essentials of huge mass and roaring upwards motion. The brick is shaped into spiky corners and turrets, and otherwise relieved only by dark-looking, tall windows. To find the C of E doing something so extreme in the interwar years is highly unexpected, making this a sharply discordant presence in these vague parkways. Unlike a lot of harsh churches, the darkness doesn't come across as meanly Protestant, but as some sort of horrible revelation, ascension through agony. Inside, the spacious structure gives some kind of uplift, but the main relief from the brown brick and brown concrete is the windows, which, narrow on the outside, reveal themselves to be pulsating slivers of blue light, the way out just about in reach. A free leaflet in the church will tell you about the building, and about how its forbidding concrete exterior conceals a lovely brick interior, which is exactly the wrong way round – but it captures well the game of inside/outside Cachemaille-Day was playing.

From north Germany to south London: the explosive brick Expressionism of St Saviour's Church in Eltham.

ST OLAF HOUSE, SOUTHWARK
H. S. Goodhart-Rendel, 1930–31
Expressionist

An intriguing riverside building, just opposite London Bridge Station, in which a traditionalist architect and historian pushes classicism about as far as it can go into an expressive, personal kind of modernism. Facing the station and its viaduct is a symmetrical office block faced in Portland stone, with jazzy stairwells, elegant but not a million miles from the contemporary norm. It is more unusual on the wharfside facade, where it faces the Thames with strip windows, gilded Vorticist signage and sculptural panels by Frank Dobson, all of it hauling up on fluted, black-granite pilotis, so that the wharf could be used.

———

PIONEER HEALTH CENTRE, PECKHAM
Owen Williams, 1935
SASSOON HOUSE, PECKHAM
Maxwell Fry, 1938
International Style, Constructivist

The Pioneer Health Centre was, if you're a libertarian of the left, one of the directions not taken by the Welfare State. It put a skilled working-class community in strange alliance with a group of biologists offering their bodies up for study in exchange for 'health' rather than simple relief of 'sickness'; preventative care and constant monitoring rather than the simple redress of illness. In the lucid, glassy building this 'Peckham Experiment' built for itself in the mid-thirties, with its strongly expressed concrete frame, Owen Williams organized the clinics and screening rooms, Constructivist-style, around the 'social condensers' of a swimming pool, roof garden and dance hall. You don't have to be convinced by the Pioneers' suspicion of state welfare to admire the way they integrated medical treatment and everyday

life to create spaces where urban life isn't compartmentalized and illness isn't confined and quarantined, something that is still visible even long after the building's 1990s conversion into flats. The social spaces are, or rather were, identifiable on the facade from the curved bay windows; if you manage to get to walk around inside, you'll find that the flats are still arranged around the preserved, grandly scaled pool. The finishes of the conversion to flats, however, are very cheap, and as of summer 2019 a little mouldy. The centre forms an interesting high-modernist group with Sassoon House next door, a crisp little design by Maxwell Fry, with a colourful surrealist relief over the entrance and a clear profile of pedestrian access decks.

———

ARNOLD, MEAKIN, NECKINGER, ST JOHN'S & ST OLAVE'S ESTATES, BERMONDSEY
Bermondsey Metropolitan Borough Architects Dept, 1930s
Viennese

These interlinked estates spread out between Tower Bridge and the viaducts that lead to London Bridge Station, and draw on the ideas of Red Vienna in a then-radical corner of south London. Each of them departs from both the usual neo-Georgian of the LCC and the Arts and Crafts cottages built nearby by the utopian socialists at Bermondsey Council, shifting instead into a more straightforward expression of unity and community. The long courtyard blocks of these estates, each with banded brickwork, long Crittall windows and access decks, are especially notable for their high and expressive archways, which lead you through the blocks from one estate to another. They're let down, as are so many imitations of Red Vienna (such as the **Ossulston Estate, p. 137**), by poor public spaces compared with their continental inspirations.

Two 1930s continental imports: the grand arches of the Arnold Estate in Bermondsey, modelled on Red Vienna...

...and the International Style of Genesta Road in Plumstead, inspired by Le Corbusier and Russian Constructivism.

85–91 GENESTA ROAD, PLUMSTEAD ✪
Lubetkin & Pilchowski, 1934
International Style

A remarkable little scheme by the hardline left-wing modernists at Tecton, using the exact same repertoire they would use for a 'vertical garden city' at **Highpoint (p. 139)** in Highgate for the purposes of a terrace in a very, very ordinary suburb of Woolwich. What is so interesting about these is how the layout uses high-modernist ideas for totally domestic, terraced-house purposes, rather than for a *ville radieuse* of flats and public open space. Although it is totally different in appearance from the high-Victorian bay-windowed houses all around, the boxed-out ribbon windows on these houses play a similar role on the street – you immediately know that these are the living rooms, even though they're on the first floor, with the entrances below. The large, black-framed bedroom windows, glittering rendered concrete surfaces and the gentle curved kink in the balconies, meanwhile, are exactly the same as in Highpoint. In showing that modernism could be adapted to the historic street without losing any of its integrity, these houses are unusual for the 1930s, but point the way to the experiments in Camden, Milton Keynes and elsewhere in the 1970s.

GRANADA CINEMA, WOOLWICH
Cecil Masey and Reginald Uren, 1937
ODEON CINEMA, WOOLWICH
George Coles, 1937
ROYAL ARSENAL CO-OPERATIVE SOCIETY, WOOLWICH
S. W. Ackroyd, 1938
Moderne

A miniature moderne town centre, at the bottom of a hill overlooking the Thames and the Woolwich free ferry, built as a result of road-widening in the 1930s as a reasonably coherent ensemble, and a good example of the priorities of the age – life organized around the cinema and the Co-op (the Woolwich one was fairly radical, offering aid to the Spanish Republic and suchlike). They display the most visually enjoyable aspects of the moderne style – sweeping, dramatic mixtures of curves and abstracted towers, either in tiles (the Co-op and the Odeon) or in Dudokish brick (the Granada), and with a scrubby public space in-between. Not long ago, these buildings (unlisted except for the Granada) were all slated for demolition, but won a reprieve largely through the combined interest of West African Evangelical churches (who have run the Odeon as the appropriately named New Wine Church (as in, 'into old bottles') for a decade, and who have restored and cleaned up the Granada as the Ebenezer Building of the Christfaith Tabernacle), and property developers turning the Co-op into flats, as the 'Wick Tower'. The latter messes up the ensemble a little through a cheap and nasty roof extension, but for me, having witnessed the building literally falling apart for many years, this is a minor quibble. The three buildings also exemplify the questionable things about art deco, streamline moderne or whatever you want to call this thirties commercial modernism, in that the back-ends are afterthoughts, grim quasi-industrial and windowless spaces that create dodgy back alleys. In the daytime, the sequence between the Co-op and the Granada is enjoyably seedy; the rest of the time I wouldn't recommend it. What upends it all into surrealism is the interior of the Granada, a shimmering Gothic stage set by the Bolshoi Ballet's old designer Theodore Komisarjevsky, an extraordinary, flimsy and dazzling succession of *trompe l'oeil* spaces; the irony of it eventually actually becoming a cathedral would not have been lost on the designer.

GREENWICH TOWN HALL
Clifford Culpin, 1939
Expressionist

A public building of great decency and monumentality, and, as Pevsner pointed out, one of the few 1930s town halls to have been built 'in the style of our time', which in this case means the style of Wilhelm Marinus Dudok, with Dutch-style brickwork and a compromise between the rectilinear geometries of Piet Mondrian and the extension of craft traditions in the Amsterdam School. In practice this means beautifully laid bricks without ornament, in an asymmetrical composition, including several distinct public functions, all of them clearly visible as separate components, in one coherent structure. The two most important sections are the Borough Hall – an essay in Anglicized modernism that combines very 'thirties municipal' detailing in wood and stone with new aspects that anticipate some of the ideas in the **Royal Festival Hall (below)**, such as the abstract but monumental convex facade to the street – and the clock tower, intended solely as an accessible campanile for the workaday, non-Royal bit of Greenwich where it edges into Deptford and Blackheath, which has sadly been closed to the public for decades.

You can see what the idea was here – a public campanile to stand proudly alongside Greenwich's famous skyline of baroque domes, a beacon of municipal pride that could be seen for miles. But today, this building is little more than a straggly, dilapidated succession of disconnected things, from Alpha course Christians to business schools. The Borough Halls still just about serve their original function as a community hall; in the ten years I lived in the borough, I went there once.

SOUTH BANK, LAMBETH: ✪
WATERLOO BRIDGE
Giles Gilbert Scott, 1939–42
ROYAL FESTIVAL HALL
London County Council Architects Dept, 1948–51
NATIONAL FILM THEATRE
London County Council Architects Dept, 1951/Avery Associates, 1991/Adjaye Associates, 2008
SOUTH BANK CENTRE
Greater London Council Architects Dept, 1966–8
NATIONAL THEATRE
Denys Lasdun & Partners, 1976–7
Modern Classicism, International Style, People's Detailing, Brutalism

There is no point in treating these four buildings as separate, so closely have they been integrated through ownership, walkways and simple logic into the cultural centre of London, or, if you prefer, the centre of south London. The earliest of them is Waterloo Bridge, which, aside from its act of making-the-difficult-look-easy (those 'effortless' arches, as Ian Nairn saw them, are held up with a lot of concrete) is interesting for the amount of functions integrated within, such as the original National Film Theatre, and its extension, the post-Archigram plastic and glass of the Museum of the Moving Image, designed in the early 1990s by Brian Avery and renovated convincingly by David Adjaye into its current incarnation as 'BFI Southbank', the underpasses beyond, and the bookstalls beneath. When the benches of the NFT's café spilled out here it was one of the best public spaces in Britain, something its gating in by Benugo has done its best to, but can't quite, ruin. From here, you can go east to the National Theatre or south-west to the Royal Festival Hall and the South Bank Centre, via walkway or riverside path. The back end, towards Waterloo and the rest of Lambeth, is still comparatively illegible, a tangle of underpasses around the drum of Avery's iMAX cinema, its Howard Hodgkin mural hidden by advertising since within a couple of years of its 1999 opening. This still doesn't feel at all like a considered part of the rest of the ensemble, more a means of covering the urban scar that used to be 'Cardboard City', but as the tents around here today make clear, that proved only to be temporary. This area doesn't have the views and riverside focus that make the three-dimensional urbanism of the front end so successful; it's also a reminder of why a good overhead walkway is preferable to an underpass.

The earliest part of the ensemble is of course the Royal Festival Hall, designed in the late forties by the LCC's first modernist team, with Robert Matthew, Leslie Martin and Peter Moro all having decisive roles. It is not now the building that people will have seen during the Festival of Britain; decorative screens were removed in the 1960s, when the rest of the South Bank Centre was built; the Portland stone facade makes it look a lot more classical than it was intended to be, a dignified frontage to a symmetrical, grandly scaled and proud public building. The 1960s redesigners also attached it to concrete walkways leading to the new concert hall and gallery, and – until the removal of part of the system in the 1990s – Waterloo Station. The Festival Hall's current reputation as one of the most loved modernist buildings in Europe dates most of all to the opening up of its foyers to all-day and all-evening use, courtesy of the radical Greater London Council of the 1980s. The public top-floor balcony view has all the longing and beauty of the 'Waterloo Sunset' the Kinks sang about, but the real attraction is the flowing space of the foyers, where admittedly delightful period detail (the famous patterned carpet, the delightful railings and doors) is subsumed into a sense of freedom and simultaneity whose importance is best realized if you compare it with the cramped, if opulent, non-theatre spaces of Victorian

buildings with similar functions, such as the Royal Albert Hall.

As to what comes next, it is in two very distinct phases, each of them showing different possible faces of Brutalism. Either the aggressive, dissonant 'architecture autre' of the GLC architects' South Bank Centre containing the Queen Elizabeth Hall, Purcell Room and Hayward Gallery, or the elegant, monumental modern baroque, as the historian Barnabas Calder conceives it, of Denys Lasdun's later National Theatre. The first part was designed by a team that included many of the pop artists and fantasists who would coalesce around the Archigram group (Ron Herron, Warren Chalk and others, in a team supervised by the older Norman Engelback). It is, both for the time and today, shockingly abstract, devoid of anything that would have identified a 'building' during any previous era; its only precursors in London are the brooding, oblique Second World War bunker beside the Admiralty and the Mappin Terraces at the Zoo, a rugged and craggy landscape rather than a discretely conceived work of architecture. Picking out details within this hillock of walkways, harsh surfaces, windowless walls and turrets is a fun game – the sensuous curved metal doors to the concert halls, the pyramidal rooflights of the recently refurbished Hayward Gallery, the curved stairwells that provide access to and from the bridge and the riverfront; unlike the Festival Hall, it is most enjoyable from the Waterloo Station side, where it is a diminutive futuristic fortress that you can clamber over like a playground; a childlike metaphor which has been taken a little too far in some of the recent temporary additions to the buildings, with 'pop-up' pavilions and shipping container fun centres regularly appearing and disappearing.

There's no bumptiousness or 'fun' in the National Theatre, and once you get over the initial shock of the windowless block of the fly-towers glaring across at Somerset

The hard stuff: lookout towers and rugged walkways at the GLC's South Bank Centre.

House, very little aggression or discordance in the design. At this distance, its classical values are obvious, the consideration with which it stands over the water, with the typically Lasdun ziggurat-like profile offering the multilevel thrills of the South Bank Centre, but with none of its disconnected, fragmentary, Ballardian perversity – there is logic, here. This was lost on the heir to the throne, but not on other architectural traditionalists – John Betjeman, for instance, wrote a letter to Lasdun praising him for this visual achievement, especially by comparison with the introverted and abrasive buildings next to it. But the NT is part of the same system, still part of the three-dimensional city, and you can, as in the Royal Festival Hall, climb up to the top of it whenever you like and enjoy the surveying perspective over the city that the wealthy pay obscene sums for. The interior, meanwhile, is tremendous, its circulation spaces and spots to linger and laze about having an angular, oblique relation to the river. There are tables and benches now, and unlike at the NFT, they are not cut off from the river and passers-by. The result is one of the great public spaces of contemporary London. A recent renovation by Haworth Tompkins has restored the exceptionally beautiful concrete work and made some subtle, non-invasive additions round the back and the sides of the building, to help give the service side of the South Bank the public activity it once lacked.

The Festival Hall, made newly accessible from the north at the turn of the 2000s through the pedestrian footbridges attached to Hungerford Bridge, has opened up too, with the 'street food market' that occupies it every weekend, while the South Bank Centre has attracted a series of more or less permanent additions to encourage constant streets-in-the-sky life on its elevated spaces. Some of these felt for a time like part of the building, such as the 'Room for London', a boat-come-singular-luxury-hotel by

a conceptual artist, which, while totally at odds with the public ethos of the building, had some sense of its surrealist design values. Similarly, the ad hoc, bolted-on stairwells, the skate park on the riverfront, and the fountains, which usually have children playing in them, all feel like they ought to be there, taking part in a dialogue with the clip-on, bolt-off, unpretentious approach of the Archigram architects. What with all the shipping container burrito bars and neon artworks all around, it has even started to become a bit much, especially when combined with the duller retail that has taken root under the Festival Hall. And – though it is not the South Bank Centre's fault – the rudely dull (and expanding) neoclassical wall of the Shell Centre is a constant, and depressing, presence, seemingly put there to exorcise what Winston Churchill allegedly called the Festival of Britain's 'three-dimensional socialist propaganda'; the new private high-rises only compound the Shell Centre's hostile presence on the site. As it exists today this is a place between retail reality and the socialist city of culture, with all the values and contradictions of both. [B.24]

THE PRIORY, THE KEEP, THE LANE & HALLGATE, BLACKHEATH
Eric Lyons, 1954–64
People's Detailing, International Style

The product of Span, the property developer co-founded by their architect, these estates were among the first after the Second World War to market modernism explicitly to a middle-class clientele. There are several other Span estates in the south of England (and a mini-New Town at **New Ash Green, p. 240**). The most perfect is **Parkleys (p. 111)**, but the sequence in Blackheath shows best what they were up to. Its earliest parts, around The Priory, are now hard to see as special for anyone who has spent much time in a minor 1950s–70s developers' or council estate, so often will you have seen the painted weatherboarding, the great open plate glass windows, the Liliputian scale ('pixie shit', as Christopher Woodward calls it), and the compromise between suburban values and modernity. You can also see what the imitations of the Span idiom lack – the planting and upkeep of the spaces between, which in so many commercial and council estates are an afterthought used for car parking. In Span estates, public spaces are always a series of self-contained squares; at The Priory, its position on a gentle slope provides memorable picturesque effects, a semi-rural city-within-a-city. Hallgate is harder stuff, with a strong, Brutalist grid of brown brick and golden concrete towards the heath and a public pond, and a self-pitying sculpture showing 'the architect' being crushed by 'society', or in this case the planning system, which for so long tried to block Lyons's modernist designs for not being 'in keeping' with this Georgian area. The villagey, somewhat unreal neo-Georgian council estate nearby is a good example of what they preferred. Visiting any Span estate can be a little unpleasant for the casual pedestrian, as there are always 'Private Property' or 'Private Estate' signs all over the grass. The intelligence and wit of Lyons's squares are usually just about worth the rudeness of being constantly told that they're not for you – though contrast the relatively laissez-faire Parkleys.

SCEAUX GARDENS, CAMBERWELL
Camberwell Borough Architects Dept, 1957–60
OROZCO GARDEN, CAMBERWELL
6A Architects and Gabriel Orozco, 2016
International Style

An object lesson in how to do public space in an inner-city council estate, courtesy of the short-lived Camberwell Architects Department, before it was subsumed into Southwark – who have since done their best to ruin it. Sceaux Gardens is a set of glassy blocks and terraces that are, unusually for any council estate, more inspired by Mies van der Rohe's luxury developments in Detroit, New Jersey and Montreal than they are by the rougher (and hence, in theory, cheaper) Corbusian example. The front facades of the buildings are in glass with colourful vitreous panels; their poor maintenance can be seen in the way that the grey mosaic cladding of the sides is barely perceptible, in the boarded-up community buildings, and in the disastrous fire that happened in one of the two tall towers, Lakanal House (there's no evidence the fire's spread had anything to do with the original design). From a distance, they're still very impressive buildings, with a brittle clarity. What happens in-between adds an unruly touch to this elegance. Sceaux Gardens was built, as the name implies, partly on the back gardens of bombed-out Victorian houses, and while the houses were removed, the gardens weren't, and the domestic nature of the pathways, sprawling trees and thickets of wisteria that run between the blocks is obvious once you realize it.

More recent additions from an unexpected source provide some neat ideas about interaction with the surrounding area. The original connection – the public pathway through Voltaire House – has been closed up by Southwark Council in their infinite wisdom, which means that the estate is effectively severed from the busy high street, which was never the intention of the designers. The South London Gallery that occupies two buildings on either side of Peckham Road has – at least during their opening hours – made major attempts to redress this, with a respect for residents which is much more humane than that of their elected representatives. Their architects, 6A, have made a break in the line of terraces on the south side of the estate, which leads past a prettily landscaped miniature square and modest, tiled ancillary buildings for the gallery, to a garden formed into concentric swirling brick terraces around a mini-ruin of London stocks with rosemary growing out of it, designed by the artist Gabriel Orozco. Walking from there, past the gallery's back entrance and café, you're on the main road. You can look at some art, too, if you like. To really see what makes Sceaux Gardens different, go to the Southampton Way Estate immediately north of it. The same slabs and maisonettes, but without either the glacial architecture or, crucially, the landscaping, reduced to a large, useless and fenced-off patch of grass.

OLD VIC ANNEX, LAMBETH
Lyons Israel Ellis, 1958
Brutalist

One of the very earliest of London's Brutalist buildings, and one of the most brusque and unpretentious, built as service spaces for the decorated shed of the Old Vic Theatre. To the street, four high storeys, two fully glazed, two bricked up but for asymmetric slit windows, a glazed internal stairwell between them, and a sculptural escape staircase at the far side, and a series of bunker-like towers to the back alley. Thick, rigid, unromantic, and a welcome bit of crankiness in the Waterloo streetscape.

FINNISH CHURCH, ROTHERHITHE
Yorke Rosenberg & Mardall, 1958
International Style

Yorke Rosenberg & Mardall were like the start of some sort of off-colour architectural joke: an Englishman, a Slovak and a Finn. This commission is one of several twentieth-century Scandinavian churches for visiting seamen around the old Surrey Docks,

ranging from the pretty, pocket Hansa-baroque Norwegian to the lurking, Brutalist Swedish. The Finnish is the finest by some way, with YRM bringing to bear their mastery of classical proportion, and the sometimes slightly prissy sense of cleanliness and dignity that characterizes their buildings for the NHS, to an apparently unsympathetic building type (who wants a church like a hospital?). In the event, it's a triumph, from the brown-brick campanile to the pure white of the main building to the street. A grid of windows for church offices suggest something a little official – but go inside, and you'll find the church itself is a perfect demonstration of the virtues of Scandinavian design. Warmth without stuffiness, cosiness without tweeness. The interior is galleried, like an eighteenth-century neoclassical church, but decorated with little more than wood, concrete, a granite panel and some well-designed suspended lamps. It's a place of purest repose, where, to quote Mies in a more literal way than he intended, 'God is in the details.' There's a sauna too.

BRANDON ESTATE, CAMBERWELL
Ted Hollamby for the London County Council Architects Dept, 1958–62
International Style

Like an inner-city version of the **Alton Estate (p. 112)**, this estate at the point where Camberwell and Kennington meet is a showcase of just how crucial the open space is to making the municipal *ville radieuse* work. Rolling greenery and mature trees surround six elegantly profiled point blocks, grids of well-detailed facing panels, with sculptural roof gardens on top, giving the estate a skyline of six pairs of concrete wings. Henry Moore's *Reclining Figure No. 3* lies on a hill below. At the north side are a rather faded shopping precinct and maisonettes, with some nice decorative touches, alongside some preserved terraces:

the first time the LCC had rehabilitated rather than demolished working-class housing. Best of all, the parkland that extends inside and around the south side of the estate is thoroughly used by locals in all weathers, especially at the weekend. It's possible these sorts of spaces were indeed poorly used and desolate in the 1960s – I wasn't there – but anyone saying that about the Brandon Estate today doesn't know what they're talking about.

EROS HOUSE, CATFORD
Owen Luder Partnership, 1960
Brutalist

The place where London Brutalism shifts from being a no-bullshit logical aesthetic into a matter of sculpture and spectacle. This speculative office and shopping complex was substantially designed by Rodney Gordon, who the commercial architect Luder had hired from the London County Council. Eros House replaced a flamboyant Victorian music hall, and retains much of the ostentation and tawdriness of that genre, although considerably more integrity. As built, it was a wing of glass offices, articulated into a staggered, sculptural arrangement, linked by a raw concrete stair tower to a Corbusian supermarket round the back. In the 1990s it was very cheaply converted into housing, meaning that the offices were shabbily clad, but the stairwell, and its various plaques and awards from the Civic Trust and the Concrete Society, was left untouched. That stairwell, and the silhouette it creates, is still extraordinary, rugged and monumental but full of subtle spatial distortions, a high-end architectural experiment made on the behest of a client more interested in a fast buck. That tawdriness has almost overtaken the building, so visiting it today is not recommended for melancholics.

FAIRFIELD HALLS, CROYDON
Robert Atkinson & Partners, 1962
People's Detailing

The only truly civic building dating from Croydon's extremely comprehensive redevelopment in the 1960s is this theatre and concert hall, set back from one of the dramatically overengineered roads that pass through this private 'Mini-Manhattan' of commercial, high-modernist office blocks. The basic idea is blindingly obvious – this is the **Royal Festival Hall (p. 84)** in miniature, a decorative, stone-clad set of flowing foyers with an 'egg in a box' auditorium at the heart of it, whose curved roof forms the building's skyline. It used to look very shabby compared to its Lambeth inspiration, but was beautifully restored in 2019 by MICA Architects – their major intervention has been to remove adverts and tat from the public foyers, which now have a glistening mid-century grandeur close to that of the **Belgrade Theatre (p. 325)** in Coventry, with its black granite columns, chic signage and elegant balustrades now emphasized rather than hidden; it's a rare pleasure to see the sixties qualities of a sixties building celebrated.

CANADA WATER ESTATE, ROTHERHITHE
SOMERSET ESTATE, BATTERSEA
WYNDHAM ESTATE, CAMBERWELL
WESTBURY ESTATE, CLAPHAM
Philip Bottomley for the London County Council Architects Dept, early 1960s
Brutalist

These small, almost identical estates all showcase my personal favourite of the LCC's various standard types for towers, which was rolled out on these four sites with only minor changes between them. Each is defined by articulated concrete-and-brick point blocks, whose living rooms have been cantilevered out from the main bulk of the buildings, creating rhythmic and distinctive silhouettes. For some reason these were built south of the river only, usually in clusters of three or four towers. At Canada Water, the brick is red, at the others it's in brown stocks; some have painted the concrete frames, others haven't. There are few great contrasts between the estates on the ground, either – stark and urban squares and low-rise maisonettes stand between the towers. But what these are most about is the creation of miniature futuristic skylines – and for some reason, they were all placed in south London, contributing to its sense of difference from the north.

___

ELEPHANT AND CASTLE SHOPPING CENTRE, WALWORTH ❶
Boissevain & Osmond, 1960–65
International Style

There is a peculiar idea that modernist buildings cannot be adapted, as if Gothic or neoclassical architecture – usually, especially in the nineteenth century, designed as self-contained, stand-alone works of art – were some sort of blank canvas for people to 'knock through' and alter to their heart's content. One way you can be sure this is bollocks is in seeing the way received opinion reacts to the successful ad hoc, gradual adaptation of a modernist building – that is, with disbelief. Such is the story with this unimpressive piece of commercial modernism, a nondescript, thinly detailed tower on a podium atop an introverted mall. After it failed as the thing it was intended to be – a typical Arndale Centre-style mall of chain stores and not much else – it slowly morphed into what it is now. This was because of the changes not to the facades – pink paint, blue cladding – but to the way that the space, both inside and outside, gradually transformed. A street market developed in the sunken walkways outside,

and the working-class British, Chinese, Latin American, Caribbean and Polish community around utilized the low rents and large, cubic glass shop units to open restaurants, cafés, hairdressers, wholesalers and much else here that would never have a hope of existing anywhere else in Zone 1. The bowling alley and bingo hall – both recently closed – were the most genuinely 'open' and democratic spaces in the whole of central London, used by people from all walks of life. The straightforward modernism of the clear, light multilevel interior is given a period charm it would otherwise lack through all of this activity, use and change. This place went from being a boring and introverted building to an important and exciting one; in modern architecture too, the 'final design' can sometimes be only the first step. Sadly, a late attempt to save the building failed; demolition commenced in spring 2021.

___

MICHAEL FARADAY MEMORIAL, WALWORTH
Rodney Gordon for the London County Council Architects Dept, 1960
METRO CENTRAL HEIGHTS, WALWORTH
Ernő Goldfinger, 1964
International Style, Brutalist

On the Elephant and Castle roundabout, this is actually an electricity substation, which Rodney Gordon – before moving from the LCC to Owen Luder – designed as an abstract sculpture of glistening metal discs as a tribute to the titular scientist and Walworth resident. About the only good thing about the recent redevelopment of the area as a suburb of Singapore is the creation of a public square around this previously ignored memorial, drawing attention to an enduringly strange urban monument. Overlooking it is the former Alexander Fleming House, now known as Metro Central Heights, built for the Department of Health as offices and turned into flats in the 1990s (hence the unfortunate 1990s magnolia paint job). Typically for Goldfinger, it has a rough and rational vigour, a multilevel skyline and, in contrast to the buildings around it – of all eras – the sort of mass, presence and confidence to hold its own against the traffic chaos all around. The rear view from the Thameslink line of the multistorey glazed walkways between the blocks is still a real thrill, making up for at least some of the estate agent clichés foisted on this place.

— — —

ST DUNSTAN'S COLLEGE DINING HALL, CATFORD
Verner Rees Laurence & Mitchell, 1961–3
Googie

A great bit of silliness, a dramatic hyperbolic paraboloid dining hall for the pupils of this Gothick public school in Catford, linked by a glass walkway but making zero concessions to context or keeping. Quite the surprise to find this from the top deck of a bus in SE6, a joke at the expense of public school pomposity – although the joke's on us, given that so many of the equally interesting state schools of the same era in the same city have been demolished and replaced with PFI tat, while this one has been preserved as well as the turreted pile next to it. *They* know what's good for them.

— — —

DINING & ASSEMBLY HALL, BRUNSWICK PARK PRIMARY SCHOOL, CAMBERWELL
Stirling & Gowan for the London County Council Architects Dept, 1961
Brutalist

The site of this building is about as spacious and eerie as you could get within inner London, occupying the space between school buildings in the interzone where Camberwell, Peckham and Walworth

all meet, an area made up of various estates of varying quality, all poorly connected to each other. Responding to that disjointed space, Stirling and Gowan created this tiny monument as a circus around which it can revolve; a circular mound has, just set slightly into it, a building divided like a piece of origami into four parts – three monopitch halls for school activities, plus a small playground with an abstracted wall connecting it to the main facade. It looks more than a little knackered now, and like practically everything Stirling designed it is much smaller in real life than in the architectural history books. Even so, it is the best building to display the way that overeducated Brutalist architects derived ideas from the ideal plans of the Renaissance, via the art historian Rudolf Wittkower; so, here, everything you see derives from an extremely clever diagrammatic plan, translated into a strange miniature landscape, a vision of celestial geometry in cheap stock brick and standard glazing.

— — —

LEWISHAM PARK
Lewisham Borough Architects Dept, 1962
International Style

A lovely essay in the oft-discussed, seldom-implemented 'towers in a park' genre: three eighteen-storey points, with nicely curved and tiled red and white elevations and deep balconies, at the edge of a little park on the otherwise rather bleak stretch between Lewisham and Catford, opposite the hospital. Lewisham, always a dormitory, isn't a place that is spoiled for monuments, and these impressive but modest markers suit the place. No grand gestures here, just a leaf-dappled enclave of municipal idealism.

VANBRUGH PARK ESTATE, BLACKHEATH
Chamberlin Powell & Bon, 1962
Brutalist

Unlike most of their contemporaries, Chamberlin Powell & Bon never did the same thing twice, so at first you might be surprised that this small estate on the other side of the heath from **Hallgate (p. 87)** is the work of the designers of the **Barbican (p. 66)**, **Golden Lane Estate (p. 55)** and the **University of Leeds South Campus (p. 381)**. It comprises a series of terraced houses around asphalted squares, with surprisingly little greenery (presumably, the acres of it on the heath were considered quite enough), around a single tower block. If you're approaching from the heath, the entrance is indicated by two otherwise purposeless brick towers, working as heraldic turrets. Then you find yourself in an irregular grid of breezeblock houses with first-floor ribbon windows, neat little drip mouldings and space-age kitchen windows on the ground floors. The houses look a little poky, and the public spaces are poor by CPB's normally high standards. The tower is excellent – two blocks of spacious and luxurious council flats with commanding views, around a central, open, Piranesian stair tower. As at Leeds, the painting of the buildings detracts from their qualities rather than enhancing them, and is probably not even cheaper than just cleaning the concrete.

NATIONAL SPORTS CENTRE, CRYSTAL PALACE
London County Council Architects Dept, 1964
Brutalist

Crystal Palace Park is the most surreal public park in Britain, centred on an absence – Joseph Paxton's enormous glass exhibition building, which was relocated to this green in suburban Sydenham from the 1851 Great Exhibition in Hyde Park – famously, its pioneering prefabricated design meant it could just be disassembled and put up somewhere else. It burned down in the 1930s, but the space where the palace used to sit is still defined by the sculptural sequence of imperial subjects, sphinxes and stairways that originally led to it. Opposite is this, the largest LCC non-housing project after the Festival of Britain that was the Great Exhibition's purported successor – a giant sports centre with several swimming pools, sports halls and, outside, an athletics track, all in one overarching structure. Reached by a long walkway across the park, it is symmetrical, unusually for a Brutalist building, with everything in the design subordinated to holding up the vast central space that serves the various different functions. The concrete columns are like thickets, creating a cathedral-like effect of organic openness. Unlike the Crystal Palace and its High-Tech successors, which aimed at being intangible, coldly logical and extendable, this is a singularly conceived one-off, weighty and grimly exciting. The difference is encapsulated outside in the absurd bust of Paxton on top of a squat square plinth of engineering brick.

DAWSON HEIGHTS, EAST DULWICH ✪
Kate Macintosh for Southwark Borough Architects Dept, 1964–72
Brutalist

One of the finest scenographic achievements of the sixties, courtesy of the then extraordinarily young Kate Macintosh. Visible across south London from its placing on the highest point of hilly East Dulwich, anyone living south of the river will know this as the pair of buildings that look like castles or battleships, the only things aside from the Crystal Palace radio towers that would make you look in this direction rather than north to the City skyline. They're placed as if directly facing each other, an irregular silhouette, in order to be looked at. It's usual for modernist buildings of this era to look a little chilling and overscaled from a distance, and more intimate close up; Macintosh was playing a different game, rejecting an architecture of systems and reproducibility in favour of one modelled, according to her own account, on the castle that overlooks Edinburgh, where she grew up.

So whereas the approach of **Park Hill (p. 370)** to its site is to attempt a continuous roofline in order to stress the systematic, repetitious nature of the estate built into the outcrop, Dawson Heights is all towers and bulges, a romantic gesture. It is in no plausible way 'in keeping' with the suburban Dulwich streets which have such a breathtaking view of it; its idea of 'context' is not based on 'What existing buildings are here and what can I do with them?', but on the rather more interesting and much more risky question: 'What can I do with this landscape?' On the ground, the craggy complexities of the silhouette have to be worked out in down-to-earth detail. Several different arrangements and types of flat are integrated into the two castle-cruisers, modelled with lots of cantilevers and staggered skylines, so as to emphasize, much more emphatically than, say, **Keeling House (p. 124)**, the individuality of each dwelling within the giant collective structure. What looks arbitrary from a distance has actually been carefully worked out on an intimate, human level. Thrilling, unique and outrageously confident. [B.13]

LAMBETH TOWERS
George Finch for Lambeth Borough
Architects Dept, 1965
Brutalist

On an inner-city site opposite the Imperial War Museum, this sparky cluster of towers was designed by George Finch under Lambeth's Borough Architect, Ted Hollamby. Like Sidney Cook in Camden, Hollamby assembled a tight-knit team of designers who created, for the most part, unique designs for specific sites. Unlike in Camden, this often meant high-rise, and George Finch had a terrific eye for skylines, rivalled in London only by his life partner and architect at the neighbouring borough of Southwark, Kate Macintosh. Here, what initially looks like several towers bunched together is actually just one, twisting and turning its way upwards, with neat boxed-out flats, as in the (pre-'renovation') **Eros House (p. 90)**, but with much finer concrete work, around a cylindrical glass stairwell; it's a lot of excitement packed into a very small space, but scaled so that it's not remotely overbearing. Shops and a doctor's surgery are built into the ground floor – a model of the currently fashionable 'inner-city mixed-use building'.

CENTRAL HILL ESTATE, GIPSY HILL ✪ ❶
Rosemary Stjernstedt for Lambeth Borough
Architects Dept, 1967–74
Brutalist, People's Detailing

If **Lambeth Towers (above)** displays Ted Hollamby's team mastering concrete urbanity, Central Hill is a perfect modernist suburb, the finest of its kind south of the river. Designed by Rosemary Stjernstedt, one of the original team at **Alton Estate (p. 112)**, it's built across a large swathe of the otherwise nondescript Gipsy Hill, with two distinct faces. Abutting the Victorian and Edwardian villas all around are grey-black weatherboarded houses, a familiar Anglicization of Alvar Aalto's Finnish rural modernism, with slightly rustic tiled paths leading you into, as it were, the 'central hill'. Mounting the slope, into which space for sports has been unfussily fitted,

The magnificent low-rise, high-density *rus-in-urbe* of Rosemary Stjernstedt's threatened Central Hill Estate.

are stepped-section concrete and pale-brick maisonettes, with nice big balconies and panoramic perspectives; the way these blocks step down and then rise up the hill, shadowed by trees, shows a rare command of the integration between townscape and public gardens. Its intimate domestic spaces gently lead to sweeping panoramas with a hide-and-seek lightness; suburban, for sure, but not at all parochial or pinched. Only the poor upkeep and the damp, deciduous trees tell you that Central Hill is not in some affluent Swiss modernist hill village. Currently, like **Cressingham Gardens (p. 113)**, Central Hill is slated to be demolished and then 'densified', though it uses its space much more effectively than the suburban villas all around – except these can't be just sold off en masse by local government in the way this can. One of the great tragedies of social housing in London is how the instruments that built it are now being used to destroy it.

COTTON GARDENS, KENNINGTON
George Finch for Lambeth Borough
Architects Dept, 1968
Brutalist

Another George Finch estate for Lambeth, as sculptural as **Lambeth Towers (p. 94)** but much more monumental and dominant. Although Lambeth didn't generally go in for standardization as such, they did use prefabricated concrete components to build this and another estate in Stockwell, where tall, thick towers have been assembled piece-by-piece into spiky and bulky Gothic skylines. Cotton Gardens is the better of the two, partly because the concrete hasn't been painted, and partly because of its relationship with the terraced houses Finch designed below, which are as miniaturized and cosy as the high-rises are proudly scaled. Note especially the way that, again, each individual flat is obvious from the elevation, as a coherent unit; it suggests the stepped maisonettes of the lower blocks at **Thamesmead Estate (below)** stacked upwards, to make full use of the inner-city site.

---

10 BLACKHEATH PARK, BLACKHEATH
Patrick Gwynne, 1968
International Style

A memorably odd modernist house in a private street round the back of the south end of the heath, and unlike many of the more personal houses of the period, easily seen by members of the public. Clad in black slate alternating with frosted glass, with a plan made up of two intersecting pentagons – and where they meet there is a low, peculiarly vaginal concrete stairwell in front with no discernible use. Someone's private pop art dream, but its client was a building contractor, rather than an artist or spy.

ST THOMAS' HOSPITAL, LAMBETH
Yorke Rosenberg & Mardall, 1966–75
International Style

You've seen this, even if you think you haven't; the fact you might not know it says something about how exceptionally quiet the radicalism of this building is. Directly opposite Parliament, this is Eugene Rosenberg designing something very similar to the Prague Pensions Institute that he worked on in the 1930s, a purist tile-clad edifice, hygienic and precise. These deep-planned hospital buildings, arranged in a courtyard on the south side of Westminster Bridge, aren't Brutalist, aren't 'sculptural', and have no interest in trying to emulate or continue the theatrics of the buildings all around, whether the Gothic of Westminster or the Baroque of the old County Hall. This is modernism as it was originally conceived in interwar Europe by technocratic socialists – buildings as smoothly running machines,

serving a rational population for egalitarian purposes, and what better for the most prominent building of the National Health Service? The fact that it has not, unlike, say, **Finsbury Health Centre (p. 52)**, become an emblem for the NHS's campaigning defenders, despite its location, maybe suggests that the heroism and sentimentality that the likes of Lubetkin brought to their version of technocratic modernism was necessary in order to form some sort of lasting public connection.

Even so. This is a great set of buildings, finely detailed, strong, and strongly public in its approach to space, but there is one feature that is on another level altogether. That is the little garden that faces the river and the Houses of Parliament, with Naum Gabo's sculpture *Revolving Torsion* at its centre (the work of another exile from 1930s Europe). An upscaled version of a work Gabo made when living in Berlin, it's a fascinating object, a steel pivot, constantly in motion, around which this Welfare State microcosm rotates.

THAMESMEAD ESTATE PHASES 1 & 2 ❶
Greater London Council Architects Dept, 1968–74
Brutalist

The third part of Stanley Kubrick's film *A Clockwork Orange* is about programmed association. A convicted murderer and rapist is being conditioned against violence via constant exposure to filmic representations of murder and rape, combined with a drug treatment that makes him associate these images with personal sickness and pain. Due to the accidental fact that Beethoven's Ninth Symphony was playing in the background of some of those images, he ends up feeling agony and revulsion whenever he hears it, despite its total irrelevance to the violence he is supposed to be being conditioned against. *Poor Ludwig Van, he never hurt no one!* It's ironic, then, that Thamesmead, the GLC suburb in which Kubrick filmed the first part of the film, has always been associated, since almost immediately after it was finished, with the violence, anomie and dystopian social engineering depicted in the film, although there's no reason to make any causal link between them. Accordingly, one of the most extensive and photogenic of the modernist schemes of the 1960s has been subjected to various drastic forms of surgery, to remove the taint of 'the old ultraviolence' from it. Maybe because Kubrick happened to film the most elegant part of the estate – the ensemble around Southmere Lake – or perhaps because this is the area that could most plausibly be rebuilt as a luxury enclave – this is the part of Thamesmead that has been most subject to know-nothing redevelopment.

The best way to see Thamesmead is to start at Lesnes Abbey, a set of ruins in front of a conserved woodland, a short stroll from Abbey Wood railway station. A walkway leads directly from the abbey through the estate, a continuous elevated route that passes the raked, stepped-section concrete panel low-rise maisonettes (with neat, legible public squares between) that dominate the estate, past grazing horses and overgrown grassland. You will eventually arrive at Southmere Lake. Fifteen years ago, you would have found integrated shops, a health centre, and a pub and community centre, overlooked by towers and the most attractive of the stepped-section maisonettes. A big chunk of these were bitten off for illiterate brick-clad blocks with silly hats, the health centre was relocated on the ground floor rather than on the walkways, because walkways are bad (the result is it's much less easy to get to), the shops were demolished, and the pub was closed. Try not to get annoyed by this, and walk across the smart pedestrian bridge under the elevated Eastern Way – an exciting multilevel trek,

London's Brutalist New Town: the towers and maisonettes of Thamesmead, built on stilts above the Erith Marshes.

SE LONDON

with movement under and above – and you can still follow the canals either to Phase 2, a relatively dull long series of interlinked grey Brutalist blocks sheltering some elegant red-brick maisonettes, or to Phase 3, where Thamesmead went Postmodernist, with fussy retro details and a transplanted Victorian clock tower to replace the promised future. This, at least, managed to continue the system of lakeside routes which had been planned for the original suburb, which was totally dropped for the foul informal Phase 4 of retail parks and Barratt Homes. And that's it – the slow crushing of an intelligent, if overambitious, idea, by the combined forces of deregulation, anti-modernism and the witless association of dystopian science fiction with mundane social democratic reality. Poor GLC, they never hurt no one.

―――

CATFORD CENTRE & MILFORD TOWERS, CATFORD ❶
Owen Luder Partnership, 1974
Brutalist

Cheap and nasty, monumental and visceral – the best surviving example of what Luder's partner Rodney Gordon called an architecture that gives you (please insert the correct genitalia if not yours) 'that feeling from your balls to your throat'. Especially after the demolition of Luder's work in Gateshead and Portsmouth and its mutilation at **Eros House (p. 90)**, this largely unrenovated building is almost an important historic survivor, security spikes, pigeon shit, spalling concrete and all. Easily spotted in Catford through the giant fibreglass cat that introduces it from the High Street, it's a minor megastructure, with a shopping parade and supermarket below, and a stack of flats above, as in the much less impressive, if equally ungainly, 'Tesco Town' built a few years ago in nearby Woolwich. This stacking of housing above shopping is 'best practice' nowadays, but the Catford Centre has still been slated for demolition for nearly a decade. The shopping segment is nothing much – a passageway logically connected with Victorian Catford – but the council flats, better known as Milford Towers, are something else, looming up monstrously in front of you as you walk past the charity shop. As you approach those beefily curved orange-brick service towers, the cylinder escape staircases in rough concrete, and the overhead walkways firing off almost at random, you are (well, I am) filled with the sort of anticipation and fear that comes with walking up to a medieval citadel. There are a lot of flats here, arranged in a long wall, cantilevered above a multistorey car park which is visible from the rear of the building.

Currently, the neglect and menace are undeniable, but there's no structural or commercial reason *in principle* why this couldn't be remade into a south London **Brunswick Centre (p. 63)**. There is a major architectural difference: that building's immediately legible plan and obvious public orientation is here replaced with a megastructural maze whose entrance and exit are opaque; a Brutalist rookery, the Catford Casbah. At the time of writing, demolition is pending, but some stairwells have been painted – it's all very mysterious.

―――

CHARLOTTE TURNER GARDENS, DEPTFORD
London County Council Architects Dept, 1930s
Lewisham Council Architects Dept, 1970s
Viennese, People's Detailing

An accidental-looking public space carved out of the industrial interzones of this most characterful of London's riverside districts. These slightly scrubby, wild gardens stand in-between two distinct moments in housing architecture. To the east, a monumental 1930s neo-Georgian/Red Viennese housing estate with grand arches, Hanseatic balconies and decks with clothes drying in the summer, an image of slightly regimented collectivity and urbane noise and clangour. To the west, a series of 1970s mews and terraces that are the product of Lewisham's then head of housing, Nicholas Taylor (the celebrated author of *The Village in the City*). Black-stained wood, good bright-red brickwork and cobbles, intimate but not cutesy. In an area that always seems to be permanently damp, these houses feel appropriately sheltered and warm. Two very different approaches to council housing, well linked by the informal green.

—

THAMES BARRIER, CHARLTON
Greater London Council Architects Dept and Rendel Palmer & Tritton (engineers), 1974–84
Brutalist, High-Tech

The last great monument of a London-wide local government architects department is, aptly enough, an engineering structure that stops London from being destroyed. Notoriously, this flood barrier has been used much more than expected. The Thames Barrier runs across the river between Charlton and Silvertown, but its public face is firmly on the south. The tall building that overlooks the Barrier consists of a visitor centre and control tower in corduroy concrete topped by a titanium crown using the same materials as the barrier below, which resembles a series of titanium shells that open out to reveal yellow pulleys and grey discs. The integration of engineering and aesthetics here is on the level of the best Victorian designers: the results are effortless, understandable to the uninitiated and hauntingly beautiful, glistening their way across the Thames. The pleasant pocket park adjacent on the south side is a recent design by Patel Taylor architects; to the north is the more complex **Thames Barrier Park (p. 132)**.

The heroic engineering of the GLC's Thames Barrier, municipal London's last great project.

CEMEX CONSTRUCTION AGGREGATE WORKS, ANGERSTEIN WHARF, CHARLTON
1990
Industrial

One of the few pieces of industrial Thames left, this is a large complex which handles concrete aggregate brought into a wharf by boat, and processes it into usable building materials. It's not much, given that this part of the river used to be nothing but industry, but it's enough to give you the impression of what this sort of landscape was like, all gantries, chutes, frames, a lightweight and daring accidental architecture resembling the Constructivist theatre sets of Vsevolod Meyerhold, but built at scale. Angerstein Wharf even has its own railway line. What's best about this surprising survival is the riverside path that runs along it, which means you can get a close-up view of a forgotten city without ever feeling like you ought not to be there. There's even a riverside pub nearby for when all that excitement gets too heady.

FORMER DESIGN MUSEUM, BERMONDSEY
Conran Roche, 1989
PRINCE'S TOWER, ROTHERHITHE
Troughton McAslan, 1990
Classical Modernism

In among the chirpy spivvy mock-warehouses and early 'stunning developments' of the part of 'Docklands' that runs from Shad Thames to Surrey Quays – much lower-rise than at Canary Wharf, and dominated by car-centred, straggly non-planning, at its worst around the Surrey Quays Shopping Centre – are these two fascinating historical fakes. What you think you see, when you look at these two Thameside buildings, are fine 1930s International Style works, smooth and elegant and optimistic and fittingly

nautical. In the case of Prince's Tower, it's an imitation of Erich Mendelsohn, with sleek glazed tubes of glass in a white concrete volume, and at the Design Museum, it's classic Corbusier with a hint of Bauhaus.

Actually the London Docklands never had any buildings like this. Aesthetic refinement wasn't necessary for dockside industry, the views from the other side or Thames Clipper boats were irrelevant, and these pure white surfaces would soon have been caked in soot and muck. McAslan's block of flats is a historicist tribute, Conran Roche's Museum a conversion and total redesign of a ragged forties concrete warehouse by Fred Roche and Stuart Mosscrop, two of the designers of Milton Keynes's **Shopping Building (p. 223)**, on the strength of which they were hired by Conran. This doesn't detract from the quality of these two buildings – both are exceptionally clever, and unlike a lot of Docklands' first, get-rich-quick, non-plan phase in the late eighties, they've actually endured well, looking rather timeless. It's all lies, damned lies, as fake as much as the many buildings of the same decade that tried to look like 1840s warehouses, and there's a lot of those around here. If you want to find the point at which modernism became just another style in the Postmodernist pick and mix, here it is.

WALTER'S WAY & SEGAL CLOSE, HONOR OAK PARK
Walter Segal, Jon Broome and self-builders, 1980s
Ecomodernist

This cul-de-sac of rangy houses off some Victorian hillside villas in one of the leafier bits of the Borough of Lewisham is so overpraised, as some sort of alternative to mass housing, a 'solution to the housing crisis', an Anarchist experiment that could somehow be a blueprint for a new world, etc., that you might be surprised when you actually visit by just how small, pleasant and obviously limited it all is. The short version of the story is that Nicholas Taylor at Lewisham Council was convinced that some throwaway, otherwise unusable bits of land owned by the local authority should be given away to self-builders, who would use the German émigré modernist Walter Segal's simple, cheap self-building system and then keep the houses. This is what happened, and it's exceptional in every respect, rather than a reproducible model. Not only in the sense that it's a programme extremely hard to scale up (shocking as this may be to many anarchists and architects, most of us don't actually want to build our own houses), but also in how well it is suited to its site. The houses are massively altered, of course, but they are still obviously the product of Segal's and his local partner Jon Broome's use of a delicate, lightweight module that makes the houses feel more like Japanese tea-houses or Case Study Houses in the LA hills than the Englishman's Castle. These sometimes gawky, sometimes stylish, always bohemian and raffish houses trace a steep hill, and it's like entering an enchanted garden. Enjoy it for what it is.

WATERLOO INTERNATIONAL TERMINAL
Grimshaw, 1993
High-Tech

A real railway terminal, on the grand scale. The International Terminal was built as an annexe to one of the most fascinatingly stupid of British railway stations – the Edwardian rebuilding of Waterloo, where a giant neo-baroque archway stuck in an alleyway leads to a vast glass hall. The Eurostar, meanwhile, was at first little more than an extension of the TGV network into southern England; journeys on it in the 1990s drew attention to the gulf between Britain's shabby, underfunded network

and the modern public transport of France. Accordingly, the International Terminal that completed this connection needed to show a modernity and confidence which had been absent from British railway architecture for a century (odd isolated successes such as **Coventry Railway Station, p. 328**, notwithstanding). Grimshaw was an inspired choice; the High-Tech architecture he represented was always about following on from the great Victorians like Brunel, and here his firm got to create a true modern equivalent of their work. Looking at the plan, it's beautifully simple – cutting away one corner of the factory-style sawtooth glass roof of old Waterloo, it inserts into it a great sweep of tubular steel and glass, long enough for its platforms to take twenty-carriage trains, while the site's sharp curve is handled with the kind of effortless grace you find in nineteenth-century stations such as York or Newcastle Central. Left disused for a decade when the Eurostar moved to a new high-speed station at St Pancras (a neo-Victorian mess, where everything except the trains themselves is crammed into a storage space originally intended for beer barrels), the International Terminal is now an incongruously dramatic terminus for commuter trains.

JUBILEE LINE: BERMONDSEY STATION
Ian Ritchie, 1999
SOUTHWARK STATION
MacCormac Jamieson Prichard, 1999
CANADA WATER STATION & BUS STATION
Buro Happold and Eva Jiricna, 1999
High-Tech

Three more of the brilliant series of Jubilee Line stations designed at the end of the nineties under the direction of Roland Paoletti, none quite as mindblowing as Hopkins's **Westminster (p. 72)** or Foster's

Canary Wharf (p. 133), but each still just about worthy of the irritant of paying extra to get in and out of a Tube station. Bermondsey is the simplest of the three to the street, a long and low pavilion built with the expectation that an office block would be placed on top, which hasn't happened yet. The escalators are what make it, placed in a vast concrete cube, with hulking concrete struts holding it up. Canada Water consists of a glass drum by the engineers Buro Happold, which serves both as a light well and a scaled-up, futuristic version of Charles Holden's rotunda at **Arnos Grove (p. 137)**. Around it is a more brittle, angular bus station by Eva Jiricna, with the shelters and lights contained in the most delicate glass frames. Southwark is the best of the three, where the veteran Postmodernist-it's-ok-to-like Richard MacCormac provided another (this time curved) unpretentious entrance to the street. It was again designed so that an office block could be accommodated above, and current proposals are so gargantuan that they envisage demolishing the entrance altogether. Underneath is an anteroom between the two sets of escalators that lead first from the surface and then down to the platform. The space between them is demarcated by a curved wall of blue glass, two baroque archways leading to escalators up or down, all held up by thin concrete supports, with a light well above. Beautiful, haunting and quietly original – I know of no other space in London quite like it.

MILLENNIUM VILLAGE PHASE 1, GREENWICH

Ralph Erskine, 1999
Postmodernist, People's Detailing

Nothing to compare with the **Byker Estate (p. 484)**, but a quietly idyllic eco-enclave, now hemmed in by impoverished versions of itself. Of some historical interest as one of the first New Labour-style 'mixed communities',

its record there is, well, *mixed* (google it, to find the residents' forum and incessant complaints by owner-occupiers about the horror of young Tom and Charlotte having to share the estate's primary school with 'chav children'). Phase 2 is in an interestingly jumbled style which has aged badly, with corroded cladding, stains and dangling tiles; Phase 3 is a denser, taller imitation of Phase 1. But that first moment was, and remains, kind of lovely. A continuous four-storey wall of concrete-framed flats, clad in stained, damp brown wood, with big multicoloured balconies and an irregular skyline created by the top-floor penthouses, curves round a purpose-designated nature reserve, with a stream coming from the Thames, a nicely contrived 'wild' place to get lost in that you can walk out of in a minute and a half. Playing fields give views of the still-extant industry of **Cemex Construction Aggregate Works (p. 100)**; and, on the riverside, a yacht club in a rougher, faintly steampunk version of Erskine's ad hoc modernism. In that ensemble somewhere is a promise unfulfilled.

TATE MODERN, SOUTHWARK

Giles Gilbert Scott, 1947–63
Herzog & de Meuron, 1995–2016
Expressionist

Tate Modern is, of course, originally Bankside Power Station, a very late Giles Gilbert Scott design, in which he hangs on to classical symmetry but otherwise strips his brick Gothic down even further than in **Battersea Power Station (p. 108)**, with a terrifying sublimity to these cliffs of brown stocks. Herzog & de Meuron's renovation inserts a frosted-glass café and viewing platform on the roof, behind the single chimney, but is actually still as symmetrical as Battersea – though there are few places where you can see this, since Foster's Millennium Bridge approaches it off-centre.

Although the glass isn't too intrusive, old photographs suggest a more intimidating building, too much so perhaps for the purposes of wandering around at the weekend glancing at contemporary art. The major changes were in the interior, where Herzog & de Meuron exploit the scale of the Turbine Hall to create something which feels more out of Albert Speer than anything else – an awesome and terrifying space that is meant to do nothing else than be awesome and terrifying, and which provokes overscaled and expensive art to try and match it. Later iterations of the same idea, like the **Baltic Centre for Contemporary Art (p. 474)**, have lacked this extreme, deliberate excess.

Today, you can make your way up the confusing system of lifts, stairs and shopping mall escalators inserted around the Hall, and take a top-floor walkway into the new Switch House, which was designed a decade ago to house the Tate's bigger bits of art and pack in loads more lucrative private conferencing facilities. The metamorphosis of the design here from Herzog & de Meuron's original crystalline, glassy proposals (something more like their Elbephilharmonie in Hamburg, perhaps) into the current brick tower says a lot about the current curious compromise in London architecture between historicists and modernists. Certainly, it satisfyingly attaches itself to the old power station, and it is similarly all about dour Gothic spectacle, with rough and fetishistic neo-Brutalist curved staircases too big even for the Tate's huge crowds and a facade of perfectly cut, stubbly bricks, more like a carpet than a mass. Best of all is the viewing platform at the top, the most accessible public view of the City skyline and a place to spite the irritated denizens of the second-rate Rogers Stirk Harbour towers adjacent, who unsuccessfully tried to have this viewing point closed.

PECKHAM LIBRARY
Alsop & Störmer, 2000
Supermodernist, Pseudomodernist

The late Will Alsop was the Richard Seifert or Owen Luder of the 2000s, a designer of big and crass buildings that were so ambitious and OTT that they ended up speaking about their time more clearly and strongly than the more serious and well-made architecture of the era. His notorious West Bromwich theatre centre 'The Public' may have been one of the worst buildings ever given state funding, but elsewhere some genuine fun is to be had. So it is with this big and bright public library, plopped into a huge public square in a dense Victorian/sixties inner-city centre. The reading rooms at the top are cantilevered far out above a Teletubbyland colonnade beneath, with the soon-to-be-'trademark' wonky skinny pilotis. This surrealist colonnade is not particularly useful – and the archway nearby already works as a place to smoke or avoid rain – but what it does is clearly denote a monumental, instantly recognizable building, exhibiting the pride in scale and presence that a good inner-city public building should. It tells you, in big letters and green cladding, 'LIBRARY'. The rear facade is an all-glass wall, stained into rainbow colours, occasionally functionally deficient for the readers, but nicely daydream-inducing, on those miserable south London winter days. Thankfully, the War of the Worlds Goes Pop reading spaces are generously sized enough that you don't have to sit by the window. When it comes down to it, not much of real enduring quality was built during the boom of the 2000s – but, at best, the populism of the era led to places that combine a pride in architecture with a sense of taking people as what they are, not as what they should be. That's what this building does so well.

LABAN CENTRE, DEPTFORD
Herzog & de Meuron, 2001–3
STEPHEN LAWRENCE CENTRE, DEPTFORD
Adjaye Associates, 2004–7
Supermodernist

These two small public buildings at different ends of Deptford Creek are roughly on the same scale, both low-rise and almost windowless structures which present decorative screens to the street, and try and create their own landscape rather than 'engage' with it in the currently popular sense. The Laban dance school is the more famous, a Stirling Prize winner and, for once, justly so – it's a limpid and perverse building. Surrounded by its own world of specially created grass escarpments, a translucent, synthetic cladding is shaded sky blue and punkish pink as it embraces the muddy trickle of the Creek. Inside, a surprisingly sombre and claustrophobic interior of black-painted rough concrete is not at all what you'd expect. At the other end of Deptford High Street, the Stephen Lawrence Centre does something more serious – named after the young student and aspiring architect who was stabbed to death in a racist attack in nearby Eltham in 1993, it houses the trust set up in his name, which runs community programmes (architectural included) largely aimed at young people, in a multicultural area, in a multifunctional building. Adjaye's design is accordingly harsher, perhaps too harsh, as a justified fear of vandalism and attacks has led to an elaborate security system, with none of the easily accessed public areas and cafés of the Laban. Adjaye's cladding screens are not translucent, but protective, jagged; the garden is smaller and, though public, feels much more for the users of the building than for stray visitors. Both interesting and intelligent buildings in their own way, these are also two poles of inner-city London – a lavish outward-aiming spectacle for the tourists and the arty types, and a more austerely financed, inward-facing parallel infrastructure for actual Londoners.

———

PALESTRA, SOUTHWARK
SMC Alsop, 2006
Supermodernist, Pseudomodernist

A big and bold piece of Alsop, near Blackfriars station's southern entrance, this is a good illustration of how to make an enormous office building enjoyable for the person who doesn't work in it but sees it a lot. The site, which would be shaped today more politely as a piece of neo-Georgian brick townscape, is treated by Alsop as the excuse for a massive, sloped, single glazed volume, linked by the 'Hi, Alsop here' wonky pilotis to a subsidiary block at the top, cantilevered as it meets the traffic crossing. As at **Peckham Library (p. 103)**, its apparent silliness belies a mastery of monumentality in scale. A fizzy, unhealthy rush, equally exciting on foot or from the train-side views on the tangle of viaducts between Waterloo and London Bridge.

———

H10 HOTEL, LAMBETH
Maccreanor Lavington, 2010
Modern Classicism, Expressionist

This currently prolific firm rose around 2010 from having lots of projects in the Netherlands, where they appreciate well-crafted, slightly staid, street-focused, brick-clad modernism, to suddenly having a dozen or so in London, due to the aforesaid becoming fashionable. This luxury hotel just off the Elephant and Castle is just right in its scale and the way its base rises to one singular cranked, bulky, angular high-rise facing a different direction, a German Expressionist experiment in angles and projections. Being a singular and coherent object, it works better than the lusciously detailed towers at '**King's Cross Central**' (**p. 154**), which, however lovely their surfaces, are too much of a clump when taken together; the H10 also compares well with the much uglier, much bigger high-rises foisted on the Elephant by the roundabout. The brick chosen here is purple clinker, which resembles nothing in the 'London vernacular'; it's as if they'd just transplanted the materials they'd normally use in Almere or Almersfoort.

_____

THE SHARD, BOROUGH
Renzo Piano Building Workshop, 2010–12
High-Tech

Is the tallest building in Britain, the highest skyscraper in Europe (outside of Moscow), really a matter of much more than superlatives? One can say that it is indeed very very big, and that it is indeed very very shiny, but is that enough? As a work of architecture, as opposed to a sign of the sort of city London has become, any assessment depends on where you're looking at it. If that place is the streets around it in Borough and Bermondsey, it's a shocker. The base of this tapering, spired, ninety-five-storey, 1000ft tower, so slender at the top, is an impenetrable, illegible glass monolith, casting huge swathes of inner-south London into permanent shadow; meanwhile, the partial breaking up of its mass into a miniature tower, alongside a second, subsidiary high-rise (the offices of News International) is clumsy. The original computer renders promised a seamless, singular 'shard of glass' scraping the sky, but the detailing is fiddly, particularly at the top, where a section of the tower is cut away to reveal its steel structure – the result simply looks unfinished.

The twenty-first-century buildings of Renzo Piano, Richard Rogers's old partner on the Centre Pompidou in Paris, rely heavily on meticulous metallic detailing, and beautifully made components, a sort of Swiss watch approach, seen at its best in the New York Times Building in Manhattan, but, here, the British construction industry seems incapable of managing such subtleties. Looked at in cold daylight, this is a bad building. Looked at in colder moonlight, however, it's a sinister and glowering masterwork. At night, a lighting scheme illuminates in reds, blues and whites the steel structure and the rough torn-off profile of the Shard's spire – the 'eye of Sauron' that has loomed over and, on special occasions, sent floodlights across, an increasingly dark and dystopian metropolis.

_____

BELLENDEN SCHOOL, PECKHAM
Cottrell & Vermeulen, 2018
Modernist Eclectic

Contemporary school architecture is a fairly depressing field, dominated by paranoia and PFI – tacky materials, bleakly metallic playgrounds, and high-security fences that make most recent schools feel like a cross between a prison and a business park. Bellenden School is a stand-out exception. Southwark Council, when not demolishing large swathes of its local-authority housing, has had a relatively enlightened policy for new schools, with some buildings of quality and seriousness presumably paid for by all the council estates it sold off – but Bellenden School is a cut above, a really delightful, light-hearted and urban school.

The school is in an alleyway, between deck-access council flats and mundane but recently lucrative Victorian terraced houses, at the point of Peckham where gentrification has become intense (cynics could argue that Southwark's programme of school building has much to do with trying to stop these new residents from moving to the suburbs when they start having kids). A curved brown-brick wall with portholes satisfies the stringent security regulations

Architecture you can read like a children's book: Cottrell & Vermeulen's Bellenden School in Peckham.

without feeling aggressive or obnoxious – quite some achievement. And then you come to an opening for a nursery, with yellow pitched-roofed pavilions poking their heads above the wall. Follow the curved wall a little further and you find a row of classrooms on pilotis, in what it has to be admitted is a fifties retro language of sans serif signage and a mix of coloured vitreous panels and stock brick. The curved path then arrives at the playground, where those classrooms on pilotis are raised partly above the play areas. This is exactly what building in a residential area in a big city should be like, and usually isn't – making walking a pleasure, and doing something imaginative and strange with the odd in-between spaces rather than shoving a slab or an icon into them. The school should also be a great place to be in as a child, when what you want is secrets, adventure, surprise, not big dumb things you can understand right away. If only there were more like it.

GOLDSMITHS CENTRE FOR CONTEMPORARY ART, NEW CROSS
Assemble, 2018
Modernist Eclectic

Goldsmiths College is in New Cross, an always slightly seedy district of early-Victorian classical streets. The college itself is never somewhere you'd go just to look at buildings. but an exception is the former Laurie Grove Public Baths, a fabulous red-and-white Jacobethan palace which has been used as studios for students of painting for the last decade or so. At an archway on its corner, the fanciful, florid detail gives way to filthy stock brick, a water tower, bins and prefabs. For Goldsmiths to pick Assemble as architects for its Centre for Contemporary Art, carved out of this building, was a smart choice, as there are few designers who could have done this organized chaos justice without smoothing it over and making it neat.

The art gallery as salvagepunk squat: the repurposed bathhouse chimney and water tank of Goldsmiths CCA.

There are two possible approaches to the building, one from the arch by the baths, the other from the main New Cross Road. Foolishly, Goldsmiths currently plan to demolish some prefabs to create a more 'formal' approach, because, as it is, the CCA is a maze you can reach via a maze.

Assemble have turned the baths' back end into a frontage, of an odd sort – a hulk of stock brick, an angular chimney and a water tank emphasized, Smithsons-style, as a found object. It resembles a Bernd and Hilla Becher industrial vignette, asymmetrical and eerie. Inside, there's the sort of montage you'd expect from the redesigners of the Four Streets in Granby, Liverpool, where the destructive effects of a botched clearance scheme were incorporated into the renovated houses. There are fragments of white tiles, soggy bricks, liquefying metal, and unexpected views outwards (into the painting studios in the main baths) and downwards (into a double-height empty space below

the ground floor). It is strange, exciting, fetishistic – and part of a major and welcome shift in British architectural culture from the facile to the tactile, as a comparison with the bumptious iconism of Will Alsop's building next door (one of his worst) should make very clear. As an alumnus of the college, I can say with some knowledge that it is Assemble's building that really captures its ethos – radical chic, south-east London squat aesthetics, and making virtues out of necessity. It is *so fucking Goldsmiths*, as people there used to say.

SW LONDON

NORTHERN LINE: CLAPHAM SOUTH, BALHAM, TOOTING BEC, TOOTING BROADWAY, COLLIERS WOOD, SOUTH WIMBLEDON & MORDEN STATIONS
Charles Holden, 1926
Modern Classicism

A clear brand: white-stone corner buildings, angular, wide glass surfaces, decorated with the London Underground roundel. Created before the mythic trip to the Continent when Charles Holden and Frank Pick found something a little more radical than Portland stone stripped classicism, these Tube stations show the architect trying to create something new from the materials at hand in 1920s London, without reference to the revolutions happening across the Channel. They are nonetheless very impressive little structures, both in the way they casually slip into the streetscape, immediately marking themselves as public buildings, and as portals to the underworld (not to mention their prescient factoring in of possible air rights – so Morden has a dull sixties block on top of it, and Clapham South a good block of thirties streamline moderne flats). The best is Tooting Broadway, where the integration of the symmetrical station with a Victorian crossroads made an appropriately municipal socialist backdrop to the intro of *Citizen Smith*. The buildings show an open-minded neoclassical architect trying to think his way out of the clichés and restraints of the style with some success; but not nearly so successfully as he did upon dumping classicism altogether a decade later. Underneath, the design of the relatively spacious subterranean stations, with their bronze uplighters, have a strange undercurrent of the sacral, one that was highly influential on the Moscow Metro.

LARKHALL ESTATE, CLAPHAM
Louis de Soissons and Grey Wornum, 1926–31
Modern Classicism, Viennese

Built as private philanthropy and taken over by the London County Council not long after completion, this estate at the edge of Clapham not inhabited by Trustafarians was designed by two classical architects in an unusual fusion of neo-Georgian at its most fey and frilly, and Central European planning at its most monumental. As at the **Ossulston Estate (p. 137)**, Liverpool's **St Andrew's Gardens (p. 425)** or Aberdeen's **Rosemount Square (p. 546)**, the arrangement of the mid-rise, long tenement blocks, with their archways leading to public gardens, is an importation of the ideas of 'Red Vienna', high-density urban drama given pride and grandeur through heraldic motifs and a fortress-like massing. The long access decks resemble those used on almost every major modernist estate in London, but the painted cherubs, Regency canopies and, most unusually of all, the well-thought-out, properly organized communal gardens make the Larkhall Estate unique among the many half-Georgian, half-Viennese estates of the thirties: tweeness and bombast, enriching each other.

BATTERSEA POWER STATION
Giles Gilbert Scott, 1929–53
Expressionist

Designed by Giles Gilbert Scott in two nearly identical phases, the first in the early thirties, the second twenty years later, this is the grandest (and certainly the largest) example of the severely reduced, mechanized brick Gothic that Scott would use for everything from universities to breweries. The power station is, as Ian Nairn pointed out in the

1960s, full of superfluities that would
have made not only a modernist but also
a nineteenth-century engineer wince,
particularly the fluting on those tall concrete
chimneys – something compounded when
they were recently replaced with replicas,
despite having no plausible use whatsoever
– but when you get up close, the raw power
of those immense brick walls is irresistible.
The building was at its most immense when
commanding a gigantic swathe of nothing
amidst the most expensive real estate
on earth. It is now reduced to a trophy
in an ugly scramble of naked property
speculation. The building will always
be worth seeing, however, and it gives
the naff new buildings around a lesson
about presence, their flimsiness making
its mass all the more powerful.

STREATHAM HILL: WAVERTREE COURT

Frank Harrington, 1933

PULLMAN COURT

Frederick Gibberd, 1936

CORNER FIELDE

Toms & Partners, 1937

CHRISTCHURCH HOUSE

1938

DUMBARTON COURT

Crouch & Coupland, 1939

International Style, Moderne

A microcosm of pre-war luxury flat building
on the busy main road between Brixton and
Streatham; it includes one major experiment
in middle-class modernism; accordingly, it is
a place to see what modernism is and isn't.
Travelling south from Brixton, the first block
is Dumbarton Court, and it is typical of the
type – tall for the period at six storeys, high
density and with a cover of greenery that
is paltry compared with the green spaces
of the post-war Rush Common council flats
on the other side of Brixton Hill. Unlike those,
though, this is full of piquant period detail,

The International Style meets suburban luxury:
Frederick Gibberd's Pullman Court in Streatham.

a tamed and Anglicized Weimar sleek of
horizontal banded brick and delicate, mass-
produced Crittall windows. A little further
south and you come to Christchurch House,
on the other side of the street, with daring
asymmetries around a monumental entrance
arch and deep, curved steamboat balconies,
commercialized Red Vienna at the seaside.

These are supposedly the unserious,
impure developer's architecture of the era,
yet Pullman Court, the first major work by
the prolific and cheerful populist modernist
Frederick Gibberd, is not as dissimilar
from them as pictures torn out of context
might suggest. It is also asymmetrical
but monumental, with two sternly towered
flanking wings; it also has green space
dominated by parking, far more dense
and tightly packed than anything the same
architect would do post-war; yet, stylistically,
the brick cladding and the illusion of
heaviness in the building's neighbours is

dissolved, with snow-white render on the concrete, and smooth access decks and balconies with just a hint of the Bauhaus headquarters in Dessau. Given Gibberd's subsequent development into the friendly face of modernism, it is telling how far this feels already from the glorious new world of the **Isokon Building (p. 139)** or **Highpoint (p. 139)** – his work is from the start relaxed and compromised. The two blocks next to it, though, reveal how much even Gibberd's modernism was needed. There is the curious deco/Arts and Crafts melange of Wavertree Court, cute but ruthlessly profit-maximizing on its site, and there's the grim, Gothamesque Corner Fielde, which looks like a model for Osbert Lancaster's caricature of 'luxury flats' – essentially an LCC block but taller and without the public space. A contemporary advert called it 'Mayfair in Streatham' and promised that 'the exclusive character of this distinguished residence has proved an irresistible attraction to many distinguished people'. How very like today's 'stunning developments'.

_____

CAMBRIDGE GARDENS, NORBITON
Sydney Clough, Son & Partners, 1949
Viennese, Moderne

The Royal Borough of Kingston-upon-Thames is not the sort of place you expect to find monumental Red Vienna-style public-housing schemes; but leave Norbiton Station to find what appears like a huge red fortress towering over the usual semis and villas, and a direct route to the estate's grand archway, where you'll find paired columns and two plaques, one to celebrate its opening, the other to celebrate its renovation fifty years later. The effect of power and pride is lessened a little at the main frontage facing the busy high street, where the inability of this axial, pomp-driven style to deal with slopes and asymmetries becomes uncomfortably clear, and the fortress-like

effect is lessened by some straggly planning – but the finishes, in Dutch brick with curved decks and streamlined glass stairwells, are still impressive. So too is the comparison with the 1960s system-built estate over the road.

_____

FITZHUGH ESTATE, WANDSWORTH
London County Council, 1953–6
People's Detailing

A dry run for the 'East' part of the subsequent **Alton Estate (p. 112)**, these towers are a particularly superb example of the LCC's architecture when it was poised between epic scale and intimate detail, joining the brave new world and the integration of the past. Nothing flash, just five brick-infill point blocks with wide balconies and a community clubhouse set in a winding grove at the north end of Wandsworth Common, interspersed with tall trees. These have grown up, so that the original idea – not so much a Garden City as a woodland city – is much clearer than it would have been when the planting was new. As soon as you stand in it you realize what it was the planners and architects were up to – bucolic, calm, modern, and with just enough of the sublime in the presence of the towers from the common to resist any accusations of cutesiness. The placement of the towers right next to a particularly OTT mid-nineteenth-century asylum shows modernism and Victoriana thrown together with neither sentimentality nor aggression. The asylum is now, inevitably, flats, and the shonky 'in keeping' new housing that has been built around it is far inferior as residential architecture to the Fitzhugh Estate. But the contrast remains, and that's much of the point here; there's another, similar early LCC high-rise estate not too far away – Ackroydon, in Wimbledon – but it lacks the wonderfully surreal effect of juxtaposition you can find here.

The fusion of landscape architecture, tile-hanging and Bauhaus proportions in Eric Lyons's Parkleys.

PARKLEYS, HAM ✪
Eric Lyons, 1953–6
LANGHAM HOUSE CLOSE, HAM ✪
Stirling & Gowan, 1955–8
People's Detailing, Brutalist

Two famous places doing the same thing – providing speculative housing for middle-class professionals between Richmond Park and Ham Common, a spacious Georgian green that feels like something out of a 1960s Joseph Losey film. They execute this task completely differently, so much so that it's amazing they were built at almost exactly the same time. Unlike at the **Alton Estate (p. 112)**, built for working-class people at the other end of Richmond Park, this wasn't the result of an explicit contest between aesthetic cliques, just pure coincidence. Parkleys, which joins on to a dull Georgian shopping parade, is the first, and for me the best, of Eric Lyons's private estates for his development company, Span. It introduces what would become the biggest clichés of post-war private housing – the zigzags of weatherboarding, the flat roofs, the neatly trimmed lawns, the northern trees and evergreens – but, here, they all still feel fresh. The landscape has a rare sense of flow – each terrace and block of flats with its wonderful (and intact) typographical and spatial touches to the stairwells, entrances and signs, is placed in a sequence of gardens, with a delicacy and poise that is more Mies van der Rohe than Bovis. Best of all, unlike at Lyons's estates in Blackheath, there are no signs telling you that you shouldn't be there – presumably this is because, in Ham, there's no Lewisham or Woolwich nearby to worry the owners.

Langham House Close has none of this ease of interlocking, abstract space; you can see it from the common as a set of flats crammed into an alleyway behind a Georgian townhouse. It's much more 'important' for architectural history, because here Stirling & Gowan took the heavy brick and concrete materials of Le Corbusier's Maisons Jaoul and fused them with the precise geometries of De Stijl, and created the 'New Brutalism' in the process. The blocks now look elegant rather than violent, particularly the low-rise 'pavilions', which are usually credited to Gowan alone.

It still feels, all these decades later, oddly cranky compared with Parkleys – narrow, personal. In this it's like a reversal of Alton; there, the Brutalists are responsible for the sublime and the epic, and the 'Empiricists' for intimacy and irrationality. At Ham, the Empiricist Lyons is in confident command of what Ian Nairn described as its 'twentieth century space', while Stirling & Gowan are doing murky things behind the bikesheds. Another important difference is that Lyons's blocks have had to be strictly maintained for them to look this good, but Langham House Close looks better the mouldier it gets, right down to the reddish-yellow mildew on the emphasized concrete drip-mouldings. **[C.9]**

——

ELLIOTT SCHOOL, PUTNEY
G. A. Trevett for the London County Council Architects Dept, 1955–6
People's Detailing

If, like me, you often go around the capital with a copy of Ian Nairn's mid-sixties *Modern Buildings in London* in your pocket, you'll have noted a lot of praise for the schools division of the London County Council (much more than the housing department), and then you'll have often found the schools he describes either unrecognizably altered or replaced with some steroidal, business park-style Academy. Elliott School, one of the most loved products of the schools division, was lucky enough to get listed. When it became the Ark Putney Academy, the new hedge-fund manager owners immediately proposed selling the playing fields, but the school was left alone. It's right next to the

very leafy Ashburton Estate, with which it forms a little enclave of thoughtful, spacious 1950s planning next to a long, dull street of phenomenally expensive yet essentially crap luxury flats of all eras from the 1910s to the present. The school is dominated by a massive curtain-walled block, with pretty blue-green spandrels and a little roof pavilion, with diapered brick patterns and wavy balconies at the gable ends, linked by a glazed walkway to a curious barrel-shaped sports hall. The buildings have all the virtues of the Lubetkin-influenced social architecture of fifties London – personality, friendliness, optimism – and none of the occasional twee vices.

The school is often noted for a striking list of famous former pupils for an ordinary comprehensive, from Pierce Brosnan to Burial; maybe the architecture inspired them just a little.

——

ALTON ESTATE, ROEHAMPTON ✪ ❶
London County Council Architects Dept, 1958–9
People's Detailing, Brutalist

The major housing cause célèbre of the 1950s in London, built on the expropriated grounds of country houses (only government intervention stopped it being built facing Richmond Park), and praised by every observer of world architecture in the 1950s and '60s – most memorably by the American photographer and critic G. E. Kidder-Smith as 'the finest low-cost housing development in the world'. In architectural history, it is the site of a showdown between the 'softs' (who started it off at Alton East) and 'hards' (who designed Alton West as a response) at the London County Council Architects Department. That is, between the proponents of a Scandinavian aesthetic and the Le Corbusier-influenced Brutalists. The latter were then seen to have won the battle, and much of what the LCC did afterwards

On the march: the slab blocks crowning the hill on the LCC's Alton Estate, Roehampton.

path from here leads to bungalows for the elderly, precise cubic houses with gardens, and eventually arrives at another hill, on to which are placed several miniaturized versions of the Marseille Unité d'Habitation, all pilotis and textured concrete. Climb up to the top of this, look out, and an entire new landscape unfolds before you, one where the world is turned upside down, and a flowing abundance of public space becomes the defining character of the city, rather than the demands of nineteenth-century speculators.

Most of the estate is listed, and is in reasonably decent condition. Its unlisted centre – including one of the miniature Unités and the estate library, a witty little design with multiple barrel roofs – is now slated for demolition by Wandsworth Council, to be replaced with mediocre twenty-first-century developer's housing. Grossly, the planning application talks about Alton's 'eighteenth-century landscape'. Eighteenth-century landscapes were for the lucky very few, and the view was that of a master surveying his property. This is a 1950s landscape, and it is for everybody. The view is for us, surveying what is ours. [A.13]

was tough and massive as a result. Yet, at this distance, the similarities seem much more obvious than the differences. Both are a matter of blocks placed into an extensive, rolling, green landscape. Both were created through the now unthinkable public appropriation of the playgrounds of the rich. Both offer very good housing, mediocre public facilities and appalling public transport links. The differences arise at minor levels of arrangement and detail.

The tall, thin 'point' blocks of Alton East are detailed in brick and tile and placed amongst tall trees as if they'd got there by accident; at Alton West, they're ruggedly textured into a concrete grid, formally arranged. All is worth seeing, but there is one sequence at Alton West that is genuinely astonishing. At the top of the hill is a country house, with its generic neoclassical sculptures still in place, looking out at the point blocks just peering out over the trees. A winding

CRESSINGHAM GARDENS, TULSE HILL
Lambeth Borough Architects Dept, 1968–78
People's Detailing, Brutalist

A simple, warm and tactile set of cottagey terraced houses in a knobbly yellow brick, around carefully planned pedestrian spaces, by the same team as **Central Hill Estate (p. 94)**, but fitted to a different site: a little corner round the bottom end of Brockwell Park rather than an all-surveying valley. Like Central Hill it has been slated for demolition, and it's even less imaginable as a 'sink estate', except by the most blinkered of traditionalists – or by a council concerned that they're not getting enough money out of these (fairly high-density) houses. Currently, the very active residents association's best hope is to take the estate out of local-authority control, which would be a tragic fate for Lambeth's municipal socialist project.

LEIGHAM COURT ROAD SHELTERED HOUSING, STREATHAM

Kate Macintosh for Lambeth Borough Architects Dept, 1972
Brutalist

A total shift in scale and register from the same architect's monumental **Dawson Heights (p. 93)**, for Southwark Council. In an extremely typical London suburban street of scrubby semis and speculative blocks of flats, this is easily missed, noticeable to the street only in the newsagent on its ground floor. This is actually the entrance to a miniature Lambeth Council estate of small houses and flats for elderly council tenants, which, without backing down from a starkly modernist repertoire of breezeblocks and complicated cubic geometries, creates somewhere urban and quiet, secluded without being mean or paranoid. The details of the blocks, and the stained-wood walkways and windows, are unshowy but with the warmth and seriousness appropriate to the task. Unlike Dawson Heights, Leigham Court Road is listed (Lambeth was keen to demolish it, as with other low-rise and exceptional estates like **Central Hill Estate, p. 94**, and **Cressingham Gardens, p. 113**), but there's no need to pit them against each other – both show the range at which a talented local-authority architect could work in the 1970s, from elemental grandeur to the tiniest details of home life. The complex was recently renamed Macintosh Court, after its architect, yet is undergoing a depressingly shoddy renovation programme, to the alarm of many residents; even so, the strength of these buildings can't be PFI'd out.

WATERMEADS, MITCHAM

R. Hodge and A. Bews for the London Borough of Merton, 1974–7
Classical Modernism

'Low-Rise, High-Density' was one of the planning innovations of the 1970s, where planners and the architects Lionel March and Leslie Martin proved you could get as many flats on to a site *and* have useful public spaces through unorthodox things like lining the perimeter of the site with housing and then leaving the spaces inside undeveloped. The most important examples of this were of course in Camden, where at, say, the **Maiden Lane Estate (p. 151)** and **Fleet Road (p. 147)** these ideas were combined with an almost retro 1920s approach to design – modern architecture as white, stark, cuboid and rational, once again. But, at the time, the similar experiments being made by the London Borough of Merton, in south-west London subtopia, were better known and more widely praised. With the return since the eighties of large populations to the inner city, they have been comparatively forgotten in the hipster reclamation of seventies housing. Merton's two largest estates, Pollards Hill and Watermeads, consisted of low-rise, wipe-clean terraces on large suburban sites. Watermeads is the one to see, as its public space is a nature reserve built around the River Wandle.

It's easy to work out what the planners were up to from looking at the unusually informative estate map, which shows a snake of housing along the river, the green spaces between, and usefully tells you that this is the appropriation of the land of what was once somebody's country house. The houses and flats are covered in a vitreous grey cladding – in need of a clean – and are very much in the Camden International Style, but they work as an unusually modern and confident backdrop to the bosky, overgrown landscape along the river, a combination of the starkly modern and the barely untamed that works as an alternative vision of what suburbia could be – it doesn't get much leafier than this, but the leafiness is wild, weird. It has to contend with an unfortunate layout, which put the back gardens facing towards the river. So a pedestrian walking the nature reserve sees the incongruous overlay of people's improvised, gradually replaced and reworked garden fences. The front doors, meanwhile, are in the courtyards, densely clogged with car parking, even with a bus and tram stop both round the corner. This rather shabby relation to the pedestrian shows how by comparison Camden architects like Neave Brown and Peter Tabori were much better at creating urban frontages. But, then, they were working with urban sites, and Mitcham is not that. A suburban dream, only slightly tarnished.

―――

SOUTHWYCK HOUSE, BRIXTON
Magda Borowiecka for Lambeth Borough Architects Dept, 1979
BRIXTON RECREATION CENTRE
George Finch for Lambeth Borough Architects Dept, 1970–84
Brutalist

Architecturally, Brixton is all about the infrastructure. There are the railways that criss-cross it, which provide exciting views of densely packed Victorian–Edwardian metropolitan spaces like the markets or Electric Avenue and the Corbusian planning of the LCC's Loughborough Junction Estate – and the motorways that were planned to slice it up, defeated by a long-running campaign that eventually convinced the GLC. Both of these buildings by the Lambeth Architects Dept were closely connected to the motorway plan, which explains some of their eccentricities – but they remain intriguing without it. Southwyck House, known to all as the 'Barrier Block' at the southern end of Coldharbour Lane, was

designed in the early seventies by Magda Borowiecka as a wall to block out traffic noise, which would then enclose an inner space that was quiet and protected – rather similar to Ralph Erskine's contemporary **Byker Estate (p. 484)**. It is much harsher than Byker, its monolithism emphasized, with a serrated profile; and the motorway it was meant to be screening was never built. It's imposing and even disturbing, until you go inside, when it all makes sense, and the sublimity runs alongside a certain communal grandeur.

Meanwhile, a short walk away, clinging to the railway line, is George Finch's 'Brixton Rec', which is this time totally windowless, at least on the front facade, with a bright red-brick volume held up on curved little pilotis connected to a flanking block with a spiny copper roof. It has that strange ability to be both warm and monumental that characterizes all of Finch's work, and features spacious, multilevel interiors which aren't treated as well as they should be, but which are far from failing either. When Nelson Mandela first visited London in 1996, this was one of the places he spoke from, and while that's because of its status as the most prominent building in the most prominent black British district, it's rather apt: a building commissioned by a Communist and designed by a socialist for a left-wing local authority, attempting to incarnate egalitarian values in one structure. Brixton Rec is for everyone.

―――

ROGERS HOUSE, WIMBLEDON
Team 4 (Richard and Su Rogers), 1967–9
High-Tech

This is one of the few exceptions to the rule in this book of 'no inaccessible private houses', because it's in a reasonably easily accessed area, and its owners, Harvard University, occasionally let the plebs in for events. Unlike Team 4's slightly earlier

Murray Mews (p. 149) in Camden, this is pure High-Tech, one of the first places where you could see that something new was happening among technophile London architects – a combination of Californian supervillain private modernism and a nerdy love for exposed mechanics. Here this is expressed through two glass bungalows in yellow-painted steel frame, with shelving and doors and everything else in curved perspex – spacious, refined and alien. The first Rogers building to be really enjoyable on its own merits rather than as first steps on the way to something else.

NLA TOWER, CROYDON
R. Seifert & Partners, 1970
International Style

Despite the intensity of building activity in sixties and seventies Croydon – the once famous 'Mini-Manhattan' of speculative office towers, a clunkier precursor to **Canary Wharf (p. 131)** whose story is told with considerable wit in John Grindrod's *Concretopia* – not that much of it is of a really high quality. Most are a matter of undistinguished corporate modernism on the cheap by journeymen British firms, impressive from a distance, occasionally interesting as an *Alphaville* streetscape, not worth much up close (though real enthusiasts should find at least something in the soon-to-be-demolished Nestlé headquarters and in the recently renovated **Fairfield Halls, p. 90**). The big exception, Croydon's seventies 'icon', is the NLA Tower, or, as it's also known, the '50p building' due to its intersecting, heptagonal plan. The way that this (basically arbitrary) shape is twisted and turned into a logical and sculptural volume is typical of Seifert in its combination of science fiction pulpiness and structural ingenuity. Like a Blair-era 'landmark building', it tells you where you are, it makes lots of money and it doesn't do much else –

Croydon futurist: Richard Seifert's NLA Tower, the symbol of the suburban metropolis.

but there should always be a place for cheap thrills in architecture, and the twists and turns of the NLA Tower have that in spades.

ST BERNARD'S HOUSES, CROYDON
Atelier 5, 1969–72
Brutalist

As a set of buildings, this quiet, low-rise housing estate is the antithesis of the high-rise Croydon. Like it, we're not dealing with state planning, but the activities of mass-market developers – in this case, the volume housebuilders Wates. Unusally, they decided to hire the cult Swiss firm Atelier 5, whose high-density, low-rise Siedlung Halen, which fits lush gardens and tightly packed terraces into a hilltop site, was the basis in many ways for later experiments in Camden, Lambeth, Mitcham, Cambridge and Sheffield.

Swiss modernism, English speculative development: St Bernard's Houses, almost hidden by vegetation.

This Croydon scheme is less ambitious, but it's well worth the challenge of finding this sheltered pair of elegant, low terraces, almost closed off from the street. It's very dense, secluded by trees, detailed in wood and stock brick to a very un-British standard of precision. When they were built, the developers marketed these as a 'New Swiss Concept in Living', but it's more interesting how the ensemble incarnates traditional suburban values of privacy, seclusion and hierarchy in a very different way from the ungainly sprawl you can see all around you here, where London meets Surrey. In fact, it resembles Switzerland much less than it does a slightly more tightly packed Southern California, with the clean lines of a Case Study House on the edges of Los Angeles. As soon as you enter the narrow yet unguarded walkway to look at the houses, you feel like you're trespassing. Nob Hill, modernist version.

KINGSTON CENTRE, KINGSTON-UPON-THAMES
Owen Luder Partnership, 1974–6
Brutalist

Like the **Catford Centre (p. 98)**, this is a megastructure, a towering, asymmetrical multistorey edifice looming over all around it, shoving car parks, offices and retail into one mass. However, it's located in a genteel part of outer south London, and so treated rather differently – its future is assured as a hotel, which has meant a smooth paint job that, while not as destructive as the cladding of **Eros House (p. 90)**, is obviously at variance with Luder's rough-arsed approach to Brutalism. As with the latter building, it's a regular grid interrupted and flanked with melodramatic service towers, sculpturally modelled. Seeing it across the large park nearby, what the paint can't hide is the flamboyantly profiled stair tower, whose presence and force still burst through.

BEDZED, BEDDINGTON
Bill Dunster and Bioregional, 2000–2002
Ecomodernist

In theory, this small Peabody Trust housing estate out in the distant ends of Sutton is 'best practice'; it's what we're meant to have everywhere, by now – a model of high-density, mixed middle/working class and sustainable living. Its unlovely name, standing for Beddington Zero Energy Development, signals its ambitions – a self-contained eco community, self-sufficient, generating its own power. Tragically, it's completely out on its own, without ever having a serious follow-up in London. The most immediately striking thing is how dense it is, on its tiny site, in a part of southernmost south London that is otherwise full of vague, wasted or underused space. These terraces and invigorating walkways would make a lot more sense in

Brixton, but then, in inner London, the price of land has been prohibitive to experiments in the last two decades. So, like a nineteenth-century utopian community, BedZed may be best thought of as 'prefigurative' – a working microcosm of a better way of building.

Some of BedZed's stylistic features are very much of their (Blair-era) period – the brightly coloured cowls, for instance, have that unmistakeable touch of Teletubbyland – but the houses are logically planned, the public spaces are a lot of fun to walk around and residents seem to expect visitors. The technology – all those panels and ducts – suggests that a really 'sustainable' architecture might be visually closer to High-Tech, with its various visibly active services, rather than the closed volumes of today's ubiquitous brick grids (though the red-brick corners of the terraces here make their own little nod towards the Victorians). More housing like this would be as visually enjoyable as it is socially useful, but the market is evidently not interested – this is fiddly to build and pricey to maintain, and requires a degree of expertise and skill that the large builders have thrived on obliterating.

NEWPORT STREET GALLERY, VAUXHALL

Caruso St John Architects, 2015
Modern Classicism

It is good to find, for once, a London building that is the poor relation of similar buildings for similar functions by the same architects beyond the metropolis. Newport Street, a private gallery owned by Damien Hirst, can't compare with the ingenuity and discovery of Caruso St John's other galleries, the **New Art Gallery (p. 322)** in Walsall, or the **Nottingham Contemporary (p. 355)**. Perhaps the architects had less interest in housing Hirst's art collection and his theme restaurant than they did in creating what

were effectively new town centres in those two Midlands cities. For what it is, though, the Newport Street Gallery is more than decent. It resembles a luxury engineering workshop, a light-industrial sawtooth joining on to some genuine industrial remnants along the Waterloo–Southampton viaduct. Inside are airy galleries and a sensuous concrete staircase. Along with their refurbishment of Tate Britain over the river around the same time, it marks Caruso St John as the most remarkable staircase designers in British architecture since Lubetkin; a grey swirl through a brick vault, a glamorous dungeon. All of this careful balance tips into unfortunate bathos in the restaurant, Pharmacy. Hirst originally designed this himself in the 1990s, and so the architects have tried to replicate it, relenting their firm, reliable grip. The space's wall-to-wall collection of medicine packets and pills is one not very funny joke repeated a thousand times, much like the man's art.

EAST LONDON

WHITECHAPEL GALLERY
Charles Harrison Townsend, 1896–1901
Extensions by Colquhoun & Miller, 1985–8/
Robbrecht en Daem and Witheford Watson
Mann with Rachel Whiteread, 2009
Art Nouveau, Classical Modernism

A building with a storied history. One of
the tiny handful of serious Art Nouveau
buildings in London, this gallery has been
at the forefront of London's avant-garde art
scene from the Edwardian era to the present.
It was, like the (more strictly Victorian)
library next door and the nearby Toynbee
Hall settlement, among several projects
to improve the health, morals and tastes
of what was commonly regarded at the
time as a slum. None of them are bombastic,
especially not the gallery. It is an instantly
recognizable design, in three clear parts
– a ground floor, with a grand, scallop-
like archway, placed off centre; a laconic
row of square windows; and two organic
towers, symmetrically enclosing a blank
space which has for many years carried the
gallery's logo (this was originally meant to
include a mosaic, like that on Townsend's
Horniman Museum, p. 79). This alternation
between abstract and organic, asymmetrical
and grand, is all crammed into a tiny space
in a bustling high street – a remarkably
vivid and powerful work, all the more so
for its shifts in scale having been executed
in the same yellow-brown terracotta, giving
the appearance of one great mass.

There have been two major extensions,
both worth mentioning. Colquhoun &
Miller's 1980s work, which extends down
the back alley that the gallery shares
with Freedom, the venerable Anarchist
bookshop/publisher (note their metal panel
gallery of left-libertarian heroes outside),
is an odd mix. The architects' neo-1930s
language of elegant balustrades and curved
metal windows is combined with Victorian
polychromy, somewhat uneasily. The more
recent extension by Robbrecht en Daem
and Witheford Watson Mann is much more
original. It is carved out of the fruitily neo-
Jacobean library next door (which moved
to **Whitechapel Idea Store, p. 134**) and,
clearly under the influence of the artistic
consultant, Rachel Whiteread, they appear
to have cast everything there in cement, so
that the outlines of a Victorian library are
still visible, but the ornament is not – a kind
of abstracted modernist palimpsest.

MILLENNIUM MILLS, ROYAL VICTORIA DOCK
1905–33
Industrial

An extraordinary industrial survival.
This complex of Flour Mills was built as
part of the development of the 'Royal Docks'
in the East End of London, which was then
the largest dock complex on earth, a series
of massive expanses of water as wide and
majestic as the Thames itself, designed
to process the produce of the British Empire,
something still remembered in the name of
the Cyprus Docklands Light Railway Station.
Built concurrently with the development
of the dock, Millennium Mills – which was
built incrementally until reaching its current
form in the early 1930s – was merely one of
several monumental concrete warehouses on
the site. Through a combination of accident,
asbestos and, latterly, conservation, the
building has never been demolished, and
so currently – still, at the time of writing –
it stands in immense, poisoned grounds,
untouched by the rampant speculative
development of 'luxury' high-rise apartments
all around it. Architecturally, it consists of
three parts. There is the ordinary functional

tradition of the original brick warehouse, the stranger D Silo, an angular, rather Vorticist presence in the wasteland, and the monumental, neoclassically proportioned concrete warehouse that dominates the site, eight storeys high and three times as wide. Its gutted structure contains within it multistorey drops, which deters all but the most hardened 'Urbex' enthusiasts. Proposals to turn it into a shopping mall, housing and an aquarium have so far come to nothing. It remains inner London's last industrial wilderness.

────

EMPIRE MEMORIAL SAILORS' HOSTEL, LIMEHOUSE
Thomas Brammall Daniel and Horace W. Parnacott, 1923–4
Modern Classicism, Expressionist

A picturesquely bleak sailors' mission, on a desolate arterial road near the redeveloped dockside in what was once London's Chinatown, before it shifted to Soho in the fifties. Not much here of the Limehouse described in *The Picture of Dorian Gray*, but this is an uncanny presence nonetheless, with a howling grimness that cleaning up and transformation into luxury flats – a fate that seems to have overtaken most of the public buildings of the East End – can't entirely efface. Mechanized Gothic, where faïence tiles outline tacked-on Gothic detail that is more James Whale than Augustus Pugin. This mass of queasy yellow brick still feels part super-cinema, part warehouse, part gateway to hell. When the Parisian cultural terrorists of the Situationist International held their annual conference here in 1960, they posed outside for a now-famous group photograph, and that faintly sinister psychogeographic air endures here still despite the change of use.

WALTHAM FOREST TOWN HALL & ASSEMBLY HALLS, WALTHAMSTOW
Philip Dalton Hepworth, 1932–41
Modern Classicism

Thankfully still serving its original function, this is the best of the clutch of halfway house moderne/classical town halls in east London, more monumental than the smaller Hackney Town Hall and more architecturally coherent than the Dutch/Georgian cross-breed of Barking Town Hall. Its commanding scale, at the centre of a large site, most likely derives from Walthamstow's independence of the London County Council, a self-governing working-class suburb. It is dominated by an elongated stripped classical portico of four tall columns, surmounted by a copper tower cribbed from the Town Hall in Ostrava, Czechoslovakia, which stands at the centre of a long Portland stone enfilade of offices, symmetrically arranged. Flanking it on the right are the Assembly Halls, the cultural adjunct to the big (local) government, whose municipal largesse is expressed through a lofty public anteroom. A stiff and conservative design in many ways, but a space of public splendour nonetheless.

────

POPLAR TOWN HALL
Clifford Culpin, 1937–8
Moderne, International Style

A confident municipal palace, courtesy of the architect of the similarly mild-modernist and brick-clad, if much larger and better, **Greenwich Town Hall (p. 84)**. The Poplar example borrows less than its south-east London cousin from the Dutch civic buildings of W. M. Dudok, and takes more from Erich Mendelsohn's department stores, like Huddersfield's **Co-operative Department Store** and Bradford's **Co-operative Emporium (p. 384)** then being built. The facade is a sweep of strip windows, aligned with a central prow, with Socialist Realist sculptures of the local industries. Both the sculptures and the architectural fearlessness were presumably a consequence of Poplar's status as a pioneering socialist council. Since it was sold off in the 2000s, this has been all defaced by a clumsy roof extension and an ugly sign proclaiming it to be 'BOW BUSINESS CENTRE.CO.UK'; so much family silver has been flogged in the East End.

E. PELLICCI, BETHNAL GREEN
Achille Cappocci, 1946
Moderne

While radical architects huddled around drawings and plans in Bloomsbury trying to work out a new, convivial modernist architecture for the East End – the Festival of Britain 'People's Detailing' style – this Anglo-Italian café in the heart of it all was the Eastenders' own modernist style. Rather than looking to Sweden or Finland, it was much more based on transatlantic glamour, a tiny Empire State Building of brown sunburst marquetry and custard vitrolite. Now a little too packed out and conscious of itself, it should still be seen – once likely considered 'common', it is now almost unique.

CENTRAL LINE:
GANTS HILL, REDBRIDGE
& WANSTEAD STATIONS
Charles Holden, 1947
NEWBURY PARK STATION
BUS SHELTER
Oliver Hill, 1949
Moderne, Modern Classicism

Four stations on the Hainault loop, a strange hidden Circle Line near the eastern end of the Central Line, and a slightly sad conclusion to the Charles Holden/Frank Pick era of London Underground design, where austerity budgets kicked in, starting a period of decline which lasted until the Jubilee Line and the Ken Livingstone era. They show how much Holden's minimalist, stripped-down architecture relied on decent materials for its grandeur.

The most famous of these four is Gants Hill, which is actually nothing at all on the surface, just a (rather nice) sign leading to an underpass and, below that, the station hall. Here, Holden returned a favour. In the 1930s, he and Pick had advised on the Moscow Metro, whose deep escalators and grand classical spaces were partly modelled on **Piccadilly Circus (p. 48)**. Gants Hill was Holden borrowing in turn from the fabulous underground vaults of Moscow stations such as Mayakovskaya; the station was even codenamed 'Moscow'. The sense of generous space comes not just from fancy materials, but from the chunky solidity of the pylons (decorated here with roundel-themed tiles, and note the roundel clock on the platforms), the size of the space, the elegance of the coffered ceiling and the atmospheric light, particularly given that Holden avoided the baroque trimmings that Moscow designers added to their halls. Combined seats and uplighters which make it look more Muscovite than it originally was, were added in the 1980s; it's a bit literal, but it makes the tribute clearer.

Redbridge and Wanstead are bleaker – the undecorated concrete of Wanstead's big square tower is especially disappointing when compared with the futuristic bare concrete hangars Holden had designed in the previous decade for **Cockfosters (p. 137)** and **Uxbridge (p. 157)**. It all helps reinforce the feeling that east and south-east Londoners might have that 'Frank Pick's London' is really a matter of postcodes with a 'W' or 'N' in. Redbridge is the better of the two, with the rotunda attached to the squat tower a fair, if reduced, continuation of the 1930s work. Both are superior to the miserable surface stations that would come in the sixties at the Victoria Line, but presage some of its meanness. Strangely enough, Gants Hill aside, the real masterwork in this cross-Essex ensemble isn't by Holden at all, but by the talented eclectic Oliver Hill, and it is actually the bus shelter designed alongside Newbury Park Station. It's a wonderfully simple, easy-looking, concrete barrel vault, with a verdigris roof coming down three quarters of the way then stopping to create a colonnade, with round rooflights behind. The budget was as low as in Holden's stations, and even fewer materials were used – but, unlike Holden, Hill knew exactly what to do with what he had, and this is a mini-masterclass in transport architecture: useful, simple and just beautiful enough to take the edge off the tedium of commuting.

LANSBURY ESTATE & CHRISP STREET MARKET, POPLAR
Frederick Gibberd Partnership, 1950–68
People's Detailing

This is Attlee's post-war London, not Macmillan's or Wilson's – a microcosm of an austere yet populist socialist capital. Named after the radical leader of Poplar Council and Attlee's immediate precursor as Labour leader, George Lansbury, this is all about the *Gemeinschaft*, a redevelopment of a bomb-damaged slum area (Lansbury used to talk about Poplar as a place where people only lived if they had to) into a cosy, self-contained working-class community. Its centrepiece and most successful space is Chrisp Street Market. The shops are in a witty style that combines Regency bow windows (their inspiration infuriatingly obscured by UPVC windows – thanks, Tower Hamlets) with Corbusian-style pilotis, which work as shelter from the miserable weather and welcoming entry points into the butcher, the baker and whatnot. Aligned to these is a fun clock tower, with a zigzag brick staircase, which has recently been restored; and in-between is a street market, now used

very well by the large Bengali population to whom all the Cockerney design references would be fairly irrelevant. The housing is duller. The original terraces and low-rise flats, with their New Town-style greensward, and the much later grid of maisonettes and towers are decent, but they lack the spark of the shopping centre. By the time of Fitzgerald House, the massively out-of-scale high-rise built at one corner of the market in the late 1960s, it seems that nobody cared much any more.

Note also in the Lansbury Estate the pleasant Susan Lawrence School by Yorke Rosenberg & Mardall (named after another once-locally famous, much-loved Poplar socialist). It dates from before they'd found their distinctive style but is airy and attractive, with its own Henry Moore sculpture, no less. There are also two churches, of which the Catholic church, a mountain of brick by Adrian Gilbert Scott, the youngest of the Gilbert Scott dynasty, is the most interesting, although not always for the right reasons; it takes the Brick Gothic-Expressionist style to the very limits of taste.

CENTRAL PARADE, WALTHAMSTOW
F. G. Southgate, 1954–8
People's Detailing

As Festival Style buildings in the East End go, this is much more fun than the **Lansbury Estate (above)** – the 1950s modernist/nostalgic mashup at its most gleeful, full of great little bits and bobs and decorative fripperies to irk the purists. It's a block of council flats, with shops on the ground floor (many of them reworked recently into an industrial chic co-working space, Walthamstow being a hot place to be right now), under a wavy concrete canopy, currently painted a fetching yellow. The flats have deep balconies and look like they'd be great places to live, surrounded by the sort of easy multicultural street life London almost casually has, where other suburban streets in other towns with much the same buildings and morphology have empty units and Betfred. The central tower, which faces the junction of the High Street and Hoe Street, is where the Borough Architect, F. G. Southgate, has really let himself go, with a decorative pattern evoking the Festival Hall carpets, a clock, a bell tower, a load of coats of arms cast in tiles, all with flats inset into it. The sort of festive, cheerful populist modernism that makes you wonder if the Brutalists might sometimes just have been puritan bores.

TATE & LYLE SUGAR REFINERY, SILVERTOWN
1950s
Industrial

Like the **Cemex Construction Aggregate Works (p. 100)** on the other side of the river, and the **Millennium Mills (p. 119)**, on the other side of the Royal Docks, Silvertown still has various enclaves of surviving industry, and they can be very dramatic. This complex is probably best viewed from across the river in Charlton and Woolwich anyway – a complicated mix of enormous great concrete volumes, tanks and chimneys, often with ships berthed, cranes loading and unloading, and smoke belching; all this activity is a reminder of the sort of things that do, beyond sentimentality, get lost when industrial buildings become ruins or loft apartments – a spectacle of noise, gas and throbbing energy. Not that it would be at all easy to fit flats into this jumbled collection of massive, mostly windowless monoliths. Tate & Lyle also have a 1930s factory a little further west, on the other side of **Thames Barrier Park (p. 132)**; Golden Syrup is still manufactured in these two buildings.

DORSET ESTATE, SHOREDITCH ✪
Skinner Bailey & Lubetkin, 1957–62
People's Detailing

In the 1950s, after the failure of his plan for the New Town of Peterlee – replaced by a dull, suburban masterplan by George Grenfell-Baines – Lubetkin famously retired to become a pig farmer, a period recalled with considerable bitterness in his daughter Louise Kehoe's memoir, *In This Dark House*. During this period, however, he actually designed three housing estates in Bethnal Green with Francis Skinner and Douglas Bailey, two of them on a truly monumental scale. The earliest of them is now in London Hipster Central, in Shoreditch, just off Columbia Road, a niche-marketing late-capitalist brandscape which contrasts ideologically with the worthiness of the Dorset Estate, with its blocks named after the trade unionists of Tolpuddle, deported to Australia in the 1830s. As architecture, they show a tortured tension between utopian aspiration, baroque planning, cost yardsticks and austerity materials. The low-rise blocks are of no interest, but two Y-plan blocks – patterned and textured like scaled-up, much cheaper versions of **Bevin Court (p. 54)** – are impressive. Their external walkways are mean, though – too narrow to fit two people passing down them abreast.

Somehow, into this cash-strapped project Lubetkin managed to force his Constructivist-baroque staircases – here, a pair of double helixes, indebted as much to Inigo Jones's tulip staircase at the Queen's House in Greenwich as they are to Rodchenko or Naum Gabo. They're well worth lingering outside for until someone lets you in. The local authority then insisted that Skinner Bailey & Lubetkin add a tower, which was completed in 1962. Here, the Caucasian patterning that Lubetkin had used since **Highpoint 2 (p. 139)** becomes a three-dimensional abstract pattern across the convex volume of the tower. The staircase

Inigo Jones meets Aleksandr Rodchenko: one of the staircases of Skinner Bailey & Lubetkin's Dorset Estate.

inside is a tight corkscrew, spiralling all the way up the tower's twenty storeys. At the centre of the estate is a community centre in a concrete rotunda, and a cutesy pub, now a West African restaurant. Given a bit of a clean, and with its public spaces spruced up, this could be an extraordinary place; as it stands, it's the best estate in London to see dreams meet reality.

USK STREET CLUSTER BLOCKS, GLOBE TOWN
Denys Lasdun for the London County Council Architects Dept, 1955
KEELING HOUSE, BETHNAL GREEN
Denys Lasdun for the London County Council Architects Dept, 1957
Brutalist

Denys Lasdun's 'Cluster Blocks' were designed to be an alternative to the 'closed' form of the standard tower block – rather than reaching your identical home through a long internal or external corridor, you would be encouraged by gentle nudges in the design to get to know your neighbours and feel a sense of identification with your part of the block. The later and better known is Keeling House. Here, the angst and yearning that Lasdun's old boss Lubetkin expressed through decorations and staircases on mean council budgets is exchanged for one simple and brilliant idea. The block is treated as four distinct towers linked by communal areas, on a stark, geometric plan. The resulting tower is unmistakeably an integral whole, but is also readable as a complex of distinct clusters of flats. Whether the cluster helped maintain working-class community is hard to prove, but by the late 1990s it had a stable and largely elderly population who liked living there. It was then sold off by the local authority to become the gated community it is now. The main architectural result of this comes in the private garden and pool around

Three of the four clustered blocks of Keeling House, in London's outdoor 'museum of housing', Bethnal Green.

the entrance, and the glass penthouses on top – which persistent rumour and urban myth claim to have been bought by various pop stars.

The lesser-known first draft is at Usk Street in Globe Town, the interzone between Bethnal Green and Bow. These funny mid-rise towers are clearer in their expression of the socio-architectural idea – you can differentiate much more easily between the 'served' and 'servant' spaces, between the individual homes and the public walkways that were meant to connect them to the street and residents to each other – but, architecturally, they are gaunt and spindly where Keeling is gutsy and forceful. It seems as if the legibility of the social idea and the coherence of the architectural expression are necessarily at variance. While Usk Street is never going to be as 'iconic' as its later cousin, it's much more easily read as doing what it's trying to do; *and* it's still council housing.

ST PAUL'S, BOW COMMON
Robert Maguire and Keith Murray, 1958–60
Brutalist

An impressive church, built according to a clear principle – a centralized design, around a polygonal glass roof, bringing light into what is otherwise a stark box of engineering brick. Unlike many modernist churches, it's not an 'exercise', and you don't feel the architects would rather be designing something else. Everything is motivated by a passionate if restrained religiosity, all organized around the alternation of darkness and light. No clichés – the exterior features neither spire nor campanile, but does carry the words, pressed into concrete, 'THIS IS THE GATE OF HEAVEN'. Ian Nairn claimed that this was better than all other post-war churches in London put together, and the only one to reflect 'any credit' on the C of E and its architects. That's not quite as true today, but it certainly remains the best.

FULWELL CROSS LIBRARY & LEISURE CENTRE, ILFORD
Frederick Gibberd Partnership, 1958–68
People's Detailing

These two buildings are very successful examples of Gibberd's attempts to take Renaissance architectural devices and make them a) vaguely modernist and b) cute – you can find very many images of this place on Instagram. The library is a rotunda with a marvellously odd fluted copper and glass roof, something between a big top, and a Persian mosque with a big *Meydan* square in front (or, at least, a Persian mosque as imitated by a Soviet architect in 1960s Tashkent). It's definitely a much more architecturally interesting mosque than the actual one Gibberd designed in Regent's Park. An arcade, almost full-scale Postmodernism *avant-la-lettre*, leads to the classically disciplined but more obviously modernist leisure centre adjacent, with which it forms a Renaissance-style ensemble of dome and box. Both buildings are similarly fun-filled inside, especially the library, where the circus dome's glazing floods a central reading room with light. A fabulous fantasy, not at all what you expect to find in Ilford.

BARKING UNDERGROUND STATION
British Railways Eastern Division, 1959–61
Brutalist

An aggressive but straightforward Brutalist terminus, designed by John Ward for the British Railways Eastern Region, whose post-war rebuilding programme was one of British Rail architecture's few successes (see also the same department's **Harlow Town, Broxbourne & Stevenage Stations, p. 188**). It's placed in a high street and displays the important 'here is the station' signifiers – you have no doubt what the big building is. Like a miniature version of

Rome's Termini Station, it's basically a big, wide, cranked concrete roof, with a glass hall beneath. It is all extremely simple – a glassy open hall under a heavy roof – but it has such strength and integrity that it can survive however many branches of Upper Crust are chucked into it.

CRANBROOK ESTATE, GLOBE TOWN ✪
Skinner Bailey & Lubetkin, 1959–63
People's Detailing, Constructivist

The biggest project Lubetkin was ever involved in, and the last – an extremely idiosyncratic and personal design bringing together geometrical baroque planning, Constructivist spatial organization, very fifties (but 'Caucasian-inspired') patterning and municipal mixed development, all, as at the **Dorset Estate (p. 123)**, on a derisory budget. It's what the young people call a 'hot mess'. If you approach it from the west on the main road, there's a row of precisely placed trees, as if you're in the Tuileries in Paris. Pass along this avenue, and most of what you see is the six towers – strange, squat twelve-storey points, lifted on daringly splayed pilotis, duplicated on the (unused) roof terraces, decorated with green panels and pale white brick, their staggered rhythms an early example of the later 'barcode facade' craze; according to the journalist and novelist James Meek's account of the buildings in the *London Review of Books*, the green panels were originally shiny and vitreous, rather than the cheap metal you see now; the barred-off stairwells were originally open, as in **Bevin Court (p. 54)**.

The gestures of openness and display that worked so well in Finsbury here come up against the harsher realities of the deep East End. It's still an exciting and at the very least utterly unique place. It is full of peculiarly formal public spaces, some of which, like

A view of Goldfinger's Brownfield Estate, ending at the controversially refurbished Balfron Tower.

the little pond around an Elisabeth Frink sculpture, at the heart of a circus of terraced houses, are as cosy and humane as the total ensemble is monumental. A good potential film set for an alternative-history scenario in which Renaissance triptychs rather than grain silos and factories provided the inspiration for modernism; currently, mainly used in 'gritty' videos, Bow being the grime heartland. Both are part of this place. [**C.15**]

BROWNFIELD ESTATE, POPLAR ☉
Ernő Goldfinger, 1963–7
Brutalist

As a piece of architecture, here everything is hewn from the same rock. As a social project, it is now a showcase of fragmentation. The LCC commissioned Goldfinger to design an estate for this slum clearance site; his proposal consisted of a grid of yellow-brick tenements and three more monumental buildings, defined by Goldfinger's use of a clear, logical grid and a total mastery of concrete as a material, both of which he had learned at the shoulder of the French neoclassicist 'constructeur' Auguste Perret. There are several distinct parts, which were designed integrally, as an ensemble – the thick, fourteen-storey Glenkerry House, the more slender, twenty-six-storey Balfron Tower, linked by the low-rise Carradale House, with modest, rational maisonettes in the gaps. Aside from their glistening, bristling concrete work – achieving the unusual feat, in Britain, of looking good in all weathers – they're formally arranged around emphasized service towers and walkways, which stick out like turrets. These dramatic features could be explained away as functional necessity – this is modernism, after all! – but the effect is one of futurist melodrama, a miniature Metropolis of intersecting and projecting volumes.

Unlike Goldfinger's later **Trellick Tower (p. 166)**, Balfron has an extremely unsympathetic site, alongside the approach roads for the Blackwall Tunnel, which it responds to as best it can, lifting flats away from the noise and blocking it off without resorting to the paranoid walls and fences used by the Smithsons at their adjacent **Robin Hood Gardens (p. 130)**. But these buildings have been treated like slums, as 'problems', and the different responses to this have been interesting, if depressing. For decades, Glenkerry House has been a housing co-operative, which has enabled it to avoid the fate of the formerly publicly owned Balfron Tower, which was offloaded to a housing association, which cleared it, then filled it with artists, then cleared out the artists, to sell it to private investors so as to 'cross-fund' the renovation of the maisonettes. Goldfinger lived in the tower for a time, gathering ideas for Trellick, and is presumably now celebrated as the first person with inherited wealth to have lived in this tower. [B.2]

___

CHALKWELL HOUSE, STEPNEY
Alina and Noel Moffett for the London County Council Architects Dept, 1964
ASHINGTON HOUSE, BETHNAL GREEN
Alina and Noel Moffett for the Greater London Council Architects Dept, 1971
Brutalist

Two very interesting miniature experiments in making a block of flats something more than a housing silo, by an Irish–Polish husband-and-wife team on commission from the LCC. Both have a raw, cranky presence that helps them stand out in a context of duller, more linear estates by the LCC's own architects, who were sadly seldom at their most creative in the East End. Chalkwell House is on Commercial Road, one of the long, wide, straight arterial roads that make

so much of the East End so bleak; it stands next to the pretty decorated shed of the Troxy Cinema, and is on much the same scale, but meets the pavement with three chunky, corrugated concrete access decks, at an angle to a zigzag of brown-brick flats, and a prow-shaped glass stairwell above; this then leads down Pitsea Street to a mass of brick, with individual flats emphasized by cantilevers, so that each can be picked out clearly by its residents. Ashington House is better known, easily seen by Overground passengers from the Victorian railway viaduct that passes Bethnal Green railway station. It resembles a kind of remix of the Stepney building, with its glazed stairwells and cantilevered flats crushed into a spiky, Gothic melange, weirder and smaller than the earlier building but using exactly the same motifs and materials. Punchy, honest architecture.

___

MIDDLESEX STREET ESTATE, WHITECHAPEL
Corporation of London Architects Dept, 1965
Brutalist

A 'Baby Barbican' (copyright Douglas Murphy) of walkways, shops and concrete flats, built into Petticoat Lane, for a lower class of City of London council tenant. Zigzag balconies to the low-rise blocks form a square around the prefabricated tower, with its sculptural concrete module. The blue paint and cheap signage make it clear that the City is investing a lot less of its pots of cash here than in the **Barbican (p. 66)** or even the **Golden Lane Estate (p. 55)** – this is Southwark Council standard – but the neglect doesn't entirely detract from this ingenious, one-off design.

Charles Rennie Mackintosh gradually transformed his design for the **Glasgow School of Art** from a striking Victorian building into a prophecy of modern architecture. In the Library wing, seen here, he launched into pure space: an abstract, light-filled room, indicated by the high, cuboid windows inserted into the stone facade.

By the end of the 1910s, a coherent modern architecture had emerged on the continent, centred in Berlin, Amsterdam, Prague, Vienna and Paris – not London or Glasgow. So the first English building to reflect these new values was by a Dutch architect, for a Dutch shipping company – **Holland House** [A.2], designed in 1916.

It combines luxurious materials with the expression of structure – the steel skeletons that were behind every large building of the time. The result is both rational and decorative – exemplifying a classical modernism later seen in the towers of **Economist Plaza [A.3 & A.4]**, whose clean lines are encased in a stone rich in fossils.

By the early 1930s, American critics had dubbed the new architecture the 'International Style'. In Britain, its finest moments are on the south coast, where the weather is most forgiving; its ultimate monument is the **De La Warr Pavilion** [A.5], a glamorous pleasure palace in Bexhill-on-Sea. A similarly rigorous style can be

found at **Dartington Hall** [A.6] in Devon, its seriousness exemplified in these minimalist dormitories. Other architects combined continental modern classicism with the British architectural context, as in the London Underground's enigmatic **Chiswick Park** [A.7] or the aggressive curves and hard corners of **Park Royal** [A.8].

← Newcastle
← ✈Airport
← Whitley Bay

Gateshead

Platform 2

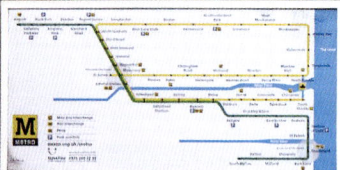

Platform 2

Between the 1930s and the 1970s, public bodies were the major sponsors of modern architecture in Britain. One of the last great moments of this age of state patronage was the **Tyne and Wear Metro**, which was planned to link Newcastle and Sunderland with their contiguous towns such as Gateshead, Tynemouth and Jarrow.

The design of trains, signs and stations was co-ordinated and lively, with the usage throughout of public art, and all information in Margaret Calvert's eponymous 'Calvert' font, which is also found throughout this book. In the urban centres, the Metro runs underground, as here, at the impressive Gateshead interchange.

After the Second World War, influenced by Mies van der Rohe, international modernist architecture shifted from white-painted concrete solids to a more technologically exacting style – as at the **Lanark County Buildings** [A.10] in suburban Lanarkshire. A more original interpretation of this idiom can be found in the University of

Sheffield's tall **Arts Tower** and low **Western Bank Library** [**A.11**], perfectly integrated with landscaped gardens. The cubic glass style was less often used for housing, but one superb example is Great Arthur House, the tower block at the centre of the **Golden Lane Estate** [**A.12**] – for a brief time, the tallest building in the capital.

The London County Council's **Alton Estate** in Roehampton, built on land taken from stately homes, was architecturally and socially the most ambitious project of the 1950s – considered by one American critic to be the 'finest low-cost housing development in the world'; and with its careful mix of low- and high-rise housing in winding paths across rolling countryside, that still doesn't seem like hyperbole. By 1959, with the construction of Alton West, a baton had passed from the decorative Anglo-Scandinavian style of the decade's start to a new, hard, continental idiom, a less outré version of the raw late work of Le Corbusier.

Britain's business districts took a while to embrace modernism, but newspapers were pioneers in this regard – especially the **Daily Express** [A.14], which commissioned three combined headquarters and printworks in the 1930s from the engineer Owen Williams, in London, Glasgow and, here, Manchester. All three of the buildings shared the same black vitrolite and sleek curves, which were often used in the paper's publicity. Norman Foster's **Canary Wharf Underground Station [A.15]**, where a curved glass entrance leads to a space somewhere between a cathedral and the skeleton of a concrete whale, has a spirit akin to the Express buildings.

Modernist architecture broke with traditional ways of emphasizing buildings through axial arrangements – instead, architects imagined structures that floated in space, paradoxically fitting with notions of landscape architecture that stressed the *genius loci*, the sense of place. At the **Pilkington Headquarters** [A.16] in St Helens, prismatic glass buildings are set among formal, man-made ponds; the halls of residence at the **University of Essex** [A.18] form a miniature skyline on the flat eastern plain. **Our Lady's High School** [A.17] in Cumbernauld, its green verdigris facade nestling in the green slopes, creates a long ridge on the rolling Lanarkshire hills.

An image of reproducibility was often at the heart of modern architecture – syncopated, repetitious facades that could seemingly extend into infinity. The first sight of **Milton Keynes Railway Station** [A.19], designed by the Development Corporation's architects and opened in 1982, is exactly this: three sides of perfectly

proportioned glass grids, and an open new city in front of you. Sometimes this aesthetic veered towards the surreal – on Tyneside, at Ryder & Yates's Engineering Research Station in **Killingworth [A.20]**, the suspended white block, with its classical Golden Section proportions, is given a skyline of almost Roman chimneys.

The 'New Universities' of the 1960s were one of the most ambitious modernist projects of the post-war years – self-contained, almost monastic, concrete communities set in distinctive landscapes, each one of them rooted in the specifics of its site. At the **University of Stirling**, the only Scottish New University to have been built from scratch during that decade, the buildings themselves are laconic and unfussy, taking a back seat to the spectacular landscape of forests, lakes and mountains, standing at almost the exact point where the Scottish Lowlands meet the wild and sublime spaces of the Highlands.

Every city has its high-rise blocks of flats, austere and minimal, which added instant skylines throughout the 1960s – but not everywhere has looked after them as well as Aberdeen. At the time of writing in early 2021, **Seamount Court**, with its clear, elegant lines, was one of several to have been listed by Historic Scotland.

The view upwards: the rooflights of Goldfinger's Haggerston comprehensive school in Hackney.

HAGGERSTON SCHOOL, HACKNEY

Ernő Goldfinger, 1967

Brutalist

A tough and generously scaled inner-city comprehensive school, and while it's another example of the category error of painting the concrete work of the architect responsible for the best concrete work in twentieth-century Britain (see also **Metro Central Heights, p. 91**), everything else about the building's upkeep is heartening, right down to the gardens and play areas. One should not lurk around schools, but if you visit when the place hosts visitors for the Open House festival, you'll see how well the disparate parts of the school have been linked together – a series of distinctive, individual spaces. The vast assembly hall and the pathway leading between the two buildings of the school are especially good – unsentimental, spacious, full of civic pride.

ARDEN ESTATE, HOXTON

Leonard Manasseh & Partners, 1967–72/ Lynch Architects, 2006

Brutalist

A good, sturdy housing estate in the most unfashionable part of what was in the 2000s London's most fashionable district, built when it was an extremely ordinary bit of the East End. Three-storey red-brick blocks, divided in a rationalist fashion through the use of grand brick pilasters and columns, are arranged around pedestrian courtyards; the estate initially appears as robust, unpretentious Brutalism, housing in a rough area that can take a few knocks. But a tiny tower of flats facing Hoxton Street takes the hints of the classical into de Chirico painting territory, blank and enigmatic. Since 2006, it has featured an elegantly ad hoc wood and glass extension on its roof, designed by Patrick Lynch, and originally used as his firm's offices before it was sold when the area's property prices went supernova. The serene rationalism of Lynch's extension is clearly linked to the classical geometry of Manasseh's designs, adding to the original ideas rather than deliberately working against them – those architects charged with adding roofs and extensions to 1960s estates should all go and see it.

─────

WATNEY MARKET, STEPNEY
Greater London Council Architects Dept, 1970–74
Brutalist

This is a red-brick, East End **Brunswick Centre (p. 63)** of step-section ziggurat flats and shops in-between, cheaper, less spatially impressive but also considerably livelier than its Bloomsbury cousin, and also rougher and readier, a real, multicultural, community space rather than an identikit mall aimed at tourists (that also means that you don't always get a sense of the flats above – all the energy is packed into the central street). It could do with being cleaned rather more often than it is, Tower Hamlets Council, but it is a strong enough building to survive neglect.

─────

ROBIN HOOD GARDENS, POPLAR ❶
Alison and Peter Smithson, 1972
Brutalist

Two long, mid-rise blocks of deck-access council housing next to the Blackwall Tunnel, and thousands of pages worth of discourse. The bulldozers have finally gone in, after ten years of an argument that has for the most part been full of smoke and mirrors. Its owners, Tower Hamlets Council, pretends that it wants to get rid of it in order to provide better housing for its people rather than in order to sell the site to developers to provide denser housing in order to help

balance the books. Its defenders claim that it's a great modernist masterpiece, rather than a neurotic, poorly planned experiment by two great modernist thinkers. Within that tension lies a tale. When Robin Hood Gardens was first slated for demolition, the design critic Stephen Bayley lamented the apparently bizarre fact that **Park Hill (p. 370)**, designed by otherwise unknown journeymen architects, was listed, whereas the scheme by the great Yale-lecturing architects who inspired them was not. There's a kernel of truth in this, in that both projects derive ultimately from the Smithsons' late-fifties competition entry for the **Golden Lane Estate (p. 55)** – but Park Hill is everything that Robin Hood Gardens is not – clear, confident, proud, complex, open, intelligible.

Robin Hood Gardens should not be being demolished. It is also full of lessons on why composing a public building primarily as a means of carrying on theoretical debates with your mates in the architecture schools is not a wonderful idea. The central 'mound', for instance, was justified with all manner of *rus-in-urbe* rising-from-the-ruins verbiage, but a steep hill in the middle of a council estate is really an ingenious means of building a public space that nobody will actually use. The combination of a Miesian grid with Corbusian concrete work, intended to cleverly unite the two poles of post-war modernist expression, is a great parlour game but results in a nerve-jangling rhythm of arbitrarily placed vertical fins. These are matters of taste, but the system of concrete fences and walls that screen the estate from noise are not – far harsher than anything designed for any other housing estate of the period, they come across as paranoid and obsessive. Sustained exploration will reveal that there was real care in the design, too. The gradation in the concrete work, which becomes smoother to the touch as you get closer to the flats, is a humane gesture, as are the unusually high ceilings in the flats.

The much vaunted, much-discussed 'streets in the sky' are not as intuitive as at Park Hill, but are still far better than the ordinary access decks which survive in their hundreds across London. The escape stairs, on the other hand, are full of blind corners, and are used much more than planned, given how often the lifts are out of order. There is absolutely nothing here that a decent architect with a decent budget couldn't fix – a RIBA competition a few years ago had particularly astute suggestions by Sarah Wigglesworth – and the buildings are certainly likely to be better than the developer's hutches that will no doubt replace them. It's just that when it came to actual buildings, Alison and Peter Smithson weren't half the architects Jack Lynn and Ivor Smith were.

At the time of writing in early 2021, one block has been demolished and another still stands; it may all be gone by the time of publication, but demolition has taken so long that it is worth checking to be sure.

———

CANARY WHARF: ONE CANADA SQUARE
Cesar Pelli & Associates, 1988–91
CITIGROUP TOWER
Cesar Pelli & Associates, 1998–2001
8 CANADA SQUARE
Foster & Partners, 1998–2001
CANARY WHARF DOCKLANDS LIGHT RAILWAY STATION
GEC–Mowlem, 1991
Postmodernist, International Style

Too big to ignore, just as the banks they house were 'too big to fail' in 2008. Canada Square is a classical ensemble of skyscrapers, planned by the Canadian developers Olympia and York as the centrepiece of the Thatcherite redevelopment of London. The original idea was for an axial ensemble surmounting the redeveloped docks of the Isle of Dogs, with lower Postmodernist offices fanning out from the centre – a despotic layout, with the central blinking pyramid on top of One Canada Square as the crowning obelisk. It has never felt like a real part of London, due to the obvious fact it is a transplant from Reagan-era New York – the American designer Cesar Pelli has simply taken one of his hierarchical stainless steel towers from Battery Park City in Manhattan and placed it in Tower Hamlets. The authoritarian, centralized layout feels extremely unlike anything else in London, feeling more like the outskirts of Paris. But it is inescapable, and it was visually improved when the original plan was completed at the start of the twenty-first century with two flanking skyscrapers. Citigroup is another of Pelli's stepped skyscrapers, but with the steel cladding replaced by a High-Tech display of structure, while Foster's totally linear, flat 8 Canada Square, originally built as the HSBC Tower, shares an aloofness with Pelli's two edifices. Best viewed while sailing through on the elevated viaducts of the Docklands Light Railway, particularly as it passes a rather grandiose, vaulted DLR station, a cold film set of a building. The underground mall beneath One Canada Square, meanwhile, is perhaps the most claustrophobic public place in London.

———

CASCADES, ISLE OF DOGS
CZWG, 1988
Postmodernist

The only residential tower built from scratch in London in the Thatcher era, and hence pretty pioneering, Cascades is the first example of what would become the main architectural typology along the Thames – the first stone placed in the wall of luxury flats that was erected alongside almost every bit of water in the metropolis is some sort of first. It's also very good, with an excellent grasp of what makes a tower – a clear image and silhouette, an understanding of height and drama, and an expressive modelling of mass. The engineering brick is a typical 'context' hostage to fortune, in that the warehouses it emulates are mostly either gone or remodelled into more luxury flats, indistinguishable from the new ones, but it helps give the tower some weight, most unlike the freeze-dried Fosterian surfaces everywhere else in **Canary Wharf (above)**. As Charles Jencks points out, it's a bit of a shame that the steep slope doesn't have any functional role – a ski lift would have been nice, or maybe a slalom to threaten recalcitrant bankers with.

———

THAMES BARRIER PARK, SILVERTOWN
Patel Taylor, 1995–9
Postmodernist

A rare good public space in Docklands, and something more poetic than that implies. Unusually, a competition was held for the design of this park, on the site of a petrochemical plant. This contest could perhaps be credited for the imaginative result – executed by Patel Taylor from the winning idea by the French designers Groupe Signes. These sunken spaces, set out to evoke miniature docks, are miles from the functional landscape architecture of granite setts and little pools so familiar in riverside regeneration public spaces. It spurns all that greyness in favour of a *Last Year in Marienbad* architecture of surreal sculpted topiary and formalistic patterning. It is multilevel, with waves of hedges and secret gardens, creating a game of hide and seek with the river, the Barrier and the bustle of luxury flats being built around it. Of these, the Barratt flats immediately overlooking the park are worth a look too: they have the right sort of scale, with their stepped sections and Red Vienna-style stairwells and flagpoles, though the cheapness of their materials means they already look stained and worn.

UNIVERSITY OF EAST LONDON, NORTH WOOLWICH
Edward Cullinan Architects, 1996–2000
Ecomodernist

We have little to show architecturally for the massive expansion of higher education (at a price) embarked upon by the New Labour governments of 1997–2010 – there are isolated gems, yet there is extremely little that betrays any sort of holistic, coherent, thought-out development; too often, universities have preferred one-off 'gateway' buildings to impress parents over any kind of unified planning. But there is this, tucked away between the Royal Docks and City Airport. It might be off-putting at first – the childlike aesthetic is more *Noel's House Party* than Denys Lasdun, and the cheap render and aluminium cry out 'Private Finance Initiative' – but spend a bit of time here, and its deep underlying individuality starts to emerge. The campus, rehousing a conglomerate of ex-polys in the East End and metropolitan Essex, is organized around two focal points. One consists of a set of halls of residence in the form of multicoloured drums, a very unusual post-seventies example of including student housing in a campus, rather than leaving it to speculators in the area around. The library and the classroom buildings are in angular, ribbon-windowed white buildings with a hint of the German Expressionist architecture of Hans Scharoun, and from the library you can watch aeroplanes take off and touch down. The public spaces between these buildings are clear, obvious and well used – a dockside promenade, a main square – but they can't make the location feel any less bizarre and implausible, especially as there's no connection with any kind of ordinary residential area around. The result is one of London's most alien landscapes, the unofficial J. G. Ballard University.

A cathedral underground: the soaring concrete vaults of Foster's Canary Wharf Underground Station.

CANARY WHARF UNDERGROUND STATION ○

Foster & Partners, 1999

High-Tech

Along with **Westminster Underground Station (p. 72)**, this is a high point of late-twentieth-century transport architecture in London, and is the best building in Canary Wharf. If you look at it from a distance, with its neon lights shimmering, or if you glide past it on the Docklands Light Railway, it's a fantastical mini-metropolis, especially for those of us who remember when there was just the one tower, surrounded by Postmodernist subtopia (and **Cascades, p. 131**). Get off the train and wander round, though, and it's surprisingly hard to find a single building that could be described in its own right, and even less a public space that could be described, as pleasant or imaginative – despite the Beaux Arts symmetry, the place's roots in 1980s

'Non-Planning' are still very visible, and the low-ceilinged underground mall beneath Cesar Pelli's **One Canada Square (p. 131)** is notable only for its sheer misery. This underground entrance point to it all, though, fills you with unwarranted anticipation. On the ground, just a glass pavilion – in the Foster-designed Bilbao Metro, they call these 'Fosteritos' – but the rib-vaulted cathedral just beneath it is breathtaking, with the commuters as the Jonahs swallowed by a concrete whale. When built, it seemed far too big, now it's crowded, but it manages its density with aplomb. There is a certain sombreness to the design, with the mandatory grey palette of the Jubilee Line extension lending itself to these Gothic, cathedral-style effects, with everything leading up to the release of the escalator and the glass exit. But as for the rest of this financial enclave, a walk brings mainly disappointment. **[A.15]**

GREEN BRIDGE, MILE END
CZWG, 2000
Postmodernist

A highly successful public space by an unfashionable Postmodernist firm (there's a hideous eighties office block of theirs nearby, so you can see just how surprising that success is). An inspiration for the mercifully cancelled Garden Bridge, it is far more logical, linking two parks so that you both feel the join (as cars on a busy road are going under you) and you don't, as the park becomes continuous. It feels completely intuitive. Underneath is the price – what were, at the time it was built, very high-end retail units by the standards of pre-gentrification Mile End, detailed in the green tiles CZWG used also at their **Public Toilets (p. 170)** on Westbourne Grove; very much of a piece with the bridge itself. Rarely has the cross-subsidy of public space with private business been done in so architecturally relaxed a fashion.

WHITECHAPEL IDEA STORE
Adjaye Associates, 2005
Supermodernist, Pseudomodernist

Like **Peckham Library (p. 103)**, this was very celebrated in its day, as a vision of a public building that would be modern and populist, and would 'spearhead' what was called 'regeneration'. Its most daring and public-spirited gesture, the escalator which goes right into the street and then scoops you into the reading rooms, was closed a very long time ago, a distant casualty of straitened municipal budgets. The New Labour nomenclature is also (thankfully) dated – not calling libraries 'libraries' did not catch on. It all feels rather tawdry now, with the shiny sheen taken off the materials, and maintenance has been poor. The basic design, though, is sound – four storeys of books, computers and a variety

of reading rooms, a bright and clear facade of coloured-glass strips, and, as at Peckham, a pride in scale that befits the importance to a working-class area of its library.

DONNYBROOK QUARTER, BOW ✪
Peter Barber Architects, 2006
Classical Modernism

Grandly named – 'Donnybrook Eighth' would be more fitting. This is a street block of low-rise, high-density housing association flats that is one of the few real continuations of the project of heroic social housing, showing a particular affinity with Camden Council schemes like the **Maiden Lane Estate (p. 151)** or **Fleet Road (p. 147)**. It is perhaps flattered by its context, for there's no getting away from the grimness that successive generations, from the 1800s to the 1990s, have foisted on the East End. And then, suddenly! – a 'Mediterranean village' of gleaming white-painted houses, clustered into a street-corner casbah, with shops at the edges. This sun-bathed aesthetic might seem unwise for the area and the weather, but, visiting it more than a decade later, I see it has kept up surprisingly well; even graffiti is just localized to the shutters of one of the shop fronts, the result either of good upkeep or of respect for the buildings, or both.

Barber has since abandoned this 1920s Le Corbusier/De Stijl look, opting at places like **Worland Gardens (p. 136)** for the biscuity 'New London Vernacular' of brick cladding. On this evidence, that's a shame, as Donnybrook combines his interest in London streets – though, above the tarmac, these are actually flats, not houses, and the ingenious plans and bay windows that maximize light into what are basically back-to-backs provide a lot of the interest on the elevations – with something that points well out of London. It's always a smart move to tell people that your modern architecture isn't inspired by Dessau or Moscow, but the Med.

The social housing of Peter Barber's Donnybrook Quarter, in the Mediterranean village of Bromley-by-Bow.

The only thing really lacking here is a café; there is a shop selling security doors instead. The very New Labour big public art, of a *Little Shop of Horrors*-like overgrown flower, is the scheme's only reminder of the deeply unheroic time in which it was built. **[D.21]**

THE FOLLY, BARKING
muf, 2010
Postmodernist

Barking Central, designed by AHMM architects, so exemplified New Labour architecture that it became the basis for parodies by artists like Matthew Derbyshire and Scott King – meanly proportioned single-aspect flats smothered in lime green barcode facade razzledazzle. Muf, hired as artists and designers of what planners insist on calling 'public realm' (a term which always ought to be prefaced with 'BEHOLD, THE') made this place a lot more interesting than it would

otherwise be, through insisting on the public colonnades that run through the apartment buildings upon the square being kept open and unencumbered. They then created, out of various pieces of waste attached to a bare gable wall, 'The Folly', a ludic and lurid piece of instant history which, by now, many people in Barking will probably think has been there for ever. It features steps to nowhere, pieces of Victorian salvage, a stone sheep at the top, and grass growing out of it. Behind, vans load and unload the goods for a supermarket.

OTOPROJECTS, DALSTON
Assemble, 2015
Ecomodernist, Postmodernist

The sort of thing they call in the more intellectual parts of the trade 'expanding the field'. Built by volunteers out of packed earth, waste and wood, it's hipster big-society rusticism, for the 'project space' of the Dalston free-jazz and experimental-music venue Cafe Oto, placed into a wasteland behind a fence, surrounded by rubbish. There is nothing else quite like it – a post-apocalyptic garden shed, built with such mob-handed clumsiness that you can imagine it housing the characters in Russell Hoban's *Riddley Walker*.

WORLAND GARDENS, STRATFORD
Peter Barber Architects, 2016
Classical Modernism, Viennese

If there's good social housing built in London in the 2010s, chances are it's tiny, ingenious and designed by Peter Barber. Rather a lot of housing has been built in Stratford since it was designated home of the Olympics in 2012, ranging from a bargain basement updating of **Cascades (p. 131)** to the severe Euromodernism of the Olympic Village, and the speculative dross foisted upon Stratford High Street. It's quite the indictment that by far the most architecturally interesting new building is a half-terrace of houses down a backstreet. These boast the currently ubiquitous stock brick, arranged into a rhythmic row of houses with arches over the doorways, showing a warmth and friendliness that feels very Arts and Crafts. A monumental tone comes from the Red Vienna-style triumphal arch, which feels like it ought to be leading you to some grand public garden, but actually just provides a useful place for residents to park their cars. This should be the basis for a district, not half a street. At the time of writing, Barber and his firm's leading partner Alice Brownfield are working on some much larger schemes in the London Borough of Newham, which suggests they know this too.

HACKNEY FREE SCHOOL, NEW PRIMARY SCHOOL & FLATS
Henley Halebrown, 2010–20
Classical Modernism, Brutalist

Two buildings close to each other on the long, wide, bleak Kingsland Road which should really never have been built, both of such high quality that they must be seen. The earlier is Hackney Free School, the first major example of the libertarian, low-budget schools programme briefly rolled out under then-education secretary, Michael Gove. While most free schools are mere sheds or converted buildings, this is a considered piece of street architecture – the main frontage consisting of a serene, classicized modern block on top of a Victorian commercial unit, with a taller, regular block of classrooms behind and a tiny playground in-between, as land costs a lot of money round here. The subsequent primary school building, meanwhile, was the result of various complicated land deals which eventually meant the entire project was funded by a private block of flats. Usually, the results of these sorts of 'cross-subsidy' – luxury flats to pay for schools and public facilities – are miserable and incoherent, but Henley Halebrown's design is so good that, somehow, they get away with it. The high-ceilinged school buildings are surmounted by a splayed ten-storey tower with a presence and monumental force that stands almost alone in London over the last two decades. Its red-stained concrete is sculpted into a column-and-frame grid that evokes equally the Italian Renaissance and the London County Council housing of the sixties – one part Bologna, one part **Alton Estate (p. 112)**. What has happened here is an attempt to make something genuinely civic out of the comprehensive mismanagement of the public sector, and, in architectural terms at least, it has worked.

NORTH LONDON

OSSULSTON ESTATE, SOMERS TOWN
G. Topham Forrest for the London County Council Architects Dept, 1927–31
Viennese

When interwar British architects wanted to do something radical and continental, they took their cue from the monumental, quasi-classical municipal housing of Vienna, not from the machine-tooled abstraction of Berlin, Moscow or Rotterdam. The Ossulston Estate is the first Viennese-style estate in Britain; there are many others in London, and a few elsewhere, from Aberdeen's **Rosemount Square (p. 546)** to Liverpool's **St Andrew's Gardens (p. 425)**. The Viennese idea was the formation of hundreds of flats into monumental courtyards, with grand, anticipation-building archways as the public access, sprawling and too big for the eye to encompass at once, but offsetting this vista-effacing length with several small vistas, miniature prospects and bombastic set pieces. It's intended to create a sense of pride and grandeur in the too often (even then) shamefaced, penny-pinching sector of working-class housing. Ossulston Street, right next to the **British Library (p. 143)**, does this well – it has a real scale and pomp, a welcome swagger. It's worth noting what it does and doesn't retain from Vienna. The flats are much bigger, with private bathrooms; it has fewer public facilities (though many more than the later LCC-Viennese estates); and the knobbly whitewash is a roughcast rusticism that is more Letchworth Garden City than Karl-Marx-Hof. The saddest difference is a comparative lack of wit in the design of the public spaces. Vienna's courtyards are always obviously planned – real gardens, with fountains and benches and flowerbeds and trees, there to be lingered in. The LCC never mastered this, and the public space here is all wheelie bins, asphalt and cars. Ignore that, though, and the Ossulston Estate is ripping stuff: our own Ringstrasse des Proletariats off the Euston Road.

PICCADILLY LINE: ✪ MANOR HOUSE, TURNPIKE LANE, ARNOS GROVE, SOUTHGATE, OAKWOOD & COCKFOSTERS STATIONS
Charles Holden, 1932–3
International Style, Modern Classicism

These six stations represent the peak of the Charles Holden/Frank Pick era of Tube design, and arguably the peak of all attempts to integrate architecture, design, art and place in Britain. For the historian Michael Saler, London Transport is what we had instead of a continental 'avant-garde' (a De Stijl, a Bauhaus, a Russian Constructivism), a notion that seems far-fetched until you've taken this route from Haringey to Enfield on the Piccadilly Line. You can begin wholly underground at Manor House, where the interest lies in the design of the platforms and the *Der Golem* UFA film-set ticket hall rather than the outside architecture, but it really gets going at Turnpike Lane. Here, you can see what Holden and Pick had gone to look at in the Netherlands and the Weimar Republic: escalators lined with German Expressionist uplighters leading to a box-like concrete hall, flooded with light from large windows, Dutch-style modernist brickwork and, above, a rectilinear campanile with the 'UNDERGROUND' logo and roundel set into it. Shops are integrated below. At Arnos Grove, open-air concrete platforms, almost proto-Brutalist, lead through a walkway to a rotunda of exceptional purity. Stockholm's

At the very end of the line: the impressive concrete hangar of Charles Holden's Cockfosters Station.

Central Library is often pegged as the inspiration, but it's of a piece with the other stations – the same warm, finely cut brick, the same concrete frame, the same sense of spaciousness and reason, albeit knocked about a bit with the usual cheap anti-pigeon netting and rush hour metal fences that mar all British transport architecture.

Beyond Arnos Grove, you come to Southgate, where the serenity of Arnos Grove has been exchanged for metropolitan motion; the lower, wider, partly glazed rotunda here is at the centre of a circus of shops and buses, and has a peculiar little futuristic light tower on top, an instant focus and monument for a new suburb that would otherwise have lacked one. At Oakwood, into what was at the time still open country (Trent Park nearby makes it feel like it still is), the ticket hall has the quality of the grandest of termini. Holden's use of classical proportions means that this wholly modernist edifice of concrete and brick has the same hushed,

time-stopping grandeur as the travertine lobbies of **Senate House (p. 51)**. And then, at the end of the line, a shock for the thousands who have fallen asleep on the Tube – the long, angular concrete hangar of Cockfosters, a fitting place to stop and take in the scale of Holden's achievement. (A larger version of the same hangar can be found at **Uxbridge, p. 157**.) [D.1]

PENGUIN POOL OF LONDON ZOO, REGENT'S PARK
Lubetkin and Tecton, 1933
Constructivist

Once an emblem of how modernism could be fun, changes at the place that insists on calling itself at all times 'ZSL London Zoo' have made the Penguin Pool into a regularly trotted out parable about the failures of modern architecture. It's a justly famous design – a tub of white concrete around two swooping ramps, one across the other, modern materials treated with great humour and freedom. Originally, penguins walked up and down these and then leapt into the pool below. The gradual changes in zoo design towards making the enclosures more comfortable for the animals, as opposed to gearing their design to public display, led to the penguins being moved to a pool that more closely approximated their natural habitat. Various other animals were tried – the first time I went to the Zoo, in 2007, there were porcupines in there. Eventually, the zookeepers gave up, and the pool now sits there as a useless listed sculpture, until eventually robot penguins are invited in. The many critics who have used this as a metaphor for modernist social housing don't seem bothered that they're comparing the reactions of human beings to those of birds.

———

HORNSEY TOWN HALL, HARINGEY
Reginald Uren, 1933–5
Modern Classicism

A seminal building, insofar as it might be the first use of W. M. Dudok's monumental version of Dutch avant-garde architecture as the appropriate style for British interwar bureaucracy. Dudok's style has been adapted to make his manner even more compromised – note the Georgian keystones on the windows to the main hall. The quality of workmanship and the sense of generous but tasteful public splendour are all very admirable, as is the scale of the tall tower that marks it out from a distance. The detailing of the stairwells, with cast-iron screens, and the fluted marble columns around, is gorgeous. Currently run as a community centre, but slated to become a luxury hotel. The Borough Architects' 1960s library nearby is also worth a visit, with its sculptural pool, abstract mosaic and clear-glass reading room.

HIGHPOINT & HIGHPOINT 2, HIGHGATE ○
Lubetkin and Tecton, 1934–8
International Style, People's Detailing

Modern architecture, as we've seen, begins in Britain as a luxury aesthetic aimed squarely at intellectuals in London's northern suburbs. The flagships of north London modernism are Tecton's two blocks of middle-class flats, overshadowing the single-family houses of Frognal, such as **Sun House (p. 140)**. Of the two blocks, Highpoint 1 is still by some way the more impressive – it's full of delightful little moments like the curved enclosures of the garden and the subtle kink in the balconies, in a pure, from-one-mould coating of icing sugar concrete. Highpoint 2 exchanges that purity for an architecture of bits and pieces, after only four years – some architects got bored with the International Style very quickly. A complicated pattern of brown and cream tiles with boxed-out flats and the famously droll use of cast caryatids from the Acropolis at the entrance, it has sometimes been treated as a surrealist building, which seems about right for its combination of Persian carpet patterns and gentle silliness (Lubetkin himself obviously preferred it, and he lived at Highpoint 2 for several years, before decamping to Gloucestershire to farm pigs). However, the comparison to the single, brilliantly realized idea of Highpoint 1 is unflattering; and Lubetkin would develop the surreal, decorative style of Highpoint 2 in a much more visually successful and socially interesting manner at **Spa Green (p. 52)**.

———

ISOKON BUILDING, BELSIZE PARK ○
Wells Coates, 1935
Constructivist, International Style

This extraordinary housing scheme by a Japanese-raised, Canadian-born architect,

A new world: the Constructivist communal housing of Wells Coates's Isokon Building in Belsize Park.

intended as a publicity wheeze for Jack Pritchard's furniture company, Isokon, was the first building in Britain to treat modern architecture as a total ethos – something much more than a new way of dressing up a building. A communal housing block – aimed at the north London intelligentsia, and notoriously inhabited by a picaresque group of novelists, Bauhaus exiles and spies – it resembles Soviet Constructivist models in its connection to social facilities (here, a raffish 'Isobar', now an art gallery), in the clever arrangements of its flats (which mask the fact that they're minuscule), and especially in its emphasis on displaying the building's circulation on its outside. The back side is a logical Bauhaus block with attractive balconies, but when you look at the street elevation, you're hit by three muscular walkways and voluptuously modelled stairwells, rising to a monumental tower. Their physicality and sensuality are

far beyond the fey abstraction of most 1930s British modernism – instead, this building is a viscerally three-dimensional experience, a new real space that you feel in your bones.

Restored in the early 2000s to its original colours – surprisingly, white with an almost Day-Glo pink undertone.

SUN HOUSE, HAMPSTEAD
Maxwell Fry, 1935
66 FROGNAL, HAMPSTEAD ○
Connell Ward and Lucas, 1936
FROGNAL CLOSE, HAMPSTEAD
Ernst Freud, 1937
International Style

A collection of what would later be called Case Study Houses in close proximity in a very affluent corner of Hampstead, the first time that north London became the place for architects and intellectuals to try out their ideas on themselves before extending them on a wider, public scale (see later, **Murray Mews, p. 149**). Of the three, the one that would stand out as a design in any era is the house by Connell Ward and Lucas (here, largely Colin Lucas), a hard and complex design with hints of De Stijl – to the street, an elemental rationalist composition; to the back, a tight mesh of railings and cantilevered concrete. Sun House, up a private path nearby, is more of a standard 1930s International Style design, like one of the imaginary houses on a London Transport or Shell poster come to life, but still not entirely feeling real. In the other direction is Frognal Close, designed by one of Sigmund Freud's sons in a brown knobbly brick, already more insular and Anglicized. In Freud's houses you can see this radical import, this 'cultural Bolshevism', attacked by Nazis and English conservatives alike, gradually becoming just a regular English residential architecture, neat brick houses behind hedges in a cul-de-sac.

2, 4, 6, 8, 10 VALENCIA ROAD, STANMORE
Douglas Wood, 1934
1–6 KERRY AVENUE, STANMORE
Gerald Lacoste, 1937
Moderne

Emerge at the northernmost end of the Jubilee Line, cross the road and you'll find a reverse L-shape of big suburban villas whose builders decided to let themselves go a little, and experiment with the new forms that had just been introduced to Britain by Central European exiles. They didn't do so in a particularly rigorous way – no free plans, no pilotis or Corbusian roof terraces here, just a shift in the design of semis towards smooth white surfaces, cylindrical glazed stairwells, an air of modernity rather than nostalgia, and, in some of the Kerry Avenue houses, asymmetrical, sprawling layouts. They exude the suburban values of exclusivity and luxury to a much greater degree than your average Mock Tudor house, because these houses are *special* – around them, the half-timbering goes on until it subsides into the green belt.

KENMORE PARK SCHOOL, HARROW
W. T. Curtis and H. W. Burchett for Middlesex County Council Architects Dept, 1938
Moderne, Expressionist

Middlesex County Council had a 'progressive' architects department in the thirties, and built many schools, libraries and suchlike in the north-western suburbs, such as the great little **Arnos Pool (p. 143)**. Mostly it's their schools that have survived best. Built just before the war, they are straightforward Dutch brick modernism, of the sort that you'll find in abundance in the suburbs of Amsterdam, Rotterdam and Utrecht. Bulky, often curved forms, beautifully detailed, pulled into asymmetric yet monumental profiles with simple playgrounds, all in very ordinary residential areas. Unusually for interwar suburbia, there are no Garden City dreams of a lost Eden, making schools like this into a glimpse of what most British architecture in the interwar years might have looked like were it not for a collective paroxysm of nostalgia and fear. All of the Middlesex schools are worth a glance, but this is the most convincing – a brick prow at the centre of a rather wan housing estate, with cubist stairwells and long flanking wings, transplanting the shabbier end of Harrow to Hilversum.

CHRIST THE KING, COCKFOSTERS
Constantine Bosschaerts, 1937–40
Moderne

Who knows (except those that live there) what delights await in the wilds of Cockfosters? One answer to the question of what you'll find if you fall asleep on the Piccadilly Line is … a Belgian Benedictine priory, designed in the purest Euromoderne in the 1930s, secluded behind a car park amongst semis and green parkways. The architect was also one of its monks, and here he designed a strikingly elegant long block for accommodation and worship. At its corner is a subtle and slightly Constructivist tower, with the red cross and the beautifully set red letters reading 'VITA ET PAX' more a matter of modernist supergraphics than anything in the tradition. As in the Bataville at **East Tilbury (p. 176)**, this isn't one of those interwar modern buildings that represent an adaptation to England, but a total transplant – suburban Liège relocated to Enfield. The interior is slightly bland compared with the striking frontage, although the corridors of the old priory feature some intriguing Expressionistic murals of saints.

Continental modernism meets the Georgian tradition at Goldfinger's Willow Road, opposite Hampstead Heath.

1–3 WILLOW ROAD, HAMPSTEAD ✪
Ernő Goldfinger, 1939
International Style

This terrace was an early attempt to demonstrate that modernist architecture could accommodate itself to commonplace British typologies – here, the Georgian street, with its externally expressed hierarchy of functions and its blunt yet civilized minimalism. Famously, this wasn't enough to please the local resident Ian Fleming, whose dislike of the buildings led to his naming a villain after the architect. There's not much that can be learned from that other than that the British upper class's hostility to modernism was deeply irrational – today, these buildings look wholly sensible and relaxed, full of stereotypically English qualities. Goldfinger's house is now managed by the National Trust, and it is worth seeing how these spaces – many of them very similarly proportioned to those in the council flats Goldfinger would later design – were treated when the architect lived in them day in, day out. There's no cold, icy high-modernist minimalism – Goldfinger's house (number 2) feels warm, lived in, and full of personality and individuality. That alternation between minimal, unfussy exterior and an inside that is a blank canvas on to which you could impose yourself as much as you liked is one of the less commented-upon aspects of modernist domestic architecture. That said, not everyone has Goldfinger's art collection. A huge amount of the appeal of this modest space is in the way it is filled with his (sometimes self-designed) furniture and books, along with scattered works by Max Ernst or Bridget Riley – you get a great sense of a modernist life well lived.

EAST FINCHLEY UNDERGROUND STATION
Charles Holden, 1939
International Style

A Holden outlier, not on the Piccadilly Line, and relatively messy in design, dictated by the need to integrate with what was then the North London Railway. Confused and blocky as an entrance, it is better on the platforms, where the stylish glass bubbles of the waiting rooms are filched from Walter Gropius's 1914 model factory in Cologne. Eric Aumonier's splendid cuboid 'Archer' sculpture is perched on the edge of the viaduct; the sculptor would later design the angels in the stairway in Powell and Pressburger's ('The Archers') 1945 epic *A Matter of Life and Death*. Here, the archer points out from the heavenly air of the suburbs, towards subterranean inner London.

BOWES ROAD LIBRARY & ARNOS POOL, ENFIELD
W. T. Curtis and H. W. Burchett for Middlesex County Council Architects Dept, 1939
Moderne

Not far from **Arnos Grove Station (p. 137)**, this is a miniature example of the very decent Dutch brick public buildings by the late-thirties Middlesex County Council Architects Dept, such as **Kenmore Park School (p. 141)**. The library is like a miniaturized version of **Hornsey Town Hall (p. 139)**, with a main block of high, slightly Georgian windows and a main tower boasting a bay-windowed stairwell, of the sort of design called 'thermometers' in Tel Aviv, here capped with a little copper crown. Across from that, the pool is dominated by a sweeping concrete canopy around a red-brick rotunda, with long, pavilion-like wings, leading to a dramatically sculpted concrete niche for an entrance. Impossibly chic in amongst all the mock Tudor.

80–90 SOUTH HILL PARK, HAMPSTEAD
Howell & Amis, 1956
78 SOUTH HILL PARK, HAMPSTEAD
Brian Housden, 1968
Brutalist

These two private buildings round the back of Hampstead Heath are great examples of the shifting meanings of 'Brutalism' between the middle of the 1950s and the end of the 1960s. Numbers 80–90 are an unpretentious glass and brick grid by the LCC architects responsible for much of the **Alton Estate (p. 112)**, for their own use, and using the same modules and proportions as their council housing. The block is easily legible, deliberately reproducible and impersonal. Next door everything has changed into an aesthetic both more introverted and more visually rich. Brian Housden's house appears to the pedestrian as three distinct grids of glass bricks, held in rough concrete frames, two inset, one boxed out, with a walkway across and a basement below – individualistic, fetishistic in its use of materials, and fascinating.

BRITISH LIBRARY, SOMERS TOWN ✪
Colin St John Wilson/Long & Kentish, 1962–99
Classical Modernism

A timeless, difficult, admirable, loveable and fudged building, designed incrementally over several decades by Colin St John Wilson and his partner, M. J. Long. Leaving aside its painfully protracted history – its site moved from Bloomsbury to Somers Town, technological troubles dragging on its construction, space restrictions meaning there are far more actual books at the BL's depot at Boston Spa in Yorkshire, plus the obligatory attacks by the heir to the throne – by the time it was finished, it was outright unfashionable, a weird half-Brutalist, half-historicist throwback in the era of Foster and Rogers being feted as the greatest British architects since Hawksmoor and Wren. It was barely even noticed; when I first started using it, in the mid-2000s, it felt like a secret, and passes were given out grudgingly.

Anyway, more fool everyone, as it's actually the most successful of all the grand projects of the turn of the millennium, both as a public space – its Lewis Carroll brick and travertine chequerboard cleverly walled off from Euston Road with a system of ingenious fairytale gates that is more Natural History Museum than Secured By Design, leading to squares within squares, piazzas within piazzas – and as a public building, with its foyers having the most flowing, generous and intuitive circulation since the **National Theatre (p. 84)**, and certainly more easily navigable than the **Barbican (p. 66)**. Typically for the time, attention focused on the Aalto-esque exterior, a barn-like roof leading to a clustered clock tower facing that of St Pancras – neither modern enough for the techies, nor literal enough for the trads, it now looks like what it is, a Brutalist building finished decades later with neo-Victorian materials, and much closer to the **Brunswick Centre (p. 63)** in its ethos than immediate appearances might suggest.

Inside, the circulation is dominated by the curved concrete stairways and the open galleries, around the library of George III, which is enclosed in the Mies tower that London never built, a beautiful metal sculpture rising the height of the building. In the reading rooms, there are lots of space, comfortable seats and an attention to the small details that is enormously welcome. It is forced to invent tradition in making lamps, seats, tables and cases that look like they could last for hundreds of years and yet aren't blandly retro or obvious, and it actually does this rather well, with Long and Wilson always knowing when to embellish

and when to stop. Now, it's almost overused, with Wi-Fi users crammed into every corridor, and, allegedly, an elaborate system of sexual codes used in the reading rooms. Although the main bulk of the building is listed – and rightly so – some of Long & Kentish's extensions at the back for storage and offices are under threat of demolition. They are integral, and should be preserved. **[D. 7 & D. 8]**

——

ROYAL COLLEGE OF PHYSICIANS, REGENT'S PARK ✪
Denys Lasdun & Partners, 1964
Brutalist

The first of Lasdun's great public buildings, marking a reconciliation of sorts between the establishment and the once insurgent modernists. The finest marbles and woods are here used in a design which is notable both for the classicism of its proportions and for its lack of conventional decorum – slit windows, an inverted ziggurat, a cantilevered escape staircase, these are what you actually see from the park. The open, glazed ground floor leads you into a radical compromise – a multilevel atrium decorated in the heavy-bronze-framed portraits of the Royal College's famous members. The extreme delicacy of the design leads to heart-in-mouth touches, as when a volume projects out through the glass wall, reaching from the heavy interior into weightless mid-air. One fork of the atrium's stairwell leads to a preserved eighteenth-century room, a trick that Richard Rogers would pull later at **Lloyd's of London (p. 69)**. There, it is a dissonant cyberpunk gesture that suggests time travel as much as historic continuity – here, it feels logical, a part of Lasdun's peculiarly Augustan version of high modernism.

Brutalism and the Establishment meet and get on rather well: the Royal College of Physicians, Regent's Park.

LONDON ZOO, REGENT'S PARK: ELEPHANT HOUSE

Casson Conder & Partners, 1962–4
AVIARY
Cedric Price and Frank Newby, 1962–4
Brutalist, High-Tech

Built alongside each other, in the second (and last) time that radical ideas for human architecture got tested on animals first, these show the extreme disparities in radical architecture in the mid–1960s, either a monumental weightiness, as heavy as a building could possibly be, or an ethereal weightlessness, where the 'building' is little more than a frame and a mesh. The Elephant House – as was, its residents having being moved out as with the **Penguin Pool (p. 138)** – is a series of fat, rugged, ribbed-concrete drums, with copper cowls on top like oasthouses, to both shelter the elephants and to display their vastness to the public. Unlike most of the zoo buildings, you can

easily imagine it being used to house humans, or, most likely, educate them, with lecture theatres and art galleries inserted into these barrels for animals to sleep and poo in. Not so the Aviary. Its usual credit as the 'Snowdon aviary' after the royal consort who was consulted in its design is forelock-tugging – this is Cedric Price and Frank Newby's Aviary, a tensile web both transparent and bafflingly complex. Unlike most of the zoo's buildings, you don't need to pay for entry to see it properly, with an extensive view – and, just as importantly, sound – available to those walking the Regent's Canal. Price, like his 1960s allies Archigram, is one of the great paper architects, endlessly celebrated in the histories. He was famously unsentimental, but here, it's hard not to feel sad at the fact that this beautiful structure is his only surviving building.

CLIFF ROAD STUDIOS, CAMDEN ✪
Georgie Wolton, 1968
International Style

Two elegant, precise blocks of artists' studios next to each other, by one of the major female architects in mid-century London. One block is a simple grid of rendered concrete and glass bricks, the other thin, symmetrical ribbon windows with a projecting central volume, both on the same scale as the houses around, a decade or so before Colqhuoun & Miller would attempt the same at **5 Caversham Road & 6–10 Gaisford Street (p. 152)**. This is a restatement, unusual in that era, of modernism's first principles – clarity, rationality and the air of the Parisian painter's studio – alongside a very new interest in London's mundane streetscape that comes from the bohemian culture of the later sixties.

ELSFIELD, KENTISH TOWN
Bill Forrest for Camden Council Architects Dept, 1968
International Style

A single stepped row of concrete flats, ushering in the Camden Council style of the 1970s – no towers, no slabs, no abstract green space, but a modernist re-conception of the street and the house, designed through the section, not the facade, which you can read from the stepped profile. This is all then given a laconic, white-walled, faintly 1920s, faintly Mediterranean appearance. Soon surpassed by larger, more ambitious schemes but well worth a visit in its own right – the tentative beginning to one of British architecture's great adventures.

GRAHAME PARK, COLINDALE
Roger Walters and Gordon Wigglesworth for Greater London Council Architects Dept, 1969–75

PEGASUS COURT, COLINDALE
Peter Barber Architects, 2015
Brutalist, Classical Modernism

Grahame Park is a large 1970s housing estate in unpretty outer north London, with Brent Cross shopping centre and the M1 in one direction, and a massive redevelopment scheme on the site of a police training college in the other. Like so many estates of its era, the worst thing you can do is walk or, worse still, drive its perimeter, where you'll find a dour collection of brick blocks with their services bunched up into hammer-shaped brick towers on top. Walk into it, however, and you'll discover that it's one of the most humane and complex GLC estates, with terraces, mid-rise blocks and maisonettes linked together by tree-lined paths, with **Barbican**-style **(p. 66)** tile-and-brick paving underfoot; at the centre is a large 'town centre' of now mostly boarded-up shops, several community centres and two churches – the design of both going in for conical, top-lit rotundas. The network of pathways (all at ground level, with a relatively sensitive Postmodernist renovation removing the upper walkways) and the dark brick unite what could otherwise have been vague and straggling.

The current 'regeneration' – a proposal to demolish has been blocked by the Mayor of London – involves new private and 'mixed tenure' blocks to provide links with an 'Aspirational' new district. Most of these are as dour as the back sides of the GLC blocks, only with a paler brick; but rather incongruously among them is Pegasus Court, the biggest of Peter Barber's London housing complexes. Clearly, the firm can handle mass – the block has a satisfying chunkiness, shaped into a complex section of setbacks, rhythmic patterns of balconies and windows, which break the volume up into a mountain rather than a monolith. It's then brought back down to earth with a very elegant tapered concrete colonnade, which the architects refer to as 'Minoan'. But it already looks rougher than the 2006 **Donnybrook Quarter (p. 134)**, with stains and scuffs belying the building's youth, and revealing its low-budget, contractor-driven 'Design and Build' construction. Meanwhile, the comparatively highly crafted paths and squares of the 1970s estate are cracking, with rubbish blowing past the benches, and nothing trickling down. Many great things here, but it leaves a sour taste.

TREMLETT GROVE ESTATE, UPPER HOLLOWAY
London County Council Architects Dept, 1964–8
International Style

An unusual little LCC estate in a close in a dense Victorian area, clipped glass cubes displaying the Americanophilia that went alongside the Dutch and Swiss obsessions in neighbouring Camden – Chicago or Montreal as a model for modern living just as much as Europe. Its lightweight, brightly coloured classical grid frames a neat green square, SOM or Mies gone municipal.

LUDHAM & WAXHAM, GOSPEL OAK
Frederick MacManus & Partners, 1974–9
International Style

Much maligned at the time and since as a harsh imposition into the early-Victorian streetscape, these two extremely long blocks of council flats now, after a recent renovation, seem closely connected to the later Camden Council culture of low-rise, high-density, faintly classical modernist housing around enclosed semi-public spaces, beginning with **Elsfield (p. 146)**

and developing into the likes of the **Branch Hill Estate (p. 151)** and **Alexandra Road (p. 148)**. The flats face the street in long, ribbon-windowed rows that, as Geraint Franklin points out, owe something to the precedent of collective housing in 1920s Moscow, an image of production-line communal luxury. Away from the street, long engineering brick facades are extended across a rolling green hill that is much more often used by residents than the silly mound at **Robin Hood Gardens (p. 130)**. A linear and strict piece of design, impressive in its clean-lined, clear-eyed simplicity.

FLEET ROAD, GOSPEL OAK ✪
Neave Brown for Camden Council Architects Dept, 1967–77
Brutalist

Inside, this is one of the nicest and most intimate of the low-rise, high-density housing schemes designed by Neave Brown for Camden Council, with a secluded, increasingly bosky public street between stepped concrete flats with lovely wooden balustrades. Humane, subtle, warm, but as precise as an engineering diagram. It is important to wait for someone to let you in to the courtyard, because facing the street around the complex is more puzzling; the houses appear as cool and slightly blank modernist terraces, with L-shaped windows and plain white surfaces, and with no street activity, which is all past the gates. The way into the main 'street' is through a curved Brutalist staircase, which has for some years been closed to all but residents. Brown's schemes are usually praised for taking their cue from the terraces and squares of the eighteenth and nineteenth centuries, but Fleet Road reveals how overstated that can be. This is a wonderful double-level streetscape of creepers and elegant maisonettes once you're inside – one of the finest civic spaces in London. The fact that

The hanging gardens of Gospel Oak: the lush vegetation and rational lines of Neave Brown's Fleet Road Estate.

it can be closed off from the street around suggests it isn't really part of the historic streetscape, it's something else. It's worth noting that Neave Brown based the layout of these on a private terrace he'd designed for himself and a group of friends in Winscombe Street; late in life, he moved from there to Fleet Road.

ALEXANDRA ROAD, SWISS COTTAGE ✪

Neave Brown for Camden Council Architects Dept, 1968–78
Brutalist

It's an occupational vice of architecture critics to worry about how their opinions could be viewed in a possible future. There are two major London schemes of the 1970s which met with an almost universally hostile reception, from left, right and centre – the **Barbican (p. 66)**, as we've found, and

Alexandra Road, a monumental street of maisonettes in a posh bit of north London, for council tenants. Aesthetic objections to this giant curve of white concrete was heightened by a lengthy and complex build process, which opportunistic left-wing councillors tried to blame on the architect, who just happened to have been the one of most conscientious designers of working-class housing in twentieth-century Britain. That aside, it's extraordinary that anyone could have treated this magnificent panorama as just another concrete housing estate by a corrupt architect. Brown was completely exonerated, and the delays were a consequence of inflation caused by the oil crisis, so the campaign against the building now appears as an incredible misjudgement. Wasn't it *obvious*? Weren't they using their eyes? Why didn't they get it? Fashion, is one answer, *doxa* another. Concrete was out, monumentality and scale were out, council housing was 'statist', and architecture was language, not space. If you wanted to make working-class people happy, you gave them houses that looked like the old ones, only cheaper and with inside loos – they couldn't be trusted to understand anything else. The people educated at the Architectural Association and Oxbridge who said these sorts of things thought they were being kind.

So, Alexandra Road. Like most Camden schemes, it was designed first and foremost in section, fitting spacious flats into a ziggurat that balances above the main line from Euston; this is shaped into a dual spine, like an elongated, futuristic Regency circus. Unlike at **Fleet Road (above)**, it's totally clear that the space between the entrances is a public street, which you can walk through as a stranger as much as you could any other. Steps lead to the lower, squarer Ainsworth section of the estate, which boasts huge outdoor terraces for residents, and a small park. There is so much to admire it's hard to take it all in – the way the complexity of the plan coincides with a totally clear single image, the richness and quality of the concrete details, the way the planting has grown up to make it all feel idyllic and exotic, and the sheer sublime thrill of it all. The way the balconies, part of the step of each row, run straight out from the flats, like an extension of each living room, should make every contemporary architect retire in shame that they will never be allowed to design anything so intuitive, so holistic. After this, Neave Brown was never allowed to work in Britain again. [B.4]

———

MURRAY MEWS & CAMDEN MEWS, CAMDEN
Team 4, Edward Cullinan, Tom Kay, Richard Gibson and David and Ann Hyde-Harrison, 1965–72
Brutalist, High-Tech, People's Detailing

An intriguing test bed for the ideas being thrown around in the 1960s and '70s, and again architects were their own guinea pigs, aided by the low price of London land and building in the 1960s (these houses would probably be impossible to build today for anyone who isn't a literal aristocrat). Murray Mews has three houses of note squeezed into what is effectively a back alley. The most interesting is Tom Kay's number 22. At the time there was a minor craze for 'casbah'-like arrangements, where small flat-roofed houses were laid out with patios, terraces and intersecting stairwells; accordingly, this house is a miniature landscape to clamber over until you get shouted at, its concrete dressed in normal, yellowy-brown London stocks. Numbers 15–19 are by Team 4, a firm made up of two couples – Richard and Su Rogers, and Norman Foster with Wendy Cheesman. These are similarly complex, though they initially look more ordinary than number 22, in a neat red brick, with bluff, windowless elevations to the street, around large, fully glazed roofs, in which you can see High-Tech's fixation with precision engineering and greenhouses emerge out of a municipal chrysalis. David and Anne Hyde-Harrison's number 33 is somewhere between a Home Counties Span house and an American Case Study House, yellow and white weatherboarding and grey tiles, with large windows on a Mondrianish grid; a few decent, if less notable, recent houses try to complement these three.

In nearby Camden Mews is found the best of all these NW1 alleyway experiments, a very early house by Edward Cullinan, then just a job architect for Denys Lasdun, showing all the qualities that he would later develop into an eco-conscious modernism in the 1980s and '90s – made from clip-together wood and steel, it's an almost rural (but not rustic) house, with a little bit of Japan, some Frank Lloyd Wright, a hint of Essex. Of the group, it's the one I would choose to live in.

HIGHGATE NEW TOWN, ARCHWAY ○

Peter Tabori for Camden Council Architects Dept, 1972–8
Brutalist

Along with **Alexandra Road (p. 148)**, this estate by a young Hungarian architect just fresh out of architecture school is among the peaks of municipal housing in Britain. Again, stepped sections, fair-faced concrete and street-like pedestrian areas which are not all that they first appear. As a former resident, the architect and critic Douglas Murphy, points out, the alleged continuation of the Victorian streetscape has been a little overstated by historians. You know here you're not just in another part of London, but in somewhere unusual, with different principles of design and layout, and that's no bad thing. There are six rows of flats, which are as much a matter of winding paths and secluded green spaces as they are of asphalt streets. One particularly interesting feature in Highgate New Town is how it straddles the sober modern architecture of the 1970s and that of the 2020s – the breeze-block terraces that make up part of the estate have the classical severity and rectitude of the better new London architecture. The imposing and elegant concrete ziggurats that face them have, on the other hand, a grandeur and confidence that we no longer seem capable of. **[B.3]**

POLYGON ROAD, KING'S CROSS

Peter Tabori and Roman Halter for Camden Council Architects Dept/James Gowan, 1971–6
Brutalist

An interesting complement and clash between the ingenious step-section planning Tabori used at the better-known and leafier **Highgate New Town (above)**,

Peter Tabori's elegant ziggurat-cum-terraces at the Whittington Estate, Archway, aka Highgate New Town.

and the demands of a rougher inner-city site. The blocks are longer, the public squares between them are larger, but the most visually striking difference is the exchange of white concrete for a rough, knobbly red brick. This facing material, evidently considered fitting in the vicinity of St Pancras Station, was actually an addition to the original designs by James Gowan, who was brought into the project late in the day. These two styles that were hostile at the time – Gowan's nods to Victorian industrial vernacular, and Tabori's pure, Central European modernism – work together surprisingly well.

―――

MAIDEN LANE ESTATE, KING'S CROSS
Gordon Benson and Alan Forsyth for Camden Council Architects Dept, 1973–82
Brutalist

Unlike all the other Camden low-rise high-density estates, Maiden Lane fell on hard times in the 1980s and '90s, and is only now being given proper care and attention, as part of the public–private deal that is also causing denser, less well-made versions to sprout around it. Low, cubic blocks with L-shaped windows, ingenious layouts and lots of fair-faced concrete are arranged in a *promenade architecturale* where a wander can present you with a series of shifting, revealing vistas. Now that the area's 1980s problems with crime and hard drugs have calmed down somewhat – these tight pathways could seem menacing in those circumstances – it is much easier to see what a good place it is. The clarity of the design has a repose and an order which coexists with a system of paths and alleyways that encourage exploration and interaction, an unusual alternation between minimalist, classical values and the virtues of complexity.

BRANCH HILL ESTATE, HAMPSTEAD ✪
Gordon Benson and Alan Forsyth for Camden Council Architects Dept, 1974–8
Brutalist

The most mysterious, magical and unknown of the great Camden Council estates. Branch Hill was once notorious as 'the most expensive council housing in the world' (not to rent, but to build), and was nearly blocked altogether by Conservative councillors in a then very Tory part of NW3. It's ironic that both this and the much wilder and more ambitious **Alexandra Road (p. 148)** were attacked so fiercely, when both are now so clearly not merely just 'good council stock', but among the finest housing ever built anywhere on the planet. That is where the similarities end. Rather than being a massive monument like Alexandra Road, visible to millions on the train to Euston, Branch Hill is secluded even by Hampstead standards, on a steep hill descending from the grounds of a Victorian lodge to one of the lushest parts of one of the plushest London suburbs. Its planning ideas and laconic facades more closely resemble those of the **Maiden Lane Estate (above)**, but the steep site makes it considerably more strange and poetic.

The estate consists of three rows of interconnected semis; it was a planning requirement, to be 'in keeping' with the villas of this part of Hampstead. Walking downwards – the recommended approach – you first see step-section houses rearing back from a steep slope, whose steps are frankly not great for anyone who isn't able-bodied; but turn around here, and you can see the huge windows of the open-plan houses, and the private walkways that lead to roof terraces, some of which have been planted with creepers. It is startlingly idyllic and Californian, built organically into the slope, with no feeling of violence or imposition. When you get to the bottom, you can see it all spread out before you, the same

The finest council housing ever built: Benson and Forsyth's Branch Hill Estate in Hampstead.

serenity and ingenuity so often found in the private modernist houses of north London, but offered at council rents, and with social intimacy rather than privet hedges and CCTV. We could have rebuilt the whole of London like this. We still could.

5 CAVERSHAM ROAD & 6–10 GAISFORD STREET, KENTISH TOWN
Colquhoun & Miller, 1978
International Style, Retromodernist

Like Georgie Wolton's **Cliff Road Studios (p. 146)**, these infill council flats are an exemplar of how quite an uncompromising modern aesthetic can be inserted into a Victorian street without any disruption. Likewise, there is a hint here of Modernism starting to become another citational style: if Wolton's work seemed like a continuity of the Bauhaus, the architectural historian

Colquhoun is glancing towards the Viennese raised eyebrow of Adolf Loos or Ludwig Wittgenstein. All that is there if you want to explore it, but for the most part this works just fine as an elegant solution to a seemingly intractable problem, and the houses and flats are well kept by Camden Council.

GARTON HOUSE, HORNSEY
Colquhoun & Miller, 1980
Classical Modernism, Rationalism

Up on the hills of Hornsey, with views down to the Arsenal Stadium below and Canary Wharf beyond, this is in one of those areas you only really get in London – Victorian bourgeois villas, interwar tenements, Brutalist complexes, seventies vernacular low-rise flats and fussy eighties Postmodernist council terraces, all threaded together with trees, pubs, grocers and streets – the sort of real but relaxed triumph that none of the narratives about urban planning have much room for. The buildings here are always decent, but only one of them is worth seeing as a major work of architecture. Colquhoun & Miller's high-rise council tower block on the top of the hill, built long after high-rise ceased to be fashionable, and accordingly reserved only for single people, uses similar materials to everything around – yellow stock brick, glass and brown wooden window frames; it was originally designed with glass brick panels, which have sadly been removed in a recent renovation. That's what it is, baldly described, but the command of proportion is masterful. Colquhoun was a theorist and historian of some renown, and here all those Renaissance architectural textbooks have culminated in this effortlessly elegant grid, symmetrical, restful and pure. Look at the private high-rise next door to see the difference; Savile Row next to Primark, and it's the council tenants that got the finest.

SAINSBURY'S & GRAND UNION WALK, CAMDEN
Nicholas Grimshaw & Partners, 1988
High-Tech

A terrific, late-space-age ensemble from just before High-Tech architecture started taking itself too seriously. Designed at the same time but distinct, this terrace of canalside housing and supermarket take different approaches to their functions and locations, but they have a similar fetishistic use of materials. Metal and plastic panels and components previously used for the space programme or for commercial aviation were repurposed to serve as the 'style of the day'. This was radical at the time, as Postmodernist architecture was rejecting the idea that there was or could be an appropriate industrial style for a post-industrial era.

Sainsbury's faces the street with grey sheeting and hardcore, fantasy-Constructivist steel trusses, rhythmic and

Luxury housing on a former industrial canal: the metal modules of Nicholas Grimshaw's Grand Union Walk.

strident; and round the back we have the housing, a row of suspended space capsules overlooking a canal. It looks like Manga-Tokyo pod-flats, but it's actually a row of spacious, single-family terraces. The photographs of the scheme on the architect's website show astonishing-looking multilevel interiors, but they've never been opened up at OpenHouse weekend, so we can only gaze in wonder at the images.

PARKSIDE, FINSBURY PARK
Sergison Bates, 2004–8
Classical Modernism

When these three small blocks of housing association flats opposite Finsbury Park were finished, the *Architects Journal* put them on the cover as an explicit provocation – I don't think the headline was 'Does it offend you yeah?', but that was the gist. The letters page was full of heated denunciations of the buildings for several issues afterwards. It is now very hard to understand quite why they caused such animus, unless you recall what new London housing was generally like at that time – for a telling example, the explosively flimsy polychrome-clad flats designed by CZWG by Arsenal stadium are very near by, and give a sense of the mid-2000s norm. This, though, is tough, dour housing recalling very ordinary post-war council housing; not the sculptural, Brutalist, coffee-table book stuff but concrete-framed boxes with brick infill and modest walkways, only with more Georgian, vertical window proportions.

More than ten years on, this has become the dominant aesthetic of London luxury living, the self-described 'New London Vernacular'. Once again, nobody is quite so obsessed with fashion and quite so in denial of it as architects. But this scheme will stand strong even when it goes out of fashion again, as it will. From the park, it is scaled to look like a pair of Victorian villas, but it's much

more clever up close, where you can see how geometrically strange it is, with what looks like a grid from a distance turning out to be a complicated system of turns and recessions to create balconies, extra sunlight, and secluded semi-public spaces for residents. Most importantly, it's nothing like the 'vernacular' that followed it, in that its 'traditional' look is achieved not via appliqué brick cladding, but through vigorous and thorough construction, with a massive yet precisely detailed concrete frame, and satisfyingly chunky warm red bricks.

'KING'S CROSS CENTRAL': CENTRAL ST MARTIN'S
Stanton Williams, 2011
SAXON COURT & ROSEBERY MANSIONS
Maccreanor Lavington, 2012
KING'S CROSS STATION
John McAslan & Partners, 2013
ONE PANCRAS SQUARE
David Chipperfield Architects, 2013
R7
Duggan Morris, 2018
AGA KHAN CENTRE
Maki & Associates, 2019
Modern Classicism

The state of the art, in contemporary London. The redevelopment of the 'railway lands' around King's Cross and St Pancras began with the **British Library (p. 143)**, followed by the transformation of St Pancras from one railway station that went to Sheffield into four that go to France, Kent, Sussex and Sheffield, badly connected via a mall carved out of vaults that were built to store beer barrels, alongside Europe's worst contemporary sculpture; but King's Cross itself has been the showcase. This is, aptly given its closeness to the trains to Paris, Brussels and Amsterdam, the place in Britain that most resembles contemporary European practice, the architecture of a tightly managed 'social market', strongly capitalist but with a more than residual culture of planning, organization and co-ordination. It was begun at a time when what twenty-first-century London had to show for concerted planning was chaotic and crass places like Greenwich Peninsula or the Olympic site in Stratford, compared to which this place was a revelation. Stanton Williams's cavernous concrete atrium for Central St Martin's art school is the least demonstrative of the lot, but even here there are a severity and rigour that you wouldn't find in the shadow of the Millennium Dome or the ArcelorMittal Orbit. It's what happened next that was truly odd – at the time.

Maccreanor Lavington's Saxon Court and Rosebery Mansions launched a thousand grids of brick slips on concrete frames across London and into Manchester, Glasgow and beyond; before this, the firm had got far more work in the Netherlands than in its home country. You can see why these high-rise flats became the flagship for the London Design Guide and the 'New London Vernacular' it legislated into being. After what felt like two decades or more of housing that wanted to be anything but tangible, but felt like constructed computer renders – barcode facades, Trespa cladding, silly roofs – this went for a then-startling tactility, fascinating surfaces of textured, decorative brick that you wanted to run your hands over, inserted into a metropolitan, classical-modernist grid. Then came John McAslan's redevelopment of King's Cross Station itself, removing the awful tin entrance pushed into it in the seventies for a very successful, albeit stark, open square, and adding a new curved entrance. Its lattice roof is a somewhat value-engineered emulation of the Coal Exchange in one of the station's destinations, Leeds.

Between the station and Central St Martin's is a development of offices on a plan by the classicist Demetri Porphyrios. Unfortunately, his own neo-art deco building

The Italian Rationalist offices of One Pancras Square, fittingly close to the trains that leave for the Continent.

is embarrassingly thin and cheap-looking, whereas David Chipperfield's emulation of the hauteur of Italian Rationalist architecture is far more convincing – today, much mainstream architecture accepts the classical critique of modernism in terms of where you put buildings in space, but Porphyrios's tawdry architecture is a reminder of why they still haven't won the argument on architectural style. North from here, you come to the unpretentious hard landscaping of Granary Square – usually absolutely packed with *Guardian* and Google employees – and, past the surviving warehouses, the plan continues with a gorgeous office block by Duggan Morris, a Chicago-influenced vertical rhythm in an alluring salmon pink; next to it is the slightly puzzling Aga Khan Centre by Fumihiko Maki, in a freeze-dried and corporate thirties International Style – it has neo-Islamic roof gardens, if you can get into them. In many ways, this place shows what London's architects and planners are actually capable of – design at least as decent, logical and attractive as anything in contemporary Europe; the Porphyrios building aside, the only bum note is Thomas Heatherwick's typically kitsch, dishonest, overengineered Coal Drops Yard, the less said about which the better. In any case, it's only when you start to consider what is missing that this place becomes problematic – it is for one class as much as is Canary Wharf, it blocks off rather than embraces the nearby council estates (the **Maiden Lane Estate, p. 151**, among them), and it is run as a private enclave, rather than as public land. It shows that planning can still happen, and can still work. Hopefully a less timid social-democratic politics will find that useful in the near future.

'JW3' JEWISH COMMUNITY CENTRE, HAMPSTEAD
Lifschutz Davidson Sandilands, 2012–13
International Style

Finchley Road, back in the days when this part of Hampstead played host to thousands of escapees from Nazi Germany, used to get nicknamed 'Finchleystrasse' – and the political right in Germany and Britain used to consider modernism a 'Jewish' style. Appropriately perhaps, then, if you want to still find north London buildings that have that Central European clarity and elegance, JW3 is a revelation. Everything about its design shows the same ethos as the luxury intelligentsia houses like **66 Frognal (p. 140)** and the elegant municipalism of seventies Camden. Modern, European architecture defined by formal purity, elegant proportion, right angles, and skilfully calculated windows letting in lots and lots of light. The fact that you have to reach it through a walkway over what is essentially a moat suggests some sad things about the present day, but the

architects have managed to create out of that a sunken square which is very lively in the summer months, and conjuring a pleasant public space out of the need for heavy security is very much a reversal of the norm. A clever, subtle and stylish building that ought to be better known.

WEST LONDON

14 SOUTH PARADE, BEDFORD PARK
C. F. A. Voysey, 1890
Art Nouveau

Voysey, a designer mainly of houses, features heavily in histories of modern architecture as a bridging figure between Arts and Crafts, Art Nouveau and modernism. His originality appears to have been a side-effect of how relaxed and functional his buildings were – comfortable, sprawling villas in the Home Counties, intended for living in rather than for showing off. The stark white facades of these houses have been claimed by historians as a source for the early modernism of the Viennese architect Adolf Loos – here, too, 'ornament is crime', though apparently Voysey was puzzled late in life to be pinned down as a 'pioneer of the modern movement'; unlike his contemporary Charles Rennie Mackintosh, Voysey did not have an adversarial relationship with the British architectural establishment, but regarded his work as just a sane and simple way of building houses. The most accessible and most modern of these houses is in Bedford Park, an arty suburb planned by the protean Norman Shaw. In a sea of red brick and tile this bright white house was evidently intended to stand out. Its two storeys, tall and thin, are completely asymmetrical; there is an almost totally glazed 'ribbon window' on the ground floor, a laconic bay with a porthole window at its corner, and an almost streamlined smaller wing to the side. Only the pitched roofs remain traditional. A crisp and elegant building, and still a visibly strange and original one, it is clearly among British architecture's roads not taken, not least by its own architect – a possible route to an angst-free domestic modernism. It can be easily seen from the main Piccadilly Line viaduct to Heathrow.

PICCADILLY, CENTRAL & DISTRICT LINES: ⊙ HOUNSLOW WEST & SUDBURY TOWN STATIONS
Charles Holden, 1930–31
CHISWICK PARK STATION
Charles Holden, 1931–2
OSTERLEY & BOSTON MANOR STATIONS
Stanley Heaps, 1933–4
PARK ROYAL STATION
Welch & Lander, 1936
UXBRIDGE STATION
Charles Holden, 1938
PERIVALE STATION
Brian Lewis, 1938
International Style, Modern Classicism, Expressionist

West London's suburban Tube stations showcase various experiments with the style Charles Holden fixed for London Transport. None of the stations – except the minimalist perfection of Sudbury Town, which was Holden's first, experimental effort in adapting continental modernism to English conditions – reach the clarity of the northern reaches of the Piccadilly Line, but they have more variety and humour. Hounslow West, of 1930, is still in a more monumental version of the south London stations of the twenties, like **Tooting Bec (p. 108)**. It's worth a visit, but it lacks the single-minded brilliance of the later work. Boston Manor and Osterley, meanwhile, show the Underground's in-house architect, Stanley Heaps, adapting Holden's new manner and taking it in a rather glitzier direction, as with the beacon on top of the otherwise impeccably minimal tower of Osterley, or the super-cinema lighting effects on the snazzy tower of Boston Manor.

Park Royal, by contrast, takes the Holden manner further and wilder, with its architects toughening and thickening the

Classical serenity, modern materials: inside the rotunda of Charles Holden's Chiswick Park Station.

style into a textured Expressionism, and twisting the volumes into intersecting brick cylinders, with a dramatic vertical presence (Welch & Lander also designed the diverting moderne housing estate adjacent). At nearby Perivale, meanwhile, everything is reduced to brick and glass, in a successful low-budget interpretation that keeps the essentials, and some neat clinker brickwork. Uxbridge, meanwhile, is the concrete cathedral of **Cockfosters (p. 137)** massively expanded in scale, like a real city terminus, and with an impressive brick and stained-glass ticket hall (the glass, showing heraldic symbols of old Uxbridge, is by the Hungarian exile Ervin Bossányi). Compared with this the symmetrical entrance is relatively stiff and under-scaled, but signals the station's presence well from the street, which is after all half the job.

Chiswick Park, meanwhile, has an unusually urban location for one of Holden's 1930s stations – it feels strangely anomalous in the relatively dense and bustling world of Zone 3, packed in with ordinary buildings rather than standing in glorious isolated space offset by Mock Tudor in Zone 5. It's excellent in any context, combining the big Stockholm Library drum of **Arnos Grove (p. 137)** with the De Stijl beacons of Osterley, and with rough, dynamic proto-Brutalist concrete canopies on the platforms. As with all of Holden's work for the Tube, it's eye-wateringly well-finished, particularly in the booking rotunda, with a huge space lined in red and black glazed brick, in a powerful concrete frame. So restrained and yet so grand, it's moving to think that public architecture was ever capable of this level of dignity; at times it can feel as if Charles Holden attained a peak for modern architecture in Britain that makes everything that happened after it look tawdry, gestural and naff. This is architecture as an Ideal-Type, the ultimate version of a particular typology that needed no further development. [**A.7 & A.8**]

RAVENSCOURT PARK HOSPITAL, HAMMERSMITH
Burnet Tait & Lorne, 1932–3
Expressionist

A mammoth project, best seen from the north side of the viaduct that carries the District and Piccadilly Lines past it – as the details and interiors don't stand up to close examination, but the effect of its sheer purple mass is overwhelming. Originally the Royal Masonic Hospital and run by the NHS since the forties, this is a cubic brick mountain in the Dutch brick modernist style borrowed from W. M. Dudok; sprawling wings with curved concrete balconies extend around a huge central clock tower. The grounds, also, are worth exploring, the placidity and precision of its gardens offsetting the stark monumentality of the hospital.

BRENTFORD 'GOLDEN MILE': SIMMONDS, COTY COSMETICS, PYRENE & CURRYS FACTORIES
Wallis Gilbert & Partners, 1930–42
GILLETTE FACTORY
Banister Fletcher, 1936
Modern Classicism, Moderne, Expressionist

At the far end of the Great West Road leading out of London, these constitute what is sometimes fancifully called the 'Golden Mile' of art deco factories. The list above is the order in which you would see them, going east to west along the Great West Road. This is not the most pleasant pedestrian experience, so given that the architecture is meant to be seen at speed, you can be forgiven for seeing them from the windows of a car or by bus. The Simmonds Aerocessories Factory (1942) is a tall tower like a reduced American skyscraper, with ten storeys of glass and brick between decoratively curved concrete uprights; it's now flats, re-named Wallis House after its architect; there wasn't a Gilbert – Thomas Wallis, an architect with an eye to advertising, just wanted to suggest a relation to one of the Gilbert Scott dynasty. Coty Cosmetics (1932) is a flat front, a miniature version of the more ambitious **Hoover Factory (below)** in Perivale, while Pyrene (1930) – they made fire extinguishers – and Currys (1936) are streamlined moderne, gleaming concrete and towers that were meant to have logos on and be seen by drivers on their way in and out of London (notably, these former factories currently serve more intangible purposes, as offices for, respectively, a private clinic, the French advertising company JCDecaux, and the recently collapsed outsourcing vultures Carillion; that's the post-industrial British economy for you).

A short walk away on a corner is the architectural historian Banister Fletcher's Gillette Building, a factory for the men's cosmetics company. It takes the same approach as Wallis Gilbert's factories – huge plate-glass steel windows, symmetry, grand entrances, with the actual factory basically hidden round the back – except in brown brick rather than white concrete, and it adds a tall campanile as a zingy visual marker. Unlike the rest, currently derelict, and hence much easier to imagine as a place of production rather than 'services'.

———

HOOVER FACTORY, PERIVALE
Wallis Gilbert & Partners, 1930–38
Moderne, Art Deco

On the Western Avenue, and on its own, thus not quite as rewarding as the 'Golden Mile' for a walk, but much more complete, is a grand suburban showcase of what German modernists called, approvingly, *Reklamarchitektur* – advertising architecture. Decorative concrete and steel gates like art deco objets d'art lead to the central neo-Egyptian block, nicely restored to all its picture palace polychromy on the outside, with a Tesco on the inside where the actual factory would have been. Flanking it on the left is a slightly later café, which is if anything even more fabulous than the main building, with enormous Crittall windows and ice-cream scoops of concrete. It was loathed at the time by the cognoscenti – for Pevsner, it was 'the worst' of west London's various 'modernistic atrocities' – and, unlike the scorn directed at the **Barbican (p. 66)** or **Alexandra Road (p. 148)** when they were finished, one can see why, at least on a theoretical level. This is facile architecture, almost literally just a decorated shed, but the decoration itself is majestic. As Elvis Costello says in his song about the building, 'it's not a matter of life or death, but what is, what is?'

COHEN HOUSE, CHELSEA
Erich Mendelsohn and Serge Chermayeff, 1935/Foster Associates, 1979
66 OLD CHURCH STREET, CHELSEA
Walter Gropius and Maxwell Fry, 1935
International Style, High-Tech

Two houses in a formerly arty and now oppressively moneyed corner of Chelsea by extremely important architects, neither in its original condition and neither in any way the architects' best work. The Gropius house is appallingly compromised by the black-grey shingles added to it some decades ago – usually a building that had been so unrecognizably damaged would never have been listed, but the Bauhaus director's authority has seen it become so. Mendelsohn's house adjacent was the more interesting of the two before they were both subjected to aggressive renovations by their owners – a spatial game of long, intersecting white volumes. Here, the owners' additions were a matter of addition rather than destruction – a cubic glass conservatory, well detailed and cleverly integrated with the house, an early design of Norman Foster.

KENSAL HOUSE, KENSAL GREEN
Maxwell Fry with Elizabeth Denby, 1936
International Style

This was perhaps the first time in London that high-modernist ideas were used for working-class housing, just as they were in Berlin, Frankfurt, Rotterdam, Moscow or Warsaw. Keeling House is a set of 'minimum dwelling' flats in two chic white-concrete crescents, around a landscaped green space and play areas. The workers in question were employees of the Gas Board – this was company housing, not council housing, as local authorities mostly remained sceptical about modernism in the thirties. Their hestitancy seems strange today,

given that these two blocks now feel cosy and humane. Their maintenance has not always been as good as it could be, but the sheltering curve created by the two blocks, and the delicate concrete details to the balconies can survive getting a little shabby. Turning the entirety of inner-city London into variants on these buildings, as the MARS group imagined in the 1930s, doesn't seem so bad an idea. Like **Finsbury Health Centre (p. 52)**, it featured as an image of the post-war socialist future in the 1943 'Your Britain, Fight for It Now' posters, irritating Winston Churchill in the process.

PETER JONES DEPARTMENT STORE, CHELSEA ✪
William Crabtree, 1936
International Style

One of the great European buildings of the 1930s, really the only interwar commercial modernist structure in London that can really contend with what was happening in Berlin, Prague or Rotterdam at that time. A sweeping six-storey curved curtain wall whips itself from Sloane Square down King's Road, a grid of windows and pale-green vitreous panels, with an inset, fully glazed floor above for the cafés and canteens, the two layers contrapuntally arranged so that their curves alternately parallel and intersect each other. Still as shiny, chic and fearlessly new as it was the day it was made, it is interesting that it took a commercial client for an uncompromised modern building to be built in such a prominent part of London – it was perhaps easier to sell modern architecture to the English middle classes as glamorous consumerism than as earnest social reform. Restored in 2004 by John McAslan, carving out an atrium which is spacious and clean but a little bland, as though it's just another John Lewis – which, I suppose, it is.

Potsdamer Platz on Sloane Square: the Weimar Republic-style Peter Jones department store, Chelsea.

WEMBLEY ARENA
Owen Williams, 1934
DOLLIS HILL SYNAGOGUE
Owen Williams, 1937
Expressionist

These two major buildings by interwar Britain's Great Engineer, creator of such masterpieces as the **Boots D10 & D6 (p. 356)** and **D90 (p. 360)** factories in Beeston and the various buildings for the **Daily Express** (Central London, **p. 50**, Glasgow, **p. 518** and Manchester, **p. 400**), are now both a little uncomfortable to visit. One, because of bigotry, the other just because of ordinary profit. Dollis Hill Synagogue was always an odd commission for such a committed functionalist, and this attempt to fuse a religious programme with his hard, glinting concrete structures has often been criticized, but I find it works rather well. Set easily among north-west London suburban semis and opposite a park with a panoramic suburban view, the synagogue is folded into a set of spiky, pyramidal roofs, with dozens of small stained-glass windows, set in gleaming Central European white concrete; it has something of the strange angularity of Konstantin Melnikov's clubs and houses in 1920s Moscow.

The synagogue is now part of an Orthodox primary school, and is treated as a fortress, with high fences and round-the-clock monitoring by security guards – even the entrance is through a security pavilion, like a military facility. How depressing that this is necessary, when it was not even in the London of the 1930s, when the British Union of Fascists was running riot. At Wembley Arena, the heavy security is less invasive, given the building is so vast. It was built as the 'Empire Pool' for an imperial expo, and the interior is not interesting for anything but its sheer size – but the elevation still suggests an impressive concrete hall, huge glass expanses between stark, straight concrete supports and two frankly industrial towers on either side. An interesting contrast, too, with Foster's new Wembley Stadium nearby, a glorious steel arch holding up a dull and corporate structure below.

———

FORMER BOAC MAINTENANCE HEADQUARTERS, HEATHROW AIRPORT
Owen Williams, 1950–55
Industrial, Brutalist

Amazing to think that this hangar was being constructed alongside Frederick Gibberd's clumsy, underscaled, timid – and now mostly demolished – original buildings for Heathrow. It does a simple functional thing – maintaining and repairing aeroplanes – but functionality can explain little of the appeal of this savage, scything arch of raw concrete, enclosing a cyclopean vastness of space. This is instinctive Brutalism of the sort favoured by young London architects bored by the prettiness of Gibberd and his comrades, only some years before they thought of it; it has also endured in functional terms, which is more than can be said about some actual Brutalist buildings. Hard to see publicly, but a plane departing from or landing at all terminals except 5 might well taxi past it; the closest terminal is 4.

———

HALLFIELD ESTATE, PADDINGTON
Drake & Lasdun, 1951–8
People's Detailing

The first major work to be credited to Denys Lasdun, this is much more the last Tecton project. Plans for a large estate near Paddington Station were ready in the firm's portfolio when it disbanded at the end of the 1940s, along with the Finsbury triad of Priory Green, **Spa Green (p. 52)** and **Bevin Court (p. 54)**, which were completed by Lubetkin, Francis Skinner

and Douglas Bailey; Hallfield was given to Lasdun and his fellow Tecton partner Lindsay Drake to complete. Although much larger simply in terms of its footprint, this is much closer to Spa Green's enjoyable and humanistic pattern-style than to the later obsessive, tortured budget baroque of the **Dorset Estate (p. 123)** or **Cranbrook Estate (p. 126)**. Certainly, aside from the last building to be completed, the tiny, complex and spatially intriguing primary school which shows traces of Lasdun's later work, Hallfield is much more 'Lubetkin' than it is 'Lasdun'. Fifteen slab blocks in complex brick-and-tile grids, with cute boxed-out concrete balconies, often at jaunty angles, in a densely tree-filled sunken space, which creates a welcome seclusion and a delightful place for a wander in an otherwise noisy part of inner west London.

———

CORRINGHAM, BAYSWATER
Kenneth Frampton for Douglas Stephen & Partners, 1961–4
International Style

The job architect on this sleek, steely block of luxury flats, Kenneth Frampton, would become much better known as a critic, like his fellow passenger from humble London architect to doyen of Marxist critique in US Ivy League universities, Alan Colquhoun; unlike the latter, Frampton wouldn't manage to combine the two in his later career. And whereas in Colquhoun's purist, classically disciplined modernist buildings (say, **Oldbury Wells School, p. 333**, or **5 Caversham Road & 6–10 Gaisford Street, p. 152**) you can find traces of his writerly preoccupations with classical tradition and city planning, Corringham doesn't point towards Frampton's later advocacy of a 'Critical Regionalism' based on vernacular materials and local topography in architecture. It's just an exceptionally high-quality development of high-end flats, with a discipline and strict elegance comparable to other projects by Douglas Stephen, such as **The Mount (below)** – although here the sources are contemporary, not 1930s. Corringham's sheer glass wall on the street side is American in its delicate proportions and lack of sentimentality, while the (private) garden frontage is more articulated and Corbusian, with projecting maisonettes and an angular, turret-like stair tower. The only obvious difference from a block of council flats of the same time is a lack of rhetoric, gesture or 'humanism' – this is just an apartment building, not setting out to solve any problems. In that sense of solving formal questions rather than social ones, you can see how the road goes from here to Harvard.

WATER GARDENS, MARYLEBONE
Trehearne & Norman, 1965
International Style

The highpoint of several multifunctional, megalopolitan complexes on the GLC–Arabic William Burroughs Interzone that is the Edgware Road. The Water Gardens are private, but to the unaware eye, this ensemble looks like a council estate – indeed, unlike, say, the **Barbican (p. 66)**, its finishes aren't noticeably better than the municipal average; a penthouse flat is on the market at the time of writing (in 2020) for several million, so you're much further here from the Lisson Green Estate than geography and aesthetics might imply. The Water Gardens 'estate' consists of three identical point blocks, with a good sweep to them, an unsubtle strength and a little bit of Mondrian-style grid patterning to the facades, enclosing a private communal garden for the residents, which is really where the difference with council landscaping makes itself known. The blocks are on a podium, under which are shops doing typical Edgware Road things, with plenty of neon. The connection between

the towers and the street is one of London's most Manhattan-like spaces, modernism as metropolitan glamour and plenty of Koolhaas's 'culture of congestion'. It could teach developers a few things today, so well does it balance extreme density, communal space and the continuation rather than interruption of a busy street.

THE MOUNT, CAMPDEN HILL
Douglas Stephen & Partners, 1965
International Style

Like Georgie Wolton's very similar **Cliff Road Studios (p. 146)**, The Mount is a small, neat and early essay in modernist historicism, a pure-white cubic apartment block inspired by the work of Italian Rationalist architects of the 1930s. Geometrical, luxurious and powerful, it is quite the surprise in a floridly Italianate part of Kensington.

CHISWICK FLYOVER
London County Council, 1959
WESTWAY, NORTH KENSINGTON
London County Council, 1964–70
GREEN DRAGON ESTATE, BRENTFORD
Greater London Council Architects Dept, 1968–78
Brutalist

The most exciting thing you can do in a car in London without going too far in re-enacting J. G. Ballard is drive the flyovers of west London, from Marylebone all the way to Brentford, a modernist landscape that shifts like a constantly rolling city-film, something that saw it put to apt use in the first sequences of Chris Petit's post-punk driving film *Radio On*. The Westway is the only urban motorway that really works as a cityscape sequence, as ostensibly similar fragments of the 'Motorway Box' that the LCC planned to encircle inner London with in Bow, Stratford and East Greenwich are grim, and allow little or nothing to happen beneath them, which is not at all the case with the Westway, which has community centres, offices and schools inserted into its multivalent, sometimes multilevel concrete viaducts. Leaving central London, you first sail past the serried blocks of standard LCC towers, reclad, and then **Trellick Tower (p. 166)**, which stands at an angle to the flyover, showing gracious proportions in the best light, and then the road descends north at White City to meet the Western Avenue.

As it does, it passes Grenfell Tower, where a fire, accelerated almost certainly by dubious cladding, killed seventy-two people. Its blackened carcass, before it was covered by scaffolding and a big heart, was a genuinely horrifying sight, and a terrible indictment of the total indifference to working-class lives that was very much a feature of the Motorway Box plan. But here that indifference to upheaval – who cares if they live in the way, we'll move them to new flats – has become something far, far worse: a lethal neglect.

A similar visual experience can be had slightly to the south, on the earlier, less ambitious Chiswick Flyover. Shortly before you leave London you pass the Green Dragon Lane Estate, also known as Brentford Towers; six corduroy concrete towers, still (thankfully for their residents) unclad, shifting like a kinetic sculpture as the M4 flyover descends to hit the Great West Road and **Brentford 'Golden Mile' (p. 159)**. Green Dragon Lane is worth an exploration on foot, also, a green and spacious Corbusian 'Radiant City', visually limpid and strange, evoking Brian Eno's *Another Green World*; it also pokes its heads out over Kew Gardens. Pedestrians who want to experience some of this landscape as it should be seen should note that any coach journey between the West End and Heathrow will go on at least some of these flyovers.

CZECH & SLOVAK EMBASSIES, NOTTING HILL GATE ✪
Jan Bočan, 1965–70
Brutalist

The south side of Notting Hill Gate was totally redeveloped in the early 1960s, by means of some fairly indifferent commercial modernism. In the process, this monster appeared, one of the most intriguing buildings of the sixties in London. It is also a deeply odd building to have emerged during the Cold War, a full-scale late-modernist Eastern European building in one of the capitals of the West. This happened because Czechoslovakia had a programme of new embassies in the sixties, showcasing socialist modernity – there are similarly ambitious structures in Berlin and Stockholm. What makes this city-block of fine grey concrete worth serious exploration isn't merely the powerful grid that faces Notting Hill Gate – though that is impressive – but in what happens when it turns the corner towards Kensington Palace Gardens, and makes various cubist plays with panels and grids. Inside, the Embassy (split now into a Czech and a Slovak half, and open every year at OpenHouse) is suffused with the surrealist modernism that thrived in Prague and Bratislava between the end of Stalinism and the Prague Spring of 1968, and which persisted to a degree right up until 1989. Tentacles of glassware to the designs of the great Czech applied artist René Roubíček have been plugged into corduroy concrete, rococo chairs stand in front of walnut walls, and a rippling white concrete wall on the exterior reveals itself inside to be a fleshy abstract relief by the sculptor Stanislav Kolíbal. This is a unique place – Věra Chytilová or Jan Švankmajer meets Paul Rudolph or Marcel Breuer in uptown West 11.

Beyond the iron curtain: the massive integrity of the Czech and Slovak Embassies on Notting Hill Gate.

LECTURE THEATRE, BRUNEL UNIVERSITY, UXBRIDGE

Sheppard Robson, 1966

Brutalist

Well known to fans of *A Clockwork Orange* (see also **Thamesmead Estate, p. 96**) for its use as the Ludovico Institute, where Young Alex is conditioned against the old ultraviolence. The campus around is middling modern, well planned, by the decent journeyman firm helmed by Richard Sheppard, but the lecture theatre, mostly windowless, is sculptural and daunting, with the projecting volumes of the interior hauled up on great concrete columns – an experience of concussive mass and power. The recent painting of the stairwells, but letting the concrete surfaces alone, has a fittingly *Clockwork Orange* pop art aspect, and doesn't ruin the harsh materiality of the rest of the building.

HYDE PARK BARRACKS, KNIGHTSBRIDGE

Basil Spence, Bonnington & Collins, 1967–70

Brutalist

Along with **Queen Anne's Gate (p. 65)**, this is Basil Spence 'ruining' the view from a major London park for fogeys both young and old. Like most of his buildings, this is populist modernism, with nearly as much historical reference as would be common later in Postmodernism. Carried on the neo-Roman concrete-and-brick arches that Spence developed for the **University of Sussex (p. 238)** from a literalization of Le Corbusier's Maisons Jaoul, this is good, vigorous work, beefy and rhythmic; the thirty-three-storey tower, with its services stuffed into a four-part concrete crown, is a good beacon, a better marker that the park is in the city than the corporate modern dullness of the Hilton nearby. Inside, the barracks are quartered for 500 soldiers and

270 horses. How much modern architecture had gone from being a marginal movement to an architecture perfectly able to express old-school power can be ascertained by Spence's own description of the thing: 'I did not want this to be a mimsy-pimsy building. It is for soldiers. On horses. In armour.'

BRITISH RAIL MAINTENANCE UNIT, PADDINGTON
Bicknell & Hamilton for BR Architects Dept, 1969
Brutalist

Familiar to the millions who have ever driven into London via the **Westway (p. 163)** – though hidden from train passengers nowadays by the kipple of Paddington Basin – this wholly utilitarian building takes the form of an extraordinary cruiser, its sinister curves justifying its current official name, 'The Battleship'. It was designed by the same British Rail employees as **Harlow Town Station (p. 188)** and the **Birmingham New Street Signal Box (p. 314)**; together, these three projects can seem like an extraordinary rearguard action against the blandness and cheapness of so much of British Rail's architecture. While Harlow is neo-Frank Lloyd Wright and New Street a particularly hairy, shaggy Brutalism, this is an outlandish nod towards the fantasy architecture of Weimar Germany – turrets and periscopes, and long ribbon windows, that run alongside your car or coach as you cruise along the Westway.

POLISH CULTURAL & SOCIAL ASSOCIATION (POSK), HAMMERSMITH
M. F. Grzesik, 1971
Brutalist

A cultural centre for the diaspora 'Polonia' of west London, exhibiting the surrealism and love of paradox in the East European modern architecture of the time. But unlike the **Czech & Slovak Embassies (p. 164)**, this isn't an official product, but one made by one of the organizations set up by the stateless exiles who wouldn't make their peace with 'People's Poland' at the end of the war. It has a unique combination – found often in Poland itself – of the outré, the high-modernist, and the extremely conservative. You can spot it on King Street through its cartoonishly overemphasized, cross-like concrete frame (surely a deliberate cross – this is the 'Christ of Nations', after all), which is dramatically recessed at the entrance, and the cross-bracing is then brought into the interior as a decorative motif. Within are a bar, a café, a restaurant, a bookshop, a theatre and, best of all, a jagged metal stairwell full of enough superb, barely known post-war painting to fill a revisionist exhibition at the Tate. Ironically, given the anti-Communism of its sponsors, it most resembles the ecumenical programme and strident design of the Houses of Culture and People's Palaces found so often in the Eastern Bloc – panto and abstraction, under one concrete roof.

TRELLICK TOWER, NORTH KENSINGTON ✪
Ernő Goldfinger, 1972
Brutalist

A taller, more elegant version of Balfron Tower, with a much more dramatically sculpted skyline, and a low-rise estate below that is as rigorous as (though less complex than) the **Brownfield Estate (p. 127)**. Trellick has long benefited from a strong tenants' association and is generally considered a well-managed high-rise, which is ironic given the public obloquy to which it was subjected when completed, despite the fact it had been built to a very high standard. Today, the 'tower of terror' is a London icon, and the flats within it, when sold on the open market, can go

London's finest tower block: Goldfinger's epically proportioned Trellick Tower in North Kensington.

WEST LONDON

for a million. To visit it is simple enough, given that unlike most council towers it has a concierge; the waiting room for the lifts has stained glass inset into its concrete, like a miniature modernist church. Mostly, however, this is experienced by people in west London as a monument and a marker, a 'city-crown' that indicates where you are. It is in its profile that the superiority to Balfron is most obvious – the slender, asymmetric, beacon-like service tower, similarly attached by flying walkways to the flats, is surmounted by a curved office, the castle turret at the top of London's most beautiful concrete fortress.

————

WORLD'S END ESTATE, CHELSEA
Eric Lyons and H. T. Cadbury-Brown, 1969–77
Brutalist

One of the very last big estates in London, and like most of those built in the 1970s, when the post-war settlement hit the rocks, it was at the time enormously controversial. As usual, now it feels much less so – a well-crafted response to the common critiques of modernist estates as being identikit and placeless, which nonetheless very much remains a modernist estate – an integral, self-contained unit designed as one entity. The towers and lower-rise blocks are clad in red brick and tile, and shaped into contorted, almost medieval towers, ceremonial campaniles, around angular squares on a polygonal pattern. As a collaboration, it exhibits both Lyons's ingenuity at planning public spaces, so obvious in his work with Span, and Cadbury-Brown's heavy, rugged version of Brutalism. From south of the river in Battersea this forms one of the more stirring of the various 'instant city skylines' of the high-rise estates.

ST SAVIOUR'S CHURCH, PADDINGTON
Biscoe & Stanton, 1973–6
Brutalist

The most confident of all the modernist churches in London – not the usual wan spike on a butterfly-roofed brick box, nor the slightly sad campanile next to a monopitch prayer shed, this is a real work of architecture. A cluster of seemingly disconnected brick shards mass around what is more obelisk than spire, it is full of concentrated energy, charging right into 'Little Venice'. It's unusual in its programme, too, joining on to a small block of Brutalist brick flats, through steps and alleyways round the back. Odd, yes, morally questionable, even (nobody is chasing the estate agents out of this temple), but adjoining a block of flats is a much more interesting and urban approach than the sad little car parks attached to so many British modernist churches.

————

HILLINGDON CIVIC CENTRE, UXBRIDGE
RMJM, 1973–6
Postmodernist

Principally designed by Andrew Derbyshire, who in the 1960s had been the brains behind Sheffield's brilliant, recently destroyed Castle Market, this is about as good as the retreat from modern architecture gets. Essentially several Arts and Crafts houses squashed, mashed and condensed into a bulbous brick mass of pitched roofs and decorative arches, it has some of the spatial restlessness and sculptural vigour of a **Dawson Heights (p. 93)**, which makes its ingratiating local suburban 'references' to Mock Tudor semis more a matter of transfiguration than boring emulation. The same can't be said of its many imitators in the supermarkets and malls of the eighties.

HAMMERSMITH & WEST LONDON COLLEGE ❶

Bob Giles for Greater London Council Architects Dept, 1969–80
Brutalist

I first saw this on a coach coming into London – usually, I'd look out at the right-hand side, a remarkable Art Nouveau terrace of soot-blackened artists' studios at the end of Talgarth Road – and I'd never spotted that there was something equally intriguing on the other side of the road. If I was on a bus, I'd have got right out at the next stop to have a good look, but you can't do that on coaches. This is an unusual building by the GLC Architects Department, and an unusual typology for this book – the Further Education/Sixth Form College, a rather neglected genre from architects. This red-brick mount of a building draws on lots of what was fashionable in the late 1960s, when it was begun – the massed mini-cities of **Lillington Gardens (p. 57)** and the industrial metaphors of the **Engineering Building (p. 348)** at the University of Leicester – and none of what was fashionable in 1980, when it was completed, after a **Barbican**-style **(p. 66)** long gestation period caused by the strikes and slowdowns of the seventies. Now, it's all gone full circle, and it looks like one of the most successful and proudly scaled of the school buildings of the sixties, which happened to have been actually opened in the eighties. The approach up Aalto-like sculptural stairwells to the asymmetrical towers and cantilevers of the entrance is ceremonial and exciting, but there's no bombast or authoritarianism about it. Currently threatened with demolition, it has just been refused listing at the time of writing. It should be saved – this stretch of inner west London would be so much bleaker without its warmth and liveliness.

THE ARK, HAMMERSMITH

Ralph Erskine, 1989–92
Postmodernist, People's Detailing

The great Sweden-based British utopian architect Ralph Erskine designed nothing in Britain for a decade after the great **Byker Estate (p. 484)** in Newcastle – and then suddenly returned with an eccentric commercial monument in the capital. This bizarre glass helmet off the Hammersmith Flyover is quite the object, once again belying the reputation that Swedish designers have for mere cutesiness and context – this is wild, a tapering, curved boatload of speculative offices (seldom a typology that inspires such experiment) around a vertiginous atrium, with an overlook tower on top of it. An original and exciting addition to west London's quotient of roadside thrills, as much hive as ark, this building always looks as if it's in a constant state of activity, at the edge of incoherence, but kept in one smooth piece.

HEATHROW HILTON

Michael Manser Associates, 1991
High-Tech

Apart from Owen Williams's **Former BOAC Maintenance Headquarters (p. 162)**, this is the only building worth seeing in its own right in the enormous city-within-a-city that is Heathrow. A similar freeze-dried, air-conditioned, perfectly controlled space to Foster's slightly earlier **Sainsbury Centre (p. 202)** in Norwich, it is a glass volume with rooms arranged around a giant atrium. In this placid span of steel and aluminium built into an artificial green landscape, sterility is a virtue, and the interior view is sublime – just don't go for a walk outside. (The nearest exit for the pedestrian who wants to see it is Terminal 4.)

PUBLIC TOILETS, WESTBOURNE GROVE
CZWG, 1993
Postmodernist

Sharp elbows can get you all sorts of things. Kensington and Chelsea had planned to put a standard, mass-produced loo here to cater for those doing their shopping on the posher end of Portobello Road; the residents' association clubbed together and got Piers Gough, Roger Zogolovitch and co. to provide an alternative design. A maximalist programme – loo, flower kiosk, a clock, some benches, shelter, with trees and plants attached – rendered into a single image of a swish pale-green-tiled pavilion, with a glass canopy recalling the Paris Metro. Easily the best building serving this basic human need in Britain, which is quite the unintended statement in a borough which cares so little about its poorer residents that it puts flammable shit on its tower blocks.

A corporate utopia of steel, glass and lawns: Richard Rogers humanizes the business park in Chiswick.

CHISWICK BUSINESS PARK
Richard Rogers Partnership, 1999–2003
High-Tech

All the contradictions in what Richard Rogers does in cities, and how he thinks about them, are encapsulated in this dreamy, limpid complex. During the 1980s, Rogers was highly critical of how the likes of **Canary Wharf (p. 131)**, or the business parks thrown up by Nicholas Ridley's 'Enterprise Zones', detracted from cities through their unplanned, car-centred, naff, sprawling and cluttered form. So, here, he designs the same typology – a privately owned, privately patrolled, easily sealed-off business enclave within (but not of) the city – and makes it really nice, with public transport links, generous 'public' spaces with plenty of exotic trees and a lake. The buildings – standardized glass grids held up in thin steel frames, with titanium louvres and escape staircases – are the Pompidou Centre gone classical and serene, with all the melodrama taken out. Unlike a lot of later Rogers Stirk Harbour schemes, it's completely convincing – this is architecture and planning of real delicacy and grace. It exhibits the important virtue of knowing exactly when to stop designing, with the clarity of the module more important than expression and elaboration. Compare it with the trashy new business district at Paddington Basin, a few Tube stops away, and it's hard to object to what Rogers did here. It's quite gorgeous, especially in autumn. But it is what it is.

RED HOUSE, CHELSEA
Tony Fretton Architects, 2001
Classical Modernism

A Chinese lacquer box of a house, in a winding side street near the Thames in the south side of Chelsea, one of the most unusual little buildings of the last twenty years. The facade is monumental, at first – a square red block with a grand projecting arch, encompassing the bay windows of the ground floor and the first floor, that takes on some of the qualities of a formal portico without using any actual classical motifs. Yet the windows are placed informally, with no obvious regularity to the facade; at the roof garden, one entrance has the blind false windows of a Georgian 'window tax' facade, the other is glazed, and both are symmetrical. Walking past, the perverse pleasures of the building's gorgeous, blushing pink surfaces, and the way the plants of the interior press right up against the black plate glass, make for memorably weird street architecture. Unfortunately, this is very much a house for living in, and not open to the public – the plans and photographs that you can find on Fretton's website show a work of great complexity and perversity, with similarities in its approach to the games of hiding and revealing in the houses of the great Viennese modernist Adolf Loos. Perhaps it can be seen as a successor to the long tradition of arty little houses in Chelsea that, in the modernist era, encompasses the likes of **Cohen House (p. 160)**; it takes a lot more money to build one now – you could probably buy an island with what this cost – but, architecturally, this is a worthy continuation.

FAWOOD CHILDREN'S CENTRE, HARLESDEN
Alsop & Störmer, 2004
Supermodernist, Ecomodernist

A building for children rather suits Will Alsop's brightly coloured Teletubbyland – unlike the overbearing crazy-tie air that often seeped into his public buildings for adults, there's not the same risk of patronizing users. This kids activity centre at the corner of the redeveloped Stonebridge Estate is one of Alsop's most radical and least-known buildings, and in its lightness of touch a remarkable contrast with the ruinously expensive and over-programmed work he was doing at the same time. Incredibly simple – a big Fun Palace framed shed and little more, with container pods for the activities inserted into it, wrapped around by coloured mesh, with a grid of dangling, brightly coloured op art panels for a facade. The sense of it being half-finished is a gift to the childhood imagination – you can imagine it to be anything you want it to be.

WESTSIDE, EALING
Gavin Leonard for Ealing Borough Council Architects Dept, 2014
Classical Modernism

From the outside, you might mistake this for a private house in the current 'New London Vernacular', a tilted grid of stock brick with a flat roof; that's to keep the planners happy. Inside, this is a council-run youth centre of intricate multilevel complexity, composed, according to Leonard, following the rules of the Functional Method developed by the Russian Constructivists in the 1920s. It's a 'social condenser' as the Russians conceived it, with a music studio, cafés, a large sports hall and much else crammed, Tardis-style, into what would otherwise seem like just another house on a suburban street, and with the routes between the parts intended to overlap and intersect, so as to encourage its users to get to know each other. It is also one of the extremely few public buildings in Britain designed by a municipal architect in the last twenty years, shockingly given just how much had been built by councils in the previous century. For all the recent talk of councils building again, after this excellent little community centre Ealing's Borough Architect was pensioned off, and not replaced.

2. EAST OF ENGLAND

Robinson College, Cambridge (p. 209)

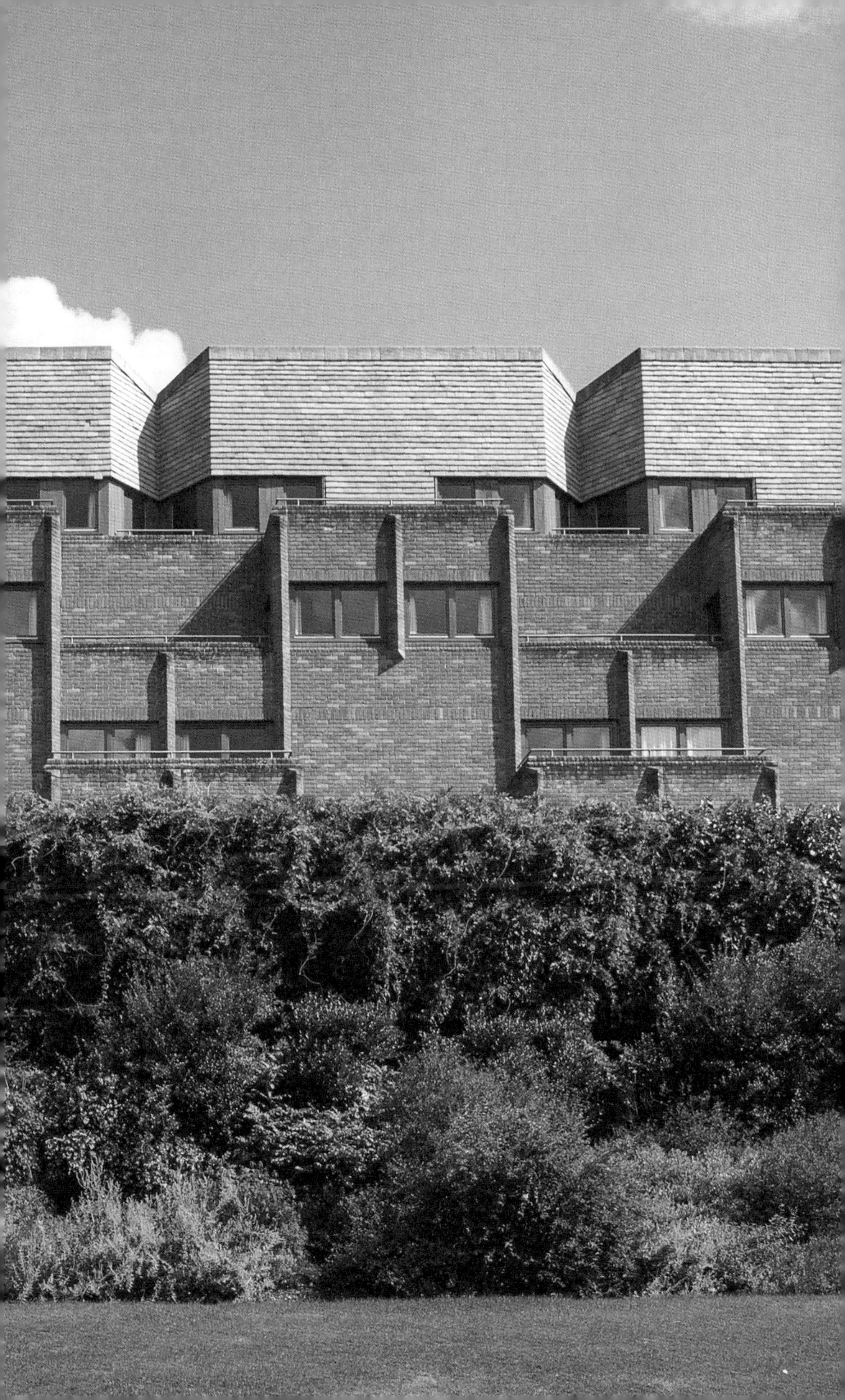

The counties north of the Thames Estuary and south of the Wash have among the richest collections of modern buildings in Europe – often in some very unexpected places. During the interwar years, Essex and Hertfordshire were used as test beds for modern architecture close to, but outside, the metropolis. Entire modernist villages such as **Silver End** and **East Tilbury** in Essex were built at the same time that nearly all London housing was Mock Tudor or neo-Georgian. These places drew on the Garden City movement, which was from the start a Hertfordshire project, based in Letchworth and Welwyn, whose industrial estates are a showcase of early modernism. The majority of the New Towns built after 1945 can be found in these two counties, which gives them an almost unrivalled quantity of modernist civic buildings.

Outside the London commuter zone, Eastern England's modern architecture is more complex. Brutalism arguably begins with the **Smithdon School** in Hunstanton, Norfolk, while Cambridge developed its own distinct rationalist 'school' of architecture from the fifties onwards, which continues in recent work like the **Accordia** housing estate. Norwich is surprisingly full of excellent council housing, carefully placed in the city centre; and the **University of East Anglia** is a remarkable integration of landscape and concrete. This is also an important area for the first examples of High-Tech architecture, with Norman Foster's three finest British works – the **Sainsbury Centre** in Norwich, **Stansted Airport** and the **Willis Building** in Ipswich – all laid out on its plains.

COMMUTER BELT NORTH

SHREDDED WHEAT FACTORY, WELWYN GARDEN CITY
Louis de Soissons, 1926
Industrial

The original Garden Cities were an inspiration to planners and architects all over the world, modernists especially – surprisingly so for places that were and are extremely English in their conservatism. Accordingly, Welwyn Garden City, built mostly in the 1920s to the designs of Louis de Soissons, is of major importance in the history of town planning. It's a more urban, neo-Georgian, faintly Tory, straightened-up 'improvement' on the charmingly rangy, proto-hippy Letchworth Garden City built before the First World War. But whereas that 'city' has no modern buildings of any importance, the more pragmatic Welwyn has a fair few, the earliest of which are the result of its strict zoning of industry on to the east side of the railway tracks. The largest, the Shredded Wheat factory, is one of the few surviving examples of pure, pre-'International Style' American Modern architecture in Britain. Soissons may have been a classicist, but, as a North American, he knew how to knock up a rigorously gridded 'daylight factory' of concrete, glass and green vitreous panels, and attach it to a giant grain silo complex of hulking concrete tubes. The result is the sort of concrete Atlantis that Le Corbusier and Walter Gropius swooned over when they gazed at the docksides of Buffalo and Montreal. It might seem bizarre that this was designed by the same architect as the suffocatingly polite Georgian 'Parkway' on the other side of the tracks, but the ruthless logic of the grid pervades both. Together, they feel more like an idealized WASP America than anywhere else in the UK.

HOUSES, SILVER END
Burnet Tait & Lorne, 1926–7
International Style, Moderne

That a pair of eerie Essex villages-cum-company-towns were the only complement in 1920s Britain to the housing estates built in the same decade elsewhere in Europe says rather a lot about how the novelty of modernism was interpreted here. As at the **East Tilbury (p. 176)** Bataville, Silver End was an advertising gimmick. It was designed around the Crittall window factory – whose works enliven many of the buildings in this book – as a living showcase of their wares and their status as an enlightened employer. Rather than being based directly on, say, the earlier modernist estates of Rotterdam or the Hook of Holland, the design of these 150 workers' houses and two managers' houses appears to have been based on the house the German modernist pioneer Peter Behrens had designed for a businessman at **New Ways (p. 345)**, the only design by a major European architect in Britain between Holland House and the Third Reich.

The workers' houses are neat little brick boxes, painted – not even rendered – in white and pastel colours, with the same diamond-like little windows that Behrens used for his only English work. As a townscape it's so memorable because it's so unexpected – a sudden little cubist Garden City on the plain. It would have been wonderful if there were more like it, but there's little more than just this place and East Tilbury. The village merits some exploration, not so much for the other buildings, like the staid brick community centre (though the gardens nearby are very pleasant) but for the beamed-from-space nature of it all. Wolverton, one of the two managers' houses, is owned by design enthusiasts who sometimes open the place up to visitors.

ROYAL CORINTHIAN YACHT CLUB, BURNHAM-ON-CROUCH
Joseph Emberton, 1931
International Style

The only British building to be admitted to the Museum of Modern Art's 1932 *The International Style* exhibition and book – a questionable but phenomenally successful project that codified what modern architecture was to Americans for forty years – just happened to be in Burnham-on-Crouch, an enjoyably scruffy yachting town in Essex. Accordingly, this small building has been given much attention over the years. Architectural history is strange. The Yacht Club certainly moves way beyond the timid art deco of most British attempts to be 'modern' at the time, and shows the influence as much of Soviet Constructivism as it does of the Corbusian/Miesian purism that MOMA were trying to prescribe, with dramatic cantilevered floors hung from a hard concrete volume, and with zigzag glazing to the side stairwells. This is all then planted on stilts, with a jetty from there to the estuary. 'The large glass area is particularly suitable in a dull, foggy climate', write Philip Johnson and Henry-Russell Hitchcock in the MOMA catalogue. I've only seen it in heavy, hazy sunshine, gleaming off the mud.

EAST TILBURY: ✪ BATA FACTORY, BATA ESTATE, BATA HOTEL & VILLAGE HALL
František Lýdie Gahura and Vladimír Karfík, 1932
International Style

Even to describe East Tilbury is to invite accusations of improbability. Divided by a green belt from Tilbury proper, it was from day one a company town for the Czechoslovakian shoe manufacturer Bata, which had become a curious modernist-

Americanist cult under its founder, Tomáš Baťa. Beginning with their headquarters in Zlín and then expanding around the world, Bata built little gridded towns of flat-roofed houses, community halls and enormous modernist factories for the purposes of family values and the mass production of high-quality footwear. The British example ascends into the category of the truly, transcendentally strange through its placement on the flattest land in the country, grasslands and marshes which you could easily imagine as part of the plains that stretch from eastern Germany to the Urals. Of the buildings, the houses are the most peculiar, because of how they're in many ways quite normal – Bata generally kept flat-building to a minimum, preferring the American model of the single-family house on its lot – but while the typology fits the suburban aspirations of the interwar years, these serene cubes couldn't be further from Mock Tudor.

Especially roughed up a bit as it is now with paint jobs, pebbledash and St George flags, East Tilbury feels extremely English. Yet in its precise cubic geometry, it's also extremely Czechoslovak, the product of a country that excelled at a huge modern architecture in the 1920s and '30s, mostly in a rectilinear, machine-made, cold-eyed style. A grid of streets, with larger, balconied houses on roundabouts, culminates at a 'town centre', which consists of a Czech Cubist war memorial, a village hall (originally a cinema, and seemingly modelled on the Bauhaus's Haus am Horn in Weimar) and two huge buildings. One of these was the 'Bata Hotel', mainly a dormitory for single workers and now a block of flats. Its restoration has been poor, and a casual glance might suggest it's just any bit of mediocre modernism; yet, look at it from a distance, and its elegant proportions are apparent. There's no mistaking the other main complex, the factory that everything revolved around – utterly timeless modern

The Czechoslovakian modernist company town of East Tilbury, Essex: cubist semi-detached workers' houses...

...and the Bata Factory, fusing continental modernism and American factory design, overlooking flat marshland.

architecture, a concrete and glass grid of purist perfection, standing as a surrealist abstraction on the Essex steppe.

East Tilbury was watered down a little after the war by some standard New Town-style conservative modernism, and recently some typically poor 'Thames Gateway' flats and houses have been erected around the 1930s buildings – uncomfortably close to the factory, in at least one instance. Mostly, the surreal effect remains. Those easily offended by Essex proletarian taste will find that the fewest alterations have been made to the cul-de-sac of big houses on Bata Avenue.

THE LABWORTH, CANVEY ISLAND
Ove Arup, 1933
International Style

The first independent work of the Danish engineer whose influence pervades the history of modern architecture in the UK is a café built as part of the sea defences in a *nouveau riche* township on an island in the Thames estuary. Originally employed as an engineer for the wall – which was replaced in the 1970s by the current design, with delightful barrel-roofed beach shelters built in – Arup's café was added as an afterthought, bearing a passing resemblance to the 'Kornhaus' riverside café in Dessau, a building which the engineer-architect will have known. The café is symmetrical, curved and glazed, with wide 'wings' that shelter al fresco tables – in the 1930s! It's now something of an icon of fun seaside modernism, along with the **De La Warr Pavilion (p. 234)** – that distinct mix of high-end aesthetics and kiss-me-quick seaside tat. Unlike the De La Warr, this listed building hasn't been treated well – the naff nineties signage and harsh security features are particularly irksome. A much more tawdry moderne, meanwhile, can be found in the Monico building just behind the seawall, improbably once a casino.

ROCHE CHEMICALS, WELWYN GARDEN CITY
Otto Salvisberg, 1938–40/
Cubitt Atkinson & Partners, 1977
International Style

In the same industrial zone as the **Shredded Wheat Factory (p. 175)**, but – curiously, given that it was designed by a convinced modern architect rather than a neoclassicist putting his mind to an uncharacteristic function – a much calmer, more rational and classical work of architecture. Salvisberg designed various buildings for the Roche company in his native Switzerland, and is best known for his contributions to the pivotal 'White City' housing estate in Berlin, one of the great meetings of socialist ideas and International Style aesthetics. Here, the politesse of the town has seeped slightly into the architecture, but it is still a finely proportioned and clearly modernist object. It consists of a rationalist multistorey grid towards the railway line, with, in front, a long office pavilion projecting towards the street on pilotis, with a classicized grille of vertical windows as public face. A gorgeously lightweight tubular glass stairwell stands to the side. Roche's later headquarters across the road is quite the contrast, a diverting piece of corporate Brutalism, with jagged layers of mosaic and gold mirrorglass. Its flash and bombast are already much further from Central Europe than Salvisberg's coolly expressed technocracy; the original Roche building stands with the **St Bernard's Houses (p. 116)** in Croydon as Britain's only examples of Swiss modern architecture, which is rather a shame. Salvisberg's building is currently derelict, but there are flats in an inoffensive emulation of it nearby. The original, closely designed to fit its function, is evidently hard to convert.

STATE CINEMA, GRAYS
Frederick Chancellor, 1938
Moderne, Expressionist

A rough bit of cinema architecture in a rough town just on the edges of London, with thick brown brick, a serrated roof and a squat tower with the words 'STATE' – it's all rather V for Vendetta, and suggests what would have happened if it were brooding churches like **St Saviour's (p. 80)**, rather than Harry Weedon's Odeon cinemas, which had become the model for interwar commercial modernism.

LOUGHTON UNDERGROUND STATION
John Murray Easton, 1940
Moderne

This Tube station at the edge of London, where most streets lead to Epping Forest, was built as part of the Underground's takeover of a looping Victorian branch line that runs through the borders of Essex and the capital. Most of its stations are in a (rather pretty) red-brick Victorian, but here the Underground started again and executed this dramatic essay in the Charles Holden Anglicized modernist style. From the street, you can grasp it in an instant – a big box (clad in pale stock brick, but actually steel-framed) with a grand glass brick oculus, flanked on the raised platforms by sleek, somewhat Italian Futurist concrete platforms. It lacks some of Holden's attention to detail, but it's not derivative either – the barrel-vaulted main hall inside the box is a paradoxical little surprise. Although here quite visibly not designed by Holden himself, Loughton has a similar ethos to his transport architecture – making sure that the station visually as well as practically links the distant suburb to the metropolis.

Streamline moderne on Epping Forest: the concrete canopies of Loughton, a London Underground station in Essex.

The stained-glass walls and thin copper spire of Harlow New Town's grandest Catholic church, Our Lady of Fatima.

MARK HALL, HARLOW: ✪
MARK HALL NORTH & THE LAWN
Frederick Gibberd Partnership, 1946–60
THE CHANTRY
Jane Drew and Maxwell Fry, 1951
OUR LADY OF FATIMA
Gerard Goalen, 1953–4
People's Detailing

In terms of its architecture, Harlow was the most praised of the first generation of New Towns. Unlike the others, it was guided by the same architect from the very start to the end – well, until the 1980s, which amounts to much the same thing. Here, Frederick Gibberd became the first of the International Stylists of the 1930s to adapt his style to 'Empiricist' English realities, with shiny white stucco exchanged for brick, ribbon windows for bows. Its centre doesn't live up to this (see the Harlow **Water Gardens, p. 187**), but residentially, a lot of Harlow is gorgeous, and nowhere more so than in Mark Hall. It is

built around the drowsily rural vernacular buildings of old Harlow, like the red-brick stables that Gibberd converted into the town's museum. The best known part of Mark Hall is The Lawn, occasionally called the 'first tower block in Britain', and certainly the first 'point block' – that is, a single tower in green space. But it makes no sense to treat it as an isolated object. Approaching The Lawn from the museum, you don't see at first that there is a ten-storey tower just around the corner. It emerges slowly through the seven oak trees that predate it, until you can see the asymmetrical red and yellow tower emerge, offset by pretty terraces – a miniature textbook of picturesque planning.

From there, it's a short walk through attractive wood-panelled terraces and three-storey blocks of flats on pilotis, with parkland flowing through them, to one of the schemes Gibberd gave to other architects – the very laconic, flat-fronted houses and flats of The Chantry, by Jane Drew and

Maxwell Fry, their only really convincing effort at designing in the new picturesque style. The way the flats are raised on pilotis to offer a green path to an Old Harlow church is exquisitely done. The thin copper spire you can see in the distance, though, is St Fatima, a modernist Catholic church with incredibly rich stained glass. It faces The Stow, a 'neighbourhood centre' with shops and a pub, heralded by another picturesque point block, and unfortunately marred by a giant Aldi.

Mark Hall is one of the places where the lush landscaping that flows through the whole of Harlow (until you reach its asphalt and concrete centre) makes most sense. There's always a corner nearby with a big tree and a winding path leading to a park, always public, always generous. There are also too many wan grass verges with nothing on them, and too few benches for it to ever really feel like you're in a town, as such – the baleful influence of Cambridge or Bath on town planning in the UK is strongly felt. But, then, the point of the Garden Cities was always to eliminate the divide between city and country, and it's seldom done better than here. Worker's Paradise, 1951. **[C.8, C.14]**

WATER GARDENS & BANK COURT, HEMEL HEMPSTEAD
Geoffrey Jellicoe, 1947–62
People's Detailing

There is a wonderfully depressing film available on the *Public Art of Hemel Hempstead*, in which a transcendentally bored estuary voiceover profiles the various artworks of its precincts. This small New Town acquired what character it has through two decisions by its main architect-planner, Geoffrey Jellicoe – to build up a large public art collection, and to define the town through its landscape architecture, Jellicoe's speciality (see his **Memorial Garden & St Matthew's Close, p. 321**, in Walsall, in a very different

context). On arrival from the railway station you're given notice of this by the lovely, maddening and totally undeveloped 'town moor' running along the Grand Union Canal. While delightful in daytime, lined as it is with some fine Berlin-style low-rise apartment blocks, nobody would ever choose to walk home here at night. Here, as in Harlow's similar (but slightly more urbane) central park, the dominant influence is Oxford and Cambridge – cows grazing on the backs, and the station placed well out of town.

You might well assume, looking at the elegant maps placed at each end of the moor (the planners of the first New Towns had a real talent for diagrams), that the canal will eventually link up with the Water Gardens. It doesn't – you have to go through a few underpasses first, and then negotiate a horrible mall. But, when you finally get there, it's rewarding. Planned in 1947 but largely built a decade later, the Water Gardens – essentially a linear pond, with public space on either side – snake through the town, parallel to the main pedestrianized street, The Marlowes. Crisp concrete bridges span the waters, and the gardens are alternately formal and bosky. Standing in the pond is a statue of dancers, by Hubert Yencesse, called *Rock and Rollers*, of 1962. Otherwise Hemel is not very rock and roll, but there are very good recent – faintly hipsterish, in fact – maps and information points on the Water Gardens telling you its history. On the hill above are the clean glass lines of a typical forties Hertfordshire School, and, parallel, the miniature formal set piece of Bank Court. Here, in Portland stone, are slightly classicized buildings which stand closer to the imperial Beaux Arts Armada Way than the modernism of Stevenage's **Town Square (p. 184)**. An array of columns and walkways creates a manual of spatial planning as the entry point from gardens to precinct. Splendid, though sadly little else here is up to this standard.

TEMPLEWOOD SCHOOL, WELWYN GARDEN CITY

A. Cleeve-Barr and C. H. Aslin for Hertfordshire County Council Architects Dept, 1948–50
People's Detailing

In terms of British modernist history, the post-war schools programme of Hertfordshire County Council is of great significance, but they are seldom worth a special visit. This is an exception. They're important as perhaps the first really independent British contribution to modernism since Mackintosh; for their free planning – derived from Bauhaus precedent to some degree but much more informal; for their use of prefabrication and factory construction, in an explicit transfer of military skills to civilian purposes; and for what is called their 'human scale', i.e. that they're generally small, and distributed in miniature glassy pavilions, in bright colours. The problem is that the prefabrication system is rather dour, and the grey panels that the schools are made up of are instantly redolent of the huts and hutches that most schools have scattered around their peripheries, which suggest more underfunding and 'making do' than they do a brave new world. But Templewood School is special for two reasons. One is its site, at the top of a gentle hill in Pentley Park, one of the most arcadian parts of Welwyn Garden City, past twee but imaginatively arranged neo-Georgian villas, tree-lined boulevards and even a couple of extremely mild flat-roofed modernist houses (late thirties, by Eugene Kaufmann and Paul Mauger), with the school's spread-out red and grey cubes placed on a hill dense with trees, giving it an almost Californian air. The other reason is the artist Patricia Tew's fabulous murals of Russian folk tales. These vivid, colourful Chagall-does-Pelican-Books panels are a little remnant of the days between 1941 and 1948 when the Soviets

were our valiant allies and good socialists would brush up on Pushkin and Gogol. Naturally, it being a working school you can't just walk in and see these, but there are occasional tours, and it is worth contacting the school, just in case.

TOWN CENTRE GARDENS & BEDWELL, STEVENAGE

Gordon Patterson and Stevenage Corporation Architects Dept, 1950–60
People's Detailing

Pevsner expressed the hope, when they were just blueprints, that Stevenage, Hatfield, Basildon, Harlow and company would be the first towns we could be proud of *in toto* rather than just in fragments since the eighteenth century and Bath. They clearly aren't, and that has much to do with the way they were built incrementally around road systems, which slice them up into chunks which can be great individually – sometimes magnificent, in fact – but which are always, as Ian Nairn tirelessly pointed out at the time, mixed up with a mess of car parks, dual carriageways and the service back ends of department stores, frequently in order to make the set pieces work as pedestrian public spaces. Yet caught in these at Stevenage is one of the grandest civic spaces of all the New Towns – bravura city planning, giving way to cosy intimacy.

So grit your teeth as you get through Stevenage's backsides between Queensway and the Gardens, because the reward is a green arc, with a pond, faintly Socialist Realist sculptures and fountains, and, just above the trees, a set of picturesquely scattered high-rises in a Scandinavian manner. From here, the space flows again into the inner suburb of Bedwell, which is very low density for an inner anything, but full of clever and warm touches, with paths and cycle lanes threading through free green squares, no petty fences or barriers, tower

Town planning at its most urbane: ponds, paths, trees and tower blocks at Stevenage's Town Centre Gardens.

blocks sparingly dotted around as markers, and simple terraces raised above on pilotis where the walker might want to get through. It's not visionary, it's not 'Utopia', and there are too often Quaker halls where pubs should be, but it's social planning of the highest order, and a sequence that explains very well why thousands preferred this place to Bethnal Green or Islington. Sort out that awful dual carriageway and it could be an eco-town.

___

HARLOW MARKET SQUARE
Frederick Gibberd Partnership, 1955–60
People's Detailing

As wonderful as suburbs like **Mark Hall (p. 180)** are, Harlow actually has one of the weaker New Town centres – a dull precinct with a fabulous sculpture collection, a mall and a retail park attached, which lacks

the enclosure and colour of **Town Square & Queensway (p. 184)** in Stevenage, the spatial drama of **East Square (p. 186)** in Basildon or the integration with older buildings in **Hatfield Market Place & The Town Inn (p. 188)**. And while many of the bad things in the New Towns can be blamed on post-1980s neglect and retail planning, this is, to be sure, Frederick Gibberd's fault, a sense of dislocation achieved through the seemingly smart idea of placing a swathe of pseudo-countryside and car parks between the centre and the railway station. This is an example of the baleful influence of Oxford and Cambridge on planning culture – an ethos where public transport was kept pointlessly distant from the people who might use it, and a chunk of the town cosplays as rural exactly in the places where what you really need is connection and continuity. Moreover, the later buildings of the New Town, like the library and the Harvey Centre, are grey, precast and dour – especially puzzling for an architect who knew – as he proved at Liverpool's **Metropolitan Cathedral (p. 427)** – the importance to a city of putting something big and special on a hill. All the good things about his town centre in Harlow are in this one market square. The pub has a great and by now deeply nostalgia-inducing decorative treatment, with a corner clock decorated with a sweet-wrapper pattern of blue and white tiles; the sculpture, *Meat Porters* by Ralph Brown, is well chosen; on one corner you can see the space-age, capsule-style concrete panels of the original Harlow Advice Centre, currently derelict, but full of the character this town centre mostly lacks; and the view is closed by a bright-yellow glass and steel curtain-walled block, which wittily combines Miesian ultra-modern materials with the picturesque recesses and balconies Gibberd uses to such impressive effect in the town's housing. Under this block is a passageway – maybe this leads somewhere interesting? Sadly, it doesn't.

ST ANDREW & ST GEORGE PARISH CHURCH, STEVENAGE

Seely & Paget, 1956
Googie

A weird little building, and the nearest thing Stevenage has to a cathedral, marooned on the same grim carriageway that divides the **Town Centre Gardens (p. 182)** from the **Town Square & Queensway (below)**. It boasts a tower that is part concrete campanile, part *Wacky Races* mishap-provoking spiral stair and part rocket, and a barrel-vaulted church hall with abstract glass inside and a quasi-medieval flinty aggregate outside. While it's hard to call this entirely successful architecture, given the lack of any obvious relation between its then-fashionable various parts, it makes a real difference to Stevenage's skyline and townscape. A welcome reminder that fifties modernism could be kitsch, silly and space-age, surrounded with much that is high-minded and restrained – a church treated like a funfair, in a town where much of the housing was designed with a religious conviction. **[C.26]**

———

TOWN SQUARE & QUEENSWAY, STEVENAGE ✪

Leonard Vincent and Clifford Holliday for Stevenage Corporation Architects Dept, 1958
People's Detailing

As with the **Town Centre Gardens (p. 182)**, surrounded by mess and planning failure, but when you're there, in the set piece, it would be churlish to object on the grounds of the tat it has made possible. This is the most – and the word is justified – *iconic* of the New Town centres, and along with Coventry the major statement of what a modernist English town would look like. So the geometry is Germanic, and the stylistic repertoire of bright colours, mosaics and colonnades is drawn partly

from Scandinavia; but the way that it's all integrated into a civic image is distinct and English, as is the use of sculpture and imagery. In fact, it's sometimes closer to the other side of the Iron Curtain, although of course denuded of propaganda and bombast. Steps from the square lead up to a raised platform, on which stands the Czech sculptor's Franta Belsky's *Joy Ride*, a jolly mother-and-child group where the child appears to be bouncing off her back. The platform is purely visual, its only purpose being for you to take in the vista. At the foot of it are the superb clock tower, with its Roman numerals, a Mondrian-like tiled pool, an announcement of a royal visit, and a relief bust of the New Towns' creator, the Labour minister Lewis Silkin. It's a summation in one object of this project's beguiling mixture of English conservatism and socialist modernism.

The street that leads from the Town Square, Queensway, shows how the New Towns differed from the stiff neoclassical parkways that passed for town planning in the interwar years (Welwyn is just down the road, for comparison). The streets are pedestrian, tightly packed, sheltered by canopies and colonnades, full of visual detail and enclosure so that you don't get bored, and are evidently popular – until the shops shut and it empties. As at Coventry, treating a city centre mainly just as a shopping centre was a big mistake, and one which runs very obviously counter to the notion that the New Towns' failure to become, as intended, the Baths and Edinburghs of the twentieth century was down to overbearing state planning. In Stevenage, the corporations evidently consider the place a low-end shopping centre, so the shops are mostly grim (excepting a few very welcome independent cafés and restaurants), the buildings are seldom if ever renovated (including the listed ones) and neglect is inescapable. The way that one of the artworks, a colourful Socialist Realist mural of the

The precinct at Queensway, Stevenage, the most socially convincing and visually enjoyable of all New Town centres.

Stevenage community (by the Hungarian artist G. Baijo) is just a fading panel above a Primark is particularly indicative. If it had all stayed in London, the whole lot would be full of craft beer startups, and a flat would begin at £900,000 for a studio.

DANESHILL HOUSE, STEVENAGE
Leonard Vincent for Stevenage Corporation Architects Dept, 1958
International Style

An elegant Miesian block by the same Corporation employees who designed much of the Town Centre, stranded in the straggly non-townscape between the railway station and the **Town Square (above)**; it was designed as the Corporation's headquarters, and now houses Stevenage Council, whose pitiful clipart logo is attached to the low, brick block that connects to these seven storeys of black frosted glass. Sharply cut, elegantly

proportioned, and now looking rather sad, in front of privatized buses and crap malls, its quality is visible despite the grime – a vision of what the better Norman Foster buildings will look like in sixty years, perhaps.

HILLE HOUSE, WATFORD
Ernő Goldfinger, 1959
Brutalist

Goldfinger meets Metroland, in a grim part of Watford round the back of Watford Junction Station. Hille House was built as a mixed-use block of offices, light industrial units and shops, and ushers in the architect's new 'tough' aesthetic, influenced by Auguste Perret's classical approach to concrete, rather than the more 'humanist' terrace at **1–3 Willow Road (p. 142)**. It works well – an irregular grid, with the left-hand corner cut away to let lorries into the back end (where there is a typically suave spiral staircase), and a cantilevered volume out over the shops which uses, for the first time, an abstract pattern of stained glass, a motif that would return at **Trellick Tower (p. 166)**. As always with Goldfinger the concrete is properly detailed, and as yet unpainted, which makes the owners of Hille House notably more progressive than those of **Metro Central Heights (p. 91)**.

─────

ST PAUL'S CHURCH, HARLOW
Derrick Humphrys & Hurst, 1957–9
People's Detailing

One of the most truly municipal of New Town churches, feeling like a real heart of a real community. Especially given the demolition of Gibberd's original Civic Centre (on the site of the **Water Gardens, p. 187**) and its replacement with business park blandness, this church feels more like a town hall than the actual Town Hall does. A tweedy mass of brick, on an interesting, decentralized free plan, leads via several entrances to a wide concrete hall, with a John Piper mosaic above the altar. Its abstract shards gradually become visible as as an outlined, halo'd Christ surrounded with Matisse-like angels. The effect is relaxed and open, more like the venue for village fêtes than a place to feel the fear (or the love) of God. It ought to have a real civic frame, a square or a garden around it, but instead it's marooned between the back ends of malls and dreadful new flats.

─────

EAST SQUARE, BASILDON ✪ ❶
Anthony B. Davies for Basildon Corporation with Basil Spence, 1957–62
People's Detailing

Another New Town set piece; this might be the best of the lot. With all the usual caveats about the messy back ends and dual carriageways, this could stand in any small city, anywhere in the world, as an exemplary piece of urban architecture. The earliest part, Freedom House, is an L-shaped street block in a very fifties style, with charming multicoloured mosaic pilotis, Expressionistic concrete colonnades, and a clock tower, set on to a blue-tiled block, accessorized with a Hepworth-esque sculpture (*Untitled*, by A. J. Poole, 1957). There are shops on the ground floor and an upper-level arcade, and a sunken square below. Viewed from above, this square, with its good, unpretentious fifties paving still in place, and a striking Brutalist staircase, starts to take on the dramatic qualities of an amphitheatre. This all falls within the conventional repertoire of New Town architecture, a pretty, Anglicized Scandinavian modernism. What is placed at the other end of the square, though, is wilder – Brooke House, a huge high-rise block of council flats, hauled up on immense, double-height splayed pilotis, more H. G. Wells than *Here We Go Round the Mulberry Bush*, holding a grid of sexily convex windows with an op art effect. Basil Spence was hired by the New Town's chief architect, Anthony B. Davies, to 'advise' on the tower, and these populist and science fiction elements are presumably his contribution. The square leads into the precincts of the rest of the town via a long pool, which features another strange modernist *Mother and Child*, this one by Maurice Lambert of 1959, with Mum lying on a plinth holding up a bowl, as baby stands on her head (at the time of writing, the pool is drained, unlike in Stevenage's **Town Square, p. 184**).

Depressingly, the 'regeneration' of the square is proceeding by demolishing Freedom House and replacing it with some typical Blair-era cladded bombast, now more than a decade out of date, and removing the multiple levels of Freedom House, so destroying exactly those things – the play of levels, the sunken square, the joy in small, pleasurably individual details within a coherent whole – that make East Square so delightful. Brooke House is a listed building,

The clear, confident high-rise flats of Basil Spence's Brooke House, at the threatened East Square in Basildon.

so won't be touched, which sums up one of the problems in the way post-war ensembles are so often treated – individual 'icons' get protected, but the conservation-area approach routinely used with pre-twentieth-century architecture is never deployed. Here, that's especially unfortunate, because this is urban design of the highest order, as any decent planner would easily recognize – a thumping 'YOU ARE HERE' that the town would otherwise lack. It should have been built upon, not erased.

WATER GARDENS, HARLOW
Frederick Gibberd, 1958–9
People's Detailing

The Water Gardens were intended to be the heart of Harlow New Town, running down from a Civic Centre in the form of a tower with a carillon at the top, placed on a gentle Essex hill, to denote 'here is Harlow' to the

country around. The gardens themselves, a series of terraces with ponds on each level, were one of the most successful parts of the town, and accordingly were among the first post-war buildings to be listed. Yet in the 2000s the council, its owners, needed money, so they flogged the lot to Standard Life, who demolished the Civic Centre, building in its place an identikit low-rise office block dominated by chain restaurants (there are council offices in there somewhere), and truncated the gardens with an Asda and a car park – a disastrous mutilation of townscape. Yet they left the specifically listed parts of the gardens – the terraces and the sculptures around them – so you can see how clever the gardens once were. Gargoyles by William Mitchell spit water fountains into a blue mosaic pool, and formal topiary cascades down the hill, enclosing miniature squares, well used by fag-smoking youth. Allowing the gardens' mutilation was a terrible failure of the listing system, but the essentials of the design, amazingly, do manage to show through in the squares and pools. Is it salvageable? Yes, it probably is. The plan is still visible underneath the naff accretions, and while the office block/restaurant complex fits the American style of Milton Keynes more than it does the Cockney eccentricity Gibberd intended for Harlow, there's much worse to be found elsewhere in Essex. When Harlow wakes up to itself, the Asda and the strip mall will have to go if this is ever going to feel like a town centre rather than an out-of-town retail park.

HARLOW TOWN STATION
John Bicknell and Paul Hamilton for British Railways Eastern Region, 1959
BROXBOURNE STATION
Peter Rainiers for British Railways Eastern Region, 1960
STEVENAGE STATION
British Railways Eastern Region, 1973
Brutalist

On reading about Harlow Town and Broxbourne in Ian Nairn's *Modern Buildings in London* – particularly his scepticism towards the former design, and boisterous praise of the latter – I assumed this was one of his bizarre drunken judgements, prompted by too much Worthington E, especially given how much better Harlow looks in photographs. On visiting them, it was impossible to deny he was right. Both stations are substantially similar in plan, they're ten minutes' train journey from each other, and both are listed. Corridors and waiting rooms are in a single concrete bridge over the tracks, punctuated by three chunky concrete towers for goods lifts and stairwells. One is in a suburban town on the very edge of London, the other is intended to herald the utopian new world of Harlow New Town. Broxbourne is unfussy and punchy, with stock brick and béton brut, elemental and immediate. At Harlow, meanwhile, the

designers (as at their later **Birmingham New Street Signal Box, p. 314**) have opted for expressionism, with the towers gone heraldic, and the bridges and cantilevered canopies stretched right out, one after the other, so that they look like an Essex version of Fallingwater. Yet Broxbourne is the more powerful and more convincing design, and it has aged much better, largely because it's so strong as to barely need maintenance. Harlow's extra elaboration and drama are justified by the fact that it needs to announce the place's importance, and it certainly does that, especially given that everything immediately around the station is horrible.

Stevenage Station pulls a similar trick a decade later, with the same system of a bridge and tower-stairwells, but taller, more monumental and more minimalist, with sharp, bright-red machine-made brickwork. Unlike at Harlow, it actually connects to the town properly, through a walkway system that threads through a spatially interesting, if badly realized, multilevel leisure and arts centre, then on to a ramp that takes you right into the heart of the town. It is shabby now, but could be brilliant with a bit of care and imagination.

HATFIELD MARKET PLACE & THE TOWN INN
Hatfield Development Corporation Architects Dept, 1960
People's Detailing

Hatfield is not one of the more exciting New Towns, partly because its project was a slightly different one. It was not so much a *tabula rasa* attached to an old village, as were Stevenage, Harlow and East Kilbride – much more, it was an attempt to tie together with a new centre, new roads and new estates a mess of suburban semis near to a historic country house and a pretty, tiny Georgian enclave, a conundrum which had grown up because of the local aerospace industry and the close proximity of the A1 (now the source of what makes the town so odd and uncomfortable, a constant hum and rumble of engine noise). The new centre joins typical New Town precincts – mediocre work by Maxwell Fry and Jane Drew, who were capable of much better – to mundane commercial architecture of the twenties. This was supplemented recently by a giant grey Asda. Hatfield's centre was commercially stricken by the decision to build a giant mall, the Galleria, over the A1, a great engineering achievement that is far less impressive on architectural and social grounds. It's the exodus of the big stores that makes the Market Place the most interesting part of Hatfield town centre. Evidently aware that HMV or H&M were never going to come back, the owners of the two-level arcade that frames the outdoor market have let it to unusual shops and restaurants, rather than just to Betfred. This works well with the little details and the copper roofs of the buildings, particularly the Festival Style Town Inn. Precisely because it isn't a run of chain stores but somewhere with some character, this corner feels more part of a 'real' town than most New Town centres.

MARLOWES CAR PARK, HEMEL HEMPSTEAD

Rex Stubbings and Rowland Emett (artist), 1960
People's Detailing

This enormously enjoyable building is one result of the public-art programme Geoffrey Jellicoe brought to Hemel Hempstead. The multistorey car park has its parking floors behind a sparky Festival Style block, with honeycomb concrete patterns, shops on the ground floor and blue mosaic pillars, a little dilapidated, as with most of the original New Town buildings. But on the gable end is a fabulous mural of Hemel and the towns nearby, in a delightful Victorian-

futurist style by the artist Rowland Emett; sputnik and Elizabeth I, penny farthings and modernist precincts. It has been slightly fancifully suggested that the way in which these images are turned into a pseudo-map, with abstract paths connecting the towns, is influenced by Guy Debord and Asger Jorn's Situationist classic *Mémoires*, but it is not for me to confirm this theory.

COCKAIGNE HOUSING GROUP, THE RYDE, HATFIELD

Phippen Randall & Parkes, 1963
International Style

The modernist cult buildings of Hatfield aren't its council estates, factories, precincts, or schools or polys, but something quite unusual for the sixties – a co-operative housing scheme by a group of middle-class enthusiasts, which included their architects, who (rather sadly) eventually became the miserable corporate firm PRP. So far, so much like the sporadic co-ops, community land trusts and self-build colonies that are scattered around the UK (**LILAC, p. 383**, being the best of them).

Yet there's nothing hippy in the way in which this group was designed – truly suburban housing, a long staggered zigzag of bungalows, with plenty of car-parking space. What makes them worth seeing is the cleverness of the layout, executed with pleasant, unpretentious detail in breezeblock and black-stained wood. Each part of the scheme is a 'patio house', which includes a garage (clearly not enough, out here in the Hertfordshire Inland Empire, as cars are parked in front of most), a private square, a garden, and a peculiar sort of winter garden, in glass and wood. Only some of this is visible from the street; it is too quiet and private for it to feel entirely comfortable to peer inside these strange and interesting houses, with their intriguing vision of sixties suburban intelligentsia life. Worth looking

Brutalism enlivening a flat landscape: the walkways and towers of Architects Co-Partnership's University of Essex.

out for when one comes on the market and you can pretend to be able to afford one, and you can have a peek.

UNIVERSITY OF ESSEX, COLCHESTER ⊙

Architects Co-Partnership, 1963–6
Brutalist

One of the most famous and notorious of the New Universities, not so much for its architecture, but for the unrest and student occupations that happened here in the 1960s and '70s. Essex was planned by its leading lights, the academic Albert Sloman and Kenneth Capon of its designers, Architects Co-Partnership, as a sort of British MIT. Its design has often been overlooked in surveys of the period – it isn't as sculptural as the universities of **East Anglia (p. 198)** or **York (p. 394)**, or as dreamlike and Arcadian as **Sussex (p. 238)**. What its designers aimed

at was the creation through architecture of an instant community. Accordingly, early surveys of student unrest noted that (however much they might have disdained 'totalitarian' modernism) the abundance of public spaces – greens, steps, walkways, passageways, squares – facilitated, as in a historic city, the use of space in a civic and politicized way. A successful community, then, whether you like it or not.

The design of the ensemble is clear and instantly recognizable. Two clusters of towers – these are the halls of residence. Their alternating stripes of dark engineering brick and vertical strips of window, and the way they rise out of the trees on the hilltop site, are a rare justified example of the overused 'Italian hill town' trope, suburban Colchester's answer to San Gimignano. In-between the towers/residences are the libraries, classrooms and laboratories. Although the raised walkways still there and the public spaces have not been spoiled, there has been some attrition of the buildings – the 'Hexagon', a sort of student community centre that stands in the middle of one of the walkway passages (the routes all spoke out from it on the plan) is currently disused, although it housed an excellent exhibition on the university's history and architecture a few years ago. The Albert Sloman Library, meanwhile, has been disfigured with cheap cladding. Even so, this is an unmissable microcosmic townscape, one of the most intense complexes of its era. **[A.18]**

CENTRAL SOUTHEND: ❶ QUEENSWAY TOWERS
P. F. Burridge, 1965
VICTORIA CENTRE
1968
International Style

Southend-on-Sea got a severe visitation from the comprehensive redevelopers in the 1960s, and while the results are generally not delightful, they have a certain scale, and some nice details. The Victoria Centre is an Arndale-style concrete megamall, whose aggressive design extends to almost Zaha-esque projecting concrete volumes and some impressively sculptural overhead walkways and multistorey car parks. The attached civic centre, designed as an integral part of the complex – showing how much council and developer went hand in hand – has a neat Festival Style clock tower and colonnade. The Queensway Towers, part of the same smash-and-grab redevelopment project, consists of a series of quite nicely detailed brick point blocks, with evocative names: Quantock, Pennine, Malvern, Chiltern. They seem to be constantly threatened with what is euphemistically called 'decanting' by local government, but they stand at the time of writing and look rather fine.

CHELMSFORD INDOOR RETAIL MARKET
1976
Brutalist

Near the collection of mediocre but vaguely impressive civic buildings in this industrial Essex county town is this puzzle: a long covered market sheltered beneath a monumental, concrete-lattice multistorey car park, with some very zippy stairwells, currently painted a dashing red, with the rest still in its béton brut. Aggressive to the exterior and atmospheric in the interior, it could be the **Barnsley Indoor Market (p. 378)**, or somewhere else that did its modernism big and brusque and then shoved medieval village commerce into it.

GOLDINGS HOUSE & GOLDINGS CRESCENT, HATFIELD
Woodroffe Buchanan & Coulter, 1968
People's Detailing

There are various experimental layouts and clever housing schemes in Hatfield due to Lionel Brett, Lord Esher, being its planner (he was later author of *A Broken Wave*, the first serious history of British modern architecture). They can feel quite suburban and wan, but this estate is central, and much more urban and convincing than most. A good Lubetkin-like council tower of brick and tile, with flats projecting out from a central core – recently renovated and looking rather des res – surrounded with much more urban housing than is the norm for a New Town. The Crescent consists of three-storey street-facing tenements with steps, as if to create a Jane Jacobs style 'stoop' for people to casually hang out on. Of course, they don't, but it does set up a snappy rhythm in a town otherwise full of vague greensward and half-designed buildings dissolving into the A1.

ARNDALE CENTRE, LUTON
Tripe & Wakeham Partnership, 1969–77
Brutalist

A miserable place in many respects, but meriting inclusion in this book for two reasons. One, the historical interest of being a rare untouched shopping centre of the high-modernist era, and, two, the sheer scale of it, which makes it grimly fascinating as an example of ordinary megastructural planning. The side facing the town centre and the competent stripped classical Town Hall has been reclad and rebranded as 'The Mall', but the dark heart of the scheme is obvious as you approach from the railway station. Three storeys of car parking, a spiral ramp, topped by a budget Mies tower, and then, deeper in, the shopping centre itself. It is labyrinthine and smelly, and possesses a monumental force that you don't forget easily. This isn't necessarily for architectural reasons as such – though the major Brutalist clichés are used well, with complex external stairways leading up to exposed waffle slab decks – but for the monumental pile-up complexity of the plan. For all its many flaws, the only one of Luton's many post-war buildings to reward exploration; the reward at the end of it is Greenfields, an excellent Swiss chalet-style greasy spoon on the upper level of the shopping centre.

EASYJET HANGARS, LUTON AIRPORT
Yorke Rosenberg & Mardall, 1970
Brutalist

When I was a frequent user of this unpleasant budget airport, I was often diverted by the large orange-painted hangars that you see as your bus pulls in to park by the gross tin shed of the terminal. Imagine my surprise, perusing a monograph on the respected modernist firm Yorke Rosenberg & Mardall, when I found that the place had pedigree. Eight huge steel girders, with a dramatic profile, like some unexecuted Russian Constructivist student project. It is painted bright orange by its current users, EasyJet, which only adds to, rather than detracts from, the pop futurism of the design.

CAMPUS WEST, WELWYN GARDEN CITY
Sheppard Robson, 1973
Brutalist

This building contains all the things that this more commercial Garden City originally lacked – library, art gallery, theatre, leisure centre. 'Planning' was so often, here in New Town Herts, planning for the market. Campus West does what it needs to do well, albeit forty years late: a rectilinear red-brick tower with low-rise wings, just at a slight tangent off the main axial Parkway, so not barging its modernity into that Beaux Arts fantasy, but providing both form and function in order to make Welwyn a much more pleasant 'city' to live in than it would otherwise be. There's even a little hint of El Lissitzky in the way the tower is suspended above the spacey geometries of the rest of the complex – a reservation of modernism and culture in a world made by Waitrose.

STANSTED AIRPORT ✪
Foster Associates, 1988–91
High-Tech

A tragic place. In design terms, Stansted is the only airport in Britain to approach the grandeur of the Victorian railway stations, but it has been beaten about by Ryanair so totally that this is almost obscured, a salient reminder that the cheapness of contemporary air travel has its correspondent in the total despoliation of the environment – the 'built environment' as much as the natural one. Stansted's planning is impeccable, especially compared with the chaos of Gatwick or Heathrow – the terminal, the bus station, the railway station and the car park are all organized with faultless logic, with easy walks between each of them. The terminal itself is Foster at his closest to his old mentor Buckminster Fuller, a geodesic module in a grid, held up on skinny white struts, offering constant natural light, creating an elegance in rippling repetition that compares only with **Preston Bus Station (p. 444)** in twentieth-century British architecture.

This is the exact place where the damage has been done, with the need to extract as much profit as possible from the airport's double existence as a shopping mall leading to artificially extended circulation routes, pointless blingy rookeries, infuriating suspended ceilings, waxy smells and tawdry kitsch. There's a lesson in this. If the best thing a railway station can do – even in new buildings, it seems – is provide a straightforward path from you to train through an airy and proud space full of the sense of arrival and departure, this is considered a problem in airports, where the main requirement, as in a mall, is to keep you wandering and shopping. So Stansted has been deliberately made less clear, less light, less pleasant; the fact that you can still make out these qualities is testament to the quality of its original design. What makes this especially sad is that Stansted excelled, until fairly recently, at something else airports need to do, considering how many people hate the experience of flying – creating a feeling of reliability and calm. That has been almost totally lost, but at least we now have multiple places to buy a large Toblerone. It is also worth noting that photography is not permitted because of 'security concerns'. Hopefully enough of Foster's original building will survive into a less ugly era.

A HOUSE FOR ESSEX, WRABNESS ✪
FAT Architecture and Grayson Perry (artist), 2015
Postmodernist

There are few greater frustrations for the modern architecture enthusiast than the difficulty of seeing – and, even more, exploring – most large private houses. Much-illustrated works by major architects lurk behind high hedges, long driveways and security gates, and are often screened from the street by trees. The charity Living Architecture can be seen as a response to this; it commissions modernist houses, usually by famous designers, that are then made available to the public as holiday rentals – though these are generally pricey. The actual houses are tasteful and sometimes excessively glossy – by far the most interesting is this diminutive house in Wrabness, on the north coast of Essex, the final project by the peculiar social Postmodernists of FAT – most of whom were Essex Boys, and it shows.

FAT's house is a collaboration with the ceramicist and muralist Grayson Perry, who had a strong dislike of the purged, 'good taste' aesthetic of Living Architecture's starchitect-designed holiday homes. This refusenik position with respect to a certain kind of middle-class modernism is here combined with an embrace of the design choices of 'ordinary people' – strange, artificial, often clashing, impurely historical, deeply personal. The site, meanwhile, is a dream. From this house secreted between bushes and trees overlooking the river Stour, you can see the barrack-room baroque of the Royal Hospital School on one side, the sprawling container port of Felixstowe on the other, and, close by, horses, marshes and fields; surprising, discrete views of these are created by the placing of the windows. But everything revolves around an elaborate cosmology, with the House being the home of the imaginary Julie Cope, whose life since the 1950s saw a trajectory leading from the edge-of-London working-class industrial hinterland in Canvey Island, up through the suburban modernism of Basildon, then the neo-traditionalist streets of South Woodham Ferrers, through Colchester and ending up in the village of Wrabness. This story is told obsessively, through almost every corner of the house, in tapestries, murals, maps, a 'tomb' just outside, and Perry's signature vases and ceramics.

But none of this would be interesting if the building itself wasn't up to the task, and here FAT's work is a bizarre triumph. Charles Holland of FAT showed Perry a book of Russian Orthodox stave churches as a model for the House, and he went with the idea – so it is divided roughly into a 'domestic' and 'religious' half, as it slopes down a shallow hill. In the 'temple' side, looking out over the river, the combination of small scale and monumentalism is explicitly sacral. The details are remarkably well-made and obsessive, from the Arts and Crafts green tiles on the facade, bearing images of the Essex coat of arms and a pregnant Julie as pagan idol, to the astonishing interiors. The double-height main hall, a magnificently detailed colour dance of patterned floors, daringly painted woods and tapestries, is dedicated to a religion of class mobility that exists only in Grayson Perry's head – a daring and totally unconvincing fusion of earth mother worship, elemental sexuality and 1970s–1980s minutiae, St Basil's meeting Stanley Spencer meeting *Abigail's Party*. The result is hard to imagine as 'living architecture' so much as a rented weekend in a gigantic three-dimensional artwork. Even the seats in this room, two ornate armchairs and two waiting-room benches, feel monumental and unhomely. This is a holiday villa as a temple, a magnificent miniature polychrome cathedral of social climbing.

A temple to the religion of social mobility: FAT's House for Essex, on the River Stour in Wrabness.

EAST ANGLIA

ROYAL ARCADE, NORWICH
George Skipper, 1899
Art Nouveau

An enormously fun Art Nouveau building, just about passing the 'proto-modernist' test. In plan, the Royal Arcade is a grandiose Victorian iron-and-glass arcade, of the sort you can find in particular abundance in Leeds and Cardiff – a high vaulted passageway, shimmering with light and glitter. But here the designer, a local architect, has obviously encountered the new style on a visit to Paris or Brussels, and has decided to take it home and use it on his new arcade. So, at the main entrance, the glass roof, with its stained-glass forest at the top straight out of Aubrey Beardsley, is flanked by two bulging shop fronts covered in flowing, organic terracotta ornament; the spaces inside are clad in a lavatorial tile and Francophile terrazzo flooring. Perverse, luxurious and piquant, an architecture of opiated decadence – very much not the usual fare in Norfolk.

ST ANDREW'S CHURCH, FELIXSTOWE
Hilda Mason and Raymond Erith, 1928–30
Expressionist

In a genre of one. The otherwise little-known Hilda Mason, Suffolk painter and architect, must have come across Auguste Perret's churches in the Paris suburbs, which continued the values of classical order in a material that the architect believed could especially lend itself to their realization – reinforced concrete (it is a measure of the conservatism of British architecture at the time that even this deliberate compromise between modernity and history was seldom emulated, even though concrete was used frequently – Perret's only real legacy in the UK is in the work of his pupil Ernő Goldfinger). Mason in turn decided to adapt Perret's post-and-beam concrete language to the form of the Suffolk 'wool church', which with its gridded Battenberg patterns would seem to be particularly suited to these mechanized techniques. The church that arose out of this experiment is strange and beautiful, though almost hidden from the suburban street by giant exotic trees. The interior, more clearly Perret-inspired than the outside, is easily seen, as the church is conspicuously friendly – and it is well kept, though there is some spalling concrete to the narthex. The church is co-credited to the classicist Raymond Erith, a cult figure among keepers of the classical faith in the post-war years, but the few accounts there are make clear that Mason was the boss.

NORWICH CITY HALL
Charles Holloway James and Stephen Rowland Pierce, 1931–8
Modern Classicism

Many of the town halls of the interwar years – which were numerous, as public bureaucracy increased in size, despite the Depression – are inspired by two town halls on the Continent. One – the shadow behind **Greenwich Town Hall (p. 84)**, **Salford Civic Centre (p. 412)** and **Hornsey Town Hall (p. 139)** – was Wilhelm Marinus Dudok's mild-modernist Hilversum Town Hall. The other is Stockholm City Hall, a design with clearer roots in the Arts and Crafts and the neo-Gothic but abstracted to a degree that would have alarmed a Victorian. Norwich, like **Swansea Guildhall (p. 286)**, is Stockholm City Hall, except rather than being placed in a commanding position on a Scandinavian archipelago it is

Pared-back classicism at Norwich City Hall, a free interpretation of Ragnar Östberg's Stockholm City Hall.

placed on a plinth above Norwich's market, offering commanding views of castle and cathedral. Like Stockholm it is in red brick with sandstone trim, asymmetrical, a grand portico and a brick-clad tower, with a copper clock and spire, but the scale and the plinth give it a truly monumental presence all of its own. The bulk of it is hard to categorize as modern (though the furnishings in walnut and mahogany, and the sculptures by the likes of Eric Aumomier, are very thirties), but its tower is absolutely of the twentieth century, a streamlined abstract beacon. Best of all, like in Stockholm it works beautifully as part of an already great skyline, worthy of the company of Norwich Castle, the Cathedral, St Peter Mancroft and the like.

SMITHDON SCHOOL, HUNSTANTON ✪
Alison and Peter Smithson, 1951–3
International Style, Brutalist

If ever there was a building whose reputation precedes it, it's this one. Along with the **Economist Plaza (p. 58)**, this is definitely the most successful of the Smithsons' British buildings, and given it was their first, it's no wonder their fame was so immediate. It is much more seen in photographs than visited, but doing so is highly recommended – it stands upon a short hill above a very ordinary, kiss-me-quick seaside town (unwisely exposing its brittle steel structure to North Sea winds), or rather it lies across it, in an extremely long, low-rise frame building, overlooking playing fields, alongside a smaller but more classically arranged sports hall, next to a playground. The school was much vaunted for the way that it was, as Reyner Banham put it, made of steel, brick and glass and *looked like it*, with no attempts to disguise or decorate the structure; but its mastery of proportion, borrowed wholesale from Mies van der Rohe's work at the Illinois Institute of Technology, is worth any amount of People's Detailing. It's not just a Mies imitation, though – they extend its module to an obsessive length, making it feel like part of the interminable flatness of Norfolk, with the school's playing fields extending out into an endless steppe.

Then there are the Brutalist gestures, as they were seen at the time, of separating the services – electrical and water – as strange ready-mades, steel-and-brick towers, standardized objects held at a remove and placed as if they were sculptures in a classical square. Whether all this is appropriate for a school has often been argued over, something encouraged both by the architects' insistence on having it photographed without any children in it, and for functional trouble – some of the glass has had to be replaced with black panels, which

Festival of Britain on the North Sea – the Never Turn Back pub, just outside Great Yarmouth.

of course makes it look even more harshly, unforgivingly modern than it did already. One can make a 'nothing is too good for state school kids' argument for Smithdon School, but unlike a Lubetkin or a Goldfinger or a Stirling building this is not the kind of avant-garde design that is likely to excite the young. The building's qualities are a matter of discipline and austerity rather than sculptural or spatial thrills. Architecturally, though, this plays what Lutyens called 'the high game' with enormous aplomb.

THE NEVER TURN BACK, CAISTER-ON-SEA

A. W. Ecclestone, 1956–7
People's Detailing

Forget all the snobbish myths about 'flat-roofed pubs' and get yourself down to Great Yarmouth. The Never Turn Back – a contender for 'best pub name in Britain'

– is one of three listed modern pubs designed by A. W. Ecclestone for the brewers Lacons in and around Great Yarmouth; the others, the Iron Duke and the Clipper Schooner, are in a quite familiar streamline moderne roadside style, but this is much more personal and original. The design is heraldic and heroic, reflecting the source of its name – the Caister lifeboat disaster in 1901, when eight lifeboatmen died after refusing to turn back from saving others; the phrase became a motto of the RNLI. Sited in the middle of a caravan park, a beer garden with a view of the beach frames a red-brick and glass pavilion. A central tower is inset with panels of East Anglian pebbly aggregate, a flagpole and the legend 'NEVER TURN BACK' in outlined block capitals that look like they're from the opening sequence of a Powell and Pressberger film. Glorious.

IPSWICH CO-OPERATIVE DEPARTMENT STORE EXTENSION
1962
People's Detailing

The Co-operative group have been responsible for some of the best urban architecture in twentieth-century Britain and show shockingly little interest in maintaining or even retaining it – countless times I've gone to find an important Co-op and found a Poundland, or, as here, an entire derelict street block. In the centre of Ipswich there is an ensemble of Edwardian and interwar moderne buildings with the legend of the Ipswich Industrial Co-operative Society Limited – 'Each for All and All for Each'. In the backyard service areas of these department stores, past curious overhead walkways between the buildings of different ages, is a decent sixties extension (and a vast surface car park). Here, above the entrance to the passageway from the car park, you'll find a gorgeous mosaic mural of the Co-op's wares, with a stylized female silhouette sifting through textiles, which fade subtly into swirling abstract shapes. The name of the muralist doesn't seem to have been recorded, although the Twentieth Century Society speculate it may have been John Piper.

Concrete ziggurat: one of the terraced, pyramidal halls of residence at the University of East Anglia.

UNIVERSITY OF EAST ANGLIA, NORWICH ○
Denys Lasdun & Partners, 1963–8
Brutalist

An unforgettable dream landscape, a bus ride away from the centre of Norwich – from Alan Partridge to *Solaris* for £1.50. Of all the New Universities, this is the peak, with everything being formed into rigorous, multilevel, three-dimensional metropolitan sculpture by Lasdun's sense of massive form and of the Piranesian multidirectional perspective. The bus drops you in the main square, where monumental steps lead down to the shops, the pub and other useful student functions; the buildings around here are huge, but regular and unspectacular. Then you get on to the walkways, which take you past the library, around snaking ribbon-windowed teaching blocks on one side, and compacted, eruptive lecture theatres on the other, until the steps lead down into a meadow, and a view of the halls of residence. These four concrete pyramids, changing shape with every inch you walk around them, with terraces at every level, look out over a stream. Rabbits dart about. Here it is, finally, the modernist Garden City, owing absolutely nothing to any previous model of settlement, a walkway mini-metropolis totally integrated with controlled nature, with no streets, no houses, no reminiscences – an alternative world of enormous power and haunting beauty, achieved just in this poignant fenland fragment.

NORWICH CITY CENTRE COUNCIL HOUSING: ✪ HEATHGATE ESTATE

David Percival for Norwich City Architects Dept, 1965

NELSON BARRACKS ESTATE & CAMP GROVE

David Percival for Norwich City Architects Dept, 1970

ST LEONARDS PLACE & LADBROOKE PLACE

Tayler & Green, 1973
Brutalist, Postmodernist

Norwich keeps its post-war council housing well hidden, but it is the most imaginative and attractive in Britain outside of London and Sheffield. The reason why this isn't better known is that, aside from one or two dull tower blocks, the estates lurk behind the retaining walls of barracks, round the back of cathedrals, in alleyways behind Victorian terraces, and are seldom tall, though they are often dense; I found out about them through John Boughton's inestimable blog *Municipal Dreams*, not through my own explorations. Obviously, I prefer the model where a city is proud of its council housing to the extent that it shouts it on the hilltops; but it would be churlish not to praise the sheer quality and, at times, even luxury of the places Norwich City Council built for its tenants in the late sixties and early seventies under the City Architect, David Percival (who, tellingly, was hired from the heroic Coventry Architects Department, who reconstructed that city). This cluster of closely grouped estates runs the gamut from heroic Brutalism to pioneering Postmodernism.

Treating them in chronological order – which is roughly the opposite order to the sequence in which they appear if you're walking to them from the railway station – we begin with the Heathgate Estate, the most straightforward 'sixties municipal' in appearance, a sort of soft Brutalism. On a hilltop site behind the pebbly retaining wall

of a former barracks, it consists of mid-rise blocks connected by overhead concrete walkways, arcing around flowing green public spaces, some of which are outright idyllic in summer, with mature trees and views over the city. The massive interlinked buildings were compared at the time to **Park Hill (p. 370)**. From it, you can see the spires of the historic city – probably the best view of it on offer, in fact – but the historic city can't see you. In any case, the estate is in good nick, with walkways and the strongly emphasized balconies currently painted an appropriate shade of yellowy cream.

A few years later, the Heathgate Estate was supplemented by something more original – the Nelson Barracks Estate, where much smaller houses and maisonettes in yellow and red brick, with wooden frames, are connected by an intricate network of pedestrian pathways. Architecturally, this is a shift towards Postmodernism, or what was called in the 1970s, 'vernacular' – more decorative brickwork, more pitched roofs – but without the tweeness or the 'in keeping' cowardice that this would soon come to mean. The defining feature is the public spaces, which are small and self-contained, marked by low, snaking walls and curved hillocks. These little squares are a reaction against the heroic open space of the earlier estate and places like it, but they're still a pleasure to walk through, with none of the 'KEEP OUT' paranoia that would dominate social housing in the eighties.

The same brickwork, and the same picturesque planning, was used at the positively bucolic Camp Grove estate, on a hilltop site ten minutes away. Here, two large high-density estates are squeezed into what is essentially leftover space in the alleyways between Victorian speculative terraces, but there is so much planting that it doesn't feel at all cramped or mean. Several different house and flat types are set in the flowing space, and you never know quite what lies round the next corner, which you frequently reach through grand archways, like a cross between Hampstead Garden Suburb and Red Vienna; cobbles and more snaking walls gently define what you are and aren't meant to walk on. After a while, if you're coming from the direction of the railway station, you reach Ladbrooke Place, and the architecture shifts into another gear. David Percival's buildings became increasingly traditional in the seventies, but there's still a Miesian clip to the proportions and materials. Yet what you now see in front of you could be in Portmeirion – several terraces of pitched-roofed townhouses, each dressed in one of sixteen different decorative facing materials, from diapered brick to pebbles to ragstone to tiles to weatherboard, with stylized pop-Georgian windows – ordinary East Anglian housing through the looking glass. As John Boughton points out, this feat of intricate decoration was achieved by Norwich Council's direct-labour organization, to the designs not of Percival's team, but the private firm Tayler & Green.

This is the only estate in Norwich by the architects Tayler & Green, who developed this abstract yet decorative manner in the rural Norfolk Loddon District Council. Fellow fans of taxonomy take note – it's to describe their work that Nikolaus Pevsner coined the term 'Postmodernism'. This is not traditional architecture, the neo-Georgian that was still limping on in the sixties before Margaret Thatcher gave it a new lease of life – it's too stylized, abstract and knowing for that, with the materials pulled out of context, as if in a photomontage. It is also far too concerned with facades and patterns to be modern architecture as it's usually conceived – it deserved a new term. Yet while a lot of British Postmodernism can be smug and overbearing, someone telling you the same joke repeatedly, here in Norwich its pioneers created buildings that are both knowing and full of uncomplicated joy. [C.7]

FEILDEN & MAWSON, NORWICH
Feilden & Mawson, 1968
International Style

The only architects' office in this book is that of the Norwich firm Feilden & Mawson, who are otherwise in this book only through **Chesterfield Library (p. 362)**, but somehow had the wherewithal in the sixties to build their own headquarters, on a pleasant riverside site near Norwich Station, between two big Victorian houses. It is set back between these two, on a hill behind a car park; the hierarchical, stepped arrangement of its two purple brick-and-steel volumes and its monumental service tower give it the slightly dynastic air of Denys Lasdun's work, or especially, **St Cross Libraries (p. 228)** in Oxford; but the scale is similar to the houses adjacent, a horizontal bridge between their Gothic spikiness. Well deserving of the 1969 Civic Trust Award still attached to it, though the big metal door blocking off the back entrance is perhaps less civic. It remains Feilden & Mawson's head office to this day.

WILLIS BUILDING, IPSWICH ✪
Foster Associates, 1970–75
High-Tech

Foster's first large-scale building – a seemingly straightforward commission, an office block for an insurance company in a very ordinary town – is still thrilling. It is one of those great modern buildings that are much more discussed and illustrated than visited, but it is not one of those where a visit will disappoint. Like so many early monuments of High-Tech architecture, it is also deeply sinister and disconcerting. Because of the Willis Building's mundane surroundings, you can still get more than a sense of how alien it must have been at the time. In the 1970s, if you were going to build an office block on a roundabout in Ipswich, it was likely to be either bricky

The imposing, sinuous mirrorglass wall of Norman Foster's early Willis Building in the centre of Ipswich.

early Postmodernism or late corporate modernism, heavy, ponderous, slow-witted architecture. And then, in amongst that tat, here comes this snaking edifice, sleek, black, blank and gorgeously expensive, with its panels of black glass clipped together with visible metal joists, boasting the sort of achingly precise and anal detailing that British modernist design has usually lacked. Approached from the railway station, it still maintains that shock, a single sinuous motion, with the greenery of the rooftop garden a surrealist apparition. From the town centre, a clutch of Victorian buildings are reflected in its opaque glass. This is the sort of thing that more simple-minded critics at the time thought made the building 'contextual' or friendly to what is around it.

It's nothing of the sort. As Simon Jenkins says, 'Foster's early buildings are like repelling magnets.' While that is clearly not meant as a compliment, it captures something of the alarming presence of this baffling, opaque thing, beamed down from another planet (or, at least, from somewhere other than Ipswich) and occupying its massive site with no relief or interruption, no ground floor shops or office workers to peer in at – just a slithering monolith. Inside – and you can go through the revolving doors without being harassed, as the security guards seem to expect it – the tasteful black is exchanged for a multistorey lime green space-frame atrium, with escalators ascending level by level – much more like the pop art spaces of a designer such as Verner Panton than the beige corporate world we know today, and that later Foster buildings helped create. At night, this strict divide between the post-punk facade and the disco interior disappears, as the building is illuminated from inside, and the glass ceases to be opaque, and the structure becomes visible as pure light.

Two revolutions: the Sainsbury Centre and, left, a model of Vladimir Tatlin's Monument to the Third International.

SAINSBURY CENTRE, UNIVERSITY OF EAST ANGLIA, NORWICH ✪

Foster Associates, 1978/
Anthony Hunt Associates, 1991
High-Tech

One of Foster's first internationally celebrated buildings; still, thousands of projects and millions in profits later, one of their best. It is linked by a walkway from the central spine of the first buildings of the **University of East Anglia (p. 198)**, and though you're still in Lasdun's multilevel mini-city, all the ruggedness, those raw tactile surfaces you're meant to run your fingers along, these have all gone in favour of freeze-dried materials, perfect form, an airport as an art gallery, or possibly vice versa. The walkway drops you into a hangar, its open space suspended via roof trusses that allow for the immense glass wall below; the metal panels and neoprene gaskets give

it the sense of a laboratory for the study (rather than a temple for the contemplation) of a superb art collection assembled by the supermarket magnate. It all looks out at the arcadian landscape around Lasdun's residential ziggurats, and below is an equally scientistic extension by Anthony Hunt, built right into the hill. Our Silicon Valley, only public; and if you want at least a sense of what poor old **Stansted Airport (p. 192)** looked like before Ryanair had at it, it's the nearest equivalent.

CAMBRIDGE

UNIVERSITY LIBRARY
Giles Gilbert Scott, 1931–4
Expressionist

What Gilbert Scott's University Library does
with classicism is amusingly identical to what
his contemporary **William Booth Training
College (p. 79)** in Camberwell did with
Gothic, and their fundamental similarity is
a good indication that what he was really up
to owed very little to conventional revivalism.
The University Library is a symmetrical
composition of reading rooms with
high ceilings, faced in brick, with strips of
American skyscraper-style vertical windows;
the book stacks are in a thick, muscular
tower, very like the one in Camberwell, and
with the same sense of mountainous mass.
The pediment between the tower and the
entrance is as superfluous as the Gothic
fol-de-rol in the William Booth College;
a meaningless gesture towards rhetorical
rather than contextual continuity, of the sort
Scott would eliminate at **Battersea Power
Station (p. 108)** and Bankside (now
Tate Modern, p. 102). This is not a classical
building, just as the Camberwell college
is not a Gothic one – both are modern
buildings, taking more from German
Expressionism and New York skyscrapers,
and the allusions are merely tacked on.
It is also worth noting how successful both
are when compared with Scott's library
buildings in Oxford, where the shift of the
material to sandstone and the alignment
from vertical to horizontal leads to a
straightforward fudge between classical
and modern. Here, however, the residual
traditionalisms are irrelevant to the raw
power of the mass and silhouette.

IMPINGTON VILLAGE COLLEGE ✪
Walter Gropius and Maxwell Fry, 1938
International Style

Impington is one of those outposts of the
'Silicon Fen' that spreads around Cambridge,
where thatched cottages and mirrorglass
office blocks intermingle, linked by a strange
'guided bus' system, where ordinary buses
move along repurposed train tracks. In one
of its villages you can find the largest and
by far the best of the three British buildings
by one of the twentieth century's most
important architects, designed barely a
decade after the amazing mission statements
of his Bauhaus buildings in Dessau. The
others, the heavily altered **66 Old Church
Street (p. 160)** and a hard-to-visit wooden
house in Shipborne, Kent, are not major
works – this is. However, Pevsner's belief
that it was the best building in Britain built
between the wars suggests the size of
Gropius's personality cult at the time.

This multifunctional school, FE college
and community centre is still an excellent
little building, from its perfectly considered
glass-and-brick bay-windowed wings,
sheltered by low trees, to the grand
curved entrance hall, which presages the
quiet, Anglicized yet subtly monumental
modernism that would emerge after the
war with the Festival Hall, and the humane
progressivism of the Hertfordshire schools.
If this is the 'International Style', it's adapted
to English tastes, English timidity, English
climate and English materials, and it's none
the worse for it, retaining some of the rigour
and freshness that must have been striking
in the musty Oxbridge architectural scene
of the thirties. It lacks the crackling shock
and excitement that Gropius's buildings had
in 1920s Germany; perhaps an adaptation
to the way that his much harder proposals
for central Cambridge had been rejected

Impington Village College, the largest British work by Walter Gropius, one of the masters of the modern movement.

out of hand. Post-war Cambridge modernism, with its yellow brick, lush landscaping and low skylines, begins right here, and has never gone away since.

––––

REGIONAL SEAT OF GOVERNMENT
Ministry of Defence, 1952
Brutalist, Industrial

The sort of building that is meant to be secret – a mean little bunker, into which the local bureaucracy were meant to escape in the event of nuclear war, and from which they would apparently continue to manage the east of England (fans of *Threads* will recall what happens to one of these when the air is blocked off) – but which development has made public. It's a fittingly menacing design, a lurking, angular construction with more than an anachronistic hint of the yet-to-be-declared New Brutalism in its modelling. There are many of these

in hard to get to locations across the country, some now listed – this one is in this book both for its unusual three-dimensionality and for its accessible location on one of the streets of **Accordia (p. 211)**.

––––

CHURCHILL COLLEGE
Sheppard Robson, 1960–68
Brutalist

At this new college just on the outskirts of the city, Richard Sheppard accidentally invented the variety of Brutalism that would become most popular everywhere around Britain – a robust, slightly dour amalgam of engineering brick, thick concrete frames, square, blunt profiles and flowing public routes under and through buildings, with attractive green space in-between. The spaces of the common rooms contain a memorably austere grandeur, there is some reasonably decent art in the grounds, and there are two notable additions – the Margaret Thatcher Archive, in the same style as the original campus, and the more recent and very different **Cowan Court (p. 211)**. The main buildings are a little banal, but charmingly so – there are a lot of housing estates designed with exactly the same materials and standards as this place that are falling apart thanks to the politician whose archive it holds.

MURRAY EDWARDS COLLEGE
Chamberlin Powell & Bon, 1962–6
Brutalist

A strange and ceremonial design for a women's college by one of the most interesting firms of mid-century Britain. I have always found Murray Edwards College (originally New Hall) rather puzzling and perturbing compared with their triumphs like the **Barbican (p. 66)** and the **University of Leeds South Campus (p. 381)** – here they seem to have let their imaginations run away with them somewhat. Like most modernist Oxbridge colleges it continues the old system of quadrangles and courtyards, here with low-rise fair-faced concrete blocks in a grid around a library and a meeting hall. The library has a curved roof and a dramatic, double-height reading room, but it is the domed hall around which everything revolves. This is a bizarre and powerful design. Outside, a quasi-Mughal dome is held up with rather phallic columns, which are themselves domed. Unlike at the library, the spacious interior lapses a little into Orientalist kitsch, with the almost Postmodernist detailing of its dome. A fascinating experiment in any case, with a peculiar, ghostly, hieratic quality – Samarkand gone Brutalist, Kubla Khan meets Louis Kahn.

WILLIAM STONE BUILDING, PETERHOUSE
Colin St John Wilson and Leslie Martin, 1963
Brutalist

The only high-rise in an Oxbridge college, and almost completely hidden. The William Stone Building is also the most interesting of Leslie Martin and his associates' attempts to create a laconic, sober modernism out of Cambridge materials – here brick, copper, treated wood, with a big green quadrangle around it. The staggered plan, allowing lots of light into each dormitory, has a lot of Aalto in it, but there's not much Finnish romanticism here – this is modernism with a stiff upper lip and a comfortable, well-tailored suit. Perhaps experiences of these kinds of mock-austere places are what spurred John Outram into the astonishing nervous breakdown of the **Judge Institute (p. 210)** nearby – but taken just as a block of high-rise flats, no baggage, this is very fine.

A residential tower block for the educational elite: William Stone Building at Peterhouse College.

The wild vegetation and furious Brutalism of Denys Lasdun's New Court has not always been popular in Cambridge.

CORPUS CHRISTI COLLEGE, LECKHAMPTON

Philip Dowson for Arup Associates, 1963–4
Brutalist

The earliest of Arup Associates' various experiments in Gothic concrete exoskeletons in Oxbridge colleges, this one combined with imposing minimalist brick towers, in an idiom borrowed from Louis Kahn's work for the Ivy League in the US. Harsh, spiky, and rather incongruous with the well-manicured lawns around it – even by local standards it feels far too clean and precise, for all its excellent qualities. Among Cambridge modernist buildings it feels like it really needs some of the mildew, picturesque ruination, UPVC and noise that a prolonged and negligent period of local-authority ownership would furnish.

NEW COURT, CHRIST'S COLLEGE ✪

Denys Lasdun & Partners, 1966–70
Brutalist

Finding this building as a pedestrian involves a harsh lesson in Cambridge's classed topography. You must enter (only in daylight, mark you) through a Gothic gatehouse, to find yourself skirting a well-trimmed lawn, then pass through another court – like everywhere in Cambridge, a mix of genuine historic buildings and various kinds of fakery and sepia repro, and there are books that can tell you which is which, but not this one – then through another, and then, eventually, you get to this. By now you will almost certainly have had to plead with a porter, in a porter's lodge, and they have every right to throw you out, in this ridiculous city where two thirds of the important buildings are in quadrangles behind highly policed gates. Lasdun's building is at the end of the sequence, and is a much more wiry, hungry-looking approach to the concrete ziggurat genre than his work at the **University of East Anglia (p. 198)**, its cubic dorms emerging tier by tier from within all the ivy and honeyed stone, scooping you up into a platform from which you can survey them. If they'll let you.

'SIDGWICK SITE':
HARVEY COURT
Patrick Hodgkinson and Leslie Martin, 1962
ARTS FACULTY BUILDINGS
Casson Conder & Partners, 1958–64
HISTORY FACULTY
James Stirling, 1964–8
LAW FACULTY
Foster Associates, 1995
DIVINITY FACULTY
Edward Cullinan Architects, 2000
FACULTY OF ENGLISH
Allies & Morrison, 2004
Classical Modernism, International Style,
Brutalist, High-Tech, Ecomodernist

One of the most infuriating things about modern architecture is its disavowed flightiness with regard to fads, particularly when it comes to condemning the people who live in the results of last year's fashion. Sometimes, however, these sharp shifts can lead to fantastic tensions and aggressions, fights at which it can be invigorating to spectate. This is very much the case with the extraordinary architectural grudge match on display at the relatively open 'Sidgwick Site' of the University of Cambridge – along with the library, pretty much the only twentieth-century university space you can walk around extensively as a pedestrian without some wanker demanding your credentials for being there; you can put this to the test by trying to get into Harvey Court, an austere and serious 'low-rise high-density' scheme of colonnades and ceremonial steps by Patrick Hodgkinson and Leslie Martin.

This is one of the major projects of the 'Cambridge School' of modern architecture, a low-key brick modernism more concerned with the creation of formal, civic spaces than spatial thrills. Yet it doesn't feel quite so civic when the porter chucks you out of it. The first part of the Sidgwick Site itself is the Raised Faculty complex for arts departments by Hugh Casson and Neville Conder, the first serious modernist buildings in the city of Cambridge; these are strong, rigorous and perhaps slightly forelock-tugging in their continuation of the quadrangular tradition.

Then, motivated by a baffling animus against these unobjectionable buildings, James Stirling decided to, in his own words, 'fuck Casson' by erecting a much more monumental, symmetrical version of his **Engineering Building (p. 348)** at the University of Leicester, a red-brick and tile-clad piece of proto-High-Tech, with complicatedly engineered (and functionally deficient) glazing in its atrium-like reading room. While Casson's buildings are modest and defined by their semi-public circulation, the History Faculty is a complete whole, a monument, a 'work of art' with complete confidence in its own genius. Like many Stirling buildings, a lot smaller in person, as if it was designed for the magazines, not for the human body. Then, after decades of disgrace and various plans to demolish, it was joined by a huge glazed building with similar overheating problems but with a much smoother, more finished and seamless appearance, by Foster; then Allies & Morrison went back to Casson's sobriety, as if that wasn't locking the stable door after the horse had bolted, in a dull, thin building that lacks the integrity of either the Raised Faculty complex or Harvey Court. The largest recent addition, Cullinan's Divinity Faculty, tries to pull it all together through a complex, fiddly but generous sweep of rotundas and welcoming curved wings, which is a much better idea than trying to put Humpty Dumpty back together again. **[B.29, D.27]**

CLARE HALL
Ralph Erskine, 1966–9
People's Detailing

The first time I tried to visit this place with a friend we were thrown out because 'this is a family college!' – so beware the porter's lodge. Once you're inside, it is ironically one of the most open and friendly *in design terms* of the Cambridge modernist colleges. Of the various Erskine buildings in Britain, it's the closest to the **Byker Estate (p. 484)** in its intimate detail, in its stained wood balconies and walkways, and in the way it has as much fun as it can with the site's topography, creating alleys, tunnels and raised plazas on the way to a green quadrangle in front of a suburban house that it subsumes into the college. A world within a world, as Cambridge colleges usually are – but here it's a world that you might actually want to live in rather than just visit, with a casual looseness that is very un-Cambridge.

KETTLE'S YARD
Leslie Martin, 1970
International Style

The ultimate instance of British modernism's insistence on both having and eating its cake. Kettle's Yard is built around the house of H. S. ('Jim') Ede, otherwise best known for *Savage Messiah*, his biography of the Vorticist sculptor Henri Gaudier-Brzeska, but the original house could not be cuter or more English. A short walk out of the town centre, what we have here is based upon a huddle of cottages, separated asymmetrically by two hilly little village greens from a rustic church – a model of the English picturesque, with the cottages' bow windows, gables and worn, crumbly, biscuity-yellow brickwork. Part of Jim and Helen Ede's impressive art collection is in these, with a Miró here, an Alfred Wallis there, and plenty of artfully arranged pebbles and shells. Yet its first-floor rooms

A miniature Scandinavia: the manicured lawns, sloping roofs and wooden details of Ralph Erskine's Clare Hall.

lead into a purpose-built extension which is an impeccable example of Cambridge School modernist architecture, designed by Leslie Martin for the unusual dual purpose of displaying the Edes' collection and as a space for them to live and work in. So Gaudier-Brzeska sculptures sit on bedside tables, and Ben Nicholson paintings are just 'there', casually among the bookshelves and the heirlooms. The spatial ingenuity of Martin's extension, with its constant shifting of downward and upward views, its mock-povera brick paving, its subtle rooflighting, and its melding together of Mies and Enid Blyton in the entrance pavilion, points the way to things like the **British Library (p. 143)** and **Pallant House Gallery (p. 242)** – mature, middle-class English modernism. There is something a little trying about Kettle's Yard; the special rope doorbell you have to ring in order to get in is only the start of it. Yet, as there are so few easily visited mid-century modern houses of such distinctiveness it would be inverted snobbery to dismiss it. Jamie Fobert's recent extension is generic, if unintrusive – big concrete rooms and 'New London Vernacular' elevations. The same architect's work for the same demographic at **Tate St Ives (p. 278)** is less conservative.

RUSSELL COURT
Peter Frost for Cambridge City Council Architects Dept, 1974
People's Detailing

One virtue that Cambridge has over Oxford is the fact that there has been some – minor, but some – overlap between the architecture of the colleges and the architecture for the rest of us, whereas the gulf there between the buildings by Arup, Stirling, Martin, Jacobsen and others and the identikit West Midlands-style council suburbia of Blackbird Leys is immense and disturbing. This is one of the most interesting of the decent little estates between the city centre and the railway station. Low-rise, high-density in the vein of **Cressingham Gardens (p. 113)** or **Lillington Gardens (p. 57)**, in the local yellow stock brick, intuitively reached from the biscuity terraces around, and on a similar scale. At its centre is a little slice of Stockholm, with tables and chairs, cobbles and small blocks of flats bunched around trees. It plays similar modern/vernacular, inside/outside games to something like **Harvey Court (p. 207)**, only you're not treated like a potential criminal if you go anywhere near it.

ROBINSON COLLEGE ✪
Andy MacMillan and Isi Metzstein for Gillespie Kidd & Coia, 1977–81
Brutalist, Postmodernist

Designed by Isi Metzstein and Andy MacMillan on one of their forays beyond Clydeside, Robinson is my favourite of the Oxbridge modernist campuses, warmer than **Murray Edwards College (p. 205)** or St Catherine's **(p. 228)** in Oxford, and much more stylish than **Churchill College (p. 204)**. It is a complete unit, a total monastic community in the city's inner suburbs, hewn as if from one mass of red brick. It doesn't look like much from the outside – evidently, it isn't supposed to, and it is almost hidden from public view by trees (perhaps this is why in my experience it has one of the most relaxed porter's lodges – they assume you're there for a reason, not because you're a tourist getting lost, a courtesy you don't receive at Ralph Erskine's much more architecturally open **Clare Hall, p. 208**, adjacent). Once you're inside, a pedestrian path on the ground and an upper-level walkway above twist their way through combined teaching and residential units. The chapel is the only note of individuality in this singular mass, perhaps unsurprisingly given that you're essentially in a cloister; the brick is pulled back like a curtain, and an immense stained-

Insurgent Postmodernism: the decorative yet beefy aggression of the Judge Institute, a monument in 'Blitzcrete'.

glass window by John Piper is uncovered. The reveals around the doors have a 'traditional' feel without being 'Gothic' or 'classical'; like all the details, they feel more part of an unexpected reconciliation between the Postmodernist and the Brutalist. Robinson tries, fairly successfully, to look like it has been there for centuries while using many of the most advanced spatial, multidimensional planning ideas of the mid-twentieth century. This is also one of Britain's great *promenades architecturales*, a walk above or below bringing about a constantly shifting craggy skyline, a surprise round every corner.

JUDGE INSTITUTE ✪
John Outram, 1992–5
Postmodernist

A ridiculous and exhilarating ride, Thatcherite sci-fi, and the most gleefully tasteless building in Cambridge. The Judge Institute is an aggressive remodelling of a minor Victorian building on the bleak road from the railway station to the historic centre, which Outram has added to with peculiar power station-like blast doors and new wings in a style both muscular and cartoonish – already a major break with the mild-mannered world of Cambridge modernism. But this can't prepare you for what you'll find inside. This isn't so much a competing aesthetic as another planet entirely, a terrifying multistorey Willy Wonka world of Piranesian staircases, giant columns in what the architect called 'Blitzcrete' and 'Doodlecrete', polychrome and neoclassical gob-ons, and complex, Expressionistic spatial effects. There is very little Postmodernism in this book, but there would have been much more if it was as fearless and excitable as this.

CENTRE FOR MATHEMATICAL SCIENCES
Edward Cullinan Architects, 2001–3
Ecomodernist, High-Tech

This quiet yet busy expanse, like an eco version of an Ideal Renaissance city spliced together with a 1960s pedway scheme, is an unusually complete and integral complex in the recent architectural history of Cambridge. A series of discrete, pyramidal blocks, dressed in brick and with various cowls and attachments to regulate their climate, revolve around a partially buried central rotunda, with a thick green roof. It is all a little eerie, with a lack of anything much else around it to stop it feeling like a laboratorial enclave, but its spatial imagination is impressive – rich, multilayered and complicated. It is a good potential set for a dystopian future in which everywhere but the likes of Cambridge and Palo Alto has subsided into chaos but an elite still lives 'rationally' in collegiate little communities of sensible people.

___

ACCORDIA
Feilden Clegg Bradley Studios, Alison Brooks Architects and Maccreanor Lavington, 2002–7
Classical Modernism

It wasn't apparent when this place was built that it would become the most influential housing estate on the residential architecture of the 2000s, introducing a tweedy brick austerity and a new aesthetic of the planned and rational that would supplant the attention-seeking barcode facades and wavy roofs of the Tony Blair era. As is so often the case, the original is much better than its imitators. This is largely because the three distinct but linked parts of this luxury private estate have the space to set up urban rhythms of repetition and regularity (the oft-photographed enfilades of 'chimneys'),

without the sense of overdevelopment that afflicts otherwise akin schemes like '**King's Cross Central' (p. 154)**. Its small scale and faint eccentricity (especially where it meets the **Regional Seat of Government, p. 204**) creates a more relaxed, pleasant effect than the uniform brick blocks that would come after, especially the miserable efforts around Cambridge Station.

___

COWAN COURT, CHURCHILL COLLEGE
6A Architects, 2016
Modern Classicism

At the corner of the luxury council estate that is **Churchill College (p. 204)** is this extremely expensive hall of residence. Low-rise and classically disciplined, it is also materially outré (clad in modular planks of wood, purportedly salvaged from shipwrecks) and spatially imaginative, with a strange grassy interior courtyard, access decks and an ingenious gridded concrete interior stairwell. This is very much the state of the art in current English residential architecture. Cowan Court has a certain coldness, and the critical excitement about it seems excessive – but this is high-quality, witty and scholarly modern architecture, and a much better model for new university buildings than the giant atria foisted upon them elsewhere – before we even begin to talk about the state of student housing.

3. SOUTH-EAST

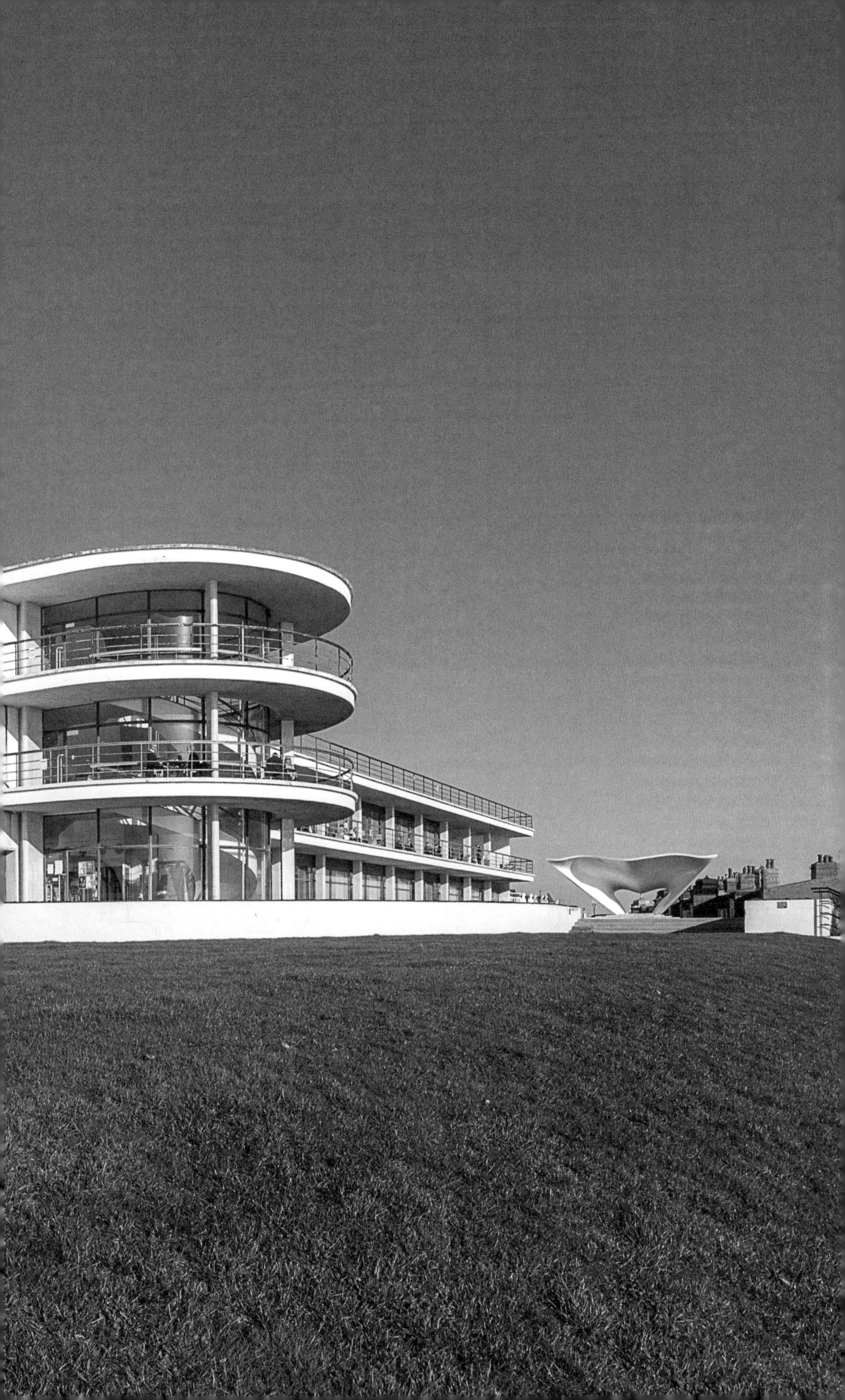

The South-East, the most affluent part of the country, is full of good modern buildings but in a much more scattered fashion than in Eastern England or conurbations such as West Yorkshire. The most continuous stretch of interesting work is found along the South Coast, all the way from Margate down to Chichester, where wealth, sun, sea, sand and stucco proved good spurs to the International Style. It is here, for instance, that you can find Erich Mendelsohn and Serge Chermayeff's astonishing **De La Warr Pavilion** in Bexhill-on-Sea, arguably the greatest English building of the interwar years, along with many other examples of seaside modernism.

The southern reaches of the London commuter belt are good for office blocks, which moved here en masse from the sixties onwards to escape London property prices – towns like Basingstoke resemble pieces of Düsseldorf and Dallas dropped on the edge of suburban housing estates. There are also three New Towns – Crawley, Bracknell and the largest and most successful of them, Milton Keynes, whose **Shopping Building** and **Station** are great achievements. Oxford's modern architecture is not as original as that of Cambridge, but it is often on a larger scale, particularly at Arne Jacobsen's impeccable **St Catherine's College**. Enthusiasts for Brutalism will find the most to enjoy in the Solent sprawl of the Southampton–Portsmouth conurbation, which boasts raw, avant-garde work such as **Wyndham Court** and **Norrish Library**, offset by the soft Scandinavian buildings of Hampshire County Council.

COMMUTER BELT SOUTH

HIGH AND OVER HOUSE & SUN HOUSES, AMERSHAM
Connell Ward & Lucas, 1929–33
International Style, Moderne

High and Over is often classed as a 'first' – the earliest International Style, proper continental modernist house in the London commuter belt – even though it is preceded by Peter Behrens's **New Ways (p. 345)**, and by the houses at **Silver End (p. 175)**. In reality, it was a first for a 1930s micro-genre – the luxurious white-walled modernist house for an intellectual who has bought a plot on the outskirts of London (and, at Zone 9, it doesn't get more outskirts than this). But what the client, the archaeologist Bernard Ashmole, got here from the New Zealand architect Amyas Connell is not so much Central European as Californian, a sprawling Hollywood villa, a commanding lair on a hilltop site overlooking the Chilterns – though the drama is lessened a little by the mainstream sixties developers' housing around. The house is on a Y-shaped plan, with the main entrance gate looking towards an even now rather futuristic cubist glass stairwell. It still looks like a film set, and although it has all the 'International Style' components such as white render, concrete, plate glass and a roof garden, one feels it would be basically the same house if done up in Spanish revival style. Harder modernism came a few years later, in the immediately subsequent Sun Houses, at the bottom of the hill – you come to these four villas first, if approaching from Amersham Tube station. Here, working with fellow Kiwi Basil Ward and the British Colin Lucas, Connell hits his stride. White walls and straight lines again, but everything about the houses is taut and sharp, set at angles to the slope. They mark the shift from Jeeves and Wooster to Fritz Lang, something that

has been lamented by admirers of High and Over. This is not an opinion I share.

———

SUNNYMEAD FLATS, CRAWLEY
Alwyn Sheppard Fidler for Crawley Development Corporation, 1949–54
THE TWITTEN, CRAWLEY
J. M. Austin-Smith & Partners, 1959–60
People's Detailing

West Green is the first of Crawley New Town's neighbourhoods, built right up against the centre, though lamentably, as so often in New Towns, cut off from it by a deadzone of fences, roundabouts, retail parks and shitty new flats. It's also, as Ian Nairn pointed out at the time, one of the most lively, coherent New Town districts, without the vagueness that takes over so many of them. Much of it is just good Anglo-Scando terraces and semis with green space, in relatively compact layouts, but these two schemes are above that standard. The Sunnymead Flats are a series of three-cornered low-rise blocks, in a rangy yet civic enclave of tree-filled parkland. Their splayed balconies and cream- and pink-painted elevations are exceptionally Instagrammable, at least so long as that Wes Anderson look remains in vogue.

A sharper, less Garden City aesthetic can be found at The Twitten, irrespective of its twee name – an estate of sheltered housing for the elderly, which is closer to something like Eric Lyons's private estates such as **Hallgate (p. 87)** in Blackheath in its clarity. You can understand this immediately looking at the groovily designed estate map – a cruciform plan, with the bungalows and houses given strong definition by dark-purple weatherboarding and tough brick gable ends, and a pedestrian path cut under and through the houses – a kind of

Bauhaus picturesque. The firm that designed it was set up by the German-Jewish émigrée Inette Griesmann with her husband, John Michael Austin-Smith; today they're a major and somewhat dull corporate firm, but this – like the similarly intriguing early work of PRP for the **Cockaigne Housing Group (p. 189)** – is a reminder of how even the most generic British modernism often derives from a very interesting place.

―――

QUEENSWAY, QUEEN SQUARE & THE BROADWALK, CRAWLEY
Alwyn Sheppard Fidler, Gaby Schreiber and others for Crawley Development Corporation, 1954–60
People's Detailing

Few of the individual buildings here stand out in their own right, but as an exemplar of fitting a New Town into an older one, this is excellent work. First of all, Queensway, a typical street of its time, mild-modernism where the aesthetic bet-hedging goes alongside lovely Mondrianish mosaic details on the pilotis, leads to Queen Square, and what was once a dashing all-glass department store designed by Gaby Schreiber (now a rather shabby Decathlon, but still a crisp design); a picturesque pathway beneath weatherboarded flats leads to the Broadwalk, where the cute pitched-roofed Anglo-modernist blocks reach a curved shop (sadly, a bookie's) to turn into the Georgian and neo-Georgian, Tudor and neo-Tudor, of the town's original high street. The quiet churchyard nearby is also quite the survival in a New Town centre. The overall effect is very like Coventry in microcosm; in the 1960s, Ian Nairn criticized Crawley for not having Coventry's bustling activity, but it has it now – one of the few New Towns that has grown up to be a real town. While here, note that the Crawley Museum, a modernist glass-entrance pavilion built on to a wooden-framed rustic house, has original models of

1950s housing estates and commemorations both of the visits of the Queen and of the formation of The Cure.

―――

BUCKINGHAMSHIRE COUNTY HALL, AYLESBURY
Fred Pooley for Buckinghamshire County Council Architects Dept, 1964–6
Brutalist

Bucks, under its head planner-architect, Fred Pooley, was one of the driving forces behind Milton Keynes; historians have pointed to it as an unusually progressive county in the Tory shires. This edifice testifies to the county's power, and was known locally as 'Fred's Folly'. It's certainly confident – twice as high as anything else in the town, with a symmetrical rhythm of cuboid bay windows and a rugged roofline, towering over what is otherwise a quiet and pleasant commuter town. What marks it out is the extreme conviction of the design – conceived clearly as a castle, a *Stadtkrone*, it puts great effort into creating both a dramatic silhouette and a sense of power and presence on the ground. This is a monument, meant to inspire and endure. And it does – the concrete is in remarkably good condition, and it is clearly looked after, at a time when most councils, regardless of political colouring, can't wait to get rid of their post-war civic centres.

―――

POINT ROYAL, BRACKNELL
Philip Dowson and Derek Sugden for Arup Associates, 1964
Brutalist

If you want to see how post-war planners thought tower blocks ought to be designed, in ideal circumstances – the benchmark, as opposed to the inner-city high-rise housing that suffered from low budgets and cramped sites – you have to go to Bracknell

Laurie Abbott's Apex Drive, in Frimley, Surrey: experimental Brutalist private houses on an outer-suburban site.

New Town. Around a mile south of the railway station, in the planned suburb of Easthampstead, a single tower stands at the centre of the neighbourhood in extensive rolling grounds, like a stately home. The park is left open, to set off the tower to maximum visual effect, and so that the landscape can be better enjoyed by the tower's residents. Around it is extremely low-rise suburban housing, in terraces, semis, bungalows and a crescent, with mature trees threaded through, and a little shopping centre with Festival Style diapered brick, a pitched roof and pilotis for the essentials. Where the hothouse Arup team of the 1960s break with an ideal plan circa 1946 is by ignoring the cutesy People's Detailing style all around and concocting instead a pure and hard modernist building, a strongly expressed concrete grid on a diamond-shaped plan. Impressive and, rightly, listed, it is let down somewhat by a poor-quality renovation by Bracknell Council, with the concrete needlessly painted, and the addition of tacky green balcony rails and cheap glass to the stairwells. An imitation – in some ways superior – of this tower in a more urban context can be found in the form of Rotherham's **Beeversleigh Flats (p. 378)**.

Fans of extremely violent and dystopian 1970s crime films will recognize Point Royal as the location of Sean Connery's apartment in Sidney Lumet's *The Offence*.

APEX DRIVE, FRIMLEY ✪
Laurie Abbott, 1965–6
Brutalist

Laurie Abbott is the otherwise missing link between the two most aggressive and thrilling moments in British modernism – Brutalism, in which capacity he worked with Owen Luder and Rodney Gordon on **Eros House (p. 90)**, the (demolished) Tricorn Centre and the like, and High-Tech, where he was one of the main designers with Richard Rogers of the crazed **Lloyd's of London (p. 69)**. This is a rare solo building, and shows him to have been a first-rate designer in his own right. Apex were a sort of mini-Span, offering shared-ownership flats to the aspirant bourgeois who might fancy a bit of modern design with their investment. But unlike, say, **Parkleys (p. 111)**, this is much tougher and stranger. The flats use a series of peculiar beefy modules, partly taken from the elemental work of the American designer Louis Kahn – powerfully expressed stair towers and projecting upper floors, and on every block a set of monumental brick arches, sometimes upside-down. These are then mixed up in each block, so that none of them are quite the same. The blocks are arranged around a communal green, with no fences or CCTV – in this exurb, they're far enough from the worry that anyone can see them. The doors have mostly been changed to standard Frimley product, but otherwise the flats are in fine condition, and so peculiar that it would be extremely hard to make them look 'normal', and with residents adding their own collections of curios around their own bit of the still communal garden. **[B.9]**

THE WHEATSHEAF & HEATHER RIDGE ARCADE, CAMBERLEY
John and Sylvia Reid, 1970
People's Detailing

There are few pubs in this book, suggesting either that the frosted glass, comfy chairs, kitschy carpets and smoky, drizzly atmos of the nineteenth-century pub is so obviously the correct space to be drunk in that anything else seems false by comparison, or, more fundamentally, that modern architecture is a sober architecture. This is one of the more convincing attempts to combine modernism and a distinct 'pubness'. The Wheatsheaf is at the end of an Eric Lyons-style shopping precinct in a big Bovis estate on the outskirts

of Camberley – not a visually exciting town – which tries its best to create a real centre out of the bosky sprawl, especially in the design of the Wheatsheaf itself. The pub is strikingly architecturally legible, on first sight – a hexagon of slate-hung volumes, spreading like spokes from a knobbly, Expressionistic central brick column. The hexagonal plan is no whimsy – inside, around that column, each of those volumes is a discrete quiet room to drink in, with the combined privacy and publicness that a good pub is all about. Whether this really *is* a good pub depends on Camberley more than it does on design, but the Reids – designers who otherwise specialized in neat, Swedish-style furniture – have done their best.

SCHOOL OF CONSTRUCTION MANAGEMENT & ENGINEERING, READING
Howell Killick Partridge & Amis, 1973
Brutalist

One of the smaller buildings on the University of Reading's sprawling post-war campus, but crammed full of ideas and energy. Known locally as 'the Lego building', this term points to its appearance as an assembly from a kit of parts – although, whereas later High-Tech architects would admit to a childhood love of Meccano, the inspiration here is traditional Japanese architecture, with its constructional techniques, delicacy and precision imitated in concrete. Among other things, that shows how far Brutalist architecture had gone away from 'truth to materials', given that concrete is not wood. But it's used with considerable skill here, with the aggregate in this stepped stack of classrooms and workshops stained several different colours – brown, yellow and orange. It's surrounded by thickets of trees and features a small pool, where the building shows off its cross-braced frame, the Katsura Palace in coloured concrete.

Red brick, High-Tech: Ahrends Burton & Koralek's Maidenhead Library, with its space frame roof.

While here, one could note the enormous contrast with the earlier university buildings opposite, at the other end of the leafy grounds – the U-shaped Edith Morley Building and the windowless main facade of the Palmer Building, both by Easton & Robertson, which cleave closely to a Scandinavian prototype. With their pitched roofs, decorative balustrades and medieval-looking clocks, they could be in Aarhus. No doubt, Howell Killick Partridge & Amis were aiming their hard, complex thing at it.

MAIDENHEAD LIBRARY ☉
Ahrends Burton & Koralek, 1973
High-Tech

A superb municipal library, one of two of the first rank designed at the same time by ABK – the other, in Redcar, was demolished some years ago. Everything is determined by a wide, spreading space frame roof, into which is inserted a two-level red-brick library full of intricate spaces, alternately secluded, with nooks for quiet reading, and spacious, with the red-brick mass cut away in places and the space frame taking over; to the exterior, it's a monolithic canalside block, with a spreading roof. A lot is happening in this building, and all of it quite unusual for the 1970s, a time when modernism was under sharp attack. The humanized modernism of Hampshire County Council's architects department can be traced to this building (see **Crestwood School, p. 250**), showing that you can maintain modernist values while abandoning both hulky concrete expressionism and glass grids. Maidenhead Library is roughly in the High-Tech genre, reliant on advanced and clearly expressed engineering, but it also has all the major virtues of a traditional civic building – monumental presence, strong materials, pride in scale – without using a single cliché of traditional architecture.

BASING VIEW, BASINGSTOKE: VIEWPOINT
1970s
FARNUM HOUSE
Farmer & Dark, 1970–73
GATEWAY HOUSE
Peter Foggo for Arup Associates, 1974–6
MATRIX HOUSE
EPR Architects, 1980–83
International Style, Brutalist, High-Tech

This is the southern sunbelt, the town once called the 'Dallas of Hampshire', all sharp suits, big business, fast cars and smoked glass. Basing View Business Park is an office district built mostly between the mid-seventies and the early eighties, when Basingstoke became an overspill town and a place for businesses to cheaply relocate to from London. A half-dozen mirrorglass office buildings stand over green roundabouts, and some are much more interesting than others. This ensemble is best known for Gateway House (now Mountbatten House), built for the paper merchants Wiggins Teape and designed by Peter Foggo of Arup Associates in 1974. It is occasionally known as the 'hanging gardens of Basingstoke', because of the way it integrates quite luxuriously crafted modern architecture – all black glass and travertine – with cascading gardens on its stepped roofs and balconies, creating a faintly post-apocalyptic image of nature overtaking modernity (in the freak heatwave of mid-April 2018, when I first set out to have a look at it, I got myself sunburnt in the process, which seemed apt).

Churchill Plaza – patriotism and Americanism conjoined, that's the South of England for you – is a very Dallas tower best ignored, but opposite lies Matrix House, a dramatic 1983 building used as offices by, inter alia, Handelsbanken and Sun Life Canada. In the then-nascent High-Tech style, it boasts a lofty glass atrium, exposed services and the sort of ambitious, sculptural detailing you'd usually have found at the

time in much sexier cities like Chicago or Hong Kong. Every block in Basing View sprawls across its site, from the red-brick Postmodernism of Snamprogetti House to ViewPoint, a block of craggy Brutalist offices that would be a cult object by now were it in London or Manchester, to Farnum House, the 1973 complex that houses the AA (here appearing in this book for the only time as the Automobile rather than Architectural Association), surmounted by a slightly sinister, slit-windowed tall tower. Basing View has a tedious beauty all of its own, revealing how much modern architecture relies for its effect on contrast: in London or Manchester, these buildings work against and with the historic city, but this concentration of the stuff conspicuously lacks tension or friction. Everything runs smoothly, or at least it does if you're driving – and if you're not, you must be either poor or a communist. Just behind Mountbatten House's tumbling foliage, through a densely planted green space, is a footbridge over a motorway, bringing you to residential Basingstoke, and Eastrop Park, with a large lake and clusters of little weatherboarded houses climbing up the hills. A town like this works well, if you don't mind all the things that are missing.

BEAR BROOK OFFICE PARK, AYLESBURY
Gollins Melvin Ward, 1982
International Style, Postmodernist

A glittering corporate oddity – Texas in Bucks. Known locally as the 'Blue Leanie', this office complex, originally built for Lloyds Bank, focuses on one bizarre, slickly delivered mirrorglass shape, a sort of monopitch pyramid turned on its side, then prevented from falling over by red-brick pylons. While most British attempts at doing American corporate HQs just feel shabby and cheap, in its lush landscaped setting this feels like

Dallas in Bucks: the slick, Americanist mirrorglass 1980s style of Bear Brook Office Park, Aylesbury.

a real analogue to the sinister mirrorglass edifices of Johnson and Burgee or Roche and Dinkeloo, something out of *Logan's Run*, or, at least, *Dynasty* – a microcosm of coked-up seventies Americana. I've only seen it under blue skies, and cannot imagine it in the rain.

PIER 6 CONNECTOR, GATWICK AIRPORT

Wilkinson Eyre, 2004
High-Tech

As Douglas Murphy points out in his book *Last Futures*, if you want to see the really existing futurist city more or less as it was imagined between 1914 and 1974, you go to an airport. Here, conservation is irrelevant – even in once-beautiful **Stansted Airport (p. 192)** – in a world where there is constant motion, constant replacement, servicing a completely transient population, and all the infrastructural rudiments of a totalitarian

state. Exciting as this might sound, the architectural results here tend to consist of big shopping malls crammed into titanium sheds. Gatwick, designed as a rationalist grid by Yorke Rosenberg & Mardall, exists now only in fragments, but it does boast this piece of astonishing futurist infrastructure. It's just a walkway with a travelator, long enough to cross a runway, high enough for a jumbo jet to go under it – but its sheer scale creates a sudden moment where the 'future-shock absorber' is removed and you can revel in the modernity of air travel, otherwise an almost wholly tedious and unpleasant experience. Wilkinson Eyre's arched, symmetrical design of the walkway has an appropriately kitsch vim; the green glass and cladding are cheap as chips, as, after all, it'll be moved and replaced sooner rather than later. You want pompous permanence, go stare at the Olympic Village.

MILTON KEYNES

UNDERPASSES & PORTES COCHÈRES ✪

Stuart Mosscrop, Fred Roche and Christopher Woodward for Milton Keynes Development Corporation Architects Dept, late 1960s to early 1980s
International Style

These two examples of simple urban design are an object lesson in how architecture can turn urban chores into pleasures. The underpasses can be found all around Milton Keynes – the most elegant are the granite-clad examples in the centre, the most verdant are in the suburbs, and the spatial qualities are the same in each. They are gentle slopes rather than canyons reached by stairs, and are wide and open enough to offer complete views of where you're going – unlike most underpasses, where pedestrians scurry like troglodytes, unable to see what is in front of them after a few paces, with motorists having priority in design terms. Here, there's peace for once between the two.

The portes cochères, on the other hand, are only in the centre, and don't have the same obvious use, but they feel as important. Their name comes from the neoclassical device of a small, gate-like shelter which was commonly used for vehicles in country houses. In Milton Keynes, they're essentially shelters, indicating where pedestrians should cross, around the administrative and retail centre, and they're detailed in black steel with the most painstakingly precise Miesian attention to proportion.

Sadly the underpasses are now often ad hoc homeless shelters, an indictment of a New Town that was once part of London's effort to deal with its housing crises.

One of the spacious, elegant, green 'Los Angeles in Buckinghamshire' underpasses of Milton Keynes.

NETHERFIELD

Jeremy Dixon and Edward Jones for Milton
Keynes Development Corporation Architects
Dept, 1975
International Style

Rather amazingly, this large housing
estate was an early project by the modern
classicists who would later redesign
the Royal Opera House. The estate was
designed when they were in an Architectural
Association clique known as the 'grunt
group', enthusiasts for interwar modernism
and classical discipline, a retromodernist
trend whose effects were felt in the great
Camden Council estates like **Branch Hill
(p. 151)** and **Fleet Road (p. 147)**. Netherfield
is one of the largest built examples of that
school of thought. It is council housing as
a means of winning an aesthetic argument –
what if you treated a hilly site and a variety
of housing types in a completely linear,
visually unified way? It is made up of several
parallel concrete terraces – an elegant
module, with a lot of Walter Gropius's Torten
estate in Dessau in it – which shift in height
according to whether the ground is sloping
or rising, giving a slightly uncanny effect.
The neighbourhood centre, meanwhile,
is a much more clearly neoclassicist design,
where an impressive stripped classical
colonnade houses Chicken Cottage
and such. In recent years, the place has
attracted much interest from architectural
historians because of how much residents –
particularly those who exercised their Right
to Buy – have altered the buildings, adding
half-timbering, new cladding, painting – but
in such a way that it still, somehow, respects
the grid. The results are fascinating, and
though the area does feel neglected, that
has more to do with the way the landscaping
has been allowed to become overgrown and
scrubby than it does the residents' changes.

EAGLESTONE

Ralph Erskine, 1975
People's Detailing

As relaxed and loose as **Netherfield (above)**
is hardline, this joins it as the most interesting
of the early Milton Keynes districts, which
otherwise include some rather overpraised
early efforts in Postmodernism and disasters
by later-to-be-famous starchitects (for
a shock, go to Norman Foster's shed-like
houses at Bean Hill). Eaglestone is similar
to the lower-rise parts of the **Byker Estate
(p. 484)** – simple houses not massively
unlike the volume housebuilding of the time,
with pleasant and enjoyable details in brightly
coloured and stained wood, particularly in
the neighbourhood centre. It is much greener
than either normal developers' housing
or Erskine's more urban work. The existing
landscape the New Town took over – oak
trees, gentle hills – is used to delightful effect.

SHOPPING BUILDING ✪

Stuart Mosscrop, Fred Roche and Christopher
Woodward for Milton Keynes Development
Corporation Architects Dept, 1975–9
International Style

Rightly extremely highly praised for
its architecture, Stuart Mosscrop and
Christopher Woodward's building here
was intended by Derek Walker, head of the
Architects Department of the New Town,
to perform a social function as well. Much of
the praise it receives is for just how different
it is from a conventional mall, because of its
abundant natural light, its serious public-art
programme, its trees, and its open, civic
and pleasant character, without the sense of
everything being channelled into spending
that is usually so much a feature of the
genre. That's because it wasn't intended to
be owned like a conventional shopping mall,
but to be a real centre, that you can walk
through at any time, just like the centre of

Public spaces in a Motor City: boulevards, portes cochères and the crystalline shopping centre in Milton Keynes.

a town, except under one roof, owned by the local authority, with M&S, John Lewis and the local newsagent all paying them rent.

Instead, barely a year after completion it was sold to a developer, which locks it at night, has added substandard extensions, and tried its utmost to stop the building being listed, thankfully unsuccessfully. Once you've discovered that this was the plan, then it all makes sense. Queen's Court, an outdoor square of stunning discipline and precision-made beauty, feels like a classical square because it is one. Double-height, top-lit galleries like Midsummer Arcade and Silbury Arcade feel like Victorian arcades because that's what they are, albeit using a Miesian (or Superstudio) grid. The covered market is there not as a concession to local colour, but because that's what a real city has. And if you explore the backways, you can see the heavy engineering that makes all this possible, with flyovers literally running above it. Now, there is a tension

between public intention and private reality, but enough of the former survives to mean this still feels like a striking and beautiful alternative to the historic city.

RAILWAY STATION & STATION SQUARE ✪
Stuart Mosscrop, Fred Roche and Christopher Woodward for Milton Keynes Development Corporation Architects Dept, 1982
International Style

My personal favourite part of the early Milton Keynes Development Corporation Architects Department's audacious combination of monumental classical geometry and American steel-and-glass high modernism, an image of austere civic grandeur that is almost calculated to present an image of the terrifying big bureaucratic state, yet which reveals a certain humanism when you've used it a few times. It was designed

There are few more spectacular examples of modernist infrastructure than the twin viaducts of **Burdock Way** in Halifax. These thin, grey flyovers are lifted vertiginously high over the town's Victorian bridges, in an area dense with nineteenth-century mills – an incredibly English retrofuturist pile-up.

The key to the Brutalist architecture pioneered in Britain during the 1950s and 1960s was articulation – emphasizing structure to create massive monuments. In Balfron Tower, on **Brownfield Estate** [B.2] in Poplar, this is performed by the full-height service tower, connected to the flats by skybridges; a similar trick can be

seen in the cantilevered lecture theatres at the University of Westminster's **Cavendish Campus** [B.5]. Meanwhile, the London Borough of Camden's justly famous housing programme included long terraces of houses and flats with ziggurat-like concrete frames, as at **Highgate New Town** [B.3] and the sweeping **Alexandra Road** [B.4].

Brutalist housing often offered an image of vastness and collectivity, with flats swept up into huge, ship-like concrete structures, dominating the surrounding landscape like a liner in port. This can be seen in the **Brunswick Centre** [B.6], a megastructure based on the unbuilt work of the Italian Futurists; and equally so in

the monastic discipline and rhythmic angularity of **Andrew Melville Hall** [B.7] at the University of St Andrews. In **Wyndham Court** [B.8], a block of council flats in Southampton, the nautical metaphors make the most sense – a huge, permanently beached concrete Cunard overlooking the Solent in the distance.

B.9

B.10

Brutalism could have an adversarial relationship to context – for while they might have been interested in landscape, Brutalist architects were seldom interested in being 'in keeping'. In the Surrey commuter town of Frimley, **Apex Drive** [B.9] sets up its own bizarre world of monumental yet suburban miniature towers.

In many cases, buildings were suspended in mid-air, floating above their townscapes. This is the effect of **Swan House** [B.10], an office block (now flats) raised on stilts above Newcastle's inner motorway on one side and the proud Victorian city on the other; and of **Beeversleigh Flats** [B.11], high on a hill above Rotherham.

Brutalist architects expressed monumentality in several ways. Where there was a spectacular site, it would be emphasized as much as possible, as with a fortress or encampment. On a steep hill in suburban south-east London, **Dawson Heights** [B.13] was modelled on the profile of Edinburgh Castle. In Wales, meanwhile,

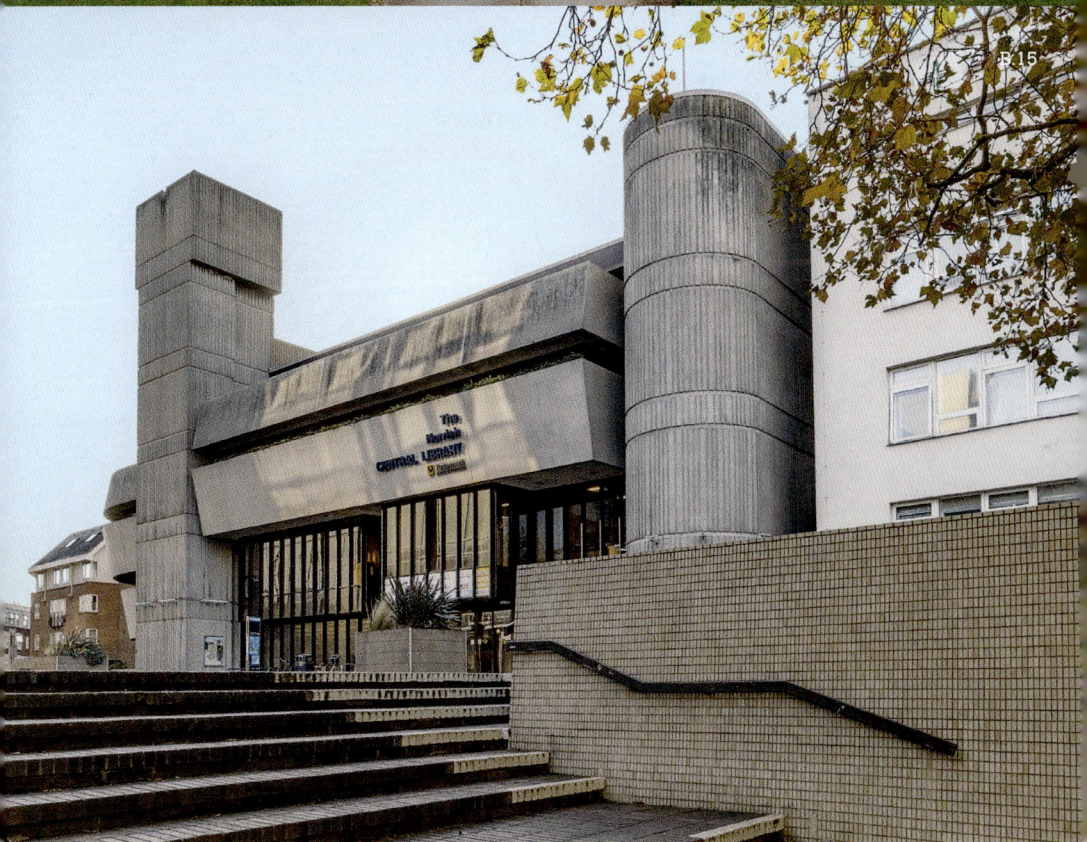

the **Swansea Civic Centre** [B.14] looms out like a bastion over the bay and the beach. On less dramatic sites, designers created their own skylines and 'castles' from scratch, as at the University of Birmingham's **Muirhead Tower** [B.12], or Portsmouth's **Norrish Library** [B.15], a miniature masterclass in grandiose power.

The green landscapes of the south of England have led to a variety of creative attempts to introduce something strange and alien to its placid lawns. Ahrends Burton & Koralek's structures at Keble College, Oxford, range from imposing brick silos to the snaking, high-tech **Hayward Buildings** [B.16]; meanwhile, in the same city, a completely different approach is taken by the **Florey Building** [B.17], raised on spindly legs above the River Cherwell, rather like an H. G. Wells Martian. But in the wilder landscape of Cornwall, buildings such as Truro's vast **County Hall** [B.18] are as shaggy and enigmatic as the surrounding hills and moorlands.

B.19

B.20

Brutalist architects often designed studios for artists; one of the most remarkable of these is Peter Womersley's concrete-and-glass **Bernat Klein Studio [B.19]**, built for a celebrated textile designer in the Scottish borders. Equally, architects often integrated avant-garde sculptures into their buildings. The concrete surfaces of

Huddersfield's **Queensgate Market** [B.20] were decorated with ceramic panels by Fritz Steller; likewise William Mitchell's sculptural walls were set into the concrete in the motorway interchange at **Hockley Circus** [B.21] near Birmingham – an extraordinary monument that will likely baffle generations to come.

The architect Denys Lasdun developed a personal interpretation of modern architecture from the 1950s onwards, favouring hierarchical arrangements of terraces and service towers, pyramidal, baroque and intimidating, but beautifully detailed and generous in their public spaces. The most famous example is one of

London's few really impressive modernist public institutions, the **National Theatre** [B.24]; the more linear side of his architecture can be seen in his **Institute of Education** [B.22]. His work was influential, especially on Building Design Partnership's **Halifax Headquarters** [B.23], an epic ziggurat built into the sandstone townscape.

A parallel avant-garde to the heavy heroics of Brutalism was the High-Tech movement, which was equally in love with the heavy iron architecture of British industrial heritage and the lightweight, tensile engineering of Cold War America. This Buckminster Fuller-meets-Isambard Kingdom Brunel hybrid style is at its most impressive in Norman Foster's showrooms for Renault – now **Kidz About [B.25]** – on the outskirts of Swindon. For an example of the architecture that presaged this fusion, one might observe the astounding scale combined with delicate steel filigrees of the Newport **Transporter Bridge [B.26]**, which was designed in 1906.

Facades in the more aggressive post-war architecture can be deceptive. **Westminster Underground Station** [B.27], scooped out beneath the stodgy Porticullis House, hides a multi-level structure that is reminiscent of Piranesi's 'Imaginary Prisons'. In the City of London, at **Lloyd's** [B.28], the services encase a full-height atrium.

Sometimes these contrasts have caused problems: the impressive glass of Cambridge's **History Faculty** [B.29] was achieved at the cost of overheating for the readers inside. But effects of intimacy could be created too, as at Bristol's **Clifton Cathedral** [B.30], where a bunker-like edifice contains a space of repose and calm.

Avant-garde rooflines are formed from the nuts and bolts of the building, as in the swooping curves of Trafford's **Imperial War Museum North** [B.31], where titanium shards are modelled with the profile of shrapnel, and the weird arrangement of pipes atop the Roger Stevens Building at the University of Leeds' **South Campus** [B.32].

by the powerhouse team of Stuart Mosscrop, Fred Roche and Christopher Woodward on a Beaux Arts U-shaped plan – a 'back of an envelope job' according to Woodward, based on **Hornsey Town Hall (p. 139)** – but blown into massive proportions, and given an abstract, gleaming, ultra-modern aesthetic that is a very long way from the tweedy world of interwar municipalism. The buildings are framed by the square that slopes gently upwards towards Midsummer Boulevard, with a modernist clock right in the centre, like a de Chirico ready-made. The office blocks that flank the square, designed of a piece with the station, are precise mass market Americana of the school of SOM and Mies, with colonnades on the ground floor. Mies van der Rohe meets Edwin Lutyens in Buckinghamshire uptown. [**A.19**]

FORMER BUS STATION
Derek Yeadon for Milton Keynes Development Corporation Architects Dept, 1983
International Style

Apparently too far from the railway station to work as a bus station as such, this now stands as a pure abstract sculpture, like the MKDC portes cochères – a long roof, a delicate grid of white tiles, is kept up by the thinnest row of steel columns, giving a view of all that space, space, space. Buses are infrequent here, and the long-promised tram and monorail systems may never materialize; but the MKDC can't be accused of having neglected the design of public transport buildings, however much its inheritors may have neglected to provide actual public transport. In the meantime, hopefully this delicate and serene building will be preserved.

The precise grid facades of Milton Keynes's railway station, as seen from the bridge over the tracks.

THE POINT ⬤
BDP, 1985
High-Tech

This entertainment centre, nightclub, cinema and general under-one-roof repository of low culture is a sort of remix of the Milton Keynes components, with a ziggurat of steel-and-glass cubes held in a whimsical Constructivist pyramid of red-painted girders, dubiously structural but adding a vertical accent to all the long, low glass, steel-and-brick pavilions all around. Its break with modernist-classical serenity irritated some of the original MKDC architects, but compared with much of what came later, it feels now like a real dialogue with their ideas, and an attempt to inject a little of the humour and verticality their work so scrupulously avoided. In fact, it's a little like a joke at the expense of the sometimes rather severe and high-minded original Milton

Buckinghamshire avant-garde: the glass cubes of The Point, suspended from a pyramidal steel gantry.

Keynes aesthetic, taking that work's motifs and transforming them into a multifunctional fun palace. It has been slated for demolition for at least a decade and has a certificate of immunity from listing, but stands at the time of writing.

―――

ART GALLERY & THEATRE
**Andrzej Blonski Architects, 1999/
6A Architects, 2018**
International Style

These two are very late additions to the 'CMK' grid, at its furthest point away from the railway station, overlooking the quasi-rural civic oasis of Campbell Park. Andrzej Blonski's original building for the MK Gallery was a concrete cube whose simple facade was regularly repainted according to whatever the exhibition was; it felt like something out of an Ed Ruscha painting,

aptly for its function and its LA-in-Bucks location. It was massively expanded in 2018 by the architects 6A, who have created much larger galleries in a shiny, steel-clad box with a grand circular window looking out at the park; the gridded cladding is a nice reference to the town's famous gridiron plan, and the generosity of the new spaces is a marked improvement. The theatre, meanwhile, is as outgoing as the gallery is introverted, with a giant order of thin concrete columns. The openness of these is responded to at the weekends by people who use it as a place to hang out and show off, giving this part of Milton Keynes the sort of outdoors street life it otherwise lacks, without doing any damage to the original grid and its ideas. It took a long time for the New Town to build these two public assets, but it would be grimly corporate today without them.

OXFORD

THE BEEHIVES, ST JOHN'S COLLEGE
Architects Co-Partnership, 1958–60
Brutalist

A big thing in the 1950s – the first modernist building in the University of Oxford, which unlike Cambridge resisted these newfangled continental ideas right until long after the war. You can see this in the fact that this place was built parallel with various neoclassical extensions and even new colleges (the freakish Beatrix Potter-meets-Mussolini style of Nuffield College, for instance). Accordingly, the designers, a socialist co-operative then best known for their Brynmawr Rubber Factory in South Wales (which was demolished in the 1990s, despite its listing), decided not to do anything too disruptive, but instead to win Oxonians over with intimacy and cuteness, without compromising aesthetically. The 'Beehives' name comes from the way these tiny, two-storey student residences are clustered into individually recognizable cells – a larger structure in which everyone has their own space with which they can do what they like. There are minuscule little copper spires on each of their six pods, a little Gothic joke amidst the plate glass windows and the staggered grid with which it meets the quadrangle – but the tough materials keep it away from tweeness. It also shows one – and the most common – route to insinuating modern architecture into the dreaming spires, by ostentatious kindness and a sensitive setting into the historic townscape. As Alex Niven writes in his poem about this building and its architects: 'We wanted something new, you see'.

Oxford's first modernist buildings, The Beehives, designed as Brutalist-Gothic Hobbit houses.

and tooled version of the Miesian volume of **Smithdon School (p. 196)**, only here, rather than being surrounded by playing fields and the Norfolk plain, the landscape itself is modernist, clipped and trimmed and right-angled. Around the main volume are wings in an elegantly ageing metal, with hedges and brick walls filed to the same modular dimensions. Capping it all is Jacobsen's addition to the dreaming spires – a haunting and exceptionally elegant concrete campanile. It is not a building which stuns or excites, but one which can be looked at and explored over decades. There are very few examples of twentieth-century architecture in Britain with its absolute integrity and attention to detail. **[D.24]**

Ceremonial International Style: the Bell Tower of Arne Jacobsen's St Catherine's College.

ST CATHERINE'S COLLEGE ✪
Arne Jacobsen, 1960–66
International Style

An enormous leap in scale from the tentative modernist enclave of **The Beehives (p. 227)**, let alone from the coy neoclassicism of Nuffield – an entire new college in pure International Style fashion, designed by one of the most feted international architects. Its significance at the time was in showing that a modern scheme could be as elegant and obsessively crafted as anything Georgian – rather than mass production, as was envisaged in the thirties (and soon to be actualized, to great controversy, in the sixties), this was a bespoke product by Denmark's answer to Robert Adam, with the design extending right down to the cutlery.

Just outside the centre, in the manicured lawns, playing fields and suburban vistas of inner suburban Oxford, 'St Cat's' consists of a long, low volume, like a far more crafted

ST CROSS LIBRARIES
Leslie Martin, 1961–4
Brutalist

Not far from St Catherine's, this is a much more municipal effort. St Cross is an intercollegiate library complex, detailed in pale brickwork, with treated wood and breezeblock interiors. It is most notable for its stepped profile from the road, rising gradually in a manner which is both classically hierarchical, yet with a modernist sense of three-dimensionality and open space in its flights of steps and stacked tiers. Astonishingly, this carefully detailed, elegantly proportioned work has been considered 'totalitarian' by generations of Oxford conservatives.

WOLFSON, VAUGHAN & MARGERY FRY BUILDINGS, SOMERVILLE COLLEGE
Philip Dowson for Arup Associates, 1964–6
Brutalist

Oxford's modern architecture is dominated by the firm of Arup Associates, founded by

Decorous brick Brutalism: the articulated volumes and grand steps of Leslie Martin's St Cross Libraries.

the engineer (and architect of **The Labworth, p. 178**) Ove Arup, but with the talented and original architects Peter Foggo and Philip Dowson as its leading designers. These works at Somerville College are typical Dowson buildings, in a kind of mechanized Gothic. Each facade features projecting cubic windows held in an elegant, precise, thin concrete frame, in a cellular style that recalls the Victorian futurism of **Oriel Chambers (p. 423)**. One side faces a small green, but the other presents its giant windows to an ordinary street, with a crumbly, spiky stone fence blocking it off. This makes it one of the few modernist Oxford colleges that can be enjoyed by pedestrians, something which is also visible at the Vaughan and Margery Fry buildings nearby. Rather than being stuffed away in a quad, these have a real public connection, so that for once they feel like proper urban architecture. Expressed, cantilevered concrete frames are projected out from a box above

a brick plinth, to the street. The little concrete arches under said plinth are much more populist than the rest of the building – hardline, high-theory Brutalism on top, lowbrow Basil Spence below – presumably a gesture connecting town and gown.

___

HILDA BESSE BUILDING, ST ANTHONY'S COLLEGE ✪
Howell Killick Partridge & Amis, 1967
Brutalist

An intimate and monumental collegiate complex on one of the main roads north of the centre. Its well-made precast concrete panels surround a central stair tower, sculptural and asymmetrical projecting windows with a capsule-like aspect, and a gorgeous Brutalist-Gothic interior, which updates the monastic affectations of Oxford's colleges for the space age. Porters are relatively friendly about letting pedestrians come in and have a wander, too, presumably expecting they're there to see Zaha Hadid's relatively inferior **Middle East Centre (p. 233)** next door, instead.

NUCLEAR PHYSICS LABORATORY
Philip Dowson for Arup Associates, 1967
Brutalist

Most of the time, the hysteria with which certain elements in the universities of Oxford and Cambridge received modern architecture seems simply ridiculous, and ungrateful, given how expensively made the buildings are, and how much the architects strained to assimilate their egalitarian ideas to the absurd hierarchies of Oxbridge. This place is an exception, so radical in its rupture with its surroundings that you can understand the reaction it caused; in fact, it is so extreme that it's probably only the possibility that an accident would

Beyond the dreaming spires: Oxford's extremely aggressive Nuclear Physics Laboratory.

make loads of tourists radioactive that has stopped it from being demolished. Right in the heart of tourist Oxford, it consists, to the pedestrian, of concrete volumes that appear to have been castellated in reverse, with a massive triangular concrete thing placed at the centre of it, like an abstract idol, baffling and incredibly sinister. Maybe the nuclear reactor is in here, you might be within your rights to wonder. Given how much of the international rep of Oxford comes from the nuclear physics and astrophysics that happens in places like this, why shouldn't it look as frightening and uncanny as it is?

FLOREY BUILDING
James Stirling, 1968
Brutalist, High-Tech

This is the last of Stirling's 'Red Trilogy' of dramatic, proto-High-Tech university buildings, along with the Cambridge **History Faculty (p. 207)** and the Leicester **Engineering Building (p. 348)**. It's also another infuriating example of Oxford's topography – there was meant to be a riverside route past this block of student accommodation, but the gown was so horrified that the town would be able to easily walk past their building that they blocked it from the start. In the Florey Building, some extraordinary geometric gymnastics is elicited by Stirling's desire to give every student a full-height glass window facing the Cherwell (a tributary of the Thames, or, as they insist on calling it here, the 'Isis'), though, in the event, stopping the hoi polloi getting in was more important than riverside views. As in many Stirling buildings, the extensive and cheaply detailed glass created major problems with regulating heat, and the reason for it in the first place was made irrelevant by changes to the site. When you approach it from the backside, you find a near-symmetrical red-tile hulk, squatting suggestively on thin, splayed legs, with a central service tower; go around it, and you see how the glass rooms are cantilevered on these legs; turn round, and the alternation between heavy and lightweight, glass and tile, are all held in a daring, thrilling suspense. The circus of rooms when you're inside is almost disappointing afterwards. [B.17]

DE BREYNE & HAYWARD BUILDINGS, KEBLE COLLEGE ✪
Ahrends Burton & Koralek, 1971–80
High-Tech, Brutalist

Ahrends Burton & Koralek were one of the most admirable firms of mid-century Britain for the way that they came to every building totally fresh, without an obvious house style or 'brand', but with plenty of imagination; what could we do here? What would work with this place? What would it be worth trying out? You can see this especially acutely in these two buildings, seemingly extremely unlike each other, placed around the polychromatic fireworks of William Butterfield's neo-Gothic Keble College. Evidently not interested in the James Stirling approach of trying to match those Victorian theatrics, it consists of two introverted but visually exciting distinct parts – a part-buried glass snake, whipping across the quadrangle, rising gradually from underground, floor by floor, into a four-storey building, all in precision-made steel and dark glass. Alongside is an almost windowless fortress of yellow brick, sculptural, inscrutable and subtly Gothic. [B.16]

ST THOMAS WHITE BUILDING, ST JOHN'S COLLEGE
Philip Dowson for Arup Associates, 1972–5
Brutalist

An intriguing, handsome collection of buildings with the projecting frames, elegant

Modernism beneath the Gothic: Ahrends Burton & Koralek's subterranean additions to Keble College.

proportions and fine materials that Dowson had developed at Arup, and probably the most successful of them, reconciling especially elegantly a modular modernity and Gothick evocations. An L-shaped series of three-storey halls of residence, unified by a beautifully detailed concrete grid and stone service towers. It is right in the heart of tourist Oxford, and, though hidden by high walls, at one point it reaches a finger into the historic zone, when the modular concrete grid extends itself into a public alleyway. Here, the concrete has weathered to the requisite Hogwarts tone, as the struts of the expressed frame come down over the honeyed stone walls. It is frequently criticized by students, dons and tourists, but there's no better fusion of history and modernity in Oxford. [D.23]

Brutalist railings and neo-Gothic houses frame Zaha Hadid's Middle East Centre at St Anthony's College.

The glass cylinders of Herzog & de Meuron's Blavatnik School of Government, crammed into Gothic Oxford.

GARDEN QUADRANGLE, ST JOHN'S COLLEGE
MacCormac Jamieson Prichard, 1994
Postmodernist

The best Postmodernist college buildings in Oxford, eschewing the twee and the merely retro for a combination of vigorous classical volumes, with 'rusticated' concrete ground floors and brick above, in a style with a little bit of Nicholas Hawksmoor, Frank Lloyd Wright, Walt Disney and, in the peculiar formal squares, integral chessboards and sunken circuses, Lewis Carroll. Like many Oxford spaces, it can be alienating if you don't have a pass, but here that rather adds to the sinister, topsy-turvy feel of the buildings; certainly the paradoxes and quirks of the neo-Renaissance planning overpower the slight hint of the twee.

SAID BUSINESS SCHOOL
Dixon Jones, 2001
Postmodernist

A building that is rare in recent Oxford architecture, in that it goes shamelessly for monumentality and scale rather than fragmentation and contextualism. Its architects, Jeremy Dixon and Edward Jones, are here a very long way indeed from their rational modernist housing in **Netherfield (p. 223)**. They have designed this Business School in an almost neoclassical manner which owes more to Giorgio de Chirico than to Bruno Taut. It is monumental, quiet, imposing and, with its funny pyramidal campanile, ever so slightly camp; it also has the virtue of being the first building to enliven the grim surroundings of Oxford's railway station.

MIDDLE EAST CENTRE, ST ANTHONY'S COLLEGE
Zaha Hadid Architects, 2015
Parametric

The last building in Britain designed by Zaha Hadid Architects before its leader's death, and without doubt the last building she had a leading role in, unusually taking personal command of this addition to a Tudorbethan house next to the terrific **Hilda Besse Building (p. 229)**. Unlike many Hadid buildings – especially the awful Sackler Restaurant in Hyde Park – it is actually well detailed, appearing to be made of a voluptuous mirrored goo squeezed out from some sort of giant tube, with some typically flamboyant Zaha circulation spaces inside, with that thrilling and unnerving feeling of being inside the body of a concrete whale. The exterior is awkward, especially compared to Howell Killick Partridge & Amis's confidence next door, but its scale is just right for where it is, as is the muted colour scheme, and its strained, structurally delinquent approach to the quadrangle says as much about the present as that building said about the 1960s. An age of anxiety.

BLAVATNIK SCHOOL OF GOVERNMENT
Herzog & de Meuron, 2015
Supermodernist

An openly oligarchical school, placed in residential Oxford. This bulky edifice is made up of a set of intersecting cylinders that don't quite align, on a long rectangular podium: a slightly kinked monumentality. Not their finest work in Britain by any means, but like many of Herzog & de Meuron's recent buildings it has a spectacular staircase, spiralling obliquely, thrilling and perturbing. It is absolutely not open to the public.

SOUTH COAST

DREAMLAND CINEMA, MARGATE
Julian Rudolph Leathart and W. F. Granger, 1934
ARLINGTON HOUSE, MARGATE
Russell Diplock Associates, 1964
Expressionist, Brutalist

Angular commercial modernism, three decades apart. Arlington House is by far the tallest building in this uneasy half-gentrified, half-desperate seaside town, a private, speculative apartment block. Originally marketed as 'luxury', it has clearly seen better days, patched up in places and with the sort of St George's flags across windows you don't find on neo-Bankside. In terms of scale it is rash to the point of being almost careless, completely dominating the scruffy beachside enfilade of Georgian and Regency terraces – but it is elegantly proportioned,

with its sawtooth plan, and adds to rather than detracts from the ensemble. If a town is going to have just one tower, it ought to make an effort. Arlington House is even, in an unusual way, contextual – its jagged forms repeat those of the brilliant cinema/entrance to the Dreamland funfair next door, which is a particularly good example of the generic Odeon style – one of the most purely (Weimar) Germanic of British thirties cinemas, right down to its *Metropolis* signage. **[C.2]**

DE LA WARR PAVILION, BEXHILL-ON-SEA ✪
Erich Mendelsohn and Serge Chermayeff, 1935
International Style

Since its restoration a decade or so ago, this has been the best place in Britain to encounter the machine-made glamour of the finest European architecture of the 1920s and '30s, with a distinctive nautical and festive twist all of its own. Mendelsohn, after making his name with the plastic, Expressionist Einstein Tower in Potsdam in 1919, became the most important commercial designer of the Weimar Republic, inventing the global 'streamline moderne' style with the curved sweeps of his cinemas and department stores in Berlin, Stuttgart, Chemnitz and Breslau; notable for us as the blueprint from which so many Odeon cinemas and Co-ops derive themselves. Chermayeff, meanwhile, was a White Russian architect and educator, who would later be better known as a theorist rather than designer.

Selected in an immensely controversial competition to design a leisure centre for this little retirement town on the East Sussex coast, they avoided the clichés that were

The dramatically serrated Brutalist silhouette of Russell Diplock Associates' Arlington House, Margate.

already seeping into the various Mendelsohn imitations being erected in the suburbs and provinces. Instead, the Pavilion idea – combined dance hall, tea room, restaurant – was taken in a much more serious direction. Compared with all the fudges, hierarchies, Dudokisms and residual neo-Georgiana of such as **Hornsey Town Hall (p. 139)**, this must have been either a shock or a revelation, depending on where you were standing. A long plane of rectilinear, white-rendered concrete, asymmetrically broken by a sudden and dramatic glass prow, leading to two storeys of glass lookouts, with a roof terrace above. No concessions, no looks back – pure form.

Inside, the fittings of the spacious public areas are of the highest quality, while never descending into the conventional luxuries of art deco – chrome and steel, not faïence or bakelite. The central staircase of that glass prow, with the ascending discs of its chandelier, is one of the single most stunning spaces in twentieth-century Britain, a churning Gabo sculpture that you can walk up and down (visitors to Berlin can see the original of this in Mendelsohn's headquarters for the trade union IG-Metall, and they can note that the British version is much freer and more open, and has a view of the sea rather than the S-Bahn). Like many arts centres in Sussex and Kent, the De La Warr has turned to appealing to hipster Londoners of a certain age to keep it going, with some success; the last act I saw there was two ex-members of Throbbing Gristle, covering a Nico album. Whether there is an event on or not, just go – this is one of the greatest buildings on this island.

Note also the concrete bandstand, by Niall McLaughlin, 2001, a fun *jeu d'esprit*, floating over the seafront with a hint of Oscar Niemeyer's sculptural Brazilian modernism. [A.5]

The sun terraces of Mendelsohn and Chermayeff's De La Warr Pavilion, leading to its curved stairwell.

DEFENCES & SHELTERS, HASTINGS & ST LEONARDS
Sidney Little, 1931–6
Industrial, Moderne

The Borough Engineer of Hastings was commissioned to modernize the sea frontage in the 1930s, with a new sea wall and a series of typical seaside promenade shelters running above it. The results are fascinating, ranging from a wall made up of pieces of broken bottles, some extremely early underground car parks, and the more conventional pedestrian canopies to cope with British seaside weather. The weirdest part of the sea wall is a beachside collection of concrete bastions and skeletal bunkers, a short walk away from **Hastings Contemporary (p. 242)** – formerly the Jerwood Gallery – and the net shops. Youth clamber up these things, seemingly undeterred by the way that they're rotting

Constructivism in Sussex: the serviced flats of Wells Coates's Embassy Court, overlooking Brighton beach.

their way into the sea. They are, surprisingly, part of the same project as the shelters that Little laid out on the seafront parade that links Hastings to St Leonards. On first seeing these, with their jolly concrete forms and the multicoloured mosaics, I assumed that they were a post-war effort, a bit of Festival Style fun, but they're actually a pre-war attempt to combine seaside levity and modernist technology.

EMBASSY COURT, BRIGHTON ○
Wells Coates, 1936
Constructivist

Along with the slightly earlier **Isokon Building (p. 139)** in London, on this apartment block rests Wells Coates's reputation as one of the major designers of the 1930s. It reverses the order of the London building, as here it's the sea frontage that is cool, continental and metropolitan,

ten square storeys curving at the eastern end, but it's the backside where Coates's Constructivist imagination really impresses – a beefy, voluptuous concrete stairwell with long, thick access galleries, asymmetrical and massive. Here, expressed in a different manner – in brightly painted render, not bare concrete – is the Brutalist interest in giant form, distortion and power. This might have been built as a block of luxury flats designed as weekend pads for theatricals, but its architecture is well beyond nostalgia.

MARINE COURT, ST LEONARDS
Kenneth Dalgleish and Roger K. Pullen, 1938
Moderne

A big and daft piece of streamline moderne – if you want to know the difference between that genre and serious modernism, compare this enjoyable, tawdry, totally overdeveloped and overscaled folly with the elegance and timelessness of the **De La Warr Pavilion (p. 234)** down the road. This vast block of flats is one of the largest buildings of the interwar years – twelve storeys and thirty bays of white-rendered concrete overlooking the beach, with a curved extension and some curved balconies at the top to make the 'ocean liner' aspect of thirties architecture goofily explicit, and shops and bars in a ground floor under a concrete canopy below. It is more Ealing comedy than German Expressionism, but good, nostalgic fun nevertheless.

BUS SHELTERS, BRIGHTON
David Edwards for Brighton Council Borough Surveyors Dept, 1939
International Style

Placed along the green boulevard where Old Steine meets the Grand Parade, these simple structures are rare and fine examples of International Style street furniture. Nothing much more than long concrete eaves with curved, metal-framed glass shelters beneath, their proportions and materials are extremely elegant. Although designed only by Brighton's Borough Surveyor, these are, like Embassy Court, emanations of the capital and its intelligentsia, Hampstead on holiday – elegant, up-to-the-minute, cosmopolitan, dashing, a little futuristic. You're a long way from Eastbourne here.

PRINCE'S HOUSE, BRIGHTON
H. S. Goodhart-Rendel, 1935–6
Expressionist

Like **St Olaf House (p. 81)** by London Bridge, this is one of Goodhart-Rendel's experiments in stretching classicism beyond its usual limits – an office block with flats above, on a corner in the main shopping street of Brighton, its steel frame construction dressed in brick, blue tile and mosaic, with square Crittall windows. The fan-like corner evokes the sort of commercial Expressionism you'd find in Hamburg, but the tweedy pattern of the red brick drags it right back to Sussex. Also in Brighton is Goodhart-Rendel's similarly Expressionistic brick St Wilfrid's Church, clumsily converted into flats.

NOTARIANNI'S MILK BAR & RESTAURANT, EASTBOURNE
1947
People's Detailing

Notarianni's was a café and ice cream chain established by Italian migrants in the thirties – there is an ice cream parlour of the same name still in Blackpool, but it doesn't have a front like this. This is the ground floor frontage of a dashing Regency building, with a bowed balcony just above, and the café's name in big sans serif capitals above a gorgeous pattern of ceramic diamonds, right out of the Festival of Britain. It was built a few years before the Festival, showing how much that populist modernism borrowed from the aesthetic of the seaside. The interior doesn't dazzle as much, with a few retained fittings, but this is one of the few great surviving modernist shopfronts nonetheless.

---

23 ST GEORGE'S STREET, CANTERBURY
Robert Paine & Partners, 1953
People's Detailing

A fizzy little Festival Style building, and by far the most interesting building in the post-war reconstruction of Canterbury. At the corner of one of the dull brick enfilades that make up the rebuilt city is a frosted-glass block with a blue stone shopfront, a jagged row of pitched roofs, and a festive zigzag canopy on top. What look at first like pilotis are actually columns holding up the roof, carried up the entire height of the facade. Simple, small, packed with dynamism and fun.

―――

ST ANDREW'S COURT, GRAVESEND
G. E. Hill for Gravesend Borough Council Architects Dept, 1961–2
People's Detailing

A pretty, small council estate in this densely packed, rowdily Dickensian Thames-side town, carved delicately into the Georgian and Victorian streets, preserving a pub and views of the river. It consists of three-storey blocks with good, big balconies and alternations of dark and pale stock bricks, packed into a small site; but despite the break with the traditional street structure these feel very relaxed in their context, particularly the row of pitched-roofed flats raised on archways, which create a fittingly

maritime alleyway to the rest of the town. The original plaque to commemorate the opening, with its delicate sans serif lettering, can still be found, and in good condition – always a sign of strong civic pride.

―――

UNIVERSITY OF SUSSEX, BRIGHTON ✪
Basil Spence, Bonnington & Collins, 1960–67
Brutalist

As the reputations of hardline modernists, the uncompromising likes of Goldfinger and Lasdun, have risen, so those of compromisers such as Basil Spence have fallen in recent years. That's a shame, as the combination of beefy presence, historical reference and monumental scenography in his best projects is very much worth experiencing. The University of Sussex is probably Spence's single best work. A long

The Attenborough Centre at the University of Sussex, somewhere between Ancient Rome and the New Brutalism.

journey out to the outskirts of Brighton (Falmer is the nearest railway station), the site is Arcadian – rolling hills, woodlands just beyond, with subtle planting and pathways by the landscape architect Sylvia Crowe. Most of the site is filled with perimeter blocks in a style which evokes both Roman engineering and Le Corbusier's Maisons Jaoul – barrel-vaulted concrete archways with bright red infill, with pedestrian paths under and through, leading to semi-enclosed quadrangles.

At a tangent to this are two detached buildings: the Attenborough (formerly Gardner) Arts Centre, a composition of intersecting, mostly windowless brick cylinders, an abstraction of the curves of the landscape; and the Meeting House, a non-denominational church in a concrete rotunda, with dozens of little stained-glass openings – like the Roman-Brutalist main campus buildings, it is a much more intense, focused, serious work of architecture than Spence is usually given credit for; at times, walking through these spaces feels ritualistic, monastic. Like all the New Universities, its coherence has been adversely affected by indifferent recent additions, which don't make it feel like it has developed into an incrementally built 'city' at all – you can clearly see the join between an original core, which has an *idea*, and later dressings, which do not.

CHICHESTER FESTIVAL THEATRE
Powell & Moya, 1962
Brutalist

Once considered very daring – it boasts a then-novel thrust stage, with seating on three sides – this uncompromising design in an attractive medieval town now seems much closer to the integration of Brutalism and English Baroque in the National Theatre than to the many provincial theatres of the sixties – Lawrence Olivier as director is the common factor. A diamond of concrete waffle slabs held up on imposing girders, it is a monumentally impressive object from the immense surface car park that rudely divides it from the historic centre. Like the NT, there are grand concrete foyers that are rewarding even if you're not catching a show there; yet I can't help but wish this rigorous work of architecture had been integrated into the rest of Chichester, instead of being sequestered in a park as a sort of modernist reservation.

FORMER THEOLOGICAL COLLEGE, CHICHESTER
Ahrends Burton & Koralek, 1961–5
Brutalist

This set of buildings – which was designed by Ahrends Burton & Koralek at their peak for a religious college – is extremely photogenic. It's accordingly a regular presence on the various 'Fuck Yeah Brutalism' type Tumblrs and photo-aggregators, where these concrete-and-brick sentinels have a shivers-down-the-spine sinister presence. Visiting it is a little different. Long since converted into an old people's home, these diminutive yet gruff brick-and-concrete towers, with their arrow-slit-like openings, are just one small corner of a larger retirement complex, sheltered from the town and reached from a suburban roundabout; this can make lurking round the site a little uncomfortable, as the people here evidently expect a quiet, undisturbed seclusion. If you're tactful when visiting, you'll find that the buildings fully reward the effort, especially for the sequence of squares between them, where each individual cell is easily distinguished. This is Brutalism not as a violent brick-bat in the public's face, but as a careful and considered way of building.

106 MELVILLE COURT, CHATHAM
**Chatham Borough Council Architects Dept,
1966**
Brutalist

On a ridge above the battlements and
barracks of the historic dockyard – itself
arguably a proto-modernist showcase, with
its huge iron hangars – this is a surprisingly
attractive modernist building amidst the
grittiness of the Medway towns. A single
tower block of fifteen storeys, it has been
carefully modelled in brick and concrete
to create an interesting silhouette, created
by its emphasized, alternating cantilevered
windows. The concrete has been painted
blue, which lessens the punchy effect,
but the elegant Mondrian pattern still
makes this a clear landmark from the
hills of the conurbation.

NEW ASH GREEN,
NEAR DARTFORD
Eric Lyons, 1967–71
People's Detailing

Very hard to reach, which is probably
part of the point – this is Span moving
from suburban enclaves into an entire
mini-New Town, placed in virgin woodland
not far from Dartford and (later) the M25.
It proved a financial failure, alas, and
was later taken over by Bovis, who added
generic seventies volume housebuilder stuff
to complete it. The centre and at least half
of the housing is still by Lyons, though,
and is often exceptional. It revolves around
an Alvar Aalto-like multilevel complex
with tactile brickwork and grey-black
tiles, with monopitch roofs. The pub here
is worth a visit, though the people in there
are aggressively normal. Of the housing, we
have familiar Span types with a slightly more
vigorous edge, and the attractive colour-
coding of the weatherboarding and the
different house-plans of each distinct area

make it clear which bit is which. The clusters
of monopitch roofs around dense trees
are rather romantic; the tiled pathways are
also of unusual richness. It's sad that so few
people in north Kent wanted to live in the
suburbs of Oslo; put New Ash Green in
north London and it'd be millionaires' row.

HOVE TOWN HALL
John Wells-Thorpe, 1970–73
Brutalist

In visual terms, this is delightfully
incongruous with genteel Hove – that
a local authority in such a (until recently)
conservative place could have commissioned
something so fierce says a great deal about
Britain at the turn of the 1970s. This replaced
a much-loved Victorian Town Hall with
an aggressive, shaggy and hairy Brutalist
bunker – at first, those not already converted
to the *jolie laide* delights of provincial
Brutalism could be forgiven for turning
away in disgust. But, ironically, it has many
of the same qualities as a Victorian town hall.
An impressive clock tower, to punctuate;
rich materials, from the bronzed curtain
walls to the quality of the corduroy concrete;
and opulent and ceremonial interiors, with
exotic materials and decorative, geometric
roofs and walls. Accordingly, after the
initial shock, you'll notice the same sense
of hierarchy, power and command of any
nineteenth-century public building. Whether
this was modern architecture being secretly
conservative or not is for you to judge.

THE LEAS, FOLKESTONE
Chamberlin Powell & Bon, 1972
Brutalist

A rare Chamberlin Powell & Bon project
not for a public client – two speculative
blocks of flats and an office tower (since
converted into flats), for a property

developer. This was only a fragment of a much larger scheme that would have totally transformed the seaside town, and which no doubt it considers itself lucky to have escaped. The two lower blocks are recognizable as Chamberlin Powell & Bon from the combination of meticulous detailing – neat little Corbusian drip-moulds – and monumentality in scale. Although the use of a stepped section makes it resemble some of the contemporary schemes of Camden Council such as **Alexandra Road (p. 148)**, the likes of Neave Brown would never have used this yellow shopping-centre brick. The tower uses similar materials, to create a strong, powerful high-rise defined to the seaside by a massive curved stair tower. The ensemble is best seen from below, on the approach from the beach up to the promenade, where there's a real drama to the way the ziggurat and tower ride the clifftop landscape. Below, you'll find various follies and remnants of the regular Folkestone Triennial, examples of a more whimsical kind of avant-garde architecture; a personal favourite is Pablo Bronstein's 'Beach Hut in the Style of Nicholas Hawksmoor'.

JUBILEE LIBRARY, BRIGHTON
Bennetts Associates, 2003–5
Modernist Eclectic

That extraordinary thing, a decent public building constructed via the British government's Private Finance Initiative, which notoriously took almost all power from architects in the actual execution of buildings and placed it in the hands of contractors. That it could survive even extensive corner-cutting is a testimony to the strength of the design. Whereas most new Brighton buildings attempt more or less successful copies of the Regency stucco style, the facade of this library borrows from the more outré seaside-facing style you can see in Kemp Town – black-glazed tiles, an

altogether more raffish material. Wings clad in these tiles frame a central glass volume. Interiors are cheaply finished and a little mean in places, but the large, top-lit spaces of the library still impress overall. It forms part of a public plaza, with the usual chain restaurants and eateries, and was clearly part of the same planning application.

TOWNER GALLERY, EASTBOURNE
Rick Mather Architects, 2005–9
Classical Modernism

The London-based American architect Rick Mather designed widely for museums and Russell Group universities, in a white walls and glass screens manner which the British construction industry usually turned into something more DoSAC than Mies. This art gallery shows another, more interesting side of his work – generous, playful, even a little baroque. A copper box connects to the International Style Congress Theatre (itself worth a short exploration for its spacious foyers, like a more conservative version of Coventry's **Belgrade Theatre, p. 325**), but then swings round the back streets, with a curved, complex play of hollows and projections in satisfyingly chunky rendered concrete. The circulation spaces between galleries offer panoramic views of a tennis court. All very Eastbourne, the H. M. Bateman genteel thirties resort meets the seaside town circa 2010, aiming at dragging the *Guardian*-reading Londoners back down south. The collection, with its holdings by the likes of Eric Ravilious, is well suited to both.

PALLANT HOUSE GALLERY, CHICHESTER

Colin St John Wilson and M. J. Long, 2006
Modern Classicism

The last built work by the architect of
the **British Library (p. 143)**, brought to
completion by M. J. Long; it's the closest
building to the BL in displaying the restrained
splendour of Wilson's late style. It adjoins
a swaggering Georgian townhouse, in which
the gallery was originally based, respecting
its scale and its logical, mathematical
approach to facade design, through a brick
grid with an austere pattern of slits, with
a grand entrance. The galleries are a great
riposte to white-cube banality, with natural
light, framed views, and unexpected paths
up and down this strongly vertical gallery.
Finishes are of the highest quality throughout.

HASTINGS CONTEMPORARY

HAT Projects, 2010–12
Modernist Eclectic

The former Jerwood Gallery stands in one of
those places where the 'Functional Tradition'
of English architecture can be seen at
its most surreal – the cluster of wooden,
tower-like, narrow-plot net shops built by
fishermen along the seafront, which in their
density, and their creation of an accidental
kind of skyline, sometimes feel as if a group
of Victorian carpenters tried to make a
model of Manhattan. They're evoked with
great clumsiness in several recent blocks
of flats, but this gallery (originally hosting
part of the Jerwood collection, and recently
renamed after a dispute at the time of
writing) steps back from these, though using
materials with a similarly murky, stained look
– black and blue tiles, with a slightly burnt
appearance, under a jagged, warehouse-like
sawtooth roof. The galleries inside are
beautifully lit and open up various views
of both the sea and the fishermen's towers.

TURNER CONTEMPORARY, MARGATE

David Chipperfield Architects, 2011
Classical Modernism

Turner Contemporary, due to the painter's
enthusiasm for the skies of Margate.
You get a lot of sky on Margate sands,
a blue-grey expanse above and beyond
the curving beach promenade and the sea.
Chipperfield's gallery tries to get as much
of this in as possible, with roof lights and
ribbon windows beaming it into a series
of discrete galleries and a café. The placing
of the gallery is ingenious, a cluster of
monopitch volumes on a slight ridge at the
end of the main promenade, clad in a grid
of blue-grey panels, harmonizing nicely
with the sky. There has been a lot of criticism
of the gallery, firstly for its role in the very
evident gentrification of parts of the town
– divided as it is between an extremely
uneasy combination of extreme poverty and
Hackney overspill, it feels very much aimed
at the latter group. More pettily, because
an elaborately 'iconic' competition-winning
design by Snøhetta was dropped in favour
of Chipperfield's simpler, more pragmatic
replacement. In architectural terms, this was
a smart move. Not solely because fashion
shifted in the 2010s away from 'icons'
towards relative classicism and sobriety, but
because their design showed little interest
in the qualities of light that drew painters
here in the first instance. This is precisely
what dominates Chipperfield's design –
it feels completely of a piece with its place.
I suspect it will endure.

SOLENT

WINTER GARDENS, VENTNOR, ISLE OF WIGHT
A. D. Clare, 1935
International Style

'A brave attempt', says the *Buildings of England*, at a miniature version of the **De La Warr Pavilion (p. 234)**, but built on a much more picturesque site. Ventnor is the town of the Undercliff, an area of the Isle of Wight given a microclimate through its placement between the sea, high cliffs, and successive landslides, a balminess enjoyed by residents who at one time included most eminent Victorians, not to mention Turgenev and Marx. The Winter Gardens are placed on one of the peaks of the landslip, with a high view of the sea, and they borrow Bexhill's curved glass prow and the white concrete cubic flanking wings.

Still highly impressive from the waterfront, where it crowns an exotically planted ridge – but marred up close by UPVC windows and cheap railings, while, inside, thirties stairwells and horrible new carpets and suspended ceilings fight it out.

———

KINGSLAND ESTATE, SOUTHAMPTON ✪
Johnson & Crabtree, 1949
SOUTHAMPTON BENCHES
Leon Berger for Southampton City Council Architects Dept, 1950s
International Style

The Kingsland Estate, known locally as Cossack Green after its main square, is the only built fragment of the utopian socialist 1943 Adshead Plan for the bombed city,

De Stijl on the Solent: the minimalist low-rise flats of the Kingsland Estate, in the centre of Southampton.

and the first landmark in Southampton's extensive adventure in modernist planning. Next to, and sheltered by trees from, the main railway line into London are several curved low-rise blocks, with nice big balconies, rendered white and pale green in the 1930s manner, and recently restored. Behind this, at Cossack Green, you can find rather formal concrete terraces around two Maillol-esque nude sculptures of Adam and Eve. The Kingsland Estate doesn't belong to the forties, visually and architecturally – it's the sort of Weimar Berlin modernist Garden City style we never really had. A placid but urbane enclave.

Note also on Cossack Green the public benches by the City Architect Leon Berger. These are typical examples of the 'Southampton bench', with rugged concrete pillars supporting planks, a simple and expressive design that you can find all over the city, which would go on to be copied all over the country and beyond.

———

OIL REFINERY, FAWLEY
Esso Engineers, 1950
FAWLEY POWER STATION ❶
Farmer & Dark, 1970
Industrial, Brutalist

Two distinct industrial megastructures on Southampton Water. Fawley Refinery is the *Blade Runner* skyline of plumes of flame, neon and steel that is visible from all raised points in Southampton and its environs. Baffling in its complexity up close, an intestinal city that looks organic and smells foul, as thrilling in its endless loops, twists and turns as **Lloyd's of London (p. 69)**, and considerably more functional. At night, it's a metropolis of haunting, fiery beauty.

Next to it, the much later power station is a massive long Brutalist volume, crowned by a glass upper storey with meticulous, cubistic rooflights, linked at ground level to a cylindrical, raised control room that has

unsurprisingly been used as a dystopian film set (I remember being taken on school trips there, and the uncanniness of its thrumming, rumbling noise). Derelict and likely to be demolished, though extant at the time of writing and easily seen. A Twentieth Century Society attempt at listing was refused and the main block was demolished in late 2019, but there are apparently still hopes to at least preserve the control room.

———

CLIFF LIFT, SHANKLIN, ISLE OF WIGHT
1956–8
International Style

Bravura engineering – a tall concrete shaft up against the high sandstone cliffs of this gorgeous Victorian seaside town, angular and monumental, with sans serif capitals set into the concrete, telling you what it is – 'LIFT'. Due to the cliff's endless erosion – a big problem in the Isle of Wight – the walkway has had to be replaced with an extended version every couple of decades.

———

NORTHAM ESTATE, SOUTHAMPTON
Leon Berger for Southampton City Council Architects Dept, 1959–60
International Style

This is the most complete, most extensive and most successful of several housing schemes designed by Leon Berger for the City Architects Department of this port city, and is a good example of the general standard of the fifties at its best – not particularly expressive or individualist, but light, intelligent, green, spacious and humane. A covered shopping centre (mostly now derelict) and a block on pilotis form the public gateway to a series of splayed five-storey blocks of purple and brown brick with blue, green and red coloured panels inset into their extensive glass facades. These sit among dense trees, and are angled to offer the top floors views (and sounds) of the adjacent wharves, the port and the Itchen Bridge, an experience I enjoyed while briefly living in one of these flats.

The intended vertical 'accent', the high-rise Millbank House, which originally used the same brick and coloured panels as the lower bocks, was clad in the 1990s with red and white plastic (in the local football team's colours, serendipitously, given that Southampton FC's ground would be moved nearby at the end of the 1990s); this has weathered reasonably well but has an unfortunate effect on the estate's coherence.

———

UNIVERSITY OF SOUTHAMPTON ✪
Basil Spence, Bonnington & Collins, 1960–70
MATHEMATICS BUILDING, UNIVERSITY OF SOUTHAMPTON
Roland Ward, 1965
HIGHFIELD BUS INTERCHANGE
Feilden Clegg Bradley Studios, 2010
International Style, Brutalist, Ecomodernist

In the city's suburbs, this is closer to a miniature New University than an extension of the somewhat forgettable brick buildings with which the place was founded in the 1920s. Spence's work here is much more in the international mainstream than the Brutalist New Delhi at the **University of Sussex (p. 238)** – concrete and Portland stone, ribbon windows, framing lush gardens and, most memorably, Barbara Hepworth's *Two Figures*. A few of the original Spence buildings stand out – the copper-clad box of the Nuffield Theatre, where Justin Knowles's sculpture *Steel Forms* stands as a sort of campanile; the Faraday Tower, suspended, like an El Lissitzky project, from a central pillar, so that it appears to float above the leafy semis around (it has been threatened with demolition for at least a decade, but stands at the time of writing);

and the glass-and-steel grid of the Students' Union, a Miesian pavilion that rests with great assurance on a small hillock. Roland Ward's Mathematics Building is something else – castellated Brutalism, with a spindly stair tower up from the hill. After Spence, buildings by Grimshaw and others are mediocre but assured, with the exception of the university's Bus Interchange, an angular wooden construction with an attached pavilion. It is small, but has real civic presence, although the fact that it's probably the best single thing built in Southampton since the 1970s says more about the city than the station itself. As it stands, Southampton University should be seen alongside the more urban likes of **Wyndham Court (p. 248)**, **Castle House (p. 247)** or **Weston Shore (p. 248)**, monuments to the period when the more vague and sprawling of the Solent's two cities punched well above its weight architecturally; a period the city should be much more proud of than it is.

———

CLARENCE PIER, SOUTHSEA
A. E. Cogswell and R. Lewis Raynish, 1961
People's Detailing

If anybody doubts that modern architecture could be just as tawdry and kitsch and embarrassingly enjoyable as anything from the nineteenth century, they should go immediately to this seedy funfair in Southsea. A blue and yellow check pattern on a glass curtain-walled tower, flanked by wings with fancy hyperbolic paraboloid butterfly roofs, it is the fifties Anglo-modernist repertoire with any hint of Scando-socialist high-mindedness removed, replaced by a naffness that derives alternately from *Thunderbirds* and Butlin's. This is the Festival of Britain if it had been organized by Benny Hill rather than Herbert Morrison.

TRINITY GREEN, GOSPORT ✪
W. H. Saunders & Son with Kenneth Barden and J. E. Tyrrell (artists), 1961
GOSPORT TOWN HALL
W. H. Saunders & Son, 1962
People's Detailing

Gosport, on the other side of a commuter ferry across a busy estuary, is geographically and economically Portsmouth's Birkenhead, although Pompey could probably only look like a Liverpool from here, with the almost charmingly gratuitous Spinnaker Tower a sort of sub-Dubai version of the **St John's Beacon (p. 429)**, and with dense barracks instead of the Pier Head. Gosport has one thing Portsmouth mostly doesn't – interesting council housing. While the big city over the water, run for much of the post-war period by a minority Labour council, scrabbled to build as much housing to rehouse slum-dwellers as it could via a massive programme of system-building, Gosport opted for something much more bespoke, with the major clearance and rebuilding of the area around the Ferry Terminal displaying an imagination and intelligent use of public space that is on the level of the Southampton housing of the time. The two major phases of the project are visible from the Portsmouth side – the Harbour and Seaward Towers, chunky sixteen-storey slabs decorated down each side with gorgeous, biomorphic abstract mosaics to the design of Kenneth Barden and J. E. Tyrrell.

Around these is an estate of unexpectedly high quality, with terraces, towers and slabs surrounding a square centred on the punchy, Hanseatic red-brick Holy Trinity Church, with a Gothic campanile and an English Baroque interior. At Trinity Close are two delightful Festival of Britain-style terraces, with tile-clad gables, blue mosaic entrances and witty, lightweight concrete canopies at the entrances; behind these is an **Alton Estate**-like **(p. 112)** picturesque setting of mid-rise towers among winding paths and trees, which now, painted in pastel colours, look even more Swedish than they must have done when they opened. Opposite these is the Town Hall, by the same architects, the local firm W. H. Saunders, who built a lot in Southampton, Portsmouth and Bournemouth. It is a good, vigorous building with an asymmetrical arrangement of curtain-walled offices, clad in tough brick and copper, around a cantilevered, curved chamber that has a hint of Lubetkin to it. A town you wouldn't expect to be full of modernist civic pride turns out to have it in abundance.

___

MARITIME ACADEMY, WARSASH
Sheppard Robson, 1962–5
Brutalist

Along with the university, the most complete modernist ensemble in the Southampton area, kept coherent by virtue of compactness and the listing system. This place began as a college to train seafarers and, especially, the Merchant Navy, and now does much the same thing with an additional focus on the oil industry – you can see Fawley **Oil Refinery (p. 244)** from the estuary here. The site is dreamy, a hill above the River Hamble, just where it meets Southampton Water, so giving a tree-shadowed view of the container ships. On this, Sheppard Robson have built what is essentially a nautical version of their slightly earlier **Churchill College (p. 204)**, unpretentious, tough modern architecture of concrete, stock brick and wood, but with an awareness of the importance of public spaces and ceremonial interiors to creating some sort of community out of an institution. The major buildings are a block of halls (originally for cadets) with cantilevered common rooms looking over the estuary and the Moyana Building, a set of common rooms and classrooms built partly into the hill, with an Alvar Aalto profile of roofs and projecting cafés with terraces emerging out of the greenery. Behind these, away from the sea, is a barracks-like parade square around the block containing the main lecture theatre, with a lovely, warm curved-wood staircase. The Maritime Academy exemplifies that early-sixties moment when modernism was adapted with relatively little compromise to venerable imperial institutions like Oxbridge and the army.

WINCHESTER SCHOOL OF ART
H. Benson Ansell, 1962–4
International Style

A delightful and too little-known building – it isn't even listed, though it would have been decades ago were it in London or Cambridge. A simple teaching block connects via a tiny little skybridge to a faceted rotunda (originally the library, now studios) with a somewhat cosmic, Expo '58 air, which sits, raised by a single concrete column, on a pond just next to the river Itchen, which has fairly untamed banks round these parts. Light and optimistic modernist *rus-in-urbe*, tucked away where nobody can get offended by it, a good distance from medieval Winchester. In sunny weather, this is one of the most utopian small ensembles in the country, with the trees, the water and the glass all in perfect alignment.

CASTLE HOUSE, SOUTHAMPTON
Eric Lyons, 1964
Brutalist

It can be hard to find commonality between what Eric Lyons did for private and public clients – the dozens of Span estates scattered around the Home Counties, such as **Parkleys (p. 111)** and **New Ash Green (p. 240)**, are tightly planned little things, with their thin-lipped facades of weatherboarding and manicured lawns. The scale and demands of the high-rise estate are totally different,

and it's no surprise that the collaborative **World's End Estate (p. 168)**, for instance, appears much more as the work of Cadbury-Brown than Lyons. So here, while the gold-on-black-granite lettering at the entrance to Castle House evokes that of **Hallgate (p. 87)**, and the vestibule is way above the usual council standard, the car park with which this meets Southampton Old Town is poor public space by Lyons's standards. Everything else about Castle House, though, is a triumph – a bravura attempt to re-create the city-crowning effect of the long-destroyed old castle within the (extant) medieval city walls, with slats of concrete along generous, **Park Hill**-sized **(p. 370)** streets in the sky. A recent renovation has made a mess of the south facade, with cheap standardized glass balconies, but it would take much more than that to ruin something this powerful.

WINCHESTER LAW COURTS
Louis de Soissons and Richard Fraser, 1964–73
Brutalist

A somewhat sombre medieval-Brutalist building, though a very well-crafted one, with its rhythm of sandstone boxed-out windows and a heavy, rough and knobbly concrete aggregate that blends well with the surrounding Gothic and neo-Gothic buildings without being patronizing or arse-kissing; certainly vastly preferable to the tedious, thin-lipped architectural Toryism of the County Hall nearby. What elevates the Law Courts from standard municipal Brutalism into something more poetic is the landscaping around it, with a grand flight of steps to the Gothic Great Hall, and an intriguing passageway into the maze-like ruins of Winchester Castle, the heart of what was once the capital.

WESTON SHORE, SOUTHAMPTON
Southampton City Council Architects Dept, 1930s/1968
Ryder & Yates, 1968
International Style

One of the strangest, most memorable set pieces of the 1960s: a row of slab blocks, **Alton Estate**-style **(p. 112)**, separated by a wild meadow from a beach on Southampton Water, with the Solent beyond. Coming into Southampton from the sea, it heralds your arrival better than any of the buildings in the city centre, a gateway to the world, right down to the names of its towers. After Hampton are Havre, Oslo, Copenhagen, Rotterdam, Canberra – places you could once go to from here. In front are shelters, similar to the **Bus Shelters, Brighton (p. 237)**, rendered curved concrete and glass moderne. The towers were never great architecture in themselves, and their recent renovation and repainting is not invasive. The tallest tower is by Ryder & Yates, though its blocky design doesn't quite compare with their work in Tyneside. The point here, though, is the landscape – a vision of the *ville radieuse* more complete than perhaps anywhere else in Britain, spacey, verdant, fishy, and with a spectacular view of the Fawley **Oil Refinery (p. 244)**.

WYNDHAM COURT, SOUTHAMPTON ✪
Lyons Israel Ellis, 1969
Brutalist

Just outside Southampton Central Station, this is one of the most audacious schemes of the time, a statement of intent from the city about the importance of its council housing, and its faith in modernity. An irregular square of mid-rise flats, with shops and restaurants on the ground floor, car parking underneath and a raised plaza between, with everything modelled in the same expensively made, fair-faced concrete, with the board marks of the shutters clearly visible. What elevates it from an extremely well-crafted estate in a prominent location into something more – into something that represents an idea and ethos for Southampton – is the undercurrent of nautical imagery, in the cruiser (or battleship) lines of the long block, and the Cunardian thrust prow of the projecting east side of the square. This is a sea city, a working-class city, and a city that is unafraid of avant-garde ideas. If only it were true. **[B.8]**

IBM COSHAM, PORTSMOUTH
Foster Associates, 1971–3
High-Tech

The northern suburbs of Portsmouth – Porchester, Paulsgrove, Cosham – are among the truly sinister landscapes of Britain. Everything is overshadowed by the forts and complex military installations of Portsdown Hill; and what is below can be surprisingly High-Tech, a reminder that the most advanced part of British industry is highly skilled workers devising interesting ways of killing people. It's no accident that IBM set up its first major offices in the UK here – the internet was invented by the US military, after all. The corporation occupies two complexes in suburban Cosham – North Harbour, a lakeside Arup Associates project along similar lines to their work for Birmingham and Loughborough Universities, which is heavily altered – and this, a very early Norman Foster building, almost untouched (bar a naff new entrance). An incredibly long, single-storey black-smoked-glass volume, it is both seamlessly, smoothly technocratic and extremely looming, surrounded by nothing but grass, car parks and the view of the chalk hills. I'm sure Foster would have justified it all with reference to the technical demands of the supercomputers that would have been placed in it, but the design virtually screams 'military industrial complex'. It's offices for the Inland Revenue now.

The thrillingly monumental articulated volumes and three-dimensional massing of Norrish Library in Portsmouth.

GRAFTON & ESTELLA, PORTSMOUTH

Portsmouth City Council Architects Dept, 1973–5
Brutalist

These blocks are quite the surprise if you come into Portsmouth from France on the ferry – rather than the dour towers and barracks that you might expect if you know Portsmouth, you instead arrive at a dramatic red-brick modernist complex. Arranged along the M275 but sheltered from it by dense trees, it's a mini-**Park Hill (p. 370)**, in its scale, a series of interlinked blocks connected by walkways, although here with **Lillington Gardens**-style **(p. 57)** articulated, sculptural brick-and-tile Brutalist profiles, much more imposing and richly textured than the standardized blocks that dominate the city. For pedestrians, best approached along Grafton Street or Estella Road.

NORRISH LIBRARY, PORTSMOUTH ○

Ken Norrish for Portsmouth City Council Architects Dept, 1976
Brutalist

There isn't much modernist architecture of quality in the centre of Portsmouth – at least, not since the totally gratuitous demolition of Owen Luder's Tricorn Centre – but there is this, and it would be enough for a lot of cities. Standing as a pivot between a raised block of flats and the civic ensemble of Guildhall Square, Norrish Library is ambitious, complex and grandiose. To the walkways behind, it presents a massive, reverse-tapering curved profile, Pompey's answer to the Guggenheim – an almost terrifyingly confident command of enormous, brute physical form. To the square, a turret-like service tower and the cantilevered upper floors of the reading rooms, with a simple glass entrance, appear remarkably restrained after all this heavy-breathing melodrama. The stair towers are in béton brut, the curved block in smooth fair-faced concrete, and the lower stairwells in the same tiles as the walkways. An astonishing achievement – a civic building both endlessly fascinating to explore and straightforward to use. The library was renamed after its architect in the 1990s, an unusual gesture which says a lot about the high regard in which this place is held. [B.15]

CIVIC OFFICES, PORTSMOUTH
Teggin & Taylor, 1976
International Style

Absurdly simple – essentially two dark mirrorglass walls to frame two dramatic monuments. These office blocks on Guildhall Square each feature a ceremonial approach of steps, echoing that of the flamboyant Edwardian baroque Guildhall and embracing the slug-like bronze of Queen Victoria, but their flat glass facades are clearly designed to reflect the Guildhall and **Norrish Library (above)**. The strongly defined pedestrian space and the alternation of straightforward blocks and wild civic buildings help form an ensemble that is one of the unheralded modernist squares of Britain.

IBIS HOTEL, PORTSMOUTH
Pierre-Yves Cochin, late 1970s
UNIVERSITY OF PORTSMOUTH LIBRARY
Ahrends Burton & Koralek, 1977/
Penoyre & Prasad, 2007
Brutalist

Ibis built dozens of identical prefab capsule hotels across Europe between the mid-seventies and the mid-eighties, and this one, on Winston Churchill Avenue, is the only British version I've come across. What it is doing in Portsmouth, of all cities, is anyone's

guess – maybe it was easy to ship it across the Channel from Le Havre. Of course, there are standard hotel designs all over the UK, and they're usually the absolute worst ingredient of a given 'regeneration' – prefab modules ineptly covered by a skein of the tackiest, cheapest cladding, the architecture of inbuilt obsolescence that 1960s radicals wrongly promised us would be interesting. But this, while indisputably one of the ancestors of that trend, was a rather chic design, with its curved concrete panels creating a wave effect, and its space pod-like toilet windows. It told you from the off that it was mass produced and prefabricated, as if that would be a selling point. The results are Fassbinderian, a landscape of hard and seedy modernity, Trans-European ennui. The first version of this building was put up in Bordeaux, in 1974, and there aren't many buildings in Portsmouth that are identical to a building in Bordeaux in 1974.

Opposite is a different kind of Brutalism altogether: Portsmouth University's library, a somewhat gaunt and grey Ahrends Burton & Koralek design of the 1970s with a contrast of heavy masonry (here, breezeblocks) and glass to that of their (much better) **Maidenhead Library (p. 219)**. Happily, the building has benefited from a good recent remodelling and a classical-modernist extension by Penoyre & Prasad.

CHANDLERS FORD LIBRARY, EASTLEIGH
Hampshire County Architects Dept, 1982
CRESTWOOD SCHOOL, EASTLEIGH
Hampshire County Architects Dept, 1985
Ecomodernist

In the 1980s and '90s, the flag of municipal modern architecture was flown by just one surviving local authority architects' department – bizarrely, this was Tory Hampshire. The County Architect (and former county cricketer) Colin Stansfield-Smith led a team which was frequently praised as proof that the idea of a social modern architecture hadn't quite died; accordingly, the department attracted talented refugees from the sixties like George Finch and Kate Macintosh. A lot of the department's activity was responding to failures of the market, providing schools, libraries and other basic social facilities for the unplanned sprawl that sprung up along the M27's 'Solent City', where houses, industrial parks and retail parks had been built without much provision for human life. These two are public buildings in what are effectively unplanned new towns on the outskirts of Eastleigh, on the outskirts of Southampton – Boyatt Wood, a collection of typical sixties/seventies houses and estates, and Chandlers Ford, a slightly more ambitious project whose 'centre' consists of two pedestrian precincts – Central Precinct, a crisp, colourful Eric Lyons-like effort, and the more grim, very vaguely Brutalist Fryern Precinct, where the central space is a car park.

Both Crestwood School and Chandlers Ford Library use deep, spreading, monopitch roofs over crescent plans, in which generous, glazed social spaces have been ingeniously created; modernist and Aalto-indebted, but with warm materials, no concrete and no scaring of the horses. The airy space of Chandlers Ford's double-height library is created by a forest of thin, tree-like columns, bolted to glass panels, a delicate, elegant space, with a hint of the strange that is much needed round these parts; outside, it forms a relatively civic square in front of the Fryern Precinct and some naff Postmodern shops. Crestwood is bigger and more ambitious. Its exterior is a Chandlers Ford-like crescent, with Aalto-esque abstract blocks of warm red brick facing a shopping precinct and a church. This only hints at what you'll find inside, which is the most impressive modernist interior in the Solent City – a lofty internal 'street', glazed in perspex, leading through brick arcades to the classrooms.

Without, unlike so many of the buildings of the era, borrowing nineteenth-century motifs, it has the feel of a utopian socialist project by some Robert Owen or Charles Fourier – the new world, under glass. The arcade was originally open to the public, and had trees inside; neither of which is the case now, but it is still worth bargaining with the receptionist for a walk through.

————

HARBOUR LIGHTS CINEMA, SOUTHAMPTON
Burrell Foley Fischer, 1997
Modernist Eclectic

In the context of the grim combination of Postmodernism and Blairboxes that is Southampton's 'Ocean Village', this building is a beacon – a cantilvered, timber-clad block with a glazed stairwell forming a 'prow', with a supergraphic 'CINEMA' at the top and a raised café overlooking the activity-free marina. Confident, public, friendly and light-hearted, it is lit up impressively at night.

————

WASTE-TO-ENERGY DOME, MARCHWOOD
Jean-Robert Mazaud, 2007
High-Tech

A combined incinerator and power station under a glistening steel dome, with a chimney placed off-centre, this is a thrilling industrial building. Framed by the skyscraping cranes of Southampton's container port, this place is an inhuman landscape of automation, distribution and disposal, chilling in its complete effacement of the remotest notion of the 'human scale', and wildly exciting for the same reason. It is not somewhere that can be visited by pedestrians, but is so unmissably sublime that a wander around the mouth of the River Test will involve it looming over you, constantly.

4. SOUTH-WEST

Clifton Cathedral, Bristol (p. 270)

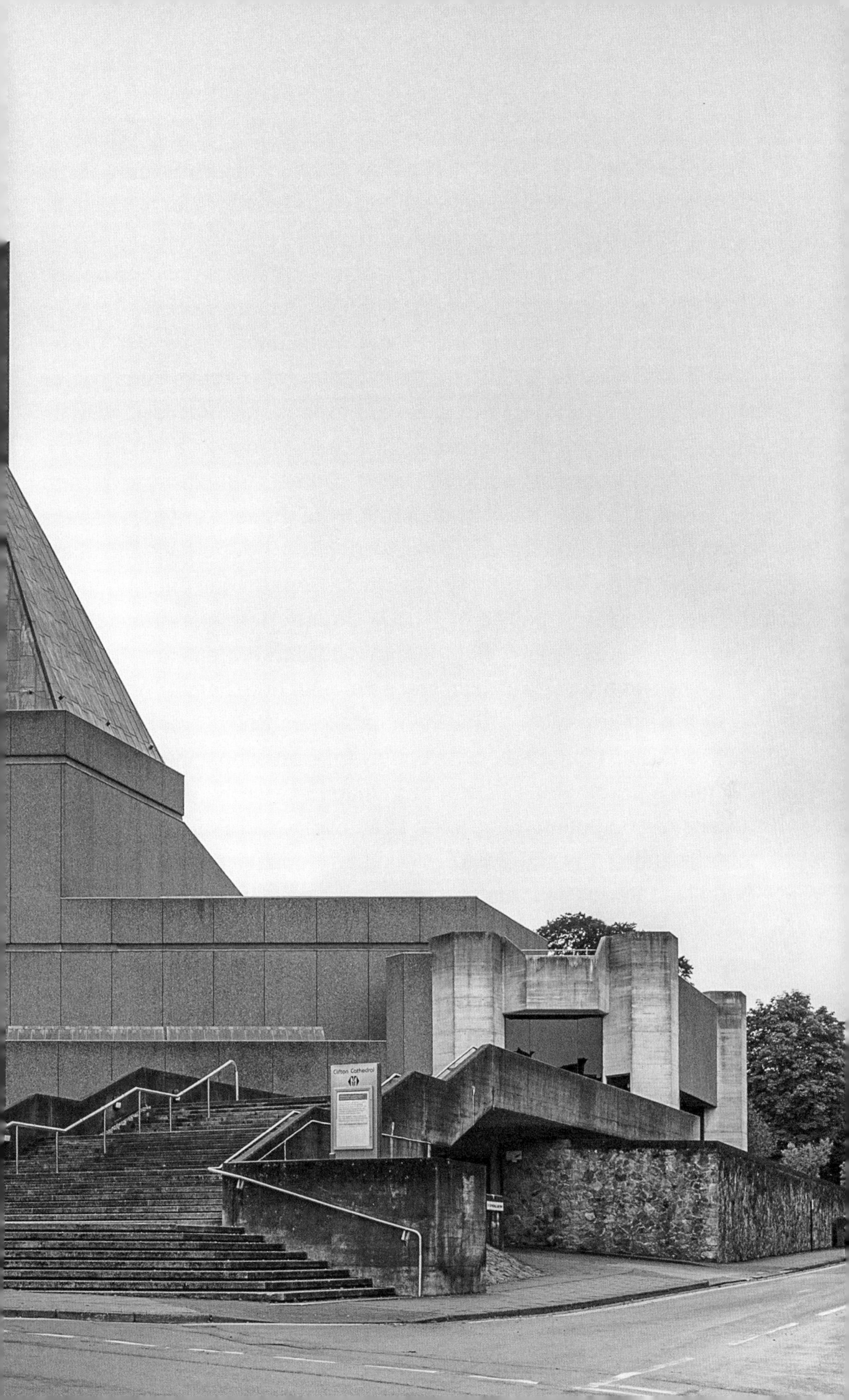
Clifton Cathedral

'If you want to like modern architecture, don't come to the south-west,' wrote Ian Nairn in 1965. This harsh judgement needs only slight revision today. The West Country is not natural territory for modernism of any kind, consisting as it does mostly of obsessively preserved stone towns and villages, with imitations of the same in culs-de-sac as the main example of modernity. There's a handful of good Brutalist buildings in Bath, Taunton and Frome, some civic planning in Exeter and a remarkable group of neo-avant-garde **Artist-Constructor Houses** in Flax Bourton, but these are exceptions. Cornwall, with its strong sense of regional identity, its rich landscape and its distinct light, is a different proposition from Devon, Dorset, Gloucestershire and Somerset, and has attracted generations of modern artists; perhaps accordingly, it has a legacy of excellent libraries and civic buildings designed by its 1960s County Architects Department, culminating in the monumental Brutalism of Truro's **County Hall**. More recently, its landscape qualities are celebrated in the **Eden Project**.

The two big cities, Bristol and Plymouth, both heavily bombed in 1940, are a study in contrasts. Plymouth is almost too rigidly planned, with its Eastern European-style boulevards, relaxing only at the lovely **Pannier Market**; while Bristol is a chaotic place where it feels like dozens of competing plans were tried over several decades and all found wanting. Central Bristol is good for housing, however, with the Corbusian **Redcliffe Flats** and the Aalto-style **High Kingsdown** built densely into teeming streets; in **Clifton Cathedral**, meanwhile, the city has Britain's finest modernist church, an intensely personal and inward work.

WEST COUNTRY

DARTINGTON HALL, TOTNES ✪
William Lescaze, 1932–4
International Style

Occasionally fancifully described as the 'British Bauhaus', this place doubles as a useful way of explaining why there was no British Bauhaus. Dartington Hall was founded by the educators Dorothy and Leonard Elmhirst in the twenties as an experimental, progressive college, centred on a picturesque, slate-grey medieval complex, with the titular grand hall, landscaped gardens, a gaunt lone church tower, and panoramic views of Dartmoor – and it would soon play a major role in everything from avant-garde ballet to the composition of the 1945 Labour manifesto. Gropius himself converted one of the hall's ancillary buildings to a cinema. But whereas the Bauhaus was in Dessau, the German equivalent of, say, Wolverhampton, its British emulation had to be set in gorgeous, misty, mammarial rolling hills, distant from the nearest city (Plymouth is half an hour by train, but you wouldn't know it). Even so, the Elmhirsts' choice of William Lescaze to design Dartington's new buildings suggested that they meant business – the Swiss-American modernist would provide for it what are extremely early International Style buildings for anywhere in Britain, let alone for Devon, then as now a backwater for modern architecture, despite the possibilities of the sea, sun, landscape and second-home-owners from London that it offers.

The earliest part is High Cross House, built for the headmaster, a ten-minute walk up and down hill from the original hall. A blunt, flat facade with a small ribbon window, painted

William Lescaze's High Cross House at Dartington Hall: an International Style house in the Devon countryside.

blue, faces the road. Open the gate – this is, along with **2 Willow Road (p. 142)**, one of only two interwar modernist houses in the country where there is easy public access – and find a geometrically complex box of modernist tricks. The blue frontage, which also contains a garage, meets a white garden facade, intricately composed and different from every angle; a single curved storey comes up against a cuboid mass, which has an open corner, a patio supported by a single spindly piloti. It was restored by John Winter in the 1990s, but at the time of writing it needs a repainting at the very least. Much better looked after are a clutch of very simple, **East Tilbury**-style **(p. 176)** cubist cottages for the college's menial staff, and. opposite them, miniature collective housing, in the form of the three halls of residence built for students, all of them slightly different, but sharing a strong horizontal emphasis, recalling the much harder, Communistic side of continental modernism. The best of these performs a delightful trick with pilotis, where half the upper floor's weight appears to be supported by three pencil-like pillars, which let you wander freely through the space, enjoying the views. And then you spot the massive concrete stairwell at the end that is the actual structural support, and realize the game being played with you. It is all very brave – a transplant of flat suburban Berlin, sitting oddly in the green Devon contours. The bright colours and hard shapes brook no compromise. [A.6]

KINGSMEAD FLATS, BATH
Corporation of Bath, 1932/
Feilden Clegg Bradley Studios, 1992
Moderne, Postmodernist

A really fine rehabilitated council estate, much more comparable to the 'Critical Reconstruction' of 1980s Berlin than the run of the British mill. Good 1930s blocks in Bath stone, with the usual afterthought public space fit only for cars and bins, were subtly reshaped by Feilden Clegg Bradley for a Housing Association, with new tiled upper storeys, walkways formed into private balconies, with square bay windows with a hint of Mackintosh affixed to the old facades. Most importantly, the scrubby land in-between was turned into a real green. Simple stuff, but such an obvious leap in quality of life.

EXETER:
DEVON HOUSE, CORN EXCHANGE, CENTRAL LIBRARY & BUS STATION ❶
H. B. Rowe for Exeter City Architects Dept, 1955–64
PRINCESSHAY
Chapman Taylor and Panter Hudspith, 2007–18
ROYAL ALBERT MEMORIAL MUSEUM EXTENSION
Allies & Morrison, 2012
People's Detailing, Classical Modernism

Exeter's reconstruction is a major contrast with Plymouth, at the other end of Devon. They share a dominance of stiff modern/classical hybrids, but there strict design rules and a clear route to the sea give the conservative planning a certain grandeur. In Exeter, a pioneering plan by Thomas Sharp was ignored, and the result can seem stifling. If you've ever wondered what would happen if you took an Erich Mendelsohn department store and tried to make it neo-Georgian, Exeter is the place for you. However, if you look beyond the Anthony Eden Stalinallee of High Street, there's actually much to admire, usually in the corners of the rebuilding – a reversal of how Plymouth has a superb main boulevard that evaporates at the edges. The Corn Exchange, at the point where chain store Exeter meets student Exeter, is notable mainly for 'period' reasons – diapered brickwork, very fifties preserved signage;

the better work reacts against the domineering classical rigidity around. The mixed-use block of Devon House, on the corner of High Street and Paris Street, begins with a concrete rotunda whose colonnade leads round to a curved red-brick shopping parade. This ends at the bus station, a simple modern block with a springy concrete canopy behind it, whose supports look like stylized hammers.

Opposite this is Princesshay, which replaced part of the reconstruction with a surprisingly architecturally confident new **St Peter's Arcade**-style **(p. 432)** 'Mall Without Walls', which features many cute references to the fifties buildings around. A corner on the other side of High Street leads to a crisp and unpretentious municipal library, beginning with a curved entrance to a side street, with the reading rooms expressed as a cube, projected out over a slope. Facing it is Allies & Morrison's quizzical, abstract extension to the Ruskin Gothic Albert Museum, a series of pavilions on multiple levels around a fragment of the Roman Wall. All of this is both much more imaginative and respectful than you'll find in most cathedral cities, but it's still notable that most of the post-war city's good ideas have had to be hidden in alleyways, behind the most banal fronts.

BATH TECHNICAL COLLEGE
Frederick Gibberd Partnership, 1956–65
International Style

Obviously you don't go to Bath for modern architecture, but you do go there for *architecture*, and if you do so, you won't fail to pass this. Absolutely loathed in the 1970s, this is now clearly by far the best of the mannered infill structures that were rather hysterically branded as the 'Sack of Bath' – the city was evidently not sacked, but few of the new buildings were much cop, evidently

too scared of conservationists to draw much attention to themselves, which of course compounded the problem. The Technical College was not nearly so fussy. A big square block, clad in Bath stone, with an irregular grid 'respecting the city's traditions' and a cantilevered lecture theatre which ignores them completely, to go off into its own world of angular geometry. The council houses at Ballance Street are also well worth a look as decent examples of what conservationists in Bath straight-facedly call 'the Sack era'.

UNIVERSITY OF EXETER: ✪ NORTHCOTE HOUSE
William Holford & Partners, 1956
PHYSICS TOWER
Basil Spence, Bonnington & Collins, 1963–7
LAVER BUILDING
Louis de Soissons Partnership, 1966
OLD LIBRARY & BILL DOUGLAS CENTRE
William Holford & Partners, 1966
Modern Classicism, Brutalist

One of the few planned spaces to do anything interesting with the rolling landscape of the South-West, the self-described 'city on a hill' at Exeter has the best site of any post-war university in England (if not quite as magical as the **University of Stirling, p. 508**). It also has two vertical points obviously intended as *Stadtkronen*. The earlier is by the staid planner-architect William Holford, who designed much of the campus – rather than the somewhat pompous classicized modernism he specialized in (exemplified by the Great Hall here), Northcote House is just a Scandinavian civic building from the 1930s, and all the better for it, with rich brickwork, pretty copper detailing, decorative rams heads, and a high campanile. The other high point, just as enjoyable, is Basil Spence's Physics Tower, a strip of workshops balanced very jauntily

The architectural joke of Basil Spence's Physics Tower, looming over the greenery of the University of Exeter.

on top of a long, low brick range – the way it peeps out from above the trees in views from St David's Station exemplifies the sense of mischief that got Spence in trouble with the cognoscenti. It also occasionally appears on 'most ugly building in Exeter' lists, which is an example, to paraphrase Mark E. Smith, of 'scientists and their bloody childish architectural tastes'. Between these, various specialized buildings, mostly in red brick, descend the steep hills, most with grand views; the best of them maximize these, as in the projecting, double-height lookout at the top of the Laver Building.

Most of the generally dull new buildings are on a separate site nearby, so the campus remains surprisingly coherent. The only addition of note on the main campus is The Forum, a flowing timber and steel roofscape by Wilkinson Eyre, intended to pull the Great Hall together with the theatre and ancillary buildings nearby. But the most

exciting addition draws less attention to itself. In Holford's Old Library, a powerful cluster of miniature brick-and-concrete towers set on a ridge, is the Bill Douglas Cinema Museum, which assembles the great Scottish director's incredible collection of cinematic tat and nineteenth-century optical illusions, laid out in vitrines under a delicate oculus. Warning: time here falls easily out of joint. [C.18]

___

BOSCOMBE PIER, BOURNEMOUTH
John Burton for Bournemouth Borough Engineers Dept, 1958
People's Detailing

A most atypical seaside pier, the diametric opposite of the mallscape of Bournemouth Pier, at the other end of the same beach. A witty, attractive entrance canopy in Festival of Britain style leads to the most laconic, unornamented pier, of wood on concrete: clear, uncluttered, just you, everyone else and the sea. It would be a great shame if all piers were like this, but the minimalism and concentrated force of this one make it uniquely beautiful.

___

BRISTOL & WEST HOUSE, BOURNEMOUTH
1958
Moderne

Bournemouth has quite a lot of modern architecture, very little of it worth looking at, but this is an exception. Taking up most of a city block, this is a good albeit conservative modern building, of a type seen much more often in the North, and in the 1930s, at that. Domesticated Mendelsohn in stock brick, with four storeys of strip windows, a curved block to one end, leading to a dramatic, partly glazed stairwell. Recently converted from offices into flats, without too much damage being done to the design.

ARNDALE CENTRE, POOLE
Leslie Jones & Partners, 1963–9
BARCLAYS HOUSE, POOLE
Wilson Mason & Partners, 1975
Brutalist

The most extreme and questionable makeovers of British towns and cities in the 1960s often happened in places where critics and conservationists weren't looking. Not in the great industrial cities like Bradford or Glasgow, nor in the allegedly defaced historic cities like Oxford or Bath, but in southern towns that were affluent enough not to be romantic, and not sufficiently historic to excite major preservation campaigns. They also tended to rebuild in a dull, parochial fashion, with the architects palpably uninterested in their task. Such was the fate of Poole, which has one of the most complete, radical and untouched multilevel city centres in the country. Of course, it is built around an Arndale Centre, albeit a low-rise one – various Brutalist and 'Contemporary' clichés thrown around a sprawling site, with flyovers for the cars and underpasses for the pedestrians and a surprisingly fetching concrete car park of intersecting cylinders. Also cylindrical is Barclays House, built as the national headquarters of the high-street bank; it consists of three great concrete drums, which look a bit pompous and banal from the front, where they're pulled into an unconvincing axial symmetry, but persist, and walk round its circumference – then you'll see how powerful they actually are, and how they're reached from a drastic upper-level walkway which connects to a rough Brutalist multistorey car park. If this ensemble was in a bigger, cooler city, someone would have made the screenprints, tote bags and mugs already.

UNIVERSITY OF BATH: THE PARADE
RMJM, 1966–75
SCHOOL OF ARCHITECTURE & ENGINEERING/NON-ACADEMIC STAFF BUILDING
Alison and Peter Smithson, 1982–91
Brutalist

It is unfortunate for Alison and Peter Smithson's reputation as architects, as opposed to architectural theorists, that their tricksy, intellectualized, somewhat ungainly and neurotic buildings are so often in close proximity to much more confident works by less feted designers who would never get to have their collected works published by Yale. So it is in Poplar, in Oxford and at the University of Bath. A lesser-known New University on an attractive green site on the outskirts of the city, the first masterplan is by RMJM, and is very closely comparable to contemporaries like Essex or Brunel, although on a smaller scale. Pedestrians and traffic are separated, with a walkway forming a continuous 'parade', which here is unusually symmetrical and channelled, like a Renaissance ideal city plan that happened to be realized after the invention of the private car. The walkway culminates in a mammoth teaching block, huge and frankly intimidating. Step off here from the walkways and you'll find yourself seconds later on green lawns, by trickling fountains.

The Smithsons were appointed as RMJM's successors at the start of the eighties, and their Architecture & Engineering School works as a gateway to the Parade. It encapsulates the problem. As always with the Smithsons' work, there are great ideas – here, particularly, the semi-secluded, semi-open walkway that runs through the building to the Parade, a much more intriguing means of circulation than the straightforward pedways built a decade earlier; but the expression of the buildings as a gaunt grid of Bath stone feels strained and clumsy. The weird heavy canopies of the verdantly sited Non-Academic Staff Building are similarly inexplicable. Throughout, the proportions are awkward, and the materials look provisional, but at this distance, it is hard to tell to what degree these are deliberate devices and to what degree simple ineptitude. These are puzzles it may be tempting to try and work out, but the architects sure didn't make it easy on themselves.

ELLENBRAY TOYS & STATIONERY, FROME

Bill Vallis, 1968
Brutalist

This punchy but humane Brutalist building is a delightful surprise in the otherwise deeply non-modernist hilltop townscape of Frome. Originally built as the town's municipal library – which was later moved to an airy but very traditionally styled Postmodernist block – it is aesthetically uncompromising, but closely fitted to the scale and the narrow streets of the town, almost right on the River Frome itself. It is broken up into two distinct volumes, unified by a strongly expressed concrete frame, with local stone in the aggregate of its fair-faced concrete. The main two-storey block features a bright, high-ceilinged main space which works perfectly in its current incarnation as a toy and stationery shop. A showcase of how to fit a modern building into a very old town without tweeness or aggression.

WYVERN THEATRE, SWINDON

Casson Conder & Partners, 1968
Brutalist

Swindon is the South-West's Birmingham, subject to what feels like a dozen unfinished post-war plans, but without

the topographical pile-up that saves Bristol. Ambitious spatial plans – walkways, overpasses, underpasses – and dozens of modern buildings of largely poor quality are overlaid on to a Victorian town centre which they batter into submission. Casson and Conder's theatre is the most ambitious part of this project, though designed in their usual somewhat dour but professional mild-Brutalist manner. Bulky shapes in stock brick, concrete and beaten metal, with spacious foyers inside – a compacted version of their Derby **Assembly Rooms (p. 362)**. What makes the Wyvern Theatre worth seeing is its connection to an overhead walkway system, with the entrances set at the second level, and steps leading to the grim surface car park below. Planning for the car rather than the pedestrian, of course, but the elevated square thus created, with its view out over the city, is intriguing, as is the porte cochère in one corner that looks like it would work as a Brutalist bandstand. Amazingly, there appear to be no current plans to demolish the building.

ARTIST-CONSTRUCTOR HOUSES, FLAX BOURTON ✪

Bob and Tim Organ, 1972
Brutalist

Modernist architecture and the countryside haven't gone together comfortably anywhere, and less so in Britain than most places. The exceptions are usually vast Home Counties private houses past long driveways, totally inaccessible to everyone who doesn't live in them (though anyone who wants to look at glossy pictures of these is recommended Alan Powers's *Modern – the Modern Movement in Britain*). So, what is this series of high-modernist custom-built houses looking out over the green hills of Somerset doing – and in what a plaque outside the parish church proudly proclaims as Winner of the Calor Gas Armstrong Cup for Avon

Small Villages 1993? One answer is 'urban proximity'. Flax Bourton is only around eight miles from the centre of Bristol, the second village out after the continuous urban area ends, and the bus service into town is more frequent than in some Bristol suburbs. Yet there's still much that can't be explained. These four houses – in a cul-de-sac off Post Office Lane, at the edge of the village – were the project of two brothers, neither with formal architectural training but with an evident interest both in Constructivism and in 1960s ideas about participation and community. They set up an architectural business under the name 'Artist-Constructor Ltd', and, somehow, they got these houses through planning. They would go on to design others, but the Flax Bourton houses are generally considered to be the best surviving examples.

Aesthetically, they are uncompromising. Each has the same basic idea – attached to a central service core, represented as a faintly hieratic tower, are cubic clusters of modular rooms, arranged differently in each house according to the needs and tastes of each resident. Some of the arrangements in the houses are deeply odd – the one window cantilevered out over a garden wall is unique. Each has been coated in white render, though originally they were apparently pastel, which is more 'in keeping' with the rest of Flax Bourton, with its typical West Country tumbledown vernacular spruced up by urban incomers. But there has been no attempt to tame the buildings and make them twee. If Britain had a saner, more honest attitude to its countryside – if everything didn't tend towards building miniature reproductions of the housing of earlier centuries, but with more car parking space – we could have had many more places like this. Somewhere rural has allowed in something modern, and both have gained from the experience.

Somerset avant-garde: the Artist-Constructor Houses, bespoke modernist villas in the village of Flax Bourton.

Brutalism in an unexpected place; the spiky concrete forms of the Arts Building in Taunton.

ARTS BUILDING, UNIVERSITY CENTRE SOMERSET, TAUNTON
Peter Hirst and Derek Rutherford for Somerset County Architects Dept, 1972
Brutalist

This is everything you could want a 1970s art college in a provincial town to be. On the edge of Somerset's county town (gorgeous red sandstone Gothic churches, the grimmest of E. Vincent Harris civic centres), this is now part of the 'University Centre Somerset', which is responsible for the generic PFI tat next to it, but also for a surprisingly intelligent restoration job. The art college itself is punchy, confident Brutalism of the Lyons Israel Ellis type, made up of big, chunky forms and articulated into clear component parts. A range of classrooms faces the main road, with a formal entrance under a square, thick concrete canopy, held up with simple steel members, with a tiny pond at one side.

On the roof, a spiky factory skyline is created by the rooflights of the studios, and at the back massive expanses of brick and glass project across and above each other, vehement and Constructivistic. Surprisingly, this has all been restored, with an unobtrusive set of new classrooms behind, in the current vernacular style – the only compromising of the building's Brutalism being the tacky gold cladding of one stairwell. Otherwise, this aggressive ensemble is remarkably well treated for a building which does not exactly say, 'I am in Somerset.'

DAVID MURRAY JOHN TOWER & BRUNEL CENTRE, SWINDON
Douglas Stephen & Partners, 1976
High-Tech

I hesitated before including this building – I do not particularly like it, although it has its fervent defenders, among them Jonathan

Meades. It is in here for its gigantic size and swagger – though the David Murray John Tower is the town's tallest, Swindon has a dozen or so towers, none of which seem to care whether anyone looks at them or not. This one does, with a symmetrical, bubbly profile of curved balconies, shiny surfaces and railway station barrel roofs – Meades suggests *Dan Dare* as an inspiration. It's all a little too tacky for my taste, but it tries to be a real *Stadtkrone* rather than just so much lettable space, and maybe that effort is enough. It joins on to the Brunel Centre mall below, which was originally in the same style, with its long barrel-roofed arcades having a similar profile to the curves of the tower. Here, horizontal rather than vertical, they serve as a High-Tech tribute to the great engineer in the town his Great Western Railway built. These arcades now survive only partially, but are rather thrilling, potentially endlessly extendable. The rest is just mallspace, and particularly bleak mallspace at that.

KIDZ ABOUT, SWINDON
Foster Associates, 1980–82
High-Tech

'Arr, the building with the yellow exoskeleton?' It's always a good sign when people know the building you're looking for, especially if it's located somewhere like the outskirts of Swindon. Foster's Renault Distribution Centre was once one of the major icons of British High-Tech architecture, helped build Foster's global reputation almost as much as the **Willis Building (p. 200)** and was extremely frequently photographed in the 1980s. That was some time ago. What it is, is a very long steel shed in a bleak suburban site of office parks and Noddy houses, most of it linear but with a side wing on a slight slope, with the structure legibly and visibly held up by a tensile structure of rods and cables. These

are detailed with a cybernetic elegance which suggests Russian Constructivism, and a lurid colour scheme and angularity which suggest one of the most frequently cited sources for early High-Tech, the 1950s children's construction kit Meccano. It's telling that this was a structure for Renault rather than for a British car manufacturer; like the Eurostar, this is the 1980s futurist France of Minitel and the Centre Pompidou crossing the Channel, and there is little else in Swindon like it, bar the space-frame of the Oasis Leisure Centre. Unlike other High-Tech icons of the period, such as the unforgettable **Lloyd's of London (p. 69)**, it is a little hard to quite see what the excitement was about, though one can still easily admire the flair of the detailing and the slashing rhythm of the rods and cables. This remains a big shed in the suburbs, converted without much fanfare after listing into a golf equipment store and, mainly, Kidz About, a giant children's play centre. It suggests that utilitarian buildings in ordinary towns could once have been regarded as being almost as prestigious as blue-chip office blocks in the City or art museums in Paris. [B.25]

TRICENTRE, SWINDON
Yorke Rosenberg & Mardall, 1991
International Style

The true believers bow out. YRM maintained a commitment to the original values of modern architecture as defined by the Weissenhof Estate in Stuttgart in 1927 – pure rectangular volumes, white walls, clear public spaces, grids and grids and grids – way beyond the point at which everyone else had abandoned them. This is the last major scheme where you can see that at work. Designed for Allied Dunbar, it consists of three office blocks with pedestrian routes passing through, by overhead walkways at one intersection and a public path at the other, with colonnades, a square and a café in the middle. The only way you can tell it was designed in the late 1980s for Swindon rather than the late 1920s for Brno is the shiny materials, gleaming white metal rather than stucco plaster. The slightly confused design of the café at the centre is the only sign of developments in aesthetics, as opposed to technology, since 1930, but the rest is all rationality and measure. Hugely unfashionable, and looking like it hasn't weathered in the slightest. The relative decay of the Brutalist and Postmodernist buildings surrounding it shows they knew what they were doing.

HOLBURNE MUSEUM EXTENSION, BATH

Eric Parry Architects, 2002–11
Classical Modernism

Every successful movement one day reaches its period of decadence; decades after the 'Sack of Bath' era of the 1970s, when conservationists saved one of the most beautiful classical cities on earth from motorways and dull office blocks, it picked silly battles such as a sustained attempt to stop this building. The Holburne Museum is an eccentric collection of terrible paintings and fascinating objets d'art pieced together by an early Victorian adventurer; since the 1910s, it has been kept in the former Sydney Hotel, which is the Palladian terminal point of the Great Pulteney Street axis, the grandest and most severe of all of Bath's planned ensembles. At the back, where it meets Sydney Pleasure Gardens – a peculiar ideal park with a railway running through it – a dull Edwardian extension was built by Sir Reginald Blomfield. In the twenty-first century, when every art museum had to 'put itself on the map' with a new building, Eric Parry was commissioned to design a replacement of Blomfield's additions, and he proposed a delicate, classically proportioned green ceramic cube, deftly sidestepping

both the demand to be 'in keeping', and the 'all-glass transparent addition to classical building' then-fashionable in the wake of Norman Foster's Great Court at the British Museum. One of the longest campaigns against a building in Bath's history ensued, largely because of the fact that Parry's proposed extension didn't use Bath stone.

More fool them – they lost, and the result is the finest example of modern architecture in Bath by a considerable distance. The facade, facing the Pleasure Gardens, is elegantly proportioned and gorgeously detailed – the ceramic cladding, evidently inspired by the Holburne's enormous collection of Japanese and Chinese vases, has some of the shimmering and organic quality of jade; and while it may not be 'in keeping' with the Bath stone of Great Pulteney Street, it is unobtrusive to the green parkland that it actually stands in. It is dated very slightly by the way the main frontage is arranged into a series of slatted fins, similar to the 'barcode facades' that were popular in office blocks at the time. Most interesting of all is the interior, particularly the narrow two-level gallery space above the café, which has been turned into a cabinet of curiosities, a dark maze of drawers and vitrines, with vases being suspended on cables from a light well. Along with Walsall's **New Art Gallery (p. 322)**, this treasure trove is the nearest thing the New Labour era had to the Soane Museum.

AUB DRAWING STUDIO, BOURNEMOUTH

Peter Cook and CRAB, 2016
Supermodernist

An extremely unfashionable building, from one of the most influential people on the architecture of the 1980s, 1990s, and 2000s, an important tutor at the Architectural Association and one of the lead fantasists in the 1960s collective Archigram, among whose unbuilt projects was the transformation

Peter Cook returns to his hometown: the bizarre pop architecture of the Drawing Studio at Bournemouth University.

of Bournemouth via an 'instant city' of collapsible and floating structures. Fifty years later, this is not that. Archigram's dreams of instantly obsolescent mini-cities of moving parts, dedicated to transience and leisure, do exist by now – as Douglas Murphy points out in his book *Last Futures*, they're called 'airports', and they're not very nice. This building showcases Peter Cook's movement away from utopia and the development of his work into an unattractively named 'Blobitecture' of arbitrary forms, which now often seems tainted by the 2000s fashion for making grown adults live in a childlike Teletubbyland. However, judged on its own merits, this drawing studio is rather intriguing. A bright-blue globule, surrounded by the clipped and functional buildings of Bournemouth's University of the Arts; inside, you find that the blobular organic formalism conceals a very clever little space, a flowing womblike hall with interestingly placed light wells producing strange effects for the students working inside, provoking fantasy rather than dour precision, as one of Cook's hated stern brick boys would have. I can't say this is a building I *like* as such – it still screams rave Grandad to me – but it's an original and surprisingly well-thought-out piece of design in a town that doesn't have much of it. An ugly little plaque at the entrance records its opening by Zaha Hadid, but does not record the fact that this was her last public appearance before her death.

BRISTOL

EDWARD EVERARD PRINTWORKS
William Neatby for Doulton & Co., 1900
Art Nouveau

Just a facade – an appliqué covering
on a factory designed by an engineer,
in the dense medieval centre of Bristol,
probably the most complex and inexplicable
townscape in Britain. But what a facade.
It basically consists of a kind of Alfons
Mucha poster draped across a Bristol
alleyway, executed in wipe-clean tiles.
In a symmetrical composition across its
four storeys, ornament is draped over the
windows, with no repetition from one floor
to another, capped by a pair of completely
original little pepper-pot towers – clusters of
Byzantine columns, capped by little copper
hats. The building's function is explained
in the imagery. Two heroes of printing,
Gutenberg and William Morris, executed
in pink, blue and green tiles, pull their
presses on either side of a stylized angel,
who is reading a magazine. Illogical, silly
and captivating: a building so fruity and
rich that it approaches the psychedelic
qualities of the best Art Nouveau. Bristol's
own back-alley Gaudí.

REDCLIFFE FLATS ✪
Bristol City Architects Dept, 1958–60
International Style

Bristol has a lot of modern buildings, and
very few of them are up to par, especially
for a city of its size and importance. What
is especially sad is that a city with so much
water has generally lined it with dross –
some of it by fine architects, like Hopkins,

Bristol's Redcliffe Flats, which drew on the articulated maisonettes of Le Corbusier's Unité d'Habitation in Marseille.

Feilden Clegg Bradley and Edward Cullinan.
The best twentieth-century complex with
a riverside frontage is, by a long chalk,
the three ten-storey blocks that make up
the Redcliffe Flats, which stand at the
confluence of the River Avon and Bathurst
Basin, just next to the spindly Victorian
Bedminster Bridge. All share a similar style
of brown-brick stair towers, strongly profiled
concrete frames and brightly coloured
panels, but there are subtle differences –
directly addressing the river, Francombe
House is the most sculptural, with
cantilevered balconies and a row of barrel-
roofed penthouses on top; the others are
more strictly rectilinear, with glass walkways
linking the different parts; Waring House has
shops on the ground floor, and a row of trees
protects them from traffic noise. Together,
these make up the most monumental, subtle
and architecturally interesting council
estate in the South-West, a sort of miniature
portside **Park Hill (p. 370)**. A recent
renovation has painted the concrete, but
the colour scheme recognizes well the
blocks' syncopated rhythms.

The Dickinson Robinson Building, whose concrete
modules invoke both neoclassicism and Brutalism.

PLIMSOLL SWING BRIDGE
**Bristol City Architects Dept with Freeman Fox
& Partners, 1962**
Brutalist

The approach roads to this bridge – four
of them in total, three of them flyovers –
are an urban disaster, cutting off Clifton
and Hotwells from the river, making what
could be a lovely riverside walk to the
Suspension Bridge a gauntlet of ludicrous
traffic, and contributing to the general sense
of the car taking priority over everything
else in Bristol, deeply at odds with its
self-image as the green and groovy British
city. And, yet, the bridge itself is a spirited
work – a steel swing bridge that can open
to let ships through, suspended between
Brutalist supports, with Goldfinger-like spiral

staircases and a futuristic lookout tower
projecting out towards the countryside, on
a thin single piloti. When, as they should be,
the approaches are all removed and the area
is given back to people rather than cars,
the bridge ought to stay, as a witty and rare
piece of Brutalist infrastructure.

DICKINSON ROBINSON
BUILDING ✪
Group Architects DRG, 1960–63
International Style

A tall high-rise and podium with arched
windows and faced with clean, marble-
aggregate concrete right in the city centre,
this is easily Bristol's finest office tower.
Along with the **Cheese Lane Shot Tower
(p. 269)** and the recent **The Eye (p. 271)**,
its quality is rare among the many tall
buildings in the centre. That's faint praise

that this place doesn't deserve – this office block (now better known as 1 Redcliffe) would look good in Cambridge, Edinburgh or London, although its sprawling nature pegs it nicely to relentlessly non-plan Bristol. Designed, unusually, by in-house architects at a paper and printing company, the tower is cool, classical and elegant, with just about enough hints of the city's warehouse aesthetic to feel 'appropriate' (not that this has always helped its appreciation). The sixteenth floor at the top has a double-height gallery, evoking the de Chirico aesthetic of Italian Rationalism; the attached low-rise block, cantilevered out over the car park, with its tubular concrete and glass stair tower, is as tricksy and sculptural as the rest is square and repetitious. A class act.

_____

BRISTOL HOTEL & PRINCE STREET CAR PARK
Wakeford Jeram & Harris, 1964–6
Brutalist

The Bristol Hotel is a modular concrete block with curved square panels around the windows, with some retro qualities but so altered internally that it's not worth a special visit. What is worth visiting, however, is the attached car park, facing what is now the culture and tourism centre of Harbourside – an op art pattern of concrete diamonds, held up on splayed pilotis, the sort of pop modernism that firms like Seifert excelled in. It now feels perfectly suited as a neighbour to the art gallery at the Arnolfini and the Bristol Architecture Centre – part of a dockside ensemble of eccentric buildings and spaces which are much more convincing as a cultural quarter than the already knackered Harbourside development, which stands just over Pero's Bridge, which has second-rate buildings by first-rate firms such as Arup and Hopkins.

DOVE STREET FLATS, STOKES CROFT
Bristol City Architects Dept, 1965–8
International Style

Not as impressive as **Redcliffe Flats (p. 266)**, these high-rises are still a diverting example of the dramatic scale that could at times be found in Bristol's high-rise housing, before preservationists caused a change of course. By comparison with the earlier complex it is more scattered, less well related to its surroundings, but has a similar clarity of design, with its coloured panels, strongly expressed concrete frame and crisp, partly glazed connecting walkways. The blocks are arranged in a line on a hilltop site, with magnificent panoramas over the city and the countryside around, but with slightly fiddly stairwells connecting them to the street.

_____

LAKESHORE
Skidmore Owings & Merrill, 1967–70
International Style

The new name of this building makes clear what the developers, Urban Splash – for it is they – are trying to do here. This is one of the few British buildings by Skidmore Owings & Merrill, a corporate firm which became, under designers like Bruce Graham and Gordon Bunshaft, the major providers of mid-century International Style glamour to American business at its moment of greatest global dominance (see also **Boots D90, p. 360**, and **Exchange House, p. 71**). They were disciples of the great German modernist Mies van der Rohe, to the point where Frank Lloyd Wright called them the 'three blind Mies'. The master's only London project was blocked largely thanks to the Victorian Society and Charles Windsor (thanks, guys), but Mies's best-known housing project, in Chicago, was called Lakeshore Drive, which is now the name of the main road running through this housing development. The developers were clearly aiming at something highly unusual in the UK – a luxury modernist housing development in the outer suburbs by the motorway, like Mies and SOM provided in Chicago, Montreal and Detroit. The failure to create this effect was not wholly their fault.

Lakeshore was originally the HQ of Wills Tobacco, later Imperial Tobacco – like much of Bristol's money, the wealth comes from the Caribbean, and so do the buildings (Wills's other famous architectural venture in the city is an in many ways equally American work, the nearly skyscraping Gothic Wills Memorial Building at the university, built only forty years before this one). The HQ stood in front of their factory, and is an L-shaped range of pre-cast concrete offices around a lake, on a sloping site. It is in two distinct parts. Two ribbon-windowed storeys directly face the lake, and above that, on a hill, are five storeys held up by an instantly legible rusty Corten steel frame, its classical proportions precisely calculated. As with most listed twentieth-century industrial buildings from the Perivale **Hoover Factory (p. 159)** onwards, only the offices were listed, and the factory itself was demolished for the grimmest kind of retail park ('Imperial Park'), with some equally nasty Noddy houses around, no public space, and loads of cars. You very much know you're not, in fact, living in the set of *Mad Men*. Yet for all this bathos, 'Lakeshore' is still a remarkable building, one of the few in UK that has all the sinister chic of the best North American corporate modernism, and the landscaping is gorgeous, a showpiece space of strictly controlled nature, walled off from the plebs (it's worth waiting until someone else gets buzzed through the gates, though). The conversion into flats by Ferguson Mann is elegantly done, and extremely subtle by Urban Splash's standards, especially compared with their mangling of **Park Hill (p. 370)**. Perhaps it just works better with this sort of architecture than it does with Brutalism – one bourgeois luxury style understands another.

———

CHEESE LANE SHOT TOWER
E. N. Underwood & Partners, 1968–9
Brutalist

Right in the city centre on the Floating Harbour, this replaced the first ever Shot Tower, of 1782 – a tube into which molten metal is thrown to make it into materiel for shotguns. Very unusually for Bristol, the modern replacement design has so much personality that it has generally been considered a fair exchange. A polygonal concrete shaft is topped by a twelve-sided strip-windowed room, which gives it the appearance of the control tower of a 1960s airport if it had been redesigned by Rudolf Steiner. It's small, but its quirkiness and monumentality make for a real modern landmark in a city that lacks for them. Now part of an office complex, it is lit up at night in a fashion that emphasizes the oddness of its science fiction geometries.

———

BARTON HOUSE & ST JAMES' BARTON
Whicheloe Macfarlane, 1969–74
Brutalist

The 'Bear Pit' is what most Bristolians call the space officially known as St James' Barton – a sunken plaza that marks the transition between the ordinary shopping streets of Broadmead and the extraordinary ad hoc alternative urbanism of Stokes Croft. Barton House is the largest of several undistinguished Brutalist blocks that line two thirds of the plaza, and is given a drama that it wouldn't otherwise have as a lumpy, cheaply renovated chunk of commercial Brutalism by its role as a gateway between two very different visions of the contemporary city. The concrete and steel circus of the block has been raised up in the middle, allowing cars and pedestrians to pass underneath. As soon as you're across, you've gone from the typical chain-store landscape that you can find in every town and city in the country, into a streetscape you can only find in Bristol – a chaos of Georgian streets and converted light industrial units, coated in political murals, multicultural and thriving, and capable of transforming any building of any era. The conversion of nearby Hamilton House, for instance, transforms an extremely mundane modernist office block into a teeming social centre. Like Barton House, buildings have little value as pure architecture, but serve to add real drama to this unique urban landscape.

1 TEMPLE WAY
Ronald Weeks for Percy Thomas Partnership, 1970–74
Brutalist

Temple Way is the pedestrian-hostile failed boulevard that leads directly from Temple Meads Station to the inner-city district of St Paul's – with a reservation of trees in one segment, with an underpass ploughing into another, this is one of Bristol's many examples of plans that seemed to have been completely abandoned and transformed mid-way through their execution. Several modernist blocks line its route, but there's only one of real quality. Built originally for the local media company Post and Press, it's a muscular Brutalist block by the same team that developed the more delicate **Dickinson Robinson Building (p. 267)**. It is broken up, in the manner of the more picturesque Brutalist buildings, into several distinct masses, composed into a hierarchical structure of windowless printworks and ribbon-windowed offices raised on enormous concrete pilotis, all wrapped in

a sleek, well-detailed skin of purple brick. It no longer serves its original purpose, but has been reasonably well renovated as a speculative office block, with pop art polychromy added to the glass facade that meets the street.

HIGH KINGSDOWN
Whicheloe Macfarlane and JT Group, 1971–5
People's Detailing

A reaction against the monumentality of the likes of Dove Street Flats, though like it the product of a wholesale clearance, this is an extremely tightly packed (to replicate tower block densities) private estate of monopitch houses, knobbly-bricked and weatherboarded in the Span style, but with a labyrinthine, rookery-like layout, with lots of paths under-and-over, on a Heathcliffian site, at the top of one of Bristol's many vertiginous inclines. Together this makes High Kingsdown feel considerably less genteel than Eric Lyons's private estates, and hence all the more interesting to explore, a strange Anglo-Danish maze.

CLIFTON CATHEDRAL ✪
Percy Thomas Partnership, 1965–72
Brutalist

A monochrome masterwork in the Vatican II genre more known for sparkling kitsch like Liverpool Metropolitan Cathedral, designed by Ronald Weeks of the prolific Welsh firm Percy Thomas Partnership. Occupying a leafy corner site in the fragmentary monumental Georgian townscape of Clifton, it can be found from the streets around by following its gaunt concrete campanile, in the shape of a prawn's tail, perhaps the most original and personal cathedral spire in Britain. When you find the cathedral, the entrance is set on a raised, ceremonial concrete plaza. Intriguing as this is, the octagonal church inside is a leap inwards, a space of extreme intensity and visceral concentration. Little more than a series of angular raw-concrete volumes, suspended above on industrial trusses. Atmospheric effects are created by the Expressionistic, sculptural ceilings, which almost – but not quite – conceal the sources of light. Above the baptismal font, the concrete roof structure is shaped into a star; the altar is asymmetrical and as hardline in its Brutalism as the National Theatre, and like it revels in the textural anomaly of the wooden traces on shuttered concrete. Not being qualified to say how this connects with the liturgy, I can only marvel at just how sharply this serious, smouldering space contrasts with the notion of Catholic cathedrals as kitsch when compared with Protestant austerity. There is no more rigorous church in England, and few that can match its intellectual and physical power. An astonishing work, and the most important twentieth-century building in the South-West.

While at the cathedral, you should take note that Clifton has another excellent piece of modernist church design a short walk away – G. E. Street's All Saints, a bombed Victorian church subsequently remodelled by Robert Potter in 1967, with a spiky Swedish spire. [B.30]

KNOWLE WEST MEDIA CENTRE
White Design, 2008
TRANSPORTABLE ACCOMMODATION MODULE
White Design, 2017
Ecomodernist

In the back garden of the community centre of the slightly Arts and Crafts council estate of Knowle West, out in the suburbs of Bristol, you can find a peculiar bungalow – modular, prefabricated and entirely ecologically scrupulous, made almost wholly out of renewable, natural materials. This 'T.A.M'

is essentially a sensible, modern house, cosy and airy without being sentimental or retro. It is intended as a means by which the residents of this estate will be able to respond to their changing housing needs by erecting new houses as and when their circumstances change – when families grow, when retirees no longer want to walk upstairs, and so forth. There should be hundreds of houses like this in Britain, but there aren't, so when they appear they're worth noticing. This is a project of the Knowle West Media Centre, a community organization housed in the other end of the estate in a simple but monumental building, constructed along similar principles; you can see here very clearly its modular system, which would be deployed by the same architects at larger scale in **LILAC (p. 383)**, Leeds.

THE EYE
Glenn Howells Architects, 2010
International Style

A simple glass-and-steel high-rise, with an eye-like ground plan (hence the name), which like most of this architect's work has a laconic regularity that avoids drawing attention to itself; yet precisely by being minimal and modern in a Floating Harbour otherwise dominated by galumphing 1980s and '90s emulations of Victorian warehouses, this stands out for its integrity and economy. A cut above the usual 'stunning developments', here and elsewhere.

Plymouth's fabulous Pannier Market, showing off its dramatic concrete canopies and upper-level walkways.

PLYMOUTH

ARMADA WAY:
DINGLES DEPARTMENT STORE
Thomas Tait, 1949–51
PEARL ASSURANCE HOUSE
**Alec French and Burnet Tait & Lorne,
1950–52**
PLYMOUTH GUILDHALL
**H. J. W. Stirling for Plymouth City Council
Architects Dept, 1951–9**
PLYMOUTH CIVIC CENTRE
**H. J. W. Stirling and Geoffrey Jellicoe for
Plymouth City Council Architects Dept,
1957–62**
Modern Classicism, People's Detailing

Armada Way, the centre of the post-war
reconstruction of Plymouth under the
direction of the planner Patrick Abercrombie,
is something between the first large-scale
effort in modernist town planning and the
last great Beaux Arts metropolis in England,
yet it often feels a prosthesis on to a messy
port city that has never known quite what to
do with it. Its stern Portland stone buildings
are often dilapidated, with activity mostly
in the lively rubble streets that survived the
Luftwaffe – though there are many personal
and intimate touches, such as the Braille
Garden midway along and the regular use
of canopies and colonnades. But there is
one great set piece, where two monumental
ziggurat-like buildings, late works of Thomas
Tait of Burnet Tait & Lorne, face each other
across a vast square. It is a rare British
analogue to the Stalinist set pieces of the
Continent, from Le Havre to Karl-Marx-Allee
to Nowa Huta, chilling, dystopian and thrilling.
   On the other side of Royal Parade from
these ziggurats is the bombed Victorian
Romanesque Guildhall and the planned Civic
Centre, allocated as part of the Abercrombie
plan but designed later along International
Style lines by Geoffrey Jellicoe. The tower has
its enthusiasts, but I've always found it rather

dour – but it's another matter at ground level,
where the pilotis lead through to a very
pretty sunken poolside square. It is being
redeveloped currently as private flats by
Urban Splash. In any case, the real municipal
splendour is in the Guildhall, whose high
campanile is the vertical counterpoint of the
sixties tower. The Guildhall was denuded of
its roof by the Luftwaffe and repaired by the
City Architect into a Anglo-socialist grand
hall, with lush glass by the sculptor F. H.
Coventry and a series of gloriously kitsch
austerity baroque chandeliers.

–––

NATIONAL PROVINCIAL BANK,
ST ANDREW'S CROSS
B. C. Sherren, 1955–8
Moderne

Like a lot of reconstructed Plymouth, this
building doesn't entirely feel part of the
'West' side in the conventional divisions
of the Cold War. A big square block with
a pompous colonnade, but beyond those
columns you'll find a wonderful triple-height
blue-mosaic gallery, and above, a similarly
delightful clock tower, which is almost
identical to that on the top of the exactly
contemporary rebuilding of the Finland
Station in Leningrad. Indeed, you could
probably have taken a boat direct from
one to the other.

–––

PANNIER MARKET ✪
Walls & Pearn, 1956–9
People's Detailing

All the things the main parts of planned
Plymouth mostly lack – innovative
modernism, civic jollity, light-heartedness
– are provided just outside the main drag
in this fabulous covered market, the sort

of complex you find often in the North but which is extremely rare in the cities of the South. The Pannier Market is a big block in Festival Style – tiles, mosaic, murals, piquant old signage ('CONVENIENCES'), under a great concrete roof, like being inside an immense whale skeleton, with natural light filtering down through each arch. Everything is blue and white, for the appropriately nautical air; cafés in the top floor let you stare at the passers-by while you have a very strong tea. Marvellous.

PATON WATSON QUADRATE
H. J. W. Stirling for Plymouth City Council Architects Dept, 1958
People's Detailing

There's a lot of decent, Swedish-style infill housing in bombed-out Plymouth, which enlivens its often chaotic townscape, and the single best part of which is this small estate in what passes for the 'old town'. Its pitched-roofed blocks are on a sloping site, with pretty, rough-and-ready slate elevations and boxed-out modernist windows and balconies. It has itself lots of fun with the hill, with exciting pathways under and across the buildings, paralleled by surprising routes via cantilevered concrete staircases; a striking contrast with the classical ramrod shoved up the rest of Plymouth.

OCEAN COURT, STONEHOUSE
Marshman Warren Taylor, 1976
Brutalist

A rare highlight in Plymouth's architecture after the completion of the Abercrombie Plan, opposite the beefy, monumental classicism of the Royal William Victualling Yard (now flats, and well worth an exploration), which provides the best vantage point. Even more than the immediately post-war work, this has staggeringly little to do with the beaten-

about working-class port, but flaunts a coastal internationalism that could be anywhere in Europe: Costa Del Devon. It's also very good, a dynamic stepped-section design without fuss or extraneous tat, full of tensile energy.

THEATRE ROYAL
Peter Moro, 1978–82
Brutalist

This is the centrepiece of one of the later squares of post-war Plymouth, an ensemble around a concrete car park, a Victorian clock tower and a bank-turned-pub in a florid sandstone baroque otherwise erased from the city. It's a good, vigorous Brutalist theatre, a complicated octagonal design with flying staircases, black bronzed glass, and pale brick rather than concrete, reflecting its completion well after the anti-Brutalist reaction had set in. The entrance forms a sunken, secluded square, which tucks it away from the vast Siberian flatness of Armada Way, a little hint of what a more spatially imaginative reconstruction might have been like.

CORNWALL

ST AUSTELL LIBRARY

F. K. Hicklin for Cornwall County Council
Architects Dept, 1959–60
International Style

Cornwall is the sort of place where a great
local school of modern architecture could
be expected to thrive, with its complex
landscape, its vernacular of harling and
granite, its vivid light, and its status as
home to many of the most important modern
artists of the twentieth century. It never
quite became that, although there are some
important (and extremely secluded) private
houses, like Richard and Su Rogers' Creek
Vean. However, it did for a time have one
of the most creative County Architects
Departments, which built some superb
public buildings in the 1960s. Following the
pattern of St Ives-based artists like Barbara
Hepworth or Roger Hilton, their work shows
a combination of questing modernity and
local particularity that is rare in the South
of England. Most of the County Architects'
buildings are decent, low-key contributions
to the townscape, but a few are very special:
St Austell Library is one of them.

A small, steel-framed building in a little
garden just round the corner from the
town's railway station, reached through low,
irregular granite walls; the same stone is
used to face the ground floor. Otherwise,
this appears as a glass building, defined
by the high, all-over glazed clerestory
windows, slightly factory-like in appearance
but detailed with a humanity and care that
you'd never find in an industrial building.
The library inside is simple in plan, an
open, accessible hall with an upper level for
researchers, lined in warm wood, and lit by
those expansive clerestories, blue-tinted so
as not to overheat, which makes the climate
seem even more lush and un-English than
it otherwise would.

SALTASH LIBRARY ✪

Royston Summers for Cornwall County
Architects Dept, 1962
TAMAR SUSPENSION BRIDGE

Mott Hay & Anderson, 1959–62
Brutalist

A stupendous little municipal library,
Le Corbusier's Chandigarh teleported to
the eastern corner of Cornwall that is
better regarded as 'Greater Plymouth'. It's
staggeringly unoriginal, a simple shrinking
down of the enormous Capitol the great
one designed for the capital of the Punjab,
zapped into the library of a very small town.
A bush-hammered set of curved ramps
as stairways, a charging bullhorn profile
roof above, and a colonnade of thin but
curvaceous pilotis framing a great glass wall,
elegantly fenestrated in an asymmetric grid.

Le Corbusier's Palace of Assembly in Chandigarh,
reimagined as a miniature municipal library in Saltash.

Concrete surfaces and wild landscapes: the headquarters of Cornwall County Council in Truro.

The two-level space inside is laid out similarly to the otherwise totally different **St Austell Library (above)**, by the same powerhouse County Architects Department. While the idea is comic – northern India come to Cornwall – the rough concrete aggregate, now weathered and smeared with lichen, fits beautifully with the slate and granite around. It also stands up to the weather much better than the fey timber and Trespa that passes for 'contemporary architecture' in the West Country. The building's setting in a car park on the edge of town wastes its monumentality a little, but that makes it feel all the more surprising.

When walking down the hill back towards the town centre, you will not fail to notice the Tamar Suspension Bridge, a design of Mott Hay & Anderson, alongside Brunel's famous railway bridge. It is graceless compared with the same firm's **Severn Bridge (p. 290)**, but exciting for its sheer height and scale, towering over this small town.

COUNTY HALL, TRURO ○
F. K. Hicklin for Cornwall County Council Architects Dept, 1963–6
Brutalist

A magnificent building, comparable only to **Newcastle Civic Centre (p. 482)** and the **Lanark County Buildings (p. 537)** in Hamilton among post-war civic headquarters, and in its massive integrity probably the most successful of the period. Unlike the more controversial modernist buildings in Truro, it doesn't barge into the historic city, which has probably helped its public estimation – it was listed some time ago, long before Brutalism came back into fashion, and it stands on a dual carriageway opposite a neo-vernacular Sainsbury's, at the edge of Truro, lying long and low in the landscape. For those who are fine with modern architecture as long as it doesn't get in the way of any of the views, this is exemplary. But this politesse in the building's location doesn't translate to the slightest timidity in the building's expression, which is distinguished by rare rigour and power. Entering from the current entrance (not the original entrance, which we'll come to) past an exotically planted garden and a car park, you come to a blunt Brutalist grid, with a lot of granite in the aggregate, rough but logically arranged. At this point, turn right, and go down the hill, and what looks at first like a decent modern office block becomes something else entirely.

As you can now see, the County Hall stands at the exact point where the cathedral city meets its countryside, and that the architects have chosen to embrace this. The three-storey grid that you've seen on the car park frontage is continued as the building descends a steep slope, with pilotis carrying the bulk, creating a partly enclosed square. This is an Oxbridge-Brutalist space, with a Barbara Hepworth sculpture and a lot of greenery, with the intensely green, flowing countryside bursting right out through the pilotis. Return to the level ground, and you'll find a heavy, granite-clad, verdigris-roofed central hall, a hulking image of power after the careful game of solid and void the architects have played up to this point. This was the original entrance, and has the most impressive of the building's expensively finished public spaces, more Scandinavian than Brutalist in character, with a lot of bright stone and wood, and plenty of light. In the cleverness and imagination of its integration with a steeply falling landscape, it's rivalled only by **Park Hill (p. 370)**, but in its setting of Brutalism with great intelligence and presence into the English countryside, it's in a genre of one. It did, however, once have a clone of itself nearby – a shrunken-down version in the model village 'Cornwall in Miniature' at St Agnes, sadly long since closed, though you can still find postcards of giant children towering over this Brutalist edifice. [B.18]

CHAPTER HOUSE, TRURO CATHEDRAL
MWT Architects, 1967
Brutalist

This is one of several modernist buildings placed in various locations in central Truro. Most are placed in such a brusque and unromantic manner as to inflame our keepers of heritage; this one is as sensitive in its scale as it is uncompromising in aesthetic. J. L. Pearson's Truro Cathedral is a late-Victorian neo-Gothic complex, easily noticeable as such due to its extreme completeness (not to mention the fashions of the figures over the entrance) but still a great thing to have on the skyline, with views from the town's hills converging on its great spiked towers. The Chapter House doesn't attempt to compete, but provides a café and information centre in a simple Corbusian building – ribbed, slightly Gothicized concrete, with a round-arched canopy above – hauled up on pilotis, with a sinister waffle-ceilinged undercroft below. It is nicely sheltered by trees in the cathedral grounds, and its refusal to compromise in aesthetics or dominate in scale is admirable and powerful – compare it with the little pitched roofs of the Postmodernist shop opposite by way of instructive contrast.

MULTISTOREY CAR PARK, TRURO
MWT Architects, 1979
Brutalist

Very much the sort of thing that 'ruined' Truro, a massive concrete multistorey car park that barges its way into the town, part of an overengineered ring-road system which is tightly drawn around the city like a noose. It's good, though, its extremely worn and mildewed textured béton brut that has worn to an interesting shade of greenish red highlighting how this is probably as convincing a bit of fake Gothic as Pearson's cathedral, just in a very different idiom. The highlight is the very sixties tubular sans serif integral signage, imprinted in concrete on each of the car park's floors, on the side visible in front of the cathedral from the railway viaduct: 'CAR PARK CAR PARK CAR PARK'.

——

TRURO COURTS OF JUSTICE
Evans & Shalev, 1986–8
Postmodernist

A difficult and overrated but serious and intriguing building, which should nonetheless be seen on any visit to Truro. Eldred Evans and David Shalev were erstwhile Brutalists of a sort, adherents of the Camden Council school of rigorous plan-and-section classical modernism; their major building in this manner, a school in Newport, was demolished a few years ago. Like many of their generation, their architecture changed radically between the 1960s and '80s, and the architects resolutely refused to admit changes in fashion had influenced them – however, suffice to say, there are no pediments with coats of arms on their 1960s work. But you can find these on Truro's **County Hall (p. 276)**, along with two rotundas with conical glass cowls, a grand classical circus, and concrete covered in the same harling of the little terraces that run up the steep hill to the courts. Most of the building's expressive facade is clustered into a corner, with some still rather Brutalist projecting windows and an air of abstraction that is far from Postmodern populism – aside from that pediment. The problem is that the building's main courtyard is not open to the public, so it meets much of the surrounding area with a high wall, though stripped classical follies visibly pop their heads over the parapet. The same ingredients are used to much more expansive and generous purposes in their immediately subsequent **Tate St Ives (below)**.

TATE ST IVES ✪
Evans & Shalev, 1989–93/
Jamie Fobert Architects, 2017
Postmodernist, Classical Modernism

There are now four Tate galleries, expanding out from the original baroque temple in Pimlico, now Tate Britain: Tate Liverpool, carved rather clumsily by James Stirling out of an Albert Dock warehouse in the 1980s; **Tate Modern (p. 102)**, of course; and, perhaps puzzlingly, Tate St Ives, in a small Cornish town. But that town became a centre for modern artists from the 1930s onwards, with Naum Gabo and Barbara Hepworth among others taking inspiration from the piercing light and raw landscape all around. (Hepworth's studio here, still much as she left it when she died in 1975, should be visited by anyone interested in modernism.) Tate St Ives now consists of two buildings, and both of them are excellent.

Evans & Shalev's original building is one of those works that fell a little between periods, and however much the architects believed that architecture was timeless, the magazines and the architecture schools evidently disagreed. This is in a sense Postmodernism after its 1980s hegemony, but classy and restrained when compared with the power suits of Terry Farrell or the polychrome plutocracy of John Outram. Yet Tate St Ives was also too historicist, nostalgic and decorative for the iconic Blairite supermodernism that would follow, so was never regarded as an 'iconic' building. More fool everyone, because this is a wonderful work of architecture, with an understanding of site, space and purpose that far exceeds most of the art galleries of the 1990s and 2000s. Built on the site of a gasworks, from which Evans & Shalev derived the shape of the central rotunda, it created a permanent, official home for the huge quantity of internationally significant art that has been made in this now tourist-packed resort-cum-fishing village.

The main frontage consists of a classical approach from the promenade over Porthmeor Beach, with grand flights of stairs approaching a grand, airy rotunda – very likely the eventual upshot of Evans & Shalev's generation's appreciation for the work of the historian Rudolf Wittkower, and his claims that the circular plans of the Italian Renaissance were motivated by sacred, mathematical harmonic theory. Certainly, when you're inside this great drum, on the upper floors of the galleries, with abstracts hung on circular galleries with an astonishing view of the sea, framed by the weird pagan rocks that so inspired Barbara Hepworth (whose preserved studio is round the corner), the sense of cosmic order is strong. This is, curiously, not the entrance, which is instead through an anteroom with two integral artworks by St Ives residents – a pulsing stained-glass panel by Patrick Heron and a Barbara Hepworth sculpture on a plinth framed by a round wall of glass bricks, as if to build up anticipation. Scattered throughout the building are little classical framing devices – in a building which, from the beach itself, looks much more Corbusian, like a giant Purist villa splayed out across the Promenade – from sudden frames of the sea view to busy detailing on the balustrades, to the slightly rickety-looking cantilevered balcony café. These are always used to emphasize the landscape and the sea, what the artists were here for. The building's recent extension by Jamie Fobert, meanwhile, is basically just landscape itself, partly as the result of planning battles (curiously, given that the poor-quality apartment buildings around here don't suggest a council that is particularly bothered about preservation). All you will see is a twist of tile and glass and a low terrace, whose rooflights shine on to a massive concrete gallery. It works well, Evans & Shalev's extrovert embrace of the sea and Fobert's tunnelling into the hills complementing each other.

Jamie Fobert's extension to Tate St Ives, piling geological abstraction on to the original neo-modernist building.

NATIONAL MARITIME MUSEUM, FALMOUTH

Long & Kentish, 1996–2003
Ecomodernist

As fitted to its rough dockland site in its own way as Tate St Ives is to its area's genteel surrealism, standing as it does where Falmouth's still extant and heavily militarized harbour meets the town's bustling, picaresque tangle of alleys. Like it, the building was designed by an intellectual, male–female team – in this case, the partners of Colin St John Wilson, who finished the **British Library (p. 143)** and **Pallant House Gallery (p. 242)** after his death. It's clearly intended to be as integral and elemental to the area around as the BL is in north London, with the shipping sheds serving as its St Pancras. There are two main parts – one gigantic timber-clad shed, with ships inside, and a curious moderne/classical 'lighthouse'. It's big and rackety, like a particularly battered pirate ship, but there is much subtlety too in the way that its corner entrance fans out in a faintly Aalto-esque manner, and in the way that the long pitched roof descends, almost informally, towards the tower. While this is a late work by veteran designers of the sixties, it is also an early example of the sort of Bernd and Hilla Becher found-object obliqueness that would characterize the work of much younger classical modernists like Sergison Bates or 6A. This intellectual energy sits slightly oddly with the populism of the building's programme, and the collection of timber-clad fishing-village-style Zizzis and Pizza Expresses around. But the public boardwalks around the museum itself focus your attention on the boats, both the yachts and the warships behind that dwarf them.

EDEN PROJECT, ST BLAZEY ⊕

Grimshaw with Anthony Hunt Associates, 1998–2001
High-Tech

One of the most famous Blair-era regeneration megaprojects, carved into a chalk pit as a series of geodesic domes containing elaborate conservatories, intended to bring purpose and jobs and even more tourism to this beautiful but extremely poor county (on some measures, the poorest area in Western Europe). Its ambitions are not so much local as cosmic, a *Silent Running*-style ark of all the plants you can stuff into a pseudo-organic growth of giant ETFE warts, set spectacularly in a panoramic, widescreen garden, full of the un-English bright foliage you find so much of in Cornwall. It's also the place where two major denizens of High-Tech architecture since the 1970s, Grimshaw as architect and Hunt as engineer, try to fulfil one of the ideas of their great teacher, Buckminster Fuller, and his dreams of encompassing all of our achievements in great geodesic domes, to protect them from the thermonuclear apocalypse. Cornwall is likely to be far away from the epicentre of that particular event, though as soon as the elaborate cooling and warming systems of these domes are no longer being tended by a skilled staff, it's hard to imagine this biosphere will last long.

These pages are not the place to ponder the Eden Project's efficacy in saving the world ('Your weapon is your wallet', signs tell you), but as architecture it is a major achievement, clearly the pinnacle of Grimshaw's career – the placement of the two dome clusters and the wooden eco-modernist visitor centres in the quarry feels intuitive and natural as well as futuristic and dramatic; the only relatively weak element is the somewhat rote lightweight Teflon theatre between them. Inside, the two clustered 'biomes' are quite different from each other, and so can't be understood without

Silent Running in St Blazey: inside the 'Mediterranean' biome of Nicholas Grimshaw's Eden Project.

a serious exploration. The smaller of the two is the 'Mediterranean' biome, and so its foliage is relatively familiar, the temperature is relaxed, there's plenty of space to see the dome's roof, which creates the possibility of quiet and empty space; and hence the Project's programmers have reacted by filling it with silly sculptures, superfluous 'Greek-style' architectural fragments, and piped birdsong (there aren't any birds here, at least not in this cluster), as if emptiness would become the megaproject equivalent of dead air – the project can't be allowed to fail, and so the possibility of children getting bored is bitterly resisted.

However, in the larger, 'Rainforest' biome, the plants (and animals – birds and lizards have been introduced here in order to 'regulate' this much more uncontrollable ecosystem against predators) are much more dense and smell much more heady, and, accordingly, the atmosphere is so intense that they've decided there's no need to hold

the kiddies' hands. Instead of theme park tat, there are elegant High-Tech walkways, overgrown with vines, leading round and up the biomes. A biosphere in paradise or **Stansted Airport (p. 192)** after the eco-apocalypse, or just an extremely elaborate greenhouse – however you want to imagine it, this is an unforgettable place that provokes fantasy, whether utopian or dystopian.

5. WALES

Proportionally, nowhere has seen as many good modern buildings demolished or left derelict as Wales. There appears to be a general belief that anything modern is not worth conserving, or can be sacrificed to development at all costs; so the inventory of demolished buildings includes work that was in fact listed, such as the Brynmawr Rubber Factory; that should have been listed, such as Newport's High School and its Chartist Mural, the Cardiff Empire Pool, Rhyl's Sun Centre or the Civic Centre in Mold; and an attrition of what still exists, such as the disgraceful dereliction of the stunning Brutalist **Coleg Harlech**. Meanwhile, large redevelopment projects such as Cardiff Bay tend to showcase contemporary design and planning at its absolute worst.

This can make searching for modernism in Wales a little dispiriting at times, but the best of what is still here has a very Welsh sense of romance and landscape. This ranges from the brilliant, punchy little **Tredegar Library** and **Brecon County Library** in the South, to idyllic private houses on the North coast, such as Harry Weedon's **Villa Marina** in Llandudno. The local firm of Percy Thomas Partnership has created excellent buildings over many decades, from the haunting modern classicism of **Swansea Guildhall** to the sublime hilltop Brutalism of **Aberystwyth Arts Centre**, from the sixties precision of the **St Fagans National Museum of History**'s Visitor Centre on the outskirts of Cardiff to the wildness of the **Millennium Centre** – which stands next to the wonderful organic design of the **Senedd**, the Welsh Parliament – in the city centre forty years later. There's a lot here to love, and it is not as loved as it ought to be.

SOUTH WALES

TRANSPORTER BRIDGE, NEWPORT ✪
Ferdinand Arnodin, 1906
Industrial, High-Tech

One of the earliest buildings in this book, and impossible to leave out – if *modernism* means anything, it means this. An absolutely astonishing structure, easily justifying a visit to Newport (and a wander through the deeply uneasy inner-city townscape of Pill) to gawp at it. A transporter bridge, for those who don't know, is one that for various reasons topographical or industrial has to carry vehicles across its length by itself, via a high-level viaduct and a suspended 'car', rather than function passively as a conduit from A to B. There is another one in Middlesbrough (**Tees Transporter Bridge, p. 466**), but it is not quite of the same startling quality, because the clanging, heavy design roots it in the nineteenth century, in the world of the Forth Rail Bridge. In the case of the Newport bridge, everything is ethereal and lightweight, with total material economy – which should be no surprise, as the designer was neither Welsh nor English, but a French specialist in transporter bridges, such as the Pont Transbordeur in Marseille, a one-time modernist icon that was destroyed during the Second World War. Newport's is nearly identical to the Marseille design, in its impressive height, in the thinness and elegance of its steel lattice, with its towering, tapering legs, and in the limpid beauty of its silhouette. It is a surprise when you walk right up to it and see just how heavy the steel supports keeping the thing up actually are – from a distance, it looks like it's floating, the cars gliding in air. **[B.26]**

Ferdinand Arnodin's magnificent Transporter Bridge over the River Usk, an ethereal proto-High-Tech monument.

Abstracted classicism: the west frontage of Percy Thomas's Portland stone Swansea Guildhall.

SWANSEA GUILDHALL
Percy Thomas Partnership, 1930–34
Modern Classicism

Like **Norwich City Hall (p. 195)**, this just falls on the side of modernity rather than retrogression (unlike similar town halls in Barking or Southampton), although it's a close-run thing, meaning this building belongs as much to the history of neoclassicism as it does to modernism. Swansea Guildhall commands a green square near the bay, and boasts a remarkable bell tower, distantly inspired by Stockholm but with a nauticality all of its own, with four sculpted prows protruding from above the clock. It is a remarkably coherent, complete work – everything looks as if it has been carved from one block of Portland stone. Interiors are more classical, but are opulent throughout, radiating pride without pomposity. The municipal fittings of the square that frames the Guildhall, such as the more strongly modernist, Charles Holden-like lamp standards, are of similarly high quality. **[D.18]**

NEWPORT CIVIC CENTRE
T. C. Howitt, 1937–64
Modern Classicism

Really an inferior version of **Swansea Guildhall (above)**, with a squarer tower and much less money spent on it, completed decades after it had gone out of fashion due to war damage to the half-completed building. It's worth seeing though, for three reasons. Firstly, the stripped, almost thuggish power of that tower, squat and severe; secondly, the way it reverses Swansea's seaside position and erects itself on to the hills above the railway station, surveying the city and providing views beyond, as much as it dominates views from the tightly packed centre, a proper civic beacon.

Weimar-on-Usk: German Expressionism was an inspiration for Odeon cinemas, such as this one in Newport.

But third and most important are the minimal yet monumental civic spaces, which fan out around the German Expressionist painter Hans Feibusch's twelve astonishing, vivid, industrial-historical Socialist Realist murals, commissioned in 1960 for the entrance hall as it was finally being completed. These pulsating, furious works are the most incredible public artworks in any building of twentieth-century Wales, and provide a fiery fulcrum to an otherwise cold building.

ODEON CINEMA, NEWPORT ✪

Harry Weedon, 1938
Moderne

Along with Harrogate's **Odeon Cinema (p. 393)**, this is probably the best preserved of the many streamline moderne cinemas designed by Harry Weedon for the Oscar Deutsch organization, and it is, happily, again working as an arthouse cinema and cultural centre, after languishing for many years either in dereliction or as an evangelical church. It's defined by Weedon's magpie-like borrowing from German and Dutch architecture of the time – a Mendelsohn curve, harsh, patterned brick detailing one part Dudok and one part Hamburg, pulled into an asymmetric Constructivist composition with lots to look at, urban scenery that is meant to put a spring in your step. Like all Odeon cinemas, it goes very very shabby indeed round the corner, the places where you're not meant to be looking – the brusque bare brick walls the Mary Anne backside to the Queen Anne, or rather, here, Greta Garbo, front. The building is now known as the NEON: 'Newport Entertains Our Nation', a cute reference to the original ODEON: Oscar Deutsch Entertains Our Nation, and perhaps also to the fact that Newport is a place that has long punched above its weight culturally – especially musically.

HOOVER FACTORY, MERTHYR TYDFIL ❶
Wallis Gilbert & Partners, 1946–8
Moderne

A very late Thomas Wallis factory complex in stock brick, but much more minimal than his **Hoover Factory (p. 159)** in Perivale, west London. It comprises a dashing curve, a monumental frontage with concave walls of Dutch brick, a grid of plate glass windows racing down an arterial road, a glamorous image of mass production, intended as display. It was recently vacated, and its future is in doubt. Merthyr, once the most important town in Wales, a militantly revolutionary industrial centre that some consider to be the birthplace of the red flag as a socialist symbol, is tragically lacking in great buildings given the wealth once generated here. If this were to go, it would have none at all of note from the twentieth century.

PORT TALBOT STEELWORKS
Steel Company of Wales, 1951
Industrial

All depends on the time of day, this one. If you come across it at sunset, with the works going full pelt, it is one of the most breathtaking landscape experiences in Wales, which is saying something. A terrifying tangle of tubes and tendrils, twisting their way around the blast furnaces, constantly belching fire, as the sky goes from pink to purple to black. Not very good for the 'environment', without doubt, but for the 'built environment' it has a level of terrible, rumbling apocalyptic activity, and a crude, overwhelming architectural force. It completely overwhelms the townscape of poor Port Talbot itself, though moderne enthusiasts should note the 1939 Plaza Cinema, whose wipe-clean faïence tiles have taken a lot of punishment.

PUBLIC TOILETS, HAY-ON-WYE
1950s
People's Detailing

In the centre of this capital of secondhand bookshops and questionable literary festivals is a public toilet, whose architect and date I cannot ascertain as it isn't in Pevsner, but its style strongly suggests the fifties. Rustic walls, a wooden upper storey in green-stained wood, and an overhanging concrete roof: an exemplary 'small architectural form', as they called them in the USSR, fitting perfectly with the historic, largely Victorian town, without tweeness or obviousness. The interiors are not quite so delightful, but given there are so few good modernist public toilets, spending a penny in here is recommended for completists.

KARDOMAH CAFÉ, SWANSEA ✪
1957
People's Detailing

The best single thing in the rebuilt post-war city centre of Swansea is this cafeteria – once part of a chain, which has managed to stay basically unchanged for decades since to the point where it's now, along with E. Pellicci in London, the best-surviving popular modernist interior, the finest example left of ordinary local craftsmen translating the modernist style of the day into a decorative and attractive space. Whereas at Pellicci the style is art deco, here it is Festival of Britain modernism – so we have a spectacular showcase of abstract multicoloured mosaics, atomic hatstands, leatherette seats on elegant little legs and tables with a checkerboard pattern which could be taken from D'Arcy Thompson's study of natural 'design', *On Growth and Form*, a fashionable book for fifties interior designers. Most of the activity is inside, but outside you'll find the best block of Swansea's rebuilding, with shimmering

The corner of the Kardomah Café: laconic post-war mild modernism above, decorative Festival Style below.

grey-green-gold mosaics between the dour curved-brick elevations and a glass door inset into the caff. Fabulous fun, and the staff know it, without feeling the need to slap a sign saying 'Come to our authentic austerity café' on the front. [C.4]

SWANSEA INDOOR MARKET
Percy Edwards, 1959–61
People's Detailing

Not much from outside, like most of the wan, sub-Plymouth redevelopment of the centre of this heavily Blitzed city into a half-modern, half-classical city of Portland stone and curtain walls, but much more exciting inside. The market is held under an enormous great steel-and-glass barrel roof with a grand clock, decorated by appropriately sky-blue sailor-suit mosaic pattern. The spirit of the place can be found in here, like a modernized Victorian railway station turned over to selling meat, veg, clothes and all manner of other curiosities.

BLAENAU GWENT CIVIC CENTRE, EBBW VALE
J. L. Thomas, 1965
International Style

This is the largest civic building in the Valleys, a modernist complex at the edge of the former steel town, in landscaped grounds; it is a little dour, but rewards exploration. The planning is strongly modernist, with the various functions (originally indicated on the historical map that still stands on the site – Clinic, Health Centre, DHSS, Municipal Offices, Leisure Centre) spread out across rolling greenery, on an irregular, asymmetrical layout. Architecturally, the most convincing part is the council chamber, a long, high-ceilinged block of Portland stone, the glass alternating with brown spandrels; this is connected by a glass walkway to a taller block of offices, which is in a sombre dark brick. The overall sense is of a miniature modernist Garden City, with free-flowing space all around, and scattered artworks which range from abstract concrete reliefs to tiled pavements with images of local steelworkers. Predictably, the council are currently considering vacating the building due to the cost of keeping it up.

WATER GARDENS, CWMBRAN
Gordon Redfern for Cwmbran Development Corporation Architects Dept, 1965–7
Brutalist

Cwmbran New Town, in the far east of the Valleys, shares its arrangement of precincts, roundabouts and low-density green suburbs with the New Towns of England and Scotland, and some of the same features turn up. But either through good sense or because of insufficient funds it has not screwed up its Water Gardens, as Harlow did with its own **(p. 187)**. The Cwmbran gardens are much smaller, later and stranger than Frederick Gibberd's Scandinavian City Beautiful approach – instead, it's a pocket Brutalist multilevel refuge amidst all the malls. In Monmouth Square, one of the town's series of shopping precincts, linked together by smartly planned routes, you'll find a sort of square within a square, lined in thick, dark Corbusian concrete, with purple tiled steps leading down to a blue pool. Standing in the pool are various sculptures, some abstract, some realist, some neither, and all contributing to a feeling of seclusion and slight surrealism. The trees are tall and rugged, as they should be up here. Aligned with the square is Monmouth House, a 1967 office block by Gordon Redfern of the Cwmbran Development Corporation, recently converted into flats; the building itself is nothing special, but its stair tower is one of the most remarkable of William Mitchell's Aztec-Brutalist concrete inventions, knobbly and rhythmic. When viewed from the bottom of the sunken gardens, it's clearly designed as part of the same scheme – from beneath the precinct to eight floors up, a piece of city treated as sculpture.

There have been proposals to infill the gardens – tellingly strongly opposed by the residents of Monmouth House – but at the time of writing it remains open and intact, though closed in winter due to the slippery surfaces, and with some tacky new balustrades. Its owners, Torfaen council, correctly note that it's hard to access for those with limited mobility, though as usual this is nothing an intelligent restoration architect couldn't sort out. Cwmbran has some nice fifties decorative reliefs, panels and sculptures tacked on to some indifferent buildings – but here the art is immersive, intrinsic to the architecture.

SEVERN BRIDGE/PONT HAFREN ○
Mott Hay & Anderson and Freeman Fox & Partners, 1966
International Style

A suspension bridge of startling purity. The Severn Bridge was until recently the main route from England into Wales for anyone coming from the south by car, and a notorious suicide spot, but seldom seems to get discussed in terms of its architecture. This is unfortunate, because it vies with the **Humber Bridge (p. 463)** for the contested category of the most elegant engineering structure in post-war Britain; it might be the better of the two, for the two stunning white steel H-shaped pylons holding up its cables, which on a sunny day make this feel like Wales's answer to the Golden Gate. Bridge design has become fussier since the sixties – partly for design reasons, with the fancy 'organic' bridges of Santiago Calatrava or, in the UK, Wilkinson Eyre; or for reasons of safety. The 1996 Second Severn Crossing is around three times the length of the first and nearly twice its width, and it negotiates a broad curve, meaning it had to be heavily reinforced with supporting concrete pillars for most of its route. Here, however, the site is simpler, and the design principles are different – the maximum effect with the minimum of materials, and effort, an analogue to the dematerialization of architecture aimed at by the likes of Mies van der Rohe. The goal is for the structure to become *beinahe nichts*, almost nothing. And, here, that's almost achieved – sea, sky, a straight line across and two straight lines above. Despite the clarity of the design, it marks debatable lands: most, though not all, of the actual structure is officially in Gloucestershire, and at the time of writing it is subject to a dispute between that county, whose council want to rename it after Elizabeth II, and the government of Wales, who would prefer it to be named in honour of Aneurin Bevan.

The sublime sweep of the Severn Bridge, connecting Gloucestershire in England and Monmouthshire in Wales.

FAIRWATER SHOPPING PRECINCT, CWMBRAN

Gordon Redfern for Cwmbran Development Corporation Architects Dept, 1967
Brutalism

The suburbs of Cwmbran consist of fairly straightforward New Town housing which is made unusually visually striking by the high hills close by, and unusually melancholic by the deep neglect and poverty so common in South Wales. The suburb of Fairwater, though, would be worth a special visit anywhere. Whereas other estates in Cwmbran loop around aimlessly as if they're in flat Essex, the centre of Fairwater is made up of monopitch terraces, with very Finnish planting around them, descending in linear strips down the hills, like Valleys terraces gone Alvar Aalto. Surrounded by car parks, its shopping precinct looks bleak from the roads around, but walk into the pedestrianized area and you'll find one of the best of all the New Town ensembles. An origami plan of two jagged blocks of turreted stock-brick flats above shops, under black-stained wood canopies, zigzags around one of Cwmbran's sunken squares. Corduroy concrete escape staircases add some Brutalist dash to the Finno-Swedish feeling of warmth and enclosure. Both intimate and dramatic, as a New Town in the Valleys should be.

PENRHYS, RHONDDA

Alex Robertson & Partners, 1966–8
People's Detailing

Right up on a mountain in the Rhondda Valley, with a heartstopping view for miles around of pit villages nestled in green bulges, Penrhys is a planned new village which has faced a grim fate. Most of this stricken place has been demolished over the decades since it was built, but just enough survives to give some sense of its total otherness. It was originally made up of both houses and flats, but these were organized in the landscape in a totally different way to the average Valleys terrace – houses and flats with monopitch roofs are dotted daringly up the hills, so that rather than the familiar Valleys sight of a row lined up along each hill and mountain, Penrhys has an integration between landscape and housing, each built into the other, much more common in Scandinavia than in Britain. It didn't work out – the energy crisis made the buildings hard to heat, aggressive slum clearance policies saw people dumped here against their will, and, my god, the wind that blows through this place is unforgiving. The flats were all demolished some time ago, but many of the houses have been refurbished, so you can just about see the picturesque plan, with an epic view for every tenant – a great idea, with the right will, the money and the technology. All were lacking. Even now, the grass is overgrown, the pavements are potholed, and if a flood or an accident were to block the place off, a pint of milk would be arduous to come by.

BRECON COUNTY LIBRARY
J. A. McRobbie for Breconshire County Architects Dept, 1969
International Style

An excellent miniature municipal library, very much in the scale of this pretty and picturesque Powys town, but refusing to be boringly 'in keeping' with its aesthetics. Two storeys, pale brick, subtly commanding concrete steps up to a corner entrance, and two distinct facades. To the side street, a strongly profiled grid, with emphasized verticals; to the main road, a fan-like plan, which gives oblique full-height views and plenty of light for the readers; the join at the corner between these has been planted with creepers. Undoubtedly modern, but warm and friendly towards its cosy

surroundings. CADW, the Welsh equivalent of Historic England, has been negligent in listing post-war buildings – many major works have been destroyed, which, given the country has so little modern architecture, has had much worse effects than similar carelessness in an English or Scottish county – an entire period here risks substantial disappearance. So it was a pleasant surprise when Brecon County Library was recently listed. It's only a shame there aren't more like it in country towns, in Wales and elsewhere.

JAMES STREET MULTISTOREY CAR PARK, EBBW VALE
1974
Brutalist

Let down a little through a naff magnolia paint job and nasty anti-suicide netting, this is a fighting-fit Brutalist car park, a tightly coiled spring of concrete floors. Its spiral ramp even has a little bit of the Welsh-American Frank Lloyd Wright in it, a sort of everyday Guggenheim, something which the paint job would actually draw attention to were it not for the netting. The building has been frequently criticized and lamented, but its design is as punchy and pugnacious as the Victorian steeltown it serves.

TREDEGAR LIBRARY
Powell Alport & Partners, 1974–5
Brutalist

Aneurin Bevan's home town has just the one bit of major Welfare State architecture, but it's a good one. Like the library in the more bougie Brecon it is small scale, like the town around, and of concrete with pale brick cladding, but that's where the similarity ends – this is a much more aggressive, strong-willed proposition. Angular, it presents itself to the round crossroads at the centre of

Tredegar as three distinct volumes, cranked, abstract and flat, with a chamfered wall secluding the entrance. The back side is more rationalist, a clear grid of glass offering lots of natural light for the readers. It's a powerful composition, abstract and perhaps a little sombre, but even those hostile to its design can surely grasp the symbolic point being made. Here, you can read books. Books are important.

SWANSEA CIVIC CENTRE ♻ ❶
C. W. Quick of West Glamorgan Architects Dept, 1979–84
Brutalist

A fascinating contrast with the witty semi-classicism of Swansea Guildhall from nearly half a century earlier. Concrete, ribbon windows and, rather than a single, instantly understandable image, a sprawling set of articulated parts like a miniature city that can never be encompassed in a single glance. A pedestrian system of circulation sometimes leads you above, sometimes below, these polygonal hulks of offices and public spaces (which include Swansea's main library and its register office). In the wrong setting this could be grimly bureaucratic, but here you're right on a beach. The contrast results in one of the most admirable examples of civic Brutalism in Britain, for the way in which these hulks stretch across the bay without dominating it. The finishes were also evidently very high quality – it has been battered by wind, seagull shit, and the belching smoke and pollution of Port Talbot, but instead of crumbling, the concrete has gently weathered, becoming part of the landscape. It is currently slated for demolition after a very contested vote by the city council, and, if it goes, I'll miss this harsh but humane thing much more than more famous absences like **Robin Hood Gardens (p. 130)**. [B.14]

Swansea Civic Centre, an underrated Brutalist public building of great complexity overlooking the sea.

INTERNATIONAL RECTIFIER, NEWPORT ✪
Richard Rogers Partnership, 1982
DUFFRYN ESTATE, NEWPORT
Richard MacCormac, 1978
High-Tech

Two remarkably different approaches out of mainstream modernist architecture, built within a few years of each other, both by famous London architects in the outer suburbs of Newport. The sprawling factory complex now known as International Rectifier is difficult to get to if you're a pedestrian – like most Postmodern industry, it's not built for you to casually chance upon – but if you can make the effort, you'll find one of Rogers's greatest buildings, left casually at the edge of Wales's third city. A sharp contrast with the coal and steel and muck and mess reputation of South Wales industry, this place promised a clean, precision-engineering future that never quite came to pass. The design idea is a very long single lozenge of production spaces, held up by a thicket of Constructivist cables, painted blue and yellow. From a distance, it has one of Rogers's Gothic skylines, spindly, busy, puzzling and exciting; up close, as always, it is gorgeously detailed, every little pipe and aluminium panel just so. In photographs the interiors look just as futuristic, bizarre and beautifully detailed as the elevations, but Newport doesn't exactly do Open House.

Surrounding the INMOS factory, so unmissable if you're visiting it, is Richard MacCormac's Duffryn estate. This was one of the largest-scale examples of the 'low-rise, high-density' trend in modernism, which resulted in London schemes such as **Watermeads (p. 114)** and **Alexandra Road (p. 148)**, and in Milton Keynes estates like **Netherfield (p. 223)** and **Eaglestone (p. 223)**. Duffryn is closer to the former in its sprawling, diagrammatic plan – look at it on a map and it's instantly legible, a 'perimeter plan' of long, linear terraces which form into consecutive loops centred on somewhat scrubby village green-like roundabouts; at the centre are an open space and some preserved woodland. An interesting experiment in planning terms, but the architecture – brick with wood detailing and little nods to mock Tudor half-timbering – shows a failure of nerve compared with the London or Milton Keynes estates using the same ideas. MacCormac would subsequently carry this into full-scale Postmodernism, which worked better than this compromise. And over it all the spiky blue skyline of Rogers' factory was giving a lesson in scale and confidence.

CHARTIST BRIDGE, BLACKWOOD
Arup, 2005
High-Tech

A minimal but grand bridge in a depressed Valleys town best known for being the home of the Manic Street Preachers, this is one of the more enduring consequences of the 'Objective One' EU money that was pumped into the Valleys and is soon to be removed from them. Cable-stayed, held up by a grand and gate-like concrete pylon, the design is simple and beautiful; it's looked over by an accompanying statue of a revolutionary, with a pike.

CARDIFF

CARDIFF CENTRAL STATION CONCOURSE
Percy Emerson Culverhouse, 1932–4
Moderne

Cardiff's main railway station was redesigned and expanded in the 1930s to largely forgettable neoclassical effect, but the interior was much more imaginative – a combination of staid exterior and moderne interior was quite common among architects who wanted to experiment a little without frightening the horses. The concourse is a spacious, vaulted and coffered space, with grey granite pilasters and, hanging low, polygonal lights, evoking late Hapsburg Vienna. The same, unfortunately, can't be said about the view of Cardiff when you leave that concourse – a parade of straggling commercial buildings of all eras. Inside, at least, you feel like you might be entering a capital city.

TEMPLE OF PEACE AND HEALTH
Percy Thomas Partnership, 1937–8
Modern Classicism

The architectural oasis that is Cathays Park, built up around the fabulous Edwardian baroque City Hall, is described by John Newman in his Pevsner guide to Glamorgan as 'the finest civic centre in the British Isles'. That all this splendour had started to go to the city's head is exhibited by this unique building. It was planned to house both the local societies for the prevention of tuberculosis, and for the support of the League of Nations; architecturally, it follows the Portland stone style of the various public edifices all around, but only in its barest essence. This is the most stripped-down, minimalist classicism imaginable, with only the faintly Georgian windows rooting it in

Britain – the ruthlessly square central portico suggests Mussolini's Rome, or even Albert Speer's pavilions in Berlin's Tiergarten. The original functions are long since obsolete, which means that the Temple of Peace (the 'Health' got dropped along the way) is now a vague ceremonial space, frequently used for weddings, which take place in the splendid Temple Hall. With its black-granite columns and polychrome coffered ceilings, it's one of the most striking interiors of its time, comparable only with Charles Holden's work in **Senate House (p. 51)**. It is ironic of course that this temple devoted to peace resembles so closely the architecture of the most bellicose states of the 1930s, but the allegedly eternal values of classical architecture have always been put to many uses.

HOUSE OF FRASER
Percy Thomas Partnership, 1965
International Style

The centre of the Welsh capital is bursting with fabulous late-Victorian, Edwardian and interwar commercial buildings, but none of them are remotely modernist – much more common is a muscular steel-framed baroque, of obvious American derivation, which you can also find plenty of around the bay in Bute Town. Unfortunately this is a book about modern architecture, so we have to sidestep the Yankee classique of Howell's department store (now House of Fraser), and follow it round the corner to find what looks like an extension of the 1930s, in the Erich Mendelsohn manner of a whipcrack curve, with three storeys of ribbon windows, all the drama of the sudden corner. It's actually post-war, but the effect is the same.

CITRUS HOTEL
Alex Gordon & Partners, 1966
International Style

The most pure modernist building in Cardiff, and easily one of the best conversions of its kind. Built as Snelling House for Cardiff's gas board, the commission was given to a local architect. But this is a much classier proposition than most of the city's office blocks, a diamond in the bleak, messy cluster around Cardiff Central Station, the only thing here to really show an engagement with the fact that designing for a capital city is different from designing for just another provincial industrial town. Its sleek eight-storey cube of glass is raised by delicate concrete struts over a podium and car park, which lifts it visually above the railway line leading to the station, a witty effect that makes it appear to float. The tower was renovated as a boutique hotel in the 2000s, first known as The Big Sleep, and currently as the Citrus Hotel. No original interiors survive, but the curtain wall has been completely retained, making it – at least from the outside – Wales's one and only Miesian mid-century modernist hotel. Whether any of this is owed to the fact John Malkovich was one of the hotel's investors it is impossible to say.

CENTRAL POLICE STATION
John Dryburgh for Cardiff City Architects Dept, 1966
Brutalist

Cardiff is one of those strange industrial cities (see also Bradford, Bristol) with plenty of great buildings, very few of which are modern. This is especially true of Cathays Park, Wales's equivalent of the Washington DC Mall, between the neo-Gothic fantasia of Cardiff Castle and the university. Dominated by neoclassical and baroque edifices of the early twentieth century – some of them, like Cardiff City Hall and the **Temple of Health and Peace (p. 295)**, of real brilliance and originality – it gradually devolves as you walk north into pompous bureaucratic blocks clad in Portland stone, much as you'd find in DC itself, no doubt. The exception is this strong Brutalist police station by the City Architect. An inset two-storey plinth and, above it, three storeys, one mostly blank, take up an entire self-contained city block, detailed with rigour and rhythm, with a welcome attention to small details, like the sculptural window reveals and the Corbusian canopy over the main entrance. It does glower, but then it houses the police – and you can always compare it with the gimcrack PFI misery of the more recent Cardiff Bay Police Station a couple of miles away.

UNIVERSITY OF CARDIFF: TOWER BUILDING
Dale Owen for Percy Thomas Partnership, 1967
ARTS & SOCIAL STUDIES LIBRARY
Faulkner-Brown Hendy Watkinson Stonor, 1976
International Style, Brutalist

At the north edge of Cathays Park, past the classical palaces and the tough Brutalism of Cardiff's **Central Police Station (above)**, you'll find the campus of the University of Cardiff, which continues the 'City Beautiful' ethos of the park's interwar buildings – space, grace, decorum – but mostly in a more contemporary aesthetic. Although the Jacobethan Main Building, opened in 1909, provides the nucleus, it was mostly built up in the 1960s in a manner that continues the palette of the earlier work but shifts style into a slightly conservative modernism. These new buildings were still clad in Portland stone, though on concrete frames, and are still sheltered behind wide tree-lined boulevards; the best are this tower and the nearby library, which show off their calm, tight-lipped aesthetic to best effect. The tower is a clear twelve storeys of ribbon windows, which become a slightly Constructivist pattern on the top storey, with a brick service tower attached – asymmetrical and elegant. The Arts and Social Studies Library uses the same materials, but here arranged into a more Brutalist expression, with heavy overhangs held up on concrete pillars, to create light, column-free reading rooms; it has something of the Japanese air you can find in Basil Spence's **University of Edinburgh Library (p. 501)**. From the street, it is almost hidden by trees.

___

CAPITAL TOWER
Sir John Burnet & Partners, 1967–70
Brutalist

By the time it was topped by a trivial tower of luxury flats in Swansea in 2008, this twenty-five-storey office tower had reigned nearly four decades as the tallest building in Wales – yet it remains a seldom-discussed building. Originally built for Pearl Assurance and renamed during the economic boom that accompanied the early years of Welsh devolution, it stands too close to the showpiece ensembles of Cardiff Castle and Cathays Park not to irritate people. But, judged on its own terms, this is a well-resolved tower with a lot of integrity. The expressed concrete frame, with the strong verticals of its mullions, its four splayed corners and its double-height top storey, creates a relaxed, elegant silhouette, while its concrete has aged very well – a sombre dark brown that complements the slate palette of Cardiff's historic buildings rather nicely. One might have hoped that the minimalism and truth to materials of this building might have provided a guide for the architects of the dozen or so recent high-rises in central Cardiff, but alas.

ST FAGANS NATIONAL MUSEUM OF HISTORY
Dale Owen for Percy Thomas Partnership, 1968–74
International Style

On the furthest outskirts of the city of Cardiff you can find St Fagans, an example of the genre of outdoor folk architecture museums that were built across Europe in the twentieth century, inspired by the example of Skansen in Stockholm. Obsolete historical buildings have been collected from throughout South Wales and assembled in a landscaped park; most of them are obviously beyond our remit here, aside perhaps from one 1940s prefab and an already dated mid-2000s eco 'House of the Future', but anyone interested in architecture will find it a fascinating place. But, given that the museum was founded after the Second World War and expanded in the 1960s, any new buildings naturally had to be modern, not pastiche. So the visitor enters St Fagans through a flat-roofed museum and café complex, with a cantilevered main hall held up on T-shaped concrete pillars; with its calm colours and low profile it fades easily into the landscape around, but not by mimicking any of the various historical vernaculars on offer round here. The interior, with its exposed concrete frame, is light and airy, a place of repose – the slim concrete beams were apparently inspired by the timber framing that can be seen in so many of the outdoor exhibits. The building was recently refurbished by Purcell Architects to impressive effect – a rare quality restoration of a modernist building in Wales.

___

ST DAVID'S HALL
Seymour Harris Partnership, 1982
Brutalist

An ingenious little theatre complex crammed tightly into a corner of Cardiff's main shopping street, to the extent that some of it is actually on top of shops, which says something about British urban priorities. From a distance, it looks chaotic, especially the massive mansard roof covering part of it, in a misbegotten attempt to be in keeping with something or other, but the street facade is strikingly clever, a set of cranked and angled concrete foyers stacked atop each other, with an oblique entrance. After that, the generous scale and grandeur of the theatre spaces themselves can be a shock, and they vindicate the efforts of the architects to somehow fit something this monumental into so tiny a space.

———

MILLENNIUM STADIUM
HOK Sport, 1999
High-Tech

No refinement or architectural good manners here, just an enormous stadium shoved right into the city centre, held up with mammoth Constructivist struts, visible from miles around, which communicate the scale and ambition of the capital far better than the dozen or so speculative towers with which it has screwed up its skyline.

———

MILLENNIUM CENTRE
Jonathan Adams for Percy Thomas Partnership, 2004
SENEDD ✪
Richard Rogers Partnership, 2005
Pseudomodernist, Supermodernist, High-Tech, Ecomodernist

Cardiff Bay is – and I hate to say this, given its symbolic importance, and the emotional attachment some have to it – a dreadful space, a blank plaza scuffed between shonky luxury flats and an appalling retail and restaurant complex, Mermaid Quay, which practically walls off both the Victorian/Edwardian commercial district at Bute Town

The organic High-Tech of Richard Rogers Partnership's Senedd, with its grand steps down to Cardiff Bay.

and the surrounding council estates – a lesson in how *not* to stitch a city together. Aside from the Liverpudlian red-brick clock tower of the Pierhead, there are two buildings that suggest how things could have been better. The Millennium Centre is much maligned by architects, largely because it replaced a thrilling, competition-winning Opera House by Zaha Hadid. By now, even the ruling 'Taffia' must know how foolish they were in spurning it in an act of cheap populism. But on its own terms Jonathan Adams's replacement is fine – a big barrel of a central volume, clad in a dun copper, and with a great supergraphic Welsh and English inscription, Expressionistic wings in the local slate and an impressive entrance hall.

The Welsh Parliament, the Senedd, is the real pick here. It is a complicated, brave, somewhat tortured building, completely avoiding the populism that might be expected. Its main frontage to the bay is deceptively simple – a public-space project, diagrammatic, in Rogers's quasi-Italian square-making manner, here executed in a minimal, rather icy fashion, with thin columns leading to a glass block and a slightly kinked wooden roof. It's as you approach up those steps that the romanticism of the project becomes clear, as the roof's billowing folds and curves rise above you, and then, as you enter the building, flow and rise up into a massive, funnel-like cowl, wild and organic. This structure is actually totally functional – it's basically a vent for cooling the building, helping to keep the energy bills down – but suddenly this rational building has tapped into those faintly irrational impulses that lie behind any national movement, even one as relaxed and benign as Welsh nationalism – an invented tradition of connection to landscape, in a city built on coal and steel. It's only a shame that the usual heavy security you'll find in any parliament makes exploration of this unique space difficult.

You can get a decent idea of it from the main foyer, before the frisking starts. [**C.23**]

ROATH LOCK STUDIOS
FAT Architecture, 2011
Postmodernist

The late, lamented cult 2000s practice FAT were adherents of the 'decorated shed' version of Postmodernism, derived from the American designer-theorists Denise Scott-Brown and Robert Venturi – buildings that are little more than canvases for surface treatments. I have my doubts as to whether this is appropriate for, say, housing or libraries, but for a huge BBC TV studios building like this one, just over the water from Cardiff Bay, it makes perfect sense – actual sheds, after all, and the decoration is joyously imaginative and kitsch. *Doctor Who* is filmed in here, and rather than the CGI dreck they use for backdrops today, they would have done better, on this evidence, to have hired FAT, whose cheap and weird pulp aesthetic runs riot here, a rave baroque of cardboard cut-out gables and Nintendo mock Tudor, leaping and twisting about over a lengthy, linear range of flat-roofed boxes.

NORTH WALES

VILLA MARINA, CRAIGSIDE, LLANDUDNO ☉
Harry Weedon, 1936
Moderne

The Birmingham architect Harry Weedon was the brand designer of the Odeon cinema chain, where he made a gimcrack version of German interwar *Reklamarchitektur* ('advertising architecture') into the picture palace vernacular. Many 'Harry Weedon buildings' were designed by others, using the repertoire he'd cobbled together out of faïence, brick and shameless thieving from Erich Mendelsohn, but this house for a Birmingham cake magnate was a personal project. It is also his finest building, and by far the most *enjoyable* 1930s modernist house in Britain, in the way that the least 'correct' version of a fashionable style is usually the most fun. It's placed in a short row of silly Victorian houses with castle keeps and conical spires, at the point where the panache of Llandudno's Victorian grand parade meets the freakish convulsions in stone of the crags. It has a street facade, but don't bother with that – approach it along the stony beach, where it gradually emerges, mirage-like, as the perfect cinematic modernist house, an abstract relief sculpture of curves and cubes set into the rock. Or rather, it is set into a purpose-built sea wall, also by Weedon, where local rubble stone is piled up into two streamlined turrets, with a little belvedere on top. The house then sails above this, its concrete sweep in sparkling condition. Suave, theatrical and thrilling.

After being sold as a house, it has been a hotel and a convalescent home, and is now a private house again. The interiors are said to be opulent; as at **New Ways (p. 345)**, it's sad that nobody at the council thought to turn it into a museum. Councils don't seem to do that sort of thing any more. **[C.1]**

APOLLO BINGO, RHYL
Robert Bullivant and Harry Weedon, 1937
Moderne

The seaside town of Rhyl has had seen all kinds of ambitious twentieth-century building projects – a monorail, a pioneering futuristic leisure centre, a 'Sky Tower' purchased from an Expo in Glasgow – and it has destroyed all of them, demolishing the first two and removing the glass gondola from the Sky Tower so that the skyline is inexplicably dominated by a lanky, dilapidated steel pole. These may all have been adaptations to reality in Rhyl, but they mean there is little to report from the Blackpool of North Wales – except for this first-rate streamline picture palace. Right next to the bus station, this follows the usual Odeon blueprint – a big brick box, with a dramatic and seedily suave curved corner prow, and grim, warehouse-like backsides – but with some original touches of its own. The fluted, Expressionistic red brick of the cinema/bingo hall, stylishly asymmetrical, is dressed at the bulging corner with cream faïence, which for once has been cleaned, and above it is a rippling faïence crest. Weimar-on-sea meets Alan Bennett uptown.

———

WREXHAM GUILDHALL
1961
WATERWORLD, WREXHAM
F. D. Williamson & Associates, 1965–7
POLICE HEADQUARTERS, WREXHAM ❶
Eric Langford Lewis for the County Architects Dept, 1970s
People's Detailing, Brutalist

It's customary in 'urbanism', ever since the work of Jane Jacobs, to scorn parkland civic centres as some sort of affront to the messy vitality of real city life. There are obviously some examples that genuinely are arid and city-dulling presences, but there are others where the idea of a civic oasis in a workaday town still has a salutary effect. One is Llwyn Isaf Park, just outside the centre of Wrexham, just before the point where the market town meets exurban retail parkland. Much here is scheduled for demolition, but the Guildhall is likely to stay – an impressively shameless Scandinavian steal, where a laconic red-brick facade with abstracted but residually Georgian arched windows features a cantilevered gallery towards the park, and to the town centre a copper tower and an obvious 'I once saw this in a book about Denmark' corner clock. The more Brutalist library next door is duller, but continues the general sense of rectitude, of having been thought about and cared over. Cross the road to the Welsh Guards war memorial and the civic parkland continues, with a couple of decent but unremarkable things like the Festival Style Memorial Hall and the vernacular-going-on-Postmodernist Magistrates' Court, and then – what's this? A tall, sculptural tower suspended precipitously on a giant T-shaped shuttered concrete column, over a sprawling podium, blocked off by fences, with the gardens overgrown. This was Wrexham's Police Headquarters, and is far and away the most exciting twentieth-century building in Wrexham – rough, daring and witty in the way that, from many angles, the tower seems to be floating.

It's hard to say budget shopping is worse even at its worst than a prison cell, but it's depressing nonetheless that a Lidl with a drive-thru coffee shop will replace this original and strange thing – an attempt was made locally to get it listed, but the Welsh conservation body responsible, CADW, is notoriously blind to modernism and predictably refused, recogizing its quality but noting that there were better tower-and-podium designs elsewhere. There are

better medieval churches than Wrexham's St Giles, too, but I doubt they'd let that be pulled down. The Waterworld Leisure Centre, just the other side of the Magistrates' Court, is also under threat. It has a fabulous hyperbolic paraboloid roof, unique in Wales – like a larger version of **Markham Moor Service Station (p. 358)**, a grand Googie swoop. A recent listing attempt by the civil society of Wrexham was also thrown out, though here the bulk of the building beneath the roof is so heavily altered along tinny nineties lines that CADW was probably correct according to listing rules in its refusal. In any case, this leafy civic oasis will be reduced soon enough to the lawn between the Guildhall and the library.

—

SCHOOL OF BIOLOGICAL SCIENCES, BRAMBELL BUILDING, BANGOR UNIVERSITY
Percy Thomas Partnership, 1969–70
Brutalist

Apparently widely despised, this unsentimental block of colonnaded concrete is the only one of many post-war buildings in the university to have any real character – it's just that its character happens to be a tad harsh. In sandstone-aggregate concrete, it has two chamfered upper storeys supported by an enormous projecting frame, which is treated as a sort of science fiction giant order of columns; behind it are red-brick laboratories. Even in 1970 there was talk in the local press of this looking like a secret-police headquarters; it was built as the Zoology Department, and has its own Natural History Museum, which is occasionally open to the public. The Brambell Building adds a bit of vigour and presence to a wan, straggling collection of schools and offices, which are insultingly dull with such a magnificent site to exploit. This one knows what it wants to do, and does it with confidence. There's even a delicacy about the way its component parts are kept together, with the massive weight suspended on these spindly supports. Bangor needs more buildings like this, not fewer.

———

COLEG HARLECH ✪ ❶
Colwyn Foulkes & Partners, 1970–73
Brutalist

A heartbreaking place, extremely hard to write about without falling into incoherent rage. Harlech College was founded as an adult education college in the early twentieth century, in one of the great historic sites of Welsh nationalism, a jaw-dropping place, with the Irish sea on one side and Owain Glyndwr's much-besieged castle on a black flint outcrop on the other – the ideal location for something like this, a site with extraordinary natural and architectural gifts to bestow. The college, closely linked with the Workers' Educational Association and preceding the Open University in its focus on giving working-class adults a 'second chance', was based around a vigorous, rough classical house by the Glasgow School architect/designer George Henry Walton, framed by arches and follies. It carried on until the twenty-first century, when a financial crisis meant that, first, it sold its rare books and its art collection, and then closed entirely, with no plan for its rescue. One would have thought that well-endowed universities like Cardiff or Aberystwyth would have been able to step in, but obviously estates departments have their minds set on more important things. It has been derelict now for half a decade, locked and fenced off from the public, though a back route along some cottages can get you there fairly easily.

The college includes the two most powerful and moving Brutalist buildings in Wales; in fact, probably the most sheerly

The theatre and halls of residence at Harlech's breathtaking Coleg Harlech, with the historic castle behind.

convincing twentieth-century buildings in the entire country – the theatre and the halls of residence, built by a local firm in the early seventies after a fire burnt down the original halls. The halls are strict late Le Corbusier, with the ascetic intensity of his monastery at La Tourette – a grid of slate-aggregate concrete, sculpturally modelled and classically proportioned, attached to the main road through a vertiginous walkway. It had relief sculptures inside by Jonah Jones, and wood-panelled walls, but all that has been stripped out, the windows mostly smashed. Juxtaposed with this square mass are the theatre's intersecting cylinders, a set of easily legible auditoria kept up by great vaulting futurist cantilevers, with heavy, brutal escape towers on either side. All extremely modern for West Wales, sure, but it fits into the black and grey of the rocks all around just as well as the castle.

The dereliction of this place is mirrored by another of Walton's buildings, the St David's Hotel, which was de-listed and demolished in 2019, with the moronic applause of the local press. There is something very disturbing in all this. It seems that anything outside Cardiff that isn't chapels, little detached houses, static caravans and castles can be freely destroyed, and that the decades after 1945 are of no consequence to the history of Welsh architecture. These college buildings are not 'eyesores', however much their dereliction may appear to make them so; but there's a horrible irony that this has been the fate of the only Welsh modern buildings to have anything like the elemental power of the Welsh landscape. Whereas the failure to list and protect, say, **Swansea Civic Centre (p. 293)** or Wrexham's **Police Headquarters (p. 300)** is unfortunate, the neglect at Harlech is up there with **Park Hill (p. 370)** as one of the real tragedies of modern architecture in Britain – a terrible collective failure, sickening in its implications.

The fusion of art and concrete in coastal Wales: the tower of the University of Aberystwyth's Arts Centre.

UNIVERSITY OF ABERYSTWYTH: ✪ GREAT HALL & BELL TOWER,
Dale Owen for Percy Thomas Partnership, 1970
ARTS CENTRE
Smith Roberts Associates, 2000
Brutalist, Ecomodernist

Aberystwyth is the only really interesting modern university campus in Wales, the only space to approach the monumentality of the New Universities in England and Scotland. Placed in the grandest romantic fashion on a hill overlooking the Victorian town and the expanse of the Irish sea, it consists of a series of simple low modern blocks leading to the sharp and punchy Great Hall and Bell Tower. The hall is of concrete, with a massive window, large enough for the circulation spaces and stairwells to be visible, and illuminated in the evening. The cantilevering of the theatre above the hallways and stairs can be seen on the facade, creating a blunt, massive composition. Outside, a purely decorative bell tower works as a cross between a grand campanile and a Constructivist sculpture. It leads to a public flight of outdoor steps, placed clearly in order for students to be able to enjoy the view. Next to this is another artwork – a torn-out-of-context stairwell to nowhere, which is used by students as a place to aimlessly hang out, as is right and proper at a university.

Lacking the integrity and drama of the Great Hall above it, the organic Arts Centre is still a very worthy addition to Aberystwyth's hilltop campus, sunken below the Brutalist buildings. A grand rotunda in green space, slightly tackily detailed but with a warmth that some might find preferable to the stark grandeur of the earlier parts of the complex.

Brutalist Revival in North Wales: the interiors of the Oriel Mostyn, Llandudno.

ORIEL MOSTYN, LLANDUDNO
G. E. Humphreys, 1901/
Ellis Williams Architects, 2011
Brutalist

The Mostyn Gallery – or Oriel Mostyn, depending on whether you're fluent in Cymraeg – is one of the grandest buildings in Wales's grandest, richest seaside town, which with its tall, rather Wes Anderson hotels and bizarre, sensual crags beyond can be a heady experience. A South Kensington-style riot of red terracotta, it was built as an art gallery (specifically, a gallery specializing in women artists, who were particularly marginalized by the local art mafia at the time), then became a warehouse, rather ignominiously – but since the 1970s it has again been a gallery, now with one of the more experimental programmes in Wales. Ellis Williams's refurb created new top-lit, white-cube gallery spaces at the back, but what is more exciting is the Brutalist revival stairwell that brings it together. Lush shuttered concrete – the architects might have taken inspiration from Walsall's **New Art Gallery (p. 322)** – is put through its paces in an angsty, jagged, maze-like composition. It doesn't *do* anything more than take you to the café, but it makes that journey unexpectedly invigorating.

PONTIO, BANGOR
Grimshaw, 2013
International Style

Nicholas Grimshaw's firm are something like the *Go-Bots* to Norman Foster's planet-eating *Transformers* – the somewhat cheaper, clunkier version of High-Tech. Like Foster, they've travelled a path from clanging, aggressive hard modernism to serene, glistening controlled environments (from Camden **Sainsbury's & Grand Union Walk, p. 153**, to the **Eden Project, p. 280**), and they've most recently moved towards the sober, stone-cladding style that has dominated post-financial-crisis Britain. They would seem like an odd choice for this ambitious combined students' union, arts centre, café, university offices and 'innovation centre' in a cathedral city. The architecture at a glance is predictable – intersecting masses, clad in honey-coloured stone so thin it looks like Trespa, PFI detailing, and an approach to context and topography that shows the application of the Alvar Aalto Guide to Designing Modern Buildings in Non-Metropolitan Areas. Walking it rather than glancing at it, however, is more rewarding. It's the only building that spans the sharp town/gown divide that is etched into Bangor's very structure, with its Gothic university perched on a steep acropolis with views out to Anglesey, the sea and the mountains, and a more ordinary town laid out below. Twisting volumes turn the ascent (or a vertiginous descent) into an approach of discovery, with surprising views out, and steep, sudden panoramas across the building from an angular, edgy five-storey stairwell. Once you've traversed it from top to bottom, an apparently dull and conformist building has revealed itself to be an ingenious topographical adventure.

turned the place into something similar to inner-London refurbishment schemes like the converted car park of Peckham Levels, or a properly Arts Council-funded spin on punkish, enthusiasm-driven renovations like Newcastle's **Star and Shadow Cinema (p. 489)**. So poured into the disused mall are an art gallery alongside a market for local small businesses, in what feels like a Welsh spin on the 'Preston Model' of municipal community wealth building. It's an ingenious, smart idea – transforming something old and naff rather than building something new and shiny. On the facade, there has been no attempt to hide the clunky original architecture, although the campanile has been given some hep new signage to indicate the new function. Inside, though, anything twee has been ruthlessly torn out, and replaced with a raw, ad hoc space of breezeblocks, bare concrete beams holding up the car parking, abstract murals and pop art screens, eventually oddly Warholian in feel. A very brave project, it deserves to thrive.

TY PAWB, WREXHAM
Featherstone Young, 2019
Postmodernist

This one comes close to summing up the British radical architecture zeitgeist – and, to be fair, you don't usually expect Wrexham to be at the height of the zeitgeist. Ty Pawb – Our House – is a remodelling of a banal 1980s Postmodernist shopping centre – the usual ingratiating stuff, neo-Victorian bay windows and red-brick pinnacles continue a polite street facade, with a whacking great car park behind and a sort of campanile at the corner. The Ty Pawb collective have

6. WEST MIDLANDS

Sports Centre Extension, Coventry (p. 330)

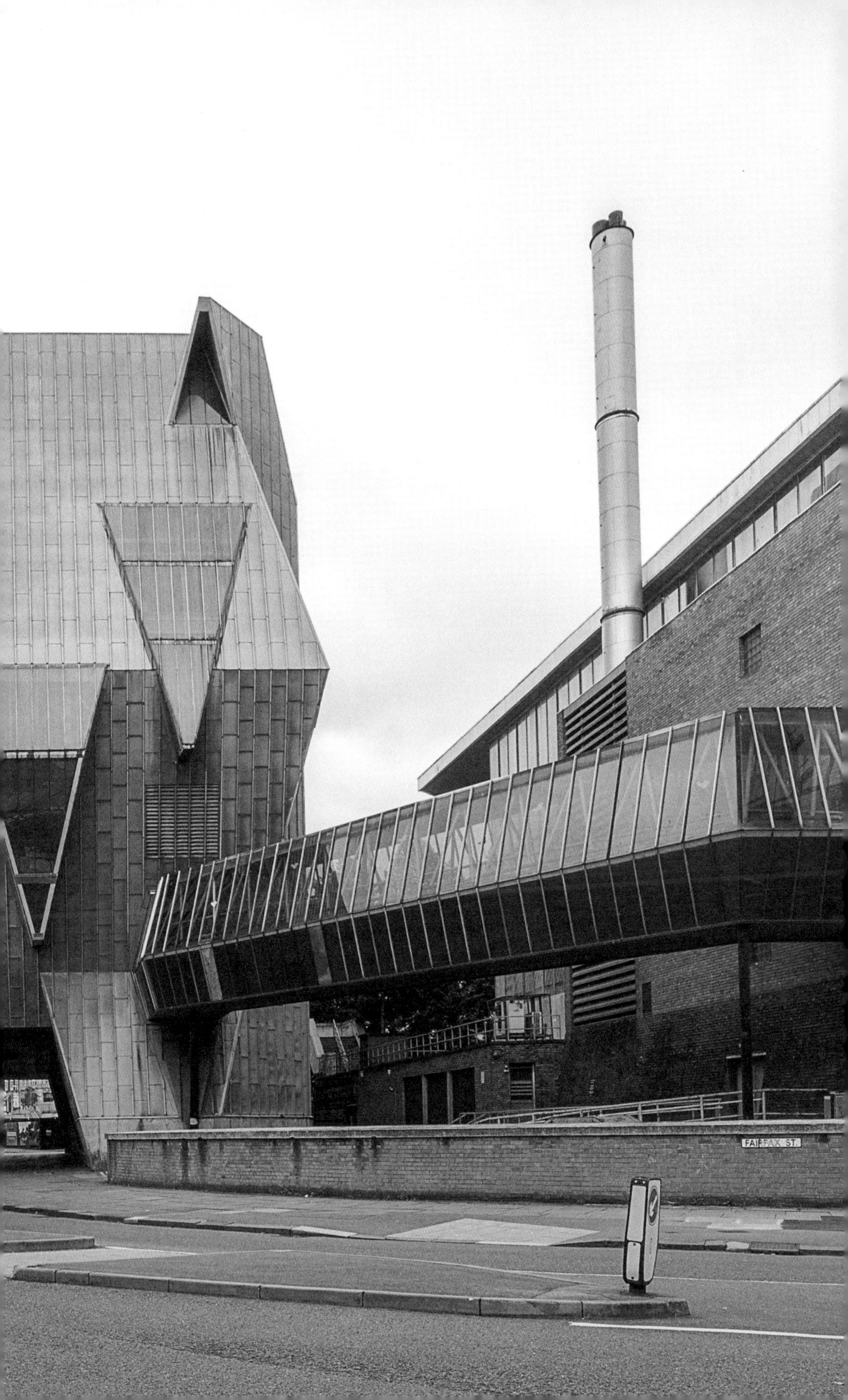
FAIRFAX ST.

The West Midlands *feels* like it should be one of the great centres of modern architecture. It is dominated by three cities – Birmingham, still the second-largest city proper in Britain (though Greater Manchester is larger), with its contiguous but fiercely independent hinterland in the Black Country; Coventry, a showpiece reconstructed city; and Stoke-on-Trent, the official name for the multicentric city of the 'Potteries'. Each of these – especially Birmingham – has built at a prodigious rate over the last century. Sometimes, the results have been genuinely wonderful. Coventry has the best modernist city centre in Britain, however neglected it might feel in places; the **Central Precinct**, **Cathedral Church of St Michael & All Angels**, the **Herbert Gallery**, the **Bull Yard** and the topsy-turvy surrealism of the **Leisure Centre** are all spaces and buildings of the very first rank, with delightful public sculpture and murals. Public esteem for these has taken a while, but many are now rightly celebrated.

Birmingham is trickier. As in Wales, too much of the best has been destroyed, particularly the three finest buildings by the local architect John Madin – the towers of the *Post and Mail* and National Westminster Bank, and the magnificent Central Library – and replacements have been poor. The best surviving work is in the university and the adjacent affluent suburb of Edgbaston, such as the **Ashley Building** or **Cala Drive**. The Black Country (and nearby towns like Kidderminster and Bridgnorth) can be a little bleak but contain some real surprises, such as the fabulous **Dudley Zoo** by the great émigré architect Berthold Lubetkin and his Tecton collective, or Caruso St John's **New Art Gallery** in Walsall, the best of its period. The Potteries in and around Stoke are even more chaotic, but here you can find the smouldering Expressionism of **Keele University Chapel** in Newcastle-under-Lyme, and the eccentric delights of the **Potteries Museum** in Hanley. The border region with Wales features the rather botched New Towns of Telford and Redditch, along with picturesque Shrewsbury, whose **Market Hall** is one of the very best modern buildings in a historic city.

BIRMINGHAM

BARBER INSTITUTE, UNIVERSITY OF BIRMINGHAM
Robert Atkinson, 1936–9
Modern Classicism

The flipside of the extreme build-it-up-knock-it-down-build-something-bigger-and-cheaper 'ethos' of inner Birmingham is some of the poshest suburbs in Britain. It doesn't get much more plush than this site, where the eclectic fantasy skyline of Aston Webb's Edwardian university buildings meets the Arts and Crafts gateways of the King Edward School. The Barber Institute is extremely borderline as a modern building – this is a deeply traditional work of architecture, closer to New Delhi than to the New Frankfurt from its heavy exterior. But if explored fully, especially inside, it can be seen much more as a European conservative-modern building of the 1930s, much more than it is a British one, classicism tempered by clean modernist lines, no fuss, no pomp, no Lutyens-style coy architectural gags. A main hall of travertine is the entrance to a concert hall, and *Kunstkammer* statues are set into specially designed niches. Exquisitely carved steps lead up to a sequence of art galleries with walnut benches and coloured Hessian walls – this is 'Swedish grace' come to Birmingham. Robert Atkinson's assistant on the Institute was a young Rosemary Smith, who would move to Sweden soon after, where she would become Rosemary Stjernstedt. Her Anglo-Scandinavia, when she came to build it in the 1950s and '60s, would be much more clearly modern, in the London housing schemes she designed at **Alton Estate (p. 112)** and **Central Hill Estate (p. 94)** – but the attention to detail, that belief that architecture needs to be humane and haptic, can be traced here.

ELMDON BUILDING, BIRMINGHAM AIRPORT
Norman & Dawbarn, 1938–9
Moderne

A rare piece of preserved airport infrastructure, off-limits to the public but easily seen from the newer airport buildings and the roads nearby, and possible to glimpse in the distance from the mainline into New Street. Birmingham's first air terminal is a complex mix of Constructivist influences and art deco chic – four long storeys, with a curved concrete corner, generously glazed with wide ribbon windows to the front, grand cantilevered 'wings' at the sides, detailed with a rawness and chunkiness that makes it quite unlike the smoother, more considered lines of the contemporary **Speke Aerodrome (p. 426)** in Liverpool. Cranky, heavy and even a little kitsch, but thrilling nonetheless.

DUDDESTON FOUR
Alwyn Sheppard Fidler for Birmingham City Council Architects Dept, 1952–4
CHAMBERLAIN GARDENS
Alwyn Sheppard Fidler for Birmingham City Council Architects Dept, 1961–4
International Style, Expressionist

These two are – were – the best-designed post-war council estates in Birmingham, which is not a good place to go tower-block spotting. This is unfortunate given that they built a shitload of them. Chamberlain Gardens is one of those schemes, like **Gleadless Valley (p. 367)**, the **Alton Estate (p. 112)** and **Sceaux Gardens (p. 88)**, that were based on the expropriation of the private gardens of large middle-class houses – full of spreading mature trees and winding paths, and other landscape effects for contemplation by their owners – and their transformation into the parkland setting for a high-rise estate. There are ten not particularly tall towers fitted into the gardens, with clipped, neat designs, no Brutalist roughness or Festival-style decoration, just fine proportions and decent materials; maisonettes and Alton West-style leaf-dappled cubic bungalows provide picturesque relief. In its quiet way, this is one of the best schemes of its period, an ordinary working *ville radieuse*. A recent render and styrofoam repair job has smothered the subtle colour contrasts of the towers' original brown brick and cream tiles, but the intentions of the designs are still clear. The same can't be said of the aesthetically disastrous cladding of the earlier 'Duddeston Four'. These four twelve-storey towers, Birmingham's first, relied on a raw, Expressionistic use of dark-red brick, shaped into craggy, Hanseatic shapes, fitting right in with the brick campaniles and spires of the industrial city. But nobody at Birmingham City Council seems to have noticed this, so they've been given a whitewash just the same as at the already rendered Chamberlain Gardens, totally effacing their design. There's a grim irony in this, in a city (and country) where new high-rises are constantly being clad in fake brick slips to be 'in keeping'. At least the cladding isn't likely to be flammable.

Alwyn Sheppard Fidler, the city architect who designed these two, was sacked from Birmingham City Council while Chamberlain Gardens was being built; his replacement was later jailed for graft. So it goes.

GROSVENOR HOUSE
Cotton Ballard & Blow, 1953–4
People's Detailing

This is the earliest surviving major building of the total transformation that Birmingham underwent between the 1950s and '70s,

a project which wasn't necessitated by Blitz damage or even particularly by slum clearance, but by the powerful City Engineer Herbert Manzoni's desire to plough massive great roads through everything. Naturally in this, architectural quality and townscape weren't much of an issue; neither, for the most part, were the sorts of spatial thrills you can find in the multilevel assault course of **Newcastle City Centre Walkway System (p. 483)**. The fact that this resulted in such a delightful bit of street architecture is quite the paradox. It's developer's stuff, pure flash – a curving six-storey office block clad in artificial stone, each bay on one side staggered into a zigzag pattern, and on the other side decorated with little fins. It's a little bit Festival of Britain, especially with the jazzy balconies, and it's a little bit op art. Generously, you could say this sort of flashy display is still often found in Birmingham architecture, in something like Make's complex, fiddly **The Cube (p. 318)** office block; but the relaxed way this slots into the city remains atypical.

ENGINEERING & ALLIED EMPLOYERS' FEDERATION ✪
John Madin, 1954–7
People's Detailing

The only one of Madin's dozens of distinguished modernist buildings in and around Birmingham to have been listed is, at first sight, the least characteristic. A modest, decorative and very fifties low-rise Edgbaston office block, it feels more like a suburban showroom. That this is legally protected while his Birmingham Central Library and NatWest Tower were demolished, the former against the repeated advice of English Heritage, feels like an act of architectural censorship, literally wiping Birmingham's Brutalist history out of the new cityscape of Trespa and Teflon. But on its own merits, it isn't hard to see why this

The well-mannered, mild-modernism of John Madin's Engineering & Allied Employers' Federation building.

building was listed. One storey of travertine offices – with, typically for its time, a special anteroom for trade union negotiators – projecting slightly above higher, more clearly modernist windows to the street, sheltered by hedges. At the entrance, a panel of green slate is incised with diamond-shaped vents, a sculptural touch that extends to the door handles and the (not usually open, but easily peered at) interiors. Everything is calm, considered, crafted, its proportions carefully calculated. Above all, this is a beautifully made building, in a city where build quality is seldom considered important; but, then, this faces Italianate Edgbaston houses, not Victorian slums or thirties semis. Madin would build widely in Edgbaston, presumably having been hired on the strength of his work on this building, going on to create several exquisite small housing schemes in the suburb.

SMALLBROOK QUEENSWAY ❶
James Roberts, 1958–62
Brutalist

The first phase of the redevelopment of Birmingham into a motorway city actually saw European-style boulevard integration of grand buildings and expressways, before it was decided, doubtless correctly, that placing a high-speed rat-run this close to pedestrians was inviting traffic accidents. But the effect of that close integration is that this terrific, sweeping curve conveys an excitement to the pedestrian as well as the driver, with a rhythm of abstract concrete reliefs and Corbusian bullhorn canopies, as the cars charge down towards tunnels and overpasses beyond. It doesn't feel like it's in Britain at all – you can imagine it in Belgrade, say, a place where mid-century modernism was truly metropolitan. Like most good modern buildings in the city, it is currently slated for demolition.

34 ARTHUR ROAD, WHEELEYS ROAD, WARWICK CREST, CALA DRIVE & ESTRIA ROAD, EDGBASTON

John Madin, 1962
International Style

To understand Birmingham – something I confess to finding difficult – you have to understand Edgbaston. Long before anyone thought of the 'Garden Suburb', that's what this inner-city district was. Only a mile or two from the city centre, these Italianate, high-Victorian and, later, Arts and Crafts houses, usually detached, in extensive gardens, are set informally in tree-lined streets, often screened by hedges and walls from the *hoi polloi*. Two things are important about this – first, that Birmingham industrialists, unlike their Northern bourgeois brethren, wanted to live in the city, and, second, that they didn't want it to look like a city. With the exception of **Chamberlain Gardens (p. 309)**, Edgbaston is also far and away the best place to see modern housing in Birmingham. That's because the landowner of the Calthorpe Estate, the owner of much of Edgbaston, decided to 'improve' his property in the 1960s, making a tidy profit while maintaining its discreet and verdant character.

John Madin argued this could be achieved by interspersing some quite dense housing – several tower blocks and maisonettes – with green ridges, groves, copses, gardens and pathways. The results are often gorgeous, green and pleasant modernism. This cluster is the spot to see each different facet of Madin and Calthorpe's project at once. Nestling next to each other at one corner are a relaxed monopitch detached house, a high-rise block made almost invisible by mature trees, some Span-style terraces of weatherboarded houses. At the cul-de-sac of Cala Drive, a set of wood-and-brick houses are laid out with great delicacy. Later parts of modernized Edgbaston reject the careful balance of modernist design and controlled nature for standard suburban development of the 1970s and '80s, with all the greenery and grace stripped away, and with a lot more car parking. As with Span estates like **Parkleys (p. 111)**, the streets are private and big signs will tell you you're not allowed to be here, but the worst I've experienced is a puzzled look.

ASHLEY BUILDING & STRATHCONA BUILDING, UNIVERSITY OF BIRMINGHAM ✪

Howell Killick Partridge & Amis, 1964
Brutalist

Two superb, interlinked buildings by the architects of **Alton Estate (p. 112)**, here putting their proficiency in the placing together of precast concrete to much more eccentric, even luxurious purposes. The Strathcona building is a faintly rustic, low-rise block curving gently around the Ashley building, an elliptical five-storey rotunda, made up of curved, convex and concave panels, articulated and visually rich with activity. But go inside the Ashley Building, and you'll find one of the truly great modernist spaces in Britain, a cylindrical, spiralling atrium under a glass dome, with the balustrades and the internal frames detailed with Mackintosh-like flair in wood and concrete. Each floor is glazed, with windows looking out into the atrium, with a cylindrical staircase running the entire height of the building. Walking around it is kaleidoscopic. Originally the Ashley Building brought together various unconnected subjects via this atrium – that's what it was there for. It is now mostly a school of languages, and you can imagine a polyglot dialogue resounding from each of the niches in its spiral, a dome of Babel.

Brutalist surfaces and landscaping at the University of Birmingham: the Ashley and Strathcona buildings.

UNIVERSITY OF BIRMINGHAM: METALLURGY & MINERALS BUILDING
Philip Dowson for Arup Associates, 1964
MUIRHEAD TOWER
Philip Dowson for Arup Associates, 1968
Brutalist

Fans of *A Very Peculiar Practice*, Andrew Davies's classic TV amalgam of anti-Thatcherite politics, anti-psychiatry and gentle eighties middlebrow comedy, will recognize these buildings as 'Lowlands University', a litter-strewn faded utopia through which the ageing alcoholic Laingian Jock McCannon, cradling his whisky, composes his opus on 'the sick University'. Both buildings are epochal images of the technocratic plate glass university, both coldly rationalist and exceptionally generous in their provision of public spaces. The earlier, and less extreme of the two, is the Metallurgy & Minerals Building. In the sixties,

it was one of the users in the UK of the American architect Louis Kahn's ideas about a 'tartan grid' of services, offices and labs. It also shows the influence of Kahn's rigorous, elemental approach to architectural expression, with a repeated module of articulated, robotic concrete parts extending right down to the angular, Cronenbergian colonnades that meet the ground floor. All this is around, of course, a quadrangle, bringing together both old-school university planning and the deployment of 'IHC PLASMA FURNACE'.

The Muirhead Tower is bigger, and meaner still, two interlinked chunks of concrete, elaborately chamfered and buttressed, in a rhythm of dual glass floors and windowless concrete floors (these were for lecture theatres and laboratories). Large parts of the design have been severely compromised by tacked-on shiny stuff and (presumably necessary) steel louvres, and a Starbucks has been shoved into the pedestrian walkway. Still, the most dramatic face of the building, where it rises above the service roads passing underneath, is untouched and decidedly pugnacious. [B.12]

THE ROTUNDA
James Roberts, 1964–5
International Style

The 'icon' of post-war Birmingham, at least since the demolition of the Central Library, is this cylindrical office block, a piece of pop architecture comparable in its effect to London's Post Office Tower (and vastly superior to Birmingham's own, half-arsed telecommunications tower). It was converted to flats by Urban Splash as part of the 'Urban Renaissance', and as the one piece of salvage from the complete transformation of the post-war Bull Ring. It is one of their better restorations, heavily rebuilt, but to the untrained eye still very obviously the same building, with the same clear proportions and uninterrupted swish curves. Compared with the massive integrity of the demolished library, it's candyfloss, but even that has its place.

BIRMINGHAM NEW STREET SIGNAL BOX
John Bicknell and Paul Hamilton for British Railways, 1964–5
Brutalist

Adjoining the consecutive disasters of Birmingham New Street – from the world's dullest megastructure to the world's cheapest bit of Parametricism, with its ETFE sagging like a cheap marquee mere months after its completion, the same miserable platforms underneath – is this tiny structure, part of the 1960s station and listed early on as a mini-masterwork of baroque Brutalism. Multiple ribs of thick corrugated concrete, asymmetrical and turreted, appear like

a toy castle, with projecting geometries recalling Frank Lloyd Wright at his most sculptural. Heavy, hardcore, surrounded by dross, from which it provides a growlingly angry counterpoint.

HOCKLEY CIRCUS ✪
William Mitchell (artist), 1968
Brutalist

The modern landscape, at its most abstract, harsh and surreal, so strange that it might appear as the result of botches in planning, but is actually wholly deliberate. The main expressway out of central Birmingham towards Handsworth rises into a flyover at Hockley. Beneath, the pedestrian underpasses lead to an expanse of pavement. Surrounding you are relief sculptures, in a Mesoamerican-cum-Abstract-Expressionist manner, by the prolific William Mitchell; some in the grey of the flyover, some of them with their concrete stained dark red. They look like snapshots from a terrifying experiment, microscope images of viruses, scales, guns (made around here after all), hair, explosions, skin, viscous and feral. Inside the underpasses, generations of graffiti painters have added their own wildstyle commentary on the space. It is like being in one of the drawings in Laura Grace Ford's *Savage Messiah*; standing here on your own, you might expect a sound system to arrive any minute and turn it into a post-punk carnival. [B.21]

BIRMINGHAM REPERTORY THEATRE
Graham Winteringham, 1969–71
International Style

A rather gimmicky civic building, with its coy semi-Gothic trimmings an echo of New York's Lincoln Centre, and when it was still there – sorry to insist on this – considerably

A close-up of the wild Mesoamerican-meets-Art Brut surfaces of William Mitchell's walls at Hockley Circus.

less convincing than Birmingham Central Library. Now that's gone, this looks a little more impressive, almost restrained compared with the monumental fripperies of Mecanoo's disastrous, pretentious and early-closing new Library of Birmingham next door, to which it is joined by a new walkway.

GRAVELLY HILL INTERCHANGE ✪
Owen Williams, 1972
Brutalist

The pay-off for the way that Birmingham has the worst public transport of any city of 1 million in Europe – for the way it is sliced into abstract slices that never properly add up but seldom acquire their own identity – is this *thing*. The main equivalent in Britain of the Piranesian, layer-upon-layer expressway stacks of Los Angeles, Gravelly Hill – that's 'Spaghetti Junction' to you – is shocking and unforgettable, not only in the way that

the flyovers are mounted atop each other, swerving away from each other at wild angles and arcs, but for the way it squats atop earlier infrastructures that carry on beneath it – rails, canals and a river, and overgrown grass and wasteland, which is how you can see it as a pedestrian. However ill-advised this is – and it is – any account of modernism that ignores or writes out places like this is as deficient as a history that sees it solely as the era of highway engineers. Here is the pure abstraction of the 1960s city – a revolutionized experience of space and time – and people have domesticated it and given it a nickname. Given that it was compared to the Pyramids at the time it was being built, one can hope that, like them, it is preserved when its original use becomes obsolete – as hopefully it will.

ALPHA TOWER ✪
George Marsh for R. Seifert & Partners, 1969–73
International Style

Another of the towers that George Marsh, partner, designed at Seifert's, and another triumph for surface flash and intelligent borrowing, and for the recognition – strangely lost on most other Birmingham architects – that if you're going to design something that everyone can see, every day, you might as well pull your bloody finger out. In this case, the inspiration is not Niemeyer, as in Seifert's best London buildings, but Gio Ponti, and specifically the Pirelli Tower in Milan. Like it, this is a skyscraper with a smooth, refined design tapering to the sides, where the services and the lifts go – not a cut-off bit of graph paper, but a complete and integral, desirably chic object. Having seen both, I actually prefer Marsh's Birmingham version to Ponti's original – he has given the

tapered shape a slinky sway, suggesting the silhouette of a well-designed cocktail dress – and that's very much the sort of metaphor they were aiming for.

———

METROPOLITAN HOUSE
John Madin Design Group, 1972–4
54 HAGLEY ROAD
John Madin Design Group, 1978
International Style, Brutalist

The last major survivals of the extensive work of John Madin Design Group in central Birmingham (aside from the neat but fairly middling Chamber of Commerce, towards which the wrecking balls are itching to swing), and while they're by no means the most interesting of Madin's work, both are decent examples of how to take a speculative mega-commission – here, giant mono-complexes of offices – and design the results with wit and flair. Both blocks are

Metropolitanism in the Second City: tramlines from the Roman temple of Birmingham Town Hall to Alpha Tower.

in the middle of a circus of underpasses and sunken plazas, Birmingham at its most interestingly alienating. 54 Hagley Road is Brutalist – alas, painted, after a refurbishment – with a precast grid of pod-like modules, zipped up with a brick-clad service tower. Metropolitan House, meanwhile, was something relatively new, an Americanist approach towards Postmodernism – purple stone cladding and mirrorglass, arranged into crystalline corner towers, shaped into an expressive honeycomb plan. Both have lower-rise blocks around them using the same modules and proportions, with semi-public spaces between, which would now be regarded as a waste of lettable space.

BRINDLEYPLACE CAFÉ
CZWG, 1995–7
High-Tech

Brindleyplace, a mixed-use project at the western edge of the centre of Birmingham, was a pioneer, of sorts – the earliest built example of what would become the typical 2000s townscape of tall but street-centred blocks, some along canals, with active frontages, coffee concessions and generally modern design, although here with the black sheep of Demetri Porphyrios's bizarre Postmodern classicism in the middle of it. Compared to the things that would happen to Birmingham after **Selfridges (below)** caused another development supernova, it appears as a model of rectitude, but the building that most repays examination is the smallest. CZWG's steel-and-glass café, free-standing at the centre of Brindleyplace's main square, marks a shift from their bumptious Postmodernism towards an organic but technophile modernism of shiny surfaces, airy interiors and petal-like openings, which can be seen elsewhere in their excellent **Public Toilets (p. 170)** on Westbourne Grove in London. Although lightweight in its construction and minuscule in scale,

and though it has had various owners over the years, the building has aged very well – an image of unfussy sophistication that can be hard to find in Brum.

SELFRIDGES
Future Systems, 1999–2003
Supermodernist, Pseudomodernist

A hard building to praise – a facade and nothing but, standing in the heart of one of the worst townscapes in Europe, hostile to pedestrians, vacuous in its design ideas, and shrill, with the adverts yelling at you constantly. But, if we have to have architecture like this, it can be done well or it can be done badly – this is done well. Birmingham Selfridges forms part of the redevelopment of the Bull Ring, mostly in a tacky manner by developer's hacks Benoy; but in order to be WORLD CLASS one corner of it was given to Selfridges, who offered it to Jan Kaplický and Amanda Levete to design (though it is connected by a bouncy walkway to Benoy's mothership). Selfridges is almost windowless, except for a cyclops 'eye' and a dumbly open 'mouth', and its blobby form is actually quite conventionally engineered, only then covered with a fancy coat of sequins. A defence of the building would run as follows. If we are going to build introverted, anti-urban shopping malls, and if we're going to have an architecture that is all about the surface decoration of a shell already decided upon by the developer, well – then that decoration, that facade, had better be pretty exciting. And here Kaplický and Levete do rise to the challenge, and that veil they've draped over the shed really is shimmering, fascinating and sometimes, especially when it is lit up by neon at night, almost beautiful.

THE MAILBOX
Associated Architects, 2000/
Stanton Williams, 2015
THE CUBE
Make, 2009
Postmodernist, Pseudomodernist

Jewels, kept in the tackiest of cases. These two interlinked buildings were, until the redevelopment of the area around the old Birmingham Central Library, the largest building projects in the city since the sixties, both of them for offices and retail, both for the same developer. The Mailbox is an extreme adaptive reuse project which involved completely gutting a Brutalist Royal Mail sorting office of 1970, right down to its concrete frame, then building around that a new symmetrical facade which resembles a Renaissance Palazzo exploded in size, denuded of ornament and executed on the cheap. What makes it worth exploring is the architects' decision to retain the complex interaction of walkways and canals that formed part of the original building, so that the main circulation space is a clear grid of multilevel arcades (recently given a glazed roof in a refined renovation by Stanton Williams architects), which lead through to canal-side restaurants with similar double-level decks. It is ironic that the most successful example of the complex three-dimensional city of walkways and skyways that Birmingham aspired to in the sixties (and then spent years dismantling) was built in the 2000s. The combination of unlovely facade and interesting interior is continued in the second phase of the same development a decade later. Make's Cube is an office tower covered in a mindbendingly complex pattern of rectilinear shapes, clearly meant to evoke 8-bit video games, *The Space Invaders Attack Brummagem* – it is ingenious but tiring to look at, even more so given the arbitrary roofscape of twisted glass volumes. But the walkways will lead you again through to a bizarrely complex atrium of (here, less successful) shops, with the shapes that are so irritating from a distance resolving themselves into an Expressionistic upwards rush to an open, uncovered sky. There was a time, once, when Birmingham architects (like poor old John Madin) could manage both exteriors and interiors, but today one will have to do.

BLACK COUNTRY

ZOOLOGICAL GARDENS, DUDLEY ✪

Tecton, 1937
International Style, Constructivist

The Second City's complement to London Zoo (well, almost the Second City – you can see the Birmingham skyline from up here), and this time designed from the very start by Lubetkin and Tecton, and on a much more unusual, topographically delinquent and historically important site, to which Tecton responded with an even more exotic set of structures. Dudley Zoo occupies the grounds of the ruined Dudley Castle, with its various pavilions and enclosures set into the winding paths that spiral up towards the half-preserved grand archway to these fragments of cylindrical fortress towers – an ideal picturesque landscape. In terms of animal welfare, Dudley was progressive for its time – no metal cages here – but not by the standards of the twenty-first century, so many enclosures have different inhabitants to those they were designed for. It has had a difficult history – for many years, Dudley Zoo was notoriously semi-derelict, with the Tecton buildings corroding into the wooded ridges. More recently, four of them have been very nicely restored, and it appears to be popular and well-run.

Dudley Zoo is the best place to see Tecton's work at its least functionalist – giant, exuberant 1930s modernist sculptures on the level of Naum Gabo or László Moholy-Nagy, which for extra effect have been populated by meerkats, llamas and lions. In the heart of the Birmingham–Black Country sprawl, the Zoo begins with a major disappointment for pedestrians.

Lubetkin and Tecton's Dudley Zoo, using the concrete experiments of Constructivism to house non-human life.

The original entrance – a restored set of wavy concrete canopies, held up with thin pilotis, on a zigzag plan – is on one of Dudley's main streets, between a couple of decent 1930s faïence-and-brick cinemas (one now derelict, one now a Kingdom Hall of Jehovah's Witnesses), and the site of a railway station, long since demolished, though it's surely an obvious choice for a tram stop for the planned Midland Metro extension to Dudley. But, for now, you get to the zoo through an enormous and extremely bleak surface car park; the ticket hall is in Tecton's original café, a simple concrete and glass box, beautifully restored by Avanti architects. From here, either paths or a cute nineties cable car take you to the upper level, with its views over Black Country suburbia and the terrace of the original Elephant House. Although it's derelict, with concrete stalactites dripping off it, this concrete strip now serves as a viewing platform for an impressive Brum–Black Country panorama.

Then follow the paths around and you can find delights such as the former Reptilarium, a straightforward concrete basin now occupied by meerkats, who look like they're guarding the castle; the Apes Enclosure (one of Tecton's cute signs is still on it, just – now saying 'PES'); three walls fanning around some relaxed-looking orangutans; the former Bird House, a drum mounting one of the slopes which is now part of the Lion Enclosure; or the restaurant, which rests effortlessly on the slope above. But the two buildings that make this worth the asking price for anyone remotely interested in British modern architecture are the Bear Ravine and the Kiosk.

The Kiosk, intended as a spot to provide both information and ice creams, is a curved concrete pod, with a jaunty hat, painted in De Stijl colours – sadly it doesn't appear to be used, standing just as an abstract sculpture. The Bear Ravine is something else. When designing the Zoo, Tecton found a cavern, part of the original castle structure, and decided to make use of it. There are two curved concrete terraces, swooping right round the ravine. The one above is held up on elegant mushroom columns courtesy of Ove Arup's engineering, and, below, a projecting tongue pokes out into the ravine – now, sadly, closed to the public. The concrete structure continues down below, to curve into a (relatively) secluded area for the bears – well, currently, the llamas – to shelter in. Regardless of which animal lives in it, the most fun thing about the Bear Ravine is in how it's a reversal of the London Penguin Pool. Rather than the animals being put on show on a set of delicate, swooping concrete cantilevers, this time it's us, put on a terrace to be stared at by the animals – an inversion the mischievous Lubetkin must have enjoyed.

———

BILSTON HEALTH CENTRE
Lyons Israel Ellis, 1937–40
International Style

The first modernist building by one of the most undervalued of the era's public-service architects (their classical Wolverhampton Civic Halls is not quite in the remit of this book). It shows little sign of the sort of tough, restrained modernism that they would become known for, but is a fine small-scale civic building. In its function – as a free municipal health centre and a beacon of clean-lined, lightweight modernity in an area of soot and messy industry – this is the Midlands answer to Finsbury Health Centre. It occupies the centre of a green wedge plunged into the middle of an industrial-village sprawl, flanked with other, later modern buildings (the Baptist Church, a punchy red-brick cube, has the look of a John Madin building, though I've no evidence it is). The most Lubetkin-like element is the witty, thin curved, concrete entrance canopy, held up on thin, angular V-shaped supports.

The bulk of the centre is yellow brick in the Dutch/Dudok manner, with a long, glazed ground floor and a recessed upper level, which originally had a Finsbury-style built-in sign, but now has a cheap canvas banner for its current users, Bilston Community Centre. At least it's being used for something close to its original public purpose.

———

CLOCK CHAMBERS, WOLVERHAMPTON
Lavender & Twentyman, 1938
International Style

A fine commercial corner building by a local firm, in the excitingly diverse centre of Wolverhampton, with its various tawdry and opulent Victorian and moderne palatial offices and emporia, now around half derelict. Clock Chambers is a low, asymmetric, Portland stone office block with fully glazed shops on the ground floor, with a dashing use of long, rectilinear ribbon windows alternating with smaller, more classical windows above and at the far side. At the emphasized corner is a coolly minimal clock and a flagpole (without a flag). In its restraint and hint of icy hauteur, it's positively European – not something that can be said about many Wolverhampton buildings.

———

MEMORIAL GARDEN & ST MATTHEW'S CLOSE, WALSALL
Geoffrey Jellicoe, 1947–53
People's Detailing

One of the places where an ideal civic plan drawn up in the most idealist moments of the 1945 Labour government actually got built (well, not quite – there were meant, apparently, to be skybridges too). This is a public-space project built around St Matthew's Church, whose tall spire stands as the terminal point of the views from Caruso St John's brilliant **New Art Gallery (p. 322)**.

From the street, steps – and a slope with a rail, an unusually accessible touch for the time – lead up to the churchyard, with a great grotesque Gothic archway at its entrance. As you ascend, you can see the Gardener's House, in a slightly Gothicized modernism with a sort of concrete lantern on pilotis, and the war memorial and gardens enclosed in the red brick walls around it – robust but evidently contextual enough with the church for English Heritage to have listed it. Most interesting of all is St Matthew's Close, a block of flats (with a good community centre at one end) in a simple, New Town style with decorative window surrounds and balconies, and a full-height archway in the middle, the town's coat of arms at the centre of the arch. It really is right off one of those poignantly idealistic watercolours of 1943, a proud civic approach towards a new, extremely English and extremely socialist world. Wonderful scenography.

———

SCHOOL OF ART & DESIGN, WOLVERHAMPTON
Diamond Redfern & Partners, 1968
Brutalist

Just on the edge of the ring road that keeps the cars out of Wolverhampton's civic heart, and right next to Wolves' ground, Molineux (art school and football, ideally suited to each other, right?), this is a powerful precast concrete slab block. Seven all-glass storeys are screened by a decorative concrete brise-soleil, creating a tough but, in some lights, rather pretty filigree pattern. Currently looking a little sad and worn, but still very much a building with presence, and, unlike most of the many purpose-built art schools of the twentieth century, it still serves its original purpose.

WALSALL CIVIC CENTRE
Borough Architects Dept, 1974
WOLVERHAMPTON CIVIC CENTRE
City Architects Dept, 1978
Brutalist

Two big civic complexes designed on the occasion of the West Midlands' 1970s reorganization, from pretending these were independent towns that just happened to be completely contiguous to recognizing the obvious fact that they're part of one metropolis; one that they really ought to have just called 'Greater Birmingham' and been done with it. While these images of bureaucratic-civic power share a very seventies brick-clad industrial-town Brutalism, they differ in interesting ways. Walsall Civic Centre is a vertical building. It begins at the back of the terrific 1902 Walsall Town Hall, a very individual, free classical design. Two tall blocks, with strips of windows placed rhythmically between heavy purple-brick volumes, are linked by a glass skyway. All this is packed into the tight townscape, with the shape animating that squeeze. Wolverhampton Civic Hall, by contrast, is a horizontal building. This time, the brick is in two tones of orangey red and the planning is Frank Lloyd Wright prairie style, leaning back to form a series of connected ziggurats, with steps between and an impressively scaled square in front. But like the Walsall building, its apparently capricious modernist design decisions are carefully calibrated towards accommodating a historic building nearby – in this case, in order to frame the brooding red sandstone of the medieval St Peter's Church. Both buildings are a tad dour, especially when compared with a more confident effort like **Sunderland Civic Centre (p. 471)** – but each has been thought about carefully, and each creates a townscape, rather than detracting from one.

NEW ART GALLERY, WALSALL ✪
Caruso St John Architects, 1995–2000
Classical Modernism

Still 'New' over twenty years later, I firmly believe this building will eventually be recognized as the finest single work to have come out of the New Labour era of lottery funding, regeneration through culture and property development through regeneration. Built overlooking a disused canal, and neighboured – though thankfully, unlike Gateshead's **Baltic Centre for Contemporary Art (p. 474)**, not crowded out – by shoddy new flats, it is of its time, and transcends it. Even at the turn of the century, though, it stood out for being at odds with the patronizing japery and icon-first-contents-second mentality that produced such edifices as the Middlesbrough Institute of Modern Art. It maybe sounds high-minded, but it isn't boring – if you want dull but worthy, there's a lugubrious pub below, by Caruso St John's partners in rigour, Sergison Bates. No, this is rigour and seriousness and pleasure, education as excitement, a world of things to discover. It is remarkable that Walsall managed to get away with it in an era so obsessed with patronizing simplification, but it did.

Two crucial things make the New Art Gallery different. The first is that it is built around an existing collection, which was previously held in the town hall, accumulated by Kathleen Garman and Sally Ryan in the middle of the twentieth century; the niches, drawers, corners and carefully arranged vistas created in the interior are meant to frame *those specific works*; and while the temporary exhibition spaces are fine enough, this collection is what the gallery is primarily about, and it has determined most of its design. The second point is that it's as much somewhere for Walsall to look out from as to look to. It's intended as an accent in an ordinary town rather than as some beacon of 'aspiration', placed at one end of the high

The finest British art gallery of the twenty-first century: Caruso St John's New Art Gallery in the centre of Walsall.

street with a spire and a hill at the other; its cream tiles don't do anything fancy with cladding, it has no non-orthogonal geometry, and its colours are not Day-Glo.

The main facade is a grid, a box, with a rhythm of windows dictated by what is happening inside, by the need for light in different gallery rooms, and by the viewing platform at the top; these are assembled into a casually classical composition. The circulation spaces are defined, aside from their generosity of scale, by an obsession with detail – the particular measure of wood that is used to clad the galleries is the same as that used for the shuttering on the concrete. Importantly, there's always a lot of natural light, so the sanitized atmosphere of the White Cube style is totally rejected – this isn't a neutral environment, it's an almost domestic space, as though you've been let in by someone to see their private collection. The ground floor is now a Costa Coffee, after the place nearly had to close because of

funding cuts, but this is reasonably well hidden. But there's no hiding the bleakness of contemporary Walsall, which has obviously never recovered from the crash of 2008, and at the time of writing has been laid waste by the coronavirus. Last time I visited, rubbish whistled around the gallery entrance. The process familiar in sixties buildings has begun, by which a great public work is gradually destroyed by neglect and austerity. Let's hope this building is robust enough to stand up to it, because this is one of the best art galleries ever built in Britain. In fact, if you don't count behemoths like the Tate as 'galleries' so much as museums, it's *the* best.

COVENTRY

BROADGATE HOUSE
Donald Gibson for Coventry City Council Architects Dept, 1948–53
People's Detailing

Coventry, not the **South Bank (p. 84)**, is the real living legacy of the Festival of Britain and of that moment in English modern architecture when Corbusian space met Regency whimsy and Scandinavian warmth. It is also a reconstruction as a scenographic, multilevel city, a sequence of distinct spaces – an approach completely at odds with the late-Beaux Arts replanning of Plymouth, Swansea, Southampton and Hull. You're constantly framed by squares, passing through arcades, under and above precincts – though always gently, with none of the Brutalist sublimity that would come later. The result is one of the most enjoyable townscapes in Britain of any era. Broadgate House is a microcosm of what Coventry's City Architect, Donald Gibson, was aiming for. Glazed lower storeys, with a shop-window projecting bay, laconic offices above, a public through-passage below, a piquant clock tower, and sculpture ranging from Socialist Realist figures to the little Lady Godiva and Peeping Tom that come out on the hour. Heroic workerism, popular modernism, games with urban perspective, bawdy nostalgia. What a bizarre assemblage!

THE PRECINCT
Donald Gibson for Coventry City Council Architects Dept, 1953–5
People's Detailing

This, cathedral aside, was the showpiece of reconstructed Coventry – built on what Lionel Esher calls the 'solecism' of a classical axis ending on the spire of a Gothic cathedral. This was the first pedestrianized shopping precinct in Britain; it vies with Rotterdam's Lijnbaan to be the first of its kind anywhere in the world. It comprises two rows of handsome brick blocks, modernism straightened up and given a Georgian suit, with two levels – this apparently twentieth-century system of dual-level circulation was inspired by the seventeenth-century Rows in Chester. As an ensemble it has been all but destroyed by a breathtakingly philistine renovation of the 1990s, which inserted a galumphing escalator into the axis and covered the rest with crazy paving. At the time of writing, these are slated to be removed, marking a long-overdue recognition of its quality and importance, and the buildings have now been listed. As if to offset this civilized change, the owners have proposed to remove all the brickwork so as to have more room for corporate logos.

CO-OPERATIVE DEPARTMENT STORE
G. S. Hay, 1954–6
People's Detailing

Viewed casually, this is just another post-war department store, like the dozen or so in Blitzed cities around England and Wales – a brick facade, with a large, emphasized glass wall inserted into it, and some nostalgic typography. Everyone knew that Coventry was special, though, so this had to have details that no other Co-op store had, in the form of the delightful decorative reliefs by John Skelton and John Trowbridge etched into the columns of its colonnade, showing scenes of work and leisure in a friendly, witty style. Like lots of fifties Coventry, it has just been listed at the time of writing.

BELGRADE THEATRE ✪
Arthur Ling for Coventry City Council Architects Dept, 1956–8
People's Detailing

The handover from Donald Gibson to London County Council designer and Communist Arthur Ling as City Architect of Coventry didn't lead to much change in its aesthetic, bar perhaps an increased clarity, a bit less cuteness. The Belgrade Theatre is a miniaturized **Royal Festival Hall (p. 84)**, built around a gift of wood from the Socialist Federal Republic of Yugoslavia (a relief panel of the Serbian capital's skyline is one of the decorative touches). It has a similar 'egg in box' layout to the Festival Hall, pale stone cladding, elegant glass details, and has a great deal of fun with its light fittings and carpets – the twisting chandeliers of the main double-height foyer are a highlight of one of the more purely enjoyable spaces in post-war Britain.

LOWER PRECINCT MURAL
Gordon Cullen (artist), 1958
People's Detailing

This mural in tiles by the designer, draughtsman and theorist of townscape is a showcase of the sheer civic pride of post-war Coventry. Everything has the same value – the council houses of Tile Hill, the churches and Tudor remnants, dinosaurs and bicycles, all drawn lovingly and inserted into an exuberant abstract pattern, interspersed with the Gibson city plan. [C.17]

―――

RETAIL MARKET
Douglas Beaton, Ralph Irredale and Ian Crawford for Coventry City Council Architects Dept, 1957–8
People's Detailing

The fatal flaw of post-war Coventry was that the most impressive spaces were part

Reconstructing across the divides of the Cold War: the beautifully crafted restraint of Coventry's Belgrade Theatre.

of a retail monoculture. Not only did this mean much of the city centre shut down at 5.30 p.m., but also that it eventually ended up being owned by ruthlessly bottom-line-driven retail developers, who were, as far as they were concerned, running a mall, not the architectural and social heart of a city. Accordingly, many buildings are in a poor state, and any post-war work that hasn't been listed is usually under threat of demolition. But the Market offsets some of the sense central Coventry has of being a poor-quality mall set in a failed utopia. Tucked away at a corner of the sequence of precincts, it is a large rotunda, with car parking on top – a simple and elegant design, replicating the double-level system of the precincts but shunning its rectilinear, axial geometry. Inside, the airy space is complemented by jovial mosaics and murals, which market stall owners have responded to with their own often attractive or simply cute signs. Note, however, that the stallholders don't always take kindly to photographers.

CATHEDRAL CHURCH OF ST MICHAEL & ALL ANGELS ✪
Basil Spence & Partners, 1956–62
People's Detailing

In right-thinking modernist circles in the sixties and sometimes even today, it was conventional to dismiss this building as little more than souped-up neo-Gothic, as sentimental kitsch – especially given it beat a much more ambitious scheme by the Smithsons in the competition that was held to replace the bombed-out ruins of the original, the highest-profile architectural casualty of the Second World War in Britain. And compared either with the austerity and rigour of **Clifton (p. 270)** or the riotous kitsch of Liverpool **Metropolitan (p. 427)**, that might seem fair enough. Yes, the way that the side elevation of the sandstone-clad hulk of the new cathedral fans out like a cutesy fifties block of flats is both fey and populist; and, yes, the canopy that links the ruined medieval cathedral and the new building is a little too pat as a gesture. But, as so often happens, time has softened the sort of fashion- and clique-based judgements to which architects are so susceptible. By now the importance of this place is obvious. It is, first and foremost, the most important, and in many ways the only, serious memorial to the victims of the Second World War in Britain. Its emotional power derives from the way the new building is aligned with the ruins of the old, an empty shell with a spire, dotted about with plaques and sculptures, some of them about peace and comradeship, others (like Jacob Epstein's thuggish, daunting *Ecce Homo*) more reproachful. Anger and forgiveness are held in a difficult balance.

This combination of firm and forgiving also lies behind the effects of Spence's new building. Yes, again, it's a fairly straighforward updated concrete Gothic nave, but the light coming into it is murky and elliptical, and all attention is focused on Graham Sutherland's tapestry of Christ, with the tortured, demonic humanoid figures around it. The copper rotunda of the chapel of Christ the Servant, on the other hand, takes a totally different approach – an overwhelmingly intense experience of multicoloured, pulsing light. It is also, I think, a church that relatively explicitly has a place for a non-believer. It is obviously devoted to a liturgy and a ritual to which you're necessarily a doubting outsider, but what has shaped this building more than anything else is an attempt to create a commentary on – and an attempt at a salve for – the experience of war, the destruction of cities and the ruining of lives. Both the Christian imagery and Spence's sequence of spaces are inextricably bound to that aim. **[C.24]**

The chapel of Christ the Servant at Coventry Cathedral, around a crown of thorns by Geoffrey Clarke.

COVENTRY

COVENTRY STATION
W. R. Headley and Derrick Shorten for British Railways London Midland Region, 1961–2
International Style

An underrated gem – even enthusiasts for Coventry's modern architecture are often surprised to find that its railway station is listed. The platforms and booking hall are minimalist, but every detail is just right. Its qualities are simple: sharp and clear and well-formed signage, high-quality woodwork and marble, and plenty of light. It has been bashed around, and the main hall is marred by snack kiosks and Virgin Trains tat. Given the spaciousness of the hall the problem is not so much overcrowding as the jarring, cheesy colours of the train companies and sandwich chains scribbling over the calm blues, greys and whites of the original building, though one addition, a plaque for Philip Larkin on one of the platforms, is more apt, with a verse on passing through here 'early on a cold new year' suiting well this fresh, bracing piece of architecture. The station's elevation, a simple glass box, once had a similarly refined complement adjacent to it in the form of the Miesian glass high-rise of Station House, but that is being demolished at the time of writing.

UNIVERSITY OF WARWICK
Yorke Rosenberg & Mardall, 1966
International Style

The geographically misnamed University of Warwick (more accurately, 'the University at the border of Coventry and Kenilworth') quickly developed a reputation as the most corporate of the New Universities – *Warwick University PLC* as E. P. Thompson called it in a diatribe, clearly unaware that such things as the University of Middlesex Maldives Campus were on their way. It is easy to discern the openly technocratic and

The technocratic Bauhaus-style modernism of Yorke Rosenberg & Mardall's University of Warwick.

businesslike nature of its founders' plans – especially when compared with the soft-socialist ideals behind contemporaries like the **University of Essex (p. 190)** – in the choice of Yorke Rosenberg & Mardall as architects, the British firm closest to mid-century US modernism. They opted for their standardized non-style, deployed in coldly rational buildings such as the vast library and the Rootes halls of residence. None of the romantic skylines and futuristic lakeside edifices of the other New Universities, just square, 1930s, purist volumes, clad in panels of white tile and metal. As a result, it feels more like a sprawling collection of buildings than a real ensemble.

The ziggurat Arts Centre of 1974 by Renton Howard Wood and the angular Students' Union of 1975 by Goodman, Short & Knowles both compound the problem through aiming at the monumentality you'll find in other New Universities, without the conviction or scale, and without coherent civic spaces between them. It has its moments, such as Howell Killick Partridge & Amis's Alvar Aalto-via-Hobbiton Houses for Visiting Mathematicians, but the main reason Warwick is in this book is Rootes. This is the earliest part of the plan, a sequence of simple Bauhaus blocks with curvaceous **Isokon Building**-style **(p. 139)** icing sugar concrete stairwells on their corners, with formal and rather Japanese gardens and pedestrian pathways threading in-between.

GRAHAM SUTHERLAND BUILDING, COVENTRY UNIVERSITY SCHOOL OF ART & DESIGN ❶
John Smith for Coventry City Council Architects Dept, 1966
Brutalist

Part of a civic quarter planned a little later than the main city centre precincts, this is an excellent Brutalist block for what was then Lanchester Polytechnic, which would without doubt have been listed were it in Cambridge and designed by somebody who lectured at the Architectural Association rather than an employee of Coventry City Council called John Smith. Four storeys in nearly black-stained concrete are surmounted by a more conventional grey-concrete range above, whose columns extend down from here to the ground, giving the appearance that it is embracing the lower part of the block. The effect is of an almost classical, imposing monumentality. The renders of a planned expansion of the School of Art and Design show the Graham Sutherland Building painted, clad and joined to shoddy new neighbours – even when listing has intervened, Coventry's institutions and civic leaders still seem deeply embarrassed by the ambition of their forefathers.

BULL YARD & CITY ARCADE ✪ ❶
Rex Chell for Coventry City Council Architects Dept and William Mitchell (artist), 1966–70
Brutalist

A fascinating contrast to the fairly traditional palette of materials in the first phase of Coventry's rebuilding – this miniature shopping precinct of low-rise blocks and squares is dressed in fins of rusty verdigris, creating a much murkier and more organic experience of light and surface than you'd find in Donald Gibson's more official style of architecture. There are also wilder decorative touches, the most interesting of which is at the Three Tuns Pub, covered in one of William Mitchell's most inspired Mesoamerican-Brutalist reliefs, as if some wildly proliferating béton brut parasites have spread all over everything – a really atmospheric and intense urban space. At the time of writing, the entire precinct is threatened with demolition.

HILLMAN HOUSE
Arthur Swift & Partners, 1965
COVENTRY POINT ❶
John Madin Design Group, 1969–75
Brutalist

In the last phases of Coventry's rebuilding – which had been based on arranging axes around medieval spires, an architectural solecism but a handsome one – it was decided to add new tall buildings at the ends of the pedestrian precincts, for much the same formal and orienting purposes. Again, the symbolic importance of replanned Coventry meant that the towers were a cut above the norm for neighbouring Birmingham. These two are – or, rather, were – the most impressive. Hillman House was originally intended as an office block and was then taken over by the council for housing, bringing a badly needed mix of uses to a centre which was otherwise far too much of a retail monoculture; it has a montage approach, with a very unusual triangular glass bay running down most of its height, a gesture which anticipates one of the favourite Postmodernist ploys for jollying up a tower. On the top, services are shoved into a concrete diamond. There is a sort of Midlands Expressionism in this one, and so too in John Madin's Coventry Point, which consists of two bulky concrete towers, modelled with flowing flair into a skyline of bluff chamfers and turret-like stair towers, connected by wide glass walkways – packed with activity and ideas. While Hillman House is right on axis, this takes a more authentically Gothic approach, oblique and imperfect, emerging unexpectedly from the corners of the townscape. Unfortunately Coventry Point is about to be demolished at the time of writing. There continues to be no justice for poor John Madin.

SPORTS CENTRE EXTENSION ✪ ❶
Harry Noble for Coventry City Council Architects Dept, 1977
Brutalist, High-Tech

Arthur Ling's listed 1950s swimming pool is nice enough and worth going to see, but this large son is from a different planet. Enormous, titanium-clad, on massive hulking legs atop a through road and connected by a brown-glass walkway to the earlier building, it is apparently meant to be in the shape of an elephant, for some heraldic reason that escapes me. It's an absolutely unique, mindboggling structure – and, in terms of its instantly eye-catching, avant-garde aesthetics, extremely close to the sort of buildings 'regeneration' usually likes, Daniel Libeskind gone pop. Needless to say, Coventry City Council is currently trying to get rid of it as an 'eyesore'. If I had to save one Coventry building from a bonfire of the modernists, it would be this one.

LANCHESTER LIBRARY, UNIVERSITY OF COVENTRY ✪
Short Associates, 1998–2000
Postmodernist, Ecomodernist

Alan Short's series of exciting, eccentric neo-Expressionist university buildings in the 1990s are now mostly forgotten, which is surely a temporary condition, as they're packed with thrills and spills. Here, several distinct towers are crammed in together at odd angles, each of them with some sort of chimney or flue on top – these are actually light wells and natural ventilation for the reading rooms below, making this one of those rare eco buildings that has fun with its technology rather than donning a straw bale hairshirt. The towers create an instant skyline that is complex and intriguing, giving the pedestrian a lot to stare at in puzzlement. (*What exactly goes on in there?*) The interiors have a bland jollity much more

Lanchester Library in Coventry, a Postmodern Gothic skyline channelling the energies of the Arts and Crafts.

common for their time, but simply as urban scenery this is riotous architecture. [C.21]

CAFÉ BAR, EARL STREET
Baynes & Co, 1998
Ecomodernist

From the outside, this purpose-built bar (originally Browns, but it has gone through several incarnations since then) is a decent if unspectacular essay in the sandstone-and-glass idiom used heavily by Richard Murphy in Scotland, derived from the Italian designer Carlo Scarpa. But go inside and you'll find the interiors are terrific – a taut barrel of wood, apparently using techniques usually reserved for boat-building. Everything is integral – the benches and booths, carved out of the same materials as the roof, giving the sense of warmth and seclusion so crucial to a good bar,

but without using any Victorian pub clichés. It has a real lightness and freshness, which connects it nicely with the carnivalesque tone of so much Coventry modernism.

HERBERT ART GALLERY & MUSEUM ✪
Donald Gibson for Coventry City Council Architects Dept, 1953–60/Haworth Tompkins, 2006–8/Pringle Richards Sharratt, 2005–8
People's Detailing, Ecomodernist

There has been a great deal of hostility or simple neglect towards the post-war buildings of Coventry, which would otherwise be seen more clearly as among the best of their era in Europe. Renovations are usually cheap and nasty, and new buildings recoil snobbishly from engaging with municipal modernism, presumably not 'aspirational' enough. This museum and art gallery is the important exception. The original gallery is one of the more obviously traditional of Gibson's buildings, brick with sandstone dressings, gentle diapering patterns and, as always, integrated art (here, *Man's Struggle*, a two-part relief sculpture by Walter Ritchie). Fifty years later, a new pavilion with factory-style serrated rooflights was inserted into the top by Haworth Tompkins, and a sweeping, faceted wood and glass expansion was added by Pringle Richards Sharratt. Neither of these is a reproduction of the style of the original, but neither does the slightest violence to it – the scale, order and rationality of Gibson's work are respected throughout. With so many aggressive and vacuous projects to 'improve' Coventry's modern buildings, this is especially valuable. A series of spaces have been created with something like the same humanity that animated the post-war reconstruction in the first place. It ought to have shown the rest of the city how it's done.

COMMUTER BELT MIDLANDS

SHAKESPEARE MEMORIAL THEATRE, STRATFORD-UPON-AVON
Elizabeth Scott, 1927–31/
Bennetts Associates, 2007–10
Expressionist, High-Tech

A frustrating, fascinating patchwork monument, the 'collage city' realized and botched. The original Shakespeare Memorial Theatre, the home of the Royal Shakespeare Company, burned down in 1926, leaving only an extremely fruity rotunda and hallway, which were to be retained in the new building. The competition winner was deeply unusual – the sole even slightly modernist public building of 1920s Britain, and the only major pre-war building by a female architect. Elizabeth Scott had worked in cinema design, and here she fused the glam prosceniums and epic circulation spaces usually used to create maximum anticipation for Hollywood product as similarly occasion-filled anterooms for the most celebrated plays in the English language. But for the exterior she brought a rugged red-brick-and-clinker Expressionism, evidently taken from Amsterdam and Hamburg, and made a craggy, unpretentious monument out of this riverside edifice. It's far from 'the International Style', but it's a powerful statement nonetheless, and one which was both denounced and praised at the time on exactly these grounds. Visit today, and Scott's building – regardless of its being listed – is by no means the first thing you will notice.

The extension by Denise and Rab Bennetts is the most dramatic intervention I've ever seen on a listed building, with the possible exception of (though far superior to) Hawkins/Brown's defacing of **Park Hill (p. 370)**. A new range along the Avon is the least of it; a huge new campanile is attached through a glass and red-brick atrium to

Scott's building and the Victorian rotunda; most questionably, a glazed café spreads all the way across the roof of the 1928 building's frontage. The changes to the stages themselves have been uncontroversial – generations of actors complained about getting lost in its cinematic spaces – but the additions outside are more uncomfortable. The tower is dominating and uncompromising, but works well as a beacon and a vertical complement to the horizontality of the two earlier buildings. What is appalling is the café on top of Scott's theatre, a gratuitously commercial and cheaply detailed imposition on to the original building, almost totally erasing its original lines. As much of the rest of the project is brave and serious, it perhaps doesn't deserve to be defined by this nasty tourist trap. But the fact remains that the first major building in Britain designed by a woman is almost hidden by what looks like a Pizza Express on its top and a massive red phallus to its side – an architectural image of a man talking over a woman.

ELGAR HOUSE, KIDDERMINSTER
1937
Moderne

Kidderminster is a small post-industrial town separated by a green belt from the Birmingham–Black Country conurbation to its east – which it resembles architecturally and culturally – and pretty towns like Bewdley and Bridgnorth to its west, for which it serves today as a giant out-of-town shopping centre, with some of the nastiest conversions of industrial landscapes to retail parks that you'll ever see. But though it is smashed to pieces by its ring road (with William Mitchell's **Retaining Wall, p. 335**, as its saving grace), it maintains one major architectural virtue. Its former textile factories – which turned out carpets until the 1990s – are right in the centre of town, forming a tight circle of Italianate mills around a messy, hilly collection of streets. In the 1930s, a very decent modern factory was added to these densely packed brick edifices – a long, chic, ribbon-windowed three-storey block, turning the street corner with a dashing Erich Mendelsohn-style curve, detailed in a pattern of dark-brown and pale-yellow brick, with large Crittall windows. There is a similar factory in Aachen, Germany, that was turned into an art museum, but the conversion of Elgar House into an office block is neatly done for Kidderminster, with a glass stairwell in a neo-thirties style clamped on to the back of the old building.

OLDBURY WELLS SCHOOL, BRIDGNORTH
Lyons Israel Ellis, 1958–60
Brutalist

So few good post-war schools survive, after the massive demolition programme that accompanied the Private Finance Initiative, that you have to take them where you can. And this is a fine example of the period, rewarded by a rare listing. Don't expect anything 'contextual' with historic Bridgnorth – a pretty Georgian town made dramatic by steep hills, bridges and funiculars – but expect good, solid modern architecture, of the sort that was supposed to suit anywhere, anytime. Oldbury Wells was actually originally two (secondary modern) schools – simple, clear, concrete-and-glass pavilions for the boys on one side of the road, and on the other side something more monumental for the girls, with a much stronger, disciplined composition around a double-height glass entrance and with the chimney and water tower treated as a concrete spire and campanile. The project architect was Alan Colquhoun, and though it would be at least another decade before he

and John Miller would classicize modernism or modernize classicism in their housing for Camden Council, this was already formal, historically erudite design.

SHEEP STREET SHOPS, STRATFORD-UPON-AVON
Frederick Gibberd Partnership, 1962
People's Detailing

One of the smartest and most unpretentious of Gibberd's compromises between modernism and historical continuity. A corner block of shops forms a small square, with its concrete frame painted black, Tudor-style, so as to be 'in keeping', with red-brick infill, and a serrated skyline; the main bulk is cantilevered out to create a secluded row of shops. Sensitive, eminently sensible and robust, and currently, judging by the green fabric hung over part of it, being run down so as to be viable for demolition.

SHAKESPEARE CENTRE, STRATFORD-UPON-AVON
Laurence Williams, 1962–4
Brutalist

A piece of pure architectural trolling, listed by some crazy person at English Heritage so that it will be here for ever. 'Shakespeare's Birthplace' is a house that may or may not have been the one where the big yin spent his childhood; all the houses around it were cleared by the Victorians as they turned Stratford into an extremely modern half-timbered tourist centre, and a garden was created from which to view the house, which is a pretty house. Then, in the sixties, this visitor centre was added. A concrete-framed block is cantilevered out over a Brutalist colonnade, and can be seen from almost all but the most direct, cropped views of the 'Birthplace'. Of course, it wasn't listed for this aggression, but for its unusually rich and intricate detailing in bronze, copper and wood, including as much public art as a particularly opulent Civic Centre. Even so, as it stands, it's a striking reminder of how history is constructed, refusing to dissemble about how artificial that process is – you are not in seventeenth-century Stratford, and this building reminds you of that with more interesting effects than the Jacobethan Patisserie Valerie behind it.

STAFFORD STATION
W. R Headley for British Railways London Midland Region, 1962
Brutalist

Oft sailed past on the West Coast mainline, this little beefcake comes under the small category of 'good British Rail stations', redeveloped by the same team that did such a good job at **Coventry Station (p. 328)**. But while that is a perfect, beautifully made International Style pavilion, this is transport Brutalism – heavy concrete hulks sheltering the platforms and linking them overhead. The street entrance has a hammerhead tower and a fine cantilevered canopy, held up with skinny pillars.

SHREWSBURY MARKET HALL ⊘
David du Roi Aberdeen, 1965
People's Detailing

The only modern presence on Shrewsbury's achingly preserved perfect Middle England skyline justifies itself effortlessly. The tall red-brick tower, like Aberdeen's **Congress House (p. 55)** for the TUC in London, is a 1930s building out of time; this time being that of those elegant Scando-Dutch campaniles that came to English towns in that decade via Stockholm and Hilversum's Town Halls, here with a spiky lantern spire on top. Not remotely 'in keeping', but so friendly that it doesn't seem to have attracted

A modern building in an old town: the curved lines and beacon-like clock tower of Shrewsbury Market Hall.

much of the opprobrium directed at anything modern in the centre of a historic British city. Below that, a sleek two-storey block with an odd sort of copper outlook post before the tower, contains the market hall. Double-height, with an upstairs gallery containing, among other things, a great record shop and second-hand bookshop, it has all you could really want from a market, unless you want to buy cheap produce – Shrewsbury is not really that kind of place.

SHIREHALL, SHREWSBURY
Ralph Crowe for Shropshire County Architects Dept, 1966
International Style

An extreme contrast with **Shrewsbury Market Hall (above)**. Instead of carefully fitting the new civic centre for Shropshire into the historic city, the decision was made to build it on a much larger site just on the edge of the centre, and build at scale, as if on a tabula rasa, though in a place where it doesn't intrude on any views. There is nothing else quite like it in the county – a long, ribbon-windowed white concrete block with a lower pavilion in front, and a glass walkway leading to a unusual rotunda, the original council chamber. The rotunda is slightly tapered, like the top of a cooling tower, so perhaps there is some inspiration from local West Midlands architecture after all. In any case, this is an excellent civic building, well-made and individual. At the time of writing, the county are planning to vacate it for a new site in a shopping mall, and there is currently a campaign to list it – a case which is surely open and shut.

REDDITCH CENTRAL LIBRARY
John Madin Design Group, 1971–6
Brutalist, Vernacular

Adjacent to the **Kingfisher Centre (p. 336)**, and using a similar red-brick-and-concrete repertoire, this was recently described in the local press as 'John Madin's *other* Library'. It's no substitute for the masterful, criminally demolished Birmingham Central Library, but if apprehended as a library in Redditch New Town, it is very good. On the same scale as the semi-Georgian straggle around, it marks a compromise between Old Town and New Town. The brick is in the knobbly, deep-red manner so fashionable in the seventies for designers who didn't want to go full raised-eyebrow Pomo but wanted to be more contextual; but the use of waffle ceilings and the excellent little concrete colonnade are both pure Brutalist. Above the colonnade are two storeys of bookshelves and, at the time of writing, a 'JobCentrePlus'; the intersecting stairwells, with each floor visible at any time, have a spatial imagination that does indeed recall the larger building in Birmingham. There has evidently been some

softening and lightening of the architecture via paint and MDF in recent years, but this remains a strong, quiet work. Opposite is a monument to John Bonham.

ROYAL SPA CENTRE, LEAMINGTON SPA
Frederick Gibberd Partnership, 1972
International Style

There are various Gibberd buildings, mostly housing estates, across the clotted-cream vistas of this impeccably planned and dislikeable Regency spa town, all of them gently adapting modernism to the Regency, or possibly the other way round. This cinema and arts centre is the most ambitious, a miniaturized version of Aalto's late, grand public buildings such as the Finlandia Hall, a glacier clad in fair-faced concrete which is in remarkably good condition, still harmonizing with the render in the classical villas around. Lacking a certain force, but a successful example of having cake and eating it.

RETAINING WALL, INNER RING ROAD, KIDDERMINSTER
William Mitchell (artist), 1975
Brutalist

Kidderminster is cursed with a 1970s bypass far too big for the town it serves – an example of the extreme priority given to cars over everything else in the West Midlands. Here, at least, there's a pay-off and, as at **Hockley Circus (p. 314)**, it comes via one of those peculiar tie-in deals where you get some William Mitchell with your heavy engineering. In this case, the retaining wall where the town was sliced open has been moulded as a sort of Indiana Jones via Frank Lloyd Wright Mesoamerican rain sculpture, streaks of concrete that originally featured water rushing down them and a lightshow. Naturally, all that drama has been cut from the council's budget, so you're just left with the sculpted wall, which is rhythmic, vitalist and bizarre, one of Mitchell's most outré integrations of utilitarian structure and abstraction.

AQUEDUCT VILLAGE, TELFORD
Eric Lyons, 1975–80
Postmodernist

Telford, like Peterlee, is one of those New Towns that were named in order to evoke an idea and an ethos rather than after a village or small town that was there already (Milton Keynes is not actually named after John and John Maynard). Telford is after Thomas Telford the engineer, in a New Town planned for the white heat of technology and all that blah, which would be built around the very birthplace of the Industrial Revolution, the tiny eighteenth-century metal-smelting towns of Coalbrookdale and Ironbridge. There are wonderful things to be found in it – especially Ironbridge itself, a fascinating if twee industrial hamlet overlooked by a whacking great set of rusting cooling towers. But it isn't unfair to say that Telford can be bleak. The plan by John Madin is so road-obsessed as to make it literally the only town in Britain that it is impossible to navigate on foot (it's not easy in Milton Keynes, but possible); it was originally meant to have a specialized busway, but that was cut, as too was a plan to put all the parking underground; more shockingly, all the civic buildings were cut. Early estates, like Woodside, with its US-style 'Radburn' layout separating pedestrians and cars, and Madin's powerful but rather lugubrious Brookside are decent enough, but marooned in roads, trees and kipple. The best parts of Telford – the industrial villages – are so badly connected to the rest that the refusal of residents to acknowledge that they live in Telford New Town when putting down their addresses may be as much an acknowledgement of reality as it is snobbery.

One exception is this excellent small estate by Eric Lyons, one of his few projects outside the Span organization. Like Madin (see **Cala Drive, p. 312**), Lyons specialized in the design of neat modernist housing estates for the affluent, but on this evidence he was more able than Madin at designing for working-class council tenants. At the end of the spine road of Aqueduct Village (the Aqueduct in question carries a canal, and is one of the industrial remnants), the optimistically named Majestic Way is a series of clusters of houses and tiny towers, clearly modelled on the gaunt dark-brick buildings of the iron villages; the two-storey towers appear as heraldic gates on the way to a relaxed circus around a village green, which incorporates an older cottage into the design. The materials and detailing – clinker and stained wood – are as fine as those in Lyons's Blackheath estates, although the neo-Victorian Right to Buy doors are not. There is an arch through the houses on the village green, and it leads nowhere.

KINGFISHER CENTRE, REDDITCH ✪
Eduardo Paolozzi (artist), 1983
Postmodernist

You know when you're approaching Redditch by car, because winding A-roads are suddenly replaced with a series of sleek seventies motorways with overpasses and high pedestrian walkways above, reminding you that you are now in a New Town Zone, which has been specifically planned to speed cars from town centre to suburb as smoothly as possible. The Kingfisher Centre is that centre, joined on to remnants of a small industrial town. The Centre was built at the turn of the 1980s, and like so many malls it has been constantly rebuilt, so that it now combines Brutalism, Postmodernism and New Labour commercialism, with the usual endlessly winding 'streets' and

Postmodern Ravenna: Eduardo Paolozzi's polychrome mosaics of high-tech life in the Kingfisher Centre, Redditch.

deliberately hidden toilets. The largest untouched parts of the Kingfisher Centre's original design can, equally typically, be seen round the back, where you can find built-in ziggurat flats and concrete skyways. There's one space inside the Mall, though, that is genuinely world class – a civic gesture as grand as any. In one of the halls, the Maecenas that was the Redditch New Town Corporation and the association of Needlemaking Employers commissioned Eduardo Paolozzi to decorate the upper-level galleries. Never mind the architecture – a Pomo galleria like a thousand others from the eighties – look at Paolozzi's mosaics. As at **Pimlico Ventilation Shaft & Tottenham Court Road Underground Station (p. 68)**, these are proof that Paolozzi, like Victor Pasmore, Mary Martin or Barbara Hepworth, was a great *architecte manqué*. They're a polychromatic pulse of commercial imagery, a computerized Pop Art Ravenna. Constructivist patterns,

images of construction, consumption and cosmic exploration, with astronauts and Soviet space dogs on the same plane as shopping for kettles, clothes and cameras. The mundane made extraordinary, or, rather, a panoramic image bank of how what is now everyday is built on a fabric of once-incredible technological innovations. Magnificent work.

CEMENT WORKS, RUGBY
Cemex, 1990s
Brutalist, High-Tech

Staggeringly crude, a squeeze of massive tin boxes, on a skyscraping scale, in a dull Warwickshire town; it achieves some sort of stunning megalomaniac grandeur at night, with its cyclopean pipes and vast silos belching smoke. Hated locally, but a lot more visually interesting than what most architects have got up to here.

POTTERIES

ODEON CINEMA, HANLEY
Harry Weedon, 1937
PEPPERS LTD, HANLEY
1937
Moderne

Two small streamline moderne buildings crammed into the interesting and chaotic centre of the city of Stoke-on-Trent (which to the enduring confusion of all non-potters is in Hanley, not Stoke). The Odeon (as was) has all the usual motifs that Harry Weedon developed for Oscar Deutsch: black vitrolite, brown faïence, Mendelsohn curves and a big brick back end you're not meant to look at, but all of it is given extra impetus by being shoved into a tiny corner, with each part fighting to express itself, a manic, packed quality emphasized by the tower running right up against the side wall of a 1960s office block. Peppers, meanwhile, was a light-industrial building with big Crittall windows, Dutch brick and more brown faïence tiles, in the late 1930s industrial-moderne vernacular. Recently converted into an office block and shops much more convincingly than is the norm, with a neat new Gropius-style glass stairwell attached.

KEELE UNIVERSITY CHAPEL, NEWCASTLE-UNDER-LYME ✪
George Gaze Pace, 1964–5
Brutalist, Expressionist

Keele is historically important as the first 'Plate Glass University', but also for the vague carelessness of its planning and architecture, which made it a cautionary example, leading to the much more coherent masterplanning and landscaping at the Universities of **Sussex (p. 238)**, **Essex (p. 190)**, **York (p. 394)**, **East Anglia (p. 198)** and **Stirling (p. 508)**. That doesn't seem like a harsh judgement when you arrive after your long bus journey from Stoke or Newcastle-under-Lyme at the main square, centred on a dull Brutalist Students' Union and, as the focal point, the library, whose combination of Festival Style, classical symmetry and a thin neo-Victorian clock tower can be most generously described as 'confused'. But there is a third building on the square, Pace's non-denominational chapel, and it almost makes up for the rest.

This is the largest of Pace's many churches, and the most impressive, with the scale if not the size of a cathedral. Like Keele's University Library, it is based on a compromise between modernism and tradition, but unlike it this is done with conviction, coherence and originality, rather than limp cowardice. The structure is of concrete and wood, the beams to the roof evoke construction techniques that are centuries old, and the raw concrete is gooey enough to convince you ferroconcrete was invented by the Tudors. The main church hall is punctuated by openings that are Gothic in spirit, not in detail, and at the front is an isolated chapel, with a kaleidoscopic opening above the altar. This was the first ecumenical chapel of its kind in the country, and a hydraulic screen can be lowered or raised to divide or unify the Anglican and Catholic spaces of that great hall. Then, all this is wrapped in purple brick, creating a Hanseatic effect using the local Staffordshire engineering stocks – so totally appropriate to the climate and the rugged, post-industrial landscape that it's puzzling more architects haven't used it up here. Smouldering, intense, warm, personal – everything about it is a firm declaration of 'this is how it should be done'. **[D.4 & D.5]**

The sculpture above the altar of George Gaze Pace's extraordinary chapel at the University of Keele.

POTTERIES

FLAXMAN BUILDING & FILM THEATRE, STAFFORDSHIRE UNIVERSITY, STOKE-ON-TRENT
1972
Brutalist, International Style

Looked at casually, this is just one of the scatter of undistinguished modern buildings at the old Polytechnic just outside Stoke's stonking Jacobethan railway station. Look closer, and at the edges this standard-issue ribbon window office block reveals subtle differences, hints that the designers had higher ambitions than just churning out another block. To the facade facing the railway line, the windows of the stair tower have been modelled into a series of polygons, and the gable end has been turned into a continuous concrete sculptural relief, like a more organic (and mercifully unpainted) version of William Mitchell's relief at **Piccadilly Plaza (p. 406)**. This block was later joined on to a punchy purple-brick Film Theatre, both of which give a bit of character to a campus that badly needs it.

———

TELEPHONE EXCHANGE, HANLEY
Ministry of Building & Works, 1975
ONE SMITHFIELD, HANLEY
RHWL Architects, 2016
Brutalist, Supermodernist

Two decorative buildings of different eras, one old and currently deeply fashionable (though perhaps not in Stoke), the other currently new and deeply unfashionable (though not with the regeneration quangos of Stoke). Things being what they are, the earlier building has far greater integrity and purpose, and its ornamental qualities are linked with its use in a much clearer way. The Telephone Exchange is, after the demolition a few years ago of the council's Brutalist-Expressionist Unity House, the tallest office block in Stoke, but it is mostly windowless – the facade presents itself as a web of concrete honeycombs, so that the lack of a need for windows in a building that originally housed technology more than people doesn't result in a blunt slab. What windows there are have been arranged with an almost baroque eye for perversity, here symmetrical, here not – and the tall columns on the open upper storeys where the wall is punched through on one side create a similarly neoclassical effect. Unexpectedly, here the Ministry of Works is playing the kind of unsentimental, intricate games with architectural history that architects like Caruso St John or Amin Taha win prizes for nowadays. It was recently cleaned rather than demolished or clad, rather extraordinarily.

I don't mean to suggest by their juxtaposition that One Smithfield – a Carbuncle Cup nominee, no less – is on the same level. Locally, this building is hugely controversial, intended originally as local-government offices but boycotted by rebellious councillors due to its offensive cost. But, for once, here the bright and bouncy facade treatment feels well thought out, more than the usual vacuous jollification stuck on top of dereliction. The curtain-walled block, just behind the **Potteries Museum & Art Gallery (below)**, is decorated in a polychrome diamond pattern, based, apparently, on the work of the cubist ceramic artist Clarice Cliff, a working-class Potteries modernist whose work is showcased in said museum. Smooth to the museum side, these diamonds then project slightly outwards as they face the under-designed Smithfield square. The colours have a real vigour and liveliness, and the pattern is more original than the commonplace efforts at borrowing 'references' from the local industry. It's unwise to speculate, but I think this one will age well – genuinely odd, where most architecture of this ilk is merely shrill.

The Potteries Museum in Hanley: a sombre Brutalist temple outside, a wonderful cabinet of curiosities inside.

POTTERIES MUSEUM & ART GALLERY, HANLEY

S. Darlington for City of Stoke-on-Trent Environmental Services Dept, 1981–2
Brutalist, Postmodernist

Perched right on the architectural cusp in the transition from municipal modernism to cowed conservationism, the Potteries Museum and Art Gallery is a municipal prestige project that houses probably the strangest and richest applied-art collection in Britain. Its architectural undecidability feels appropriate rather than compromised, caused by the building's need to pay tribute to the workmanship and craft of the local population. Approached from the front, a strongly horizontal Brutalist pavilion has at its centre a basically Socialist Realist ceramic frieze, depicting the workers of the Potteries – men and women, coal-mining and pottery-firing, intricate craft and heavy labour. A bridge leads from the street to the formal entrance, while the wings have a more openly Brutalist asymmetric compositions of cantilevers and walkways, with ceramic details supplementing the béton brut. Inside, the extensive galleries spread around a central atrium, and are in a similar mix of local reference and abstraction – neo-Victorian archways leading to vitrines full of everything from Wedgwood to Anglo-Bauhaus, in glass cabinets that suggest the Italian modernist Carlo Scarpa had taken a break from designing museums full of Renaissance paintings, and had opted instead to take tips from the Gateshead Metro Centre. A place to get lost in.

7. EAST MIDLANDS

Engineering Building, Leicester (p. 348)

The East Midlands is less clearly defined as an area than the West Midlands. Northamptonshire, for instance, is far more similar to a southern county like Buckinghamshire than it is to Derbyshire, which is far closer geographically and culturally to South Yorkshire; the flat rural expanse of Lincolnshire, meanwhile, has nothing in common with either the North or the South. But within the East Midlands there are four sizeable, interesting towns – Northampton and Leicester in the south, Derby and Nottingham in the north – and a hinterland around each of these, with Lincoln, as a cathedral city, boasting a surprising amount of unusual modern architecture.

Leicester and Northampton each have some of the most famous modern buildings in the country – Charles Rennie Mackintosh's **78 Derngate** and Peter Behrens's **New Ways** in Northampton are more significant than anything of the period in much bigger cities like Manchester or Leeds, while the skyline of the **University of Leicester**, with its three towers by Arup Associates, James Stirling and Denys Lasdun, is unrivalled. Nottingham, the biggest city in the East Midlands, has Owen Williams's breathtaking factories for **Boots – D10 and D6, D90** – on its outskirts in Beeston, but the city itself has had some of its best years in architecture and planning over the last two decades, with a sleek, light rail system that can take you from Caruso St John's **Nottingham Contemporary**, a powerful statement of the *genius loci*, to the fresh new space of Hopkins's **Jubilee Campus**. Among the most striking and original buildings in the East Midlands are those of the local architect Sam Scorer, whose concrete shell structures can be found used both in service stations, like **Markham Moor Service Station** on the A1, and in churches, such as **St John the Baptist**, in a Lincoln council estate.

SE MIDLANDS

78 DERNGATE, NORTHAMPTON ✪
Charles Rennie Mackintosh, 1916–17
NEW WAYS, NORTHAMPTON
Peter Behrens, 1926
Art Nouveau, International Style

The modernist 'myth' of Charles Rennie Mackintosh – one to which I fully subscribe, unconvinced as I am by the currently fashionable notion that he was just another Edwardian eclectic designer – rests on the curtailment of his architectural career after the completion, in 1917, of the remodelling of 78 Derngate, an early-nineteenth-century terraced house near the centre of Northampton. What a strange and parochial way to end, only a decade after completing a revolutionary building for the Art School of what was at the time one of the biggest and most powerful cities in the world. In Northampton, this intersects with another 'myth' – which architectural historians have recently tried to dismantle, but which I have no objection to – whereby the fully modernist architecture which Mackintosh was inching towards had to be imported from Germany, due to the lack of interest in a deeply conservative Britain. This process of importing modernism began when 78 Derngate's owner, the model-maker, industrialist, Labour councillor and municipal sponsor (he devised Northampton's **Public Baths, p. 348**) Wenman Joseph Bassett-Lowke commissioned his next house not from Mackintosh, but from Peter Behrens.

These two commissions were both a result of Bassett-Lowke encountering German and Austrian design on his extensive business trips. Certainly, he was enthusiastic about the Deutscher Werkbund, the industrial design unit where Behrens was prominent; and if you wanted to commission something in Britain during the First World War that would have the modernity, originality and clarity of Central European design, it made sense to commission Mackintosh, given his strong links to the Austrians – and equal sense to drop him, after the war, when you could go direct and commission Behrens himself. Yet the comparison of the houses shows what was lost in that transition.

The street frontage of 78 Derngate has few hints of what you'll find inside, bar the eerie black and white diamond pattern on the door at the original entrance (though various bits of naff Mockintosh signage on Derngate will prepare you). John McAslan's restoration project – which for the first time opened up public access – first pushes you through a cold, neo-modernist visitor centre and gift shop, and then up some narrow steps suddenly into the house. Many of the rooms are mild, with some still residual Arts and Crafts touches, flowery wallpaper, lush woodwork and lots of light; all of them are relatively small, crammed into the narrow but high-ceilinged spaces of a Georgian terrace. Two rooms, however, are so original, so powerful, so personal, that they practically invite the notion of Mackintosh as protomodernist. The first-floor reception hall is utterly baffling. Almost entirely black, it is dominated by the diamond patterns previewed on the front door, etched in yellow on black marquetry; the grid of a Japanese screen, like at **Willow Tea Rooms (p. 516)**, divides this from the narrow stair. That then leads to the guest bedroom, where this strangeness is almost burlesqued, with strident migraine stripes behind and above the two beds, and a clock that could be a Soviet Constructivist design of a decade later, were it not so well made.

If this is violently Expressionistic, with the *Sturm und Drang* of German work from the same period, on the rear facade, Mackintosh unintentionally pointed towards what would come next. The white-rendered

Hiding behind the Georgian doorway of 78 Derngate...

...you can find a proto-op art bedroom on the top floor...

...reached from the stairs of the Hall Lounge, Mackintosh's most radical experiment in cubist geometry.

remodelled back end of the house, with its grid of outdoor terraces, stands somewhere between the stripped-down Art Nouveau of Willow Tea Rooms and New Ways, the house Bassett-Lowke would move into ten years later. Located at 508 Wellingborough Road, it is around half an hour's walk partly through a delightful park, or fifteen minutes on the bus into the suburbs from Derngate – the staff are very happy to give directions. On the journey, there's a sharp shift from the still urban context of the first house into typical leafy interwar territory, sprawling houses spread around big driveways – and in the middle of them this puzzling little box, on a similar plot but somehow feeling much smaller and more modest than everything around it; compare the Hollywood Hills pomp of that other 'first International Style house in Britain', **High and Over House (p. 215)**, three years later. As German modern architecture of the twenties, it's transitional – the cubic style shows Behrens moving towards the laconic white right angles of De Stijl and the early Bauhaus houses, but the V-shaped projecting glass lantern (immediately borrowed by that other Glaswegian, Thomas Tait, at **Silver End, p. 175**), the odd semi-castellated spikes and the '1926' sign show some residual Expressionism. The house was recently on the market, and the extensive photos on the property showed how sensible and straightforward the sequence of rooms is, especially compared with Mackintosh's ferocious intensity; just a nice, clutter-free suburban house. But they also revealed, as did many of the photographs that appeared in the press in the 1920s, that the rear elevation is a horizontal version of 78 Derngate, white walls, open verandas and an airy view out over suburbia. Behrens, incidentally, never went to Northampton – but then neither did Mackintosh.

BEDFORD MANSIONS, NORTHAMPTON
John Brown and A. E. Henson, 1934–5
Moderne

A neat and chic interwar four-storey block of flats, conveniently just opposite **78 Derngate (p. 345)** – red brick, Crittall windows, and very elegant stair towers protruding out of the brick like thermometers. Conservative by international standards, dashing by Midlands ones – evidently Bassett-Lowke's effort to introduce modern design to Northampton paid off just a little.

ATHENA CINEMA, LEICESTER
Robert Arthur Bullivant, 1936
CURVE THEATRE, LEICESTER
Rafael Viñoly Architects, 2007
Moderne, Supermodernist

A dual-corner composition, made up of a former Odeon (now a conference centre), with a great contrast of curves in brick and tile, exciting every time you see it, deliberately mirrored (in a more ostentatious way) by Rafael Viñoly's recent Curve Theatre. Unlike many of its kind, the way it fits into the streetscape doesn't leave room for a miserable sheer brick wall where the pedestrian isn't meant to be looking, so it has by accident much more integrity than most thirties cinemas. Compared to the Athena, the Curve is over-engineered, fussy and expensive, but unlike Viñoly's lamentable other British buildings – the FirstSite gallery in Colchester, the unforgivable 'Walkie-Talkie' in London – it genuinely has some character. Its sweep of metal fins aligns well with the curves of the cinema opposite, creating a dramatic little urban vortex made up of two dramatic buildings interacting with each other. **[C.3]**

PUBLIC BATHS, MAGISTRATES COURT & POLICE STATION, NORTHAMPTON

J. C. Prestwich, 1936
Moderne

A very striking civic centre catering to Justice and Leisure built in the thirties in an Americanist moderne manner, with cream stone cladding around massive ziggurat-like forms – the central block, the police station, is almost out of 1930s Moscow, Northampton's Lubyanka. The baths, on the other hand, are deceptively forbidding – within its aloof shell is a glorious, lightweight vaulted pool, with delicate concrete arches.

––––

UNIVERSITY OF LEICESTER: ✪ ENGINEERING BUILDING

Stirling & Gowan, 1959–63

CHARLES WILSON BUILDING

Denys Lasdun & Partners, 1961–6

ATTENBOROUGH BUILDING

Philip Dowson for Arup Associates, 1968–70
Brutalist

A wonderful miniature Brutalist skyline, a kind of neo-Tokyo set into manicured lawns in the suburbs of Leicester. Only one of the three is famous, but each is equally exciting in its own way. The earliest and by far the best-known outside Leicester is the Engineering Building. Depending on your historical perspective, this is either one of the great monuments of Anglo-Brutalism or the first Postmodernist building in Britain. The latter interpretation is supported by the amount of historical references crammed into its tiny space. A small, slender tower with a lecture theatre connected to a low-rise glass workshop, it takes the glazed cylindrical stairwell from Barshch and Sinyavsky's Moscow Planetarium and plugs it into a lecture theatre swiped from Melnikov's Rusakov Club; the red tiles and red brick are a deliberate reminiscence of the nineteenth-

century industrial North, the service tower is taken from Louis Kahn, and the delicate faceted rooflights of the workshop are Stirling & Gowan's own glimmering invention. Unlike in Stirling's later work, all this formal exuberance, citation and cleverness is focused by Gowan's sobriety and rigour, not to mention restrained by its low budget. The sheer diversity and ingenuity of form is breathtaking, but the result is strangely cerebral. It lacks the physical and emotional punch of most Brutalist structures; exploring it is closer to admiring the workings of a Swiss watch than the more elemental experience of a Denys Lasdun building. There is one of his towers nearby, so you can be very aware of the difference.

Lasdun's mastery of mass and assemblage made him a natural fit as a designer of towers – always plenty of visual interest, always a dramatic, fully three-dimensional silhouette – so it's a shame he didn't design more. There is pretty much just this thing and **Keeling House (p. 124)**, and unlike the latter this one hasn't been penthoused and whitewashed. A wide five-storey block is surmounted by three cantilevered storeys, with the services shoved into a blank attic and a semi-detached stair tower, which gives the complex the requisite machine-Gothic ambience. Students being students, there have been proposals to paint the tower red and blue, so as to make more clear its resemblance to the head of Optimus Prime; the historian of Brutalism Barnabas Calder would be scandalized, and he'd be right, given how much the effect is of a single form poured from one mass of concrete – but the students' proposal shows they understand the science fiction qualities of this oblique, powerful, imperturbable building much more than they would by treating it as if it were by Christopher Wren.

This is much harder to do in any case with the latest and tallest of the three. While the Engineering Building and the Charles

Two of the University of Leicester's three towers: Denys Lasdun's complex, articulated Charles Wilson Building...

....and the repeated space-age glass and concrete modules of the Attenborough Building, by Arup Associates.

SE MIDLANDS

Wilson Building are fine art architecture, finely wrought, one-off, visionary, impossible to repeat or extend, the Attenborough Building is much more of a mass production experiment – interlinked, bunched volumes of precast curved concrete, inset with jewel-like, angular, protruding windows. It has the usual Arup attention to the detailing of its precision-engineered components; and, like the other two towers, it repays repeated viewing, with its tapered form much less simple than it looks, the reflection of the jagged glass never quite as you expect.

――――

CARLSBERG BREWERY, NORTHAMPTON
Knud Munk, 1970–74
Brutalist

There is a reason why this is much more impressive than most industrial buildings of its era in the Midlands – the elusive but all-important lure of Scandinavia. Carlsberg is of course a Danish company, and so when commissioning a brewery to churn out gassy lager, the decision was taken to make it a showcase of Danish design. You might expect the results to be an elegant, precise and formal work of buildings in landscape, such as **St Catherine's College (p. 228)** in Oxford – and Knud Munk's Greig Hall in Bergen shows he could certainly work in this idiom – but, instead, the design was massive and Brutalist. Like the **Express Lift Test Tower (below)** on the other side of town, it is best seen from a distance, a dark-brown ribbed-concrete ziggurat standing impassively over the marshlands around the River Nene, alongside two beefy, squat chimneys. Up close, lower, stepped-section blocks, a green-painted big shed and several metal canisters and pipes lead towards the main, pyramidal brewery, which stands in front of the walkway along the river, allowing, at night, pedestrian inspection of the lager-making process.

HAYMARKET THEATRE, LEICESTER
Building Design Partnership, 1973
Brutalist

This was produced by the BDP offices at a time when they were almost routinely churning out works as brilliant and as disparate as **Preston Bus Station (p. 444)**, the **Halifax Headquarters (p. 388)** and the Leeds **Bank of England (p. 382)**: a theatre built into a retail megastructure, pulled off with effortless aplomb. Unlike those, this is not listed, but after a period of dereliction was reopened a couple of years ago. It takes up an entire street block, and with its cranked and angled red-brick colonnades and stairwells it borrows freely from both Lasdun and Stirling, while never seeming like an imitation of either. The main cantilevered theatre volume is above a row of shops, which then leads to a small public square with trees, a Constructivist sculpture and a flight of stairs, good for sitting on.

――――

EXPRESS LIFT TEST TOWER, NORTHAMPTON ✪
Maurice Walton, 1980–82
Brutalist

A Lift Test Tower does what it says it does – you test lifts in it. This one has been treated with considerable sculptural vim, a curvaceous, tapering concrete shaft, with a split-level tower at the top, modelled with the same conviction as, say, **Trellick Tower (p. 166)**, though it is a lot simpler. Along with **Emley Moor Telecommunications Tower (p. 389)**, it's the only really interesting example of the non-inhabited urban tower we have in Britain. It's surrounded today by a staggeringly bland executive-housing estate, which creates a formal circus around it, but it can be seen from any vantage point in Northampton or the area around.

A most unusual structure: the Express Lift Test Tower in Northampton, now surrounded by speculative housing.

QUEEN'S BUILDING, DE MONTFORT UNIVERSITY, LEICESTER ✪

Short & Associates, 1991–3

Postmodernist

Perhaps the richest example of the ideas-packed neo-Arts and Crafts Alan Short specialized in during the 1990s. This is very much Postmodernism, so the forms really are meant to evoke Victorian diapered red brickwork and tiled attics, alongside a set of towers that try to mimic a Gothick skyline through 1990s means. Inside, the Piranesian spaces are thrilling, spindly green metal walkways in a stockbrick silo, a Terry Gilliam Carceri. None of it feels facile or facade-deep – like the best Victorian Gothic buildings or the Dutch Expressionism that grew out of them, this is an architecture of weight, and of the interiors these eldritch forms make possible – it isn't a 'decorated shed' but a real physical and spatial *experience*. [C.22]

NATIONAL SPACE CENTRE, LEICESTER

Grimshaw, 1997–2001

High-Tech

A wonderfully odd museum of spacecraft and rockets, in a bulbous pupa of ETFE 'pillows', like an extruded version of the same designer's **Eden Project (p. 280)**, scaled precisely in order to fit various rockets inside as prize exhibits. Its incongruity comes partly out of the extremely English setting – a cheap and crap neo-Georgian housing estate, an ex-industrial canal, some wasteland – but this would be a surreal skyline object just about anywhere, and its bumptious lack of deference to any conventional notions of civic architecture is highly appropriate to its function – a balloon filled with Vostoks, Apollos and Blue Streaks that might float away at any moment.

CITY OF NOTTINGHAM

YMCA
T. C. Howitt, 1937
Expressionist

A classical architect trying to move with the times without throwing all he's learned overboard, and taking pointers from bricky Expressionist Hamburg rather than the Med – in terms of climate and context, always a sensible idea in Britain. A black vitrolite ground floor, with a lattice of diapered light-brown brickwork above, around a strongly vertical central tower, evidently inspired by Giles Gilbert Scott. An eccentric thing, good to have in the townscape.

NEWTON BUILDING, NOTTINGHAM TRENT UNIVERSITY
T. C. Howitt, 1956–8
Modern Classicism

It's often forgotten just how much neoclassical architecture was still getting built after the war, before in the 1960s modernism carried all before it for the first and last time. This is one of the most fascinating of these very late free-classical buildings, like **Wood Street Police Station (p. 57)** in London a phantom of what would have happened if we'd had a Socialist Realist architecture in Britain. In plan it's modernist – a high-rise on a podium – but the podium is a stripped classical pavilion and the tower a mass of faïence cladding and vertical strip windows. It shouldn't work, but it does – a little Gotham, a little Stalinist Warsaw, in the centre of the Midlands metropolis; a monumental image of a road not travelled. Refurbished a few years ago by Hopkins Architects, it is now mainly used as a conference centre. **[D.10 & D.11]**

NOTTINGHAM PLAYHOUSE
Peter Moro & Partners, 1961–3
International Style

A well-liked and strongly civic building, framing a purpose-built square just at a tangent from the city centre. A concrete drum holding the theatre inside it stands above a long, Miesian rhythmic screen of glass and steel, with the paving of the square subtly shifting into the stairs towards the entrance. The foyer, with its thin concrete supports, is lapidary and impressive, and the theatre within, as previewed by the drum visible from the street, is sweeping and curved, and conjures an appropriate sense of anticipation and occasion. Definitely the most sheerly enjoyable of Moro's various modernist theatres, though see also the heavier, more complex and anxious **Theatre Royal (p. 274)** in Plymouth.

VICTORIA CENTRE ✪
Arthur Swift & Partners, 1965–71
Brutalist

A gigantic Arndale-style complex, hard to forgive on straightforward town-planning lines – replacing a railway station closed under the Beeching cuts, and turning everything into a massive enclosed mall, with the baroque clock tower of the station held up as a trophy, the severed head of the enemy – but any discussion of it has to reckon with the council high-rise towers that Nottingham City Council got as their share of the Faustian planning bargain, which are absolutely awe-inspiring. They are on the same cyclopean scale as the Mall itself, and run its entire length, with the staggered heights creating an instant metropolitan skyline. They're reasonably simple, if broken down into their component

The relaxed, civic modernism of Peter Moro's Nottingham Playhouse, contrasting heavily with...

...the 'comprehensive redevelopment' of the Victoria Centre, skyscrapers of council flats above a shopping mall.

CITY OF NOTTINGHAM

parts – linear, square, flat-roofed, ribbon windows, no Brutalist fancy stuff, and insulated with pink- and grey-painted render – but what that would miss is the way that the flat roofs fall and rise into a series of incredibly tall interlinked blocks; from the front axial approach in front of the clock tower, the central block is modelled like a castle. The overall effect is rivalled here only by **Park Hill (p. 370)** in using high-rise housing as an elemental image of ruthless modernity. I challenge anyone to see it rise up unexpectedly in Nottingham's workaday townscape and not be just a little bit thrilled.

—

UNIVERSITY LIBRARY
Williamson Faulkner-Brown & Partners, 1971–3
Brutalist

Like Arup's John Player Factory built around the same time nearby – which was in the first draft of this book, but has since been demolished – this small library is a tough Brutalist building with a low profile, set deep into the landscape, with a similar logicality and linearity of plan, and roughly tactile surfaces. Seen on its own terms, the vertical windows and the chamfered corner give the library its own quite specific monumentality, especially conspicuous in the mainly neoclassical – right up until the seventies – Nottingham University campus.

—

JUBILEE CAMPUS, UNIVERSITY OF NOTTINGHAM
Hopkins Architects, 1996–9
High-Tech, Ecomodernist

This is an extension of the University of Nottingham, built on the site of the bicycle factory where Arthur Seaton works in *Saturday Night and Sunday Morning*. It's in two halves, one decent, by Hopkins, from

Hopkins's Jubilee Campus for Nottingham University, a rare 1990s example of a coherent plan, properly executed.

the 1990s, and one reprehensible, by Make, from the 2000s. The Hopkins section is relaxed ecomodernism, by now showing its age a little bit – the wood hasn't matured terribly well, and everything looks a little dirty – but as a campus, and as a public space, it's excellent, with the airy timber-framed teaching blocks around major buildings detailed to look like forts or, in the case of the circular block facing the lake, a unique form of eco-Brutalism. Worthwhile on its own terms, but also if you go and look at phase two next door first, it looks like a masterpiece. One of the best juxtapositions of a contemporary architect really continuing the modernist tradition, and one who isn't – Hopkins has designed here from the outside in, and Make have designed from the inside out, uninterested in anything but 'impact'.

IBIS HOTEL
Benson & Forsyth, 2005–8
Constructivist

A delightful surprise – one of the chain hotels which foist endless dross upon British cities hired the true-believer-modernist architects of the **Maiden Lane Estate (p. 151)** and the **Museum of Scotland (p. 503)** to give them a 'design hotel' in an infill site along the tram line. There's one conventional gesture, the glass atrium facing the street, but everything else is treated as an experiment inspired by the unbuilt architectural projects of the Soviet painter Kasimir Malevich, with abstracted volumes almost hanging in space, detailed in the De Stijl primary colours, arranged at strange angles to the street. You can nevertheless just about tell it's an Ibis – some of the finishes are cheap – but, still, a vindication of the possibility that even one of the grimmest typologies in contemporary Britain, the prefab budget hotel, can be done with style and wit.

NOTTINGHAM CONTEMPORARY ✪
Caruso St John Architects, 2006–9
Classical Modernism

While Caruso St John's **New Art Gallery (p. 322)** in Walsall is a simple monumental block, with a clear relation to the rest of the town, this is a deliberate puzzle, placed between the scrape and noise of rapid-transit tram lines on one side, and the classic townscape complexities of the Lace Market, with its mix of (ex-)industry, warehousing and Victorian churches on the other; and all that while negotiating a steep slope. It responds to all of these challenges with great intelligence and considerable deadpan wit. It is built of corrugated concrete, which has been stained and imprinted with lace patterns, then tinted green and gold. Its different sides have their own character; from the tram, the results are rather classical and logical, as is usual with Caruso St John. But from the stairs that lead up to the Lace Market, facing sheer brick walls, it evokes a pile-up of shipping containers, a much more avant-garde and dissonant mass; but, even here, the entrance is straightforward and civic, inset and glazed, with the 'containers' cantilevered out above. The gallery spaces are clear and well lit, though there's none of the fancy business with concrete shuttering that you'll find in Walsall. It is a fascinatingly harsh and eccentric building, and like Walsall it has aged well; of all the buildings of their era, these two are among those we can be most sure will still be remembered decades hence. **[D.15 & D.16]**

NE MIDLANDS

BOOTS D10 ('WETS'), BEESTON ✪
Owen Williams, 1930–32
BOOTS D6 ('DRYS'), BEESTON ✪
Owen Williams, 1935–6
Constructivist

If you're unconvinced by the idea that architecture has revolutions, go to the Boots Factory. In this sprawling site between Nottingham and Beeston are three factory buildings in a row. There's the original 1928 factory, built when a US drug corporation bought up the Nottingham cosmetics and pills company – a hulking and stodgy concrete building, with architecture confined to some dressing around the edges to make it look more monumental. Next to it, built just two years later, is the 'Wets' (creams, perfumes and pastes) factory, an astonishing leap into the unknown, a wholly original, utterly confident construction of pure concrete and glass, completely functional (the factory is still working to this day) and visually scintillating. Here in one place the real, shocking difference between, say, the **Hoover Factory (p. 159)** in west London and the Dessau Bauhaus, between G. K. Chesterton and James Joyce, between Duncan Grant and Piet Mondrian; two buildings on different planets, a couple of years apart. And then the third building, the 'Drys' (pills and powders), is different again, exchanging lightness for weight, dissonance and abrasive bare concrete.

Conveniently, this view of the three buildings in a row is one of the views of the Boots Factory that you can see as a member of the public – you can survey these from a roundabout in Beeston, and possibly lurk a little bit; the adjacent canal path allows

The mechanical sublime: space and structure in Owen Williams's still-operational 'Wets' factory for Boots.

a slightly fuller view. If you can bargain your way inside or if you have a friend who works there, there is not so much to see in 'Drys', with a lot of the production spaces turned into offices and meeting rooms; but 'Wets' has some of the most remarkable modernist spaces in Europe. The long factory building is flush with glazing, inset into, rather than a curtain wall across, a complex structure of concrete mushroom columns; the corners are tapered, giving it a subtly cubistic feel, with no mannerisms. The structure creates the possibility of a four-storey open space inside for the factory itself, with galleries and walkways running around it, with, originally, a space for Mr Boot to survey all that was going on (and, below him, a truly bizarre glass brick structure called the 'Perfume Dome'). The roof above has tens of thousands of little glass prisms set into the concrete structure, to avoid too much glare and overheating – giving the effect of a gossamer constellation, a concrete sky. It resembles most of all the shopping arcades and 'trade fair palaces' built in distant Prague around the same time – whether Williams was aware of these I have no idea, but the fact that there's a hint of Czech Cubism to the tapering concrete arches around the lifts suggests he might have swiped an idea or two from Constructivist Central Europe – a good few years before the wave of emigration from Hitler brought that architecture with it, too.

After this, D6, built a few years later, isn't quite as thrilling, but it does something else, in many ways equally influential. The lightweight spatial effects of D10 are absent, but in engineering terms the D6 building is actually more pioneering, with various kinds of complicated cantilevering to create the column-free (but, this time, separated) interior spaces. Like Williams's contemporary **Daily Express** buildings (Central London, **p. 50**, Glasgow, **p. 518**, and Manchester, **p. 400**), there are also some incongruous art deco touches in the interior,

echoed in a thirties-style staff café. It's in walking around the outside of the factory where you can see what is original and exciting in the design – the monumental heft of the rhythmic concrete Z-beam supports extending all the way along are of such raw power that Reyner Banham put D6 into his book on *The New Brutalism*, 1960s architecture thirty years before the fact. Of course, Williams would have denied all of these aesthetic effects and resonances, and explained everything all in terms of the demands of the different jobs of making the wet goods and the dry goods. Opposite is a cute little fire station, also by Williams, a miniature version of D6. It's the architect-engineer relaxing from all that strenuous pioneering to have a little joke at his own expense. He clearly deserved the rest.

_____

ECHO BUILDING, LOUGHBOROUGH
1931
ODEON CINEMA, LOUGHBOROUGH
Harry Weedon, 1936
Moderne

In the 1930s, this fairly shabby industrial town carried out ambitious plans for road-widening and boulevard-building, and then rendered the effort aesthetically nugatory by letting landowners do as they liked when they rebuilt. The result is typically interwar, with much faïence, banded brick and zigzag patterns, but very little of it is any good – precisely the sort of careless planning that led to such a strong counter-reaction after the war. Two buildings stand out. The Echo Building is a symmetrical cream-tiled commercial palace, with good graphics – Gothic lettering and a horseshoe motif – a recessed entrance and plate glass shopfronts. The Odeon – still an Odeon, happily – has a strange polygonal tower and spivvishly suave blue-green deco tile patterns. None of it is any more than decoration, but it's very pretty decoration.

LEE LONGLANDS, DERBY
Sidney Bailey, 1938
International Style

It seems that local architects could do the Erich Mendelsohn streamline style as well as anyone actually born in Central Europe, and here the otherwise unknown Sidney Bailey provides a Midlands equivalent of the great Co-ops of the North, in the dense and diverse shopping streets that have to cope with competition from the vast Intu megamall that defaces Derby. The plan and the aesthetic are Weimar Republic commercial modernism at its most swish and svelte, three long ribbon windows whipping right round, but as it's in Derby, the facing materials are red brick and cream tiles, like the Victoriana all around. The results are so successful that it's a shame commercial architects in provincial cities abandoned this seamless fusion of international and local, contextual and glamorous – none of the post-war retail buildings in Derby can match it.

––––

MARKHAM MOOR SERVICE STATION
Sam Scorer for Denis Clarke Hall, Scorer & Bright, 1959
Googie

This wasn't originally a building as such at all, but a hyperbolic paraboloid shell roof to shelter cars at a petrol station on the A1. It's in the fizzy, sugary speedfreak style of the fifties that Americans called 'Googie', strikingly engineered shapes designed to be seen at speed – 'Ducks', as the Postmodernist architect-theorists Denise Scott-Brown and Robert Venturi called them. This one is sleek as can be, a bird swooping down to snatch away the Little Chef that was inserted below it. This is not by Scorer, but leaves his roof alone, meaning that you can still very much see his roof structure as intended while you eat your fry-up

(it has recently become a Starbucks, but the same applies). The combination of ambitious engineering and mundane Englishness is piquant – *Carry On Santiago Calatrava*.

––––

LINCOLNSHIRE MOTOR COMPANY SHOWROOMS, LINCOLN
Sam Scorer for Denis Clarke Hall, Scorer & Bright, 1959–61
Googie

This is on Brayford Pool, a waterside enclave in what was an industrial part of Lincoln, lately reshaped into, on one side, the decent if not-to-write-home-about campus of the University of Lincoln and, on the other, a cheap, cheesy retail 'n' restaurant district. In the making of that otherwise dull zone, the planners retained these showrooms by Sam Scorer, on which two hyperbolic paraboloids are suspended from thin supports. Here, the infill to insert a Prezzo and a Nando's is a bit more invasive than at **Markham Moor Service Station (above)**, but it is striking how much the building fits into a typical 'regeneration' space, making clear how much twenty-first-century Iconic Architecture owes to the roadside design of the fifties.

––––

ST JOHN THE BAPTIST, ERMINE ESTATE, LINCOLN ✪
Sam Scorer for Denis Clarke Hall, Scorer & Bright, 1963
Googie

The low-rise, New Town-style Ermine Estate is a model of its kind – pleasant, green and well kept, a great example of how this medieval city was quite a patron of modern architecture. Most of its really notable modernist buildings were by the local architect Sam Scorer, who combined in his work an ability to work in both rationalist modes (as at Lincoln's Barclays Bank) and, more often, in a 'Googie' style, an American,

Municipal Googie for the Church of England: the shell roof of Sam Scorer's St John the Baptist in Lincoln.

high-speed architecture of engineering spectacle. What is so astonishing in St John the Baptist is that he has successfully converted this approach to the needs of a church, without it seeming at all forced, facile or Vegas-like. From the outside, you're looking at something similar to his **Markham Moor Service Station (p. 358)** – a concrete hyperbolic paraboloid, lurking strangely among the trimmed lawns and trees of the Ermine Estate. When you're inside, this apparently self-effacing design suddenly makes sense – the swooping concrete shell, lined inside with lush woodwork, is completely focused on a spectacular, bright and completely abstract stained-glass window. The artificial bright light of that window and the barrel-like concrete hall create together a sort of psychedelic ark. One of the best-kept secrets in modern architecture in Britain; I wonder how many people even in the Ermine Estate know that there is this firework at its centre. **[C.25]**

UNIVERSITY OF LOUGHBOROUGH: HERBERT MANZONI BUILDING
Sheppard Robson, 1964
COMBINED PHYSICS BUILDING
Arup Associates, 1964
THE TOWERS
Gollins Melvin Ward, 1965
PILKINGTON LIBRARY
Faulkner-Brown Hendy Stonor, 1975
Brutalist

There is much to see at the University of Loughborough, a former engineering college around a pompous Jacobethan house on the edge of the industrial town, but it takes effort. Unlike its contemporaries, Loughborough lacks a unifying idea or a conception of public space – a masterplan by Arup was commissioned but abandoned in the early sixties, so there's nothing resembling what other universities of the period have to offer: the lush gardens of **Southampton (p. 245)**, the lake at **York**

(p. 394) or **East Anglia (p. 198)**, the walkways at **Bath (p. 259)** or **Essex (p. 190)**, or the Roman Forum of **Sussex (p. 238)** to bring it all together, and there's no vantage point where you can take it all in at a glance. Instead what we have here is some interesting buildings around asphalt squares, surface car parking, business park-like new buildings and bleak greens – all scattered around some first-rate public sculpture. The first building the bus drops you off at is the Herbert Manzoni Building – named, tellingly, after the famously architecture-sceptical Birmingham engineer. It's a Portland stone lozenge projecting out on concrete legs, with some Lynn Chadwick sentinels in front. It's very easy to get lost here – the layout is not intuitive and there are few maps – but you should be able to locate The Towers, due to their being at least twice as tall as everything else. This hall of residence consists of two prefabricated concrete hives linked by a service tube, a sort of low budget metabolist architecture, the sort of building that would have been described at the time in excitedly dystopian terms as a concrete hive for the engineering student as termite.

From here, a walk along car parks and lawns will lead you to the later halls of residence, which are basically seventies/ eighties low-rise housing estates set among trees and linked to common rooms. Some of them are quite pleasant, especially when the windows are open and the music is blaring out (the red-brick clusters of Falkner and Eddington Court, in the style of **Lillington Gardens, p. 57**, are the best). The most notable building aside from The Towers is Pilkington Library, the only other attempt at creating something monumental and memorable, an upturned pyramid linked to the street by a walkway at the top floor. Unlisted, presumably because little of the original fabric survives inside, but very impressive, akin to a Denys Lasdun building without the integrity but spiked with an enjoyable dose of sci-fi kitsch. At the edge

of the site, furthest from the town, are the executed fragments of Arup's masterplan, modelled on the 'tartan grid' of their stern concrete blocks at the **Metallurgy & Minerals Building (p. 313)** in Birmingham. These blocks, the largest being the Combined Physics Building, stand on a grass ridge, and they make a very appropriate use of the aggro neo-Constructivism of Paul Wager's metal sculptures. Arup's blocks march along until one crosses the access road, and then it all stops. From there, it's playing fields, woodlands and farms as far as the eye can see, and the heavy-engineering world ends abruptly.

BOOTS D90, BEESTON
Skidmore Owings & Merrill, 1960–62
International Style

At the Nottingham edge of the Boots site, with very different values to the sublimity of Owen Williams's astonishing 1930s industrial Valhalla; a cooler world, where production was quiet and automated, and the buildings were just clipped together. D90 is American corporate modernism at its smoothest and most elegant, without the stray angles and rough edges that most British firms would have added. A two-storey Miesian pavilion is ingeniously nestled in a landscaped hill, dazzlingly and meticulously detailed – the way the glass offices are slotted in just behind a projecting black steel I-beam at the corners is particularly perfectionist. It's better outside than in, where the grey carpets, suspended ceilings and wood partitions are original, but make clear how much today's corporate blandness is the extension of that of the sixties – as you can see if you compare SOM's original to DEGW's blander 2000s extension. At the time, of course, offices like this were new and exciting – a newspaper feature on this place asked the question: 'Would you let your daughter work in an open plan office?'

COURTHOUSE, CHESTERFIELD
**S. Allen and Roy Keenlyside for
Borough Architects Dept, 1963–5**
People's Detailing

Chesterfield has an unexpectedly grand feeling with its statues, its Dutch market square and its neo-Georgian Town Hall – a real centre for the small mining communities that surrounded it. Chesterfield Courthouse stands on a ridge in parkland, set to the side of the crisp porticos of the Town Hall. Its plan is roughly an outstretched fan, with thin, semi-Gothic windows and jagged pitched roofs, facing the Town Hall. Materials are exceptional throughout, with granite and marble set into its concrete frame, and there is great exploitation of the fall of the land, with the courthouse treated as a picturesque object in a formal garden. The courts themselves have moved to a business park-style block elsewhere, and the building is now derelict and up for sale; demolition would have been a certainty if it wasn't listed, and one of the most subtle meetings of classicism, modernism and landscape in the Midlands would have been lost.

Opposite the Courts is a dispiriting office building called 'Future Walk' – an example of the depressing things that can happen when a building isn't listed, but a sculpture that was part of it is. Barbara Hepworth's *Rosewall*, a rare stone carved work, was commissioned for a specially designed pool in front of a Miesian office block. It now sits decontextualized and scale-less in the car park of 'Future Walk'. Listing is a blunt instrument, but without it…

RATCLIFFE-ON-SOAR POWER STATION
Building Design Partnership, 1965–8
Brutalist

An awesome complex, familiar to millions from its placement next to East Midlands

The sinister cooling tower skyline of Ratcliffe-on-Soar Power Station, the most accessible of its kind.

Parkway Station, on the main routes from London to Sheffield and Nottingham. Eight colossal cooling towers (a standard design, but what a design – 'iconic' architects would love to have come up with something so organically monumental) and a pulsating, throbbing great coal-fired power station behind it. At night it is breathtaking and apocalyptic, a truly villainous headquarters.

BARCLAYS BANK, LINCOLN
**Sam Scorer for Denis Clarke Hall,
Scorer & Bright, 1968–70**
International Style

When walking around Lincoln for the first time, it is natural to be surprised by just how many good modernist buildings there are set into the historic townscape. Consult your Pevsner, though, and you'll find that until very recently each one of them was designed by Sam Scorer, who was able to shift when required from the Googie that has made him a minor cult figure in recent years to Brutalism, Postmodernism and, in this superb bank building, scaled perfectly to its Georgian neighbours, a restrained, high-end Miesian corporate steel-and-glass high modernism. Its luxurious sobriety is closer to the originals than all the Mies imitations in London.

ASSEMBLY ROOMS, DERBY ❶
Casson Conder & Partners, 1971–6
Brutalist

Casson and Conder were long-standing adversaries of the more gestural, wilfully spectacular post-war modernists – see the fight between them and James Stirling at the **'Sidgwick Site' (p. 207)** in Cambridge. They won a competition for the Derby Assembly Rooms against an early Postmodernist scheme by Stirling, which is now probably more famous (outside Derby) than the completed building. That's a shame, as it's an exemplary, if rather conservative, Brutalist cultural complex, whose main value is in the way it brings a civic space together. Replacing a classical design that burned down in the 1960s, Casson and Conder's building is broken up into distinct parts, with a complexity that in places is like a Midlands microcosm of the **Barbican (p. 66)**. There is a long glazed circulation area facing the Market Square, held up by a grand, rectangular concrete colonnade, and a distinct block currently housing a Tourist Information Centre, which is scaled to match the fey Swedish classical council buildings behind; the corner between these two blocks provides a surprising concrete frame for the clock tower of the Victorian Derby Town Hall. A multistorey car park round the back connects the Assembly Rooms to Derby's horrible, over-engineered road system. A so-so (by their standards) recent arts building by Feilden Clegg Bradley has

closed the square, so now it's a very decent classical-modern-contemporary space, full of buildings responding to each other. Currently the ground floor of the Assembly Rooms is let out for council rent-raising purposes as an 'Ask Italian', although its jazzy, angular light fittings and chairs suit Casson and Conder's building surprisingly well. Predictably, despite being by some distance the best twentieth-century building in Derby, it is currently slated for demolition.

CHESTERFIELD LIBRARY
Feilden & Mawson, 1985
Brutalist

A surprising James Stirling tribute some time after his 1960s architecture ceased to be fashionable, and an early and very successful example of Public–Private 'planning gain', where a public service is paid for by retail. Chesterfield Library is part of The Pavements, an ingenious bit of retail planning that fitted a mall almost imperceptibly into the historic city, created a little enclave of small alleys of independent shops out of the leftovers, and linked the lot via a glass walkway to a big Postmodernist car park at the back. In amongst this was a replacement library. It has stepped mirror glass volumes to the street, with service areas in neat, bright-red engineering brick, and several floors tucked into the slope below – an instantly exciting topographical experiment, an alleyway that suddenly has a view of the green Peak District all around. Beneath, a café is tucked below a pedestrian pathway, with two projecting metal bay windows, a lovely little detail. It is apparently one of the most used libraries in the country, and you can see why – a real part of the town's everyday life.

A rural factory of modernism: the rotunda of Hopkins's works for the designer David Mellor in north Derbyshire.

DAVID MELLOR CUTLERY FACTORY, HATHERSAGE

Hopkins Architects, 1988–90

High-Tech, Ecomodernist

A promotional leaflet for the David Mellor Factory lists its address on the front as 'Hathersage, Derbyshire', and on the back as 'Hathersage, Sheffield', so that should give an idea of the geography – the Peak District borders of north Derbyshire and South Yorkshire, with their darkly picturesque mill towns turned retirement villages for the Sheffield intelligentsia. David Mellor himself was one of these – a Bauhaus-influenced industrial designer who moved production of his cutlery out here in the 1980s. The factory was built on the site of a gasholder, which necessitated laying it out as a rotunda. The steel structure has some of the mesh-like, grid quality of a Victorian gasometer, with the production process laid out logically as an A to B to C carousel. There are regular tours where you can see Mellor's elegant, mildly quirky knives and forks being made, a rare example of modernist cottage industry.

This was the first place a firm of British High-Tech architects adapted their designs to local context and historical architecture; so the rotunda is clad in the local stone, and it is kept low, among a thicket of trees. It's a stone-and-steel combination that Michael and Patricia Hopkins would make their own in somewhat stodgy buildings of the 1990s, such as the Inland Revenue HQ in Nottingham or Portcullis House in London, but it's still light and fresh here. Today, the factory stands next to a slightly glassier shop and café in a similar style, also by Hopkins, and with a delightful outdoor exhibition of objects Mellor had a hand in designing, such as the standard traffic lights and pedestrian crossings found in their thousands across the UK. Seeing these familiar objects taken out of context makes their Bauhausian abstraction that much more clear.

8. METROPOLITAN YORKSHIRE

Odeon Cinema, Harrogate (p. 393)

The West Riding of Yorkshire is one of the best areas for modern architecture in Britain, especially if you prefer your modernism cranky, personal and topographically specific, and have less interest in the clean lines of the International Style (with the notable exception of Sheffield's pure, minimalist **Western Bank Library** and **Arts Tower**). Both the conurbations of the south, around Sheffield and Doncaster, and of the west, around Leeds and Bradford, are full of brilliant, often gigantic works of the post-war era. These include such masterpieces as the **Halifax Headquarters**, **Park Hill** in Sheffield, **Queensgate Market** in Huddersfield, and Chamberlin Powell & Bon's **University of Leeds South Campus**. Each of these combines quirkiness and monumentality, a dual quality that pervades so much of the sublime landscape and nonconformist townscape round here.

The main actors in Yorkshire were local architects' departments – which were capable of turning out work of serious quality, like **Beeversleigh Flats** in Rotherham and the staggering **Gleadless Valley** in suburban Sheffield – local building societies and banks, and universities, particularly in the two biggest cities, Leeds and Sheffield. But credit is also due the Co-operative movement, whose sleek, streamlined 1930s department stores brought a dash of modernity to the Victorian townscapes of Doncaster, Huddersfield and Bradford. The regional capital, meanwhile, has one of the most impressive of the 'New Universities' of the 1960s, the **University of York**, where space-age concrete buildings stand enigmatically around an artificial lake. Although much has been demolished, including important work like Leeds's Quarry Hill flats, the Bradford and Bingley headquarters in Bingley and Sheffield's Castle Market, and recent architecture can be shabby (especially in Leeds), urban Yorkshire has more than enough to remain one of the most rewarding parts of the country for modernism enthusiasts.

SHEFFIELD

REGENT COURT, HILLSBOROUGH
Edgar Gardham, 1936
Moderne

The steel city's incredible adventure in modern architecture – which made it the city with the largest number of truly first-rate modernist buildings outside the capital – begins a little inauspiciously with this ultra-high-density private-housing complex. Looking marooned now in mostly low-rise surroundings, its scale in the 1930s must have been outrageously domineering. Long, symmetrical and tall, with cream-rendered wings and a brick front, its nine storeys enclose a mean courtyard, and flats are reached via meaner walkways. The lack of public space around this giant block is precisely what post-war local-authority architects strained to avoid. But its rude scale means that Regent Court boasts a totalitarian drama, a pungently urban contrast with picturesque, humanist arrangements of towers, hills and trees such as nearby Netherthorpe (late 1950s, clumsily reclad in the 1990s). The typically thirties clock at the top of the central stair tower is especially 'period'.

CHURCH OF THE SACRED HEART, HILLSBOROUGH
C. M. E. Hadfield, 1936
Expressionist

Like **Regent Court (above)** on the other side of Hillsborough Barracks, this is strong, if conservative, interwar architecture. Essentially splicing together ideas from Cachemaille-Day (the swelling brick curve at the back, recalling his smouldering **Church of the Epiphany, p. 380**) and Giles Gilbert Scott (the rising, stepped Gothic-cubist tower), with a little bit of Dudok in

the precision-cut Dutch bricks, it's a powerful example of suburban Expressionism, none the worse for its lack of originality – in the straggling townscape of Hillsborough it is an imposing presence.

GLEADLESS VALLEY ✪
J. L. Womersley, Braddock & Martin-Smith, Peter Jackson and John Taylor for Sheffield City Council Architects Dept, 1955–78
People's Detailing, Ecomodernist

This is one of the greatest modernist housing projects in Europe. I have seen people genuinely gasp out loud as they approach this place from the hills around, as they suddenly go from the squat semis carelessly tossed into the vertiginous Arcadia of the south of Sheffield where it meets the Peak District, and then, this – a council estate as a South Yorkshire Southern California. The way the hills and the buildings interact allows each to be experienced with rare intensity, as one complete unit. In order to fit into the complexity of this incredible space, a dozen or so different house and flat types are employed. There are terraces in a pretty normal fifties style, which, as Ruth Harman and John Minnis point out in their Pevsner city guide, resemble Span housing, with relaxed weatherboarding and brickwork; there are split-level maisonettes, some of which sprawl elegantly across the drops, others of which straddle the slopes with the monumental power of one of Richard Neutra's Los Angeles houses; there are stark tower houses, resembling the medieval-modernist work of Wheeler & Sproson, **Somerville Square & Coltburndale (p. 507)** in Burntisland and the **Langlee Estate (p. 493)** in Galashiels; there are neo-Victorian terraces with precipitous sliding inclines; there are two clusters of point blocks, one of them in an almost forested area; there are neat, New Town-style shopping precincts; there are churches, one of which, the Googie rocketship of Holy Cross (Braddock & Martin-Smith, 1965), is absolutely superb; and there's a network of pedestrian pathways that makes it a pleasure to walk through, at least for the reasonably fit.

So visually rich is Gleadless Valley, that it's baffling that it isn't better known and more popular. One explanation is that it needs to be *seen*; photographs seldom convey the panoramic, widescreen nature of Gleadless Valley as a totality. Of course, it's poor, and, as a member of the Tenants' and Residents' Association once pointed out to me, people who have grown up here don't realize quite how extraordinary it is (unlike those who moved here in the 1950s and '60s, who had Victorian slums or indifferently planned suburbs to contrast it with). It is also poorly treated by the local authority. Right up until the eighties, new parts of it were being added, with shifts in style, but no drop in quality. The warm, organic ecomodernist step-section flats by the Sheffield City Council Architects' Department's Peter Jackson and John Taylor are the most interesting 1970s works in Sheffield (there are also clones of these on a less dramatic site in Derby Terrace, Heeley). Yet, more recently, there has been attrition: the green spaces are poorly maintained, one of the three towers on the highest hill was demolished, and the cluster of towers was reclad with an appallingly unsympathetic black and Day-Glo green colour scheme, which among other things took their balconies away – hopefully they aren't now flammable. All that said, in large part this astonishing place survives as it was built, for the working-class people for whom it was intended – unlike its inner-city counterpart at **Park Hill (p. 370)**. It is unmissable.

Peak District Palisades: the glorious hillside townscape of J. L. Womersley's Gleadless Valley, Sheffield.

METROPOLITAN YORKSHIRE

UNIVERSITY OF SHEFFIELD: ✪
WESTERN BANK LIBRARY
Gollins Melvin Ward, 1955–9
ARTS TOWER
Gollins Melvin Ward, 1961–5
International Style

More superlatives, I'm afraid. You simply won't find better American-issue International Style buildings anywhere in Britain than this masterful pair. As with the **Golden Lane Estate (p. 55)**, these are the result of one of those competitions where Alison and Peter Smithson submitted some interesting paper architecture which made it into the history books while a lesser-known firm got on with creating an enduring work of real architecture. The extension to Sheffield's Victorian–Edwardian campus counts as the first planned modernist university campus in Britain, predating the New Universities of the mid-sixties – though it is too dense and urban to really resemble the surrealist future-villages that are the universities of **Essex (p. 190)**, **East Anglia (p. 198)**, **York (p. 394)**, **Sussex (p. 238)** and co. Instead, it's part of another lineage, from Mies van der Rohe's work in Chicago for the Illinois Institute of Technology – metal and glass grids, clear and unpretentious, laid out logically – except, here, their arrangement around the Victorian Weston Park, with its picturesque trees and stream and its stern Grecian museum, makes for something distinctly English.

The twenty-storey tower is a singular monument of steel and glass, crowned with Portland stone, an elegant shaft of light that was until very recently the city's tallest building. Contrary to appearances it's a concrete-framed tower, something that only becomes clear to the eye from up close. Inside, there's a Paternoster lift, which is lots of fun, and the university is accommodating to visitors. If the tower is merely a very fine piece of architecture, the library has a breathtaking concentrated intensity of vision

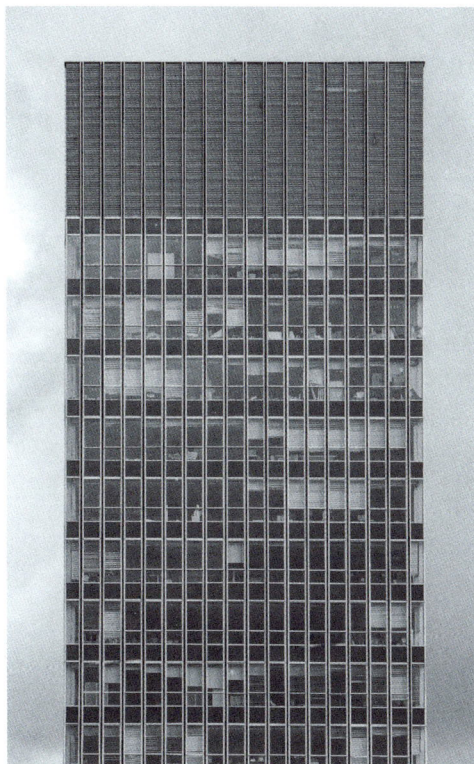

Precision engineering, Sheffield steel – Gollins Melvin Ward channel Fifth Avenue in the city's Arts Tower.

that could almost seem inhuman were it not for the care with which the small details are treated. Walk into the mezzanine connecting it to the tower, through lush marble spaces (and a plaque recording its opening by no less than T. S. Eliot), and you soon come to the upper level of the reading room, looking down on the students, who look out on to the park. Ian Nairn compared this view to one of Brueghel's snow scenes. Both buildings have been scrupulously renovated in recent years for their original purpose, a privilege never granted to equally important Sheffield buildings of the era such as **Park Hill (below)**, or the scandalously demolished Castle Market. At least here, the listing system has worked as it should, and two wonderful pieces of architecture have been preserved for generations to come to enjoy in all their complexity. [A.11]

PARK HILL ✪
**Jack Lynn and Ivor Smith for Sheffield
City Council Architects Dept, 1961**
Brutalist

It's hard to know where to begin with this unforgettable, tragic building. Placed on a hilltop above Sheffield Station, this was intended, like Denys Lasdun's **Keeling House (p. 124)**, as a means of re-creating working-class community in a new form. It is immensely long, and visible from almost anywhere in Sheffield – as an abstract image, it is a ridge of rock, a geological formation, integrated into its hill. The guiding principle was the series of continuous walkways that snake through the entire building, which the designers imagined would become 'streets in the sky'. Actually, they're access decks, of the sort that social housing has had since the 1860s, but here, they not only connect different blocks together, they're also made much more pleasurable through their width,

around five times the norm, allowing people to linger and talk, and for milk carts to drive along them; and, most importantly, through the fact you can (or could) walk on to them from street level, without going up any stairs. On the ground are trees, a green and playgrounds, and, as built, pubs, shops, public toilets and community centres, none of which exist today.

This sort of high-density, mixed-use housing is actually pretty close to 'best practice' in the twenty-first century, but was alas built for the 'wrong' people. Though regarded as a successful estate until the 1970s, the collapse of the steel industry hit it hard, and like most high-density estates it was run down over the 1980s and '90s. It was then emptied, block by block, in the 2000s, as part of a publicly funded transfer to the developers Urban Splash, who have marketed it to the city's lecturers and its 'creative class'. One fifth of the complex is now luxury housing, its original fabric

A tragic monument: the mangled collective dream of Park Hill, ruined by social cleansing and shiny cladding.

ripped out at enormous expense, reclad with tacky (and already dated) aluminium panels; but given that that project hasn't sold well, the systematic aesthetic as well as social destruction of the estate has been paused at the belated 'phase two', where at least the original fabric of one of the blocks was preserved in its renovation by Mikhail Riches as student housing. The rest of it, three-fifths of the complex, is still derelict in 2021. Because of the close proximity of the offices of Warp Films, it is regularly used as a film and TV set, or for music videos. The entire process of 'regeneration', still ongoing, has already taken four times as long as it took for the complex to be built; as this whimsical game was played with Sheffield's largest inner-city council estate, the city's waiting list has spiralled and spiralled. It is a scandal, and the fact that this moronic project has been so celebrated – probably the first unfinished building to be nominated for the Stirling Prize – indicates an awful moral vacuum at the heart of British architecture.

But if you visit, you will still find an extremely impressive work of architecture, of such physical power that it would be breathtaking even as a ruin. There is nothing else outside of medieval castles or Georgian Bath that compares with the sheer confidence in Park Hill's negotiation of its steep slope, with its concrete grid going from being on the scale of terraced housing at the south end to a sheer fourteen-storey monument at the north, all with a continuous flat roof line and (until recently) a continuous public walkway, and that modular concrete grid clanging relentlessly along like a 4/4 beat as the hill rises and descends. It is a masterpiece – one of the most moving works of architecture of the twentieth century, anywhere. What will happen to it in the next decade is anybody's guess. I hope to one day see the people who 'regenerated' it tried in a court of law.

JOHN LEWIS ❶
Yorke Rosenberg & Mardall, 1961–5
BARKER'S POOL
Sheffield City Council Urban Design Team, 2005
International Style, Postmodernist

John Lewis, originally Coles Brothers, is a standard-issue Yorke Rosenberg & Mardall building of the sixties, a clear and classically proportioned grid of tiles and brick, commanding one side of a square opposite the twenties neoclassical City Hall, and matching it for presence – almost palazzo-like in its golden-section frontage, with a car park with the same proportions attached at the back. It is slated to be demolished as part of plan for a megamall without walls in central Sheffield, currently indefinitely stalled. It is a piece of the old modernist Sheffield that currently has in front of it Barker's Pool, one of the Postmodernist squares created by Sheffield Council in the New Labour years as part of what they called the 'Golden Route' of public spaces between the railway station and the university. These squares were hard to praise at a time when the council was bent on destroying its superb modernist legacy, and they do tend towards Yorkie kitsch – big steel balls, sandstone furniture – but they work very well as public space, and always have people sitting on them or generally hanging out. Barker's Pool is the best of these – simple, intuitive, as if it has always been there.

___

HYDE PARK
Jack Lynn and Ivor Smith for Sheffield City Council Architects Dept, 1965/1991
Brutalist

When you look at the Sheffield skyline from a distance, you can see that its prodigious – and in some ways unbroken – affair with avant-garde modern architecture brought out something latent in the city's landscape. These hills were just waiting for monuments, and as they weren't built when John Ruskin used to lecture here, praising the landscape and blasting the dullness of the buildings thrown carelessly into it, it had to happen between the fifties and sixties. Some of the towers that were erected on the slopes are gone – Woodside, Norfolk Park, Kelvin; others, like Upperthorpe and Netherthorpe, have been reclad tackily though they retain their extravagant planning; and **Gleadless Valley (p. 367)** and **Park Hill (p. 370)** we know. The crown of it all was once this place, where a gargantuan 'Castle Keep' flanked by two slightly lower Park Hill clones and a long row of terraces were set into Sheffield's highest hill. Unfortunately, unlike at Park Hill there was no easy access from the street, and the sheer size was considered daunting and relentless quite early on; it never had the success as an estate that the earlier building indisputably did. The 'Keep' was demolished in 1991, leaving the fragments you can see today – the two miniature Park Hills and the terrace, which has been reclad in brick with pitched roofs, which is best ignored.

Looking at photographs of the original Hyde Park, it was clearly architecture of almost insane daring; considered simply as sculpture, it is the saddest of all the losses of modern architecture. But, then, housing is not sculpture. The two Park Hill clones have been reclad in a vaguely High-Tech manner, which looks better than the naff patterns on Upperthorpe and Netherthorpe. At night, especially with the lights on, you can still capture here the grandeur described in Pulp's 'Sheffield: Sex City', where 'the whole city is your jewellery box – a million twinkling yellow street lights'. But in any case, if I were to get the choice to see any demolished post-war building reconstructed, it would be the original 'castle keep' of Hyde Park.

TINSLEY VIADUCT
Freeman Fox & Partners, 1965–8
BLACKBURN MEADOWS BIOMASS PLANT
BDP, 2014
Brutalist, Supermodernist

This story starts with another demolition of a Sheffield modernist 'icon' in the 2000s. Tinsley Viaduct is part of the M1, and is an unusually ambitious bit of road engineering, with two levels carried on a complex steel mesh. Whether you drive into (or out of) Sheffield or see it by train, the twin levels of the viaducts have a dramatic, Expressionistic effect, the gateway into the city of the future. They were originally neighboured by Blackburn Meadows Power Station, which had two tall, thin cooling towers, a different design from the more squat type you can see at, say, **Ratcliffe-on-Soar Power Station (p. 361)**. Together, these slotted together into an accidental composition, like a Düsseldorf School photograph. The demolition of the towers when they became functionally obsolete was opposed locally – frustratingly, much more vigorously than the campaign to save the amazing Castle Market – but the less grossly polluting replacement by BDP is really very decent. Clad in black steel, like the immense Forgemasters steelworks nearby, its component parts slot together with the angular rightness of a Constructivist sculpture, and a glazed section is tinted orange, which at night appears as a tamed glimpse into the inferno. Unfortunately it's set back, no doubt for very good environmental reasons, further from the viaduct than the old cooling towers were, meaning they never quite appear as a unity. Even so, this is an unusually fair exchange, the only one of the many removals of one of Sheffield's post-war landmarks that has seen something of equal interest taking its place.

Sheffield Brutalism at its most avant-garde: the ruthless, bunker-like facade of Moore Street Electricity Substation.

MOORE STREET ELECTRICITY SUBSTATION ✪
Jefferson Sheard & Partners, 1965–8
Brutalist

Unlike many of the other Brutalist buildings in Sheffield this doesn't have to serve any sort of social purpose – it just needs to sit there. The very specific requirements of the substation subgenre – windowless, deliberately baffling – have been fulfilled with even more obsessive tactility and punch-in-the-guts Brutalist power than in the **Birmingham New Street Signal Box (p. 314)**. Concrete is put through its paces in several different surface treatments – rough, smooth, patterned, ribbed, corduroy. The skyline of the building suggests a miniature fortress, with its asymmetrical frosted glass maintenance stairwells feeling practically heraldic. Disdained for years, it has been a beneficiary of the newfound fashionability of Brutalism, and is now celebrated and lit up in the evenings with neon floodlighting. Sheffield, where the people look good and the concrete is loud.

EPIC DEVELOPMENT
Jefferson Sheard & Partners, 1968–9
International Style

Designed by the same firm as the **Moore Street Electricity Substation (above)**, at the same time but totally different in style and approach, this is a complex megastructure whose multiple functions are resolved elegantly into a series of gleaming boxes. This group of largely windowless spaces was a comprehensive redevelopment of a big chunk of the steep slope between the city centre and the railway station, with things that don't need windows, like discos and cinemas, on the higher level connecting with the city centre and a car park on stilts connecting to the ground level and the bus station. Architecturally, this is an essay in the delicate white-tile formalism pioneered by Yorke Rosenberg & Mardall – it still looks futuristic, though it is in dire need of a clean and was, sadly, denuded a few years ago of the 'ROXY' sign for the disco inside. Like the best Sheffield buildings, it is all about the levels, the ways in which a mundane slope can become an architectural adventure.

CONCOURSE, UNIVERSITY OF SHEFFIELD
Arup Associates, 1968–9
Brutalist

This two-level public-space project is the sort of thing architects and planners insist today on calling 'public realm' – an elegant flyover, with something of the combination of delicacy and strength of Arup's **Kingsgate Bridge (p. 470)** brought down to earth, is gently raised above, and thereby creates, a square. An interesting contrast with the 'Golden Route' of the 2000s such as **Barker's Pool (p. 371)**, or the amusing Gaudí parody of nearby Devonshire Green, in that the concrete, brown-red tiles, multiple levels and modernist hardness feel much more appropriate to Sheffield as a modern city. This non-twee space is certainly not used any less than the twee spaces are.

GEOGRAPHY & PLANNING BUILDING, UNIVERSITY OF SHEFFIELD
William Whitfield, 1968–71
Brutalist

One of the better schemes by a prolific and usually slightly stodgy establishment modernist, placed in a bosky corner of Weston Park away from the library and Arts Tower. Interconnected hexagons of sandstone-inflected concrete framing brown brick, it has a bridging effect visually, aptly

given that this is where students of space and place are working – shifting the eye from the glinting Chicago of the modernism on one side and the Mock Tudor on the other.

MAGISTRATES' COURT & SOUTH YORKSHIRE POLICE HEADQUARTERS
B. Warren for Sheffield City Council Architects Dept, 1968–78
Brutalist

One of the lesser known of Sheffield's Brutalist buildings, almost hidden behind the old Town Hall and the building site where Castle Market once was. Unromantic and bureaucratic (well, obviously), these are a faintly intimidating pair, well crafted in corrugated concrete and red brick, which has worn extremely well despite the usual minimal-to-non-existent maintenance. The Magistrates' Court is reached via a concrete bridge, as though miscreants should be thrown off to the crocodiles after a guilty verdict. The boxed-out brick volumes towards the back and the great concrete cylinders of the towers of each of the two buildings have an appropriate Gothic quality given the many many dubious things the South Yorkshire Police have got involved in, with Hillsborough and Orgreave in their jurisdiction.

MOORFOOT ❶
Property Services Agency, 1978
Brutalist, Vernacular

Moorfoot is an office block made up of two enormous and asymmetrical red-brick polygonal ziggurats that spread across the south of central Sheffield, at the end of the bland, pedestrianized Portland stone parade of the Moor, marking its terminus. The complex was built as a bureaucratic castle and is currently used by the city council as offices after plans to replace it (as part of a shopping mall scheme) with something less weird have come so far to nought, although the area around it is still half derelict. It is very strange, far too big and captivating in its endlessly puzzling geometry, both domineering and self-sabotaging, never allowing itself to be seen as one single coherent image. At one point, there was meant to be a monorail going from this to Castle Market at the other end of the city centre.

WINTER GARDENS & MILLENNIUM GALLERIES ✪
Pringle Richards Sharratt, 1995–2001
Ecomodernist

The surroundings of this – the arse end of Hallam University, Millennium Square, the most corporate of the 'Golden Route' public spaces, and Conran's cheap, pitifully underdesigned St Paul's Tower – are not encouraging. Contain your revulsion, however, and you'll find two humane and modest public buildings, the best of their era in Sheffield. Approached from Millennium Square, you start at the Winter Gardens, with its succession of soaring, taut wooden archways, with the foliage crammed into a small space, with pathways running through it. Then a side door leads you into the galleries, barrel-vaulted with glass bricks, and an escalator running down to a glazed café looking out over the university. Both parts link intuitively together while being very clearly separate, and have aged very well – unusually for an era of flimsy, cladded buildings. But the Gardens achieve more than just competence – there's a real poetry to them, a surreal irruption into the Regeneration landscape. They also constitute an important public through route from the 'lower' and 'upper' parts of Sheffield, one of the richest of short cuts.

Pringle Richards Sharratt's elegant, organic Winter Gardens, the best Sheffield building of the 'Millennium era'.

PERSISTENCE WORKS
Feilden Clegg, 1998–2000
Supermodernist, Brutalist

A real outlier – a neo-Brutalist building, begun in the late 1990s well before the re-evaluation of that era and manner had begun in earnest. It's not just Brutalist in the sense of its using lots of concrete, although that was unusual enough at this point, but for its gruff approach to townscape. While too much architecture of the New Labour era was bright and tacky, this accepts that it will be bashed around a bit – as a block of art and craft studios, many of them doing metalwork, it could hardly not be. That sense of roughness and provisionality has been embraced, to form hard, abstracted concrete volumes thrown into the streetscape. Inside, a top-lit arcade showcases the artists' work, while the glazed ground floor has an obvious 'active frontage' by contrast with Sheffield's sixties modernist buildings, strongly connecting to a linear traditional street. A welcome building which recognizes that this is a city of modernity, labour and crags.

CHARLES STREET CAR PARK
Allies & Morrison, 2008
Supermodernist

Next to, and designed alongside, Conran's dreadful St Paul's Tower – which is the tallest building in Sheffield and an utterly trivial piss-weak extruded grid of brown luxury flats – this is much more the sort of building that Sheffield deserves. Its facade is made up of dozens of faceted stainless steel panels providing a screen across ten floors of parking. These give glimpses of the city's panorama from inside, and create an intriguing pattern for the pedestrian; pure décor. On the face of it an unusually visually centred, flashy product of the usually ultra-sober Allies & Morrison, but its alternating grid, with each steel panel

on the same module, is close in principle to something like **City Lit (p. 74)** in London. A strange combination of discipline and flash.

SOUND HOUSE, UNIVERSITY OF SHEFFIELD
Carey Jones and Jefferson Sheard & Partners, 2008
Supermodernist

Carey Jones build a lot in Yorkshire, much of it bog-standard developers' housing, student flats and office blocks, but now and again a project comes out of their office with a personality that suggests they could create much more interesting work when given the chance (**Candle House, p. 382**, in Leeds is another example). This project for Sheffield's Department of Music is remarkably fresh and original. It's the size of a large house and encased in rubber for soundproofing purposes, which looks rather plush, like a giant square black sofa. The overall effect is of a marvellous little surrealist object, sitting in a mundane bit of Sheffield, resembling more a conceptual artwork than a functional building.

SOUTH YORKSHIRE

CO-OPERATIVE DEPARTMENT STORE, DONCASTER ✪
T. H. Johnson & Son, 1938–40
Moderne

In the South, tentative interwar modernism is about lidos, luxury flats and Tube stations. In the North, it's about labour movement institutions: co-ops and pithead baths, in particular. Most of the latter have been demolished and those which survive are usually inaccessible, but every big town or city north of the Trent (and a few south of it, like **Ipswich, p. 198**, or **Woolwich, p. 83**) has its grand co-operative department store, great structures that once included shops, reading rooms, dance halls and conference halls, at the very heart of the city. Indeed, one way of understanding the decline of the labour movement in the North is through the

fact that although the Co-operative group still very much exists, they have sold off every single one of these wonderful, proud buildings. However, they can still be admired architecturally as a statement of collective confidence. Doncaster has one of the very best. Right in front of the station, it embraces the 'relentlessly advancing streamlined battlecruiser' aspect of Erich Mendelsohn's work and adapts its materials to a South Yorks industrial language of brick and faïence. It consists of a city block of brick, with a dramatic curved 'prow' with two lower wings in vitrolite swaying around it, framing a cylindrical glass stair tower in the middle. Suave, sexy and beefy – glamorous, even, and there's not a lot of that in Doncaster. The same can't be said of the way it is currently subdivided into multiple uses – charity shops, flats, a branch of Peacocks.

Still powerful: the sweeping curves of the Co-operative's Weimar-style department store in Doncaster.

BEEVERSLEIGH FLATS, ROTHERHAM ✪
Maurice Dakin for Gillinson, Barnett & Partners, 1970–71
Brutalist

Rotherham once had a large cluster of Brutalist public buildings in its town centre, but these have all been demolished and replaced with nothing of note. However, it does still have this first-rate piece of work, a superb, isolated point block, beautifully made and positioned, and Rotherham's only high-rise. If you're going to do something only once, you might as well get it right. It stands on a hill just outside the town centre, at the edge of a very pleasant municipal park and a Palladian local-history museum, and is best approached from these, where the framing by mature trees gives it an **Alton Estate (p. 112)** or **Gleadless Valley (p. 367)** feel. But the tower itself is not at all in the friendly, Scandinavian manner, but a much

more hardline proposition – a rhomboid plan with a strongly expressed, projecting frame, resembling the work of Ove Arup and Philip Dowson in Oxbridge, Birmingham and Bracknell. It was actually designed by a local Yorkshire firm, which otherwise seems to have been limited to minor work like Leeds's unlovely Merrion Centre. A walkway leading from the street, with car parking below, provides a pedestrian podium with views right across the town and the moors beyond. Ingenious as its planning on the slope is, what is really important is the integrity and elegance of the tower itself – easily one of the finest of its era in the country. [**B.11**]

BARNSLEY INDOOR MARKET ❶
1960s/IBI Group, 2016–19
Brutalist, International Style

Barnsley had the misfortune of being designated an 'Italian Hill Town' in a

The impressive Beeversleigh Flats, an elegant council high-rise on a quiet street in Rotherham.

The complex arrangement of offices, car parking and concrete structure at Barnsley's Metropolitan Centre.

whimsical plan by the architect Will Alsop at the height of the New Labour years; the main upshot of this has been a series of poor buildings in imitations of Alsop's style, such as Interchange Station, which are sometimes interestingly planned but incessantly tacky and shrill. This plan was then abandoned, and IBI Group architects proposed instead building around the Arndale-style Metropolitan Centre, a complex 1960s comprehensive scheme including council offices, a multistorey car park and the Indoor Markets. At the time of writing around half of this has been demolished, with crisp, modern-classical new market buildings gradually taking their place, which are much more disciplined and coherent than the baubles that were built here a decade ago. The car park and the covered market hall have a certain post-punk Northern municipal grimness, right down to the modernist clock tower; the rough way it has been treated,

incrementally slicing bits off and piecing new parts together, works rather well, as a sort of montage architecture. But the eventual plan is to replace the Metropolitan Centre completely, which will lose some of that sense of contrast; but at least the new buildings are good.

―――

MAGNA SCIENCE ADVENTURE CENTRE, ROTHERHAM
1955/Wilkinson Eyre, 1999
High-Tech

Built as the Steel, Peech and Tozer steelworks, Magna is an adaptive reuse project making a dramatic industrial theme park out of this huge factory at the point where Sheffield and Rotherham meet (it is just on the Rotherham side of the invisible line). It's the modernist, heavy-industry equivalent of all those Victorian industrial museums you can find across the North, and accordingly is a much less sentimental proposition than those olde worlde efforts – a big shed, where you can get a sense of the scale and Miltonian pandaemonium of steelwork without having to do any of the actual work. And here, Wilkinson Eyre, so ill-suited to the museums it has done attached to classical buildings (such as the awful SeaCity in Southampton), is in its element, stripping back parts of the original building's frame to reveal its spindly High-Tech construction, creating ravey lighting effects inside and otherwise leaving these harsh, futuristic forms well alone. It is also one of the few places you can take a six-year-old to on a weekend day out and, given it is periodically used by Warp Records for raves, go dancing until six on a Sunday morning.

LEEDS

CHURCH OF THE EPIPHANY, GIPTON ⊙
N. F. Cachemaille-Day, 1936–8
ST NICHOLAS'S CHURCH, GIPTON
David and Patricia Brown, 1965
Expressionist

Leeds was a centre for large-scale planning in the interwar years, much more than Sheffield, an order that was reversed from the fifties on. Today this is hard to spot, given that one of the grand plans, the high-density Red Vienna-style Quarry Hill Estate, was demolished at the end of the seventies and replaced with a lumpen Postmodernist office block. The suburban side of thirties Leeds's socialist plans still survives at Gipton, a very low-density cottage estate with broad green parkways and Beaux Arts layouts that are mainly only noticeable to pilots. At the centre of it is this incredible church from the most interesting religious architect of interwar Britain. A militaristic assemblage of intersecting drums, held up in the interior by tubular concrete columns, it is dressed in a smoother version of the red brick of the council semis around, and has no spire or ambition to be a 'City Crown'. It's brooding, almost crouched. It's usually locked, so you should email or telephone the church first, or of course attend a service. Rather than feeling like the heart of the community, it feels embattled, with plastic strips to guard the stained glass. It just sits there and burns away, a lurking monument of startling introverted intensity.

For a relief from this ominous rumble, the jolly sixties Catholic church nearby (architects Patricia and David Brown, who designed several across the North) takes a more populist approach to modernism, all fun concrete arches and abstract patterns, but naturally lacks its thuggish power. [D.2 & D.3]

LEEDS CITY STATION CONCOURSE
W. H. Hamlyn, 1938
Moderne

Underneath the P. G. Wodehouse-visits-Stalinist-Moscow opulence of the Queen's Hotel, a giant lump which screws up the tortuous circulation of Leeds's railway station, is this nice concession to the public. Built as part of the first of the station's many rebuildings in the late 1930s, it's a lofty, grand concrete hangar, dressed in icing sugar render and black marble pilasters, with elegant, low-hanging deco lamp standards, well restored recently by Carey Jones. Its contrast with the nastiness of the rest of the station, with horrible work from both the 1960s and 2000s, is striking – if only it had served as a model.

―――

LEEDS INNER RING ROAD, WOODHOUSE LANE SECTION
1964–9
Brutalist

Leeds's touching and wholly fulfilled ambition to become 'Motorway City of the Seventies' has had pretty deleterious effects on its urban coherence, with huge and complex roads severing the tightly packed centre from the inner-city districts, and with no serious public-transport investment to alleviate it. However, it has given us this Piranesian piece of hardcore post-war townscape. As at Glasgow, a lot of dramatic engineering has gone into ensuring that the connection with the university in the west of the city is maintained, whereas everywhere else is cut up into fragments through sprawling dual carriageways. The result is this sunken concrete cutting between Leeds Infirmary, with its power station-like chimneys, and Woodhouse Lane car park, which stands as a fragment of a futurist city, in a city with a Victorian or neo-Victorian heart. It is hugely exciting to walk across the pedestrian upper level, and hopefully when this terrible planning mistake is rectified, some of it will be retained for its sheer spatial melodrama.

UNIVERSITY OF LEEDS SOUTH CAMPUS ⊙
Chamberlin Powell & Bon, 1967–70
Brutalist

After the **Barbican (p. 66)**, this is the most comprehensive scheme by one of the most consistently brilliant and scrupulous firms of the post-war era. Forming a complete pedestrianized campus at a visual and spatial remove from the pompous deco and bumptious Pomo that otherwise defines the university, it is best known and most photographed for its upper-level circulation

in a long series of Constructivist concrete and glass bridges. These are every bit as exciting as those in **Park Hill (p. 370)**, and much better detailed. Most of the teaching blocks are in long, clear four-storey rows, with lots of glass and a complex roof line of exposed services. In between is an asphalt square (somewhat lamely prettified in the nineties) – and a pool, with parades of steps nodding towards a certain classicism. The result is a fascinating labyrinth which you could happily explore for hours, every turn revealing a different view, the geometries shaking themselves into different alignments, with contrasting views into the other buildings and across the city.

At the centre is the extraordinary Roger Stevens Building, a richly sculptural lecture theatre, a tricksy and vigorously articulated mesh of exposed concrete pipes and a Corbusian staircase. It is one of the very few lecture theatres of its day not to borrow (via the **Engineering Building, p. 348**, at

The thrilling multilevel megastructure of the Roger Stevens Building at the University of Leeds.

the University of Leicester) from Konstantin Melnikov's Workers' Clubs in 1920s Moscow, instead creating an original and incredibly dramatic design all of its own. It is not complete – the miniature brick-and-concrete high-rise estate that formed the university's original halls of residence was demolished a decade ago, which is fairly outrageous given the shocking quality – and quantity – of Leeds's recent student housing blocks. But the bulk of the complex remains as it was built. In its spacious internal organization and its approach through a bridge over a pond, it anticipates many features of the Barbican itself. However, this is no sort of a first draft, but a project of such integrity and power that even the know-nothing painting of its high-quality concrete in estate agent magnolia can't seriously damage it. [B.32]

The Bank of England in Leeds, designed as a gleaming inverted ziggurat by Building Design Partnership.

BANK OF ENGLAND ⊙
Building Design Partnership, 1969–71
Brutalist

A Brutalist branch of the Bank of England, located in the high-density, high-tension Ruskinian Gothic world of business Leeds. In the 'upturned ziggurat' genre initiated a few years earlier by Boston City Hall in the US, but in a nod to the wealth inside and the opulent craft of the Victorian blocks around, béton brut is limited only to a cantilevered canopy, intended to be part of a walkway system like the **Pedways (p. 60)** in the City of London and the **Newcastle City Centre Walkway System (p. 483)**. Most of the facade is made up of lush, polished-granite modules, which project outwards, creating a cellular effect not dissimilar to that of a nineteenth-century warehouse, but there's no interest here in being 'in keeping' – placed on a corner, this is both a continuation of the street and a clearly differentiated monument. It's part of a group of Building Design Partnership buildings of the late sixties and early seventies, including

Preston Bus Station (p. 444) and the **Halifax Headquarters (p. 388)**, of extraordinary sculptural quality and urban interest, all of them completely different in form and materials. The BDP office at that time must have been a fantastic place to work.

CANDLE HOUSE & GRANARY WHARF
Carey Jones and John Thorp for Leeds City Architects Dept, 2005–9
Classical Modernism

Puzzlingly, given the paucity of its public space and the often extremely poor quality of its modern architecture, Leeds had a City Architect in the 1990s and 2000s, John Thorp. Just before he retired, he was finally given free rein to design an integral miniature district of the city, and Granary Wharf was the result, part of the canal and riverside lands behind the back of Leeds Station. As in London, the idea of how to make things coherent and civic has been to use a lot of brick cladding. This felt refreshing in 2009, but now feels rather like an austerity straitjacket. Yet these are fine, robust buildings – albeit yet more hotels, luxury flats – firm, well composed and with a reddish-brown brick that corresponds nicely with that of the derelict Italianate factories nearby. One part of it is more than just 'quite good' – the high-rise of Candle House, a fine cylindrical tower, every floor of which has been slightly twisted away from the other, like the architects were turning the world's most sensible kaleidoscope. Highly unusually, it looks superb both up close and from a distance. Contrast it with the shoddy mess of the earlier Clarence Dock, a more compromised project by the same architect/planner team, and you'll see how good it is.

———

BROADCASTING PLACE, LEEDS BECKETT UNIVERSITY
Feilden Clegg Bradley Studios, 2008–9
Supermodernist

One of Feilden Clegg Bradley's occasional and usually welcome shifts out of sensible modernism and into something more sculptural, this consists of an arts faculty and a student housing tower for the other Leeds university, both functions cranked into what appears to be an inhabited Richard Serra sculpture, an angular and angry chunk of rusty red Corten steel. And where many other recent towers – in Leeds, especially – seem like computer-generated 3D patterns more than real buildings, this one has a civic presence on the ground, with the tall tower and the lower teaching blocks in the same rough idiom, framing a convincing pedestrian square. A good combination of the harshly eccentric and the humanistically civic. The puzzling name comes from the BBC Studios that previously occupied the site.

LILAC, BRAMLEY ✪
White Design, 2013
Ecomodernist

The single most interesting eco-housing scheme in Britain, and the most convincing experiment in co-operative ownership for several decades. The acronym stands for 'Low Impact Living Affordable Community', and it consists of a communally owned estate of two-storey blocks of flats, built out of zero-carbon materials – packed straw bales in a timber frame. Solar panels heat the water and a little common-room-cum-tea-room-cum-community-centre is attached.

All very nice. But what makes it different is the size of the project – it is on the scale of a small council estate, its deep-balconied flats around an attractively overgrown green square (open to the public) with a pond in the middle and allotments round the back. This is a far more urban and extroverted proposition than the eco norm. The modular design, meanwhile (aside from the already rather dated gestural roof at the common room), avoids the embarrassing techno-hippy aesthetics so common in the genre for a simple modernist grid, with a frame construction that recalls the fifties early Brutalism of a Lyons Israel Ellis, right down to the L-shaped windows. Because it never feels exclusive or haughty, it lacks that irritating sense of being an enclave, somewhere where those in the know get to live decently (although of course, that's what it is). Instead, it's a logical and serious proposal for housing which could, and should, be rolled out everywhere; not lifestyle smugness, but a better kind of ordinary. This feeling also comes out of the very unpretentious area it's placed in, a scruffy lower-middle-class Leeds suburb with a rudimentary bus service. Most importantly of all, it's just lovely – a fine piece of sweetly convincing propaganda for the communards' ideals. If we're lucky, this is the future.

WEST YORKSHIRE

CO-OPERATIVE EMPORIUM, BRADFORD ✪ ❶
W. A. Johnson and J. W. Cropper, 1935–6
CO-OPERATIVE DEPARTMENT STORE, HUDDERSFIELD ✪ ❶
W. A. Johnson and J. W. Cropper, 1936–7
Moderne

These two excellent urban buildings, both built by the Co-operative movement, make clear something distinctive about what happened to modern architecture when it reached the textile towns and cities of the West Riding – that, for all the demolition and clearance that went with it (especially in Bradford), the new was assimilated to the old in a remarkably relaxed way. Usually faced in the same warm brown sandstone as the Victorian and Edwardian classical, baroque and Gothic department stores, office blocks and warehouses that define their city centres, they merely shift emphasis – flat roofs rather than spiky skylines, horizontality rather than verticality, a sense of freshness rather than the familiarity of tradition – within a common polyphonic collective composition. This pair both draw on the same source – Erich Mendelsohn's department stores in Weimar Germany – and insert them into the mill town cityscape to the point where they're seamlessly part of their fabric.

The slightly earlier is the store in Bradford, better known locally as Sunwin House, which is closer to the German template in its ribbon windows and the two strongly modelled, cylindrical steel glass turrets that mark the two corners of the sprawling, uneven chunk of the city it sits in. It's currently derelict, and the windows are blocked up, but the quality

Huddersfield's art deco former Co-op, one of many excellent Co-operative department stores in West Yorkshire.

The commercial corruption of modern architecture usually known as 'moderne' or 'art deco', with its vanilla ice cream curves and sunburst motifs, was always best suited to the seaside, as at the **Villa Marina** [C.1] in Llandudno, built by the Odeon cinema chain's chief architect, or Margate's **Dreamland Cinema** [C.2].

Moderne architects borrowed forms from continental 'high' modernism – the curves of Erich Mendelsohn, the brickwork of German and Dutch Expressionism – and made an architecture of surfaces, as seen in the former **Athena Cinema** [C.3] in Leicester. After the war, the super-cinemas were superseded by television, but

C.6

the colourful modernist vernacular was continued in Italian cafés, such as Swansea's **Kardomah Café** [C.4]. This play of decoration and space was nowhere more important than at **Bevin Court** [C.5 & C.6] in London, where a simple Y-shaped plan conceals the most remarkable staircase in twentieth-century Britain.

Local traditions often inspired architects who attempted to Anglicize modernism and introduce elements of decoration and pattern-making. Frederick Gibberd's terraces at **Mark Hall** [C.8] in Harlow New Town, with their warm wood and brick, look like they could have been there for centuries; the same could almost be said

COLERIDGE COURT

of Tayler & Green's flats at St Leonards Place and **Ladbrooke Place** [C.7] in Norwich. The most successful modern decorator was Eric Lyons, whose 'Span developments', such as **Parkleys** [C.9] in Ham, south-west London, combined weatherboarding, tiles and patterned screens with a modernist sense of abstract space.

The Byker Wall is the largest part of the **Byker Estate** in Newcastle, which was built incrementally to the design of Ralph Erskine from 1969–81 and represents a thwarted revolution in housing, where socialist planning and public participation might have been reconciled. An area of Victorian flats was gradually cleared, with residents given a say in how the design would unfold as it continued. The 'wall' was the architects' idea, though – an irregular, snaking block with painted balconies and walkways to protect the estate's houses from traffic fumes and noise. The result is one of the great roads not travelled – an Anglo-Scandinavia on the Tyne.

C.11

C.12

The great north-eastern metropolis of Newcastle is full of sudden changes in scale and powerful, heavy architecture with a rare richness and grandeur being smashed up by gigantic infrastructure. At the art deco **New Tyne Bridge** [C.11], designed by Mott Hay & Anderson and built from 1925–8, the steel viaduct literally leaps over the rooftops; L.G. Ekins' **Co-operative Department Store** [C.12] is a mini-Manhattan of vitrolite and sandstone; George Kenyon's **Newcastle Civic Centre** [C.13] combines a comprehensive programme of modern art with a lantern-like spire designed to harmonize with the city's medieval cathedral.

The planning principles of modern architecture have shifted over the years, but these all show alternatives to the existing city that aim at being quiet and humane rather than bombastic and aggressive. Britain's first true tower block, **The Lawn** [C.14] in Harlow, owes its irregular profile to a plan giving each flat a view, and

preserves as many trees as possible. The tabula rasa of the **Cranbrook Estate** [C.15] in Bow, East London, uses techniques from the Baroque to give a sense of both epic scale and decorative intimacy. In Pimlico, the materials and proportions of **Lillington Gardens** [C.16] follow those of the adjacent Victorian Gothic church.

The architectural draughtsman Gordon Cullen was an exponent, with his *Architectural Review* colleague Ian Nairn, of 'Townscape' – that is, the sensitive juxtaposition of picturesque old buildings with new ones, favouring the eccentric over the futuristic. In his 1958 **Lower Precinct Mural** in reconstructed Coventry,

Cullen showcased the results in one city, a patchwork of new modernist buildings – patterned high-rise flats, new precincts, and of course Basil Spence's Cathedral – that aimed to have every bit as much character and charm as the historic buildings which had been destroyed in the Blitz of 1940.

While Brutalist or International Style architects used landscaping to create epic, imposing compositions of monumental forms in abstract space, the more populist modernists who emerged after the Festival of Britain took an intentionally picturesque, paradoxical approach. Forms could be deliberately humorous and

surreal, as with the volumes projecting out over Devon hills in the University of Exeter's **Laver Building** [C.18].
The most creative landscape architect in this trend was G. P. Youngman, whose pathways, underpasses and
bridges in **Cumbernauld** [C.19 & C.20] were clever, surprising, and often distinctly odd.

Postmodernism can be traced back to the post-Festival of Britain architecture of designers like Tayler & Green or Basil Spence. The latter's **Cathedral Church of St Michael & All Angels [C.24]** in Coventry is almost Postmodern, but stops short of it through its burning, moving earnestness. One Postmodernist firm that managed to avoid

the flimsy, patronising limits of this 1980s style was Alan Short Associates, in works like the **Queen's Building** [C.22] at De Montfort University in Leicester, or the **Lanchester Library** [C.21] at the University of Coventry. A similar mix of heft and pop art picturesque can be found at the **Millennium Centre** [C.23] in Cardiff.

Modernism came out of the same rationalist, Enlightenment circles as atheistic twentieth-century movements like psychoanalysis and Soviet Communism, so it unsurprisingly took some time for pure modern architects to design a convincing church. The best examples either burrow into an Expressionist brick intensity or favour joyous kitsch, all pulsating stained glass and wildly ambitious concrete superstructures. Stevenage's **St Andrew & St George Parish Church** [C.26] does this impressively – but a true one-off is **St John the Baptist** [C.25] in Lincoln's Ermine Estate, a fusion of American roadside engineering and Abstract Expressionism.

Liverpool's **Metropolitan Cathedral**, a utopian techno-spiritual space suffused with light artificial and real, was built over the crypt of an unfinished Baroque megastructure. Frederick Gibberd's design rejects any obvious tributes to Liverpool's abundant monumental architecture, but complements it in an ingenious way.

of the building is obvious. Also derelict is
the smaller Huddersfield Co-op, which has
similar ribbon windows and sandstone
(with demolitions around it revealing the
red-brick warehouse backside), and with
the glazed stairwell replaced with a more
classical, heavy tower with vertical windows,
a little like the Americanist style of the
Co-operative Department Store (p. 479)
in Newcastle. Best of all is the corner on the
street side, at the point where it neighbours
the cornucopia of Victorian commerce all
around. Here there is a dynamic modernist
composition of cubistically detailed
stairwells and the starkly carved sandstone
Neue Typographie of the Co-operative logo.
For no logical reason, it is not listed, unlike
the Bradford Co-op, and there are currently
proposals for several storeys of banal
student flats to be piled on top. The
Co-operative's neglect of its architectural
legacy is not the greatest of its problems,
but it's a depressing one nonetheless.

HUDDERSFIELD LIBRARY & ART GALLERY
E. H. Ashburner, 1937–40
Moderne, Modern Classicism

With its strange fascist/Assyrian figures
by James Woodford facing the bustling
markets of Huddersfield, this is an unusual
mixture of the imposing and the ordinary.
It is in a very severely stripped classical
manner, with everything reduced into a
massive symmetrical plinth, grand stairways
downwards to the markets, and a lofty
if badly treated interior, with a first-rate
art collection, much of which is in storage
because Kirklees Council can't afford to
insure it. A little like the Co-ops, what makes
the building successful is the way that a new
(here, new-ish) style and spatial approach
is assimilated into the scale and sandstone
of the city; here, evidently, people believed
they could be modern and local at once.

SUGDEN'S MILL SILOS, BRIGHOUSE
1959–63
Brutalist

Grain silos – vast, silent, minatory – are of
major importance in the history of modern
architecture as one of the major inspirations
for Le Corbusier and Walter Gropius.
Here, you can see their engineers adapting
their design to modernism's ideas about
abstraction and monumentality. The edges
of the two bunches of linked, tall silos have
been filed to jagged points, their repetition
turned into an optical effect, presumably
to give some visual interest to by far the
tallest buildings in Brighouse. They've been
recently painted, and turned into a suitably
forbidding climbing wall.

MARKET & CLOCK TOWER, SHIPLEY ✪
1961
People's Detailing

A very pretty Festival of Britain structure
in this small mill town in the City of Bradford,
with the sort of gaiety and pleasure in
detail cuteness that is so commonly found
in Coventry, but rarer in the hard townscapes
of West Yorks. An elegant clock tower,
a black-tile-clad concrete market hall with
lots of mosaic fun inside, and at the top
of the tower a little ceramic man who comes
out to ring the bell. There are various routes
into the market, but the most enjoyable is
to enter through the base of the clock tower
itself, where a cubic glass passageway,
treated like a Mondrian grid, has inset into
it a stairwell to the market below. Sometimes
modern architecture was about innocent
joy, and that's what differentiates it from the
ponderous Victoriana that dominated towns
like Shipley. You could, the last time I went
there, buy badges with the Jeremy Corbyn
slogan 'FOR THE MANY NOT THE FEW' in

The Festival of Britain reaches Shipley: the patterned clock tower and canopies of the town's market.

a ring around the clock tower. The market was opened by Bruce Forsyth.

MONTE CARLO CAFÉ, HALIFAX
1960s
People's Detailing

In the Victorian Valhalla that is central Halifax, there are a few untouched bits of modernist signage, particularly in the markets and arcades, and there's this one very pop-sixties caff interior. Pink leatherette booths, brown Formica tables, and purple archways subdivide these small rooms, in a permanent fug of steam from fry-ups and hot cups of tea. A neon sign outside gives the café's aspirational name and a hint of the glamour inside.

HALIFAX SWIMMING POOL ❶
F. H. Hoyles for Halifax Borough Architects Dept, 1964–6
People's Detailing

Surrounded on three sides by Halifax's spectacular townscape – classical terraces that would sell for a million apiece in Bath or Oxford, hills beyond, and the astonishing neo-Constructivist **Halifax Headquarters (p. 388)** in the near distance – this is by comparison a modest, self-effacing modernist public building, on a sloping site. Its rectilinear volumes, broken up into distinct circulation spaces around glazed swimming pools, are nicely detailed with the local sandstone, but the main event is inside. Within the swimming pool itself are two remarkable ceramic murals representing *English Pond Life* by the artist Kenneth Barden, who also designed the tower block gable-end murals at **Trinity Green (p. 246)** in Gosport. These murals are brighter and more organic, a gorgeous semi-abstract assemblage of plants and crustaceans, in vivid pastel blues, greens and reds. The swimming pool is slated for replacement, and, bafflingly, a recent application for listing was refused – the murals in particular are in the first rank of the period, but they would make no sense if they were torn out of the building, as is currently proposed.

BUXTON HOUSE, HUDDERSFIELD
Bernard Engle & Partners, 1965–8
RAMSDEN HOUSE, HUDDERSFIELD
1960s
Brutalist, International Style

Huddersfield was quite the city of culture in the sixties, judging by the art collection it amassed, and the way that reliefs and murals were integrated into its new buildings throughout that decade. This resulted not only in the concrete reliefs that are on the low-lying shopping centre that takes up too much of the town centre, but also these two interesting integrations of art and architecture. Buxton House is a vigorously modelled high-rise, brown-brick infill and concrete with an almost castellated silhouette, reached through the very sixties (still, in terms of signage) arcade of Buxton Way; at the end of which, a gorgeous abstract mosaic mural of flying triangles, overlapping each other with a dynamism that recalls the more famous art/architecture work of Victor Pasmore; it works as a sort of oblique entrance to the tower. Ramsden House meanwhile is a more basic glass tower on a podium, with a shopping arcade set below it. So above Betfred and Max Spielman Portraits is a glittering continuous mosaic by Richard Fletcher, in very bright primary colours, showing the workers of Huddersfield (gender-balanced!) and their labours, in a modernized, slightly cartoonish version of Socialist Realism – you can imagine it in a post-'56 town centre in an industrialized part of Eastern Europe. Katowice comes to Huddersfield, something which must amuse some of the Polish migrants to the town.

INTERNATIONAL WOOL SECRETARIAT, ILKLEY
Richard Collick and William Mitchell (artist), 1968
Brutalist

The International Wool Secretariat – designer of the surely iconic wool logo on every label, among other things – had its headquarters in the poshest part of the Greater Bradford Worstedopolis. It's in a dull suburban street, where the big houses are just at the foot of the Expressionistic crags of Ilkley Moor, and it's hidden from these by a high hedge. British business, with its usual confidence in urbanism. The building, when you find it, is straightforward sixties modernism,

Heaps of sheeps: William Mitchell's relief sculpture over the entrance to the International Wool Secretariat, Ilkley.

an emphasized concrete grid, currently painted, but the action is all in the lecture theatre, a massive bronze volume decorated with rams, sheep, abstractions. This relief is called *The Story of Wool*; it's not immediately obvious, but it's actually narrative-based, with series of horned beasts at the concave front, and at the flat sides the production of wool and what the Historic England website calls 'the scientific analysis of wool', which is a cue for Mitchell's vital, original, lurid Mesoamerican version of Abstract Expressionism to go wild. All this, and in bronze-faced glass-reinforced plastic.

Mitchell's relief is listed, but the building around it isn't, being apparently 'not of special interest'. If you want to see the results of assuming that public artworks are some sort of gallery exercise, which could happily be moved anywhere, go to the main building of the University of Bradford down the road, and see another strange and beautiful relief on a lecture theatre ruined by the ugliest blue cladding imaginable.

The imposing grandeur of the Halifax Headquarters, with offices cantilevered over a Constructivist sculpture.

HALIFAX HEADQUARTERS, HALIFAX ✪

Building Design Partnership, 1968–74
Brutalist

If the embrace of place means something more than a craven form of aesthetic cowardice, then the Halifax HQ is one of the most magnificent pieces of contextual architecture in the country. An enormous dark-glass volume suspended on a concrete plinth, angled towards the town centre, taking up several city-blocks, it is extremely ambitious and shudderingly powerful – a power which is much more passion than aggression. The ingenuity with which it angles and twists its vast bulk into the hilly former mill town and the way its blacks and browns mirror and spark off the blackened ashlar of the Victorian commercial architecture nearby are all about embracing and enhancing the place where it has been placed, without the slightest bit of arse-kissing. It feels, at least to a visitor, not so much a building that is in Halifax as a building that *is* Halifax. The way the town is crammed into a gorge in the middle of the Pennines, the nature-defying scale and melodrama of the Dean Clough Mills, the Piece Hall or Charles Barry's Town Hall; all of these are taken up and extended without being merely cloned.

Comparing this building with, say, the Alsopification of Barnsley, what is unusual in Halifax's HQ is that it represented a large investment in the town, yet resisted the common notion that the worst thing a post-industrial town could be is itself. Better this than an 'Italian hill town' of trivial Teletubby baubles — though the brightly coloured plastic automated machinery inside the Halifax building could surely satisfy even the most bumptious of 1990s architects.

If these evidently down-to-earth architects had only read and quoted some continental theory, it could have been included as part of Kenneth Frampton's 'critical regionalism', refusing at once kitsch, retro and placelessness. As architecture, the Halifax HQ is still a magnificent model of local modernism. But what of its function? It was listed abruptly because of the instability of its owner, a mutual that has transformed itself into a part-nationalized gambler in derivatives. The excellent Bradford and Bingley headquarters in Bingley, a terrific Lasdun-esque complex by John Brunton, wasn't listed, and was demolished. However remarkable and local their architecture, the buildings of the mutuals and co-ops all over the North are very much a remnant of the past, not an enduring tradition. Hopefully a new generation of co-operators could learn something from the Halifax building's pride and power. [B.23]

EMLEY MOOR TELECOMMUNICATIONS TOWER ✪
Ove Arup & Partners, 1969–71
Brutalist

The only serious TV tower in Britain to even approach the grandeur of those placed in practically every city in Central Europe, the Soviet Union and North America. Rather than being in an urban centre, it tellingly stands in moorland near Wakefield, which in turn is the city that gives the best views of the tower in the distance. However, it is worth trying to go closer – this is superb engineering work that, unlike most of its kind in the UK (Liverpool's goofy **St John's Beacon, p. 429**, Birmingham's cheap BT Tower), is also superb architecture, a smooth and sensually curved concrete spike, with a control post near the top that really ought to have a revolving restaurant on it, but doesn't.

West Yorkshire's modernist beacon, the Emley Moor Telecommunications Tower, on its rural site near Wakefield.

HIGH POINT, BRADFORD ❶
John Brunton & Partners, 1970
Brutalist

Hardcore. This headquarters for the Yorkshire Building Society is a sort of giant concrete Gundam helmet on top of a hill in the half-derelict, recession-battered centre of Bradford – a staggeringly daring building, even for its time. Strips of red windows in a sandstone-aggregate mass, modelled into something between medieval fortress and supercomputer, this is an unbelievable work, that has obviously come from somewhere deeper and more primal than most architecture of any era, the 1960s included. When things get dark in Bradford, they are very dark indeed, and this piece of machine-Gothic is a sort of Edinburgh Castle of commercial Brutalism. Once almost certain to be demolished, there is now, hearteningly if implausibly, a movement to conserve it.

QUEENSGATE MARKET, HUDDERSFIELD ❷
Seymour Harris Partnership, 1970
Brutalist

The demolition of Sheffield's Castle Market makes this place the finest British market building of the twentieth century. Huddersfield already has a very good covered Victorian market, so it gets to have the best of both worlds. The Queensgate Market is sunk into a sloping site in front of the City Art Gallery, and access is a little oblique: but once you're inside, you realize just how extraordinary and odd a place you're in – the inspirations all seem Latin American or Polish rather than English or French, a series of massive, swelling concrete supports, fanning out into cave-like triangular pillars, arranged in a peculiar order so that the strips of window let in light constantly, although never quite in the places you expect them to. Spatially, it's incredibly

The ribbed concrete and blunt forms of the diamond-hard High Point office block in central Bradford.

dramatic, but because all of the oddness is going on well above the eye level, it never distracts or detracts from the stalls. Exit at the end furthest away from the concert hall, and you can see how the complex meets the streets around: steps lead you down to a sort of stone city wall, dressed to the street by a series of Mesoamerican reliefs by Fritz Steller. Flamboyant and spatially extravagant, yet totally suited to its purpose, it's extraordinary that this building could ever have been controversial – it's an absolute joy to use. Yet, like the **Halifax Headquarters (p. 388)**, it had to be listed to avert threatened demolition, and the shoddy new signage suggests that its owners still have little idea of what an amazing thing they have here. Self-hatred runs deep round these parts. **[B.20]**

BURDOCK WAY, HALIFAX ✪
1970–73
Brutalist

A rash and thrilling mix of the extreme and the contextual, similar to that at the **Halifax Headquarters (p. 388)**, this thing is a bypass on two motorway viaducts suspended high above the city, in order to surmount its sudden drops of level. It crosses vertiginously over the ornate Victorian North Bridge below, with the gruff 'functional tradition' slabs of the Dean Clough mills adjacent (intelligently refurbished as a mix of offices, studios, arts venues and small businesses, and worth visiting in their own right). As thrilling to walk under as to drive over, you can approach it via some of the atmospheric snickets once photographed by Bill Brandt, where it appears as an irruption of totally confident modernity into the industrial townscape. Both futuristic and very Yorkshire, without feeling the need to clad anything or paint it pink. **[B.1]**

KIRKGATE CENTRE, BRADFORD
John Brunton & Partners, 1974
Brutalist

Hated for replacing enormous chunks of the Victorian city, from this distance in time the Kirkgate Shopping Centre feels much less disruptive of Bradford than the dull Portland stone of the civic complex around the library and its attendant dual carriageway. This is totally of its place, rammed into dense streets, with local sandstone in the concrete aggregate, and the chunky forms in concrete and black glass close in mass as well as palette to the moderne, baroque and Gothic of the city. Far too big, of course, but the identity of Bradford is strengthened, not weakened, by this beast. The cafés in the market on the basement level, with its concrete reliefs and old seventies signage, are excellent.

WAKEFIELD MARKET ❶
Adjaye Associates, 2008
Supermodernist

This spindly market hall is a surprisingly unpretentious building from a fashionable London architect called upon to 'regenerate' the least architecturally interesting of the West Riding cities. The brick facades to the market's service areas have a little of the bluff warehouse-chic of Adjaye's Dirty House in Shoreditch, but the bulk of it is a great open hall, more like a Victorian market than the more modernist examples such as Huddersfield's **Queensgate Market (p. 390)**. Simple, airy and meeting the street with an open gesture of tall black-steel columns, meaning that it always feels permeable, even when the market has closed for the day. Budget cuts have made Wakefield Council look at closing it, but if austerity allows it to survive, this is a sensible and enjoyable building that should become an inextricable part of Wakefield.

HEPWORTH GALLERY, WAKEFIELD ✪

David Chipperfield Architects, 2009
Brutalist, Classical Modernist

A brave location for the city's main effort in culture-driven urban regeneration, and equally a brave choice of building, as this is nobody's idea of a flashy icon. The surroundings are derelict mills, some in brick, some covered in corrugated iron, in a canalside landscape which has gone overgrown, creating a gently Tarkovsky-esque feeling of nature overtaking urbanism, although there are banal distribution sheds, light industry and bleakly looping roads around to dispel the illusion. Chipperfield's response to this was a design that draws on that slightly eerie, slightly abandoned post-industrial atmosphere rather than shifting it all into the Blairily grinning world of regeneration. Discrete concrete gallery spaces are treated as independent volumes, like a cluster of tiny Brutalist towers, and look especially imposing and enigmatic when reached from the bridge over the sluice that cuts this industrial enclave off from the city centre. Straight on, it's all concrete and hard lines; but other views display it sheltered by willow trees. As time goes on, it's likely that the concrete, too, will start to go green and mildewed, and rather than being a sign of failure, that roughed-up, organic modernism will be highly appropriate, both to the site and to the work of the Wakefield-born sculptor who the building is named after. As it is now, a decade on, it's still relatively shiny and smooth, which is a tribute to the project, especially in an era of ubiquitous shoddiness.

The stark landscape of David Chipperfield's Hepworth Gallery, in a canalside post-industrial corner of Wakefield.

YORK & ENVIRONS

ODEON CINEMA, HARROGATE ✪
Harry Weedon, 1936
Moderne

This is the best preserved 1930s Odeon in the country, just at the edge of the centre of the attractive Victorian spa town. The usual stuff – a Mendelsohn-influenced assemblage of prows and towers, dressed in cutely period tiles and mean brickwork – but here you can see that generic type almost untouched, right down to the lush foyers and the very chic neon 'CINEMA' sign at the top of its Al-Bowlly-meets-El-Lissitzky tower. And on top of all that it is actually still an Odeon cinema. Not only is this evidence of how good an extremely common type can look when it's in a town whose self-importance means that everything gets obsessively preserved, it is also the nearest thing you can get to the actual experience of visiting a 1930s modernist cinema, even if it is to see *Avengers 12*.

RADOMES, RAF MENWITH HILL, RADIO CORPORATION OF AMERICA, NEAR HARROGATE
Buckminster Fuller, 1954–8
FYLINGDALES SOLID STATE PHASED ARRAY RADAR, RAYTHEON, NEAR HARROGATE
1989–92
High-Tech

Most of the places in this book can be visited by public transport, but it is worth finding someone who can drive you to this bizarre and disturbing surrealist landscape. Both of these are on the outskirts of Harrogate, where the West bleeds into the North Riding – lovely, bright-green rolling countryside, much more lush than the murky moors around Leeds and Bradford, which you

can pleasantly sail through until oh, what's that there on the horizon? Both of these are essentially American spy bases, and have been run as such since the 1950s; each is tied strongly into the command networks of the nuclear war that we're ready to launch at any moment. They're known for their 'radomes', a design developed by the RCA company from Buckminster Fuller's tensegrity geodesic domes, but only Menwith Hill still has a full set of these giant golf balls, shaken out almost randomly, the single strangest integration of architecture and landscape in England. Nearby Fylingdales demolished most of theirs in the 1980s and replaced them with a giant angular radar station, a giant steel version of the concrete 'acoustic mirrors' you can still find in Dungeness and the **Sound Mirror (p. 466)** at Redcar. It is wrong to admire structures set up to spy on you or to help incinerate you in a civilization-destroying thermonuclear apocalypse, but you go to these (not too close, naturally) and try not to be flabbergasted.

BYRON COURT, HARROGATE
1960s
International Style

I once had the unusual pleasure of judging a 'best modern building in Harrogate' contest, in what is probably the worst large Yorkshire town to have to choose in. I opted, out of an impulse for trolling, for the Conference Centre, a fairly poor, sub-James Stirling mirrorglass and red-brick edifice sheathing a thrilling Frank Lloyd Wright imitation spiral staircase, but you will note that is not in this book. The honest answer, however, would have been this elegant block of parkside luxury flats – a simple, Bauhaus-inflected design in Portland stone and concrete, rational, serene and finely made, the sixties equivalent of an elegant early-Victorian classical villa.

WALMGATE BAR HOUSING, YORK
York City Council Architects Dept, 1960s
People's Detailing

A small close of council flats tucked in behind one of the gates of York's preserved city walls, an attractive enclave of pitched-roofed brick-and-glass blocks, some of them on pilotis, around faintly Georgian-feeling squares, like a miniature **Lansbury Estate (p. 122)**. It is deliberately unspectacular and unfussy, but with its relaxed scale, strong materials and modest proportions, it's a pleasant and humane exemplar of building modern housing in a well-preserved medieval city.

UNIVERSITY OF YORK ✪
RMJM, 1964–7/BDP, 2009–11
Brutalist

In his quasi-Thatcherite cultural history *English Culture and the Decline of the Industrial Spirit*, Martin Weiner points out that the naming of the English 'New Universities' in the 1960s betrayed a rural and medievalist bias – **Sussex (p. 238)**, not Brighton, **East Anglia (p. 198)**, not Norwich, **Essex (p. 190)**, not Colchester, Kent, not Canterbury, **Warwick (p. 328)**, which is actually in Coventry, with the only exceptions being York and **Lancaster (p. 452)**, where presumably these celebrated medieval cities deserved to have the word 'University' alongside their names, although each is in geographical terms as peripheral to its town as the 'county' universities are to theirs. This is questionable, in that, Coventry aside, this is a list of historic or spa towns – the major industrial cities already had their universities, which were founded in the

nineteenth century. Where Weiner may be accidentally on to something is that out of that list (all of which, with the exception of William Holford's mediocre work at Kent, are in this book) York is absolutely the most urban. Whereas East Anglia, Sussex, Essex and Warwick (and Lancaster) are all surreal bucolic-futurist environments, mostly owing little visibly either to colleges or cities of the past, York is a piece of 1960s city, with a very obviously collegiate layout of squares and quadrangles.

The relative 'normality' of the original campus at Heslington West owes much to the decision of its architect – Andrew Derbyshire, one of the great unsung designers in an otherwise anonymous collective, previously the designer of Sheffield's Castle Market, later of **Hillingdon Civic Centre (p. 168)** – to use the CLASP system of modular concrete construction. It was otherwise used for local-authority schools at the time, many of which have since been demolished, but used here the system becomes a series of concrete classrooms and teaching blocks, with oddly Georgian-feeling vertical windows, some of them projecting outwards like abstracted, cubist Regency bays, and delightful portes cochères connecting the various green and asphalt squares. These frame the only monument here of the kind the other New Universities went in for, the lakeside Central Hall, a fabulous piece of Pop Futurism of the sort pioneered by American architects like John Lautner, a display of flamboyant concrete construction, with a hexagonal hall supported on angular, splayed columns and a central support, detailed like a little suspension bridge.

The later additions, all by BDP, are a typically mixed bag. They are unable to rise to the original campus's level of vigour and power, with the usual congeries of cladding, big atria and tacky extraneous gew-gaws, but you can still find some spatial thrills here, such as the flying walkways of the

Patrick Gwynne's delightful Theatre Royal in York, an interpretation of Gothic in concrete and plate glass.

snaking Berrick Saul Building; or in the way the new campus extension at Heslington East frames a lake in a much more informal, woody, Scandinavian manner than the original buildings. What Brutalism's new neighbours always seem to lack in comparison is integrity.

THEATRE ROYAL EXTENSION, YORK ✪

Patrick Gwynne, 1967
Expressionist

The architect Patrick Gwynne was one of the most individual of the first-generation modernists in Britain. He mostly designed hard-to-visit private houses, but this thoroughly accessible public building is also his most eccentric work. It's a delightfully perverse café and booking hall, attached to a Victorian–Ruskinian theatre, which completely goes off in directions that could never plausibly be imagined as In Keeping,

though it is certainly Gothick of a sort. Stalagmite-like concrete columns create a faintly camp modernist crypt, a good possible set for an episode of *The Avengers*, and a twisting spiral staircase in the middle feels fittingly theatrical. Although it uses the constructional and structural ideas common at the time, which you might find in, say, a Peter Moro theatre like **Nottingham Playhouse (p. 352)**, it takes them in a totally different direction, Brutalist Grand Guignol.

9. GREATER MANCHESTER

College Bank Flats, Rochdale (p. 415)

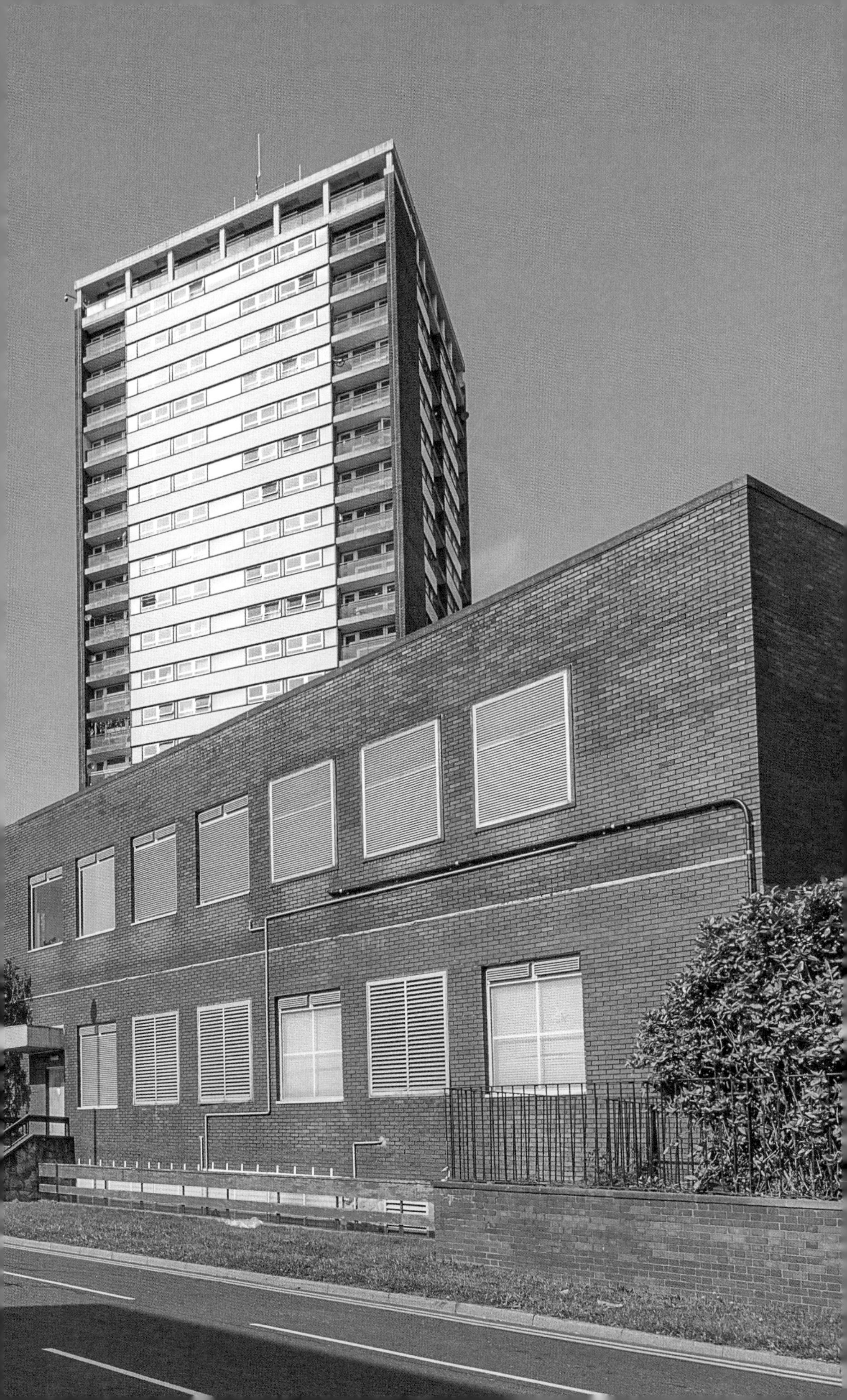

The borders of the city of Manchester are surprisingly tight, but it stands at the centre of the most powerful conurbation in England outside London, with a self-confidence and pride built on its role as the driver of the world's first industrial revolution. It is unexpected, then, that a place which punches so far above its weight in so many other respects lacks the sort of strongly individualistic modern architecture you'll find in such abundance on the other side of the Pennines. However, interwar architecture is strong here, especially in suburban places such as the huge Wythenshawe estate in south Manchester, around the powerful church of **St Michael & All Angels**, Northenden, by the Expressionist N. F. Cachemaille-Day, and in central Manchester too, with the grand **Kendal's Department Store** and the black-glass curves of the **Daily Express Building**; while, later, L. C. Howitt's work as City Architect resulted in fun sixties buildings such as the famous **Hollings Building**. The extensive regeneration architecture of recent years is a mixed bag, but more confident than in Leeds or Birmingham, with gems such as **Chetham's School of Music** in amongst all the barcode facades and the cladding. Meanwhile, subversive traces of the city of post-punk and pop cults can be found at the **Exchange Theatre** or **Homes for Change**.

Outside the City of Manchester, there's a lot of surviving civic Brutalism, particularly in places such as Stockport and Leigh, with its terrific **Turnpike Centre**; meanwhile, as befits places where 'civic pride' has often been a rallying cry, there are strong modernist town halls in Oldham, Wigan and Salford. The appalling housing left by the Victorians was redressed through grandly scaled city centre housing schemes, of which the best survival by far is the **College Bank Flats**, a complete skyline right in the heart of Rochdale. The Metrolink tram/ light-rail system makes Greater Manchester a relatively easy place to get around, though, as with so much here, development and design quality do not go together as much as they should.

CITY OF MANCHESTER

LEE HOUSE
Harry S. Fairhurst, 1928–31
Moderne, Chicago School

The last of the great textile warehouses in
Manchester, and the only one where modern
methods of construction are expressed
on the facade rather than hidden behind
a grandiose imperial frontage. Moreover,
Lee House is the eight-storey base of
a never-constructed seventeen-storey
skyscraper, cancelled when the
Great Depression hit mid-way through
construction. Harry S Fairhurst was the
architect behind the superb canyon of tall,
steel-framed Edwardian warehouses on
Whitworth Street, such as India House,
Bridgewater House and Lancaster House –
but the word 'warehouse' shouldn't imply
that they were merely used for storage.
These were showrooms, grand, palatial
buildings at the front, where the wares
of Cottonopolis could be displayed in
comfortable, luxurious settings, with High-
Tech steel or concrete framed blocks at
the back for storing, loading and unloading.
Here, Fairhurst abandoned the baroque
frontage/functionalist backside dichotomy
for a more repetitive, Americanist aesthetic
of huge bay windows in a modular grid,
between very faintly Expressionistic brick
mullions, with a white stucco base. The
building is very obviously unfinished –
after the eighth storey it is just suddenly
truncated, with a bit of art deco folderol
to hide the fact. The main facade and
the rhythm of the windows are impressive
by themselves, however, especially when
framed by the Bridgewater Canal. An end
of the warehouse tradition in Manchester,
for sure, but also the start of an honest
modern architecture in the city.

ST MICHAEL & ALL ANGELS, NORTHENDEN, WYTHENSHAWE ✪
N. F. Cachemaille-Day, 1935–7
Expressionist

The same story as Eltham's **St Saviour's
Church (p. 80)** and Gipton's **Church of the
Epiphany (p. 380)** – a modernist church of
burning intensity amidst low-rise, low-density
interwar cottage council housing. While
those two churches resemble each other,
St Michael, Northenden is quite distinct,
with a star-shaped plan unique for its time,
and a richer, redder texture of brick. To the
street, you see what looks like a bare-brick
ground floor and a latticework of Gothic
arches above, but, inside, all the energy
in the star is forced towards the triangular
protrusion of the altar, with its full-height
glass wall filled with numinous modernist
angels and cherubs, swaddled in abstract
arabesques of pure colour. More than any
of the other Cachemaille-Day churches,
it's startling for the soft/hard, light/dark
alternation between harsh austerity – the
slightly ribbed, bone-like concrete frame
that runs down the length of the church, the
frankly industrial dark-red and black bricks
– and the release of sudden moments of fierce
beauty, in that gorgeous glass wall. **[D.28]**

———

CO-OPERATIVE WHOLESALE SOCIETY
W. A. Johnson and J. W. Cropper, 1936
Expressionist

An early and unassuming part of the distinct
'co-op quarter' in the north of the city
centre, dominated by the masterful Miesian
CIS Tower (p. 403) and its galumphing
recent complement by 3DReid. By the same
Co-op in-house architects who designed
the excellent sandstone department stores

in Bradford **(p. 384)**, Southport **(p. 435)** and Huddersfield **(p. 384)**, this is five storeys of plate glass and pale-yellow Dutch brick, rooting it in the work of Dudok, but with a faint little Mendelsohnian curve at the street corner, and a CWS logo with a built-in moderne holder for a seemingly permanently absent flagpole. A faint but elegant echo of the socialist architecture of interwar Europe.

DAILY EXPRESS BUILDING, ANCOATS ✪
Owen Williams, 1936–9
International Style

Placed at that distinct point where the centre of Manchester suddenly stops and the straggling, impoverished, blasted and half-derelict landscape of Ancoats begins, this is a suavely metropolitan brother to Williams's other two blocks of combined offices and printworks for the paper in

Fleet Street **(p. 50)** and Glasgow **(p. 518)**. As a complete work of architecture, it might be the best of the three, confidently occupying an entire block, whereas the others involve a certain squeeze to see them properly. No reminiscences, no masonry, no nostalgia, just a steel frame wrapped around with black vitrolite and blue glass, beautifully artificial, with a double-height glass ground floor where you would once have been able to spy into the printworks printing away, and a stair tower and reclined extension, both of which give the composition a coolly Constructivist asymmetry. **[A.14]**

KENDAL'S DEPARTMENT STORE
J. A. Beaumont, 1939
Expressionist

Of central Manchester's two great thirties buildings, this is not as structurally radical as the **Daily Express Building (above)** on

A dash of glamour on Great Ancoats Road: the finest of Owen Williams's three headquarters for the *Daily Express*.

The strikingly original glass bricks and Portland stone facade of Kendal's Department Store on Deansgate.

the other, lower-rent side of the city centre, but this department store on Deansgate is more original, a Chicago-via-Berlin one-off. Steel-framed, then clad in vertical strips of stone, it might seem to be similar to the Selfridge's approach of masonry/frame baroque of which there's plenty to be found along Deansgate; but it strips its materials down to their essentials, with the stone strips divided up by immensely high windows of glass brick, a feature which can't be found in any of the American or Weimar sources. Kendal's is one of the few buildings in pre-war Manchester that presages the particularly Gothic and commercial approach it would take to both modernism and music. Well, you can certainly imagine a teenage Ian Curtis mooning around these crystalline floors on a miserable Sunday, the opalescent walls setting him dreaming of Fritz Lang. It's currently a House of Fraser, and no original interiors survive.

PREFABS, WYTHENSHAWE
Frederick Gibberd Partnership, 1946
People's Detailing

There are few complete housing estates left of the factory-built prefabs intended to provide an instant solution to the homelessness caused by the Blitz, so this little cluster in south Manchester's sprawling, impoverished Garden City is a particularly welcome survival. Especially so, because these aren't Nissen huts but real houses, using one of the better government-commissioned designs, sketched out by Frederick Gibberd before being put into mass production by, as the propaganda used to say, the same factories that had been making munitions just weeks earlier, swords-into-ploughshares fashion. You can see exactly what they are – pieces of corrugated sheet metal, clipped together – but they're also neat little designs with a lot of Sweden in them, big windows and good proportions, and often attractively painted by residents. Grouped around green closes with a lot of trees, you can see this as a warm-up for the architecture of the New Towns. All surviving clusters of prefabs are interesting, but this is the only one which is worth seeing in its own right as an integrated work of planning and architecture.

HOLLINGS BUILDING, FALLOWFIELD ⊙
L. C. Howitt for Manchester City Council Architects Dept, 1957–60
People's Detailing

Better known to generations of students of the University of Manchester as the 'Toast Rack', because of the way that this triangular tower's concrete frame superfluously but very enjoyably shoots upward and then hooks itself back in a loop, so that it looks as if everything is suspended from a row of concrete arches, whose tops are visible and hence could fit giant slices of toast.

Pop art architecture in inner suburban Manchester: the so-called 'Toast Rack', with its expressed structure.

The metaphor is silly, but the building is all success – a rhythmic op art architecture that is both fun and vigorous, and a reminder that the populist strain in modernism ushered in by the Festival of Britain wasn't just about diapered brick and neo-Victorian typography, but could also be about a display of structure as sheer pleasure, with none of the machismo of Brutalism. A child could instantly look at this building and see how it's made, but there's considerable class in the way those concrete arches are modelled. This sort of unpretentious joy in structure was a hallmark of Howitt, Manchester's City Architect at the time. Built as the university's Domestic Trades College, it is currently being refurbished as, predictably, flats. Hopefully, the precedent of **Park Hill (p. 370)** won't lead to the 'iconic' concrete structure being preserved and the rest of the fabric being replaced with shiny tat.

TENNIS & BOWLS PAVILION, WYTHENSHAWE

L. C. Howitt for Manchester City Council Architects Dept, 1959
People's Detailing

Nothing fancy – just a neat and clever design for a pavilion in Wythenshawe's main park by Manchester's talented post-war City Architect. Two parts, one in brick, the other clad in tile and suspended on one large column, so that you can shelter under it. The result is gently radical, a showcase of modern construction – look, it doesn't fall down! – that doesn't make too much of a fuss of itself, the sort of laconic and slightly surreal structural wit that the likes of OMA tend to strain for nowadays. The designer, being one of those modest civil servants who were responsible for so much of the best twentieth-century architecture, would probably have regarded it as merely a good day's work.

The grand timber vault of Manchester's Oxford Road Station, a pioneering work of ecomodernism.

OXFORD ROAD STATION ⊙
W. R. Headley and Max Clendinning for British Railways London Midland Region, 1960
Googie, Ecomodernist

A possibly apocryphal anecdote has Walter Gropius visiting Manchester for the first time, taking the train along the viaduct that runs between Piccadilly and Oxford Road, seeing the rear facades of the Edwardian warehouses that the railway line and the canal used to serve, and realizing that these abstract glass grids meant that Manchester's engineers had done what the Bauhaus was trying to achieve, years before. Of course this is based on the rather gauche idea that Gropius, who had worked on the design of several factories, hadn't seen the back end of one before, but it does point to the excitingly modern effect of that short ride even today. But the new station built at the end of it in the sixties takes a completely different approach to modern architecture,

not repetitious or mechanistic but unique and organic. Steps up from Whitworth Street lead to a great, oyster-like wooden canopy, in a Googie style similar to (much heavier) buildings such as the Haus der Kulturen der Welt in Berlin. The platforms are sheltered by taut wooden barrel roofs, warmly and gorgeously detailed. The horrible signage and clutter of privatized rail tries to do its best to disrupt the simplicity of this design, and fails.

CIS TOWER & NEW CENTURY HOUSE ⊙
G. S. Hay with Sir John Burnet, Tait, Wilson & Partners, 1959–62
International Style

Without doubt the best tall building in Manchester, and the most convincing facsimile of American modernism at its most *Mad Men* in England (Sheffield's **Arts Tower,** another frontage, clearer from a distance, which has a service tower initially clad in mosaic tiles, which gave a slightly more angular, angsty accent to the Platonic geometries. Around ten years ago it was covered in solar panels, which fit well with the blue of the curtain wall – a drastic change, but successful in my view. The lower, fifteen-storey New Century House, part of the same complex, is untouched.

WILLIAM TEMPLE MEMORIAL CHURCH, WYTHENSHAWE ✪
George Gaze Pace, 1963–5
Brutalist, High-Tech

Quite how the new suburb of Wythenshawe ended up with two first-rate churches in a not conspicuously religious city is a bit of a puzzle. There were no Victorian churches to rely on here, of course, on virgin territory, but this is still a curious statement about the civic fathers' idea about what working-class Mancunians needed, especially given that it took decades to provide a shopping centre, and a rapid-transit link to the rest of Manchester was built only in 2014. All spiritual needs were catered for, few others. Both of Wythenshawe's great churches are by very personal architects – here, the individualist is G. G. Pace, who shared a liking for dark-red brick, heaviness and lurking profiles with Cachemaille-Day, but had a much more oblique approach to the interpenetration of light into his stark, heavy solids. So here we have a concrete-and-brick barn with a copper roof, with several irregular rooflights set into it, sombre enough. But, inside, the roof is held up with Meccano-like steel supports, which unexpectedly pushes it into the lightweight territory of early Foster and Rogers. It's a bizarre choice, but it works, with the Meccano pieces painted black, along with the organ, creating a strange techno-brutalist space that also works as a primitive hut.

Manchester Mies: the glinting steel and glass of the CIS Tower, modelled on 1960s Chicago.

p. 369, is a much more enjoyable effort in the extruded-glass grid genre created by Mies van der Rohe and Gordon Bunshaft, but it's too eccentric to really feel like it would be at home on Madison Avenue). The twenty-five-storey CIS Tower could easily be on the Upper West Side or on the Chicago Loop, and is the direct result of a research trip to the US to find out how to make one of these towers. It is amazing that the most impressive emulation of American high-capitalist design came via the Co-operative, and now stands next to a statue of Robert Owen, as if the end point of the experiment in uniting equality and mass production that he'd embarked on at New Lanark took us here.

That's as may be, but the tower is undeniable. It's a building of two distinct sides – a frontage which is a shimmering, glorious tribute to New York's Lever House, with a slightly darker blue to its panels, and

Ecclesiastical Arts and Crafts meets High-Tech: George Gaze Pace's remarkable William Temple Memorial Church.

OWENS PARK, FALLOWFIELD ❶
Building Design Partnership, Mitzi Cunliffe (artist), 1964–6
International Style

Near to the **Hollings Building (p. 401)**, this forms halls of residence for Manchester University students, in the form of low-rise courtyards and a elegantly splayed tower, detailed well in smoothly faced stock brick and concrete. There is floor-to-ceiling plate glass for the communal spaces, up the centre of the tower, and smaller windows for the bedrooms, a good choice easily read from the facade. What makes it absolutely worth seeing are the series of black fibreglass panels placed at ground level around the complex. These are *Cosmos 1*, by the American sculptor Mitzi Cunliffe, and they're a grid made up of repetitious modules, part biomorphic surrealism, part engineering diagram; the door to the dry riser is built in. Altogether, this is one of many superb works by the sixties/seventies Building Design Partnership collective, and it is currently slated to be replaced with pitched-roofed blocks in the 'vernacular' by BDP's current team. They look decent enough in the renders but they lack the captivating spaciousness and specificity of this place.

111 PICCADILLY
Douglas Stephen & Partners, 1965
International Style

An impressive tower by one of the most interesting commercial architects of the 1960s and '70s, eighteen clear, strong ribbon-windowed storeys supported by great trusses of concrete, which divide the facade into distinct parts, apparently inspired by the work of Louis Kahn. Subtly sculptural, and impressive in engineering terms – it's all cantilevered above the Rochdale canal. A refurbishment by the ubiquitous developers Bruntwood keeps it looking spick and span but the painting over the concrete takes away some of its physical heft and presence. Although there are far worse things you can do to a concrete building than paint it white, it still shows a certain failure of imagination.

___

PICCADILLY PLAZA
Covell Matthews & Partners, 1965
Brutalist

This near-megastructural complex is the most immediately obvious result of Manchester's aborted experiment in multilevel corporate modernism. On a long podium taking up one quarter of the blocks around Piccadilly Gardens, there are three semi-separate buildings: a slab (now the Mercure Hotel), dramatically raised on hulking concrete pillars from the podium for no obvious reason other than that it looks amazing, and that it means it can be visually separated from the low glazed block under it; a tower, with a sculptural relief up the side based apparently on early computer printouts; and a third part, originally a low-rise block with a hyperbolic paraboloid roof, which was supplemented by a dull Blair-era piece of cladding-and-wavy-roof submodernism via another Bruntwood refurbishment. The concrete has been painted everywhere, and today it feels very much an integral part of the nasty, aggressively commercial centre of Manchester, where horrific levels of homelessness and the transformation of any available space into luxury flats coexist extremely uncomfortably. Even for its time, it's overscaled and domineering. But there are serious thrills to be had, if you can grind your teeth through the rest.

MANCUNIAN WAY FLYOVER
G. Maunsell & Partners, 1965
Brutalist

Part of the inner motorway Manchester foisted upon itself, this two-mile flyover is a segmented design of prestressed concrete components, slicing south Manchester off from the centre. As architecture, it's as dramatic as the **Westway (p. 163)** and much better detailed – there's even a plaque from the Concrete Society on one of its pillars. As with the **Leeds Inner Ring Road, Woodhouse Lane Section (p. 380)** and Glasgow's **M8 (p. 526)**, it opens up where the pedestrian might want to walk from the centre to the university, and doesn't give much of a toss about anyone else, although a good redesign of the spaces underneath and a rerouting of the traffic could probably do something about that; the sinkhole that opened up on it recently might help that process along.

___

MATHS & SOCIAL SCIENCES BUILDING, UMIST ❶
Cruikshank & Seward, 1968
Brutalist

Young Mancunians can get very excited about their modern architecture, which they richly showcase in magazines like *The Modernist*, to a degree that's sometimes a little puzzling. There are no masterpieces here compared with Sheffield or Coventry, but there is a lot of good solid journeyman work, of which the campus of the University of Manchester Institute of Science and Technology is a particularly good example. The Maths and Social Sciences Building is a blunt tower, assembled into a faintly fortress-ish skyline, with well-detailed concrete work; it is a decent and punchy Brutalist building, well worth having around, and well integrated with public spaces and lower-rise buildings in a similar style. It is particularly dramatic when seen from the

Mancunian Way flyover – moody concrete lines, horizontal and vertical , surviving hints of that seventies Factory Records city of Gothic modernism, now so often buried under barcode facades and shiny cladding. It is slated for demolition but is still used by UMIST at the time of writing, unlike the same architects' almost Postmodernist Chandos Hall, which, with its small windows, fully glazed escape staircase and curious roof sculpture, was a light-hearted pop modernist tower until its demolition at the end of 2019. *The Modernist* has called for preservation of the UMIST campus, with backing from luminaries such as Johnny Marr.

GATEWAY HOUSE ✪
R. Seifert & Partners, 1969
International Style

Low-rise Seifert, but every bit as good as the firm's best towers, a sinuous tile and glass office block with shops on the ground floor, sashaying its way round the corner from Piccadilly Station. Smooth and calming, it is an interesting companion piece to the heavy-breathing theatrics of **Piccadilly Plaza (p. 406)**, fulfilling its function as a dramatic speculative building designed to make an impression on visitors without drama – mods and rockers, these two. So confident is its curving design that it hasn't dated at all – you could mistake it for one of the sleeker products of what used to call itself 'New Emerging Manchester' in the New Labour years. Of all Seifert buildings, it has the least caveats, no moment where you can smell the money – it exudes an effortless metropolitan excellence. Manchester occasionally likes to compare itself to certain other European second cities with a reputation for coldness, arrogance and footballing supremacy, and this is one building which actually does feel like it might be in Milan.

The sinuous curve of Richard Seifert's Gateway House, slinking its way towards Piccadilly Station.

PRECINCT CENTRE, UNIVERSITY OF MANCHESTER ❶
Hugh Wilson and J. Lewis Womersley, 1972
Brutalist

Dour, powerful and properly urban, this is one of the major survivals of what was once a multilevel campus, by the former municipal architects of Cumbernauld and Sheffield, respectively. Although it hasn't been swept away completely, like the same architects' contemporary Hulme Crescents nearby, and hasn't been bombed, like their lavatorial Arndale Centre, it is now just a fragment of what was once a wider podium-and-walkway campus. It's big – tall, wide and hulking – in red brick and a concrete frame painted black, with projecting glazed stairwells and a lone walkway now going nowhere in particular. One of the Mancunian spaces to take the temperature of the era, a remnant of the aesthetic whose looming atmosphere eventually produced Joy Division.

ROYAL EXCHANGE THEATRE ✪
Levitt Bernstein, 1976
High-Tech

An extremely original, ambitious and strange design, with more personality than most Manchester buildings put together. This H. G. Wells Martian tripod was inserted in the high-Victorian Royal Exchange, which became disused when Cottonopolis finally collapsed economically in the 1970s. Manchester at that point was on the eve of a cultural renaissance – with the explosion of post-punk just round the corner – and this building marks a rare triumph of authentic post–1968 radical architecture, a temporary-looking nodule with a 'democratic' theatre in the round inside, suspended by a network of gantries and pulleys, with steps and walkways upwards. The other aspect of the seventies – the newfound respect, not quite become genuflection, towards historic architecture – means the space around

Radical architecture of the 1970s: the high-tech pod of Levitt Bernstein's theatre within the Royal Exchange.

is opulently imperial, only adding to the time-out-of-joint, steampunk air of Levitt Bernstein's addition. Its prolific architects would never do anything nearly so thrilling again, and for Manchester architecture generally this interest in the punkishly ad hoc is the road not travelled. More than this, the Royal Exchange Theatre is almost unique in post-war British architecture in the way it resembles the most out-there utopian schemes of the era; its only real cousin is perhaps Preston's **Plastic Classroom (p. 445)**. The nearby IRA bomb of 1996 apparently made the structure wobble a little, and some additional work by the architects dates from its aftermath.

HOMES FOR CHANGE, HULME
Mills Beaumont Leavey Channon, 1997–2000
Ecomodernist

Between 1976 and 1997, no modern building worth looking at was built in Manchester. This is an extreme version of a common fate in the North, as large cities outside London depopulated and deindustrialized, with new development usually in the form of lowest-common-denominator 'enterprise zones'. Yet it's especially glaring in a city which had, in those precise years, become arguably the most important in England in terms of music and pop culture. Maybe this is not coincidental. Much of that culture was based on the reuse of space rather than its creation anew (they didn't have access to that sort of capital). Nowhere was as reused as Hulme, where the Wilson/Womersley-designed Brutalist 'Crescents' gradually devolved into a crumbling, labyrinthine playground about which ageing Mancunian punks can be alternately vitriolic and sentimental. As the Crescents faced demolition, one group of residents banded together into a co-operative to make sure that they weren't rehoused in Barratt Homes. The result is this strange, cheaply made, faintly elitist (it is locked at

night, so its eccentric courtyard spaces can only be explored at certain times) but nonetheless inspiring place. Ground floors of brick-panel workspaces and community facilities with four storeys of timber-clad flats above are connected by metal walkways, an intriguing insistence on the deck-access that was so condemned in the old scheme, with a scrubby but well-used green square inside. By no means great architecture – it's too confused and cheap for that – but a fascinating, rare and by all accounts highly successful planning experiment.

EPPING WALK BRIDGE, HULME
1969
HULME ARCH
Wilkinson Eyre, 1997
Brutalist, High-Tech

These two excellent bridges are sixties Manchester and post-Blair Manchester in a nutshell, both traversing the dual carriageways that were originally intended as a pleasant, green link from the centre to Wythenshawe, but were de-greened in the sixties into the current high-speed asphalt assault course. Epping Walk Bridge on Princess Parkway is one of several spindly footbridges that were intended to make sure Hulme wasn't completely cut off from the world (it needed more than that), and it's quite a sexy design, resting on a kinked concrete leg. It's best known for a view taken from one side of the bridge across it, a snowscape press photo of Joy Division, by Kevin Cummins. The Hulme Arch is another footbridge over the adjacent Stratford Road, and was intended to de-Joy Division Manchester by replacing a bleak, spacious and mute modernism with one that 'spoke' to people through iconic gestures – here, through the way that it obviously frames the new skyline (and the **Beetham Tower, p. 410**, in particular), as a sort of slick modernist triumphal arch.

CONTACT THEATRE, CHORLTON-ON-MEDLOCK
Short Associates, 1999
Postmodernist

An exciting building, absolutely bursting at the seams with ideas and weirdness – if we're going to reassess Postmodernism, this is a much more interesting way back to it rather than all those tedious pink-stone-and-pediment office blocks in London. What makes Alan Short's Postmodernist buildings so unusual for their time is their physical presence and scale. At the time, perhaps this missed the point of a genre which professed to be a matter of decorated sheds, signs and signifiers – but if you're interested in buildings as things that exist in space rather than as theorems, you're in luck. This youth theatre is a series of brick auditoria and foyers, modelled with an Arts and Crafts-like attention to the texture of brick, metal and wood, which have exited the world of modernist good taste through the bizarre rooftop extrusions that make up their skyline, twists of chimneys and cowls that apparently have an energy-saving function yet could just as easily be there for sheer effect. In a city that tends to the relentlessly utilitarian and seems to find any notion of fantasy some sort of sign of weakness, the freakish skyline of this thing veering into view as you leave the precincts of the university is most welcome. A friendly apparition.

BEETHAM TOWER ✪
Ian Simpson Architects, 2008
International Style

Somebody once described this skyscraper as the work of 'a mediocre architect at the top of his game'. There was a compliment alongside this insult. The Beetham Tower is by far the best thing Ian Simpson has ever designed – compare it with the same firm's new towers nearby, and you can see

The beacon of the repopulation of central Manchester: Ian Simpson's distinctive Beetham Tower.

an unfortunate combination of over-slick glass gloop and a fumbling approach to form. Here, however, Simpson struck exactly the right note. The forty-seven-storey tower is in two distinct parts: the lower section of hotel rooms (a Hilton, of course), and above it flats for footballers, oligarchs and other assorted masters of the universe. There is a bar in the join. What makes it such a superb tower is the way Simpson has demarcated these three parts in the section, so that the flats are cantilevered out at the level of the bar above the hotel rooms, which gives it a distinctive, immediately recognizable shape. It's neither here nor there that the decorative fan placed at the top was put there to lift it above the height of a (far inferior) skyscraper being topped out in Leeds at the same time. It gently mirrors the shape created by the cantilever, completing it.

The slenderness of it all, no doubt intended to avoid the bulky look of sixties towers, is perfectly ethereal, the Miesian 'almost nothing'. Mies wouldn't have approved of the curtain wall's barcode facade, and hopefully in a couple of decades a new facade treatment will replace it, as it's the only sign of the firm's usual flash nonsense; in rainy weather, the pattern is almost invisible, which is useful in Manchester. In every other respect, this attempts something ambitious – being the Mancunian *Stadtkrone*, built very consciously with the knowledge that it will be the tallest thing in sight – and gets it exactly right. Not only is it by a long distance the finest of Simpson's buildings, it is well above the standard of the rest of the non-stop succession of towers foisted upon Manchester in the last fifteen years. Apart from this, and perhaps John Assael's nearby Great Northern Tower, a Richard Rogers-imitating glass slalom, pretty much every one of them could be demolished tomorrow without anyone missing them.

CHETHAM'S SCHOOL OF MUSIC
Roger Stephenson Studio, 2012–13
Classical Modernism

Manchester's seemingly unstoppable post-1996 construction boom has given it more new public spaces, public transport and public buildings than anywhere outside London, but it all seems to have been made possible by the acknowledgement that the government wasn't going to pay for quality – so better that they pay for something rather than nothing. So from hospitals to arts centres to stadia to schools to Metrolink stations, it has all been blunt, bluff, brash and frequently incredibly tacky, as if flash will make up for poverty. This makes the new extension of Chetham's School, based in seventeenth-century buildings in the north of the centre, a surprising stand-out. It compares especially well with other major public buildings in the centre, which

range from vacuous (Urbis, the hideous redevelopment of Victoria Station) to well-meaning but generic (the People's History Museum, Mecanoo's HOME). Where some cities (hello, Edinburgh) are so obsessed with context as to cripple themselves, the Chetham's School of Music is valuable for being a rare new Manchester building to address its surroundings in an intelligent way. It is directly opposite the ashlar range of the original Victoria Station, and meets its gentle curve with another, clad in a brown brick which isn't the same as, but harmonizes well with, the station's sandstone. Windows for the classrooms and the foyers of the concert hall inside are in thin strips, in a dynamic, Mendelsohnian composition, moving to a whipcrack corner curve. Interiors are very decent too, with a gracious brick atrium; they're open to the public, but zealously enforced 'safeguarding' procedures mean you should ask nicely before taking a look. [**D.25**]

WHITWORTH ART GALLERY EXTENSION
MUMA, 2015
Classical Modernism

A relaxed second addition to the existing parts (one Victorian, one post-war municipal), of Manchester's main modern-art gallery. Cubic concrete galleries with plenty of natural light, dressed in good, textured red brick and copper, attached to the back end of the florid Gothic original, with a sawtooth roofline behind, which has obvious industrial reminiscences, looking out over a very pleasant green, with a sculpture park nearby. The café, meanwhile, is a brick-and-glass pavilion, right in the trees. Humane, well crafted, a little high-minded – what it's doing in contemporary Manchester is anybody's guess.

CITY OF SALFORD

SALFORD CIVIC CENTRE, SWINTON
Percy Thomas and Ernest Prestwich, 1935
CIVIC CENTRE EXTENSION & COMPUTER CENTRE, SWINTON
Cruikshank & Seward, 1973
Moderne, Brutalist

This was originally Swinton and Pendlebury Town Hall, before being repurposed as the home of the expanded Salford Metropolitan Borough when Greater Manchester was created in 1974. It consists of three very distinct parts. The first is a typical town hall, no better or worse than the average, by the Welsh firm of Percy Thomas – the usual symmetrical melding of Dudok, Stockholm Town Hall and residual neo-Georgian, with a great big clock tower; the way you can tell it's not in South Wales is that it's in brick rather than Portland stone. It has been made a lot more interesting by two interconnected buildings, both built in the early 1970s. The main extension is straight-up authoritarian Brutalism, in a harshly rhythmic march of angular vertical fins, and with grey, well-detailed pebbly concrete – from the rear in particular, with some kind of command room at the top corner, it is exceptionally paranoid and relentless, but in an excitingly grim way, a tradition of ugly-captivating that has always been big in Cottonopolis. Yet the other extension is something else entirely – a virtual clone of Norman Foster's machine-tooled brown-glass **IBM Cosham (p. 248)** in Portsmouth, to a litigation-inviting degree. Regardless of provenance, it looks terrific, sleek and low between these sharp-elbowed monuments.

FORMER SALFORD TECHNICAL COLLEGE, UNIVERSITY OF SALFORD
Halliday Meecham Architects, William Mitchell (artist), 1967
International Style

Part of Salford University's scattering of newly unified colleges and polys, the old Salford Tech is a decent but minor piece of municipal modernism – brown brick, a mid-rise tower and a lecture theatre. It's not at all bad, but wouldn't be in this book but for the fact that the main square boasts three upright and literally totemic figures by William Mitchell (he decided not to name them), so outré in their form that they led an appalled Prince Philip to blurt: 'What the hell are they?' at the college's royal opening.

What they are is one of the more extreme examples of Mitchell's fusion of Mesoamerican ornaments and masks with the messy montage art-architecture of the New Brutalism. As with the motorway square at **Hockley Circus (p. 314)**, concrete is shaped into wild and organic forms, with mosaic touches to the eyes of one of the figures. They look out over the A6, a landscape totally transformed by Salford Council in the sixties into a spacious world of dual carriageways and towers, with Barratt Homes and a drive-thru McDonald's appearing at random. A narrow, unpleasant bridge 'connects' the college to the flats; these serried high-rises, undoubtedly quite daunting, over-scaled, system-built things, were refurbished recently with what is now called 'Grenfell-style cladding', which at the time of writing is being removed. Mitchell's three sentinels stare at it all disapprovingly.

LANCASTRIAN HALL & CENTRAL LIBRARY, SWINTON ❶
Leach Rhodes & Walker, 1968
Brutalist

Opposite the civic complex at Swinton, this is a massive exercise in fully expressed power. Next to a very bleak post-war precinct, it overcompensates for its wan neighbour through assembling a step-pyramid of brown ribbed-concrete masses, one slab of services and a cantilevered block with some marvellous sixties signage, with walkways going across to offer access from the street and the precinct. A much more impure version of the heavy heroics of Denys Lasdun or James Stirling's buildings of the same era, looking as if a gifted student had looked at them and thought; 'Ha, I can do that.' Apparently the plan bears little relation to this heroically gestural exterior – it's hard to tell, as the building is currently derelict – but in any case this is fine urban sculpture.

WEST RIVERSIDE & HIGHLAND HOUSE
Leach Rhodes & Walker, 1969–75
Brutalist

A striking set of buildings, and a notable example of Greater Manchester's geographical anomalies. These two sets of sculptural office blocks, clinging to the River Irwell, were constructed from curvaceous space-age bachelor pad precast panels, by the local firm of Leach Rhodes & Walker, who are still active; they built their own small glass headquarters here too, though it is currently slated for demolition. Both groups of buildings have otherwise survived the shifts in fashion; the low-rise cluster of Aldine House, Baskerville House, Cloister House and Delphian House (all named after typefaces – the original client was the *Guardian*) has been rather over-refurbished by Bruntwood as West Riverside, and the nearby high-rise on a podium of Highland

The extremely space-age moulded concrete modules of Highland House, on the riverside in Salford.

House, built for the Inland Revenue, has become a Premier Inn. In each case, the interesting profiles of the concrete panels are strong enough to make an impression despite their timidly tasteful painting over. Both are very obviously part of central Manchester, a stone's throw from the Town Hall and the cathedral. There's no obvious marker between each side, just the trickle-like river. Except that's the boundary between Manchester and Salford, see! So it's actually somewhere totally different.

─────

LOWRY ARTS CENTRE, SALFORD QUAYS
Michael Wilford & Partners, 2000
IMPERIAL WAR MUSEUM NORTH, TRAFFORD
Daniel Libeskind, 2001
Supermodernist, Pseudomodernist

Some of the world's most important designers have come to do some of their worst work in Greater Manchester. Tadao Ando's appalling – and by the time of publication probably demolished – piss wall at Piccadilly Gardens, Santiago Calatrava's needlessly fussy bridge over the Irwell, Foster's bland office blocks at Spinningfields: none of these are worth your attention. These two large-scale public buildings by James Stirling's former right-hand man Michael Wilford and perma-memorializing 'self-igniting Yahrzeit candle' (as Martin Filler put it) Daniel Libeskind are a partial, but only a partial, exception. One is in 'Salford', one is in 'Trafford', but tourists know they're in 'Manchester'. They face each other on either side of what is called for a reason the Manchester Ship Canal, and they are both faced in titanium; a High-Tech bridge by Wilkinson Eyre (no Gateshead **Millennium Bridge, p. 477**, but fine nonetheless) links them, and a massive flour mill looms in the background. Both use a style of abstracted shapes and non-orthogonal geometries,

and both have ends you're supposed to look at and ends you're not. Each might look pretty silly on the outside but has a spatial rush as soon as you're inside, whether through the alternation of dark and murky alleyways and precipitous walks of death in the War Museum (they're supposed to simulate the experience of war, which is of course preposterous) or the polychrome explosion of colour and the flying walkways in the Arts Centre.

They're more than nice to have, and it would be a great shame if they disappeared. But as a public-space project this is a disaster. The Lowry faces a shoddy outlet mall and is poorly connected to clusters of 'luxury flats'; the War Museum is surrounded by an eighties-style surface car park, as if it's a TGI Friday's; and next to it is the Poundland Canary Wharf of Salford MediaCity, a massive complex that is a good idea appallingly executed, with the cheapest materials and the most 'cash the cheque and run' of architects. The eventual effect is 'iconic' architecture as cargo cult, as if a couple of buildings that could be in Barcelona or Bilbao can substitute for the public infrastructure of a Spanish city. There is real revulsion against all this now, and rightly so – Manchester has been its flagship. These two will find their place in the affections of future generations, and it doesn't really matter if it'll be as 'serious architecture' or just period kitsch. [B.31]

SE LANCASHIRE & NE CHESHIRE

THOMAS LINACRE CENTRE, WIGAN
A. E. Munby, 1937
Moderne, Expressionist

On the edges of Wigan's central Mesnes Park is this red-brick art deco health centre, previously part of a grammar school, and then, after selection was abolished, a high school. It is executed in a slightly fey municipal moderne, with neo-Georgian details taken to the point of abstraction, with the sash windows made tall and thin, as in a Giles Gilbert Scott building. Overlooking the town centre is a commanding, chunky tower with an octagonal clock. Very much of its time – a compromised building, but one which people here would surely miss if it disappeared.

———

COLLEGE BANK FLATS, ROCHDALE ✪ ❶
W. H. G. Mercer, Rochdale Borough Surveyor, and E. V. Collins for Wimpey, 1962–6
International Style

This estate of standardized towers, known locally as the 'Seven Sisters', is by far the finest among the very few examples of system-built housing in this book; between them, Rochdale's surveyors and Wimpey managed to come up with a twenty-one-storey tower that had a well-profiled brown-brick and cream module with elegant rooflines created by dramatic top-floor penthouses. This block they then built seven times, right in the centre of town, a short walk from – and visually rivalling – the justly famous neo-Gothic Town Hall. Incredibly monumental and not for the faint-hearted (what is, round here?), the estate also pays unusual attention to the experience for pedestrians, with the blocks set on podiums with wide, well-made walkways and built-in benches, and a clear underpass link to the unlovely pink Postmodernist shopping centre that dominates the town, currently still with some 1980s quasi-modernist murals. This is one of the great municipal skylines, which perhaps predictably is now being threatened with demolition in favour of 'town houses' and recladding, something that hopefully the Grenfell Tower disaster might make the authorities think twice about. There is at the time of writing a campaign against this – 'Save the Seven Sisters'.

In the lobby of the furthest of the seven from the shopping centre, the block called Mitchell Hey, is a fabulous polychrome ceramic mural. It is made up of what look like dozens of pieces of smashed crockery, transformed into an Abstract Expressionist bricolage – a thrilling thing to find en route to the lifts. This is one of originally seven by lecturers at the college of art, here George and Joan Stephenson. When the lobbies were refurbished in the early 1990s, residents voted on whether they wanted to keep the murals – sadly, only this one won the vote. The others, equally abstract and equally wonderful, can be easily found on Miles Glendinning's *Tower Block* website.

———

MERSEYWAY CENTRE, STOCKPORT
Bernard Engle & Partners with Alan Boyson (artist), 1965
Brutalist

As Adrian 'Jones the Planner' points out in his excellent essay on the town, Stockport is a place for people who enjoy urban terrain – stairwells that range from civic and formal to Bill Brandt-style snickets, walkways and iron bridges, sudden slopes and revealed views of a higgledy-piggledy townscape. It's all in a valley, plunging down towards the astonishing red-brick viaduct that carries

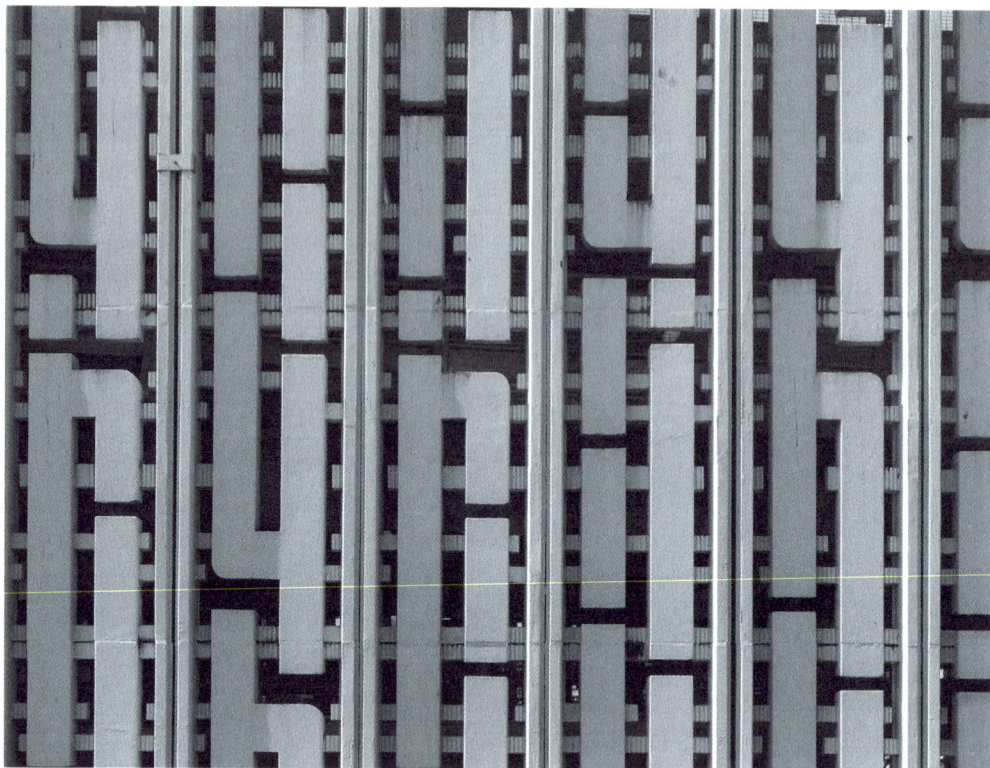

Abstract patterns relieve the facade of the sprawling Merseyway Centre in the heart of Stockport.

the trains over it towards Manchester – yet the immediate view of the town from the bus or railway stations is of a shopping mall and office block dross-scape which resembles Swindon more than anywhere else. But, up close, it's a lot more interesting; the mall is the Merseyway Centre, a megastructure which plugs itself into this irregular townscape, rather than obnoxiously shoving itself on to it.

Coming from **Stopford House (p. 418)**, the first part of the Merseyway Centre you notice is the concrete road bridge which goes across it; there are four floors you can walk around, two of which have – increasingly depleted – shops, and the whole is brought together through the motif imprinted on the concrete facade, a fascinating op art pattern of vertical strips, written in what looks like an imaginary concrete script – created by Alan Boyson, of **Hull Co-operative (p. 461)** fame. If you want to see it in its pomp, a particularly delightful historic image can be found in Martin Parr's *Boring Postcards*.

A chunk of the complex was given a Pomo makeover in the 1990s, and the decline of the chain-store high street makes it rather bleak at times. But if it ever gives up on being a third-rate mall there's an **Elephant and Castle Shopping Centre (p. 91)** here in the making, a concrete souk, a modernist maze made from of a worn-out Arndale.

VICTORIA SQUARE, BOLTON
Shankland Cox, 1965–73
People's Detailing, Brutalist

This square was designed by Graeme Shankland, the Communist planner, *New Left Review* contributor and, for some, 'destroyer' of Liverpool; I came across it in Otto Saumarez Smith's great book on sixties comprehensive redevelopment, *Boom Cities*. He shows how Shankland's plan for Bolton entailed actually conserving the grand Victorian buildings of a vigorous provincial city and building the plan around them – so, here, public spaces link together William Hill and George Woodhouse's stupendous 1866 baroque Town Hall, and Bradshaw Gass & Hope's epic 1930 Vittorio Emanuele civic circus behind it, and frames them with a new square around the War Memorial. New buildings were added by the Borough Architect, mostly clad in Yorkshire stone. These frame the side facades of the Town Hall with colonnaded blocks; the most interesting of these is in a peculiar pre-cast Brutalist-via-Victorian idiom, reminiscent of the weird mass-produced vernacular of East Germany (which is a compliment, sort of). Shankland's work here might not seem like much, a mere paving and repair job, so if you want to see how good it really is, go to Leeds, where the miserable setting of an even better Victorian Town Hall seems to sum up that city's depressing feeling of unplanned, moneygrubbing waste. Here though, it feels as if you're in a real city, like in Europe, and can drink your cup of tea in repose while admiring the monuments.

WIGAN CIVIC CENTRE
Borough Architects Dept, 1970
Brutalist

Wigan, like most Outer Manchester towns, is great for Victorian proto-modernism – here, several iron-and-glass arcades and cyclopean cotton mills – but not so much for post-1918 modern architecture. Perhaps tellingly, the civic fathers of many of these towns (see also Oldham, **p. 418**, Stockport, **p. 418**, Swinton, **p. 412**) were much more adept at building themselves interesting headquarters than they were at building similarly considered schools, housing, libraries and health centres for their overwhelmingly working-class population. Wigan is a case in point, as the only post-war modernist building worth lingering around in its centre is the Civic Centre.

Its concrete is painted white, but there's no mistaking the Brutalist nature of these offices, with a horizontal three storeys to the street, with shading for the wide windows provided by angled concrete panels; there is another floor below, with concrete bridges going excitingly across, and strong Corbusian canopies leading to the entrances. Impressively lurking and powerful for such a small complex, it is currently derelict, and with, no doubt, an 'uncertain future'.

TURNPIKE CENTRE, LEIGH ⊘
J. C. Prestwich and William Mitchell (artist), 1971
Brutalist

Far, far better than the Greater Manchester civic norm – a truly impressive example of municipal modernism and an intelligent and original completion of a civic square, in a place that could still seriously do with

William Mitchell's vivid sculptural relief, dominating the front facade of Leigh's Turnpike Centre.

a lift. The Turnpike Centre was a local project by its borough council, supplemented by William Mitchell with riotous Mayan-Brutalist reliefs both inside and out; it was built as a combined library and art gallery, which opened with a show by Henry Moore. After a period of what one member of staff has called 'watercolours and paintings of Johnny Depp', it's currently trying to revive this experimental spirit. In any case, it's embodied in the building. On the square the Turnpike Centre forms a U with an Edwardian baroque ashlar Town Hall on one side and a red-sandstone Gothic church on the other. Its facade is faced in around four distinct concrete treatments, raw, tactile, creating different rhythms and textures, and is dominated by projecting concrete bay windows, like a harsher **Oriel Chambers (p. 423)**. Heavy and vehement but full of subtleties, generous without being patronizing or overbearing, this is a first-rate civic building.

————

STOPFORD HOUSE, STOCKPORT
J. S. Rank for Stockport Council Borough Council Architects Dept, 1975
Brutalist

A tremendous, little-known Brutalist civic building of exquisitely domineering formality. Stopford House is an extension at the back of Alfred Brumwell Thomas's Stockport Town Hall (beefy Portland stone Edwardian baroque, with a splendid tower and unlovely, bulky wings), and the juxtaposition of the two shows the shift in the expression of municipal power from expressions of imperial grandeur and architectural continuity to abstraction and dissonance better than anywhere else I know. At the side of the old building, steps lead up to a vast concrete plaza, which apparently is ferociously guarded against skateboarders, bikers or anyone who might want to use it for anything other than sucking their

cheeks in and contemplating it in a long raincoat. The square is flanked by a strange concrete winter garden, overgrown and faintly post-apocalyptic. The main block is a regular, rhythmic poured-concrete march of moulded fins, part of it hauled up on massive pillars, with similar frightening confidence to Truro's **County Hall (p. 276)** or John Madin's demolished Birmingham Central Library; though Madin wouldn't have fudged the building's resolution, as J. S. Rank has here with the pointlessly ugly left-side stairwell. In most other respects, though, this is memorably imposing stuff, almost parodically sinister – looking every bit like the Town Hall of the town where *Unknown Pleasures* was recorded. I had thought of the adaptations of David Peace's *Red Riding* on first seeing it – but, it transpires, it's actually used in the parodic spin on the same seventies police brutality themes, *Life on Mars*.

————

CIVIC CENTRE & QUEEN ELIZABETH HALL, OLDHAM ❶
Cecil Howitt & Partners, 1976
International Style

Amazingly dated for its time, this appears to be a prestige project of the early fifties somehow realized more than twenty years later. Nothing necessarily wrong with that, of course. A series of offices arc around an eleven-storey tower, clad in a brown-white reconstituted stone, with black-framed square windows, rather solemn but powerful, with its strongly emphasized lift tower. On the supporting podium are rich black and brown marble panels, incongruously luxurious and classy opposite the 1980s Pomo Oldham Markets, which looks like it was made by the in-house designer at Aldi.

Much more than just classy is the Queen Elizabeth Hall, adjacent. At first glance this blocky concert hall, a composition of stone volumes and rectangular beaten-metal sculptures, looks a little stodgy; but, up close, the sculptures reveal themselves to be complex, gorgeously wrought lights, with faceted golden lamps at their ends; these continue into the interior foyer, which also has similarly odd, almost fetishistic metallic discs running along the booking offices. It has something of the H. R. Giger quality of the other Queen Elizabeth Hall on London's South Bank, though the similarities are mostly in the interiors. Inevitably, there are plans to demolish the buildings, most imminently the hall; Oldham's recent crop of public buildings includes the terrific **Art Gallery & Library (below)**, and the truly appalling PFI hospital opposite the Civic Centre, so it's hard to be confident that what replaces it will be better. It's certainly unlikely to be as weird and intense as the Queen Elizabeth Hall. It is worth noting that underneath the Civic Centre there is also a nuclear bunker, which was recently revealed to the public.

—

FORMER CO-OPERATIVE BANK HEADQUARTERS, STOCKPORT
Maxwell Hutchinson & Partners, 1987–92
Postmodernist

A hard entry to justify on strict grounds of 'quality', whatever that means, but so extraordinarily weird it would seem churlish not to include it. On the other side of the viaduct from the town centre is a giant speculative mirrorglass pyramid (taken over after its initial commercial failure by the Co-op – what a contrast with the brilliant architecture it once built all over the North! – though the Co-op vacated it more recently), designed by the 1980s architectural TV celebrity Maxwell Hutchinson. It can be seen clearly from the train to Manchester Piccadilly, and is also highly visible from the M60, and may be best appreciated from there – context is not really an issue here. Yet, somehow, a giant blue pyramid in the middle of Greater Manchester's sprawl of disused mills, motorways and retail parks feels very appropriate, a dose of sinister 1980s corporate evil, a palace for the giant lizards that rule the world. At its crown, a clear glass point is flanked by what resemble gun emplacements. Originally, a whole development of these pyramids was planned – the mind boggles.

—

OLDHAM ART GALLERY & LIBRARY
Pringle Richards Sharratt, 1999–2005
High-Tech

Pringle Richards Sharratt is one of the great unsung architectural firms of recent years. Its formal repertoire is standard to post-1997 New Labour architecture – here, lightweight metal trimmings, red terracotta tiles and whacking great atria. But they're always assembled to create generous, logical, easily used public spaces. Here, an art gallery with lots of natural light is joined on to a municipal library. The latter has barrel-vaulted spaces on the top floor expressed as a great glass tube, with particularly notable paintings placed at the entrances to the concrete stairwells, and with a walkway going into the old municipal buildings opposite. On the ground floor, an atrium links to a four-square library, with alternately open and intimate spaces; peculiar polychrome frosted-glass lights illuminate the space between. Nothing feels done for effect, everything is easy, pleasurable and well made. Being able to do this on a PFI budget must have been an art in itself.

10. NORTH-WEST

Preston Bus Station (p. 444)

Bus Station

The North-West of England is, after the South-East and the West Midlands, the most densely populated part of Britain; it is a larger region than either, though, stretching from the dense conurbations of Merseyside to overwhelmingly rural Cumbria. The metropolis here – excising Greater Manchester, which has its own chapter – is of course Liverpool, which vies with Newcastle to be the most straightforwardly beautiful big city in England. It is bursting full of pioneering architecture, including what has plausibly been described as the first modernist building in the world, **Oriel Chambers**. Liverpool City Council was a rare municipal sponsor of progressive design in the interwar years, as can be seen in the **Philharmonic Hall**, in **Speke Aerodrome**, at the **St Andrew's Gardens** housing complex and with the remarkable Expressionist edifices of the **Mersey Tunnel**, which can be found in both Liverpool and Birkenhead.

Post-war architecture is much weaker in Liverpool, but the architects of both the city of Preston (in the form of locals Building Design Partnership, whose major work in their hometown is the staggering **Preston Bus Station**) and the county of Lancashire produced some superb work. Under Roger Booth, the county built such disparate works as the pop art **Plastic Classroom** in Preston and the hardcore Brutalism of its police stations/headquarters in Blackpool and Chorley. There are some notable corporate offices in this once heavily industrial region, of which the finest is **Pilkington Headquarters** in St Helens. Lancashire and the Wirral have a lot of excellent religious architecture, especially the cathedrals in Liverpool and Blackburn, and the eccentric Expressionism of F. X. Velarde's Catholic churches. In the north of the region are found the resorts of Blackpool and Morecambe, which have some splendid thirties buildings such as the **Midland Hotel**, and the industrial Cumbrian coast, where the most interesting outpost is the intense island townscape of Barrow-in-Furness. Near the border with Scotland, Cumbria's county town, Carlisle, has an excellent International Style **Civic Centre**, currently under threat of demolition.

LIVERPOOL

ORIEL CHAMBERS ✪
Peter Ellis, 1864
16 COOK STREET ✪
Peter Ellis, 1866
NORWICH HOUSE
Edmund Kirkby & Sons, 1973
Uncategorizable

Ask a silly question, and you'll get a silly answer. The most plausible entrants for the 'what is the first modernist building in the world' contest are two Victorian office blocks by the architect Peter Ellis in the centre of Liverpool. What about – you may ask – all those functionalist warehouses of the nineteenth century, without ornament, often steel-framed, sometimes entirely of steel and glass? But then most industrial buildings have always been built largely for their purpose. The Romans built plenty of concrete warehouses. So the first modernist building has to be about more than just function, but also a new way of making architecture, one which tries to create some sort of fusion of new technologies and consciously embrace new aesthetic possibilities. All this is true of Oriel Chambers and 16 Cook Street in a way it isn't about Liverpool's many extraordinary high-Victorian warehouses. What these two make of their technologies and ideas is obviously not what 'modern architecture' would do with them, but the decisions made here about structure and space are different answers to the questions that would define them in the twentieth century.

Oriel Chambers is a grid of huge bulbous glass windows, described by Liverpool's great early-twentieth-century classicist Charles Reilly as 'a cellular habitation for the human insect'. It is iron-framed, and you can see it is iron-framed, without any decision to hide this fact with a classical or, given its date, Italianate dressing; and the idea that

the freeing up of the facade that the frame created could be filled with glass feels very twentieth century. But, then, the elements of the facade that aren't of plate glass are made up of a strange invented gabled Flemish style in sandstone; and the frames of those glass globules have little spikes to help that upwards, Gothick motion. These feel integral, not tacked on, with the architecture and the technology working together.

Ellis's slightly later 16 Cook Street, meanwhile, is less resolved architecturally and is much more of an eccentricity. It is another fusion of gables and great expanses of glass, which here resembles the bastard child of Louis Sullivan and mundane Victorian commercial design; but at the back is a cylindrical glass staircase that would have been contemporary a century hence. Steampunk architecture.

Steampunk architecture: the iron, glass and stone office pods of Peter Ellis's Oriel Chambers.

Across the road from Oriel Chambers, Norwich House tries with some success to continue the 'cellular habitation' motif while using the Brutalist means of raw corrugated concrete, mass-produced panels and an even greater sense of repetition. The inspiration from Oriel Chambers is obvious in the slightly projecting bulbous windows, though you'll find a much more inspired high-modernist tribute to Peter Ellis nearby at **4 Dale Street (p. 429)**.

─────

ROYAL LIVER BUILDING
Walter Aubrey Thomas, 1908–11
Chicago School

Yes, really. Of course, the Edwardian pomp of the Pier Head's 'Three Graces' is exactly the sort of imperial bombast that modernism placed itself against, and, of course, this 'grace' is clearly not modern architecture as it emerged out of the First World War. Yet there's another line of modernism's emergence, which derives from Louis Sullivan and the Chicago School of the 1880s and '90s, where framed construction was treated as an organizational principle for the architecture applied to it, not as something to be ignored or cloaked (though while Chicago's towers were steel-framed, that of the Liver Building is concrete). The repetition and scale it made possible could be emphasized, and organized into a distinct base, shaft and crown, as with a Greek column. So, yes, much of the granite ornament on the Liver Building is strictly Edwardian, but the long, determinedly monumental side elevations are almost a direct crib from Sullivan and Adler's Auditorium Building in Chicago. The crowning towers are of the twentieth century, too – tiered and cupola'd in a way that anticipates the abstracted hierarchies of art deco. More importantly, as the only true early skyscraper in Britain, with its thirteen storeys and its twin towers, the

Liver Building carries all the thrill of the early twentieth century's rush of change. Looking at it either crowning the city from a distance, or as a sheer cliff of masonry up close, you can clearly see it's part of the world of the great steamships, the first aircraft, the Model T and the telegraph. Electricity crackles through it.

─────

THE MATCHWORKS
Mewes & Davis with Sven Rylander, 1919–21
Industrial

Near to the splendid **Speke Aerodrome (p. 426)**, but easily missed, is this classic Americanist industrial building, one of the purest examples of the glass grid, Midwestern 'Daylight Factory' genre then being celebrated by the likes of Le Corbusier and the Bauhaus (while being phased out in the US itself). It's an unfussy example of the genre, without the cyclopean scale of the **Shredded Wheat Factory (p. 175)** in Welwyn Garden City – a long, low-rise range of glass and concrete with a tall water tower, and faintly Egyptian details added by the nominal architects, otherwise best known for the (steel-framed) French baroque of the Ritz in London. Renovated as offices reasonably well by Urban Splash, with a little High-Tech whimsy added round the edges by their architects, Shedkm.

─────

MERSEY TUNNEL VENTILATING STATION & MERSEY TUNNEL ENTRANCE
Herbert J. Rowse, 1931–4
Moderne

Liverpool at the interwar peak and/or twilight of its imperial grandeur. Most of what was built in this period in the centre consists of magnificent American-classical edifices like the India Buildings, a genre which goes right up to the fifties, in the form of Lewis's Department Store; admirable in its way, but not modernist. Like the **Royal Liver Building (above)**, these sit at the midpoint between modern and classical – Rowse improvised his own part-Americanist, part-Parisian art deco solution to the engineering problems of the (first, known as Queensway) Mersey Tunnel. The Ventilating Station is the politer version of the enormous masses Rowse designed for the other side in Birkenhead **(p. 434)**, with Portland stone dressings and naughtily moderne sculptures, in order to harmonize with the great Edwardian mammoths of the Pier Head. The entrances, meanwhile, round the back of the Victorian civic buildings at William Brown Street, combine lovely moderne fittings in copper and vitrolite – kiosks, lamp standards – with faintly Egyptian picture palace pavilions and a grand archway. The golden road to Birkenhead.

ST ANDREW'S GARDENS ✪
John Hughes for Liverpool City Council Architects Dept, 1935
Viennese

Liverpool is a great problem for those (hello) who want to set up an isomorphism between radical politics and radical architecture; a sectarian Tory council in the 1930s went to Red Vienna and built a dozen or so collectivist superblocks in its image, while a Trotskyist council in the 1980s demolished almost all of them in favour of council-owned Barratt Homes. At this distance we don't have to worry about that, so we can just gaze in awe at the only one left of formerly Blue Liverpool's Red Megabuildings, marooned on a hill above Lime Street, surrounded by low-rise cul-de-sacs. Known locally as the Bull Ring, and now student flats, St Andrew's Gardens is an irregular circus of concrete and well-made, sculpted brick, reached, as in Vienna, through grand

Red Vienna reimagined in red brick in Red Liverpool at John Hughes's St Andrews Gardens, aka the 'Bull Ring'.

archways – high and Expressionistic to the side entrances, wide and triumphal in the centre. The brick decks inside are a grand sweep, with Mendelsohnian curved, open stair towers at the corners. These enclose a well-tended green space with benches and community buildings. Its private security doesn't take kindly to visitors, but it's worth being shouted at to see, for once, an estate of 1930s tenements with a convincing central (semi-)public space at its heart rather than a car park or a wasteland. Irrespective of its provenance it *looks* like an idea of socialism, an image of collective abundance and communal pride, so it's apt it stands in what is today the reddest city in the country.

———

PHILHARMONIC HALL
Herbert J. Rowse, 1936–9
Moderne

Hope Street is one of the great streets of England, between the two cathedrals – neo-Gothic on one side, the bizarre invention of the **Metropolitan Cathedral (p. 427)** on the other, with superb, mostly Georgian and Victorian, buildings in-between. Mid-way along is this excellent piece of Dudokery, which displays how the Dutch dilution of Constructivism and Expressionism could create traditionally civic statements of power and pride. You can see this in the strongly symmetrical elevation, based on two curved stair towers, with its fine brickwork and American-style high strip windows, and more obvious residues of De Stijl radicalism in the composition of the side wings, where cubic windows and planes of bare brick alternate like the solids and voids of a Mondrian painting. As at Birkenhead's **Mersey Tunnel Structures (p. 434)**, the hall shows Rowse to be one of the most talented and open-minded of interwar official architects, able to take his sources from the Continent and the USA and then transform them into something distinctly Northern and English.

SPEKE AERODROME ✪
E. H. Bloomfield for Liverpool City Council Architects Dept, 1937–40
Moderne

Airport archaeology. Air travel is brusquely unsentimental about its buildings, and only a handful of important examples of its architecture survive globally (the **Elmdon Building (p. 309)** in Birmingham and the **Former BOAC Maintenance Headquarters (p. 162)** are a rare exception, while even more recent buildings like **Stansted Airport (p. 192)** are already struggling to retain any integrity). But next to the contemporary John Lennon Airport – with its rather poignant slogan, 'Above us only sky' – is Liverpool's original aerodrome. It was designed by the city's own architects in the second half of the thirties, and feels very much part of the municipal project, at the edge of the city council's lush suburban parkways and the neo-Georgian Speke council estate, though the area is now marred with retail park dross. Architecturally, Speke Aerodrome is very much in the Central European manner of thirties Liverpool monuments like the **Philharmonic Hall (above)** or **St Andrew's Gardens (p. 425)**, a suave metropolitan brick expressionism derived from Vienna, Hamburg and Amsterdam. Approach it from the grim retail parks around and you don't quite get the buildings' full import, with a classical symmetry and a bulky central block in purple and red brick; it's more avant-garde and much more exciting if admired from the rear facade you would see when alighting from a plane – a hexagonal glass control tower with a clock, and spreading concrete and brick wings, long and elegant, befitting what was then a luxury mode of travel. Here, evidently, Liverpool's planners and architects thought that air transport could give rise to structures of the same beauty and grandeur as those built for its ocean liners. Their mistake. Much as the terminal has become a hotel,

The very late architecture of the Port of Liverpool: the concrete arch of the Tate & Lyle Sugar Silo.

the Crown Plaza Speke, the brick hangars, with their deco reliefs, symmetrically flanking the aerodrome, have been repurposed – one is a fitness centre, the other something called 'Shop Direct'. As a result of their preservation, the aerodrome still feels like a coherent ensemble, especially with the sad and beautiful old aircraft left out on the tarmac. A form of infrastructure that usually acts like it has no history is here enriched by it. [**D.17**]

TATE & LYLE SUGAR SILO
Tate & Lyle Engineering Dept, 1955–7
Brutalist

Close to the derelict expanses of Stanley Dock – a mammoth brick complex now used mainly as a film set – this is a simple industrial structure, part of a refining industry which clung on here until the 1980s. It is straightforward enough, with its raw concrete, barred windows and hulking proportions, but it has been given considerable grandeur by the ribbing of its concrete barrel roof and its finely profiled concrete mullions. Temporally, it's the last industrial edifice of any architectural note in the city, but it's very much a twentieth-century structure – a hangar, not a shed, which has been conceived as a building to look at as well as simply to stuff things in.

METROPOLITAN CATHEDRAL ✪
Frederick Gibberd Partnership, 1962–7
People's Detailing

Liverpool's Roman Catholic cathedral – the most prominent in any British city – has always had a hard time from the critics. Classicists might lament the way that it replaced Edwin Lutyens's New Delhi-style mammarial baroque design (the crypt of which was built, and still stands);

Charles Jencks, in his once-influential book *Modern Movements in Architecture*, used it as an example of the decadence into which modernism had fallen, arguing that its various registers and integrated artworks didn't 'speak' coherently. The sectarian term 'Paddy's Wigwam' has stuck. None of this is fair. Kitsch, you say? Have you ever *been* in a Catholic church before? Cluttered with artworks, is it? Ever set foot in Westminster Abbey? Too large? Not while facing that cyclopean neo-Gothic Anglican cathedral at the other end of Hope Street it isn't.

Today, opinions are softening towards the building, and it seems to be gradually joining the Pier Head and the Anglican cathedral in the city's pantheon of tall buildings, appearing on the usual tourist paraphernalia: which is good, because it's brilliant. Like the more stark **Clifton Cathedral (p. 270)** in Bristol, it's very obviously a response to the reforms of Vatican II, bringing formal experiment and an intimacy of arrangement to the hierarchies of Catholic architecture. But whereas the Bristol building uses the new freedoms that designers of Catholic architecture had gained in order to push into an intense, personal, stripped-back experience of the ineffable, Liverpool's cathedral is a populist experience that feels like some extraordinary collision of Oscar Niemeyer and Las Vegas. The basic idea is instantly readable as soon as you see the building – a sort of 'altar in the round', carried up by concrete columns into an immense funnel-cum-crown. Inside, the circular plan is lit by thrilling pulses of blue light through stained glass. The way the interior is lit by natural light, so that it alternates between murk and celestial bursts and shafts of colour, is captivating. The artworks – outside, the typically cryptic and brutish concrete reliefs by William Mitchell; inside, John Piper and Patrick Reyntiens' glass, and Gibberd's own rather freakish, spiky baldachin – are all worth exploration, and, whatever Jencks might have said,

they all feel of a piece, pulled together by that spiral upwards. Modernism against minimalism. [C.27 & C.28]

———

ALLERTON LIBRARY
R. Bradbury for Liverpool City Architects Dept, 1963
WYNCOTE SPORTS PAVILION
Gerard Beech, 1961
International Style, Brutalist

Deep in the Garden City southern suburbs of Liverpool, you can find this wonderful modernist library, in a wedge between a broad parkway of semis. The site is used with subtlety and flair, with the library lodged in-between mature trees. The building itself is Brutalism as in the **Smithdon School (p. 196)**, rather than in terms of big concrete monuments – precise, clipped-together steel-and-glass volumes, with an abstracted water tower on top as 'found object' – Mies on a municipal budget, with a layout evidently modelled on one of his spaced-out, Malevich-via-Schinkel plans. Then there's something that is all the architect's own, a wing of the building covered entirely by a repeated concrete grid pattern, like an op art sculpture.

Close by in Allerton is Liverpool University's Wyncote Sports Pavilion, designed in 1961 – a (listed) glass cube overlooking a very neat lawn, a curiously successful modernization of the *Daily Mail* England genre of the cricket pavilion, refined, curt and elegant.

———

UNIVERSITY OF LIVERPOOL SPORTS CENTRE
Denys Lasdun & Partners, 1963–6
Brutalist

One of Lasdun's smaller buildings, but a masterclass in his firm's remarkable ability to be architecturally aggressive and spatially generous. Placed in the middle of the urbane Georgian residential inner city of Liverpool, this attracted the usual criticism for not being In Keeping, and although it maintains the scale and height of the Georgian terraces, a raked, exposed-frame concrete sports hall was never going to try and look like a Georgian terrace, at least not until the 1980s. But the way the building is placed on the street is far from careless – the way that its raked frame continues down to the pavement creates a fine civic gesture, effectively becoming a pedestrian colonnade.

LIVERPOOL PLAYHOUSE EXTENSION
Hall O'Donohue & Wilson, 1968
ST JOHN'S BEACON
James A. Roberts Associates, 1965–9
International Style

When the appalling St John's Centre, a scar on the centre of Liverpool, is finally demolished, hopefully these two will be salvaged, much as its designer James Roberts's **Rotunda (p. 314)** was retained when Birmingham's Bull Ring shopping centre was pulled down. St John's Beacon, now known as the Radio City Tower, is a fun and goofy example of the telecommunications tower genre, with concrete shaft and disc-like crown – though the revolving restaurant inside is sadly closed. It's probably the only *direct* British example of the type that compares with those in inner cities in Europe and the US; the **Post Office Tower (p. 59)** is in its own world, **Emley Moor Telecommunications Tower (p. 389)** is on a hill near Wakefield, and the **Express Lift Test Tower (p. 350)** is in a Barratt Estate. The St John's Beacon was originally built just as a clever way of providing ventilation into the mall below, and the fact that it wasn't designed as a TV tower points to its greatest problem – it's far too short. The tower doesn't raise itself high

enough above the more mundane high-rises of Liverpool to have the effect that it ought to, though views of it from the north – say, from Everton Park – are more impressive than those from the Mersey. By different architects, but part of the same project, the Playhouse Extension is similarly a matter of confident curved forms, daringly attached to a music hall baroque decorated shed: two intersecting cylinders, one entirely glazed, one with ribbon windows, and each supported on a single column – exactly the sort of pop architecture you would think Liverpool ought to specialize in but doesn't.

4 DALE STREET ○
Bradshaw Rowse & Harker, 1971
High-Tech

In his Pevsner city guide to Liverpool, Joseph Sharples describes this building – built as a Midland Bank and at the time of writing

Bradshaw, Rowse & Harker's bank at 4 Dale Street: Oriel Chambers updated for the high-tech age.

partly used as a restaurant – as a modernist attempt to emulate the nearby **Oriel Chambers (p. 423)**, which gives some sense of its bizarre presence. It is some measure of the extreme radicalism of Oriel Chambers that a building designed a century later should look ultra-modern while following it closely in both structure and style. The tribute is explicit – these offices with a street frontage are crammed similarly tightly into the Victorian grid, it is roughly the same size and scale, and it boasts a similar series of giant glass cells for some sort of species of giant insect. Here, though, all the residual Victorian historicism has been stripped away, leaving only the bubbles, this time angular and spiky rather than gently curved; each black-glass module is shaped into a flat-sided diamond, which is then repeated right round the corner facade. It's a fragment of a world in which Oriel Chambers was truly the birthplace of modern architecture, rather than just a local eccentricity.

KINGSWAY TUNNEL VENTILATION TOWER ✪
Bradshaw Rowse & Harker, 1971
Brutalist

In the same fascinating if depressing post-industrial wasteland as the **Tate & Lyle Sugar Silo (p. 427)**, this monumental work of engineering is made up of three distinct volumes on a brick plinth – two big hexagonal grilles and, between them, a biomorphic concrete tower, straddling it all in the manner of some terrifying Futurist monster, straight out of the imaginary drawings of the Italian fantasist Antonio Sant'Elia. These ventilation towers for the second Mersey tunnel are a total contrast with the Queensway towers of the first; ironically, the firm that designed them was founded by the same architect, Herbert J. Rowse. Liverpool architecture of the early seventies could be seriously dystopian, as if the start of the city's sharp decline pushed designers into producing

The monumental, Italian Futurist-style ventilation towers of the Kingsway Tunnel, the second across the Mersey.

images of fantastical domination and surreal aggro. This is one of the results, and it has fun with its malevolence, a comic horror.

NEW HALL PLACE
Tripe & Wakeham Partnership, 1972–6
Brutalist

Built as the offices of Royal Insurance, this is the major Brutalist building of Liverpool, near the Pier Head, and it's a pretty jarring edifice – a thirteen-storey concrete sandcastle, made up of stacked, staggered and jenga'd chunks of yellow-tinted concrete. The projections and set-backs of the design were intended to accommodate planned concrete walkways, interconnecting the office blocks in the centre; although partially constructed, most of the system has been removed, unlike the City of London **Pedways (p. 60)** or the **Newcastle City Centre Walkway System (p. 483)**. Whatever the rationale, the effect is of a completely three-dimensional space, one that pedestrians can climb about and around, and where the office workers can take their fag breaks with up-close views of one of the greatest skylines in Europe. It doesn't genuflect to that historic skyline, instead combining a real grandeur of scale with zero compromise in aesthetics – and much more impressively so than recent bungles like Mann Island or the Museum of Liverpool, on the other side of the Pier Head.

MERSEYRAIL: CENTRAL, HAMILTON SQUARE, JAMES STREET, LIME STREET & MOORFIELDS STATIONS
1977
International Style

Liverpool has what couldn't quite be called a Metro – more a German-style S-Bahn, a comprehensive suburban train service that covers most of the city and its surroundings.

These five Underground stations – four in Liverpool, one in Birkenhead – were opened in the late seventies, with a common design of curved brown-plastic and white-metal panels, which have an enjoyable futurist feel to them, and a good system of signage; all are unpretentiously placed in the ground floors of existing buildings, Central now at the bottom of a rather grim mall, Hamilton Square in Birkenhead within the original Victorian Underground station surmounted by a Gothic tower, and the others in post-war office blocks. Not quite a fair exchange for the destruction of the Liverpool Overhead Railway, an elevated north–south route that could easily have been brought into this network, as per the viaducts in Berlin, but a decent little system nevertheless, which could be so much more if it hadn't been sold off. It is now so badly managed that nobody who doesn't live here seems to know that Liverpool actually has a Tube – and between the first and second drafts of this book most of the fittings described have been removed without protest or comment. Although the tunnels and signage remain reasonably elegant, there is much less of note to see beneath Liverpool than there had been before the stations' refurbishment. A disappointing contrast with the far better design record of the roughly contemporary **Tyne and Wear Metro (p. 486)**, but worth seeing nonetheless.

QUEEN ELIZABETH II LAW COURTS
Farmer & Dark, 1973–84
Brutalist

Along with **New Hall Place (above)**, one of the city's few efforts in Brutalism – evidently, it was more of a Manchester thing – not emotional or grandiose enough for Liverpool. The long gestation period of these law courts corresponds precisely with the collapse of the city's economy, and the government's treatment of Liverpool as a sort of urban enemy within. Accordingly, it must have felt a grim place, an immense castellated edifice in which to punish the city's trangressions. In a way, that's still the effect it has now – it's humourless and heavy, and frames, rather appropriately, a stodgy statue of Queen Victoria. But, by its own brooding lights, it's a powerful design, ship-like in its feeling of surging force, and the asymmetrical skyline and pulling together of disparate elements is audacious and successful. Brutalism like the FBI did it.

ONE ARTHOUSE SQUARE
Austin-Smith:Lord, 2004
High-Tech

This was built as offices for an NHS trust, as part of the redevelopment of the Ropewalks into the natural place for the 'creative class' to come and transform Liverpool as it has so obviously transformed Manchester. It didn't quite work out like that, although the area itself, with its spindly warehouses, cobbled alleyways and sudden gusts of sea air, has far more atmosphere than anywhere in Manchester. It was always a strange idea to put NHS offices here, given that the 'programme' is always meant to be luxury flats, start-ups and vertical drinking, rather than ordinary people doing normal public-sector jobs (although they of course played a far bigger real role in the New Labour period's brief revival of the Northern economy). So this place got sold off and is soon to become a hotel, which is a shame, but doesn't detract from the ingenious design, by the architects of the lumpier FACT arts centre nearby. It's built into the back end of an old warehouse, and creates a (now very boozy) public square out of what would have been just bins and rats; on to the brick wall they've affixed big glass bays and a stair tower with a hint of Constructivism about it. The best of a few similar small-scale schemes in the area.

UNITY TOWERS
AHMM, 2007
Pseudomodernist

Part of a generally dull cluster of luxury high-rises in a city that needs few things less, these are good examples of the architecture of their period, now receding into history – the refusal to believe the good times will ever end in what Jonathan Meades called the 'soufflé economy' – a sort of architectural Superlambanana. There are two Unity Towers, both for the same client and designed by AHMM, one of the main firms of the period, best known for the lurid Day-Glo cladding of their Westminster Academy and Barking Riverside projects. One of these two, an office block, is an extruded barcode facade that is unbearably of its time, but the other, taller, residential tower is more interesting, striped in an approximation of Vorticist dazzle-painting, with a faintly unnerving metal-clad outlook post at the top. For some lucky Merseyside master of the universe.

ST PETER'S ARCADE, LIVERPOOL ONE
Dixon Jones, 2008
THE BLUECOAT
biq, 2008
Modern Classicism

Liverpool One is barely defensible – the blanket privatization of a swathe of the city centre, transforming it into what is effectively a shopping mall, owned, policed and legally treated as such – but it has more spatial imagination than most architecture of its era, with some enjoyable multilevel walkways and elevated parks, and some !!!FUN!!! facade treatments which are now dating with extreme rapidity. Dixon Jones's suave St Peter's Arcade, with its terrazzo floor and **Oriel Chambers**-style **(p. 423)** futurist aquarium shop windows, has aged best of its various components.

Continuity on Hope Street: the Everyman Theatre, next door to the neoclassical Liverpool Medical Institution.

At its edges is an arts centre by the Dutch designers biq, connected to a very early English classical building of 1716, the Bluecoat School. It was intended partly as a polemical contrast with Liverpool One – biq were keen to stress a continuity in scale and materials with an idealized (rather than actual) idea of Liverpool as a city of red brick and black granite. The building is detailed to an extremely high standard, and its high gable is appropriately maritime. When it was built, the Bluecoat felt like a real holdout, a piece of scrupulous, long-term architecture standing in the kitchen of a particularly insufferable party. Now, in cities that have money (i.e. not Liverpool) cheaper, paler versions of biq's attempt to use a modernized English vernacular are everywhere. They seldom possess the grace of this excellent little building.

EVERYMAN THEATRE
Haworth Tompkins, 2011–14
Modernist Eclectic

Like many of the better recent buildings in Liverpool, this is about continuity rather than the *tabula rasa*. What you notice first is the facade of glinting silvery panels, embossed with photographs of local figures – a low-budget but clever and attractive device that feels popular rather than populist. Four decorative brick chimneys crown this, and give the auditorium natural ventilation; they're detailed in a similar fashion to the rough Georgiana all around, with many of the bricks salvaged from the chapel that previously housed the theatre. Behind this is a deep-planned building, partly retaining elements of the blocky 1970s theatre on the same site. A subtle and strong urban block, able to hold its own on the architectural premier league that is Hope Street. It won the Stirling Prize in 2014, for once deservedly so.

MERSEYSIDE

WARRINGTON TRANSPORTER BRIDGE
William Henry Hunter, 1913
UNILEVER DETERGENT POWDER PLANT, WARRINGTON
1920s–1980s
Industrial

It's almost quaint to see a working, noisy factory right next to a major railway station (Warrington Bank Quay) – this must be pretty much the only place left in Britain where this is possible. The site, built up incrementally since the 1920s, hasn't noticeably had an architect anywhere near it, and is a sprawling collection of silos and puzzling halls, which bubble and smoke and rumble at all times of the day. The silos have recently been painted with some cutesy Unilever branding, but this is smelly, unpleasant industry, the price Warrington pays for our washing powder; as townscape, it's a rare and very likely temporary survival of inner-urban, un-zoned industry. Nearby is a Transporter Bridge over the Mersey, heavy and rusty compared to its cousin in Newport **(p. 285)** but worth seeing. The rest of Warrington is a sprawling expanded New Town, a sort of Merseyside Corby.

MERSEY TUNNEL STRUCTURES, BIRKENHEAD: ✪
WOODSIDE VENTILATION TOWER, SIDNEY STREET & TAYLOR STREET VENTILATION STATIONS
Herbert J. Rowse, 1931–4
Expressionist

Three absolutely astonishing structures, just the other side of the Mersey from Liverpool. These are part of the same project as the **Mersey Tunnel Ventilating Station (p. 424)**; the evil twins of the Portland stone-clad,

dignified art deco shafts and entrances in the heart of the metropolis. While the shafts on the other side of the river are detailed in Portland stone and stand amongst the monuments on the Pier Head, their Wirral cousins are placed instead in the scrubby light-industrial alleyways of central Birkenhead, where they appear as sentinels. For pedestrians, the best route is a short walk from the Hamilton Square Underground station, where they provide a drastic contrast with the smart classical square that gives that station its name. The largest of the shafts, the Woodside Ventilation Tower, is easily visible from the Pier Head on the Liverpool side, and from there is impressive enough, but from close by it is overwhelming, the most powerful brick architecture in twentieth-century Britain, surpassing even **Battersea Power Station (p. 108)** in its roaring gutsiness. Proportioned like a skyscraper, it is stepped upwards to form a thuggishly successful skyline, where the decorative brick details leading up to and then crowning the top add to its physical strength, like sinews on muscle.

The other two are almost as amazing. Sidney Street is like one of Cachemaille-Day's explosive, compacted Expressionist churches transposed to the purpose of getting people from one side of the Mersey to the other; whereas Taylor Street is a miniature power station in its own right, a huge brick volume with two squat towers, with all the thrilling force of Bankside (now **Tate Modern, p. 102**). Unless you already live in the Wirral, the prospect of crossing the river at Liverpool to see some ventilation shafts might not sound tempting, but I could not recommend it enough. **[D.19]**

Sturm und Drang in Birkenhead: the brick cliffs of one of Herbert J. Rowse's Mersey Tunnel ventilation towers.

CO-OPERATIVE DEPARTMENT STORE, SOUTHPORT

J. W. Cropper and W. A. Johnson, 1934
Moderne

Another of the impressively Central European department stores built by the Co-op in the thirties across the North and the Midlands as images of 'progressive' commerce, alongside Bradford **(p. 384)**, Huddersfield **(p. 384)**, Newcastle **(p. 479)**, Derby **(p. 358)** and the southern outlier in Woolwich **(p. 83)**. Like its cousins it compromises its sources – the streamlined stores designed by Erich Mendelsohn for Berlin, Chemnitz, Stuttgart, Wrocław, etc. – by adding sandstone cladding and a little light decoration. This is one of the largest and plushest, befitting its location in the commercial centre of Southport, a grand coastal emporium built for the Northern bourgeoisie of the nineteenth century to flash their cash in. Accordingly, here

Cropper and Johnson go for more ornament, with sandstone pilasters and stick-of-rock pastels – and for more tech, with a full four-storey all-glass cylindrical stair tower creating a very dramatic corner. It's also, sadly, the most depressing example of the after-effects of the Co-op's firesale of its own history; today the subdivided building is one half Poundland, one half derelict.

———

ST MONICA'S CHURCH, BOOTLE ✪

Francis Xavier Velarde, 1936
Expressionist

Pevsner gives this a supremely back-handed compliment – 'an epoch-making church for England, though not of course for the continent'. Well, since this is a book about British architecture, it'll have to remain epochal. As British churches of the 1930s go, the only one to bear comparison to this overwhelming brown brick mass is

The delightful combination of Expressionist emotion and kitsch decoration in F. X. Velarde's St Monica's, Bootle.

St Saviour's Church (p. 80) in Eltham, and it derives from the same source, the German Expressionist brick churches of Dominikus Böhm. But whereas the single-minded burning intensity of Cachemaille-Day's London church feels decidedly Protestant, Xavier Velarde's approach is very Merseyside Catholic in its combination of scale, sweep and sentiment. St Monica's – usually locked when there isn't a service – can be found on a totally ordinary street of bright-red terraced houses, overshadowed by container cranes. The parsonage ends the terrace, but breaks with its palette, opting for sombre dark-brown brick instead, and shifts the street's linearity into an angular Expressionist composition of spikes and curved bays, like a thirties house in Belgium or Holland. A small square then frames the church itself, an immense surge of masonry, with three huge windows surmounted with stylized, sexless etiolated art deco angels. The harshest facade faces a park rather than the street, where the brick becomes hard and industrial, a factory-like repetition of buttresses and high windows.

——

HOYLAKE STATION
William Henry Hamlyn, 1938
Moderne

The railway station for this genteel Wirral seaside town is an atypical emulation of Charles Holden's London Underground stations outside the South-East – its red-brick rotunda a miniaturized **Arnos Grove (p. 137)**, but with suave curved concrete canopies reaching out to frame a bus stop and a taxi rank. It lacks Holden's integrity but has some delightful details, especially the little curved Crittall-windowed pod of a ticket office – placed right on the line where the platform meets the booking hall, so that one of its curves faces into the building and the other out towards the trains.

REFLECTION COURT, ST HELENS
Herbert J. Rowse and Kenneth Cheeseman, 1937–41
Moderne

This was the original HQ of the glass manufacturers before they moved to Fry and Drew's luxurious **Pilkington Headquarters (below)**, and it's now marooned in what must, facing extremely tough competition, be the most unpleasantly overengineered ring road in Britain, a baffling hellscape of retail park slurry and incomprehensibly placed pedestrian junctions. Waiting to cross the road here does, however, give you lots of time to contemplate this block. Alternating lines of strong Mendelsohnian ribbon windows and very Amsterdam red-brick details lead to what is evidently a repeat of the same architect's heavy, ceremonial entrance for Liverpool's **Philharmonic Hall (p. 426)**; but what that building lacks is the excellent asymmetrical clock tower on this block, a clever and intricate Constructivist–moderne assemblage of brick masses and curved projections.

CHURCH OF THE ENGLISH MARTYRS, WALLASEY
Francis Xavier Velarde, 1953
Expressionist

Xavier Velarde, evidently unaffected by the shift from Brick Expressionism as the 'progressive' language of churches in the thirties to the concrete experiments of the sixties, carried on doing very much his own thing, developing an increasingly personal language out of the massive structures he'd pioneered at **St Monica's Church (p. 435)** in Bootle, and **St Gabriel's Church (p. 442)** in Blackburn, always fitting with wit and intelligence into the mundane places they're built into. Here, we're in Wirral suburbia, and the scale is less industrial than in Bootle or Blackburn; there is a similar

personal style of vast masonry halls and elongated figures, cleverly given a structural role as mullions; but the detached campanile, red brick with an open bell tower and a conical copper cap, is from somewhere else entirely – a strange, timeless abstract Renaissance, of the kind you could imagine in a fifteenth-century painting.

SILVER JUBILEE BRIDGE, RUNCORN
Mott Hay & Anderson, 1956–63
Industrial

An ambitious piece of engineering – like a more delicate, pared-back version of the Victorian melodrama of, say, the Forth Rail Bridge – it spans the Mersey suspended by a great arched mesh of thin steel. It's as good in its way as the **New Tyne Bridge (p. 479)**, but, unlike that structure, looks out on the panorama of industrial Runcorn and Widnes rather than the heart of a city. It's also a last great hurrah for the heavy metal bridge style; subsequently, all the interesting bridges are in the minimalist, International Style of the **Severn Bridge (p. 290)** and **Humber Bridge (p. 463)** crossings, making Runcorn's bridge feel like a last magnificent monument of Victorian technology.

PILKINGTON HEADQUARTERS, ST HELENS ⊙
Maxwell Fry and Jane Drew, 1959–63
International Style

Along with the **CIS Tower (p. 403)** in Manchester, the glass manufacturer's new HQ was and is the purest and most confident statement of mainstream modern architecture in the North – lesser-known because of its location, but no less its equal. In fact, it is one of the most sheerly impressive complexes of its kind in the entire country, a project of unusual completeness, rigour and spatial generosity. The buildings occupy a campus-like site a mile or so outside the centre of St Helens – it's a sort-of public park, in that you can wander or cycle through the grounds, although you're certainly not allowed into the buildings. The landscaping is the centrepiece, by the underrated G. P. Youngman, and as calm and ordered as his work in **Cumbernauld (p. 535)** is craggy. Green hillocks with mature trees frame a lake – a (currently derelict) glass block marks the end of the water. A straightforward concrete bridge leads across to a tower, accessed from a mezzanine, with lower offices at a right angle to it and a glassy canteen pavilion alongside, creating a series of subtle levels, a *promenade architecturale* that is a joy to walk through. Then, leading to the car park and back out on to the street, are a series of lower administrative blocks, with glass walkways calmly criss-crossing overhead.

There is more visual excitement and event in this walk than you'll find in most modernist ensembles, but the buildings themselves stay cool, without the slightest hint of any Brutalist sculptural heroics. It is expensively made, with plenty of granite and limestone, but placed into a straightforward articulated grid, stressing the concrete frame beneath, especially in the tower. This is a late work by a pair of architects who had learned their trade in the 1930s, when modern architecture was classical and Platonic, not Gothic and romantic; and while there are no thirties motifs to be found here, these buildings show complete fidelity to the idea of modern architecture as a rational, logical project. The irrational has its place, and that's in art – and, accordingly, inside there are various works of real significance. The easiest one to see is in the foyer of the tower, a set of opalescent glass murals by Avinash Chandra. Placed on multiple levels in this open-plan space, these are the equivalent of the Abstract Expressionist canvases in a Fifth Avenue HQ, except much more integral

with the building's own materials, which here are twisted into surreal and organic shapes. There is a security guard working here who is an enthusiast for the building – if you're lucky, he'll be on duty, and if not there's just time enough to admire the murals before being told you're not allowed to.

What disturbs about the complex a little is a factor shared with any Victorian or art deco factory administration building. In one direction is the factory, still plugging away, just, its smoke billowing into the air, in utterly utilitarian grey metal sheds; in another direction, big suburban houses for the management in what was for a time effectively a company town – and on the long bleak roads back to the centre, terraces, big and bay-windowed for the deserving, mean two-up two-downs for those not. The North of England remained what it was, even when its industrialists briefly experimented with being patrons of high modernism; now, of course, they don't bother. [**A.16**]

SOLAR CAMPUS, WALLASEY
Emslie A. Morgan for Wirral Corporation, 1962
People's Detailing, High-Tech, Ecomodernist

The real avant-garde, the true pioneers, are not always to be found where you most expect them. Readers of Reyner Banham's classic 1969 study of architecture and its heating, cooling and conditioning technologies, *The Architecture of the Well-Tempered Environment*, might remember that he ends the book with a school in Merseyside, the first completely solar-powered building in existence. You might wonder how many of the top-flight architects and academics who have read this Yale-published book have ever bothered to visit the place he was writing about. The Solar Campus – for that is what it is – is a comprehensive school on a long straight road at the edge of Wallasey, just where suburbia starts to become semi-rural.

From that road, you can see a completely normal early-sixties municipal building, part of which is used by Tranmere Rovers FC as a training ground. Hard to see what the fuss is about, although the listing because of said fuss has preserved the crisp, ingeniously planned qualities of the typical post-war school much better than in most places. What you must do is walk to the playing field, and then take a good look round the corner for what looks like a great High-Tech garden shed, clad in timber, of which one end is completely glazed – a completely bizarre combination of rough-arsed artisan construction and Californian advanced modernism, a sort of Charles and Ray Eames lean-to. That all-glass facade deliberately overheats, in order to power the building. It is one of two glass walls – one is opaque so as to reduce the heat and glare that are being accumulated by the other. The way the result looks so ad hoc and shabby is common to a lot of major advances – if you've ever been to Bletchley Park, you'll recognize that scruffy alignment of sheds and cybernetics. There's a lovely poetry to the fact that the sort of passive-energy technology that will hopefully save us in the future was first developed for a suburban school in the North of England; and you can't fully understand that without going to see this building. For navigation purposes, it's near to Wallasey Lidl.

14 WATERGATE STREET, THE ROWS, CHESTER
W. Campbell & Son, 1970
Brutalist

The Rows in Chester are a marvellous fake, a set of streets of half-timbered emporia, most of them reconstructions dating from the nineteenth and twentieth centuries, with upper-level internal galleries running through them, like some accidental foretaste of the multilevel cities of the sixties.

In a couple of places these actually collide, as frankly modern infill meets the Tudor and the mock-Tudor, and this is the most interesting, a spindly (and, sadly, painted) Brutalist frame, with well-detailed boxed-out windows, and a continuation of the upper-level walkway above the shops.

TRIAD BUILDING, BOOTLE
Hind Woodhouse Partnership, 1971–4
Brutalist

It can be a shock to chance upon this twenty-three-storey rude boy next to Bootle New Strand Station – here is one of the most aggressive Brutalist buildings in the country, unheralded and unnoticed. Its level of blaring noise and violence really cannot be gainsaid. The Triad, an office block for the Inland Revenue by a firm otherwise lost to history, is so called due to its complex three-part plan, which resembles three Richard Seifert buildings having a fight with each other – the sort of strange splayed layout you can find in, say, the **NatWest Tower (p. 66)** combined with the obsessive, polygonal modelling of the concrete modules in **Centre Point (p. 60)**, only here in a dark-brown concrete rather than Portland cement. The whole dissonant mass is held up on pilotis above a sculptural podium, a solid base to a warped, twisted tower. No denying the machismo in this one: strictly for the hardcore.

RUNCORN SHOPPING CITY ✪
Fred Roche, 1972
International Style

A failure, on any measure, but a fascinating and heroic one. In the sixties Runcorn was placed in that uneasy category of New Towns that were quite sizeable actually existing towns already before they became New. The results of this questionable process – more one of planned suburban expansion than anything else – generally tend to be less ambitious than the thrilling experience of creating something out of nothing. Runcorn 'New Town', bolted on to the Victorian industrial town on the south side of the Mersey, is better known for James Stirling's extremely outré and long-demolished Southgate housing scheme than for anything still there. 'Runcorn Shopping City' is the exception, an entire new centre to serve the expanded town, enclosed, climate-controlled and integrally linked with both civic buildings, and, unusually, its own public transport network, a partly elevated specialized 'Busway'. Catch this from the old town, and after faffing around at complicated junctions and in suburban streets it suddenly glides on its own dedicated roads through Span-style terraces in dense trees, then rides up on to a concrete viaduct, from which you emerge into the 'Shopping City'.

The architect, Fred Roche, would a few years later be one of the designers of Milton Keynes's **Shopping Building (p. 223)**, and this shares a lot of its preoccupations. It expresses an American modernism of precision and order, clad in what were alleged to be 'self-cleaning tiles' (they don't entirely self-clean). One side of the shopping centre is divided by the columned Brutalist enfilade of the Busway viaduct from the library, various office blocks, the council offices and the police station, and here the elegant, wipe-clean style is very like that of Yorke Rosenberg & Mardall, particularly **St Thomas' Hospital (p. 96)** – neat, if a little too sanitary. Get underneath – there are stairs, but they're not used now except by pigeons as a concrete shithouse – and the procession of walkways and paths is unusually spatially ambitious; in Milton Keynes, this sort of thing is hidden from the public, in the service areas behind the glass cubes.

The Shopping Centre has been painted blue and grey, but is obviously of a piece with all the rest. There's nothing much to see inside – it's run as a very very low-end mall, and narrowly escaped demolition in the 2000s – but follow the paths to the South Bus Station, emerge from the escalators on to the viaducts and you're in a real fragment of Milton Keynes's seamless, crystalline mirrorglass *Logan's Run* world, with the buses gliding as smoothly as monorails. The main difference between this place and Milton Keynes is economic – while Buckinghamshire thrives, Merseyside struggles, and my god you can tell, as you scuttle through the Poundlands. The forward-thinking and humane planning of the Busway is obviated by retail parks and deregulation, creating a bleak, exurban landscape. Whereas most malls couldn't care a damn about bus users, pedestrians or planning, this one made a huge amount of effort for all of these; it's lost in shabbiness now, but a good planner, a conscientious council or a sensitive developer should be able to piece it all back together.

ORMSKIRK STREET UNITED REFORMED CHURCH, ST HELENS
APEC Architects, 1976
Brutalist

A weird and cranky combined church and community centre, dominated by its exceptionally ungainly and angular metal roof, creating probably the most poignant combination of futurism and dilapidation of any building in the North, a region which can sometimes specialize in exactly that. The roof is almost brown with rust, but the sheer oddness of this object in the streetscape is inescapable – it resembles one of the 'Deconstructivist' buildings of the 1990s and 2000s implemented on a parsimonious dissenting church budget. Not a 'good' building as such, but a unique one.

High modernism on the River Dee: the cubic, Bauhaus-style Salmon Leap Flats in suburban Chester.

SALMON LEAP FLATS, CHESTER ✪
Gilling Dod & Partners, 1976
Classical Modernism

An excellent small estate of luxury, low-rise middle-class flats on a weir of the River Dee (salmon apparently swim the weir, hence the name). Its ownership structure imitates the Span model developed first at **Parkleys (p. 111)**, with the housing and public spaces maintained by the joint action of the owner-occupiers. But its design – three short terraces, cubic, regular, coolly poised, in front of a delightful natural waterscape – owes much more to the 'Grunt Group' at the Architectural Association (see here especially **Netherfield, p. 223**, in Milton Keynes), or the work of Camden Council, than it does to Eric Lyons' language of tile-hanging and neat little lawns, which was by then a ubiquitous style of suburban housing. Instead, these are elegant homes,

with a hint of De Stijl, modernism itself becoming retro. You can imagine it attracting art lecturers, say, as a place to return to after lecturing on Mondrian or Barnett Newman. Originally in salmon pink, the flats were repainted white recently, which makes their connection to the classic modernist revival even more obvious. A sane and restrained model of high-density housing by a river, worth a thousand of those overdeveloped waterside 'stunning developments'.

CENTRAL LANCASHIRE

ST GABRIEL'S CHURCH, BLACKBURN
Francis Xavier Velarde, 1932–3
Expressionist

The earliest of F. X. Velarde's massive brick churches, borrowing from German Expressionism – imposing, convulsive, cinematic, full of rumble and horror – but in an appalling state. On a suburban site of semis and council houses at the edge of Blackburn, near the improbably named Ramsgreave and Wilpshire Station, it rises up from a slope with a huge rectilinear tower, barely dressed up with the slightest of Gothic recollections, with a simple brick barn to the back. A heavy concrete roof was shoved on to the tower in the sixties due to leaks, and the building is currently considered unsafe due to subsidence – services are held in a Nissen hut next door. This is raw and bare in any case – a rare Protestant edifice from an architect who devoted his life to the Catholic church. A more complete example of Velarde's Brick Expressionism can be found at **St Monica's Church (p. 435)** in Bootle.

—

LANTERN, BLACKBURN CATHEDRAL
Laurence King, 1960–67
People's Detailing

The designer of this lantern, the architect and church restorer Laurence King, once claimed that 'it is traditional to be modern'. Cathedrals, in theory, should be one of the places where this is most evident, because they're almost inherently additive – with a few exceptions such as Salisbury, our medieval cathedrals are all a mish-mash of differing styles, Perpendicular or Decorated laid over Romanesque – although the Victorians tended to remove the Renaissance

and Baroque additions that a more enlightened age had bolted on to the barbarous Gothic edifices. Which makes it all the more odd there are so few things like this. Blackburn Cathedral is a late-Victorian-into-Edwardian expansion of a late-Georgian Gothick parish church, transformed into a cathedral through a century of incremental building; in the post-war years it was rather daringly decided to place a modernist lantern dome at its centre. The design is jagged and discordant, with a tall, thin aluminium spire of the sort you can find in dozens of suburban fifties churches, but it is placed on the Gothic melange with considerable skill, feeling both seamless and distinct; it helps that its dark concrete and stone harmonize with the bulk of the building. Inside, the transition extends to the way that the original high windows have been filled by King with abstract glass, making it less clear what is modern and what is traditional, while the lantern works much like an ordinary dome, with a light play of hexagonal polychrome beaming down on to the altar below.

Beside the cathedral is a decent new chapter house, in a Mackintosh-esque style, by Purcell architects; a strong, non-ironic Postmodernist building, let down by some rather PFI materials in the interiors.

—

ST MARY'S CHURCH, LEYLAND ✪
Jerzy Faczynski for Weightman & Bullen, 1961–4
Brutalist

The Polish contribution to modern architecture in Britain is pretty significant, due to two generations of exiles in the 1930s and '40s, but this is the only building that could easily be *in* twentieth-century Poland, and almost nowhere else. Invigorated by the 1956 post-Stalin 'Thaw', the reforms of

The Polish Catholic modernism of St Mary's, Leyland: a spectacular building for a suburban housing estate.

Vatican II and the example of Le Corbusier's Ronchamp chapel, architects in Poland created a series of hallucinatory Brutalist-baroque churches, where the kaleidoscopic spatial effects of the high Baroque, the structural daring of high modernism and the physical intensity of the most lurid Christian artworks were fused to absolutely thrilling effect. Here, a Polish exile has provided one of these churches for a leafy housing estate in a dull former industrial town. A tall concrete campanile, with abstracted windows for the bell-ringer that are taken right from the Unité d'Habitation, stands in front of a grand drum of a church, with a terrifying, hard Expressionist polychromatic relief of the Last Judgement by Adam Kossowski over the main entrance. Inside is a mindboggling panoply of Expressionistic sculpture; a highlight is the spindly, Giacometti-like stations of the cross that are placed in the niches of the V-shaped

concrete supports of the drum; furious with anxiety and pathos, but neatly and precisely arranged. It is often locked, but the chaplaincy next door is not, and they'll let you in if you ask nicely.

REGISTRY OFFICE, PRESTON
Roger Booth for Lancashire County Council Architects Dept, 1965
International Style

Round the back of the indigestible Edwardian stodge of Lancashire County Council's offices just outside Preston Station are two really excellent small office blocks by the same council's Architects' Department in the sixties – a slit-windowed, granite-clad volume of council offices, and this exceptionally crisp three-storey block, housing Preston's births, marriages and deaths. Resembling the Bauhaus-true-believer rationalism of, say, Yorke Rosenberg & Mardall, but by municipal employees, its glass grid is framed by a clearly expressed, projecting concrete frame, clad in stone. Modern architecture as it's seldom done in England, especially in the North – lucid, beautifully machine-made, serene.

POLICE STATION & MAGISTRATES' COURT, CHORLEY
Roger Booth for Lancashire County Council Architects Dept, 1968
Brutalist

How many ideas were sparking in Lancashire County Council Architects Department! Here, just behind Chorley's Gradgrind-Venetian Town Hall, is a local cop shop treated as a microcosmic essay in hardline Constructivism. Six storeys of simple sixties materials – concrete, glass, engineering brick – are stacked up and then expressively pulled out in three dramatic cantilevers, creating an overwhelming monumentality, dynamism and power with the simplest of means; a similarly stylized projecting flight of steps leads up from the pedestrian square. Who knew that the ideas of El Lissitzky in the utopian aftermath of the Russian Revolution would end up informing the design of a police station in Chorley? Between the two larger structures, the Magistrates' Court is a good example of the other LCC's more standardized buildings – white brick, slightly stripped classical, crowned by what became something of a signature, two steep copper roofs.

PRESTON BUS STATION ⊙
Keith Ingham for Building Design Partnership, 1969
Brutalist

It's incredible to think that this building – the only piece of transport architecture in twentieth-century Britain that has the scale and grandeur of the Victorian railway termini – was seriously proposed for demolition by Preston City Council as recently as 2014. Some of the criticism was fair – the building is far too big for the actual quantity of buses that travel in and out of Preston, and the system of underpasses and walkways that connect it to the town centre is far from perfect; it's just that much the same thing could be said about many nineteenth-century railway stations; Hull Station, for example, is at least three times too big for that city's present-day needs. It's the perennial problem of modernism and preservation. If you present something as purely driven by functional motives, when it ceases being entirely functional in the way it was envisaged, your building has no self-defence other than the things you didn't mention, like commodity, firmness and delight – and Preston Bus Station has all three in magnificent abundance.

The plan is simple – it's very long, with a high-windowed bus station on the ground floor and four storeys of car parking on top, an intelligent integration of public and private transport; and it's the car parking that is responsible for the aspect of the design that has made it so successful and popular. And popular it is, topping even a local press poll of the best building in Preston, which, given that it's near to the Greek temple of the Harris Museum, means something. That precast concrete module, a curved profile with fins cut into it, produces a rippling, shading, rhythmic effect when repeated across the bus station's prodigious length. This is an architecture of flowing repetition as pleasing to the eye as that to be found in any eighteenth-century terrace. The station hall below was intended by the architect, BDP's Keith Ingham, to be like 'an airport', revealing that it was designed in the distant days when airports were more pleasant than railway stations. It remains a clear, high space with a logical and elegantly designed system of signage and imperishable, shiny materials.

One of the more depressing things about the building was once the needless attrition of these remarkable qualities, but a good, simple restoration has repaired it, cleaned it and added an updated version of the 1960s signage system, so that you might almost think you were in somewhere that actually valued and regulated its public transport, like London, or Europe (the bus companies, of course, are still awful). The bus 'apron' facing the city centre is being turned at the time of writing into a public square. Like the repair of the city's Victorian market, the bus station has become a showcase for the new wave of municipal socialism coming out of the city, a 'Preston Model', based on rejecting outsourcing, cap-doffing, arse-kissing to developers, shame and self-hatred, in favour of building on the qualities of what we already have, and the latent desire for co-operation and collective action. There aren't a lot of happy endings in British modern architecture, but here's one.

UNICENTRE & GUILD CENTRE, PRESTON
Building Design Partnership, 1969
Brutalist

These two office blocks can be found at the back of **Preston Bus Station (above)**, and were designed by the same architects as part of the same ambitious comprehensive redevelopment project, here extended into an attempt to give Preston an instant new skyline. One is wide and grey, with a silhouette that evokes some of the ripples of the bus station; the other has a peculiar pinkish-brown tint to its concrete aggregate, and a glass stair tower. These two are not as impressive as the bus station by a long chalk – not much is – but the richly modelled, craggy towers still feel in many ways integral to this coherent modernist city centre ensemble. Unlike the bus station, the towers currently have no protection.

RMJM's Guild Hall: the second, less known of central Preston's two great modernist public buildings.

GUILD HALL, PRESTON ✪
RMJM, 1973
Brutalist

After **Preston Bus Station (p. 444)**, this is the most interesting of this city's remarkable crop of good post-war public buildings. Designed to replace a Victorian Guildhall and of course hated by the usual suspects for the same reason, it's actually a very intelligent, architecturally monumental and even contextual response to its site and function. The building can be reached from walkways via the bus station itself, but the main civic face commands a square next to the rear of the glorious neoclassical Harris Museum. The elevation to the square consists of a strip-windowed, polygonal cantilevered concrete volume, hauled up on great columns over a red-brick plinth; there's even a choice of entrances, either via ground floor or via walkway. When you're inside, the Guild Hall's foyers are in the form of a grand red-brick arcade with a glass roof, clearly in tribute to the Victorian arcades nearby. A clumsy partial refurbishment when the building was briefly in private ownership placed wood panels over the red brick on the ground floor for no obvious reason; but the city council has recently reclaimed control over it so wider plans to mess it up are likely to be abandoned. In any case, the building is an obvious candidate for listing – a vigorous, imaginative civic edifice that is absolutely of its place.

PLASTIC CLASSROOM, KENNINGTON ROAD PRIMARY SCHOOL, PRESTON ✪
Roger Booth for Lancashire County Council Architects Dept, 1973–4

An absolutely wild building, the most far-out work of architecture produced in Britain by a municipal architects' department – a sort of geodesic Buckminster Fuller dome, made

Science-fiction architecture in Preston: Lancashire County Council's freakish and fun Plastic Classroom.

up of self-supporting jagged plastic modules, with a classroom inside. This is formally radical, not just putting the old wine into a shiny new disposable plastic bottle – it creates a new kind of space altogether, a sort of classroom in the round, encouraging both attention and fantasy. Despite being clearly part of that late-1960s sci-fi-utopian consumer moment where, as Archigram put it, 'buildings are the same as frozen peas', it has aged impressively, a well-kept little thing. It's part of a very ordinary suburban Victorian primary school, red brick and Gothic roofs, to which it is linked by a small walkway – everything on the small child's scale – to this spiky explosion of energy. It must spark huge excitement and engagement from the kids there, an adventure every time you walk into it from the old corridors.

PAVILION CAFÉ, AVENHAM PARK, PRESTON
Ian McChesney, 2008
Ecomodernist

A pleasant café, secluded in a corner of Preston's beautiful riverside park; there's plenty of glass, so you can feel like you're in the trees without being rained on, under an umbrella of wood, fanning out as the building curves round the park's edge. In a better country there would be dozens of little public works like this, which would make my job much more difficult. Alas there are very few, so you can admire this light and dignified building as a one-off, given ex-industrial towns are more likely to have a boarded-up public loo than an optimistic Ecomodernist café. Amazingly, this one has even survived austerity – at the time of writing.

NORTH LANCASHIRE & CUMBRIA

MIDLAND HOTEL, MORECAMBE ✪
Oliver Hill, 1933
Moderne

One of the truly grand buildings of the thirties, and one of the few to be located in the North, is initially a disappointment – it is one of those stars which, like a Hollywood actor, look much smaller in real life. The 'iconic' facade – two sweeping wings of icing sugar rendered concrete around a strongly horizontal, partly glazed stair tower, with two stylized seahorses sculpted by Eric Gill at the top, in a manner that is pure Paris-via-LA glamour, without any hint of Central European high seriousness – is fine enough, but it looks pint-sized when you arrive in Morecambe on the little branch line from Lancaster. Then, when you go to the seafront promenade, you note that Urban Splash, who restored the building, have been typically invasive, with an upper floor of blue glass penthouses and a naff Pizza Express-style glass café on the ground floor. But go inside, and all is forgiven. Especially admirable – and admirably restored – are the canopied, streamlined café pavilion, a Mendelsohnian block asymmetrically projecting out of the far corner, with a gentle English surrealist mural (by Jonquil Cook, paying tribute to a destroyed original by Eric Ravilious) and nice neo-space-age red seats, and the fabulous main hall, where the nautical artworks by Eric Gill and Marion Dorn are held within an airy, pure space dominated by a gorgeous chrome-and-concrete spiral staircase. This is provincial glamour at its best.

The grand staircase of Oliver Hill's Midland Hotel in Morecambe, with a 'medallion' mural by Eric Gill.

ST JOHN'S CHURCH, BARROW-IN-FURNESS

Seely & Paget, 1934
Modern Classicism

An eerie thing, metaphysical Barrow. A Cézanne picture of a whitewashed Mediterranean church has been dropped in the Glasgow-style high-density hardman shipyard townscape of Barrow Island. It feels like bits of churches stitched together, its whitewashed concrete beamed in from thousands of miles away from all this rainy sandstone. Unnerving, like a mirage.

———

LITTLE BISPHAM TRAM STATION, BLACKPOOL

John Charles Robinson for Blackpool Corporation, 1935
Moderne

Blackpool's paradox as a place devoted to bright High-Tech spectacle and mass-culture leisure, as well as a place which can feel deeply stuck in time, is encapsulated well by the fact that it's the only town in Britain never to have dismantled its tram network – an amenity that Sheffield, Nottingham, Edinburgh, Manchester, Birmingham and Croydon have all had to rebuild. Now, with the old double-deckers replaced by sleek, Metrolink-style vehicles, it's all rather modern. The Blackpool Tramway was evidently already a little special, though, as you can see in the unique series of tram stations that Blackpool Corporation built in the thirties. They're like miniature Tube stations crossed with beach shelters, with toilets and kiosks, to serve the new suburban areas then being built. Little Bispham is one of the most impressive – an open colonnade to the tram line and a curved moderne canopy facing out to the sea, in red brick and cream faïence – a miniature sundae of a building.

PLEASURE BEACH CASINO, BLACKPOOL ✪

Joseph Emberton, 1937–9
International Style

Not a lot of people talk about the fact that at the entrance to Blackpool Pleasure Beach is one of the largest and most dramatic International Style buildings of the thirties. But if the South has the **De La Warr Pavilion (p. 234)**, the North has this – similar scale, confidence and grandeur, but with a rather different purpose and a concomitantly divergent fate. The Pleasure Beach, with its Coney Island-style rusty rollercoasters, stands at the opposite end of Blackpool Promenade to the Blackpool Tower, a steel filigree proto-modernist High-Tech edifice of astonishing beauty and piquancy which is disqualified from discussion here since it's really a giant spire on top of a grand Victorian eclectic palace (you don't get that at the Eiffel Tower). The Casino, which marks the start of the Pleasure Beach, was designed by Emberton on the strength of the **Royal Corinthian Yacht Club (p. 176)**, but his direct application of Central European modernism to the seaside doesn't at all result in a clumsy incongruity, a clash of high-mindedness and vulgarity. The design is a great stepped rotunda in white rendered concrete, and a tall, thin tower with a looping, tumbling concrete corkscrew all the way up. If that seems like a concession to commercialism, you can find an almost identical tower at the echt-functionalist Olympic Stadium in Helsinki. It's a very pure building, its sweeping lines picked out perfectly by the piercing Blackpool light.

This being Blackpool, it's not a polite dancing-and-tea-type affair but a shrill casino, with a Costa built into it, and although some elegant original signage remains, there are few remnants of the original interior. But well-maintained architectural heritage is not what anyone comes to Blackpool for. What people come

Hedonistic functionalism: Joseph Emberton's Pleasure Beach, where International Style meets the funfair.

here for is thrills like the Pasaje del Terror next door, and the crazed-looking web of girders of the rollercoasters, currently behind a bizarre Postmodernist fibreglass 'street'. Rather than an embarassing juxtaposition, the glamour of Emberton's Casino embodies the combination of banality and aspiration in a place like this – you could win big! Or you could go on a rollercoaster! Or you can just stare at other people doing these things, and at the rich, vivid and surreal environment they're doing them in.

BRUCCIANI'S CAFÉ, MORECAMBE
1939
Moderne

From the same Lancastrian family as a lovely but pre-modernist café of the same name in Preston, this is a first-rate piece of demotic art deco. Bentwood chairs of a quite original design, equal parts Patrick Hamilton and

Gio Ponti with red leatherette upholstering, are scattered in a bay-windowed building which looks moderne from a distance but is most likely Regency. The best features are the frosted-glass representations of Italian cities placed on the windows in niches along the side wall of the café, leading to a glass relief of Venice; some *pittura metafisica* with your bacon barm.

RADAR STATION, FLEETWOOD ✪
Roger Booth for Lancashire County Council Architects Dept, 1961–2
Googie

On the beach at Fleetwood, with a panoramic view of the bay and of Barrow-in-Furness's Devonshire Dock Hall glistening through the haze, you can find this ingeniously odd little building. Designed for the training of naval personnel in radar technology, it's placed in front of the colonnaded, folly-like

At the end of the line: Fleetwood's Radar Station, overlooking a pebble beach and the Irish Sea.

Lower lighthouse, one of several designs by Decimus Burton in the town, behind which is the sweeping crescent of the North Euston Hotel. Being a modernist building, the Radar Station copies neither, but responds to them, and to the beach, in various subtle ways. Hauled up on pilotis above the beach, the small curved building, with its bizarre skyline of dishes and aerials, is rendered to one side, and clad with seaside pebbles on the other. As in the later **Plastic Classroom (p. 445)**, there's a wit and lightness about the building which has a faintly pop art feel, alongside a careful attention to context in a rather battered historic town. Thoroughly worth the hour's journey on the tram from Blackpool. It's further evidence of just how creative Lancashire County Council's Architects Department was in the 1960s under Roger Booth – one of the few examples of a county commissioning a similar quantity and diversity of interesting modern buildings as you'd find in a city such as Sheffield, Southampton or Norwich.

GOLDEN MILE AMUSEMENTS, BLACKPOOL
1960s
Googie

Of the many captivatingly odd 'decorated sheds' – in Robert Venturi and Denise Scott-Brown's phrase – containing penny arcades that face the sea along the 'golden mile', this one is the stand-out. A concrete frame rises up into a series of giant hoops, above neon signs, bright and lurid, everything designed to stir the senses and baffle the eyes. A little piece of 1960s Vegas, roadside futurism just like the Americans did it in their moment of glory.

CARLISLE CIVIC CENTRE
Charles B. Pearson & Partners, 1964–6
International Style

Cumbria is absolutely a place to go to for architecture and townscape, but not of the recent past – the twentieth century has done little but build roads and clean up the old buildings, and not much else. As is common in the UK, the county town has devoted itself seemingly solely to shopping, mainly in the form of BDP's early Postmodernist Lanes centre, a pleasant but fussily designed and introverted mall. And then … what's this elegant thing on the bottom of the hill, at the edge of the ring road? Why, it's a high-end International Style high-rise, with its visible frame coated in marble and mosaic, infilled with patterned panels, and a set of delicate balconies and a roof garden adding a slightly whimsical, English touch. You could almost miss it – tower as it may be, the city council in its wisdom sited its only major modern building at the bottom of a hill, so that it doesn't appear in any views of the historic skyline – I guess if you're going to get pure modern architecture in Carlisle, that was always going to be the only way in. The self-cleaning materials are so impeccable that you have to look quite hard to see how much the Civic Centre is being run down, with the main entrance turned into an impromptu cop shop, the landscaping shabby, and the council chamber, in a separate 'rotunda' (more a hexagon), being emptied, in preparation for … being demolished and replaced with a surface car park, which Carlisle Council boast will earn it £80,000 a year. I have tried to avoid nostalgia in this book, but the progression from commissioning a local firm to design you a top-of-the-range work of architecture to knocking bits of it down for car parking does tell a story.

The simple and monumental planning of Lancaster University, with squares, colonnades and a tower.

LANCASTER UNIVERSITY: ✪
ALEXANDRA SQUARE
Shepheard Epstein, 1964–71
COUNTY COLLEGE
Roger Booth for Lancashire County Council
Architects Dept, 1967
CHAPLAINCY
Cassidy & Ashton, 1968–9
RUSKIN LIBRARY
MacCormac Jamieson Prichard, 1997–9
LANCASTER INSTITUTE FOR
THE CONTEMPORARY ARTS (LICA)
Sheppard Robson, 2011
Brutalist, Postmodernist

Lancaster University, like the **University of York (p. 394)**, has a quite traditional Oxford/Cambridge/Durham structure, organized into separate but interlinked colleges, each made up of discrete quadrangles and sheltered spaces. As in the lush, comfortable green-and-grey landscapes of the **University of East Anglia (p. 198)** or of **Sussex (p. 238)**,

the form of Lancaster University comes from the landscape – and in this case its inhospitability. The site the architect-planners at Shepheard Epstein were given by the local authority was a hill above the M6, around five miles out of Lancaster; apparently, the map they unfurled when they reached the top was immediately blown away. So what they built here is a sequence of squares connected by relatively narrow, surface-level walkways, surrounded by a relief road to accommodate the buses and cars. The landscape views are not inwards, as with the bucolic Brutalism of the southern New Universities, but outwards, to the hills around. The architecture is disciplined and civic, moderate modernism without the coldness and vagueness that mar the **University of Warwick (p. 328)**.

The low-key set piece is Alexandra Square – a rectangular plaza, with steps along one side, a tower at one corner, the main library in the other, a complex and well-used public space in-between, and stairs down to a bus station hidden below. The buildings framing the plaza are architecturally laconic in yellow brick, with concrete frames and sun-screens, and new concrete benches running along the edges. There is nothing spectacular or sculptural, but it is all scrupulous, coherent and complete, with the experience on foot clearly paramount. The County College, meanwhile, was given to Lancs Council's powerhouse architects' department under Roger Booth, who provided a much more vehement surface treatment of precast, rhythmic concrete modules in the then-fashionable 'egg-box' manner – but when you're inside its quadrangle, the underlying idea is clear – futurist Oxbridge. Much more than in most sixties universities, subsequent additions have not marred the essential structure – some cheaply built and poorly designed halls of residence face lovely landscaped greens, closely connected with the old squares, and at the edges of the County College the LICA arts centre by Sheppard Robson is a timber structure clad in a brittle blue rain-screen, linked to the walkways by a lake and wooden bridge, lightweight and elegant. But there are two buildings separate from the sequence of squares that are worth treating alone.

The first is from the university's early years, the Chaplaincy, one of those non-denominational churches that so many New Universities had. This is a rare attempt at something 'iconic' here, like the theatre in York or, well, everything in Essex, East Anglia and Sussex – a Corbusian organic concrete sweep upwards into a writhing concrete spire, and, below, three concrete, brick and timber halls, with the Protestants in one, the Catholics in the other and the Jews upstairs. The other curio is Richard MacCormac's extraordinary Ruskin Library – the name is a slight misnomer: this is a gallery with a tiny reading room in a grey-stone rotunda, reached by a processional walkway via a miniature granite maze (no, really). Inside,

this puzzling chapel is rather poetic – a miniature version of the **British Library (p. 143)**, with a collection housed in a sort of treasure chest, suspended in a gridded atrium. Ruskin would hardly have approved of all the right angles, but would have surely noted the craftsmanship of the rare stones and metals. Around it, the civic bustle of the squares and quadrangles feels very distant, leaving just a strange little chapel on a desolate Lancashire hill.

As with the Universities of Birmingham and Keele, Lancaster has some notability in British television – the skyline of the chapel and the tower forms the looming modern citadel from which Antony Sher's Howard Kirk inflicts his reign of terror in *The History Man*. [D.14]

FORTON SERVICES, M6
T. P. Bennett, 1965
Brutalist, Googie

The architecture of twentieth-century infrastructure has survived poorly, reflecting an era that – in Britain – was fixated equally upon consumer disposables and upon the belief that everything that looks new is shit. You'll find fewer motorway complexes and airports in this book than train and Tube stations, and that doesn't just reflect the fact that it's written by a pedestrian, but also the fact that a lot of the good stuff – plenty of which was built, as you can see in David Lawrence's compendious book *Food on the Move* – has been destroyed or irretrievably altered. Here's an exception, one of the surviving motorway structures with a claim to that overused epithet 'iconic'. A few miles south of **Lancaster University (above)** on the M6, Forton Services combines its grand concrete and glass walkway over the roadway with a tough, futuristic observation tower looking out at the surrounding countryside – a proud and alien beacon, which has managed to survive being painted cream, and has even managed to get listed, which is unusual for a structure in such poor condition. There is no public access today to the tower, and non-drivers should note that you can see it on the West Coast mainline, just south of Lancaster – look east.

POLICE HEADQUARTERS & MAGISTRATES' COURT, BLACKPOOL ✪ ❶
Roger Booth for Lancashire County Council with Tom Mellor & Partners, 1966–7
Brutalist

'Blackpool', as someone once said, 'stands between us and revolution'; and much in the same way as, say, Victorian Sheffield has an enormous barracks near the centre, here, just behind the **Golden Mile Amusements (p. 451)**, opposite the Central Pier, is a bitterly forbidding Brutalist fortress, to keep an eye on all the goings-on (though,

in fairness, I doubt suppressing insurrection has been among its major functions). The Police HQ tower is one of a series designed by the Lancs County Architect Roger Booth, all using a standardized kit of parts. Thin vertical strips of windows and concrete imprinted with rough abstract patterns are artfully arranged alongside boxed-out, elegantly detailed square bay windows, all juxtaposed in a manner close to the bluff yet meticulous compositions of contemporary minimalist architecture. There are others in Skelmersdale, St Helens and Morecambe, but while this still stands (not for long – it is derelict at the time of writing), this is the one to see, so complete is it as a miniature citadel of crime and punishment. From the seafront, steps lead up to an overhead walkway, which then connects to a raised plaza, linked by walkways to the police station's tower and the serene, ashlar-clad, low-rise law courts (these by Tom Mellor and Partners) at the edge of the site, where steps descend back

Behind the bright lights and the sea frontage: the harsh, enigmatic Brutalism of Blackpool Police Headquarters.

down towards the scabby backstreets. Like **Stopford House (p. 418)**, it seems to deliberately court accusations of totalitarian chic, but there are meticulous details, like the benches and (now empty) planters arranged perfectly as events within the grid.

COUNTY LIBRARY, MORECAMBE
Roger Booth for Lancashire County Council Architects Dept, 1967
Googie

In a tatty, neglected corner of Morecambe between the main roads and the high street, secluded by trees, you can find this complex, intimate municipal library. Intersecting hexagonal boxes, connected by a glass entrance pavilion, contain discrete reading rooms, with spreading copper butterfly roofs bringing the design together, like a fifties roadside diner gone civic. It was originally clad, like Fleetwood's **Radar Station (p. 450)**, in nautical pebbles, but leaks have meant a reclad of much of it in purple brick, which works well, and a few panels of the original have been retained, so you can get a sense of what it once looked like. As renovations of post-war buildings by cash-poor local authorities go, this is remarkably sensitive, and shows the esteem in which this friendly, quirky design must be held.

THE ROUND HOUSE, BARROW-IN-FURNESS
1970s
Brutalist

A strange object at the edge of Walney Island, on the outskirts of the shipbuilding town. With plenty of pillboxes and silos nearby, it very obviously takes these as its inspiration, for the purpose of what was originally a council-run seafront café but which has for some years been a Chinese restaurant. Intersecting concrete and brick cylinders on a ridge looking out over the Irish Sea, resembling (a little) the Art Gallery at the **University of Sussex (p. 238)**, but in a very different locale: the result is eerie, minatory and gently witty.

DEVONSHIRE DOCK HALL, BARROW-IN-FURNESS
McAlpine, 1982–6
High-Tech

Barrow-in-Furness, originally purpose-built as a steeltown in the second half of the nineteenth century, has something which, after decades of de-industrialization, no other large town in Britain has – a gigantic working factory right in its centre, overwhelming its townscape. You can go round and look at Barrow if you like Victorian architecture – a good Gothic town hall, some statues and parks, an enclave of Glasgow-style tenements – but looming over it, in every corner you look, is this building, perhaps the single most dementedly over-scaled structure in urban Britain.

Like the **Radomes (p. 393)** of RAF Menwith Hill and Fylingdales, it is hard to praise as such – it's one of the most unforgettably horrifying architectural experiences in Britain. This is where the submarines that carry our, cough, 'nuclear deterrent' Trident are built; it's a rare example of the Thatcher government investing in industry in the North. Ships, steel, coal, even cars and computers were allowed to decline or disappear, but when it came to nukes, lame ducks were worth bailing out, whatever the cost. 'DDH' is an immense, ugly, grey and black windowless metal shed, the size of an entire town in itself, like Cape Canaveral laid on its side. Its unbelievable scale is emphasized through the fact that it doesn't stand in the middle of nowhere by a motorway, but in the middle of a Victorian town, which it dwarfs and dominates like a death star.

11. NORTH-EAST

Kingsgate Bridge and Dunelm House, Durham (p. 470)

The North-East is all about its great rivers, which divide the region neatly into four conurbations. Probably its finest works of all are bridges: the heavy steel clangour of the **New Tyne Bridge** and the elegant, organic span of the **Millennium Bridge** at Gateshead over the Tyne; Ove Arup's spindly Brutalist **Kingsgate Bridge** over the Wear in Durham; **Tees Transporter Bridge**, lifting cars across the Tees at Middlesbrough; and the magnificent sweep of the **Humber Bridge** in Hessle. In the south the Humber divides East Yorkshire and North Lincolnshire; the dominant city here is Hull, where the great buildings of the Victorian and Edwardian era sit seamlessly alongside post-war reconstruction efforts such as the **Hull Co-operative**, with its *Sea and Ships* mural. The Tees is less obviously rewarding, but enthusiasts for dramatic industrial architecture will find much to enjoy. Wearside's largest town is heavy-industrial Sunderland, but the river also passes the acropolis of Durham, where the Brutalist **Dunelm House** nestles below the Romanesque cathedral. In County Durham, meanwhile, is one of the most interesting and least known New Towns, Peterlee, with its extraordinary **Apollo Pavilion**.

Newcastle is in a category of its own, with its planned early-nineteenth-century city centre and tradition of strong civic pride. In the 1960s and '70s, it was arguably the most ambitious city in Britain – the humane and exciting **Byker Estate**, the best of its kind in Britain, is one obvious result, and the excellent design of the **Tyne and Wear Metro**, the only system of its kind in England outside London, is another. The industrial riversides have mostly been turned over to commerce and housing in the last two decades, reasonably impressively in Gateshead around the **Baltic Centre for Contemporary Art**, and with more mixed results on the Tees between Middlesbrough and Stockton. The best recent work is in inner-city Newcastle along the Ouseburn, with bohemian spaces such as the clustered mini-towers of **The Malings** housing complex, or the anarchic **Star and Shadow Cinema**.

HUMBERSIDE

POST OFFICE, SCUNTHORPE
John Haswell for the Office of Works, 1939
Moderne

On a corner near the railway station, this is a rare interwar moderne building from the Post Office, which generally, like the banks, preferred images of stolidity. Not as radical as the work being put out by the cinemas and the Co-ops at the same time, it balances a facade of sharp curves and rectangles (all the usual nods to Mendelsohn and Dudok) with faintly Georgian windows. Beautifully made, with expressive, Dutch-style brickwork and black vitrolite tiling to the ground floor. If only more post offices were like it.

HAMMONDS OF HULL
T. P. Bennett, 1950–52
People's Detailing

The reconstruction of Hull after the heavy bombing it suffered in the Second World War was more or less like the **Armada Way (p. 273)** in Plymouth, only stylistically even more conservative – a masterplan prepared by New Delhi's architect-planner Edwin Lutyens, completed just before his death in 1944, was mostly ignored. Accordingly, it lacks the centrifugal nature of Plymouth's great boulevard carved out of the historic city, a messy compromise for which many people in Hull are probably grateful. Some of the 1950s' bloodless neo-Georgian edifices have a certain BBC English clip to them, with a lot of flat roofs and canopies to protect from the rain and wind, but this is the only one of the reconstruction buildings that really need detain those interested in modern architecture. Hammonds of Hull stands as the main monumental building on the ceremonial Paragon Square, near the railway station; and although various

owners have come and gone (it was a House of Fraser until 2019, and is currently disused) it has always been a department store. It is a mix of modernist motifs – big wide and long ribbon windows to show off the wares, alongside bands of Portland stone – and more traditional remnants, with its entrance block featuring both plate glass and pilasters. Conservative, but grand, and in good condition by Hull standards.

QUEEN'S GARDENS, HULL
Frederick Gibberd Partnership, 1958–9
HULL COLLEGE
Frederick Gibberd Partnership and William Mitchell (artist), 1960–62
People's Detailing

I once walked around here with someone whose grandfather was a Labour councillor; admiring its trees, flowers and sculptures, the glorious domes of the Edwardian civic buildings on one side and the monumental modernism of Hull College on the other, she commented: 'This is what my granddad thought everything would be like.' Queen's Gardens are a public space made out of the infilling of a dock that previously occupied this site; they were landscaped by Gibberd after the war in a final passing of the baton from classicists to modernists. The result is gorgeous, and very well used. Perhaps egotistically, Gibberd then filled one entire side of the axis he'd created with Hull College, which is unusually Corbusian for his decorative, Festival Style tastes – a punchy concrete frame with an irregular grid of offices and studios, a sculptural roof terrace and, best of all, William Mitchell's frieze of polychrome nautical creatures. As good a civic space as any that Hull's planners created in the city's imperial pomp, and much more relaxed and democratic.

The domes of The Pods leisure complex, adjoining the more modest North Lincolnshire Civic Centre.

NORTH LINCOLNSHIRE CIVIC CENTRE, SCUNTHORPE
Charles B. Pearson & Partners, 1960–62
THE PODS, SCUNTHORPE
Andrew Wright Associates/Space & Place, 2010
International Style, Ecomodernist

I came here to see the Civic Centre, with Elain Harwood's guide to post-war listed buildings in hand, but it was the newer building next to it that really caught my attention. This happens often, but seldom in a positive sense. These two buildings stand in a linear central park running out of the steel town – you can see the blast furnaces from the upper storeys – lined on the other side by big 1930s semis, a sharp turn from urban to suburban. The Civic Centre is set deep in the park, surrounded by trees, and consists of an L-shape of cellular offices, attractively detailed and colourful, with red window frames and dark-green marble, and a stylish concrete escape staircase, framing a more classical double-height colonnade and a drum for council meetings. It is in a good state, another one of those instances where listing has helped retain something that would otherwise be very probably passed over, sold and demolished.

But, next to it, the 'Pods' swimming pool is a new Ecomodernist building of considerable aplomb. Reached via a winding path off the park, it boasts four low wooden-framed domes, two with diamond-shaped rooflights, one with a green roof, and one glass dome containing the entrance. Its slightly rum profile and faceted glazing (some panes of which are now cracked) are an obvious nod to Foster's **30 St Mary Axe (p. 73),** but, that aside, this is a fresh and bucolic modern building, without clichés, elegantly integrated into a town and a landscape that lazy thinking might hold to be totally alien to it. One of the least known but

The icon of post-war Hull: Alan Boyson's glittering 'Three Ships' mural on the front of E. P. Andrew's Co-op.

most successful – and, judging from brief acquaintance, one of the most well-used – of the New Labour regeneration projects.

CAFÉ INDIE, SCUNTHORPE
Derek Brown (artist), 1963
International Style

Built as a Co-operative Pharmacy, this is striking evidence of the Co-operative movement's progressive role in architecture outside the big cities. A big glass emporium, its facade is dominated by a huge mosaic, representing science, pharmaceuticals and the pharmaceutical industry, and as so often in North Lincs (see also **Grimsby Central Library, p. 462**) the artist was local. A kind of mosaic frieze in black, white and red, stretched out in long blocks of colour, what looks at first like Abstract Expressionism is subtly figurative, with phials, test tubes and pills all thrown into the mix. It's now

an independent café, serving craft beer and vegan food of the kind that some appear to believe is exclusive to inner London.

HULL CO-OPERATIVE ✪
E. P. Andrew and Alan Boyson (artist), 1955–63
People's Detailing

Hull's Co-op, like **Hammonds of Hull (p. 459)**, straddles modernism and classicism – a big, symmetrical city block, with a well-detailed grid of windows but which otherwise could easily have been designed thirty years earlier. What makes it into one of the most valuable and important buildings in Hull is the great mosaic mural by Alan Boyson on its convex front facade, which is now the city's best-known piece of modern design, because of a successful attempt to list it (after several refusals), the direct consequence of a lively local campaign.

Grimsby Central Library, which integrates sculpture and decorative panels into its rigorous concrete grid.

On a glittering gold and green background, the mosaic depicts three ships, because this is Hull, and ships go from here. It has the lucid simplicity of a sixties children's book illustration, and is one of the most locally appropriate and worthwhile integrations of art and architecture in Britain.

GRIMSBY CENTRAL LIBRARY ✪
J. M. Milner for Grimsby Borough Architects Dept, 1966–8
International Style

This little-known building is a small masterpiece – a concrete jewel box in a neglected town. Viewed from the street, it's incredibly simple, a classically inspired grid made up of prefabricated concrete panels. The application of system-building to a public building like this is rare in the UK aside from the CLASP system, responsible for some decent schools, dreadful railway

stations and the **University of York (p. 394)**. As a result of its use of faintly Eastern Bloc-style concrete panels combined with Socialist Realist sculpture, Grimsby Central Library is very Baltic, fittingly given its context in the tall brick warehouses, cold seas and plains of North Lincolnshire; it could be on the northern coast of East Germany, in Rostock or Stralsund. The ceramic abstract reliefs on the building's right flank are especially *echt DDR*. That isn't to suggest that this is a utilitarian building – quite the reverse, and that's where the building's classical discipline comes in. At the front, you can understand everything that's going on here. A double-height ground floor for ordinary reading rooms, rooms above for researchers, then a partially blank floor for services, and offices above, all symmetrical. That blank, windowless floor is decorated by five willowy, Gothic sculptural figures. These are the *Guardians of Knowledge*, and are by one Peter Todd, who was head of Grimsby College's art department at the time.

The entrance is not through that classical facade, but from the side, under a sculptural honeycomb grid, past a colourful swirling mosaic incorporating the medieval seal of the town of Grimsby (this is partly obscured by ineptly designed disabled access, the only lapse in care in an otherwise very well-maintained building). Then you're in a hall decorated with abstract tapestries, leading to the double-height main reading room. This is elegantly laid out, with square marble columns, chic sixties lighting set into sets of clustered tubes, and a finely carved wooden balustrade on the stairwell up to the mezzanine. This is civic design of the highest order. Aptly, a plaque records its opening by Grimsby's MP, Tony Crosland. It exemplifies the sort of anti-Fabian, anti-Victorian conception of public good as a matter of art, fun and enjoyment rather than 'improvement' that Crosland wrote about in *The Future of Socialism*. Bafflingly, the library is not listed, but its owners know what they have here; in 2018, there was an exhibition celebrating the library's fiftieth anniversary.

UNIVERSITY OF HULL: BRYNMOR JONES LIBRARY
Castle Park Dean & Hook, 1966–9
GULBENKIAN CENTRE
Peter Moro, 1969–70
Brutalist

At the University of Hull you can see the unexpectedly modernist results of Philip Larkin's tenure as chief librarian – the Brynmor Jones Library, a dramatic and rather American cantilevering of multistorey stacks, in the 'giant robot head' genre of gestural educational Brutalism. The rest of the campus, by Leslie Martin, is decent if undemonstrative, with the exception of Peter Moro's typically original and personal Gulbenkian Centre, a cranky little theatre

with a red-brick ground floor, a Brutalist second floor containing the auditorium, and a bulky copper roof. A little defensive perhaps, but the interiors boast Moro's usual sense of grand three-dimensional space.

ABBEY WALK MULTISTOREY CAR PARK, GRIMSBY
Harold Gosney (artist), 1970
Brutalist

Between **Grimsby Central Library (p. 462)** and the railway station sits this small, three-storey car park, with a concrete spiral ramp at one end. It may not look like much from a casual glance, but look closely and you'll find six sets of four low-relief sculptural panels set into the concrete. Curvaceous abstracts, bodies and industrial assemblages, they nod towards Fernand Léger and, especially, towards Le Corbusier's paintings (rather than his buildings). The sculptor was a local artist, Harold Gosney – other works of his are scattered around the town, a little known legacy of modernist public art. The car park apparently has a bad reputation, and is due to be renovated and aesthetically 'improved' – hopefully this will mean cleaning rather than erasing these panels.

HUMBER BRIDGE, HESSLE ✪
Freeman Fox & Partners, 1972–81
International Style

Like the **Severn Bridge (p. 290)**, one of those works of a cold-water-in-the-face freshness that engineers seem incapable of these days. Perhaps they're pressured to avoid this clarity in favour of the arbitrary creation of iconic shapes. Two graceful concrete suspension towers, cables and a road. Tall and elegant, it makes all the Santiago Calatrava imitations cities like to foist on themselves, where tiny spans are crossed with a self-infatuated display of effort,

The Humber Bridge, a masterclass in minimalist engineering, its wide span achieved without fuss.

Bruce Grobbelaar-style, look embarrassing. A rush of clarity and purity, performing an extremely difficult task – spanning a wide estuary, high enough for ships to go along – while carrying a major road, while looking completely easy and logical. Beautiful.

SCUNTHORPE CENTRAL LIBRARY
Derek Parkes for Scunthorpe Borough Architects Dept, 1974
Brutalist, Postmodernist

A unique design, with all the gruff monumentality of Brutalism but with a pitched roof and decorative diapered brick patterns that push it much closer to Postmodernism – as if someone were designing with a Paul Rudolph building in one eye and a Robert Venturi in the other. Scunthorpe Central Library commands a good civic square opposite a sprawling mall on one side, the indoor market on the other, with tower blocks to its left and a good, very seventies low-rise high-density estate to the right. The library's design is dominated by chunky flanking stair towers, and the aforementioned brick patterns – windowless, the effect is extremely monumental, both a 'decorated shed' and a hulking, weighty chunk of masonry. The only problem is the lack of natural light and ventilation (was this something to do with the air from the nearby steelworks?), causing a bleakness compounded by a cheap and nasty interior renovation in 2018. During the latter, 'improving quotes' were scribbled ineptly on to grey walls; one of them reads: 'Work gives you meaning and purpose and life is empty without it', as if it were personally chosen by Iain Duncan Smith. It's hardly 'knowledge is power' – but, seen from the square, the building conveys that still.

TIDAL SURGE BARRIER, HULL
Shankland Cox Associates, 1980
Brutalist

Although the two are contemporaneous, the Tidal Surge Barrier on the River Hull is a jarring, cranky building compared with the purist magnificence of the **Humber Bridge (p. 463)**. It's made up of two towers, concrete angles clashing, fully glazed at the corners but otherwise formed of proper Brutal concrete, unusually late for the UK. Its immensity is necessary to hold up the barrier itself, which descends from here to prevent floods. It's both a clangorously impressive work of engineering and a monumental city gate.

THE DEEP, HULL
Terry Farrell & Partners, 1998–2002
Pseudomodernist, Deconstructivist

Terry Farrell was once Britain's major Postmodernist architect; this deliberately 'iconic' building showed it was possible to move on from Postmodernism's historical references, in-jokes and 'complexity and contradiction' without in any way returning to modernist notions of form following function or structural integrity; instead, you could float freely, creating arbitrary, spectacular form for the purposes of encouraging tourism. Not that there are many tourists here today. But what Farrell did is now indelibly part of the landscape, if more as sculpture rather than architecture. The function (the building is a Sea Life Centre-style aquarium, with uninteresting interiors) is much less important than the way it occupies the small peninsula that juts out from the River Hull into the Humber. It takes that little inlet and turns it into a Caspar David Friedrich crash of steel, glass and titanium, its prow upturned like a sinking ship, marooned for ever off the North Sea.

HULL TRUCK THEATRE
Wright & Wright Architects, 2009
Brutalist

A dour but rigorous theatre from the urban regeneration era, which did some bad things here – the shopping mall around this building being one of the worst. A low corner block, detailed in purple-black engineering brick, with a glazed foyer and a bare-brick interior – you could easily imagine it was a Lyons Israel Ellis building of the late fifties, making it one of the very few examples of Brutalist Revival. This gives it an enormous (comparative) integrity, as a looming dark presence in the midst of so much Trespa trash – secluding itself into a punchy little box rather than playing with the wankers. Sadly some of the naffness around has seeped into it, as the very stylish red and white signage at the corner was recently replaced with a rubbishy little sign, much more redolent of the general standard of modern local-authority clipart design.

SCALE LANE SWING BRIDGE, HULL
McDowall Bendetti and Alan Fraser, 2013
High-Tech

Fussy, for such a short span – a good example of the meretricious approach to bridge design shown up by the **Humber Bridge (p. 463)** nearby – but this gets away with it through superior gimmickry. It has a circular café built into it, and like the **Millennium Bridge (p. 477)** on the Tyne, it opens up when ships and boats need to pass, with a cute and dramatic outward swing – a clever and genuinely fun example of urban scenography and ingenuity.

TEESSIDE

TEES TRANSPORTER BRIDGE, MIDDLESBROUGH
William Arnot & Co., 1911
Industrial

In scale, the grandest of the Transporter Bridges, and the only one to have been accepted as an emblem by the town it serves – despite being a fair walk from the centre this is Boro's equivalent of the **New Tyne Bridge (p. 479)**, its own icon of industrial modernity, and unlike the Tyne Bridge it actually does stuff, still lifting cars across the Tees. Its shape is peculiar, especially compared to the proto-Foster lightness and delicacy of Newport's **Transporter Bridge (p. 285)**; the pillars on either side of the river are almost triangular, and the two sides of the bridge itself seem to cascade downwards, giving it a rather friendly, almost cute silhouette; you can read what it does, instantly. It is painted bright blue, and is today surrounded on the Middlesbrough side by some very bumptious new buildings and a giant sculpture by Anish Kapoor, products of an over-ambitious regeneration plan of the 2000s. However the Transporter Bridge remains by far the most impressive work of art in the area.

―――

SOUND MIRROR, REDCAR
Royal Engineers, 1916
Industrial

A real oddity, a piece of advanced First World War technology and concrete engineering marooned in a bland housing estate on the outskirts of Redcar. Pre-dating radar, sound mirrors – the most famous are on an island in Denge, north Kent – were scattered around eastern England, designed as devices to detect incoming aircraft, essentially on the principle of giant concrete satellite dishes.

Like bunkers without slits, they are intriguing proto-Brutalist objects, angular, aggressive and puzzling – you wouldn't know what one was unless you'd been told. This one has become especially surreal because of its preservation in a completely identikit developers' housing estate. By coincidence it is the same size as the bungalow next to it, and is treated as if it's an independent house.

―――

WILTON POWER STATION ✪
ICI, 1952
SOUTH BANK COKE OVEN TOWER, MIDDLESBROUGH ✪
Simon Carves Otto, 1956–7
Industrial, Brutalist

The train or car journey between Middlesbrough and Redcar provides a front-row seat for a spectacle of industry with little rival anywhere else in the country; most of this is not 'architecture' but the sort of abstract-looking but completely functionalist objects that the photographers Bernd and Hilla Becher went round Europe photographing in the 1970s, carefully cropping out the mess and waste around them. You can't miss the mess, but the things you will see on the way are well worth it. These are two of the most interesting. The Coke Oven Tower – a gruff 'DORMAN LONG' logo carved into it – is a symmetrical, stepped concrete block which has the proportions, if not the size, of a particularly outré Brutalist skyscraper in an American university, but all this is by accident. Wilton Power Station, meanwhile, is a staggering hulk, an immense swell of concrete and brick without the slightest hint of design or beauty; but its sheer mass arising out of the North Yorkshire landscape is mindboggling.

Stark and imposing: the Dorman Long works on the industrial and post-industrial outskirts of Middlesbrough.

STATION HALL, MIDDLESBROUGH

John Dossor, 1954
International Style

The main bulk of Middlesbrough Station is a Ruskinian Venetian-Gothic Victorian building, interesting in its own right, but a large chunk of it was bombed by the Luftwaffe, leading to the insertion of two fine steel-framed halls between the entrance and the platforms. There are barrel-arched rooflights on each side, one of which clips on to the Victorian buildings, with marble panels and lots of light – an exemplary fusion of two completely different styles that neither compromises nor disrupts. There are currently proposals to redevelop the station that will emphasize the canopies at a new entrance, as a modernist face for a town so often seen in terms of decline.

FORUM, BILLINGHAM

Elder Lester & Partners, 1967
Googie

This leisure centre and concert hall in the new town ICI built for its workers is one of Britain's rare Googie buildings. This is a very fancy bit of engineering, a hyperbolic paraboloid roof suspended over a wide space in the oyster-like shape that was enormously popular at the time in the US and Eastern Europe – a vaulting, spectacular style that in many ways prefigures the 'wow factor' architecture of regeneration in the 2000s. It also one of those places, like **Park Hill (p. 370)**, where you can see how very different rules are applied to listed modernist buildings than to any other era; not long after the Forum was listed, it was clad in the cheapest, nastiest blue and yellow panels, defeating the entire point of listing. At least it's all cosmetic, so can presumably be removed in some more enlightened future.

DARLINGTON TOWN HALL
**Williamson Faulkner-Brown & Partners
and E. A. Tornbohm for Darlington Borough
Architects Dept, 1967–70**
Brutalist

Darlington stands out on Teesside as a
pleasant and vigorous industrial market
town, with a perceptible medieval plan
around its market square, very unlike the
Gradgrindian gridiron of Middlesbrough.
This civic centre at a corner of that square
is modest in scale, especially compared with
the substandard recent retail development
behind it. In the main section, a raised plaza
frames a rather dour office block cut into
sharp vertical concrete strips – what makes
it worthwhile is two other aspects. One is
the sculpture in front of two clasped clusters
of steel beams, *Resurgence* by John Hoskins;
it is meant to commemorate the railways
on which the town was built, but can be
experienced simply as a minimalist welded-
metal sculpture, between the utopian clarity
of Naum Gabo and the clanging Gothic of
Richard Serra. At right angles to it is the
block of the Town Hall containing the council
chamber, a formal, faintly classical Brutalist
volume on pilotis, with something of the
Golden Section repose of the demolished
Birmingham Central Library. One boring
thing, one exciting thing, one serious thing,
adding up to an ensemble worth keeping.

CENTRE NORTH-EAST, MIDDLESBROUGH
1971
International Style

Currently up for sale to be transformed
into flats, so while it's entirely likely to
be clad in something horrible by the time
you read this, at the time of writing you
can still see the best International Style
block in the North-East, and probably the
best modern building in Middlesbrough

– certainly a much more successful one
than the Middlesbrough Institute of Modern
Art nearby, a meretricious design by Erick
van Egeraat. Built as council offices, and
originally known as Corporation House,
it was clearly designed as a complement
to the neo-Gothic Middlesbrough Town Hall
next door, an 1889 block with a tall clock
tower that you could imagine in Albertopolis
or central Manchester – but here, in a coal-
black stone so as not to be destroyed by the
atmosphere of what was at the time a very
heavy-industrial town. This well-detailed
two-part tower uses a similar tone for its
smoked glass, but the architects had the
good sense not to try and offer a gestural
equivalent to the spikes and spires of the
earlier building, continuing it only in terms
of height and colour. It can err on the bleak
side, but this is Middlesbrough after all;
better to be unashamed about what you
are than paint yourself purple in the hope
that a creative cluster might open in your
undercroft. For some evidence of the farce
that happens when you try this, a visit to
the Middlehaven regeneration area half
a mile north of here is recommended.

DAWSON HOUSE, BILLINGHAM
Elder Lester & Partners, 1973
International Style

As a sort of unofficial New Town, like
Killingworth (p. 475) just north of Newcastle,
Billingham had a very ambitious town plan
in the 1960s, which was largely executed –
a covered mall with a bullhorn entrance
nicked off Chandigarh, Lubetkin-esque
patterned tower blocks, the aforementioned
Forum (p. 467), an elegant little art gallery
in the Festival Style, and this, a circular tower
block. Some of these have gone – the art
gallery very recently – and the towers have
been marred with hopefully not flammable
cladding – though they were severely
dilapidated beforehand. Treated properly,

this could be a fabulous space-age ensemble, and Dawson House, the circular high-rise, still makes that clear – witty, simple, a pop art architecture like an SF illustration come to life.

NORTHGATE HOUSE, DARLINGTON ❶

1975
Brutalist

You can see this as the East Coast line sails through Darlington's astonishing Victorian station – a black-glass cube with a concrete services tower, the main vertical feature in the town along with the Gothic church and the spiky market tower. This sort of sombre Victorian–Brutalist skyline combination is common in the West Riding, but more unusual in the North-East, with only Corporation House in Boro as an equivalent; and it works well. Up close, the derelict building's Gothic approach to form is more obvious, broken up as it is into several distinct volumes, and reached from a seedy labyrinth of patterned cast-concrete underpasses. Currently for sale, so the smoked glass is likely to be replaced with the usual Trespa barcodes.

IMPERIAL CHEMICAL INDUSTRIES, WILTON

Building Design Partnership, 1975
Brutalist

ICI's 'Wilton Centre' was built as an integral business park and office block for its white-collar staff, next to one of its sprawling Teesside refineries – the pipework skyline here, lit up and throwing up plumes at night, was local lad Ridley Scott's first inspiration for the cityscape of *Blade Runner*. But there's no attempt to create a mini-metropolis; instead the always-conscientious Building Design Partnership created a series of red-brick and black-painted concrete pavilions with strongly expressed Brutalist service

towers, walkways over lakes and park-like planting. This is the state-of-the-art office environment of 1975 – much more holistically designed than most of what you'd find now, but still downwind of the gases and fumes of hugely polluting industry. Now broken up and used by a variety of different companies, it's still in good condition. Unlike most places in this book, it is not straightforward to visit, though it's worth contacting its current owners (easily googled) to try, since it has the kind of powerful coherence in a single integrated complex that is otherwise only found in post-war Oxbridge colleges.

CENTRAL AREA HOUSING, MIDDLESBROUGH

Dixon del Pozzo for Middlesbrough Borough Architects Dept, 1980
Postmodernist

An unexpected find, just off the rigid grid of Victorian Boro – a vernacular/Postmodernist council estate of very high quality, a sort of Teesside answer to the **Byker Estate (p. 484)**. The Central Area, as it is glamorously called, is made up of low-rise crescents of flats, with deep balconies, private gardens and green public squares, detailed in good red brick to the main bulk of the structure and stained wood for the windows and the little pitched roofs over the bay windows. A little bit of Aalto, a touch of **Lillington Gardens (p. 57)**, and a certain amount of Pomo Victorian nostalgia, adding up to an underrated, undervisited but very pleasant inner-city estate, showing how adaptable and humane local-authority housing had become at its best by the end of the seventies, a decade in which it was relentlessly criticized for its inflexibility and inhumanity.

WEARSIDE

MUSEUM & LIBRARY, SUNDERLAND
City Architects Dept, 1963
WINTER GARDENS, SUNDERLAND
Napper Architects, 2001
People's Detailing, High-Tech

A happy marriage of ideas from three different eras about how you design a civic building. The first is a neo-baroque palace of the 1870s, with the ideal-type Victorian municipal landscape of Mowbray Park behind it. Bombed in the war, the side facing the park was redesigned by the City Architect in a very enjoyable amalgam of Festival of Britain clichés – an asymmetric facade of brick, blue-glass panels and slate, with the city's coat of arms and a wavy concrete canopy providing shelter from the rain. The juxtaposition stresses the neo-Victorian qualities of so much fifties design (although the building is sixties, the ideas are not). The ceramic tile murals under the canopy are by Walter Hudspith; a polychrome riot of semi-abstract industrial and cosmic shapes emerging out of a calm black grid is a fair exchange for Victorian allegorical sculpture. Calm civic dignity, richness of materials – but not too much! – and a certain ennobling optimism. Next to that, a somewhat clumsy new entrance, best ignored, and on the other side the Winter Gardens, added in the twenty-first century. This was not a good time for Sunderland architecture, as you can note via the miserable slab of flats that overlooks the Wear and blocks most city centre views, but the Winter Gardens are housed in a simple glass drum whose only touches of wilfulness are in the curved walkway leading you up into the roof – otherwise, it's Foster-esque late modernism, filled with a sweaty mass of ferns. It does its job admirably, and is ageing well.

UNIVERSITY OF DURHAM: KINGSGATE BRIDGE ✪
Ove Arup & Partners, 1963–5
DUNELM HOUSE ✪ ❶
Architects Co-Partnership, 1966
Brutalist

A dual masterpiece, senselessly treated as separate by idiots. The first part was personally designed by Ove Arup himself, rather than simply engineered by the firm – there probably isn't any other individual who was involved in so many important modern buildings in Britain, and this was his personal favourite of all his works. You can see why Arup wanted to take this project on himself, as it's the sort of site any designer would kill to be able to work on. The footbridge across the Wear is suspended at a high level (with balustrades for the vertigo-prone), on two sets of two delicately poised, angular supports, and is clipped together in the middle with a little steel clasp. From above, it's a clear path to the craggy mass of Durham Cathedral, from below it's a fantastic lightweight construction, firm and delicate, with materials that are starting to fade and mould into the same colour as the trees and the Cathedral. The ashes of Arup, who died in 1988, were scattered here.

It then connects, with a slight kink, using the same materials – and passing a little bust of Arup himself – to Dunelm House. This is a Students' Union for the collegiate University of Durham, again placed on an absolute dream of a site on the other side of the Wear, with steep, overgrown banks just a short alleyway's walk from the Georgian streets around. Given the bosky surroundings, the design by Architects Co-Partnership is, in their own words (to describe their work at the **University of Essex, p. 190**), 'shaggy' – a rough collection of béton brut spaces stepping down almost arbitrarily to the river, topped by a strange roofline of ceramic concrete cylinders. It has a wonderful sense of being both hewn from the same mass of material and of being deliberately perverse, a slightly accidental tumble of rooms and halls, with concrete louvres and unexpected rooflights adding to the jumbly appearance; the stepping of the arrangement allows patios and roof gardens at multiple levels. The spaces inside have been battered a little by use, and its owners, a university interested only in 'heritage' and 'icons', have criticized this excess of circulation space, not noticing that this was exactly the point, a flowing freedom of non-prescriptive places to hang out; perhaps the reason why it is under threat is that these spaces that would be so suited to a university in, say, Sheffield, Bristol or Manchester happen to be in the Oxbridge of the North – although it's hard to imagine any building so totally built into its site.

SUNDERLAND CIVIC CENTRE ✪ ❶
Basil Spence, John Bonnington & Partners, 1968
Brutalist

There are a few Basil Spence buildings (or rather, by this point, John Bonnington buildings) that superficially resemble this one – among them Kensington Town Hall, an unlovely red-brick mulch that may be recognized by those who watched the news around the time of the Grenfell Tower disaster. Explore this one on foot rather than via Google Streetview, and you'll find it is in a different class altogether, as interesting and as serious as **Newcastle Civic Centre (p. 482)** – a rare example of Sunderland not being the poor relation. In fact, the Sunderland municipal buildings are usefully understood as a reaction to the way Newcastle's Civic Centre is a pretty traditional Guildhall, with its tall spired tower and its formal gardens. Sunderland is something

One of the purple-and-red, brick-and-tile courtyards of Basil Spence's sprawling Sunderland Civic Centre.

else – horizontal rather than vertical, egalitarian rather than hierarchical, sliding unobtrusively into the townscape rather than standing as a monument, and hewn from one material as a total environment, rather than treated as a series of episodes.

Although you should certainly go and see it, much can be learned from looking at the building on a map. There are two open hexagons of offices, enclosing within them public squares; and as if as spokes to these, two distinct blocks, one of which is the public Civic Hall. An overhead walkway connects it to Mowbray Park – it didn't have to, but it would be nice, so they did it. Walking round, you see how this plan has been translated into an endlessly intriguing *promenade architecturale*, taking you under, above and through a sequence of spaces. The surfaces and the visuals, meanwhile, are meticulous. The offices are laconic in expression, but clad in rich, dark-red glazed bricks. Above you, when you pass beneath one of the hexagons, is a concrete gridded waffle slab ceiling; and under your feet are hexagonal red tiles, running through the whole site – it has something of the radiating intensity of a Victorian terracotta office building or law courts, but without any intent towards being intimidating or grandiose; it is, to quote one local, all For Your Pleasure. Most memorable is the treatment of the many steps that accommodate the building's hilly setting, which create an effect of erosion, of building picturesquely subsiding into landscape, that takes centuries in a cathedral but is replicated here by clever design and wit.

Currently Sunderland Council is running the place down, according to a local press report hoping it'll be able to sell the site and demolish before it is listed. Hopefully by the time you read this either it'll have had a change of heart, or Historic England will have forced the issue – because while calling this 'the best modern building in Sunderland' may sound like faint praise, the city would lose something special if it did go.

APOLLO PAVILION & SUNNY BLUNTS, PEERLEE ⊙
Victor Pasmore (artist) and Peterlee Development Corporation Architects, 1969
Brutalist

Robert Hughes, in his enjoyable if fraudulent TV show on modernism, *The Shock of the New*, claimed that however much we might enjoy Mondrian's paintings, 'none of us would want to live in one'. This is the nearest point we ever got to this being a reality; except it was 'living in a Pasmore'. The story is convoluted. Peterlee is one of the North-East's two official, government-designated New Towns; the other, Newton Aycliffe, is not of architectural distinction, while Killingworth and Billingham are 'unofficial', independent projects of ICI and Newcastle City Council, respectively. Unlike most other New Towns, Peterlee had aspects of a grass roots project, and was named after Peter Lee, a local miner and activist in County Durham. Its first architect-planner was Lubetkin, who quit after a row with the coal board, which wanted to mine under the high-rise blocks he had planned as a *Stadtkrone* for the town centre. After that, it became a less successful Crawley or Hatfield of the North, until more radical ideas once again took hold, and it was decided to invite Victor Pasmore – who had recently developed from a realist into an abstract painter – from his teaching post in Newcastle to help design a housing estate, the evocatively named Sunny Blunts.

Not only were the colour schemes of the houses – in Pasmore's habitual intensely Northern colours – and the arrangement of the estate, around a central green, designed in collaboration with the artist, but so too was the landscaping of the stream that ran through the estate, with knobbly, Abstract Expressionist concrete aggregate banks. Shadowed by strangely imposing but low-rise black-brown mini-towers of three storeys, the semis and terraces frame a concrete bridge, designated on completion

The Apollo Pavilion in Peterlee, a utopian work of architectural sculpture in a coalfield New Town.

the 'Apollo Pavilion'. This is one of the single most extraordinary spatial and architectural experiences in Britain, a Constructivist sculpture in béton brut with all the complexity and power of Gabo or Malevich but on a far larger scale, and that is intended to be walked through, and that shifts constantly, as a three-dimensional play of heavy, but freely floating, abstract forms. It's very exciting, a real statement of the incredible things that were considered possible at the end of the sixties. What happened next is a decline, fall and surprising rise.

The first and most important factor was the crushing of the miners and the destruction of mining communities, which plunged the area into a deep poverty from which it has not recovered; the second, more trivial question was that the flat-roofed houses were not particularly well built to resist the damp weather of the North-East. So a 1990s renovation saw them given pitched roofs, while Pasmore's colour experiments on the original wood panels were covered up with brick, turning them in appearance into 'normal' fifties New Town houses, exactly what the designers at the time wanted to move away from – though, of course, it was better not to have rain in your house. The Pavilion was derelict and worn, and there was even talk of demolition. Around 2010, regeneration money finally arrived, and the Pavilion was restored to its current, close to original, state, and it's now popular, played on by children but also with a new trickle of modernist tourists going to see what is surely one of the most remarkable things built in England in the twentieth century. It transpires that people don't mind having a giant Mondrian in front of the garden of their council house to look at every day; they just don't particularly want to live in one that has dry rot and rising damp.

TYNESIDE & NORTHUMBERLAND

JAMES KNOTT MEMORIAL FLATS, TYNEMOUTH
Charles Holden, 1938
Viennese

Charles Holden's only major building outside London and Bristol has a site to die for – a high scrubby ridge between Tynemouth and North Shields, on the north bank of the Tyne, looking out to where the river meets the North Sea. Like the builders of churches and castles round here, he recognized that the correct approach is to build something monumental that commands the site rather than fades into the background – that Tyneside tradition where a fearless grandeur of giant buildings stands boldly up to the grandeur of the landscape. The James Knott Memorial Flats are a set of interconnected blocks of council housing, placed on land donated by the eponymous Tory shipping magnate to be used in perpetuity to house working-class people – municipal urbanism as noblesse oblige, sure, but not too affected by it; this is nobody's model village. Similar, architecturally, to Liverpool and London's Anglicizations of Red Vienna, with stock brick, epic archways, long access decks, and here with much bigger balconies than was the norm, to get a proper lungful of that bracing air. A large, square asymmetrical ceramic clock tower gives this otherwise quite classical composition a Gothic skew, suggesting a social castle. The complex is seen at its most imposing from below, on the seafront, which is reached by three sets of concrete staircases (one of them badly spalled). Up close the condition of the flats is decent, with a recently renovation providing external lifts at the rear access decks, for its mostly elderly residential population.

BALTIC CENTRE FOR CONTEMPORARY ART, GATESHEAD
Gelder & Kitchen and Mouchel, 1950/
Ellis Williams Architects, 1998–2002
Industrial, Moderne, High-Tech

Until very recently most big British port cities had monumental concrete flour mills on their docksides, but after demolitions in Hull, Glasgow and Southampton, the Hovis mill next to the **Imperial War Museum North (p. 414)**, London's **Millennium Mills (p. 119)** and this place are the only major survivors. They shared a common aesthetic – an industrial art deco, with flanking towers and their names picked out in brick, and they all had a rare combination of period piquancy and raw power. Gateshead was smart to use the Baltic Flour Mill of 1950 as the starting point for the transformation of the south side of the Tyne into a space of consumption, vertical drinking and gallery-going, mirroring the Newcastle Quayside opposite. The renovation as a contemporary art museum by Ellis Williams was quite a tricky task, compared with that which Herzog & de Meuron had to contend with at Bankside (now **Tate Modern, p. 102**): there is no grand turbine hall-type space in a flour mill, and any large expanses that do exist are vertical rather than horizontal, so not particularly conducive to even big and spectacular art. Instead, the building has been treated as a shell, with a new High-Tech gallery inserted into it. This has been done mostly very stylishly – the viewing gallery boxed out from between two of the four towers is particularly well judged. The way the gallery uses its vast brick exterior as a backdrop for giant artworks promoting current exhibitions always works well; the less said about the shonky flats behind that ineptly imitate the style and scale of the building the better.

FERNDALE AVENUE NURSERY, WALLSEND

Williamson Faulkner-Brown & Partners, 1965

International Style

This was once Wallsend's main library, and was designed with a very similar approach to the same firm's **Jesmond Library (p. 482)** – perhaps the first and last time that the leafy inner suburb of Newcastle and this dense and depressed shipbuilding town got the same treatment. Delicate steel-and-glass prisms on a concrete podium, everything light, crisp and sharp, with its sheer facade of windows folded like a concertina. The building was derelict for years after the council moved the library into a bleak shopping centre, but its recent reuse as a nursery seems to be working well – coloured panels to screen some of the glare of the glass give it an attractive Mondrian-like face. If the building had not been listed, it would surely have been demolished, given Tyneside dignitaries' historically brusque reaction to architectural heritage.

TYNE TUNNEL VENTILATION SHAFT, JARROW

Ryder & Yates, 1967

International Style

Based, apparently, on the upturned cone of a Venetian chimney pot, this enigmatic concrete sculpture must be the strangest of all of Ryder & Yates's surreal modernist objects. The Tyne Tunnel is a thrilling ride, very much part of the extraordinarily ambitious modernization of the Tyne–Wear metropolis that also entailed the **Tyne and Wear Metro (p. 486)**, **Newcastle Civic Centre (p. 482)** and **Sunderland Civic Centre (p. 471)**, the **Byker Estate (p. 484)**, the **Apollo Pavilion (p. 472)** and so forth – the pedestrian tunnel is also widely praised as a Festival Style engineering effort but has been closed every time I've tried using it.

You can just about see its slightly Charles Holden-like entrance near to the Ventilation Shaft for the road tunnel in Jarrow, but the shaft is best seen from the other side of the river in North Shields or Wallsend, where it appears to be the same height as the town's church spires and tower blocks, a giant abstract cowl.

KILLINGWORTH: ENGINEERING RESEARCH STATION ✪

Ryder & Yates, 1967

LAKESHORE ESTATE

Ralph Erskine, 1968

International Style, People's Detailing

Killingworth, a new town essentially for British Gas and its workers, was part of that strangely confident era in Tyne and Wear architecture and planning when it was probably rivalled only by Sheffield for the intensity of municipal experiment, although not always with such enduring architectural results – even when the buildings were of serious quality, they haven't always survived the economic collapse of the North-East's industrial economy after the seventies. The Engineering Research Station is the only one left of a series of office blocks in low-rise pavilion style by the highly talented local firm of Ryder & Yates, ex-Lubetkin designers who had settled in the North-East after the initial failure of the **Apollo Pavilion & Sunny Blunts (p. 472)** at Peterlee. Thankfully, the surviving office building was always the finest. Highly abstract, it consists of a long, low white square, a ribbon window sandwiched in the middle, held up on pilotis with a bridge entrance reached through an oversized, extremely elegant concrete arch, and, on top, a strange surrealist roofline of biomorphic chimneys and cowls. It seems to float above the landscape, and presumably this is why these ideas above their station have been so comprehensively punished.

Killingworth's Engineering Research Building: drawing on both modernist architecture and metaphysical painting.

In terms of housing, Killingworth was originally dominated by an enormous, system-built, deck-access housing complex, long demolished; Ralph Erskine's Lakeshore estate is the survivor – not a masterpiece, like Ryder & Yates's office block, but a very decent work nonetheless. It's a grid of terraces and bungalows on one side of an artificial lake, with some neat shape-making around the windows and pleasant, faintly nautical stained woodwork. The way it meets the lake with nothing but asphalt pavements feels disjointed, as if it were never quite finished. That many of the houses' doors open right on to the lake suggests exciting possibilities – an integration of boats and council homes that hasn't, as yet, happened. Presumably it might have in Sweden. The success of the estate led to Erskine being hired for the much more monumental **Byker Estate (p. 484)**. [A.20]

COASTGUARD STATION, TYNEMOUTH
Ministry of Works, 1968
Brutalist

Daring stuff – a Brutalist building placed in one of the most magnificent and atmospheric medieval ruins, the remains of Tynemouth Priory and Castle, a clifftop ensemble overlooking the mouth of the Tyne. It doesn't quite match up to it, but it makes a pretty spirited attempt at marrying these two quite different aesthetics of the sublime, the fragmented and the uncanny – Brutalism and Romanticism. It is positioned there for reasons of simple utility. The site of the priory and castle had been used for military purposes during the First World War, as a station for monitoring and shooting down Zeppelin raids, and the part of the castle that faces the sea directly is full of remains of concrete bunkers and emplacements, and guarded by an impressively Vorticist gun. So there was a tradition of using these ruins (which are genuinely awe-inspiring – the priory must have been on the scale of Durham Cathedral), so why not build the coastguard station here? And why not do it in the contemporary style, which with its asymmetries, rough materials, turrets and general air of latent, compressed violence already has an almost medieval approach to architecture? The resultant building is just slightly too functional to pull it all off, but a sight of its angular visor, looking out over the sea, right up against the priory's high crumbled vaults, is not something anybody is likely to forget.

Visitors to this extraordinary place should also note in the distance what looks like a streamline moderne outlook tower, visible over the bay windows of the Victorian B&Bs lining the seafront. This, with the address of 47A Percy Gardens, is actually an outlook tower built during the First World War to monitor the gun emplacements on the castle. It is now used as a six-storey house.

___

GATESHEAD METRO STATION ✪
Williamson Faulkner-Brown & Partners, 1980
International Style

Not much to see on the ground – there was, once, when it faced Owen Luder's astonishing Trinity Square car park, rather than the Trespa pish it abuts today – as here, Faulkner-Brown's (as it was generally known for short) went for a megastructural retail and transport complex rather than the elegant, small-scale pavilions that otherwise dominate the Tyne and Wear Metro. It is a little too close to the ultra-utilitarian big-shed genre for comfort – aptly, much of it is a giant Wilko. But persist, because underneath is the finest underground space of the Metro – in fact, it vies with Westminster and Gants Hill to be the most elegant Tube station in Britain. Crystalline mosaic murals on either side of what look like pixellated Hokusai murals, and then two sets of escalators rise through a limpid, red and white framed grid. One of the most imaginative and exciting statements of the clear bright future promised for Tyneside, which was alas delivered only in disconnected fragments like these. **[A.9]**

___

MILLENNIUM BRIDGE, GATESHEAD
Wilkinson Eyre, 1995–2001
High-Tech

Taut as a bow, this is the most elegant of the many thin, curvaceous footbridges of the New Labour era, a legible and beautiful essay in tension. Partly its quality derives from the fact that the form, however obviously aesthetic, has arisen as a way of meeting the demands of function, i.e. to deal with the reason why there hadn't been a footbridge on this part of the Tyne before – ships. So rather than simply swinging open, as some of the bridges upriver do, the entire construction snaps together, like a clam shell; this, too, dictates the curve of the pedestrian path. Viewed in enfilade, the resulting arch fits perfectly with the parade of the **New Tyne Bridge (p. 479)**, the High Level Bridge and the swing bridges beyond as the most architecturally impressive riverscape in Europe.

___

SAGE MUSIC CENTRE, GATESHEAD
Foster & Partners, 1996–2004
High-Tech

The **Baltic Centre for Contemporary Art (p. 474)**, the **Millennium Bridge (above)** and this, a multifunctional concert hall, were all projects of Gateshead rather than Newcastle, although they all face the same problem, created by topography and railway engineering, that they're far easier to reach from the centre of Newcastle than they are from the centre of Gateshead.

The result feels almost selfless – Gateshead's sacrifice for the greater good of the Tyne. All three buildings are individually wonderful, and fully deserving of the somewhat brief fame that they enjoyed in the 2000s, but they're badly disconnected, as if after the grand gesture everyone (apart from the property developers) just gave up. So the Sage meets the Millennium Bridge and the Baltic with a surface car park. This is especially frustrating, because the view of them all together, with the earlier bridges and the Newcastle skyline, reveals just how coherent and cohesively they've been created of a piece – the three bulbous bulges of Foster's hall appear precisely calculated to complement the curves and arches of the **New Tyne Bridge (p. 479)** and Millennium Bridge. Also very nicely done is the way that the glass skin that they've stretched across these bulboes is opaque from the top, becoming translucent halfway down to show off the stairwells and circulation spaces of the concert halls. But, despite all this high drama, how you walk into it on foot has been treated as an afterthought.

SEGEDUNUM ROMAN FORT VISITOR CENTRE, WALLSEND
PreFab Design, 2000
High-Tech

Reader beware: this building does not fit many definitions of 'good architecture', but it is so peculiar and memorable that in the end I couldn't help but put it in this book. Get off the Metro at Wallsend and you'll notice signs in Latin – 'Suggestus II. Noli Fumare'. There is a reason for this. That gigantic viewing platform you can see in front of the river and the remains of the shipyards is part of Segedunum Roman Fort Visitor Centre, which was Wallsend's big Millennium Project – an 'iconic' lookout bolted on to a Jacobethan office block, which looks out on to the underwhelming *Time Team*-esque very small walls and uncovered foundations of the fort that guarded the eastern end of Hadrian's Wall; a park with some reconstructions is behind. There's quite a lot of Michael Hopkins in the way the High-Tech glass and steel are clipped on to the red brick, and real drama in the scale of the tubular lifts shooting up to the great glass outlook pod, but it's also deeply naff and inappropriate to the function the building is meant to serve. If seen as a memorial tower for the remains of Tyneside industry, it starts to make a lot more sense – a sci-fi launchpad for grounded steamships.

BERWICK WORKSPACE, BERWICK-ON-TWEED
Malcolm Fraser Architects, 2008
Ecomodernist

It's fitting that this rare modern building in the Anglo-Scottish border town is by a Scottish architect, given that this has always been somewhere that isn't quite England. This intriguing set of council offices is fitted with some ingenuity into a backyard behind historic buildings, with a serrated roofline, and a serene classicism that sits peculiarly with the rough planks of wood used to clad it, as if it's intent on upending its own ordered elegance. Without performing any 'look how in keeping I am' gestures, the results feel highly appropriate to this neither-here-nor-there landscape.

NEWCASTLE UPON TYNE

NEW TYNE BRIDGE ⊘
Mott Hay & Anderson, 1925–8
Moderne

Here is the Tyneside Metropolis, a spatial experience of such extremism as to be without parallel in Britain, or probably anywhere else in northern Europe. The heavy metal clatter of the Tyne Bridge, irrespective of the mannered dressing of its art deco granite supports, crashes across the tops of tall Victorian office buildings, with the cars roaring across – none of the pedestrian-and-traffic-separating walkway systems of the sixties are so violent as this, including Newcastle's particularly dramatic examples of the genre. Aggression is the tradition here, with Stephenson's High Level Bridge being rammed through a castle as long ago as the 1840s. But this bridge is about more

than just that multilevel melodrama, it is a matter of the magnificent arch at its centre, a parabolic curve – resembling the same engineers' Sydney Harbour Bridge – that works as a truly triumphal entry to Newcastle. Welcome! [C.11]

CO-OPERATIVE DEPARTMENT STORE ⊘
L. G. Ekins, 1930–31
Moderne, Chicago School

Quite different from the Mendelsohn imitations of Co-ops in Lancashire and Yorkshire, this one, much more the product of a feverishly imagined America. Like them, it uses the local sandstone, so that this irruption of modernism (of a sort) doesn't disrupt the coherence of the nineteenth-

Britain's finest riverside townscape, centred on the heavy engineering and art deco detail of the New Tyne Bridge.

Metropolis-on-Tyne: the twin towers of the 1930s Co-operative Department Store in central Newcastle.

century cityscape – arguably the finest in urban Britain, in the form of the classical coherence achieved by the early Victorian developer Richard Grainger and architect John Dobson, so one where continuity makes more sense than rupture. But if it's not a change in either materials or palette, it's definitely a leap in scale – curving in from the side streets, it consumes an entire city block and boasts plate glass windows set in abstracted pilasters with a balcony colonnade on top, two tall towers, convex glass vertical strip windows, and a copper and brass clock on each of the grandiose symmetrical towers. This is the only interwar building that rivals the extraordinary things Newcastle did before 1914 and after 1955: glamorous, bombastic and, today, a Premier Inn. [C.12]

GIBSON STREET FLATS
Newcastle City Architects Dept, 1939
MELBOURNE COURT
Newcastle City Architects Dept, 1965
HADRIAN TRUNK SWITCHING CENTRE
Ministry of Works, 1968
International Style, Brutalist, Moderne

On the hill above the restaurants and bars of the Tyne Quayside is a weird, scattered area of truncated social-housing complexes, lone office blocks, decontextualized Victorian remnants and poor-quality student housing. Presumably it is their chaotic character that means these streets are completely absent from Grace McCombie's Pevsner guide to Newcastle and Gateshead, despite sitting between two areas described at length. If you can stomach the empty sites, spiked fences and shonky student complexes, it can be very rewarding. If approaching from the Quayside, the first buildings you will come

In the early 1930s, inspired by a trip to Germany and the Netherlands, Charles Holden unveiled his version of the new style on the outer reaches of the Piccadilly Line. Stations such as **Arnos Grove** were deployed to serve a civic idea, with each one intended as the focal point for a new suburb, its miniature town hall.

Architects wishing to combine historical continuity with modernism would turn to the brick Expressionism of Amsterdam or Hamburg, which combined new forms with familiar materials. In the 1930s, this became the style of N. F. Cachemaille-Day's churches in new suburbs and council estates like **Gipton** [**D.2 & D. 3**], in Leeds, where

powerfully modelled facades intended to stand as 'city-crowns' for the new areas conceal airy halls. After the war, this ecclesiastical Expressionism was continued by George Gaze Pace at **Keele University Chapel** [**D.4 & D. 5**], in the Staffordshire Potteries, with its beautifully made clinker turrets and organic, barn-like hall.

The later work of Alvar Aalto, with its warmth and gentle monumentality, was the beacon for civic-minded architects in the post-war decades. It was clearly with Aalto in mind that Andy MacMillan and Isi Metzstein asked the builders working on **St Bride's Church [D.6]**, East Kilbride, to lay the bricks however they liked,

lending a deliberately rough finish. The largest-scale attempt at emulating Aalto was the **British Library** [D.7 & D.8] in London. Its exterior design suggests an enclosed civic square; inside a succession of interlinked spaces, featuring meticulous attention to the smallest tactile details, encourage loitering and lingering.

In 1932, Charles Holden was commissioned to design a campus for the University of London in Bloomsbury. Dropping the brick which he had favoured for his tube stations in the suburbs, he designed **Senate House**, a skyscraper of Portland stone that was clearly intended to stand for centuries. For some film and TV buffs,

this edifice has been an image of totalitarianism, the 'Ministry of Truth' of *Nineteen Eighty-Four*; for students it has been the only unifying point of a sprawling federal university; and for many Londoners it is the only real interwar skyscraper in the capital, a place that instantly evokes the atmosphere of the 1930s.

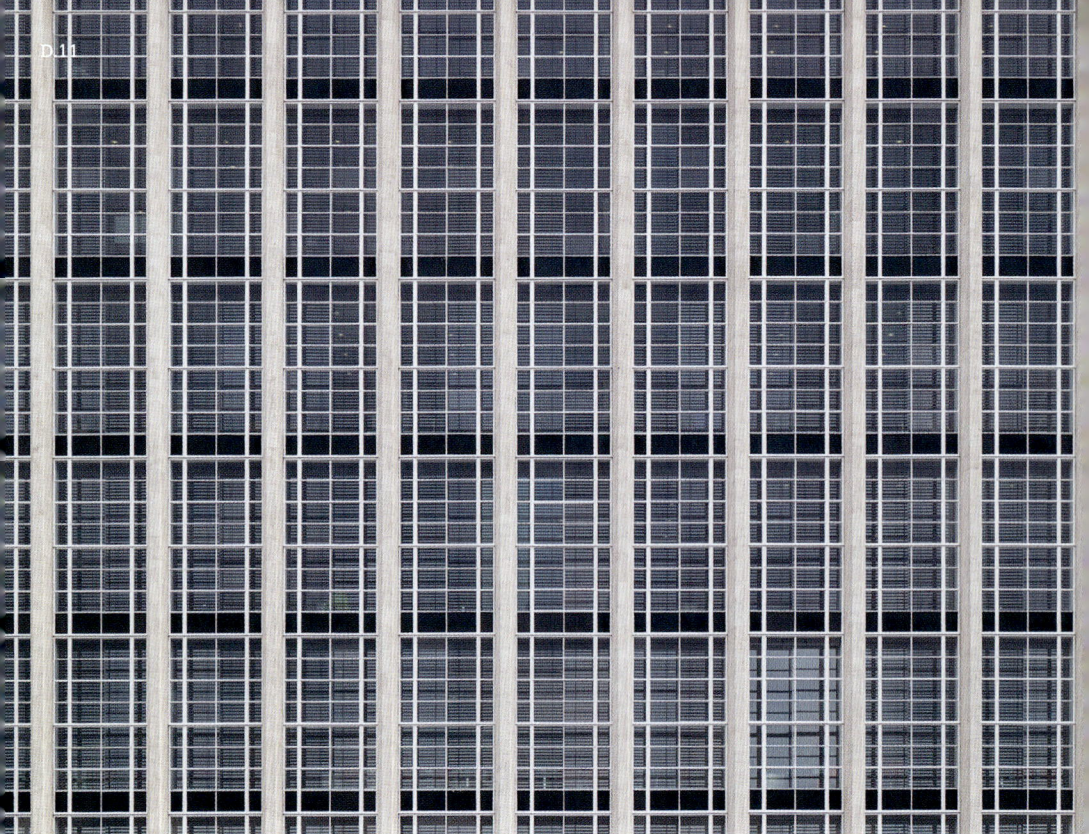

The alternation between imposing silhouette from a distance and complexity on the ground can connect seemingly disparate buildings. Nottingham Trent University's **Newton Building** [D.10 & D.11] displays a powerful upwards motion but also attention to small details, such as the metal frames of the vertical grid of windows.

At the **Barbican** [D.12] in the City of London, built over three decades, a baroque approach to urban planning – with its high-rises and slab blocks framed by grand circuses, formal squares and lakes – extends to the brass handles, tiled floors and the meticulous bush-hammered finish of its concrete surfaces.

A civic building can accommodate itself to what already exists, create a new context altogether, or try some combination of both. **Greenock Central Library [D.13]** is a formal, stone-clad building, reached from a square dominated by a massive Victorian Town Hall, which it defers to without genuflection. Similarly, **Nottingham**

Contemporary [D.15 & D.16] elegantly references the industrial townscape of the historic Lace Market with the print on its green concrete facade. But some buildings are designed for everything else to revolve around: consider the swirling rotundas of the University of Lancaster's non-denominational **Chaplaincy** [D.14].

The 1930s was arguably when municipal power came into its own, with everything from council housing to theatres to schools to airports being designed by in-house teams at the town hall. **Speke Aerodrome** [D.17], Liverpool's first airport, was designed as a brick-and-steel edifice both rooted and winged; the astonishing

Parking strictly for the
use of Royal Mail

brick roar of the **Woodside Ventilation Tower** [D.19] in Birkenhead was built as part of the Mersey Tunnel project. Such statements of civic power were influenced alternately by the architecture of social democratic Scandinavia and of fascist Italy, and none of them were so elegant as the famous **Swansea Guildhall** [D.18].

A village-like scale is one obvious way to encourage a friendly, intimate townscape – as at the **Pier Arts Centre** [**D.20**] in Stromness on the Orkney islands, where refurbished old buildings house a first-rate modern art collection. The architect who has most attempted these townscapes in recent years is Peter Barber, in whose

work the street-and-alley aesthetic appears as Mediterranean, in the social housing of Bow's **Donnybrook Quarter** [D.21], or as extremely English, in Finsbury Park's private **Moray Mews** [D.22] – both interpretations of what an actual village might look like in the twenty-first century, not kitsch reproductions.

What Philip Dowson of Arup Associates has done with the **St Thomas White Building** for St John's College is, seen one way, a dramatic and overconfident assertion of modern architectural values in the back streets of Oxford – the concrete frame that repeats throughout the sprawling building extends so far that it actually

surmounts and pulls in a section of the college's Victorian wall. But viewed more sympathetically, this is one Gothic style meeting another – Gothic Oxford and modernist Oxford both sharing an architecture of expressed structure, rich materials and maze-like layouts, piled on top of each other, layer on layer.

Coherence is often a matter of repetition – disciplined, syncopated facades, with powerful rhythms across a large scale. In Oxford, **St Catherine's College** [D.24] stretches its modules of glass, copper and brick across the college lawns; the **'Sidgwick Site'** [D.27], in Cambridge, takes a similarly quadrangular approach.

On urban sites, this can result in buildings that defer to their context, as at **Chetham's School of Music [D.25]** in Manchester. Few architects would dare to attempt something like **60 Queen Victoria Street [D.26]**, whose almost fetishistic mesh of copper and steel is part nineteenth-century office block, part set design for *Alien*.

Wythenshawe is a council estate the size of a town in south Manchester. With few shops or pubs and no railway station, it was the churches – notably the miniature 'cathedral' at **St Michael & All Angels**, with its spindly, organic concrete vaults and multicoloured light – that became the civic focus for the new suburb.

to are the low-rise brick 1930s council tenements on City Road, leading up to Gibson Street, Blagdon Street and Granville Terrace, with their elegant, long concrete access decks – unspectacular but robust, these have been given a renovation with wooden balconies, gates and trellises borrowing extensively from the aesthetic of the **Byker Estate (p. 484)**, a mile to the east of here. The blocks frame a well-looked-after green square. Opposite is a similarly low-rise but more strongly modernist estate, the cubistic, International Style Melbourne Court, whose crisp, white-painted maisonettes are connected by overhead walkways around another green public space. Then in the middle of all this is the Hadrian Trunk Switching Centre, a high-rise telephone exchange, with a dramatic, space-age concrete frame. Four times the size of everything else, it has somehow beamed down here from the more grandly scaled world of the city centre a mile to the west. Surrealist townscape – a collection of pieces that don't quite fit together, made much more interesting through their rude juxtaposition.

The Herschel Building: International Style modernism and abstract art arrive in Newcastle at once.

HERSCHEL BUILDING, NEWCASTLE UNIVERSITY

Basil Spence & Partners and Geoffrey Clarke (artist), 1957–62
International Style

There is a good cluster of modern buildings at Newcastle University, interspersed with some decent neo-Tudor and neo-Georgian, across asphalt squares and quadrangles. This is one of the best, tellingly because of its integration with sculpture, which would become a hallmark of the years in which Trotskyist-turned-technocrat T. Dan Smith presided over the city council. The Herschel Building marks Spence's move from semi-historicist, populist modern architecture into something more sober and American, with ribbons of sky-blue panels and expanses of window, and a marble-clad lecture theatre like a clenched fist. In the forecourt is Geoffrey Clarke's *Spiral Nebula*, a tense coil of what looks like salvaged shards of metal, on a properly large scale, dominating the space around the building – it isn't a bauble, but a complement, a dialogue about modernity between the rationalist tower and the seething abstract sculpture. The Spence team would build on this combination of well-crafted International Style modernism and well-chosen sculpture at their **University of Southampton (p. 245)** at the other end of England, on a greener, more suburban site. Meanwhile, Clarke's work would be the first of several integrated modernist artworks in or around public buildings across the city and its region, from **Newcastle Civic Centre (p. 482)** to the **Apollo Pavilion (p. 472)**.

NEWCASTLE CIVIC CENTRE ✪
George Kenyon, 1958–68
People's Detailing

This is complete design, the grandest civic complex anywhere in post-war Britain. The combination of rousing spaces, meticulous details and a declarative skyline makes this our closest equivalent to great twentieth-century city halls, like that of Oslo – a connection that the patrons of Newcastle Civic Centre were fully aware of, to the point of having the King of Norway open the building when it was finally completed, in 1967. It immediately came in for some attacks by critics, largely because by then its decorative, populist version of modernism was out of fashion in favour of the sculptural gestures of Brutalism. Nowhere (aside from maybe the **Barbican, p. 66**) is the misjudgement of buildings on the basis of fashion more conspicuous than here, as this is a building of genuinely moving splendour and generosity, which did not deserve to be dismissed because it no longer chimed with what the hipsters were doing at the Architectural Association.

Newcastle Civic Centre is basically made up of a glazed slab block, like an elongated UN building, with a ceremonial tower at one end; a long glazed linking block, with a clipped rhythm of copper slats, raised on faintly classical arches in the manner of Spence's work at the University of Sussex, arches which you can walk under into a sunken square around a pool; and the concrete rotunda of the main meeting hall. These are the spaces you feel most powerfully on the ground, though it's the tower that dominates views. The halls and interiors are grand, with all the doorhandles and lamps designed as integral artworks, warm and pleasant, as welcoming as Newcastle itself. Of the many sculptures and reliefs built into the architecture, David Wynne's river god on the tower, the frosted-glass goddesses at the main entrance doors and the seahorses on its copper crown are all obvious nods towards Scandinavia, allying the Northumbrian coast with a sort of greater Scandinavian Social Democratic North Sea network. But the artwork that sticks most in the mind is quite far from these attempts at historical reverse-engineering. It is in what was built as the Rates Hall, and is now the Customer Services Centre. Everything is clad in the richest granites and marbles, planes of veined and ribbed stone illuminated by the plate glass windows; at either side are abstract vitreous panels by Victor Pasmore, perfectly calculated to frame the space. T. Dan Smith claimed that all this luxury, this useless beauty, was meant to infuriate the wealthier taxpayers paying their rates. Now it's part of one of those spaces where cash-drained councils try to act as a last line of defence. It stands as a reminder of what these now skeletal institutions were once capable of. [C.13]

————

JESMOND LIBRARY
Williamson Faulkner-Brown & Partners, 1962–3
International Style

A great little branch library by a firm that built a lot of very classy modern architecture in and around Newcastle. Jesmond Library, in a well-heeled and studenty area north of the centre, is a glass rotunda of black-painted steel with reddish-brown panels, which fan out around its circumference in a zigzag pattern; the reading rooms inside are relaxed and airy. The serenity and civic virtue of this and Wallsend Library (now the **Ferndale Avenue Nursery, p. 475**) made their architects a natural choice to design the Tyne and Wear Metro's buildings a decade later.

NEWCASTLE CITY CENTRE WALKWAY SYSTEM: ✪
A167(M) PEDESTRIAN BRIDGES
Various architects, 1963–2018
SWAN HOUSE
RMJM, 1963–9
MANORS CAR PARK
D. T. Bradshaw for Newcastle City Engineers and Planning Dept, 1971
MEA HOUSE
Ryder & Yates, 1974
HADRIAN BRIDGE
Newcastle City Engineers and Planning Dept, 1975
International Style, Brutalist

The east side of Newcastle city centre was the largest test bed of the separation of pedestrians and traffic anywhere outside the City of London's **Pedways (p. 60)**, but is far more radical, with people and cars brought perilously close together, seemingly deliberately to heighten the contrast and excitement of the two levels working in parallel, with the noisy conduits of engines and metal below and the airy new metropolitan space above; this is, of course, as the **New Tyne Bridge (p. 479)** makes clear, a local tradition. Much of this has been dismantled over the subsequent years, but a lot still survives, and it is sometimes even added to, as in London.

Swan House is the most central, and the most notorious part of the system, and has been rightly criticized for its role in the destruction of a Victorian arcade that was one of the most important elements of the classical city centre built by the developer Richard Grainger and architect John Dobson. On its own terms, it's strong stuff, an immense volume of concrete units suspended above a multilevel circus of circulation, sublime and a little terrifying; it has since been turned into flats, which is either a vindication of the concept or proof that in the 2000s people could be sold anything as 'luxury living in the heart

of the city'. Just beyond it is the seventeenth-century Holy Jesus Hospital, a rough red-brick complex hard up against the underpass, and then the dramatic sweep of Manors Car Park, which swings alongside a two-level inner-city motorway; its laconic concrete grid is like a set of go-faster stripes. Seeing this from the pedestrian walkways is one thing, but hurtling towards the Tyne on this racetrack makes for the most exciting architectural motorscape in Britain.

Going north from here, the unique Hadrian Bridge crosses the motorway, a pedestrian conduit enclosed in concrete, with porthole windows to watch the traffic. Its ribbed concrete is the same as that of the motorway cutting. The cluster of walkways around MEA House is more sober, prioritizing the pedestrian rather than the amphetamine-addled driver in a concession to logic and humanism. They originally encompassed a library by Basil Spence, and now enclose a decent enough late-modernist replacement by Ryder Architecture, the successor firm to Ryder & Yates. The original partnership's talent for abstracted, slightly surrealist, biomorphic ensembles can be seen at its finest near the end of the walkway network, at MEA House, an office block for charities that meets the ground with a great brick drum, and above meets the walkway with a row of mirrorglass. From the section you can see how elegantly Ryder & Yates have put together the walkways and stairwells, and the little Phrygian cap at the top.

These are the strictly *architectural* moments, but it's the experience of the other things you see from unexpected angles, into backsides and backyards, non-Civic Trust skylines and accidental ensembles, that really makes this so much fun. There is, however, no obvious plan either for maintaining or for destroying the network. So metallic new walkways span the motorway to make life easier for students at the University of Northumbria, and some concrete walkways have been supplemented with more

The most complete multilevel cityscape in Britain: layer upon layer in the east of Newcastle City Centre.

fashionable materials such as wood; but an upper-level shopping arcade has been left to rot, without a single unit still open. Like a grand project of the Soviet Union after 1991, it has been 'Balkanized', split up into little pieces. But the totality can still be felt if you walk round here for long enough. **[B.10]**

___

BYKER ESTATE ✪
Ralph Erskine, 1969–81
People's Detailing, Postmodernist

As with Sheffield, it's all superlatives here. If **Park Hill (p. 370)** is the great masterpiece of the 1960s, then Byker is the peak of the 1970s, and speaks of its priorities and values every bit as eloquently. Today, Park Hill is treated as a problem best managed by a property developer (with abundant state subsidy, naturally), whereas Byker is managed and looked after by the people that live there, as a Community Land Trust.

Yet both are massive schemes based on the monumental spaces of deck-access 'streets in the sky' and moments of great intimacy; both were unusual for their time in rehousing much of the local community in a new building without dispersing them all; and both are, above all, spaces where you can feel the idea of collectivity and urban living as a communal endeavour. But while Park Hill is socialism in concrete, here the same ethos is expressed in brightly stained wood.

Byker stood against the idea of solving a slum's problems with a sudden big bang, a violent clearance; famously, Ralph Erskine and his partner, Vernon Gracie, set up shop in what was then an area of dilapidated Tyneside flats and back-to-backs, so that they could work with the residents day in, day out; a part of the new scheme would be built, opinions and experiences would be canvassed, and then they'd plan the next part accordingly. The only element of the estate that didn't come out of this sort of consultation was the 'Wall', the long, sinuous deck-access block that meets you outside Byker Metro Station, with a pattern in red and yellow brick, but which, inside, transforms into a brightly coloured world of typically Scandinavian woodwork details and sheltered, warm-looking flats, shaded by trees. The rest of the estate, aside from one very stylish high-rise block (the most Swedish part of all, with its red wood balconies and its serrated blue roof), is made up of terraces, arranged into distinct squares and neighbourhoods, often with pieces of salvage from the old place mixed in, and they step down towards the Tyne in picturesque little huddles, at one point framing a Victorian church spire.

Throughout, the grand and metropolitan shelters the small-scale and local, but these poles are not divided or fragmented – all is part of the whole. That this would be the last large-scale council estate to be built in Britain is heartbreaking, as it shows a degree of wisdom and balance had been achieved beyond anything which preceded it. Maybe that's why it had to be stopped. [C.10]

VALE HOUSE, JESMOND ⊙
Douglass Wise & Partners, 1966–8
International Style

Not far from a cluster of decent but minor system-built towers is this lone point block, almost skyscraper height, in its own little park downhill from the terraces of Jesmond. System-built, like most high-rises after council leader, T. Dan Smith, made some dodgy deals in order to get things done, it is one of the great examples of the high-rise block as a singular monument, placed just at the edge of a hill, like a concrete-panel beacon, and reached from the green by an impressive concrete walkway which seems to almost plunge into the second floor. The sides are a continuous abstract

A more humble side of Newcastle's modernist townscape: modest terraces and the point block of Vale House.

relief sculpture like a computer printout, a *jeu d'esprit* added when the architects realized they could systematize sculpture, too. Last time I visited, a spring day, the green around had flower boxes, informal little benches and birdbaths, all in very good nick.

ST JAMES'S PARK STADIUM
Faulkner-Brown Hendy Watkinson Stonor, 1973
Brutalist

There are lamentably few football stadiums really worth visiting solely for their architecture, given their importance in most towns and cities. They usually fall into one of two categories – interchangeable new arenas by international megafirms, which you can find in, say, Middlesbrough, Southampton or Old Trafford, and more commonly ad hoc patchings up of Victorian stands and 1990s post-Taylor Report additions. St James's Park involves a fair bit of patching up too, but it exhibits so much of Newcastle's flair for the extreme juxtaposition that it has to be seen. It stands just behind one of the city's dignified classical ensembles, The Leazes, sandstone sobriety in front of a manicured green; to this it presents a massive Brutalist backside, towering, chunky great concrete cantilevers, tilted to a jauntily Constructivist angle. Usually this sort of brusque throwing together of concrete and ashlar generates heavy criticism; not here, so important is St James's Park to the life of the city; it's almost as if nobody notices how extreme a montage it is.

SALVATION ARMY HOSTEL
Ryder & Yates, 1976
International Style

Another clever, original and strange Ryder & Yates scheme, and one of the first buildings to engage properly with the formerly industrial Quayside. This is a hostel, now run by the Salvation Army, that nestles in the steep slope from the scruffily residential east end down to the Tyne; it is formed into a crescent of smooth purple brick, with one of Peter Yates's surrealist biomorphic rooflines, and a small but pleasant park in the middle. As always, the details are impeccable, like the boxed-out, kinked common-room window, or the curved canopy at the main entrance, held up on little pilotis, which shows a delicacy and awareness of the importance of the 'special' that the architects must have learned in their apprenticeship with Lubetkin. Humane and warm, and with none of the Noddy House crap usually insisted on by the contemporary providers of care homes and hostels; these inhabitants are treated like adults, capable of using a real modern building.

TYNE AND WEAR METRO: ✪ JESMOND & ST JAMES'S STATIONS
Faulkner-Brown Hendy Watkinson Stonor, 1978–80
BYKER VIADUCT
Arup Associates, 1979
VENTILATION SHAFT ('PARSON'S POLYGON')
David Hamilton, 1982–5
International Style, Brutalist

The Tyne and Wear Metro is a superb project, one that shames England's cut-price rapid-transit networks like Manchester's Metrolink or the Sheffield Supertram. Both of those were nineties budget replacements for more expensive proposals for a Metro and a sort of Docklands Light Railway, respectively, which makes it all the more strange that Newcastle managed to get its own proposals past the Treasury in the seventies – presumably it was a busy day in Parliament. So like the London Underground – like a European city! – Newcastle, Gateshead and Sunderland got to have a real Tube, with real stations, and

The concrete supports of Arup's Byker Viaduct, part of one of the best-designed engineering projects of the 1970s.

NEWCASTLE UPON TYNE

The elegant, spacious Jesmond Metro Station, a glass cube secluded in trees just off the ring road.

a real design effort, with integrated artworks and Margaret Calvert's excellent typeface. Faulkner-Brown's aesthetic is very much in the seventies Anglo-Miesian moment elsewhere epitomized by Milton Keynes – cool, elegant, a bit West German, a bit North American, with a consistent black, white and yellow colour scheme.

The interiors of the wholly subterranean city centre stations like Central, Manors and Monument are decent seventies modernism, a little like the pre-renovation **Merseyrail (p. 431)** or London's Victoria Line, but there are stand-alone stations here too – on match days, Tubes run to St James's, a box covered by foliage, surrounded by a sunken square. The station to see, though, is Jesmond, a handsome Miesian pavilion forming a square around abstract sculptures by Raf Fulcher, and with a late-Matisse-style multicoloured enamel mural below, by Simon Butler. Other bits of the Metro's infrastructure worth seeing – aside from its reuse of old stations,

like the moderne Longbenton and iron-and-glass Tynemouth – include Arup's incredible Byker Viaduct, a snaking design with ribbed, tall concrete pillars which taper upwards in a captivatingly organic fashion; it joins the Victorian Ouseburn Bridge and Byker Bridge in a Piranesian ensemble of high-level bridges charging above the pubs of the Ouseburn Valley. In the centre, meanwhile, look out for 'Parson's Polygon', a ventilation shaft not far from Monument shaped into a piece of *art brut* sculpture in red tiles and brick. In recent years, standards have slipped somewhat, as the relatively tacky extension to Sunderland and the clumsy, PFI-style rebuilding of Haymarket (a deserved Carbuncle Cup nominee) shows. But, still, this is a remarkable achievement, and, as with the **Byker Estate (p. 484)**, a tragic one, in that nowhere has ever been allowed to follow it. Not only that, but Tyne and Wear's initial, London-style integration of its Tubes with its buses was dismantled by central government, and a recent bid to take them back in-house was defeated. In Britain, only London is allowed to have good public transport.

OUSEBURN FARM
Newton Architects, 2005
THE MALINGS
Ash Sakula, 2015
Ecomodernist

Underneath the Byker Viaduct is an urban farm, an appropriately bohemian, hippy use for this area of craft beer pubs and cottage industries in old warehouses, run by a charity. The farm's buildings are in an attractive eco style, with a faintly Japanese post-and-beam construction. Not far from it, you'll find The Malings, abstract, miniature brick residential towers on the Ouseburn itself, square and dense. Close together, these are the only entirely new buildings of the last twenty years in Newcastle (rather than Gateshead) that are worth a detour, both of them gentle and optimistic little places, with no 'regeneration' bombast.

STAR AND SHADOW CINEMA, SANDYFORD
MawsonKerr, 2018
Ecomodernist

Like a lot of the really interesting urban projects of the last few years, this is a raw, anarchic adaptive reuse project for an unusual client rather than a new building. Compared with the expensive, tourist-oriented projects like the **Sage Music Centre (p. 477)** and the **Baltic Centre for Contemporary Art (p. 474)** it suggests both a shift towards a new political and social radicalism, but also the bleak stringency of 'austerity' and David Cameron's 'Big Society', which slashed the municipal arts budget in Newcastle by, literally, 100 per cent.

The Star and Shadow Cinema has been around for a while in various temporary locations, but for its permanent building it took over a disused MFI warehouse – seventies, corrugated iron and glass, opposite a park – and converted it into a cinema and social centre. The conversion is spacious and comfortable (especially by the standards of anarchist social centres) but still has an eye for the makeshift – there is something very Dada about the bolted-together window frames (donated by enthusiasts) that make up the entrance facade, like a functioning *Merzbau*. Meanwhile, the cinema itself received Arts Council funding purely through having it decorated in neo-Constructivist style by the artist Annette Knol – they would never have paid just for a cinema. The toilets, meanwhile, are coated in more donations, this time decorative tiles. If the future is like this it can't be all bad, just so long as people actually get paid.

12. EDINBURGH & EAST COAST

Gala Fairydean Stadium, Galashiels (p. 193)

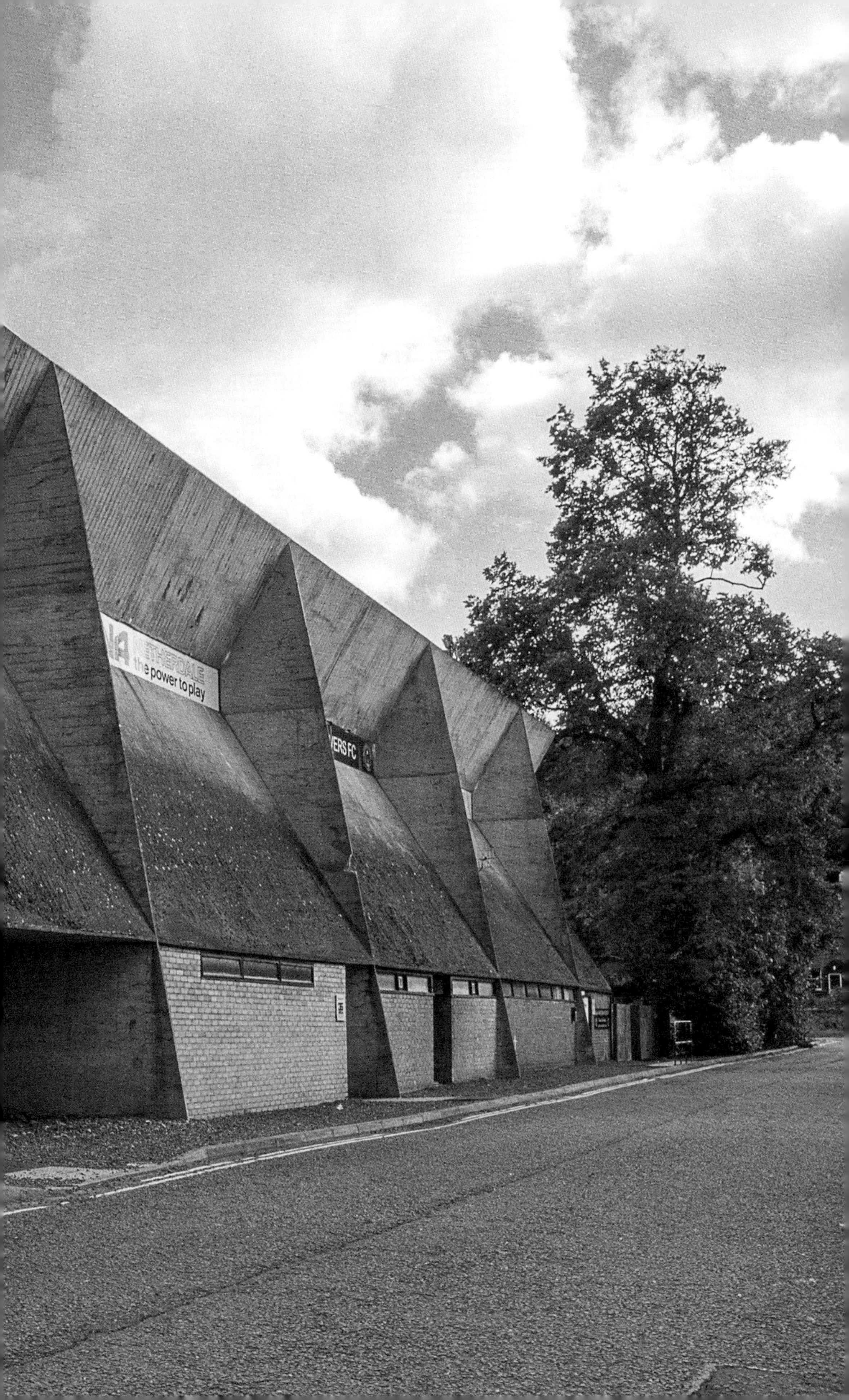
the power to play
VERS FC

Scottish townscape, historically, is nothing like English. The tightly packed, tall tenements of Edinburgh's Old Town have no analogue south of the border, and the Enlightenment capital of the New Town is unlike anywhere – except possibly Bath – in the sheer scale and drama of its planning. Partly because of its undeniable beauty, Edinburgh faced a quite different kind of post-war rebuilding to cities of its size elsewhere. While there was a little new housing in the centre, such as Basil Spence's historicist-Brutalist **Canongate Redevelopment**, most slum clearance led to the creation of large, low-density estates on the outskirts, many of which are currently being demolished. Edinburgh has consistently built excellent modern buildings in every decade since the 1930s, but each has been carefully placed so that it doesn't barge into the postcard views. This is what links such apparently unlike structures as the monumental art deco government offices of **St Andrew's House** in the 1930s, the elegant, high-modernist **Royal Commonwealth Pool** in the 1960s, the extension of the **National Library of Scotland** in the 1980s, and the rhetorical, complex and personal **Scottish Parliament** in the 2000s. More hardcore modernism is confined to the port at Leith, with impressive results, such as the grandiose concrete crescent of **Cables Wynd House**.

Perhaps due to the strict demands of conservation, the eastern part of the Scottish Central Belt and even the rural Borders are actually better for really great modern buildings than the capital itself. The Borders region features some of the most interesting and individualistic Brutalist architecture in the country, through the work of Peter Womersley – the pick of the bunch being his ingenious **Gala Fairydean** football stadium in Galashiels, which would be globally famous were it in Boston or Tokyo. The conurbation, meanwhile, includes perhaps the greatest New University of all, the **University of Stirling** in the suburbs of that city – a one-of-a-kind meeting of lakes, mountains, forests and elegant, restrained modernism. The former Fife coalfield, meanwhile, has an impressive legacy of council housing, in styles which combine Scottish vernacular forms and the more enigmatic side of Brutalism.

BORDERS & LOTHIANS

GALA FAIRYDEAN STADIUM, GALASHIELS ✪
Peter Womersley, 1963
Brutalist

The Scottish Borders, a historically conservative and rural area, have an unusually large quantity of interesting and pugnacious Brutalist architecture – certainly far more than you might expect. That what they have is of such quality, rather than the usual developers' dross or the dour tiny-windows council vernacular most Scottish local authorities favoured, is largely due to the work of one architect, Peter Womersley – though the Fife firm of Anthony Wheeler and Frank Sproson has contributed its share of important work as well. This is probably the strangest of a strange crop, resembling no other sports building in Britain, or, really, anywhere else, with a bizarre but intuitively brilliant approach to its concrete construction. Detailed in shuttered béton brut, the one grandstand of Gala Fairydean FC appears to have been the result of an origami experiment with concrete, a series of folded and faceted volumes to the street, and to the pitch one great jagged grey cantilever. Exhilarating, sculptural and unique.

LANGLEE ESTATE, GALASHIELS
Wheeler & Sproson, 1965–9
Brutalist

An obvious cousin of their work near their office in Kirkcaldy for historic burghs like Dysart **(Saut Girnal Wynd & The Towers, p. 508)** and Burntisland **(Somerville Square & Coltburndale, p. 507)**, the Langlee Estate is on a hill above Galashiels, from which it appears as a small-scale but imposing and hieratic presence. Much of it comprises terraces of maisonettes, rendered in red, resembling the bleak housing of much of suburban Scotland, but around half of the estate is made up of the fascinating 'tower houses' that the architects pioneered in Fife. These are peculiar beasts, three storeys, mostly just two flats in each, with deep, elegantly detailed balconies, and greyish-white harling over the elevations. They genuinely feel 'tower-like', despite their diminutive size, and have a haunting and monolithic presence in the townscape, split by stairwells into craggy skylines. It feels like a crossover between the Scots vernacular and Mediterranean hill town, boasting some of the stern Italian Rationalism of a designer like Aldo Rossi – lessons in how to look both modern and eternal.

BERNAT KLEIN STUDIO, SELKIRK ✪ ❶
Peter Womersley, 1969
Brutalist

Womersley designed two buildings on this site in Selkirk for the textile designer Bernat Klein. The earlier, designed in the fifties, is High Sunderland, one of a genre of houses he'd designed as a sort of northern analogue of California's sunkissed Case Study Houses. I've not included it because there is no public access – I have no interest in leading people to places they can't explore; those interested are recommended *The See-Through House*, a memoir by Klein's daughter, Shelley. The designer's studio, on the other hand, is on the main road, at the bottom of a hill, and was designed from the outset as a public showcase for his products. Accordingly, it is strongly outward facing, one of the most visually arresting and complex modern buildings in Scotland. Two daringly cantilevered bronze balconies in a dramatically articulated concrete frame,

The studio of the modernist textile designer Bernat Klein, secluded in woodlands just off a main road in Selkirk.

with a careful monumentality comparable to the best work of Denys Lasdun, suspend fully glazed rooms that would once have been filled with beautiful modernist textiles. The building is listed, but is currently empty and deteriorating. Although this makes it a dreamlike place to walk – with the concrete walkways through the forest into the showroom covered in leaves and wisteria – it would be a tragedy if it ultimately led to the destruction of this wonderful building. **[B.19]**

DISTRICT ASYLUM BOILER HOUSE, MELROSE ❶

Peter Womersley, 1977
Brutalist

One of the weirder of Peter Womersley's buildings. This industrial, straightforwardly functional structure was designed in a similarly formal, Japanese manner to **Gala Fairydean Stadium (p. 493)**, employing the

same shuttered concrete and rigorous proportional systems, except here the pieces, rather than projecting inwards and outwards, have all been collapsed, like a house of cards that has been dismantled and its components laid out on a table. An intriguing little bit of gameplaying, it is one of those places where an architect has used a windowless functional box as a place to try out ideas, knowing that it only had to protect and shelter machines, rather than people – so it has a similar stridency to, say, Sheffield's **Moore Street Electricity Substation (p. 373)**, though it is much more personal and oblique. It is currently slated for demolition, though its deadpan formalism is so fashionable right now that if you commissioned some photos for a glossy magazine and said it was by a famous Swiss architect it would probably have an Airbnb inside it soon enough.

TORNESS NUCLEAR POWER STATION, DUNBAR
National Nuclear Corporation, 1980–88
Industrial

Nuclear power stations tend, for obvious reasons, to be located in depopulated areas – places where nobody is looking. In Scotland, Dounreay is a typical example – as far north of the island of Great Britain as you can possibly go, on the outskirts of Thurso. Torness is unusual, then, for having been built close to the East Coast mainline, on a dramatic site resting on the Lothian coast. Most of all, it's simply a very dramatic work of minimalist, monumental architecture. Made up of shiny white cubes, stepped and staggered with a central projecting volume, which at night can be seen lit up from within, it resembles a vast 1920s modernist sculpture – one of Kasimir Malevich's 'Architektons', built to house thermonuclear reactors.

ABBOTSFORD VISITOR CENTRE
LDN Architects, 2013
Ecomodernist

This is the ticket office, café and shop for Walter Scott's house, a Baronial castle so over-designed, technically ambitious and generally foolish that he had to churn out historical novels at a Stakhanovite rate so as to be able to maintain it. Sensibly, the visitor centre makes no attempt at being 'in keeping' with either house or gardens, but opts for a dialogue with the forest around. Placed in-between pines, a strongly horizontal low pavilion clad and furnished in high-quality wood is relaxed and idyllic, with none of the naffness that is often a feature of Historic Scotland's visitor centres. It's strange there are not more Scottish buildings like this, given the country's aspirations to Scandinavian social democracy; and seeking out other work by the Edinburgh-based LDN Architects on the strength of this will tend to disappoint.

Abbotsford Visitor Centre, an incongruously minimal and calm entrance to Walter Scott's very silly house.

EDINBURGH

SOUTHSIDE GARAGE
Kininmonth & Spence, 1933–4
International Style

The first important building by twentieth-century Britain's premier populist modern architect is this fetching concrete garage inserted into a row of tenements, painted white with a cute moderne sign. One plate glass storey is dramatically cantilevered above what was originally the space to fill up your car, but is now a niche leading to a Majestic Wine Shop. Pretty standard if slightly advanced for the time, with few flashes of individual personality – perhaps the fact the space for the cars is narrow but the facade for pedestrians impressive might suggest a favouring of image over boring functional integrity that would define Basil Spence's career.

IMPERIAL DOCKS GRAIN ELEVATOR, LEITH ✪ ❶
A. H. Roberts, Kinnear & Gordon and M. C. White, 1933–57
Industrial

Highly visible – for now – from Edinburgh Castle, where it stands on the edge of the city facing the North Sea, this is Leith's castle. Built over several decades, it is Britain's major equivalent to the sprawling grain silo complexes of North America, in Montreal, Buffalo and so forth, that so inspired the heroic age of modernism. That is: monumental concrete engineering, in elemental forms, standing pungent (in both senses) and hard against the water. As structures for the grain import industry go these are so much more abstract and modern than the relatively coherent, classicized monumentality of the

The white concrete and glass Southside Garage, an early work by Basil Spence in an affluent Edinburgh street.

The other Edinburgh: the cyclopean concrete grain elevator at the old imperial docks in Leith.

Baltic Centre for Contemporary Art (p. 474) in Gateshead or the mill complex next to the **Imperial War Museum North (p. 414)** – one lower block with a rhythm of repeated concrete supports, and then a tower-like edifice facing the water and the city centre. Grain silos are notoriously hard to convert – there are examples, but not only do they tend to lose their uniquely imposing qualities in the process, it is expensive to do. So while it is listed, the owners, Forth Ports, have successfully applied for listed-building consent for demolition, and at the time of writing fully intend to remove the complex for a biomass power station. It would be better if they demolished the pathetically shonky flats that they've foisted upon Leith and Granton, but there's priorities for you; fairly obvious evidence too of the patent fact that the leaders of one of the most obsessively preserved cities on earth couldn't give the slightest toss about what happens to the architecture of its working-class periphery.

ST ANDREW'S HOUSE ✪
Burnet Tait & Lorne, 1934–9
Moderne

Before the **Scottish Parliament (p. 504)**, there was this thing, built into the southern flank of Calton Hill and dominating the skyline, whereas Miralles's building burrows downwards at the lowest point of the Royal Mile. This headquarters for the Scottish Office – the result of some minor devolution after the First World War – is the nearest thing interwar Britain had to a modernist government building, at least not counting town halls. Thomas Tait's architecture had developed from Chicago School blocks like **Kodak House (p. 47)** to a Dutch-influenced monumental moderne, at **Ravenscourt Park Hospital (p. 158)**. This edifice shows his mastery of the fusion of stripped, residual classicism and elemental forms derived from De Stijl and Constructivism, here executed in Edinburgh's sombre, patrician-grey ashlar.

The moderne edifice of St Andrew's House: built into the rock of Edinburgh, surrounded by Victorian monuments.

St Andrew's House is two rather different buildings, depending on your direction of approach; the main entrance is its most conservative side, with black-granite moderne gateposts in a super-cinema style leading to a vast neo-Egyptian colonnade, with everything symmetrical and domineering. But if you see it, as most do, from below – easily done, as it overlooks the main railway approach into Waverley – the feeling is of a giant, daunting mass of stone built right into the rock, a castle out of Franz Kafka rather than Walter Scott; authoritarian, without doubt, but thrilling. It is so extremely Edinburgh that it's almost parodic, which makes it all the more remarkable that Miralles decided to do something so different for the actual, elected Parliament that finally arrived in the 2000s – breaking with tradition in a city that bitterly resists ruptures. But of the two buildings, this is one whose power you can feel in your bones.

ST CUTHBERT'S CO-OPERATIVE
T. Waller Marwick, 1937
International Style

Obviously, Edinburgh being Edinburgh, it doesn't have much in the way of interwar modernist architecture, and it has even less in its historic centre, which makes this small piece of infill all the more unusual. In the middle of the sandstone row of Broad Street, where the Old Town meets the unlovely Postmodern bank complexes of Tollcross, is a single glass frontage, on the same scale as everything around it, with its glazed grid offering views of the concrete frame inside. Now a conference centre, whose lettering tries to emulate that of the old Co-op it was built for, not much survives on the inside – but the facade is an interesting early attempt to show how a pure modernist building could stand as a part of a classical townscape – certainly with a lot more restraint than the average Victorian building.

DOMINION CINEMA
T. Bowhill, Gibson & Laing, 1937–9
Moderne

A typical streamline moderne picture palace, in the well-heeled southern Edinburgh burb of Morningside. In such places, architecture gets thoroughly pickled in aspic, with local-amenity societies and civic groups keeping a beady eye on the smallest change. So buildings like this, which can lose their lustre very easily when turned into evangelical churches or business schools or through sitting derelict, tend to look at their best in Edinburgh. It's generic, with the usual gestures taken here from Erich Mendelsohn, there from Hollywood, and with a bit of Dudok, with a piquant curved tower and chic ashlar cladding, but it has survived unusually well – and, what's more, it's still a cinema.

———

UNIVERSITY OF EDINBURGH: ✪ 40 GEORGE SQUARE
RMJM, 1960–63
APPLETON TOWER
Reiach & Hall, 1966
International Style

The start of the rot, for some, in that, here, this heartland of hardline conservation began to opt for high-rise modernity. Of course, it was well out of any of the historic views, in neither the Old Town nor the New Town but at the start of the Scottish capital's southern suburbs, but it did entail the partial demolition of one of Edinburgh's earliest squares, and for that this tower, and Spence's slightly later **University of Edinburgh Library (p. 501)** on the other side, have never been forgiven. Nonetheless, the high-rise here – built as the David Hume Tower and recently renamed following the Black Lives Matter protests – is a serious, vigorous and well-crafted modernist building, with meticulous attention to detail and material The model is American university campus

Edinburgh Mark III: after the Old Town and New Town, the modernist squares of the University of Edinburgh.

architecture, and in this case the work of Josep Lluís Sert at Harvard, which moved towards a 'new monumentality' after the war. Fifteen storeys, with a sandstone-clad spine and a black-tile grid of windows, both very much in the city's pre-existing colours, and with the tower's bulk articulated into distinct asymmetric parts, make this something of a mix between Old Town cragginess and New Town rationalism.

Reiach & Hall's shorter, white-walled, ribbon-windowed Appleton Tower is slightly more generic, lacks the same degree of elegance and has just been reclad, but it's still a very decent modernist high-rise, well calculated in its relations to the rest of RMJM's miniature campus around the former David Hume tower, with its raised sandstone squares and walkways. In most places, this would be thought a triumph – in Edinburgh, many act as if working here is like being forced to live in **Ratcliffe-on-Soar (p. 361)**.

Le Corbusier in Leith: the Brutalist grid and circus-like sweep of Cables Wynd House, aka the 'banana block'.

CANONGATE REDEVELOPMENT
Basil Spence & Partners, 1961–9
People's Detailing

Basil Spence on home territory, with the firm's warm, populist and attention-seeking brand of modernism a very good choice for the site. The post-war rebuilding of Edinburgh Old Town, more a question of slum clearance and rehousing somewhere less reekie, was under the star of the planner-polymath Patrick Geddes, whose notion of 'conservative surgery' offered an alternative to the slash-and-burn *tabula rasa*. Instead, the old would be improved, and the sensitively new built alongside, an enlightened and humane approach which arguably culminates in the **Byker Estate (p. 484)**. The first part of this project at the bottom of the Royal Mile is by the classical architect Robert Hurd, and it's decent enough, but is complemented by Spence's more confidently modern work; the height stays the same, and so to a degree does the language, with harling and rendering in warm colours and rubble stone gabled walls, but these are interspersed with heavy concrete lintels and cantilevered balconies, and even some faintly Brutalist stairwells, creating a visually exciting little maze. As with Wheeler & Sproson's work in Burntisland **(Somerville Square & Coltburndale, p. 507)** and Dysart **(Saut Girnal Wynd & The Towers, p. 508)**, the result is a relaxed integration of history and modernity that is rare in England, but which Scottish architects seem to have found easy.

———

CABLES WYND HOUSE, LEITH ○
Alison Hutchinson & Partners, 1962–5
Brutalist

If you are going to do large-scale clearance, as opposed to the 'conservative surgery' of the **Canongate Redevelopment (above)**, you may as well do it properly, with a sense of the Promethean grandeur of sweeping away the noxious and planless old and building confidently and optimistically anew. Cables Wynd House, in the centre of Leith, is best known as the 'banana block', for entirely obvious reasons when you see it. It's enormous – nine storeys and incredibly long, sweeping around its site as if nothing would stand in its way, but with a sinuousness that belies its bulk; and, unlike much Scottish modernist housing, it's well detailed too, with decent concrete work, deep balconies and a rationalist syncopated rhythm to its grid that suggests a thorough reading of Le Corbusier's *Modulor*. It has recently been listed, and quite right too, although reports on this new status tended to mention that people had been known to take drugs in here, which evidently nobody had ever done before in a Victorian tenement.

UNIVERSITY OF EDINBURGH LIBRARY
Spence Glover & Ferguson, 1965–7
Brutalist

I don't know who led the project at Basil Spence's Scottish office for this building, but I find it hard to imagine that it was Spence himself or his usual close collaborators. There is none of the vernacular of the **Canongate Redevelopment (p. 500)**, the Roman references of the **University of Sussex (p. 238)**, the emotive Gothic sentimentality of Coventry's **Cathedral Church of St Michael & All Angels (p. 326)** – just a totally logical modern building with an evident Japanese influence in the trabeated-concrete post-and-lintel construction of these large, spacious bookstacks and reading rooms, the beams exaggerated beyond functionality, and all then slightly cantilevered so that it floats when viewed from George Square. Strange for these purveyors of enjoyable kitsch

to have produced something so hardline, which unsurprisingly has provoked the usual hostility directed at modern buildings in Edinburgh. Its formal discipline, however, is deeply classical, and much more so than those Spence buildings that make deliberate classical references.

BRITISH HOME STORES
RMJM, 1964–8
THE NEW CLUB
Reiach & Hall, 1966–9
International Style

Princes Street is one of those terrible misunderstandings that 'historic' cities are so prone to. For architects in the twentieth century, whether modernists or not, this boulevard was widely regarded as a terrible mess, buggered up by the Victorians with silly eclectic piles, interspersed with the scattered stumps of the original Georgian street. Although some of the Victorian additions, like the department store Jenner's, are now much loved, looking at 1930s pictures of Princes Street it's clear a chunk of Birmingham had been placed in one of the most beautiful cities in the world. So a panel was set up to redevelop it with a concerted series of modern buildings – all for the same purposes and the same people, of course, with shops on the ground floor, *haut bourgeois* clubs and offices above – using a common palette of ashlar, granite and, curiously, upper-level walkways. Space for the latter was allocated before the plan was abandoned, which explains the cantilevered projections of the buildings that resulted.

After that, you can guess what happened. The planners hadn't realized that what heritage enthusiasts and enthusiastic reactionaries liked about old buildings wasn't that they were ordered or disciplined or part of a coherent vision, but that they were old. The new buildings were stopped halfway through the plan's execution, so only about half of today's Princes Street results from the 'panel'. These are the best two fragments, with RMJM's BHS as elegant as their other Edinburgh buildings and with a justified pride in scale, and Reiach & Hall's club an interesting mix of Constructivist geometry and classical serenity. Both are now listed, but so, of course, are the buildings around them that they were intended to be a battering ram into.

ROYAL COMMONWEALTH POOL ✪
RMJM, 1967–70
International Style

Edinburgh's best modernist building, the only one perhaps of the first rank, and it is widely accepted as such, probably due to the fact that it lies low in the landscape, not interrupting anything – plus, everyone loves a swimming pool. It has its cake and eats it, through refusing to compromise in aesthetics, but lies low enough, with its rectangular, horizontal profile, not to offend the zealots. Actually its response to the site is rather unusual – its stretched out glass-and-aluminium pavilions draw some attention to the fact that there's a volcano just behind it, and not every city can boast one of those.

But it's the interior qualities of this building that people love it for. There are very few experiences quite like the bracing clarity and spatial openness of entering the Royal Commonwealth Pool, walking from its terrace into vast glassy foyers, with everything focused on the huge blue box of the pool, viewing platforms and cafés beautifully arranged above and around. If **Lanark County Buildings (p. 537)**, Sheffield's **Arts Tower (p. 369)** and Manchester's **CIS Tower (p. 403)** have our best stabs at the vertical side of high-end American modernism, this is the closest equivalent to the horizontal side of Mies, SOM and the like, a play of interlocking

The Royal Commonwealth Pool: a laconic, restrained building with a joyously open and airy interior.

glass surfaces that is absolutely captivating, an open space without prescriptions or preconceptions, where you can forget about all the weight of Edinburgh.

SCOTTISH WIDOWS
Spence Glover & Ferguson, 1976
International Style

Like Seifert's **NatWest Tower (p. 66)** in the English capital, this is financial architecture as aerial advertisement, a series of intersecting glass hexagons, a plan which is much more readable through aerial photography than on the ground, where security features and the idiosyncratic layout make for an uncomfortable pedestrian experience, though Sylvia Crowe's landscaping makes up for this to some degree. Architecturally, it lacks the confident mastery of the **Royal Commonwealth Pool (above)** next door, but is still worth a visit, with bronzed-glass volumes raised on pilotis above a pond giving an image of seventies corporate serenity.

NATIONAL LIBRARY OF SCOTLAND CAUSEWAYSIDE BUILDING
Andrew Merrylees Associates, 1982–9
Postmodernist

An interesting part-vernacular, part-Brutalist branch office of the National Library (the main building is in the Old Town). Its placing at the edge of a Victorian corner is one of the better results of the collective loss of nerve of Scottish architects in the 1980s – preferring to join on to the existing townscape rather than form its own, but retaining a certain jagged aesthetic vigour that elsewhere was supplanted by cap-doffing neo-Victoriana. Those who know the **Halifax Headquarters (p. 388)** might feel this to be a strange remix of it, with similar grids of black mirrorglass and punchy chunks of sandstone arranged into a craggy assemblage rather than a vast suspended volume. Some of the detailing is a tad 'Mockintosh', which is one way to date the building, but it's a tensely exciting block nonetheless, particularly its skyline of bunched towers. Recently renovated and looking very spruce.

MUSEUM OF SCOTLAND
Benson & Forsyth, 1998
Classical Modernist, Postmodernist

A brave montage, classical yet abstract, contextually sandstone-clad, with separate parts – jagged Constructivist shards, a neoclassical drum – projecting inwards and outwards in unexpected places. It might at first surprise those familiar with the architects of the **Branch Hill Estate (p. 151)** and **Maiden Lane Estate (p. 151)**

Gordon Benson and Alan Forsyth's Museum of Scotland, effortlessly fusing Baronial, Brutalism and Mackintosh.

to realize that this is a late example of their work. Unlike many of the architects who got their fingers burned designing Europe's finest social housing in 1970s Camden – Neave Brown, for instance, would never work again in Britain after **Alexandra Road (p. 148)** – Gordon Benson and Alan Forsyth continued designing excellent buildings. Like their contemporaries Evans & Shalev in **Tate St Ives (p. 278)**, they adapted the parts of Postmodernism that already fitted with their conception of the city as rational project, combined it with their erudition in architectural history, and discarded the flash and commercialism – a sort of intellectual Postmodernism. The conduit from the crystalline perfection of their London housing to this heavy, reference-filled architecture appears to be the 1920s and De Stijl, with many of the strange projections and geometries having their roots in the likes of Gerrit Rietveld's Schröder House in Utrecht or H. P. Berlage's Gemeentemuseum in The Hague. Here, this is fused with planner-pleasing classicism; yet note how at the far corner the sandstone is pulled back, and a startling white-walled modernist building is revealed.

On the contents, I can't rival the description of its complexities in Neal Ascherson's *Stone Voices* – and particularly of the interesting questions raised by the collection, where the richest exhibits date from before there was a place called 'Scotland'. Because it houses this peculiarly non-nationalistic national collection, Benson and Forsyth's deployment of abstraction and montage is far more fitting than any Baronial nostalgia or New Town reproduction could ever be – an idea of Scotland that encompasses everything that has happened on its territory, not just the seventeenth and eighteenth centuries.

SCOTTISH PARLIAMENT ✪

Enric Miralles, Benedetta Tagliabue and RMJM, 1999–2004
Postmodernist

Such an overanalysed building that it is better just to visit it first, have a good look around and then read something about it, rather than go there with preconceptions or, worse, a booklet or a tour guide telling you what Enric Miralles was 'trying to say' in each meticulously crafted, personal and peculiar little corner. And there are a lot of corners – there is no building in post-war Britain that is so obsessively detailed, so full of decorative flourishes and fragmentary pieces. The story of this building makes the tortuous gestation of other public buildings of its era, like the **British Library (p. 143)**, look positively easy. Enric Miralles and Benedetta Tagliabue won the competition to design the Parliament in 1998 partly because of geopolitical analogy, given their status as Catalan innovators and localists, carving out their own niche in the devolved Spanish state; but also because Miralles sold the building as a personal project, with every little detail making some sort of reference to the landscape, history and identity of Scotland – apparently, he threw down a pile of twigs at one meeting and said 'this is the Scottish Parliament'. Then Miralles died, and RMJM had to actually build this poetic and weird object, or rather set of objects.

It went overbudget, and while this is common in Britain – the system of competitive tendering enshrined in the Private Finance Initiative means that it's legally imperative to choose low bids, which of course are usually ridiculous underestimates – this one really was profligate, due to the bizarre complexities of the design. In the scale of its controversy, it's rather as if one of the famous unbuilt projects of the era, like Zaha Hadid's Cardiff Opera House, actually did get built, in the face of all the tabloid venom and

Enric Miralles and Benedetta Tagliabue's enduringly strange landscape in their epic Scottish Parliament.

preservationist ire. Completing it was a struggle, but now we have it, it's nice to have. Unlike other famous budgetary disasters of the time – Will Alsop's preposterous The Public, in West Bromwich, being my personal least favourite – what we have now is a fascinating building, and one which will last.

So what is it? It's a series of concrete 'crags', set down at the end of the Royal Mile, opposite the royal Holyrood Palace (the Crown in Parliament represented as the Crown, opposite Parliament), and, crucially, with the volcanic mass of Arthur's Seat looming just above. These crags are then split into distinct segments, in organic, curvaceous shapes, and are then decorated with wooden and metallic screens and louvres, in patterns that reference something or other; a long wall facing Canongate has poetic fragments on Scottish cussedness and distinctiveness (independence, even) set into its concrete. Even the spiked fences and concrete blast walls to guard against terrorism are treated as the pretext for Gaudí-cum-Corbusier sculpture. Everything is low and sprawling, refusing to erect any kind of monumentality – a rather startling thing to avoid doing in a Parliament. This absence, as much as its sensitivity to landscape, is key to the building's radicalism, as is the slightly scruffy location – it's opposite a royal palace to be sure, but it's also round the corner from the council estate of Dumbiedykes. And compared with, say, Parliament Square in London, the green circus in front of the main entrance is genuinely public and communal, with many places to sit and relax or to assemble. No other European Parliament I know of has overgrown grass terraces in front of it. It is a fussy building, pretentious and sometimes whimsical, but also a great one.

Richard Murphy's Cowgate Housing towers, following the scale and materials of Edinburgh's Old Town.

OLD FISHMARKET CLOSE HOUSING & COWGATE HOUSING
Richard Murphy Architects, 2004–6
Classical Modernist

Richard Murphy is one of the most talented architects working in post-seventies Scotland, but aside from the fact that he clearly knows it, his work aims at a Caledonian version of the obsessively detailed, perversely over-articulated historically minded modernism of the Italian museum designer Carlo Scarpa. Doing this in the render and nasty bits of timber that make up contemporary British construction materials can be rash. His various housing association schemes, mostly in Edinburgh with a couple in Glasgow, are often a battle between ideas and materials, with a tendency to age badly. But they're usually worth seeing, and these two in the Old Town show an architect confident enough to emulate the tall, thin profiles of

the historical tenements around, without simply reproducing their facades; both are fitted tightly into the dense, teeming townscape, in a way that could seem like overdevelopment elsewhere, but here feels exactly right. At Fishmarket, a private scheme, the two tall tenement towers are given wood-clad gables, outlook points in the jumbled skyline; in the social housing at Cowgate, three interlinked towers step down a slope, and have a pleasant internal courtyard to offset the crowdedness, something the private flats lack. Like the original tenements of the Old Town, both blocks balance giant size with complexity, surprise and picturesque irregularity. There's been a lot of talk about 'high-density living' in the last two decades, yet these are among the few buildings that show real thought about how to use urban concentration to create an intense civic life, rather than just a profitable one.

FIFE & STIRLING

TOWN HOUSE, KIRKCALDY
David Carr and William Howard, 1937–56
Modern Classicism

A curio – a typical 1930s 'progressive' Town Hall on a small scale, a slightly Scotified Scandinavian stripped classicism, with a rigid entrance colonnade and integral sculpture, in a style that recalls the likes of **Huddersfield Library & Art Gallery (p. 385)**. Due to the intervention of the war, it wasn't completed until well into the fifties, by which time it was enormously unfashionable, yet this doesn't seem to have caused either any change of track or any scrimping on the minimal but elegant details. Its best feature is the tall copper clock tower, which resembles that in the Town Hall of the Czech city of Ostrava – also a coal-mining area, a Socialist Realist association that rather suits the political allegiances round here (from 1935 to 1950, the colliery towns of West Fife were represented by the Communist MP Willie Gallacher). It commands a pleasant square which gives Kirkcaldy a strong civic focus that most of the scattered industrial towns of Fife lack.

———

SOMERVILLE SQUARE & COLTBURNDALE, BURNTISLAND ✪
Wheeler & Sproson, 1955–62
Brutalist, People's Detailing

These two housing estates are the best surviving examples of Wheeler & Sproson's unique fusion of Scottish vernacular, Rationalism, Brutalism and Civic Trust picturesque. By the railway station you'll find a cluster of tower houses, harled in

Council housing in Burntisland, inserting modernism into a historic townscape without any cringing.

brown and grey, proud, imposing and eerie; running between them is a zigzag of houses going down a hill to the town centre. These showcase the more abstract side of the firm's work, but in the centre itself they've weaved modernist flats with old fishermen's cottages, with a treatment of decorative stonework and warm purple rendering that resembles Basil Spence's housing in the **Canongate Redevelopment (p. 500)**. The intuitive and ingenious use of the port atmosphere is very well done, with partial views of the Firth of Forth in surprising places. The direct juxtaposition of old and new here never feels forced or cloying; architects could still learn a great deal from this place.

SAUT GIRNAL WYND & THE TOWERS, DYSART
Wheeler & Sproson, 1958–67
Brutalist, People's Detailing

Originally, the most celebrated of this firm's work in Fife, with 'The Towers' in the inner-town area of 'Dysart 2' often featuring in books and articles about the distinctiveness of Scottish modern architecture. For Ian Nairn, in 1965, their work in Dysart was 'a remarkable tour de force on the cliff... gesticulating at the sea as though the town around the corner was Cannes, not Kirkcaldy,' adding up to 'the best in the country for the re-interpretation of the existing character and the effortless combination of old and new'. This makes it all the sadder that this was the Wheeler & Sproson estate to be given a crass Regeneration in the 2000s. These miniature three-storey high-rises are still recognizable, it's just that everything has been cheapened, with naff pitched roofs on top of the originals (which had a more subtle, shallow pitch), a tacky playground and fences, and naff gables to the lower-rise blocks. Obviously everyone likes their buildings to have money spent on them and

to be cleaned up, but the crassness is totally unnecessary – given the subtlety with which Wheeler & Sproson approached historic architecture, it's the facile replacing the immanent. However, the earlier 'Dysart 1' on the hillocks overlooking the Firth is still in place, and is, as at **Somerville Square & Coltburndale (above)**, an intelligent and nuanced stitching together of old and new, with council houses and cottages assembled into a friendly montage, grouped around a civic square, with little steps down to a green.

UNIVERSITY OF STIRLING ✪
RMJM, 1966–72
International Style

The University of Stirling is a remarkable integration of landscape and architecture, of the highest international standards – and nowhere near as well known as it deserves to be. It is set, like so many New Universities, in the grounds of an appropriated stately home, where the picturesque landscaping has been retained and extended, with uncompromisingly modern buildings set intelligently into it, with both working to mutual advantage. The feature that makes it most interesting is perhaps partly why it isn't as famous as its English counterparts such as the Universities of **Essex (p. 190)**, **East Anglia (p. 198)**, **Sussex (p. 238)** and **York (p. 394)**; the buildings themselves are in no way gestural or extravagant, without, say, East Anglia's ziggurats or Essex's hill-town high-rises. Instead, the architecture is laconic and logical, taking a back seat to nature – and there's no nature quite like this in urban England. There is no better-sited university in the whole of Europe, a concrete utopian monastic community surrounded by mountains, set into forests, sat by a lake, under wide, open sky.

Reached – inevitably, as with the other New Universities, by car or 'Uni-Link' bus – as a walled complex, you come first to

The perfect integration of landscape and modernism at Stirling, perhaps the finest of the New Universities.

the Pathfoot Building. Looking on plan like a Suprematist painting, with its asymmetrical block bars, it stands a long volume on a ridge, and houses the art gallery and various offices. Inside is a communal 'Crush Hall', decorated by the great Constructivist sculptor Mary Martin. This is just a taster. From here, the ridges and wooded pathways lead through a cluster of mid-rise tower residences, surrounded by forest. These face the university's central space; above you are hills crowned by the spiny Victorian clasp of the William Wallace monument, visible for several miles around. And in the near distance, the rugged purple and green crags of the Ochil Hills, as astonishing a sight in an urban environment as Arthur's Seat in the centre of Edinburgh. A clear, linear footbridge held up on high, thin struts leads from here to the combined Library/Arts Centre/Students' Union, held up on pilotis, a wonderful place to survey the whole complex.

Throughout, the buildings are unfussy – good, clean modern architecture in rubbly concrete panels, not making too much of itself but having a lot of fun with the shifts of level, creating patios, skyways and courtyards. For all its restraint, it doesn't kowtow to the historical importance of the town or the elemental power of the landscape. Look, for instance, at the way the tall halls of residence stand nobly in the forest, and imagine how much would be lost without the juxtaposition. Catch the University of Stirling on a clear autumn day, with the concrete reflected in the lake and the sun catching the mountains, and it's not just the most breathtaking modernist ensemble in Scotland, or Britain, but anywhere on earth. [A.21]

Systems and complexity: the tricky geometries and concrete modules of James Stirling's halls for St Andrews.

ANDREW MELVILLE HALL, UNIVERSITY OF ST ANDREWS ✪
James Stirling, 1968
Brutalist

Far better known, but if compared (as nomenclature and geography might tempt one to) with the contemporary buildings at the **University of Stirling (above)** this is a great building in a dispiriting part of the historic town. As with the Smithsons, Stirling's was an intellectual and highly innovative architecture, accordingly given much importance in the architectural history books. His buildings, taken on their own merits, are always fascinating in and of themselves, but sadly that doesn't always translate to *places* that are that much worth visiting. Andrew Melville Hall is a hall of residence at the periphery of an attractive if haughty ancient university town; it stands at the furthest edge of a cluster of desperately uninspired Postmodernist and Pseudomodernist buildings on a straggling, ugly campus. These make walking to Andrew Melville Hall a rather grim trudge – but, when you get there, it's worth it.

This is a fascinating building, cranky and overwrought but packed with action and event. The ingenious original plan consists of two multistorey 'fingers' of student residences, each of which use the same discrete prefabricated ribbed-concrete module, in an angled pattern creating a rippling effect. A fully glazed walkway runs between these modules, with a glazed common room at the centre, whose monumental profile is reminiscent of Stirling's **History Faculty (p. 207)** in Cambridge. Their placing on the slope, closing a view, creates a staggeringly impressive perspective in photographs, which typically disappoints slightly in the flesh, but it's bravura nonetheless, with the rough grey concrete fitting St Andrew's palette of ashlar and ruins as well as the red brick fits the University of Leicester's **Engineering Building (p. 348)**. Originally, these halls were meant to be the centrepiece of an entire suburban campus, but they leaked, so are now just a distant explosion at the edge of an education subtopia. **[B.7]**

MAGGIE'S FIFE, VICTORIA HOSPITAL, KIRKCALDY

Zaha Hadid Architects, 2001–6
Deconstructivist

A baffling work, for the charity that builds cancer care centres attached to NHS hospitals. Surrounded by interwar municipal suburbia, this is in a vast site, serving much of Fife, with a tall tower and a galumphing new megahospital by BDP, straining to disguise its mass via cladding, twists and turns. Hadid's building – her first to be completed in Britain, after many false starts – glowers darkly, set low amidst all this tat, tiny, sharp and raven black. You might indulgently view this as an admirably unsentimental way to approach its function – as serious as cancer, as it were – but it could also conceivably be quite frightening for the recently diagnosed, who are its main intended users. Like most Maggie's centres, it is secluded in its own small garden, a diamond drained of its colour set among trees, reached by a concrete bridge across the undergrowth. One glass wall faces the greenery, so that the interior is less daunting than it is on approach – a sense of the building-in-the-forest that is achieved much more successfully by OMA at their **Maggie's Glasgow (p. 532)**. Even so, this is a ruthless way to approach a project that is supposedly intended to be a showcase of 'signature' architecture's alleged ability to be more reassuring and humane than the giant bureaucratic medical machines of large hospitals. Caught just before ZHA exchanged these taut, angry right angles for billowing computerized curves, it gives some hints as to why they may have considered that shift necessary. In any case, this disconcerting building is a stark statement about the status of high architecture in the public sector; perhaps, you might wonder, the era when a good local firm of architects built dozens of examples of good modern council housing and good modern schools across the industrial towns of Fife had a saner way of seeing architecture than the era which prefers the periodic hiring of globe-bestriding geniuses to drop a building or two in the interstices of the products of the value engineers. As it is, Hadid's work here is relegated to the dark corner of a mountain of tat. It smoulders, bitterly.

13. GREATER
GLASGOW

Lanark County Buildings, Hamilton (p. 537)

Glasgow has a real big-city energy which is comparable with nothing else in Scotland, let alone England and Wales – much more like Berlin, St Petersburg or Manhattan than Edinburgh, Manchester or Birmingham. Everything here is bigger – the buildings are taller, the streets are wider, the views are panoramic; and the social problems have been on a similarly vast scale. Before the First World War, when it was 'Second City of the Empire', this was the only British city to produce a first-generation modernist architect of the same significance as an Adolf Loos or an Auguste Perret – Charles Rennie Mackintosh, whose **Glasgow School of Art** is one of the great buildings of the world. This era also saw the creation of the most overcrowded slums of any rich country, which were finally cleared after 1945, and replaced with high-rise estates of staggering size. Many of these have been cleared in turn, but the best survivors are **Moss Heights** and **Hutchesontown B**, south of the Clyde. Today it is a badly planned city with many indifferent new buildings, though it has also brought in a few world-famous architects to build 'signature' icons; ironically the best of these by far is OMA's tiny, beautiful **Maggie's Glasgow**.

The conurbation has similarly dramatic vistas and intractable problems, whether in the industrial towns along the Clyde that are Glasgows in microcosm, like Paisley and Greenock, or in the New Towns set up to alleviate Clydeside's overcrowding, which include East Kilbride and the much more impressive **Cumbernauld**, whose imaginative housing and landscaping are usually ignored for its much-derided megastructural **Town Centre**. The most interesting Clydeside architectural firm after the war was Gillespie Kidd & Coia, who specialized in churches and schools. Their largest scheme, St Peter's Seminary in Cardross, is derelict and inaccessible, and even their best church, **St Bride's** in East Kilbride, had its campanile removed in the 1980s, but their buildings are now a bit of a cult, and deservedly so. The single most surprising modernist building of Clydeside, though, is in Hamilton, by a fairly obscure architect – the **Lanark County Buildings**, a stunning clone of the United Nations headquarters that exemplifies the American dreams round here.

CITY OF GLASGOW

GLASGOW SCHOOL OF ART ⊕
Charles Rennie Mackintosh, 1897–1909
Art Nouveau

It was once a commonplace to argue that modernism in Britain both started and ended with Mackintosh's work at the Glasgow School of Art, at least until it returned as a continental import in the thirties: a sort of architectural version of the 'British invasion' thesis of American musical history, where something is invented, forgotten and comes back, reinterpreted, from elsewhere. This viewpoint has been criticized more recently for overrating Mackintosh's own radicalism – as if all he really wanted to be was another Edwardian neo-Baronial designer, and his 1920s self-exile from Britain to become a modernist painter and his scathing comments on British modern architecture

('there isn't any') were some sort of accident. The people who want you to believe this are bent on making the extraordinary boring, and should be ignored. Revisionism be damned – there's nothing in early-twentieth-century British architecture, and very little in European or American architecture from the same time, that compares with the spatial extremism and gleefully uncompromised invention of Mackintosh's major buildings. What's more, in the two phases in which the School of Art was built, you can watch Mackintosh push and push at the limits of his time, and then heroically break free of them. *Revolutions happen.*

What follows is necessarily a sketch – entire books have been written about this building, and more will be, especially as it is finally fully repaired from the second of two devastating fires in recent years. Much of

Two views of the School of Art: the front facade, with factory-style windows and art nouveau decoration...

...and the unforgettable Library, perhaps the first truly modernist space in northern Europe.

the fun of Glasgow School of Art derives from how it exploits the accidents of topography, with the building set on the steepest slope of Garnethill, the highest elevated part of the inner city's magnificent Americanist grid. Start at the earlier east wing, and you can see how we begin with Mackintosh's personal, Secessionist version of the Scottish Baronial style – a mountain of heavy brown sandstone, with turrets and glass oriels carved into it. A seemingly straightforward if asymmetrical street frontage bridges the two distinct parts – big windows like a factory, their bulk offset with railings of iron roses, and with an upper level above of completely glazed studios and a heavy masonry entrance, hefty, curvaceous and heraldic. Then you're at the west wing, which is where the sudden leap into space happens. You can get a preview of that on the west side of the building, visible to shoppers and strollers on Sauchiehall Street; carved into the rock and harling is an extraordinary facade of high windows, cubic and repetitious, with smaller oriels flanking them, alternating with more sheer walls of stone. This was always the side that would be shown in the histories of modern architecture, to prove that we, too, had one of the Pioneers of Modern Design, working as a journeyman architect at the firm of Honeyman & Keppie. And, you know, the historians were right. This is a facade as abstract, original and endlessly fascinating, endlessly re-readable, as anything by Behrens, Hoffmann, Horta and others.

This is the library wing, and it is that interior – in the psychological as well as spatial sense – that is the pretext for the experiment. I'll condense it into two spaces. One is the haunting glass silo that leads into the library, already a sudden shift into the cosmic. The second is the library itself, a place which is redolent of the moment in Tarkovsky's *Solaris* when the gravity on the spaceship is switched off and everything floats. After that first experience

of weightlessness, in the multiple levels of this light-infused, cuboid, galleried space, you can admire something that modern architects in Glasgow would seldom get right again – a richness of material, with the black-painted wood of the fittings and the rectilinear light-sculptures of the chandeliers worth a lifetime's worth of visits.

The two fires' destruction of the original fabric of one among a tiny handful of places worldwide where you can see a shift within one building from traditional space into modern space is an incalculable loss. The school is currently being rebuilt to mirror its original state, which is absolutely right – there are places to try new interpretations and to have dialogues between the contemporary and the historic, but this is not one of them; it would have been like getting Foster to redesign the inside of St Paul's. The custodians of the building in the 2010s, however, should be regarded with much the same undying contempt as Donald Rumsfeld is with reference to the Iraq Museum in Baghdad. **[A.1]**

WILLOW TEA ROOMS ✪
Charles Rennie Mackintosh, 1903
SCOTLAND STREET SCHOOL ✪
Charles Rennie Mackintosh, 1903–6
Art Nouveau

Neither of these is as shattering an experience as the **Glasgow School of Art (above)**, but both provide plenty of evidence that it wasn't a fluke. The Willow Tea Rooms, located on the now rather dowdy commercial thoroughfare of Sauchiehall Street, is typical small-scale Secession architecture; more than any other of Mackintosh's buildings, you could easily imagine it in Vienna or Budapest, a simple street building without traditional references in white render, with its long window defining an interior of strongly vertical, emaciated elegance, filled with Charles

Mackintosh's Scotland Street School, at the cusp between Victorian monumentalism and the Bauhaus.

and Margaret Mackintosh's furniture, which in its formal experiment and posterior discomfort set a precedent that would be enthusiastically followed by De Stijl. The best part is the open gallery in the middle, with its logical and elegant wooden frame in the Japanese manner that Frank Lloyd Wright was then making his own in the US.

Scotland Street School, meanwhile, is at first more obviously a Victorian building, a board school, wide, tall and turreted. Two things place it outside the Glaswegian or London norm – its railings, which, as Ian Nairn pointed out, have angular decorative motifs that would still have been considered modern sixty years later, and its almost fully glazed, strongly expressed twin stairwells, which would later be emulated in Walter Gropius's Model Factory in Cologne of 1914, and hence are the first iteration of the streamline style in modern architecture. Here, you can see how Mackintosh has developed something that looks and feels

extremely modern, spacious and fresh, using the standard materials of this most impressive and metropolitan of nineteenth-century industrial cities – red sandstone and wide expanses of glass. The building is now a museum, so public access is easy.

ST VINCENT STREET CHAMBERS
James Salmon, 1899–1902
LION CHAMBERS
James Salmon, 1904–5
Art Nouveau

Many of the most interesting buildings of the 1910s and '20s in the 'Second City of the Empire' were, as in Liverpool, in an American sort of neoclassicism, with pediments in front and steel frames beneath. But just before that in the 1900s, the city was a centre of Art Nouveau, which made impressive use of new technology without sticking great Ionic columns all over it. These two buildings by James Salmon Jr demonstrate this in steel and concrete, respectively. The Hat Rack, as it's known, is one of many tall steel-framed blocks in the city centre grid, where eight storeys is fairly normal; unlike most, it uses the frame not as something to drape masonry over, but as a means of elongating and stretching out its plate glass windows, topped by sandstone spikes. The results are best described as spooky. The slightly later Lion Chambers is concrete Baronial, asymmetrical and made up seemingly of splicings of different buildings into a faintly creepy mini-skyscraper. It has been derelict for some considerable time.

___

LEYLAND MOTOR COMPANY
James Miller, 1933
Moderne

Glasgow's topography is peculiar, and takes a while to get used to. There are two areas of monumental townscape which are absolutely of the first rank, the grid-planned inner city and the flamboyantly picturesque West End, which are sliced off from each other by the most dramatic motorway surgery. But in a ring around the inner city, intersecting partly but not completely with the motorways, was once a tight circle of industry, which was the source of Glasgow's conspicuous, if unusually tastefully displayed, wealth. The fact that a motorway – a big chunk of it built, shockingly, in the 2010s – crashes across it makes it hard to explore, but there are some gems to be found. This derelict chunk of a car factory just south of the river is one. The buildings consist of a Detroit-style 'daylight factory' of wide windows in a concrete frame with brick infill, and some serrated-roofed garages behind them – but what you notice is the dramatic sandstone corner, a streamlined curve rising to a fluted, florid tower, like an Italian Futurist drawing come to life, in miniature.

ROGANO'S ❶
1935
Moderne

Glasgow is full of excellent moderne and mid-century Italian cafés in various states of repair and preservation, but while it's no **Café d'Jaconelli (p. 521)**, this is one of the most visible and most celebrated. Whereas the others tend to be proletarian in location and design, this oyster bar and restaurant right in the city centre clearly aims at something classier. The sign, with its angular lettering and lobster mascot, is pure 1930s Italian design, from when Futurism had melded with art deco and advertising; the interior, said to be modelled on the Queen Mary, is tawdry, opulent and atmospheric, all chrome, vitrolite, plush wood and glass.

Fans of demotic modernist signage and shopfronts are also recommended the University Café in Hillhead, Queens Café in Govanhill and Central Café on Saltmarket; though I can't vouch for the continued survival of any of these, they've lasted longer than their once numerous Soho cousins. Rogano's itself is currently boarded up after its closure during the coronavirus lockdown, though its owners insist this is temporary. It ought to be protected nonetheless.

___

DAILY EXPRESS BUILDING ✪
Owen Williams, 1936
International Style

The third of Owen Williams's trilogy of streamlined glass office blocks for the 1930s major mass-market paper, and closer to Manchester's **(p. 400)** than it is to Fleet Street's **(p. 50)** in its height and extent. It's built tightly into the dense fabric of the 'Merchant City', in the east of the monumental grid, a red and blond sandstone mass into which this artificial, jarring irruption of black and blue glass is still a wonderful piece of architectural advertising.

The former Daily Express Building, the most cubic of Owen Williams's three headquarters for the newspaper.

This much-extended building is far more obviously industrial than the other two in its harsh angularity, with a tall multistorey block and a lower wing, asymmetrical and futuristic. While so much Glasgow architecture is a matter of heaviness and masonry heft, this was a rare irruption of the machine aesthetic without the classical dressing, right into the heart of the city – vitrolite and steel amidst all the sandstone, industry and commerce shown openly, without the frills and the fol-de-rol. It remains a great little toy in the townscape.

BERESFORD HOTEL
Weddell Inglis & Taylor, 1938
Moderne

It's easy, and was once popular, to lament central Glasgow's interwar decline in architectural originality, but there's very little decline in actual *quality*, with a ton of superb classical architecture, which is sadly outside our remit. Unfortunately its interwar modern architecture, when it finally got built, was nowhere near on the level of the cities that Glasgow could otherwise compare itself to, like Vienna, Berlin, St Petersburg, Shanghai or Chicago. Generally speaking it's a little kitsch, and none of it is more tawdry and glamorous than this high-rise hotel, built at the bottom of Garnethill so that despite its height it doesn't actually rise out of the grid. The nine storeys of cubicle-like rooms (now flats) are symmetrically organized around curved, streamlined bays, with ice cream fins up the middle, a little prefiguring of the post-war Scottish-Italian style responsible for so much of Glasgow's best demotic design. The side elevations, though, visible from the west side, are grim, all the cheapness of a cinema backside stretched up to ten storeys. The hotel was built for the 1938 Glasgow Imperial Exhibition, a streamline moderne expo masterplanned by Thomas Tait; the only other notable remnant of the exhibition is the De Stijl via neo-Georgian Palace of Art, south of the river in Bellahouston Park.

LUMA LIGHTBULB FACTORY
Cornelius Armour, 1938
International Style

A fascinating little complex in the southern industrial zone, just round the corner from the exit of the Clyde Tunnel; like many Glasgow places, very easily accessed by car, more trickily by public transport. A simple white-rendered concrete factory, with some very interesting things going on round the back, in a manner that recalls the French moderne of Robert Mallet-Stevens, all curved stairwells and porthole windows, which is lifted into something much more interesting by its central block. This cantilevered, full-height glazed pivot, visible from quite far away despite not being that tall by Glasgow standards, is a marvellous piece of pop-Constructivism, designed, of course, to showcase the bulb factory's wares. They were restored as flats in the nineties, which, like the similar residential refurbishment of Peckham's **Pioneer Health Centre (p. 81)**, now look very much of their time, a Terence Conran version of the thirties. That fabulous tower remains undimmed.

GOVAN LYCEUM
McNair & Elder, 1938
GLASGOW FILM THEATRE
James McKissack and W. J. Anderson, 1939
Moderne

Two well-preserved streamline cinemas, built into dense cityscapes, that have fared differently given Glasgow's extreme-even-by-British-standards inequalities. The lesser of the two, architecturally speaking, is the Glasgow Film Theatre – now the main repertory cinema in the city, but originally

Moderne on Garnethill: the Glasgow Film Theatre, a new style built with Glasgow's old materials.

the glamorously named 'Cosmo' – in Garnethill round the corner from the Art School. It is a somewhat confused fusion of Dudok and Odeon in shabby brown brick, albeit with a great, preserved and plush interior which makes it worth seeing. The Govan Lyceum is ship-style, sleeker and cooler, expanses of brick for poster display, arranged around a central prow of glass bricks. In the context of Govan, it's a dramatic and sweeping presence, a lively modern building in the brooding Victorian shipyard cityscape. Derelict, but with plans to be restored as a community arts centre.

MOSS HEIGHTS
Ronald Bradbury for Glasgow City Council Architects Dept, 1946–53
International Style

The first of the big Glasgow estates of 'high flats' has been reclad and messed about, but it is still the best place to capture some of the cyclopean scale and monumental ambition of the city's rebuilding between the 1940s and the 1970s. Planned immediately after the war and then built at the start of the fifties, Moss Heights is on a suburban site south of the Clyde, and consists of three immense slab blocks, which, from below, appear as a dramatic citadel, surmounting a hilltop; their arrangement is informal, but their mass – especially of the extremely long middle slab – is imposing. At the time, like other early high-rise estates – a useful comparison is **Churchill Gardens (p. 53)** – they were described by the council as 'luxury flats' for the working class, with the lifts and mod cons that were lacking in the Victorian tenement flats most people lived in. The original elevations lacked the relief and composition of a Churchill Gardens, relying instead on repetitive power and mass, broken up by curved balconies. In a recent renovation, the blocks have been tidied up and given concierges, and they look like decent places to live, but any trace of the 1940s in their design has been removed; the way you can date it is through the north-facing access balconies, which appear as great interlinking arms, giving Moss Heights something of the heroic socialist imagery of a Karl-Marx-Hof. Red Clydeside finally gets its own Red Vienna. In the film of Alan Bennett's play *An Englishman Abroad*, they stand in for Guy Burgess's Moscow flat.

CAFÉ D'JACONELLI
1950s
Moderne, Googie

A parallel story to the one told in this book about the public acceptance of modern architecture could be told through demotic design, ordinary things and non-architect-designed places. In the 'high modernist' version of the story, the interlocutor is France, Germany, the Netherlands, and sometimes the USA and USSR, and in the 'low modernist' one, it's Italy, and its modern clothes, designs and coffee machines. Glasgow is the heart of Italo-British modern design. The University Café in the West End, the Central Café in the East End, Queens Café in Govanhill or the more luxurious **Rogano's (p. 518)** oyster bar in the centre are all worth seeing, but Café d'Jaconelli, in Maryhill, just round the corner from the Partick Thistle stadium, is the don. An ordinary-enough-looking caff from the outside, built into the ground floor of a tenement, disguises an extraordinary interior. There's some moderne woodwork and wallpaper, and the sign says 'EST. 1924', but the curved purple-leatherette booths with space-age, conical lamps suggest that the place had at some point a post-war futurist makeover, looking as if one of the Jaconellis stopped off at Expo '58 on a business trip to Brussels. The bubble-like fishtank built into the wall adds the space capsule effect. Oh, and the Knickerbocker Glory is very good.

ST CHARLES BORROMEO, KELVINSIDE
Andy MacMillan and Isi Metzstein for Gillespie Kidd & Coia, 1959
Brutalist

Gillespie Kidd & Coia have a cult status in Scotland (and especially Strathclyde) comparable to Goldfinger or Lubetkin in England; that fame is such that everyone knows that their best buildings were not generally by anyone called Gillespie or Kidd, and seldom by a Coia, but by the Glaswegian duo of Andy MacMillan and Isi Metzstein, two atheist intellectuals whose main client was the Catholic Church. They became the lead designers of a firm built up before the war by Jack Coia as mildly experimental church-builders; Coia gave the duo carte blanche to pull things in a much more vigorous direction. This is one of the first fruits of that, a small Brutalist church built on a difficult site on a corner next to a stairway in the romantic red-sandstone world of the West End. The church itself is a simple enough hall – apparently planned by Coia – but the rest is much harder stuff. A brick-and-concrete cylinder leads you round into the big concrete-framed church itself, with a béton brut campanile, now spalling somewhat, to the side. Best seen from below, where its complexities and craggy, physical approach to the townscape are most easily appreciated.

HUTCHESONTOWN B
RMJM, 1962
International Style

Hutchesontown in the Gorbals was the flagship for Glasgow City Council's comprehensive redevelopment programme, which set out to solve the problem of the city's consistently overcrowded and dilapidated housing, which was considered (puzzlingly to a superficial contemporary glance, given how handsome the surviving tenements look), to be the worst in the country, at one fell swoop, in a massive programme of high-rise building. The city acquired more tower blocks than anywhere else in Western Europe. In order to achieve this, they used system-building on a practically Soviet scale, and sadly often with a very Soviet build quality, or lack thereof. But Eastern European cities have specialized in repairing and renovating their blocks in recent years, while since the 1990s Glasgow seems to have detonated a complete high-rise 'scheme' every year. Among the first to go were the huge slabs of Basil Spence's Hutchesontown C, and the story of that – well told in John Grindrod's *Concretopia* – has overshadowed the much simpler and much better built Hutchesontown B, by the major Anglo-Scottish firm Robert Matthew Johnson-Marshall, which was (like Building

Design Partnership, Lyons Israel Ellis or Yorke Rosenberg & Mardall) one of those great unsung post-war firms, whose work is seldom spectacular, but always of high quality. It has also tended to survive.

So, there are no theatrics in this estate facing the south side of the Clyde, just a grid of simple, well-detailed cubic low-rise maisonettes and precisely calculated towers with a slightly Constructivist dash to the pattern of glazing on their flanks. They look rather utopian when seen from Glasgow Green on the other side of the river, but importantly they also convince up close. The only problem is the horrible, horrible landscaping – the renovation by the 'arm's length' company that runs the city's housing has been good to the blocks, preserving their shape while insulating them from the reliably appalling weather, but in the process of removing the pedestrian walkway system that once connected them, they've surrounded the buildings with a security system of fences and CCTV so mean and paranoid that it feels distinctly prison-like, the horrible result of the 'Secured by Design' policies insisted upon by the police force. Puzzlingly, at the less architecturally interesting but multilevel and highly complex **Dundasvale Court (p. 525)** on well-heeled Garnethill, Glasgow Housing Association ignored these directives, yet the place hasn't collapsed into crime and social breakdown.

GLASGOW COLLEGE OF BUILDING & PRINTING ✪
Wylie Shanks & Underwood, 1964
International Style

A great Corbusian block overlooking George Square, currently used by Glasgow City College and turned ill-advisedly into a billboard for the city's 'PEOPLE MAKE GLASGOW' marketing campaign, which has turned the crisp, elegantly detailed curtain wall of this tapered glass tower half pink.

Whereas a lot of the corporate modernism in Glasgow can be rather grim and Presbyterian, this development, with its tower facing the square and a lower block up on the hill, has real confidence and generosity, with both parts of the building well articulated in their details and still unaffected by the UPVC glazer or the cladder. Each part features terraces that are an amusingly transparent ripoff of the roof garden of Le Corbusier's Unité d'Habitation, an organic and sensual assemblage of curved forms. The idea may have been someone else's, but it's used very well. As you know when you walk around the hills of the West End or climb to the top of Queen's Park, this is a city of spires and towers, so to finally plant a real high-rise (not a compromise like the **Beresford Hotel, p. 519**) in the giant eight-storey mass of the Glasgow grid called for something sculptural, a modern interpretation of the idea of a campanile or the cupola. It's delightfully odd that one of the grandest and rainiest

Victorian spaces in Britain has this approximation of a surrealist Mediterranean concrete garden as its tallest building.

———

OUR LADY & ST FRANCIS SCHOOL
**Andy MacMillan and Isi Metzstein
for Gillespie Kidd & Coia, 1964**
Brutalist

This powerful brick-and-concrete Catholic school by MacMillan and Metzstein (long since turned into offices), at the edge of Glasgow Green, was incorporated in the late 1990s into a *Millennium Project* called 'Homes for the Future', the first step in the 'regeneration' of the East End. These homes are a well-meaning collection of low-rise apartment blocks, appallingly badly built, where a variety of talented architects tried out ideas that would have worked well on a larger scale and with a bigger budget, but which here looked like a poorly constructed

Glasgow College of Building & Printing, Glasgow's first curtain wall office block, with its Corbusian rooftop.

architectural zoo. One side effect of its (very laudable, and rather ahead of its time) incorporation of this Brutalist school-turned-office-block into the new development was that it draws your attention to the gruff integrity of the 1960s building. Architects tend to get very excited about the way that MacMillan and Metzstein's buildings express their section, and you can see this especially strongly here – a subtle set of cantilevers expresses each spacious, glassy floor as an individual unit, pulled into a punchy and pugnacious composition, with no fat, nothing superfluous.

GRAPHICAL HOUSE
Rogerson & Spence, 1964–5
People's Detailing

A miniature of industrial modernism overlooking the Clyde, just north of the Portland Suspension Bridge. Graphical House combines a logical concrete-framed block with plenty of glass and visible stairways, with its brown-brick infill treated by the architects as an excuse for enjoying themselves with plenty of (by then, already dated) Festival Style *lettres ornées* signs and sculptural wall panels, which makes this into a sort of typographical museum in the streetscape. Its name has been borrowed by a nearby graphic designer housed in a sandstone Victorian building, but this derelict building is surely dying to be given some sort of fashionable use.

SCOTTISH AMBULANCE SERVICE
Skinner Bailey & Lubetkin, 1966–70
People's Detailing

One of the very few Lubetkin and Tecton (or, here, post-Tecton) projects outside England, but a very interesting one, largely designed by Francis Skinner with Lubetkin adding the staircase and the supergraphics. The result doesn't really resemble anything else they did, although the ideas are all traceable to their late work like the **Dorset Estate (p. 123)**, and even to their youthful **Finsbury Health Centre (p. 52)**. The Ambulance Service building is in the fragmented, somewhat windswept area of Cowcaddens, near the Metro station and opposite **Dundasvale Court (p. 525)**. It consists of two blocks, one of them a straightforward mid-century modern chunk of concrete-framed offices, the other a more unusual cantilevered block, clad in white mosaic, with an interesting symmetrical window pattern and a salvaged Victorian Ambulance Service emblem, a good example of late Skinner/Bailey/Lubetkin's love of heraldry. Turn the corner, and you can see a big red cross, illuminated at night – this pop art supergraphic was Lubetkin's contribution, and suggests there was plenty of life left in the old man, even in his sulk as a Gloucestershire pig farmer. Inside, there's one of his incredible Constructivist staircases, where the main waiting room opens out into a diamond-shaped atrium. An odd and somewhat gaunt building, currently very worn, but full of good ideas.

UNIVERSITY OF GLASGOW: QUEEN MARGARET UNION
Walter Underwood & Partners, 1968
RANKINE BUILDING
Keppie Henderson & Partners, 1969
BOYD ORR BUILDING
Dorward Matheson Gleave & Partners, 1972
HUNTERIAN ART GALLERY
William Whitfield, 1977
Brutalist, Postmodernist

The University of Glasgow supplemented the thrillingly Heathcliffian Gothic of George Gilbert Scott's campus acropolis with a series of co-ordinated Brutalist buildings in the 1960s and '70s, expanding right up to the edge of Byres Road; most of them are worth exploring, although what used to be the best of them, the tower cluster of William Whitfield's library, has had a bad attack of the cladding. Start with Queen Margaret Union, a bulky student centre making full use of its hilltop site, defined by the surging lecture theatre and a well-articulated, complex office block next to it, with a very dramatic concrete escape staircase, projecting outwards and, fortuitously for fag-smoking students, protected from the rain by its own roof. Then move on to the Rankine Building, which uses grey aggregate panels in a city of the finest sandstone, but gets away with it through the elegantly Japanese suspended slabs of its storeys and the turret-like flanking tower, attached to which is an excellent stainless-steel sculpture by Lucy Aird, its explosive forms held prisoner by its hard lines.

The next two buildings are the most interesting. The recently renovated Boyd Orr Building is a twin tower of high and wide ribbon windows and glinting concrete, with a Melnikov-via-Stirling Constructivist lecture theatre, while Whitfield's Hunterian Art Gallery is in a genre of one, Brutalist Postmodernism. It begins in the expected manner with great tubular forms in baroque, textiled London Zoo **Elephant House**-style **(p. 145)** ribbed concrete, but then transforms itself into a cast-concrete Art Nouveau tenement, housing the gallery's Mackintosh collection. Long before Rachel Whiteread made a career out of it, this is powerful evidence of concrete's ability to take the imprint of, and preserve the ghost of, something that has disappeared – and to do so in the heaviest and most present of materials – a wilfully perverse and haunting paradox.

ANNIESLAND COURT

J. Holmes & Partners for Glasgow City Council Architects Dept, 1968
International Style

Glasgow's **Trellick Tower (p. 166)**, say the history books, and you can see quite easily where they're coming from – the way that the service tower is separated from the rest of the block, with glass walkways connecting them, and the way that the maisonettes are expressed as a rationally subdivided grid, clearly seen at the rear of the elevations. It's also a way of seeing the enormous difference between Goldfinger, an architect with the scrupulousness, talent and personal authority to insist on the absolute highest possible standards of concrete construction, and the average Glasgow architect of the sixties, unable to challenge the bean-counters and the desperate call for more housing, faster. But if considered just as what it is, rather than unfairly compared with Goldfinger's masterpieces, this is an excellent tower, carefully positioned at a major junction as the West End starts to fade into suburbia, elegant and sparky, with red mosaic cladding and a spiky upper-level shopping parade below (sadly, mostly derelict). At the time of writing, flammable cladding is being removed from the tower.

DUNDASVALE COURT

Laings with Glasgow City Council Architects Dept, 1968–78
International Style

Unlike **Anniesland Court (above)**, **Hutchesontown B (p. 522)** or **Moss Heights (p. 520)**, this was never 'great architecture' and had no pretensions in that direction. A huge, dense estate just south of the motorway tangle, next to Cowcaddens Subway Station, it vehemently marks the divide between the Victorian centre and the city around it. All systems, all grids –

a maze of low-rise deck-access blocks and several tall, bluff towers, and not much else. And yet it works, and has always been one of Glasgow's most popular estates, a fact which has been variously put down to its few constructional problems, a city centre location, and the fact that there's a large police HQ nearby. A recent renovation has cut the grass, properly paved the squares, insulated the blocks and added naff mirrorglass screens on the deck-access blocks, but, in striking contrast to Hutchesontown B, it has added no gates or fences or aggressive CCTV. Perhaps the way to make housing estates work is by making their public spaces more pleasant, rather than by treating those who use them as criminals. Maybe it's that simple.

ANDERSTON CENTRE
R. Seifert & Partners, 1968–72
Brutalist

A failure, without doubt, but an intriguing one. This was the Scottish Seifert office – on this evidence, a tad less sophisticated than the London one, preferring Soviet bluntness to Braziloid sculpture – doing a big-bang speculative project to fill one of the sites to the west of the centre cleared for the **Kingston Bridge & M8 (below)**, assembling offices, shops and high-rise council flats into one multilevel megastructure. In the end, it was badly built, left unfinished (creating the notorious 'bridge to nowhere') and, more recently, clad in a hugely unsympathetic, although no doubt thermally improved, manner. Approaching from the Victorian grid you come first to the best part, the offices, where a textured, fully three-dimensional block surmounts the road on tapering pilotis; above that, the shopping parade is still interesting in multilevel terms, creating some surprising views, but it has been wretchedly treated, with the tackiest of pediments and dressings gobbed on in the nineties.

The flats, already overbearing, are covered in the usual tat, which at best maintains their basic articulated shape. So why visit it? Largely because this is still a strange and invigorating place to walk, where you move quite suddenly through a simple step upstairs from John Betjeman's 'finest Victorian city in the world' into a complex alternative, a city of the future which never quite worked but which still exists because nobody has got round to demolishing it.

DEE OF TRONGATE
1960s/1970s
Brutalist

This narrow shopfront on the eastern side of Glasgow City Centre is straight out of *A Clockwork Orange*, the sort of pop art street architecture that intensity of development has long since expunged from London, Birmingham or Manchester. Dee of Trongate were once the main Glaswegian purveyors of Mod clothing, and the red bubble lettering inset into concrete, with a large plate glass window displaying the clobber, is sexily Mod-ish. Its survival is especially impressive given that the Victorian building above it is in a horrendous state of disrepair.

KINGSTON BRIDGE & M8
William Fairhurst, 1970
Brutalist

A very bad idea. The M8 is probably the most extensive inner-city motorway in Britain, and unlike many (Birmingham, Nottingham, Bristol) the damage it did is not being repaired or undone, but instead extended, with the construction of the hideous, low, blue-painted flyovers of the M74 only a few years ago – especially insulting in a city where the level of car ownership is amongst the lowest in Britain, and with one of the most extensive (although not necessarily reliable) public transport systems outside London. But seen purely amorally and spatially, there are parts of the M8 that are outright thrilling – the approach into the city, flanked by high-rises that are neon-lit at night; the high-arched Kingston Bridge over the Clyde, a constant hiss of activity, held up on a sort of municipal Brutalist version of Waterloo Bridge; the multiple flyovers just north of Cowcaddens; and the section of the M8 that ploughs between the West End and the western part of the city centre, which, while turning major monuments like the Mitchell Library and Charing Cross into meaningless fragments, is quite an experience to either drive along – where eighties oil-boom office blocks surmount it, and you drive under them – or to walk over, where there are wide and logical pedestrian links, something that is rare in inner-city motorways. As with the **Leeds Inner Ring Road, Woodhouse Lane Section (p. 380)**, the obvious planning rationale was to maintain a connection between the centre and the university, while wilfully mangling much of everything else. Still, these moments are exciting, whereas the M74 is too low-slung to ever give those metropolitan thrills – which also adds an extra 'fuck you' to the areas like Govanhill that it carves up – and too bland in its design to be worth looking at.

BRITISH OVERSEAS AIRWAYS CORPORATION ✪
Andy MacMillan and Isi Metzstein for Gillespie Kidd & Coia, 1970
Brutalist

MacMillan and Metzstein's only major commercial commission was a tiny office block for BOAC on Buchanan Street, Glasgow's pedestrianized equivalent to Oxford Street or Deansgate. Their usual austere brick and concrete wouldn't be suitable for such a site, so instead this

is an example of their highly original use of metal. Three storeys of high, tinted medieval-modernist windows, projecting out from above what was originally a BOAC showroom and is now a Pretty Green, all of it encased in a black-green copper screen – modest, contextual, yet futuristic and even a little fetishistic.

SAVOY CENTRE
Gavin Paterson & Sons, 1971–9
Brutalist

Commercial and harsh, this is nonetheless a much better speculative megastructure than the **Anderston Centre (p. 526)**, although it was less ambitious at the time as well as being less drastically altered afterwards. The Savoy Centre consists of a shopping mall, a music venue and an office block, all hewn out of the same ruggedly textured yet clearly aesthetically patterned concrete,

Modernism in the Victorian grid: Gillespie Kidd & Coia's BOAC, slotting into Glasgow's townscape.

into which is cut a dashing bit of seventies signage, cast into the concrete so that it can't be removed. The skybridge over Renfrew Street that connects it to the Royal Conservatoire (a very late work of Leslie Martin, civic but staid) is pretty dashing too.

NORTH WOODSIDE ESTATE
Glasgow City Council Architects Dept, 1970s
Brutalist

This estate is one of the earliest and best attempts to conserve and extend the local tenement tradition. When Glasgow, like everywhere else, started to become sceptical about high-rises and started to renovate its Victorian buildings, it tended to go for attempts at emulating and imitating these streets of flats, which after the soot was cleaned and the blinkers removed were finally revealed as one of the great urban typologies in Britain – if well treated, that is. This began a long-running trend which has never quite ended of trying to replicate the effect with new buildings. The problem with these imitations was that they missed precisely the two things that made Glasgow tenements most interesting – the high windows and the opulent use of ashlar – and exchanged them for brick cladding and poky PVC windows. The results are worthy urbanism, but usually dull architecture. Here, the low-rise flats are clad in a shiny red terracotta which harmonizes with the red sandstone; the massing attempts to continue the modernist project, in its dynamically articulated cantilevered maisonettes and its sense of a continuous, sculptural form. It also engages with the Victorian city by framing a preserved, still-used bathhouse.

HILLHEAD PUBLIC LIBRARY
Rogerson & Spence, 1972
Brutalist

Easy to miss on the notoriously bougie Victorian parade that is the Byres Road, this is a classically proportioned grid of concrete pilasters and wooden spandrels, with a projecting abstract concrete relief over the entrance, housing a spacious, double-height library and a zigzag carpet in Glasgow subway orange. What with the NHS and the University of Glasgow's apparent collective determination to clad and/or demolish anything made of concrete, this will soon be the major Brutalist edifice in the West End.

GLASGOW SCHOOL OF ART, BOURDON BUILDING
Keppie Henderson & Partners, 1979
Brutalist

One of those later buildings of the art school which make the cardinal mistake of not being Mackintosh's **Glasgow School of Art (p. 515)**, which to be fair is an extraordinarily high bar. This once formed part of a Brutalist ensemble with the underrated Newberry Tower, replaced recently by Steven Holl's intriguing and 'problematic' **Reid Building (p. 533)** for the school, but it appears to be staying; ironically enough, it's by the successor firm to Mackintosh's own employer on the original buildings, Honeyman & Keppie. This is typical Glasgow Brutalism, roughly textured and ribbed, bulky and a little *dreich*, and with a neo-medieval eye for townscape scenography. These two storeys on stilts surmount Renfrew Street, like a shabby realization of one of Sant'Elia's Italian Futurist cities; it's best seen from the other side to the Art School, where a range of tenements-turned-B&Bs frame its spindly, brackish profile.

GLASGOW SUBWAY:
GOVAN STATION
SPT Architects, 1980
HILLHEAD STATION
Alasdair Gray (artist), 2014
ST ENOCH STATION
AHR Architects, 2014
Postmodernist, High-Tech

The third Underground system to have been built in the world, and the only one never to have been extended – much about Glasgow can be gleaned from this fact, though it's only a half-truth, as the construction of the Argyle Line 'Low Level' in the seventies provided a second Underground line. The Glasgow Subway's current form is mostly owed to its reconstruction in the late 1970s, before which, shockingly, the city considered dismantling it completely. There are only a couple of Victorian surface buildings left, most notably the neo-Baronial old entrance to St Enoch Station. This is now a Caffe Nero, but it has been recently supplemented with neat if value-engineered imitations of Norman Foster's glass bubble canopies from the Bilbao Metro; and there is an entrance built into a grand circus of tenements at Cessnock. The rest of the line is in the brick-and-fibreglass turn-of-the-eighties style that the Glaswegian critic Douglas Murphy calls 'Brutalomo', fusing Brutalist abstraction and Postmodernist historical reference, though it also features some excellent signage and typography. Many stations, especially in the south, are surrounded by wasteland as a result of slum clearance and industrial collapse, which means the open spaces have been used as bleak surface car parks (the Subway is in places effectively a Park and Ride system). Another, more recent, renovation has increased the light to the tiny underground halls bequeathed by the 1890s, and involved commissioning a wonderful Alasdair Gray mural at Hillhead. Govan, one of the larger late-seventies stations, is a tubular fibreglass capsule like a space vehicle about to take off, suspended on brick piers. Although it has been messed up of late with unsuitable glass canopies and extrusions, its combination of beefiness and cuteness is still very Glasgow.

———

BURRELL COLLECTION ✪ ⓘ
Barry Gasson, John Meunier and Brit Andresen, 1971–83
Postmodernist

This museum in Pollok Park, three miles out of the centre, contains the collection of a Glasgow shipping speculator, and nothing else – its entire purpose is to house William Burrell's accumulated medieval doorways, Renaissance tapestries, Buddhist statues, Chinese porcelain, Mughal carpets, Post-Impressionist paintings, and so forth. It's a fabulously odd collection, easily the most interesting in Glasgow – some of it came from William Randolph Hearst's own stash, and you can tell, as there's much that is colourful and lurid. It posed a question that many architects in the early 1970s were unable to answer. As Barnabas Calder explains in an essay about the 1971 competition for the building, the main ideology of the time – High-Tech, with its fetish for the inflatable, adaptable and collapsible – was totally unsuited for a building which was meant to cater for one, static thing, and to do it once, integrally. Postmodernism was suited to such an idea, however, at least in the 'Collage City'/'Townscape' version of these ideas. It's well-mannered Postmodernism, though, without a trace of kitsch – no learning from Las Vegas here.

When approached from the park, the first thing you see is a sprawling expanse of glass, not hugely unlike the Victorian Botanic Gardens in the West End. To get in, you pass through a sandstone gable, to which one of Burrell's medieval doorways has been fitted. The components are those of nineteenth-century Glasgow, but spatially this is new;

Pomo in Pollokshaws: the glass roof, miniature trees and historical fragments of the Burrell Collection.

CENTRAL MOSQUE, GLASGOW
Coleman Ballantine, 1982–4
Postmodernist, Brutalist

Unless you're very enthusiastic about the prospect of seeing the designers of out-of-town Asdas and Barratt Homes trying to evoke the glories of Isfahan and Istanbul, most British mosques are of spiritual and cultural rather than aesthetic interest. This is by some measure the most interesting – much more so than Frederick Gibberd's extremely tentative Regent's Park Mosque, the other contender. It is also one of the few Glasgow buildings to make much use of the Clyde – there is no clear path to the river, but its dome is a clear monument as you cross the bridges. The design is based on a single motif, an angular, faceted module which repeats in the brick-and-red-sandstone porches, in the elegant gates, in the panels of the glazed dome, and in the peak of its tapering concrete minaret. It is more a late-Brutalist design than a Postmodernist one – punchy, physical, a little municipal – but for the exoticism of its dome, especially evocative when lit from within at night.

BRITOIL BUILDING
Hugh Martin & Partners, 1986
Postmodernist

Oil boom architecture seems to be the same everywhere in the world, whatever the climate – the glass is mirrored, the buildings are big, the materials are smooth, the suits are sharp. This exemplar has a similar smoked-glass and ziggurat profiles thing to **Gateway House (p. 220)** in Basingstoke, or, closer to home, **Shell UK Exploration & Production Ltd (p. 548)** in Aberdeen, but gains immensely from being integrated with Glasgow's metropolitan cityscape rather than business park blandness. Monumental and imaginatively modelled, it has a sombre murkiness and opacity that fits rather well

the two levels of long, wooden-roofed arcaded galleries, held up with thin concrete pillars, have a quizzical abstraction to them, relaxed and informal, with comfortable, slightly Aaltoish furniture and fittings akin to those of the **British Library (p. 143)**. Best of all is the constantly surprising, subtle way the architects have fitted parts of the collection integrally into the building, with Gothic doorways and portals everywhere, and the stained-glass fragments inset into the plate glass, with its views of the park. A humane and inexhaustible building, one that repays frequent visits.

The building is listed and undemolishable, but the recently commenced renovation threatens to carve new entrances and add more retail and coffee. These are pretty ill-considered – this is a complete work that would seriously suffer if bits started being removed. A separate pavilion would be a much more sensible idea.

with Glasgow, and it marks well the point where the Victorian grid is just about to get smashed to pieces by the infrastructure of the petrol economy.

ST ENOCH CENTRE
Reiach & Hall and Gollins Melvin Ward, 1989
Postmodernist

Like the **M8 (p. 526)**, this falls into Glasgow's specialized category of 'nice structures, terrible ideas'. This is on the site of the demolished St Enoch railway station, and is surrounded by a bombsite of surface parking, next to the Clyde and in the heart of the city – criminally wasteful. The building, however, is extreme and dramatic, a gigantic glass pyramid that very obviously tries to emulate the Victorian structures that preceded it on the site; seeing it suddenly rear up from the lanes and alleys around is memorable, a chunk of Dallas embedded in a rainy Montreal. Sadly, there's little inside that matches up to the promise of this extraordinary roof.

THE LAURIESTON
1960s
HUTCHESONTOWN
CZWG, masterplan 1990–2005
FRIARY COURT
Page/Park Architects, 2006
LAURIESTON
Page/Park Architects and Elder & Cannon Architects, 2015
Postmodernist, Classical Modernism

The housing here consists of replacements for Basil Spence's Hutchesontown C, in the Gorbals. They are driven by a questionable ideology – people can't live in towers, modern urbanism never works, etc. – which places like **Dundasvale Court (p. 525)**, **Moss Heights (p. 520)** and **Anniesland Court (p. 525)**, not to mention the adjacent

Hutchesontown B (p. 522), all contradict. But taken for what they are, rather than as a polemic, these are very decent examples of contemporary planning and architecture. The first two phases, by London Postmodernists CZWG, consist of a series of circuses and tenements, detailed a little cheaply but opening up vistas and promenades, especially in the ways they frame the remarkable 'Greek' Thomson church adjacent; the grand classical planning suggests the likes of Kelvinside, but the pedestrianized public spaces in-between are of the moment, and are a rare acknowledgement that relatively few residents of inner-city Glasgow own cars. The recent Queen Elizabeth Square is the most impressive part, with better brickwork and a more flamboyant approach to form than the 1990s work.

The other recent redevelopments in the Gorbals, which replace the mammoth slabs of Norfolk Court, are by the always conscientious local firms Elder & Cannon and Page/Park. Rather than any Glasgow precedent, they resemble the 'New London Vernacular' pioneered at **'King's Cross Central' (p. 154)** – severe grids of brick tenements, impressively coherent and robust, in purple, red and yellow brick. Worthy as all this is, none of these projects represents what Glasgow really needs, which is a serious project of urban repair to link the residential areas severed by industry and motorways – something much more important than replacing decent tower blocks with decent tenements. The best thing here isn't trying to convince anyone of anything – it's The Laurieston, the flat-roofed, grey-mosaic-clad pub built to serve the original estates. Still here, still with the same dusty, carpety décor, popular with young folk and – remarkably – recently listed.

BBC SCOTLAND
David Chipperfield Architects, 2001–7
GLASGOW SCIENCE CENTRE
BDP, 2001
International Style, Pseudomodernist

With their alternation of a severe glass block with a bulbous, digitally engineered monument and a wonky swing bridge, these dockside developments are an incredibly obvious attempt to replicate the Gateshead ensemble of the **Sage Music Centre (p. 477)**, **Baltic Centre for Contemporary Art (p. 474)** and **Millennium Bridge (p. 477)** – slightly further upriver, by some bland yuppie flats, the 'Clyde Arc' is almost actionable in its 'tribute' to Wilkinson Eyre's Gateshead bridge. Many of the buildings here are poor, even those by major architects, such as Norman Foster's 'Hydro' concert hall and Zaha Hadid's back-of-an-envelope-scribble-shed of a Transport Museum, but the Science Centre and the BBC headquarters are a cut above. The Science Centre is in the officially approved regeneration style of organic objects clad in titanium, but it deploys this style with more coherence and integrity than most, with the shiny metal grubs relating well to each other, and to a rather elegant steel lookout tower, currently disused because of safety concerns. The BBC headquarters, though partly disowned by Chipperfield due to cost-cutting in the building process, is still an admirably serious building, with its stern, almost Brutalist ziggurat atrium encased in a logical, rationalist glass screen. It looks very fine in drizzly weather, which is the minimum a Glasgow building ought to do.

These shiny, professional buildings are in shabby working-class Govan, not that you'd know it. Although the enormous Govan Town Hall is a few yards away as the crow flies, there's no way of walking between the two. As in Newcastle/Gateshead but without sloping topography as an excuse, it's easier to get here from the city centre than the residential area around. The fact that if you could walk to it from Govan, you could do so *from a fucking Tube station*, is more evidence of twenty-first-century Glasgow's maddeningly elitist non-planning.

———

RADISSON HOTEL
gm+ad architects, 2008
International Style

The most prolific architects of the Blair Boom in Glasgow, Gordon Murray and Alan Dunlop were good at big city centre bombast, like the Apex Hotel or the Sentinel office block, and terrible at masterplanning and housing, on the evidence of their bland 'Glasgow Harbour' development. This is the most interesting of their flash and brash inner-urban projects – scaled well to the slightly chaotic area south of the Central Station, but with its verdigris screen like a coked-up MacMillan and Metzstein, and with the more expensive rooms boxed out in odd corners. Its materials mean it should age well.

———

MAGGIE'S GLASGOW, GARTNAVEL GENERAL HOSPITAL ✪
OMA (Office for Metropolitan Architecture), 2011
International Style

The most architecturally and socially convincing of the Maggie's centres, the charitable cancer care outposts attached to various big NHS hospitals, first in Scotland, then more gradually in England and Wales (see also **Maggie's Fife, p. 511**, **Maggie's Dundee, p. 545** and **Maggie's Highlands, p. 555**). Gartnavel is a complicated place even by NHS standards, with grim PFI blocks, never-dismantled prefabs and general kipple around a Brutalist slab and a mostly derelict Gothick castle, originally an asylum. OMA's response to this is seclusion, taking a wooded part of the green and sloping site,

Maggie's Glasgow at Gartnavel General Hospital, the most beautiful of these cancer care centres.

and nestling a Miesian Farnsworth House into it all – a wonderful fantasy in this dense part of the West End. Relaxed, but precise and appropriately medical, it is tiny, calming, and unlike practically everything else built in Glasgow since the thirties, beautifully made. Most importantly, OMA seems to have given the brief more thought than many Maggie's architects. This is, first and foremost, a space for people who think they might soon die, where they can be reassured and cared for. Here, reassurance and comfort are provided with the slightest of means – glass, steel, wood, trees and no clutter, so that in these delicate, limpid foyers you can feel like you're in a forest rather than in the middle of Glasgow. Yet there's plenty of architectural ingenuity here, no matter how simple the plan and the elevations are, and the fact that OMA has managed to fit all of this into a little patch of grass by a hospital car park is hugely impressive. Absolutely exemplary hospital architecture.

GLASGOW SCHOOL OF ART, REID BUILDING
Steven Holl, 2014
Supermodernist

Hold me tight and spit on me, but I think this is a worthwhile building, albeit a deeply flawed one. One of a clutch of buildings by big international architects – Foster, Zaha, OMA – built in Glasgow in the last decade, it has been harshly criticized for the way that its main south-facing facade, with its drizzly opaque glass screen and its rectilinear bulk, straddles a 1930s students' union and glares at Mackintosh's building to the extent that it spontaneously combusted soon after. I also have my doubts about that facade, which seems needlessly aggressive, but there is much to admire if you give it some patience. The north-facing facades, for instance, which step down from the slope, are both abstract and industrial, with the long rows of glazed studios dominating, as they should. The blue opaque cladding that is used throughout the exteriors, while being a completely new material for Glasgow, looks good in its abominable climate, particularly in the rain in an early evening when the studios are being used and the lights are on, when it appears as a ghostly factory of art. The interiors are based on what Holl calls 'voids', circular whorls of stairwells that provide views up, across and beyond the various spaces where students are making things. These are spacious enough to have benches placed in them, a good recognition of the importance to art students of accident and blether. The problem, again, is that it has all been done on the cheap – heavy use may prove to be unforgiving of the white rendered concrete and the brittle glass. Even so, a place to be explored, and not dismissed for not being by Charles Rennie Mackintosh.

THEATRE ROYAL EXTENSION
Page/Park Architects, 2015
Supermodernist

Here, Page/Park for once do 'dramatic' rather than 'sensible', and very successfully too; this is basically a new entrance appended to a music hall-like Victorian decorated shed, which is not one of Glasgow's more inspired classical buildings; the response is a gilded stairwell and foyer placed at a surging corner, swishing with considerable confidence, lined in red – plush, glam, and vertiginous to walk up and down. Sadly it is rather cheaply made, a problem which afflicts so much contemporary architecture in Britain, but, curiously, Glasgow in particular – the construction industry here seems incapable of detailing a building well, with **Maggie's Glasgow (p. 532)** the only exception.

CITY OF GLASGOW COLLEGE: RIVERSIDE CAMPUS
Reiach & Hall and Michael Laird, 2015
CITY CAMPUS
Reiach & Hall and Michael Laird, 2017
Classical Modernism

Two imposing, formal but unpretentious buildings for a recently amalgamated city-wide Further Education College, an unusual example of this most frequently ignored part of the education system getting proper buildings. The Riverside Campus is that bafflingly rare thing, a Glasgow building that actually addresses the river; its twin towers of severe gridded facades have below them an attractive colonnade for everyone, and a semi-public square for the students; inside is everything from industrial workshops to elaborate boat simulators to mundane classrooms, around an impressively scaled but shoddily detailed atrium. The City Campus, in the north-east of the centre near the blackened Cathedral, uses a similar classical-modernist language of columns and vertical fenestration, but is a little looser in its plan and all the better for it, its splayed massing giving its central atrium a welcome sense of sublimity and drama. Both should be seen.

CUMBERNAULD

PATHWAYS & LANDSCAPING ✪
G. P. Youngman for Cumbernauld
Development Corporation Architects Dept,
1957 onwards
People's Detailing

Cumbernauld is an enormous leap from the
dullness of the earlier East Kilbride, with a
much greater sense of place. A great deal of
this is owed, very unusually for the post-war
era, to a landscape architect, G. P. Youngman.
Place yourself in any of the town's housing
estates except for the very recent, and you'll
find his work – pathways, underpasses,
tunnels, parkways and squares, all executed
in a very Northern series of cobbled and
mottled spaces, with heavy rocks to denote
where you ought to walk, paths taking
desire-line-like shortcuts through trees,
and portal-like funnels into the underpasses;

Northern landscape architecture for a New Town:
trees, steps, paving and housing in Cumbernauld.

all of it is done with loving care, and imparts
a faintly magical, Tove Jansson feel to a
town made up largely of council estates.
[C.19 & C.20]

——

CARBRAIN
Derek Lyddon and James Latimer for
Cumbernauld Development Corporation
Architects Dept, 1963
People's Detailing

The earliest of Cumbernauld's housing
estates you see as you exit the railway
station. First, a long, linear row of harled
maisonettes, some of them in impressively
clustered tower houses, evoking Scottish
tradition; these are pulled together into
a 'wall' with red terracotta trim, apparently
in reference to the fact the Antonine Wall
ran through what is now Cumbernauld.
Behind this frontage you'll find cubic
terraced houses, with hard paving rather
than greenery between them – this was
intended as the 'urban' bit of the town, with
the tree-studded Seafar being the 'suburban'
part. But being urban didn't preclude
being green, so Youngman's thoughtful
landscaping flows alongside all of this, with
a lovely park leading from here to the town
centre. Nothing is vague, everything has
a precise role to play – no New Town feels
as warm or as intimate.

——

SEAFAR ❶
Cumbernauld Development Corporation
Architects Dept, 1963
People's Detailing

Cumbernauld housing at its most relaxed,
with clusters of terraces in bosky, dense,
almost forested landscaping. It originally
had a cluster of towers, which were recently

demolished – senselessly, as the views and landscaping around (rotunda-like car parks, and great hill fort-like swathes of pebbles) were integrally designed with them; if there was ever a case for renovation rather than demolition of high-rises, it was here. However, most of the rest still survives – best of all are the steeply pitched-roofed houses on Liddel Road, tumbling down the hill, a little piece of suburban Oslo – and why not? This is north-western Europe after all. The new houses that have nibbled away at its edge, on the other hand, are pure north Kent or south Essex, like most new developer products in Clydeside.

———

CUMBERNAULD TOWN CENTRE
Geoffrey Copcutt, 1967
Brutalist

A terrible mistake. The idea was as follows: the town centre would consist of a long concrete spine that would have a shopping mall, a bus station, some housing, and whatever else its users and owners fancied inserted into it or removed from it at will in the manner imagined by the Metabolist movement of architects in Japan, who imagined buildings as constantly growing and morphing organisms, a much-discussed image of adaptability. Well, it did get adapted, by shopping mall developers who didn't care much for Copcutt's sculptural Brutalism, and so they inserted various kinds of tat into it before they decided to eat away at the original building, until all that was left was a tatty and gaunt fragment, with the rather optimistic penthouses uninhabited. Cumbernauld is full of good things and good ideas, but its most famous building is not among them. However, in the remnant that exists, with its pile-up of industrial forms, like a gantry crane and containers cast for ever in immovable concrete, you can see both the seduction of the Metabolist idea – the city as a gigantic self-renewing machine – and

its disastrous reality when applied to a bluff capitalist reality, where aesthetics and Tesco Extra pull in opposite directions.

———

OUR LADY'S HIGH SCHOOL ✪
Andy MacMillan and Isi Metzstein for Gillespie Kidd & Coia, 1968–74
CUMBERNAULD TECHNICAL COLLEGE ✪
Andy MacMillan and Isi Metzstein for Gillespie Kidd & Coia, 1978
Brutalist

Two excellent MacMillan and Metzstein buildings, showing the poles of their work, from the quasi-Scandinavian 'humanist' to the futuristically Brutalist. Our Lady's, in Seafar, is the former. Although its long volume, its finger-like plan, looks factory-like from a distance, up close everything is beautifully made, in tactile copper, with the main classrooms cantilevered gently above green hillocks. The college, in the centre, meanwhile, is one of MacMillan and Metzstein's 'section' buildings, made up of two symmetrical stepped volumes, completely readable by the passer-by, hauled up on concrete stilts above some more Expressionist landscaping. Its relentless grey breezeblock elevations are closer to, say, **Thamesmead Estate (p. 96)**, a fearless rush of new space, ill-served by owners and weather, than they are to the Scandinavian and Italian references the architects were moving towards in places like **Robinson College (p. 209)** in Cambridge. Given it is so close to Copcutt's **Town Centre (above)**, it is likely that the dramatic length and harsh materials were a response to it – two long walls, among the New Town's many references to its former status as a bastion to keep the Picts out. With the Town Centre so mangled, it now carries on its own the raw, monumental, somewhat unforgiving aesthetic that originally defined it – a romantic, futuristic Metabolist fortress on a hilltop in rural Strathclyde. **[A.17]**

STRATHCLYDE

NEW CIVIC BUILDINGS, PAISLEY
Hutchison Locke & Monk Architects,
1959–63/Collective Architecture, 2015
Brutalist

A sprawling civic complex at the heart of what could be one of Scotland's great townscapes, between an early multistorey textile mill, a medieval abbey, a muscular Victorian Town Hall and the River Cart, which is instead cut up with roads and aimless greensward. This vast multipart complex, now used by Renfrewshire Council, is made up of long, ribbon-windowed ranges with roughly corrugated concrete towers and a modular, cantilevered debating chamber at the far end, the most picturesque part of the ensemble. Most of the blocks have recently been slightly tackily clad, close to the original colour scheme but losing some of its physicality; there seems to have been little logic to the renovation, with different parts clearly assigned to different architects. However, this fragmentation has one good upshot, as the 'Community Safety Hub' next to the police station was redesigned by the Glasgow practice Collective Architecture, which retained the texture and grain of the Brutalist aesthetic as much as possible, albeit with a certain whimsy in the replacement of a pyramidal rooflight with a nouveau Postmodernist golden cowl.

Nations building, standing amidst the Barratt Home and business park wastes like it had been beamed down from space. This is also very much how it feels when you disembark right in front of it, at Hamilton West Station – there, in front of a row of typical Clydeside middle-class tenements, and with a miserable system-built tower block with a ridiculous hat on behind, is a precision-engineered sheer slab of glass encased in Portland stone. Carry on round the corner, to the front facade, and the apparition doesn't disappear or congeal into a grim reality. Framing it is a formal square – no seats, so to be contemplated only in movement – with a network of rectilinear walkways over an abstracted pool, and a Portland stone rotunda as the 'public face' for the births, marriages and deaths. Everything has such cold elegance that you can hardly quite believe it's real. Only the poor-quality logo of South Lanarkshire Council, the building's current owners, tacked on at one corner gives the game away. Yes, it's real.

What is it doing here? How did the Scottish construction industry, which otherwise mangled most everything it touched during the sixties, manage to build an International Style tower complex of the absolute first rank? How is it in such good condition, in a town which otherwise is conspicuously neglected? So many questions. [A.10]

LANARK COUNTY BUILDINGS, HAMILTON ✪
David Gordon Bannerman for Lanarkshire County Architects Dept, 1959–64
International Style

I first glimpsed this from a minibus en route from Glasgow to the Utopian Socialist factory village of New Lanark – what appeared in the distance to be a clone of the United

ST BRIDE'S CHURCH, EAST KILBRIDE ✪
Andy MacMillan and Isi Metzstein for Gillespie Kidd & Coia, 1964
Brutalist

A lot of Andy MacMillan and Isi Metzstein's buildings are cult objects for architects, as they're full of what architects value most: legibility, integrity and an obvious knowledge of architectural history. Not all of these things are always so important to the laity. This New Town church, however, has such richness, strength and ingenuity that it could quite easily convert the unconverted (to the GKC strain of Caledonian Brutalism, rather than the mother church, though that's always a possibility). Two thick brick boxes – one facing the dual carriageway – have been detailed in the most wilful and creative way by their masons. MacMillan and Metzstein just told them to lay the bricks however they liked, and this fascinatingly irregular, fluted and fanned Gothic box is the happy result, a rare modern example of taking Ruskinian theories on architecture and the dignity of the manual labourer seriously. Finding the entrance is a bit of an adventure – you'll discover that it's in a tiny niche in-between the two boxes, and that the high brick wall curves around you as you enter. Inside, there's a vast prayer box, obliquely illuminated by strips of pulsing stained glass. Headspinning, intoxicating architecture, achieved with a ruthless economy of materials, expressed with great generosity.

Around that entrance, the paving is formed into a faintly pagan red and black pattern, and its points spur you towards the rectory. Its play of surfaces – brick, copper, concrete – and its imaginative play with the levels on this steep site point the way forward to the spatial and material richness of GKC's **Robinson College (p. 209)**, making this into a turning point between their earlier Brutalism and the sensuous, Aalto-influenced Arts and Crafts work that would follow. The campanile was removed in the 1990s, despite the building being listed. This doesn't detract too much from the church, but it detracts a great deal from East Kilbride, a town which badly needs vertical features of identification, without which it blurs into a pleasant enough but indifferent spread of greenery and roundabouts. [D.6]

DOLLAN BATHS, EAST KILBRIDE
Alexander Buchanan Campbell, 1968
Brutalist

The other building worth going to see in East Kilbride, like **St Bride's Church (above)** surrounded by green space in a housing estate that you wouldn't otherwise look twice at. It's in the town park, between the town centre – basically a nondescript enclosed mall, and with this weather who can blame them – and one of the first housing estates in the New Town, the decent little maisonettes of Park Terrace, with an organic, Moore-esque concrete sculpture by Jim Barclay at their centre. Looking at the Dollan Baths from the outside, what you can see is pure structure, with the concrete arches supporting the repeated curves of the bulbous roof giving the thing an insectoid appearance. Fascinatingly odd – more like one of those strange Soviet objects that appear in coffee table books than a municipal baths in a Clydeside New Town. Relatively unscathed by a cheesy renovation, with the new glass canopy entrance at least making some effort at a dialogue with the curved and freakish forms of the original.

GREENOCK CENTRAL LIBRARY ✪
James Watson, Burgh Architect, and Charles Anderson (artist), 1970
Brutalist

Like Paisley, Greenock is a miniaturized, condensed emulation of Glasgow's architectural qualities – Victorian civic buildings of staggering opulence and scale, truncated but hugely ambitious modernist experiments, general neglect. But its riverside site makes the Clyde embankments in the parent city look pinched and paltry – a stunning panorama of mountains and hills, and the river widening dramatically as it meets the Firth of Clyde and the Irish Sea beyond, foregrounded by the container

The remarkably futuristic expressed concrete structure of the Dollan Baths, in East Kilbride New Town.

cranes of a working port. The Central Library is a replacement for a Blitzed part of a nineteenth-century civic ensemble, with an excellent pink-sandstone Palladian church on one side, a spindly market cross in the middle, and H & D Barclay's stupendous late-Victorian Municipal Buildings dominating everything, with its fantastical and phallic, almost skyscraping tower, in an impure imperial baroque as lurid and overripe as, say, the Brussels Palais de Justice – and, pointedly, taller than Glasgow's contemporary City Chambers. Even before the bombing, the building was unfinished, with a shop owner refusing to shift, leaving a peculiar provisional space at the base of the tower.

The post-Blitz library wisely refuses to attempt any sort of emulation of the verticality of the Municipal Buildings or the church, and is instead determinedly horizontal; while it completes the square, it tries to create its own civic space rather than compete, at the same time remaining a decidedly monumental building. You reach it via a dramatic spiral concrete ramp, which frames the towers around, and come to an empty plaza and the entrance to the library – a symmetrical, almost classical facade, with a concrete relief of art brut figures by Charles Anderson in the middle, and panels of pearlescent green slate. On the side facades, these are formed into vertical strips, like pilasters. Most importantly given the Clydeside weather, these panels look gorgeous in the rain. The library was recently renovated, but is currently closed, with some of the stock moved into council buildings nearby, a move that is presumably austerity-related. The green panels have been recently emulated at LDN Architects' (relatively inferior, but not bad) Beacon Arts Centre on the riverside. [D.13]

14. NORTHERN
SCOTLAND

Kylesku Bridge (p. 555)

Scotland north of the Highland boundary fault is another world – wild, inhospitable and sublime; it approximates to the far north of Sweden, Finland or Norway, with rugged, not necessarily pretty small towns and villages loomed over by an unforgiving but captivating landscape. However, the region does include two big lowland cities, Dundee and Aberdeen, each very idiosyncratic. Dundee feels like a refugee from the Central Belt, with a tight and exciting city centre penned in by massively over-engineered roads; it has built some of the more worthwhile civic buildings of recent years, two of them – the **Victoria & Albert Museum** by Kengo Kuma and **Maggie's Dundee** by Frank Gehry – being interestingly peculiar works by famous names. But more typical of the city's qualities are crowded, montage-like buildings such as **Dundee Contemporary Arts**, or the university's **Bonar Hall**. Aberdeen, meanwhile, is a wealthy oil city of uniform grey-granite facades, few trees, and a port right in the town centre; paradoxically, it is most notable for its council housing, the best kept in Britain, whether the 1930s Red Vienna style of **Rosemount Square** or the Brutalism of **Seamount Court**.

The only city within the Highlands proper is Inverness, which has a messy suburban sprawl with a lovely riverside promenade at its heart, enlivened by the attractive and airy **Eden Court Theatre**. Most of what is of interest up here is a matter of heavy infrastructure, not public buildings. That means hydroelectric dams, such as the massive **Glascarnoch Dam**; it means dramatic bridges over lochs and inlets, like **Kylesku Bridge** and the **A9 Bridge, Helmsdale**; but it also means personal dream-projects, of the sort you can only really create when very far from the seats of power, like the **Hermit's Castle, Achmelvich**, or Orkney's 'Italian Chapel' at the **Scapa Flow Fortifications**. The islands too are something distinct – especially Shetland, which has used its oil revenue to build a Swedish-style social democratic state-within-a-state, with great public buildings and attractive social housing, both still being built up to the present day, such as at **Endavoe & Undirhoul** in Scalloway.

DUNDEE

UNIVERSITY OF DUNDEE: ✪
TOWER BUILDING
RMJM, 1958–61
BONAR HALL
Andy MacMillan and Isi Metzstein
for Gillespie Kidd & Coia, 1969–82
DUNDEE REPERTORY THEATRE
Nicoll Russell Studios, 1982
International Style, Brutalist

A fascinating tangle of modernist buildings of various styles and scales, tied together at the western edge of central Dundee's intimate grey Victorian townscape. The one you'll notice first, the city's main tall landmark, is the university's Tower Building, originally the Arts Tower. The first major high-rise building in Scotland, it's still one of the best. One sheer side faces towards the city centre, and a more articulated

facade towards the rest of the university, with an asymmetric composition featuring a dramatic balcony at the top and a cantilevered volume four storeys up, both with elegantly proportioned windows and the first hint of nativism in hardline Scottish modernist architecture – rubble cladding and varnished wood panelling, currently in very good condition. To the ground floor, the wood becomes warmer, and darker, and a public passageway pulls you underneath. Linear as it may look from a distance, on foot, the building is a superb townscape, creating a sequence of nooks and views in a complex part of the city, something that later modern buildings nearby continued.

Adjacent is a rather later university building, much smaller, by Gillespie Kidd & Coia, that exhibits a less visceral, more intellectual response to the questions of site and material. Clad in a precise, machine-made yellow brick and black-stained wood, it consists of several cascading modules, crammed hugger-mugger into a corner, with a walkway link from the street, and a secluded plaza below – a huge amount of activity and visual interest stuffed into a tiny space. Its rear facade, meanwhile, faces an alley which leads to the back end of the roughly contemporary Dundee Repertory Theatre, where black corrugated globules housing service areas for the theatre jut out above a heavy, breezeblock base – an excitingly weird composition which, if you follow it out on to the street, resolves itself as a more conventional, punchy, bunker-like Brutalist theatre with a glazed foyer facing an urban square. Three totally different sites, three totally different buildings, and a far better model for stitching together this fragmented city than the current one of plonking icons on the Tay.

Local materials, International Style: RMJM's crisp, elegant Tower Building for the University of Dundee.

DC THOMSON HEADQUARTERS
T. Lindsay Grey, 1960
Chicago School

At the back of the four-storey Americanist Edwardian red-sandstone palace of the *Beano* publisher's original offices, this tower is the real Chicago School skyscraper that Glasgow never actually managed to build, despite several attempts, in the Edwardian era, and that just about qualifies it for inclusion in this book. There was plenty of classical work built up until the early sixties in office districts across the country, but very little of it is like this – drawing not on England circa 1690, but upon the USA circa 1890. If it had been built a few decades earlier, this giant edifice would be utterly pioneering work, but it just happens to have been built at a time when its design had become retrograde. Its facade consists of three bands of three bays, strung up into a strongly vertical composition through Louis Sullivan-like bands of sandstone surging upwards, divided into a classical three-part facade. It is marred in long views by an illiterate recent roof extension, presumably to make it financially 'viable', but still imposing and exciting from the street, and from the graveyard of The Howff opposite – it has that punchy, giddy feeling of upwards motion that denotes a true skyscraper, even though here it has only nine storeys.

DUNDEE CONTEMPORARY ARTS ✪
Richard Murphy Architects, 1996–9
Modernist Eclectic

The most fully realized of Richard Murphy's intricate, clever, fiddly buildings. Begun just before the 1997 election and opened by none other than Donald Dewar, as a plaque at the entrance records, it's the New Labour civic endeavour before it became tarnished, lucky enough to fall in that sweet spot when a public building could be lavished with lottery money and built to a finish that two decades of neglect can't quite spoil. With typical ingenuity, it takes the shabby brick wall of a light industrial building, holds it up as a screen, punches an irregular system of cantilevers and balconies into it, and builds a new structure of cream rendered concrete, glass brick and green copper above and behind it. From there, steps, with tables and benches, lead up to a prowed streamline moderne entrance. Inside, stairs descend from that sweeping entrance pavilion (currently used as a shop and for print sales) to a two-level space, lined by obsessively detailed balustrades, with a café and restaurant below, and leading to spacious galleries in the shell of the old industrial building. Unfashionable at the moment, but this is an impressive tightrope walk – the only one of Murphy's attempts to emulate the Italian museums of Carlo Scarpa in a British context that really comes close to its inspiration.

Richard Murphy's Dundee Contemporary Arts: top-lit spaces, delicate steel supports and meticulous details.

NINEWELLS HOSPITAL
RMJM, 1964–73
MAGGIE'S DUNDEE, NINEWELLS HOSPITAL
Gehry & Partners, 2003
Brutalist, Deconstructivist

Maggie's Dundee is the only building in Britain by the man who is, using appearances on *The Simpsons* as a barometer, the most famous living architect on the planet. Rather than being a flashy, photogenic monument, it's a pleasant surprise, humble and humane (though, at the time of writing, there's another building in progress, a block of luxury flats in Battersea, which tells you 'HELLO I AM A FRANK GEHRY BUILDING' with tedious logo-flashing vehemence). This Maggie's centre for cancer care, courtesy of Charles Jencks's voluminous phonebook, is a real response to a brief and a place. On a green, wooded ridge overlooking the Tay, it has a glorious setting, to which it pays tribute with subtlety and grace. An organic, lighthouse-like main block faces the river (with a view for the patients), a jagged skyline of low, wooden-framed pavilions, with a computer-engineered titanium roof being the only 'signature'. Compared with the main hospital, it's like a Deconstructivist farmhouse for an avant-garde Little Miss Muffet.

Ninewells itself is one of the few Brutalist hospitals not to have been entirely PFI'd, which makes it worth a look in its own right. Designed by RMJM using a similar rough grey stony concrete module to their **University of Stirling (p. 508)**, it has had one corner given the tacky cladding treatment, but the rudiments are still very clear, as is the undeniably institutional hulk of the thing, swept up into a grey parade of repeated units rather than exploiting the grandeur of the site in a more imaginative way. The curvaceous, sculptural chimney of the complex, though, is very impressive, with the same sort of heraldic quality as the clock tower of a Victorian asylum.

VICTORIA & ALBERT MUSEUM
Kengo Kuma & Associates, 2018
Modernist Eclectic

First, caveats aplenty. Yes, it's based on the by now surely discredited 'Bilbao Effect' idea that the best way to sort out a depressed post-industrial city is by plonking a big cultural building on a waterfront – and, naturally, this comes without the huge investment in public-transport infrastructure and public spaces that the Basque city made at the same time. Yes, it's marooned in dross, the bauble on top of an unplanned and grim riverside regeneration subtopia, seemingly oblivious to the fate of so many of these places after the financial crisis of 2008. And, yes, the design is literally facile. Anyone interested in structural honesty would be maddened by the construction – a black-clad concrete-framed box, which has had concrete ornament bolted to it with metal clips.

The V&A's Dundee outpost does, however, feel wholly of its place, never doing that awful thing of trying to jazz up the city it sits in to be somewhere else. Kuma has realized three important things about Dundee – bad weather, a grand estuarine setting and a context of Victorian buildings, and responded to each of these. Inside, too, there are many smart and subtle ideas, from the shift in the jagged structure from concrete to wood to the very well-used 'living room' café, and, most of all, the way the views are framed through tiny openings in these wood modules to create little postcard-sized vignettes. So go look at the way these two upside-down step pyramids of galleries relate to the Tay, on their artificial island, the way they lurk, fearlessly grey in the grey weather, around the grey Victorian buildings, and, especially, walk the inverted pyramidal blocks to see how they frame views of the river and the hills around with the water running between, and you may find this building much less easy to dismiss.

ABERDEEN

ROSEMOUNT SQUARE ✪
Leo Durnin for Aberdeen Burgh Architects Dept, 1937
Viennese

During the interwar years, the more 'progressive' local authorities all sent their delegations to Vienna, to report back on what was then the widest-scale construction of public housing in the world, as the Austrian capital rolled out all-mod-cons integrated communities of flats, bathhouses, squares and childcare facilties, in monumental, bombastic crescents and courts. In the 1970s and '80s, many of the Vienna imitations in cities like Leeds, Liverpool and Manchester were demolished for their lack of lifts, their density, and sometimes the small size of their flats, so this is a large part of housing history which survives only in tiny pockets.

Red Vienna in grey granite: the monumental Socialist Realist council housing of Rosemount Square.

Some fine examples remain, like London's **Ossulston Estate (p. 137)** or Liverpool's **St Andrew's Gardens (p. 425)**, but Aberdeen has perhaps the most complete of the Vienna imitations. Built at the edge of Rosemount Viaduct, a nineteenth-century 'improvement', Rosemount Square follows the Viennese in refusing to break completely with local traditions – so this, like everything else in Aberdeen, is coated in the shiniest grey granite, meaning it feels very much part of the historic city. But it also copies Vienna's planning ideas completely, with tenements in a grandiose circus, entered through a triumphant archway, with integrated modernist figurative sculpture (a naked woman atop a flying horse in an Eric Gill style) over those arches. It is so obviously continental in inspiration that it even has wooden shutters that can cover the balconies, although in Aberdeen the necessity of keeping the sun out is optimistic at best. Even so, the materials root this completely in the granite city, making it is a very successful localization and miniaturization of Central European heroics. Like all Aberdeen's council housing, it is in excellent condition.

SEAMOUNT COURT & PORTHILL COURT ✪
Aberdeen Burgh Architects Dept, 1964
International Style

Aberdeen, like Glasgow, was erecting system-built high-rises right up until the 1980s. Unlike Glasgow, it is very rich, due to being the main port for North Sea oil, and, perhaps coincidentally or perhaps not, it has treated its blocks with vastly greater care than has Scotland's metropolis. Most of what Aberdeen has is just the standard product of the time, notable mainly for the fact that the city council washes the stairwells, cleans the elevations and mows the lawn, proving that such things are indeed possible. However, the twin towers of Seamount Court and Porthill Court, just outside the city centre, would be distinguished in any city. The elevations are made up of strong concrete frames with glinting, flinty rubble infill, connected by two elegant glazed skyways shooting between the blocks, which are held up on expressionistic splayed pilotis; the grey is offset with subtle, Corbusian notes of red, white and yellow. Coolly luxurious, these towers are an image of what Scottish high-rise housing should have been and mostly wasn't. **[A.22]**

TRINITY HALL
Mackie Ramsey & Taylor, 1964
Brutalist

Providing an HQ for the 'Seven Incorporated Trades of Aberdeen', this is one of Scotland's more inexplicable Brutalist buildings. Clad throughout in precast panels where the concrete has been mixed with granite aggregate – hence fitting into Aberdeen's relentlessly grey palette – it combines abstraction with decontextualized remnants of Aberdeen's bourgeois trading history. Long wings with shops on the ground floor are punctuated by expressed rooflights, with a central block dominated by stained-glass windows taken from an earlier incarnation of the Seven Incorporated Trades, which are cantilevered above the stairwell, with a waffle-slab ceiling above. Together, this creates a puzzling and perhaps unique fusion of corporate Brutalism and Victorian nostalgia. Behind it is a nineteenth-century cemetery, shiny granite gravestones perfectly aligned, the pure Aberdeen experience.

JOHN LEWIS
Covell Matthews Architects, 1970
ST NICHOLAS CENTRE
1985
Brutalist, Postmodernist

Unlike in, say, Lerwick, where public spending has been lavish and evident, you can walk around the centre of Aberdeen never really knowing that you're in a place made phenomenally rich by North Sea oil. The streets have been kept reasonably clean, the historic buildings don't need cleaning because they're made of granite, and the council flats that come right up to the Victorian centre like **Seamount Court & Porthill Court (p. 546)** are kept in unusually good nick, but other than that the late twentieth century contributed nothing except several malls which are just as grim and forgettable as they would be in much poorer towns, revealing the real secret of the poor-quality public space of the UK – a matter of culture and procurement more than the simple availability of cash. But it would be amiss not to note that there is one exception to this rule right in the heart of Aberdeen – the St Nicholas Centre, now part of the multisection 'Bon Accord Centre' but easily identifiable as a separate work of architecture. To the street, it's an arcade, within which there are the usual shops and low ceilings; above that, it's much more interesting. A flight of stairs leads up to a roof garden, with granite planters, a colonnade of elegantly proportioned shops, and even a copper-roofed bandstand, all finished to a level of detail unusual in Scottish modernism; a Presbyterian mini-**Barbican (p. 66)** in polished granite.

If this follows local traditions in a modernist form, round the back, serving John Lewis, you'll find something very different – the former Northern Co-operative. This is an absolutely ferocious Brutalist building, bristling with spiky aggression and raw, corrugated surfaces, roaring into

Public space in the Oil Metropolis: the raised roof garden of Aberdeen's St Nicholas Centre.

the polite streetscape. With its strange serrated profile, its layers of concrete resemble something like **Preston Bus Station (p. 444)** turned upside down; it is like nothing else in Aberdeen, a vehement rejection of all these good manners.

SHELL UK EXPLORATION & PRODUCTION LTD
McInnes Gardner & Partners, 1975–85
Brutalist

Best seen looming over the oil industry straggle along the railway line as you approach Aberdeen from the south, this is a straightforward Brutalist pyramid – stiff, slick and steroidal as its American inspirations. The tinted glass in particularly evokes the famous mirrorglass oil company style that anyone who grew up with *Dallas* will know well. But if examined more closely on foot, you can see how this office for

Shell's operations in the North Sea combines the Texan corporate style with something rather closer to the Denys Lasdun version of modernism, where functionalism is made into monumental, eternal sculpture. It sprawls across its suburban site, with the facades made up of several distinct stepped sections; the effect is particularly close to the bluntness of Lasdun's IBM building next to the **National Theatre (p. 84)**, with fewer airs and graces. This is a ceremonial ziggurat of pure power, and one that would probably have worked better in the centre of Aberdeen, where it could serve as a reminder of where all that money went.

HIGHLANDS & ISLANDS

SCAPA FLOW FORTIFICATIONS, ORKNEY

War Office, 1940–44
Industrial

Of the various landscapes thrown up by war in the twentieth century, those around Scapa Flow, the base for the British fleet in both World Wars, are most worth exploring, even if you're not interested in the extremely morbid worlds of ordnance tourism and urbex. The 'Flow' itself is a bay lying between several of Orkney's islands, just south of its mainland, and easily reached on buses from Kirkwall and Stromness. The key sites can be found between the villages of St Mary's and St Margaret's Hope. The largest of the surviving fortifications are known as the 'Churchill Barriers', and were built immediately after the German conquest of

Norway (a country closer than England to Orkney and Shetland, which were actually part of the Kingdom of Norway until the fifteenth century) in order to block the bay from German invasion. They consist of enormous hollow cubes of concrete, piled up on the seabed high enough to reach the surface, looking like bridges constructed out of randomly dropped bunkers; the line of cubes is deliberately irregular and jagged, to prevent the Barriers from being flooded.

Alongside these, several towering concrete gun emplacements and pillboxes were scattered to defend the Barriers, now made, if anything, more surreal by the way that life has carried on around them for generations, with livestock milling about among the concrete. The Barriers survive *in toto*, converted after the war into causeways linking Orkney's mainland

Prefab and craftsmanship at Orkney's 'Italian Chapel', made from a Nissen hut in a POW camp at Scapa Flow.

with the islands of Lamb Holm and South Ronaldsay; they provide views of another even more grim remnant, with many visible fragments of blockships, wrecks put here to deter submarines – below these are remnants of the German fleet scuttled here in 1919. If all this is a little too unnerving, you can visit the 'Italian Chapel' on Lamb Holm – a Nissen hut which Italian POWs working on the Barriers converted into a pocket baroque church, which is open to the public. It's sentimental but delightful, especially the *trompe l'oeil* decoration inside the hut.

___

GLASCARNOCH DAM
James Williamson & Partners, 1946–57
Industrial

The North of Scotland Hydro-Electric Board, set up by the Clydeside socialist Tom Johnston, was the nearest thing Clement Attlee's government had to FDR's Tennessee Valley Authority – a massive showcase of central planning and modernist engineering designed to revive the economy of a historically depressed and impoverished rural area – in this case, the northernmost parts of the Highlands, which had never fully recovered from the clearances of the eighteenth and nineteenth centuries. This was achieved, as in the US, through huge, high-modernist hydroelectric projects – the rerouting of the lakes and rivers that run through the north Highlands into dams and power stations, and which provided cheap electricity, at a substantial loss, to every village and croft. Glascarnoch Dam is the easiest seen of the Board's structures because it stands midway on the A835 between Inverness and Ullapool, right next to the roadhouse of the Altguish Inn. It's an epic structure – a curved concrete wall rising out of earthen mounds between hills, framing looming mountains; an access roadway for the engineers runs across it, with a control tower in the middle of the main dam structure, and another overlooking it, held up on thin concrete piers above the Loch. If most interactions between landscape and architecture in fifties Britain were 'picturesque', this is something else – the rawest, most Wagnerian sublime.

___

63 HIGH STREET, NAIRN
1950s
Moderne

The relatively slow pace of development in Scottish provincial towns compared with English ones can result in survivals like this, on the high street of a windy seaside town. The street block that now houses M&Co. is a distinctive and piquant example of twentieth-century retail design, where the entire frontage of a Victorian building has been replaced by black granite and plate glass, arranged into a jagged rhythm of inset windows – an aesthetic which seems distinctively Scottish, elegant and patrician.

___

HEDELL'S PARK ESTATE, LERWICK, SHETLAND
Moira & Moira, 1954–5
People's Detailing

Two decades before the oil money bonanza hit the Shetland Islands, this was the first in several interesting municipal experiments there. On the hills above the sternly Victorian slates and turrets of Lerwick town centre are several lanes and 'closses', cobbled, steep and interconnected; here is where Shetland's slums – now a very hard thing to imagine – were once clustered. The housing scheme that replaced them aimed to recapture some of the intimacy and community of these tenements and closes, taking an approach similar to Wheeler & Sproson's **Somerville Square & Coltburndale** in Burntisland **(p. 507)** and **Saut Girnal Wynd & The Towers (p. 508)** in Dysart – miniature tower

Council housing in the very far north: Moira & Moira's Hedell's Park Estate in Lerwick, Shetland.

houses with irregularly placed windows, rendered with grey and red harling – aiming to look enigmatic and necessary, like folk architecture. The walk through and around the blocks, many of which are on pilotis, is very enjoyable, with old chapels and houses left around to make clear that this isn't a *tabula rasa*. In the main square of the estate, terraced houses step up the hill in front of a curious nautical playground, with concrete lilypads and a 'boat'. One of the blocks carries a Saltire Society plaque, commending it for good design, as it should.

HERMIT'S CASTLE, ACHMELVICH ✪
David Scott, 1955
Brutalist

The strangest and most poignant Brutalist building in Scotland, and one that is still very little known – I first came across it via Barnabas Calder's description of camping out inside it, in his book *Raw Concrete*. The story is as follows: David Scott, a young architect from Norwich, was on a Highland holiday at Achmelvich caravan park, a site which overlooks a gorgeous sandy beach, framed by rocks, with views of the sea and the islands in one direction and some of the most imposingly alien mountains in Europe on the other. Falling in love with this place, Scott convinced the local crofter to let him build a bothy on one of the rocky inlets that descend to the sea next to the caravan park. What he made there, mostly with his own hands, mostly out of a concrete aggregate mixed from the limestone rocks all around, was something between a primitive hut, a pyramid and one of the cranky, organic Le Corbusier buildings of the period such as the church at Ronchamp or the monastery at La Tourette. The story then told is that when he had finished it, Scott slept there for one night – moulded concrete beds and bookshelves were part of the structure –

A Brutalist bonsai fortress: the castle of Achmelvich, one of post-war architecture's great eccentric monuments.

and then never returned. According to the crofter's family he did come back – once.

The story is extraordinary enough, but as a building this is in a genre of one; a landscape experiment where the most apparently modern material – concrete – and the most futuristic style – Brutalism – are used for a structure which appears to grow completely organically, like a fungus, from the rock. The problem is getting there. The caravan park is one thing – if you don't drive, request buses go, albeit rarely, from nearby Lochinver – but when you get to the beach, the castle, which is not signposted, is just the other side of the hill with the cairn on top to your left, along the fence of the campsite. You will have to do some climbing and leaping over rocks, bog, sheep and sheep shit in order to get there, but it is barely a ten-minute 'walk'. When you do get there, you'll find the castle is tiny – barely taller than an adult person – and so closely linked to the landscape that you could even miss

it if you weren't looking for it. The tall, thin entrance portal is built into the rocks that fall down to the sea, which makes it inaccessible for anyone who hasn't done a little climbing before, but the other three sides are more easily explored – a miniature step pyramid, with a Corbusian grid of windows and a hammerhead chimney, cute and strange, monumental and minuscule. If anyone tells you modern architecture is technocratic, destructive of natural landscapes or inhumane, show them this – the world's only Brutalist bothy.

POST OFFICE, KIRKWALL, ORKNEY
Ministry of Works, 1960
People's Detailing

Nobody visits Orkney for its modern architecture, obviously, but even so, it can be surprising what you'll find there. In the tight townscape of its tiny capital is this post

Longboats and the Post Office: a sculptural relief at the 1960 GPO in Kirkwall, the capital of Orkney.

office, in a far-north version of the Festival of Britain style, with white harling, faintly modernist fenestration, a pitched roof and a wonderful doorway, with a stylized Viking longboat in stone relief over the entrance, flying the flag of the Royal Mail. The nearby recent Visitor Centre and bus station are a more ungainly attempt at regional modernism, trying to emulate the **Museum of Scotland (p. 503)** on the cheap, but function well.

OLD LIBRARY, LERWICK, SHETLAND
Zetland County Council, 1966
International Style

Designed originally to provide museum, archives and library in one small building (before they moved to the dockside), this lively and clever pure modernist building is no longer Shetland's Central Library, which moved a decade or so ago into the large Victorian church next door. However, it's still used for library services, and there are reports that the books might be moved back there in future, which is heartening, as many councils would just have demolished an old sixties library. You can see the demarcations of the plan easily at a glance – a fully glazed, Miesian upper storey in blue steel and glass, raised on a rubble stone base, with the museum originally above, the library below. Details are lots of fun throughout, but the best feature is found at the entrance. Each side of the doorway has been given carved panels where Viking tracery and heraldry frame a post-war boy and girl immersed in a book. Delightful.

THE HORN, ERROL, NEAR PERTH
1970
Googie

A surrealist pop architecture fragment on the A90 that connects the Central Belt with Dundee, just outside the city of Perth. The Horn was originally a shed providing sandwiches and cups of tea for travellers, but it was redesigned in 1970 as a single-storey glass block connected to a rotunda, obviously in emulation of the more high-end motorway service stations of the era such as **Markham Moor Service Station (p. 358)**, but with some personal touches that the big firms would never have gone in for – in this case, the fibreglass cow on top of the rotunda, which has black spots in the shape of the continents of the world. No, really. The original big red serif signage survives, and the interiors are largely untouched too; TripAdvisor hosts fervent arguments about the quality of the sandwiches and the all-day breakfasts. The owners have proposed moving to a larger café further up the A90 to a much duller design, but at the time of writing The Horn still stands, as strange as ever, in the Perthshire countryside.

The diamond-shaped foyers of Eden Court Theatre, the largest modernist public building in the Highlands.

A9 BRIDGE, HELMSDALE, SUTHERLAND

Babtie Shaw & Morton, 1972
Brutalist

Helmsdale is a 'clearance village', made by the landowner to resettle some of those ethnically cleansed in the Highland Clearances of the eighteenth and nineteenth centuries. It stands at the foot of the mountains, right on the North Sea, divided by a river that is crossed by an elegant stone bridge designed by Thomas Telford. Next to that is this concrete and steel supplement, built to take the A9 trunk road that runs from the Central Belt up to Thurso, the northernmost town in Great Britain. In other circumstances, you might not look twice at it, a fairly typical motorway bridge of its time, lightweight concrete on a springy, surging steel support. But there is something oddly majestic about the way this one frames the sea, between rough hills, with the river

below, as if deliberately placed to create a haunting vignette. This subtle (if possibly accidental) meeting of modernity and landscape involved the demolition of the ruins of a castle, but, then again, modernist bridges are rarer up here than ruined castles.

EDEN COURT THEATRE, INVERNESS ✪

Law & Dunbar-Nasmith Architects, 1976/ Page/Park Architects, 2007
Brutalist, Vernacular

The 'capital of the Highlands' faces the river with a confidence rare in British cities. Here, the sorts of things that other cities have had to build from the 1990s onwards – buildings that face the river, attractive footbridges, green spaces – were already put there in the nineteenth century. There's not much in the way of good modern architecture, though, with this single first-rate exception. At one corner of the riverside boulevard, a Baronial building was supplemented in the 1970s with this excellent theatre and cinema complex, which has sustained an admirably varied programme. You can read it quickly from the facade – four bays of diamond-shaped, tile-roofed steel-and-glass prisms, with a rusty black fly tower behind, an appropriately murky use of material given the local climate. This makes an impressive frontage, but it's inside, in the generous, spacious foyers which feed the large main theatre, that the building's quality and originality really shows itself.

Those prisms, lined on the inside with oak, offer views of the cityscape and create a dynamic sculptural pattern in their own right. As you walk up the steps, it's like being in a vast scaling-up of Mary Martin's sculptures at the **University of Stirling (p. 508)** – no wonder it fits rather seamlessly with a demonstratively non-orthogonal extension by Page/Park, which introduced cinemas and a smaller theatre, making this a multifunctional space. In the extension the original geometries become a lot more wilful and digital, but the extravagant interlocking space is maintained, as is the relaxed palette of greys and blacks. The walk between the two parts, in the upper-level foyers, is an unusually smooth connection between two different approaches. The building must have been well respected, as very few buildings of this era in small cities have been treated with such sensitivity.

KYLESKU BRIDGE ✪
Ove Arup & Partners, 1982–4
Brutalist

One of the great modernist bridges, little known because of its position in the very furthest part of the Highlands, in the far north-west of Sutherland, close to Caithness and the northern limits of the island of Great Britain. The landscape here is harsh, thrilling and, frankly, terrifying – sheer bog and freakishly proportioned mountains, whose shapes are owed partly to an asteroid strike nearby many millions of years ago (it's nice to realize that there's a geological reason why this feels like another planet). Approaching from the south – as you likely will be, unless you live on Cape Wrath – the A894, forking off from the main north–south road, sweeps at wild gradients and in wide curves through the area, and at the hamlet of Unapool swerves suddenly to cross an inlet, Loch Cairnbawn. On the other side, you'll find a car park and viewing point, with a monument to the local submarine crews (a good place to hide things, this was) and another to the construction of the bridge you can now see in front of you. A drastic sweep across the loch is held up by two tall, steeply inclined supports, each formed into two curved Vs, beautifully detailed with the same elegance and flair as Arup's earlier **Kingsgate Bridge (p. 470)** in Durham. These splayed concrete legs are designed so that the bridge can withstand the high-velocity winds that blast the site, and which will be blasting you if you go to see it.

MAGGIE'S HIGHLANDS, RAIGMORE HOSPITAL, INVERNESS
Page/Park Architects with Charles Jencks (landscape architect), 2005
Ecomodernist

One of the more cramped Maggie's cancer care centres, at a corner between a main road and a car park, so lacking the bosky surroundings that enliven **Maggie's Dundee (p. 545)** and **Maggie's Glasgow (p. 532)**. But Maggie's centres are meant to excel in creating intimate enclaves of warmth and calm in places that are so often grimly institutional and utilitarian, and here Page/Park's building does a very decent job. Raigmore is an immense brown concrete monolith standing steadfast against driving rain and winds coming in off the North Sea and the mountains; the centre is a tiny verdigris and timber building, curling like a hibernating animal into the ridges of Charles Jencks's maternal, mammarial landscaping, with a garden, a library and a patio. Much less spectacular and much more 'eco' than the Maggie's norm, with its wooden frame, and a world away from the sinister architecture-as-cancer-metaphor in **Maggie's Fife (p. 511)**. Not so photogenic, but better suited to the job in hand.

The concrete and glass galleries of Stromness's Pier Arts Centre, framing boats and the bay.

PIER ARTS CENTRE, STROMNESS, ORKNEY ⊙
Levitt Bernstein, 1979/Reiach & Hall, 2007
Classical Modernism

A jewel of a building, architecturally the finest art gallery in Scotland that isn't in Edinburgh or Glasgow – and in terms of its collection, too. The Pier Arts Centre, like **Tate St Ives (p. 278)**, is an emanation of the interwar alliance of Hampstead and Weimar in Exile, via the collection of the Anglo-German artist, socialist and anti-fascist Margaret Gardiner. She hated the term 'collector' (considering it faintly bourgeois and possessive), but whatever you want to call this, it's a very impressive assemblage, with major sculptures by Naum Gabo and Barbara Hepworth and good work by local artists like the film-maker Margaret Tait. Gardiner founded the centre in 1979 some years after moving to Orkney, with Levitt Bernstein converting a house and a warehouse (originally the local offices for the Hudson Bay Company – this place is perhaps less peripheral than it feels) and linking them together.

This was extended in 2007 – two years after Gardiner's death at the age of 100 – by Reiach & Hall. Their extension is a volume on the same scale as the historic buildings which is completely different in its treatment. The steel-and-glass aesthetic evokes an unlikely fishing village version of Mies van der Rohe – completely appropriate to this fusion of continental high modernism and intense, geographically peripheral localism. The interior spaces with their subtle play of light, their strategic placing of particular works from the collection in their own niches and spaces, and their exquisite wood and concrete finishes, are all of remarkable grace and delicacy. This is the only gallery to have really learned from Caruso St John's majestic **New Art Gallery (p. 322)** in Walsall – like it, this is not an art gallery as an 'iconic' 'regeneration' bestowed from on high, but a project that is personal and public, idiosyncratic and generous – and, most importantly, you couldn't imagine this building being anywhere else but here. **[D.20]**

LERWICK:
SHETLAND MUSEUM & ARCHIVES, HAY'S DOCK CAFÉ
BDP, 2007
SOLARHUS
Richard Gibson Architects, 2009
MAREEL
Gareth Hoskins Architects, 2013
Modernist Eclectic, Ecomodernist

Since the cat was let out of the bag in Andy Beckett's history of the 1970s, *When the Lights Went Out*, the one thing left-wing people in Britain know about Shetland, a part of Norway until the fifteenth century, is that it's the only area of the country to have done with North Sea oil what Norway did. That is, it extracted as much tax from it as possible and kept the proceeds in a sovereign wealth fund to be spent on a variety of social projects. By the twenty-first century this had made it the second-wealthiest local authority in the country after the City of London, and created in reality the Scandinavian social democracy that so many Scottish Nationalists aspire to (support for the SNP has always been low here, though – the distant unaccountable capital here is Edinburgh more than London). The first wave of public buildings, dating from the 1980s/1990s, were unfortunate enough to coincide with a low ebb in Scottish architecture. The many community halls, leisure centres, sports centres and council houses (the Clickimin Centre in Lerwick is the biggest) are in a grey pebbledash and big pitched-roof style that isn't exactly aesthetic, though their interiors can be vast, and maintenance is impressive. Surprisingly it has only been in recent years – with the fund starting to run low, and some more normal Scottish problems creeping in – that Shetland architecture has started to look as Norse as its politics and economics. This dockside ensemble of public buildings, near to where the boats from Aberdeen come in, is a little showcase of this. Here, you really

could be in Bergen or Trondheim, in a place where the Scandinavian obsessions of British architecture and Scottish politics are much more than cosplay.

Approaching from the town centre, you first come to a business park which looks nothing like any other business park in the country, by the local firm of Richard Gibson Architects. Rather than the steroidal Trespa groundscrapers of Edinburgh or the blank sheds of everywhere else, there are several brightly painted, chalet-like buildings modelled after the surrounding dockyard structures, housing various companies, around a dramatic solar-panelled 'Solarhus', which was initially criticized for its unsuitably lightweight materials in the punishing climate – though it looks excellent at the time of writing. Nearby are some dull, Blairite council offices, the only indicator that you are still in Britain. Then there are the two showpieces. The earlier is BDP's Museum, which is formed out of several old dock warehouses, in a manner which suffers in comparison with, say, the delicate poetry of the **Pier Arts Centre (above)** in Orkney, but is nonetheless very nicely arranged, especially the main addition, a tall wooden tower formed out of what looks like randomly arranged panels from ships, containing various boats and mannequins. The 'high architecture' here is Mareel, a huge arts centre of the kind that many towns twenty times the size of Lerwick would kill for, containing a cinema, theatre, café, gallery, bookshop and much else in two dramatically sloping volumes clad, like so many buildings in the Northern Isles, in grey corrugated metal, one of the more daringly unromantic gestures towards 'context' you're likely to find. Linking these is a harbourside pedestrian promenade which might be a wee bit narrow in a high wind, but is otherwise delightful, and it ends at an artwork by Lulu Quinn, rusty gramophone-style speakers playing recordings, interviews, stories and sound artworks that change with the wind and the weather.

ENDAVOE & UNDIRHOUL, SCALLOWAY, SHETLAND

Richard Gibson Architects, 2010s
Ecomodernist

One should not overpraise Shetland's municipal endeavours – many of them are simply about making an inhospitable archipelago liveable – but it is still striking how more social housing is built here, proportionally, than in any big city in Britain. Today, most of it is built by the Hjaltland (the old Norse name for Shetland) Housing Association, and designed by Richard Gibson Architects. It all seems to continue the 'Are you *sure* we're not in Norway?' vein of the dockside in Lerwick, except even more so, because this is ordinary everyday stuff, nothing 'iconic'. My pick of the estates is these two on the outskirts of Shetland's second town. There are two groups, one of big A-framed houses, another of lower houses with cubic rooflights and a series

of chalets above, all built of timber – an interesting choice in a place with hardly any trees, however authentically Norwegian it looks – and placed at the foot of a mountain, with a quarry behind and small factories all around. A productive landscape, extremely harsh, but softened in the way the Swedes, Norwegians and Finns have done repeatedly for the last eighty years – bright colours, good materials and a sensitive settling of buildings into the landscape rather than simply plonking them on top.

On the opposite side of the Voe is the bizarre and comprehensive Scalloway Museum, designed in 2012 by the same architects, which is not as well resolved as the housing in architectural terms, but similarly celebrates Shetland–Norway links, this time through the 'Shetland Bus' that sent fishing boats and submarines to occupied Norway. One of the oddest and most moving museums you'll ever visit. Outside are a ruined castle and a salmon-packing factory.

A panoramic view of new housing in Scalloway, Shetland, currently being rebuilt in the style of suburban Bergen.

A GENERAL GLOSSARY

Note that architectural genres such as 'Brutalism' are defined in the introduction.

Aalto, Alvar (1898–1976): Finnish architect, whose use from the 1930s onwards of natural materials and organic, irregular layouts was influential on much post-war building.

Active frontage: in contemporary town-planning, businesses such as shops or cafés on the ground floor of an apartment building or office block.

Aggregate: the chosen material, usually stones of various kinds, in a concrete mix.

Architectural Association (AA): influential and elite school in Bloomsbury, London, generally the location of the architectural avant-garde at any given time.

Ashlar: finely cut stone.

Axis: in town planning, an imaginary line used to arrange buildings as an ensemble – usually used here to describe the arrangement of buildings culminating in a symmetrical view.

Barcode facade: a form of *curtain wall* with a randomized pattern, popular in the 2000s.

Baroque: a particularly extravagant development of *Renaissance* architecture.

Bauhaus: an important school of art and design, active in Germany from 1919 to 1933. Often slightly inaccurately used to describe any international modern building of the interwar years and sometimes later.

Beaux Arts: a grandiose form of nineteenth-century official architecture, especially in France, based on neoclassicism, the Baroque and the creation of grand *axes*.

Béton brut: a French term – 'raw concrete' – for the deliberately untreated, unpainted concrete work common in the late work of *Le Corbusier*, then borrowed by Brutalist architects worldwide.

Brise-soleil: an inbuilt projecting frame or a series of louvres or blinds to shade windows from sunlight; literally a 'sun-breaker', though the nearest English term is 'sun-screen'.

Bush-hammering: a means of treating wet concrete by hitting it with a kind of hammer to produce a gnarled, textured effect.

Cantilever: a projection where an upper part of a building is thrust out above the one below, without a supporting column.

Carbuncle Cup: annual prize for 'worst building by a British architect', an anti-*Stirling Prize* awarded since 2006 by the journal *Building Design*. Its name derives from a term used by Prince Charles in 1984 to describe a mooted extension to London's National Gallery by Ahrends Burton & Koralek, which was cancelled after his intervention.

Cladding: the material that makes up the outer facade of a *framed* building.

CLASP: a *prefab* building system, mainly used in schools from the late 1950s onwards, developed by the Consortium of Local Authorities Special Programme.

Classicism: the architectural styles derived from Ancient Greece and Rome; as a revival, known as neoclassicism.

Coffering: a pattern of inset panels, often used in ceilings and domes, especially in classical architecture.

Colonnade: a system of covered columns on the outside of a building, widely found both in the architecture of the Italian Renaissance and in the postwar colleges of Oxbridge.

Corten: a form of steel that gradually stains red as it rusts without the structural material degrading.

Cupola: a small dome.

Curtain wall: the facade of a *framed* building, applied as a skin, particularly in glass towers.

Deck: a pedestrian walkway, in the open air (as opposed to an internal corridor), usually above the ground; hence the 'deck-access' of many twentieth-century apartment buildings.

De Stijl: a Dutch art, architecture and design movement of the 1910s and '20s, committed to right angles and primary colours.

Diapering: a kind of brickwork laid in a diamond pattern, usually in two colours.

Dudok, Willem Marinus (1884–1974): Dutch architect whose rectilinear brick designs were extensively copied in interwar British architecture, especially of the *municipal* variety.

Elevation: the external view of a building.

Faïence: a finely glazed ceramic, here particularly when used as *cladding*, especially in art deco and moderne buildings of the interwar years.

Fenestration: windows, and where they go on a building.

Formwork: the moulds into which concrete is poured during construction, often determining the building's eventual finish or form.

Frame: here, meaning the steel or concrete skeletons that are the structural basis for most modern buildings larger than the scale of a house; can also denote the timber frames of Tudor or, sometimes, 'eco' buildings.

Gabions: loose stones held in a metal cage.

Gallery: a space that is open on one side such as a walkway or *deck*, a *colonnade* or an upper-level interior balcony.

Gothic: the high architecture of the Middle Ages.

Hyperbolic paraboloid: a delicate, shell-shaped thin concrete *vault*, largely in the 'Googie' architecture of the 1950s and '60s.

Infill: the facing material sandwiched vertically or horizontally within a *frame*, as opposed to an exterior *curtain wall*; usually brick inset into a concrete frame.

Le Corbusier: pseudonym of the Swiss architect **Charles-Édouard Jeanneret (1887–1965)**, probably the most influential of the twentieth century, which is why so many modern buildings appear 'Corbusian'.

Malevich, Kasimir (1879–1935): visionary Ukrainian/Soviet painter, influential on architecture particularly via the work of *Mies van der Rohe*.

Masonry: stonework or brickwork, often bearing the weight of the building but sometimes, especially today, used as *infill*, as *cladding* or as a *curtain wall*.

Massing: the particular three-dimensional form of a building.

Melnikov, Konstantin (1890–1974): Soviet architect, whose work is particularly celebrated – and plundered – for its use of dramatic *cantilevers*.

Mendelsohn, Erich (1887–1953): German-Jewish architect whose streamlined buildings were frequently plagiarized across the world in the 1920s and '30s, and who lived and worked in Britain during much of the latter decade.

Mies van der Rohe, Ludwig (1886–1969): enormously influential German architect, best known for his post-war steel buildings in the USA, with their precise and elegantly emphasized *frames* and *curtain walls;* hence 'Miesian'. In 1964 he designed a tower for a site in the City of London that was never built due to a preservation campaign.

Module: the repeatable individual components of a building, usually but not exclusively one that is *prefab* in its derivation.

Mondrian, Piet (1872–1944): Dutch abstract painter, linked with De Stijl; from the 1920s on, his primary-coloured grids became a source for everything from the facades of office blocks to the floor tiles of cafés.

Mullions: the vertical bars in *fenestration*.

Municipal: of an elected local authority or council. Crucial to twentieth-century architecture, given the extensive role of local-authority architects' departments, especially between 1945 and 1979.

Narthex: the entrance hall of a church.

Niemeyer, Oscar (1907–2012): Brazilian architect whose use of curved concrete forms and *brises-soleil* was an important source for much commercial architecture of the post-war years.

Pediment: in Ancient Greek architecture and its derivatives, the usually triangular gable suspended on columns above a *portico*, sometimes filled with sculpture.

Penthouse: a smaller, separately roofed housing unit on top of a larger building, usually a residential tower.

Pilaster: a usually ornamental vertical pillar, designed to resemble a column.

Piranesi, Giovanni Battista (1720–78): Italian architectural draughtsman. His dramatic, detailed etchings were influential on *classicism* and the *Beaux Arts*, but also on modernism, particularly via the fantastical multi-level spaces of his 1750 series *Imaginary Prisons*; the latter are what twentieth-century critics usually refer to when using the term 'Piranesian'.

Porte cochère: a *portico* not directly connected to a building.

Portico: a columned and roofed projection, usually at the front of a building.

Portland stone: a white limestone, quarried in Dorset, widely used both in English Baroque architecture and in the first phase of post-Second World War reconstruction.

Prefab: made in a factory rather than on a building site, so 'prefabricated'. In Britain it usually refers to the factory-built houses that were used during and in the immediate aftermath of the Second World War; can also be used to describe the factory-made components in high- or low-rise *system-building*.

Private Finance Initiative: or 'PFI' – a public–private funding mechanism used in public buildings from the early 1990s to the mid-2010s which became notorious for poor build quality, particularly in *cladding*.

Renaissance: in architecture, a free and creative development of ideas found in Roman ruins, combined with new mathematical and scientific knowledge; subsequently developed into neoclassicism and the *Baroque*.

Rendering: either (a) a smooth, coloured plaster covering a building, especially popular in the international modernist villas and apartment blocks of the 1930s; or (b) the painted or computer-generated image of a building produced during the planning process.

Ribbon windows: the continuous, wrap-around windows made possible by *frame* as opposed to *masonry* construction.

Roughcast: a coarse pebbly cement, used as a facing material; sometimes also called pebbledash or (when combined with lime, usually in Scotland) harling.

Rudolph, Paul (1918–97): American Brutalist architect, known for richly textured surfaces and complex, almost *baroque* arrangements.

Scott Brown, Denise (1931–) and **Venturi, Robert (1925–2018)**: a pioneering partnership of American Postmodernist architects and theorists, particularly notable for their study of Las Vegas, their embrace of 'complexity and contradiction', and their classification of buildings into either 'decorated sheds' or 'ducks'. The designers of London's National Gallery Extension, which is not in this book.

Secession: a movement close to Art Nouveau in early-twentieth-century Vienna, with some similarities to the work of Charles Rennie Mackintosh in Glasgow and Northampton.

Section: a view of a building as if it has been cut through, so that the internal layout can be seen. Often implied in post-war architecture, especially through the use of a descending 'stepped' layout.

Services: the various pipes and chimneys and cables carrying a modern building's electricity, gas, water and suchlike; visually emphasized in both Brutalist and High-Tech architecture.

Shuttering: the boards placed on a concrete mould; these usually retain the imprint of wood, an effect particularly popular in Brutalist buildings of the sixties.

Socialist Realism: a form of *classicism* favoured by authoritarian regimes in Eastern Europe between the 1930s and 1950s.

Space frame: a complex horizontal *frame* made up of many small parts, suspending a building's structure from the ceiling; widely used by High-Tech architects and by British Rail in the 1970s and '80s.

Spalling: in concrete, deterioration of the *aggregate*, with small pieces crumbling away from the steel reinforcement.

Spandrel: in modern architecture, the (usually coloured) non-structural panels in a *curtain wall*.

Stirling Prize: an annual prize for 'best building by a British architect', given out every year since 1996, and named after the architect James Stirling (1926–92).

Stock brick: the mass-produced brick of a particular area; here, usually the brown-yellow brick used in London, historically made in Bedfordshire, or the bright red brick of the Midlands and North, historically made in Accrington, Lancashire.

Streamline: the aerodynamic styling used in cars, aeroplanes and ships during the interwar years, extensively borrowed in the architecture of the time.

Structural: the parts of a building that make it stand up.

System-built: buildings made from *modular, prefab* components, usually of the 1960s, usually of large concrete panels, particularly controversially in council housing towers. Still used in hotels and student housing.

Tile-hanging: the ceramic tiles placed in patterns on the more middling modern housing of the fifties and sixties.

Trabeated: using a horizontal and vertical form of construction, rather than using *vaults* and arches.

Travertine: a yellowy-white limestone, popular in luxury architecture of all eras since the Romans.

Trespa: a cheap but versatile *cladding* material of the 2000s and 2010s.

Truss: an expressed support or strut, suspending part of a building, here particularly in High-Tech architecture.

Upright: a vertical structural support, as a column or as part of a frame.

Vault: a self-supporting, usually arched structure.

Vernacular: a linguistic term misappropriated to indicate an architecture either in or deferring to the local building tradition of an area, widely popular in the 1970s and '80s and the 2010s.

Vitrolite: a once-popular but now obsolete brightly pigmented factory-made glass used to delightful effect on many buildings of the 1930s.

Wright, Frank Lloyd (1867–1959): prolific and protean American architect, highly influential on *De Stijl* and, via it, most modern architecture.

Ziggurat: a form of pyramidal structure where the different levels are emphasized rather than smoothed away, as in many Egyptian pyramids.

A MODERNIST READING LIST

There is an enormous literature on modern architecture, and while much of it is for specialists only, a great deal of it crackles with the polemical excitement of a movement constantly redefining itself and its history. Listed below are my suggested starting places. But first, I'll recommend the most obvious handbooks to explore the British architecture of the last hundred years (or indeed the last thousand) – the multi-volume, constantly updated series begun by Nikolaus Pevsner in the 1940s, *The Buildings of England*, continued in the last few decades with *The Buildings of Wales* and *The Buildings of Scotland*, and augmented by the beautifully designed *Pevsner City Guides* that concentrate on inner-urban areas. These are the most impressive attempt to create a complete topographic and architectural mapping of anywhere in Europe, if not the world, and I would have found it absolutely impossible to write this book without them; there is little in this book that cannot be found in 'Pevsner' (as brand, not as person), although my judgements and recommendations are obviously my own. Almost as useful have been the publishing projects of the campaign and research group The Twentieth Century Society, whether through the issues of its journal *Twentieth-Century Architecture*, its *C20* magazine, and the series of accessible, illustrated monographs on *Twentieth-Century Architects*, with indispensable volumes on John Madin, Chamberlin Powell & Bon, Ryder & Yates, Alison and Peter Smithson, Arup Associates, Powell & Moya and Frederick Gibberd, among others. A more youthful and wilfully eccentric complement to these can be found in the beautifully designed issues of *The Modernist*, the journal of the Manchester Modernist Society. The first thing I would recommend anyone starting looking at modern buildings for the first time to do would be to get a pile of these and a pile of Pevsners, then go for a walk. But to go further than this, start with …

OPERATIVE HISTORIES

The historiography of modernism in Britain is controversial. Conventionally, it's a matter of thesis/antithesis, and of what Manfredo Tafuri has called 'operative histories': in other words, accounts that are as interested in bringing something to being in the present as they are in telling an accurate story about the past; now they are themselves of historical interest. Globally, the main example of this is Sigfried Giedion's *Space, Time and Architecture* (1941), but in Britain everything starts with Nikolaus Pevsner's *Pioneers of the Modern Movement: From William Morris to Walter Gropius* (1936), later retitled *Pioneers of Modern Design*. This subtle and humane book is a *longue durée* history of modernism which roots it firmly in the Arts and Crafts movement and Art Nouveau. The first attempt to challenge it was Reyner Banham's *Theory and Design in the First Machine Age* (1960), a much more academic text – those who want a more accessible and lively history by him should start with *The Age of the Masters: A Personal View of Modern Architecture* (1975). Banham downgraded the importance of the Arts and Crafts and gave far greater attention to avant-garde movements like Futurism and Constructivism, and to industry. After him, Charles Jencks's intriguingly odd *Modern Movements in Architecture* (1973) veers into a Postmodernist interest in fragmentation and paradox, while his book *The Language of Postmodern Architecture* (1977) is straightforward advocacy for modernism's alleged successor. The early Jencks is worth reading, but his pop-semiotics are trivial when compared to the work of a generation of architectural historians who shared both a certain pessimism and a grounding in Marxism.

The most read of these is Kenneth Frampton's regularly updated *Modern Architecture: A Critical History* (1980), which is sophisticated, panoramic and sharp in its historical judgements; it draws on the often dark assessments of the Venetian Marxist Manfredo Tafuri, translated into English in the gnomic and bleak *Architecture and Utopia: Design and Capitalist Development* (1976) and the two volumes (with Francesco Dal Co) of his *Modern Architecture* (1976), then an unparalleled historical and theoretical achievement. Those that appreciate Godwin's Law and New Right polemic might enjoy David Watkin's *Morality and Architecture* (1977), a frontal, sometimes scurrilous attack on Pevsner's Hegelian histories and the notion of modern architecture as zeitgeist. Less conservative counter-histories than Watkin's *Daily Mail* laments can be found in the combination of media theory and feminist critique in Beatriz Colomina's *Privacy and Publicity: Modern Architecture as Mass Media* (1994) and Katherine Shonfield's fusion of film studies, sociology, interior design and engineering in her account of British and American housing and workplaces, *Walls Have Feelings* (2000) – notably, both are rare women in this company. Martin Pawley's attempt to continue the Futurist project in very unsympathetic circumstances in *Terminal Architecture* (1998) is the anti-Watkin, and the sombre, Marxian cadences of Alan Colquhoun's *Modern Architecture* (2002) is the anti-Pawley. The most interesting recent interventions into modern architecture's history in the UK are two books by Douglas Murphy, *The Architecture of Failure* (2012), which traces modernism's emergence not out of the Arts and Crafts, but out of the florid techno-arcadia of Victorian iron-and-glass exhibition halls, and *Last Futures: Nature, Technology and the End of Architecture* (2016), a fascinating history of the radical movements of the 1960s and '70s. My own stab at intervening in this history was *Militant*

Modernism (2009), a blatantly operative and syncretic attempt to concoct a socialist modernism out of various disconnected fragments, from Constructivism to the London County Council to Bertolt Brecht and grime.

KEYS AND GUIDES

The Pevsner to Banham to Jencks to Watkin to Frampton to Pawley narrative of polemic and counter-polemic can often ignore the various guides to modern architecture that people were actually reading and relying on at the time, which can reveal a much more complex story. My personal favourite is one of the earliest, the great German Expressionist and utopian Bruno Taut's *Modern Architecture*, translated into English as early as 1929; it is less influential but vastly more enjoyable than 1920s manifestos like Le Corbusier's mistitled *Towards a New Architecture* (translated 1928) or Walter Gropius's *The New Architecture and the Bauhaus* (translated 1935). Even more fun than Bruno Taut, though only occasionally discussing architecture directly, is László Moholy-Nagy's *The New Vision* (translated 1932).

Later translations of foundational texts of the 1920s and '30s include the Soviet Constructivist manifestos of El Lissitzky, *Russia: An Architecture for World Revolution* (translated 1970) and Moisei Ginzburg, in *Style and Epoch* (translated 1982 and again in 2018) and *Dwelling* (translated 2017), along with two similarly radical books by the Czech critic Karel Teige, *Modern Architecture in Czechoslovakia* (translated 2000) and *The Minimum Dwelling* (2002), both useful for revealing just how close to the political far left the early modern movement often was. From the centre, meanwhile, worth consulting are Adolf Behne's *The Modern Functional Building* (translated 1996), and Walter Curt Behrendt's valedictory *The Victory of the New Building Style* (translated 2000), an obvious source for Pevsner. From the political right, meanwhile, Philip Johnson and Henry-Russell Hitchcock's

The International Style (1932) is questionable on dozens of levels but is of huge historical importance and gorgeously illustrated. For a history of the depoliticization of modernism from the 1920s to the 1930s, Eric Mumford's *The CIAM Discourse on Urbanism* (2002) is the book to read. A useful global survey is Jean-Louis Cohen's *The Future of Architecture since 1889* (2016).

In Britain, J. M. Richards's excellent *An Introduction to Modern Architecture* (1944) is perhaps the best place to see how modernism was sold to people here (his later *The Functional Tradition*, 1968, is a fine bit of operative history); more specialized, but with a similar aim, are F. R. S. Yorke and Colin Penn's *A Key to Modern Architecture* (1939), and Thomas Sharp's *Town Planning* (1940). A good place to take the temperature of the technocratic sixties, in terms of both built projects and paper architecture, and the dizzying possibilities of both, is Royston Landau's *New Directions in British Architecture* (1967), and for an elliptical take on the aftermath Theo Crosby's *How to Play the Environment Game* (1973).

The first of many retrospectives is Lionel Esher's *A Broken Wave: The Rebuilding of England, 1940–1980* (1981), which is nuanced, calm and informative, especially compared with paranoid nonsense like Alice Coleman's *Utopia on Trial: Vision and Reality in Planned Housing* (1985). Those looking for a condemnation of 1960s modernism by someone who has few architectural prejudices and actually likes people ought to try Nicholas Taylor's passionate and useful *The Village in the City* (1973). The nineties were fallow years for modern architectural history in the UK – the only major work is Miles Glendinning and Stefan Muthesius's fittingly monumental history of system-built points and slabs, *Tower Block: Modern Public Housing in England, Wales, Scotland and Northern Ireland* (1994). A good general history can be found in Alan Powers's *Britain: Modern Architectures in History* (2007),

and his lavishly illustrated book on the International Style in London and the Home Counties, *Modern: The Modern Movement in Britain* (2005) is fun. The largest quantity of retrospectives have been published since around 2010, and they're an interesting bunch, aside from the many vacuous photo-books. The most complete history is now Elain Harwood's gargantuan *Space, Hope and Brutalism* (2015); after Pevsner, Harwood is probably the most important popularizer and defender of modern architecture in this country; her *Guide to Post-War Listed Buildings* (2016) is also essential, as is John Grindrod's wonderful *Concretopia: A Journey around the Rebuilding of Post-War Britain* (2013), which combines giddily non-academic descriptions, serious social history and interviews with everyone alive he could find. Barnabas Calder's *Raw Concrete: The Beauty of Brutalism* (2016) can be empiricist and parochial but remains a first-rate architectural history, with beautifully considered and meticulously researched descriptions of, in particular, the work of Denys Lasdun. Otto Saumarez Smith's *Boom Cities* (2019) is a brilliant, morally and politically complex history of comprehensive redevelopment and the inner-city 'architect-planners'. It suggests there's still a lot more to be found out about this era.

PLACES AND PEOPLE

One of the best ways of understanding modern architecture in the UK is through the work of topographers who dip in and out of modernism – these would include Jonathan Meades's *Museum Without Walls* (2013) and *Pedro and Ricky Come Again* (2021), Gillian Darley's *Villages of Vision* (1975), *Factory* (2003) and *Excellent Essex* (2019), and of course Ian Nairn's *Modern Buildings in London* (1964), *Nairn's County Durham* (1964), *Nairn's London* (1967) and *Britain's Changing Towns* (1966, republished in 2013 – with an introduction and updates by me – as *Nairn's Towns*). All have sharp, eccentric and often convincing judgements. Similarly, the assessments of modern buildings in the various volumes of Edward Jones and Christopher Woodward's *A Guide to the Architecture of London* (most recently, 2016) are never less than thought-provoking, as are Adrian Jones and Chris Matthews's two topographic surveys *Jones the Planner* (2012) and *Cities of the North* (2014). A useful and sometimes harshly critical guide to 1980s (sub)urbanism is Stephanie Williams's *Docklands* (1993), and there are very insightful comments on modern, especially recent, buildings in Rowan Moore's *Why We Build* (2013) and *Slow Burn City* (2016). Historic Scotland's *Building the Future* (2009) is a very good illustrated history of Scotland's modern architecture. Also notable for their insights into how two theoretically minded modern architects saw a historic city and the motorway landscape, respectively, are Peter Smithson's *Bath: Walks around the Walls* (republished in 2017) and Alison Smithson's *AS in DS* (1982).

Many monographs exist, sometimes self-published, about major British modern architects, such as Connell Ward & Lucas, Ahrends Burton & Koralek, Wells Coates, Yorke Rosenberg & Mardall, Gillespie Kidd & Coia, Lyons Israel Ellis, Owen Luder Partnership, Alison and Peter Smithson, Ernö Goldfinger, Building Design Partnership, Sergison Bates and Zaha Hadid Architects, and sometimes on local authorities like Sheffield and the London County Council. These are mostly just photography with occasional textual padding, and are for fans only. Exceptions to this include John Allan's remarkable *Lubetkin: Architecture and the Tradition of Progress* (1992); David Lawrence's *Bright Underground Spaces* (2008) and Michael T. Saler's *The Avant-Garde in Interwar England* (2001) – both on Charles Holden, Frank Pick and the London Underground; Rowan Moore's *The New Art Gallery Walsall* (2003); Thomas Howarth's *Charles Rennie Mackintosh and the Modern*

Movement (1953); Andrew Saint's *Park Hill: What Next?* (1996); Alan Berman's *Jim Stirling and the Red Trilogy: Three Radical Buildings* (2010); and Jeremy Gould's *Plymouth: Vision of a Modern City* (2012) and *Coventry: The Making of a Modern City* (2016). The Smithsons' vigorous self-description in *Ordinariness and Light* (1970) is the sharpest book by these architects-as-theorists. Possibly the best serious history of a modern building in Britain is Alison Ravetz's *Model Estate* (1974), about the demolished Quarry Hill, in Leeds. Similarly, Celia Clark's picaresque *The Tricorn: The Life and Death of a Sixties Icon* (2008) is bursting with personality, on the failed and destroyed Brutalist mall. On housing, I strongly recommend both Lynsey Hanley's *Estates: An Intimate History* (2007) for the history from below, and John Boughton's *Municipal Dreams* (2018) for the view from above.

ONLINE

Instagram is bursting with images of modernist buildings and great specialist accounts, but the format of the scrolling feed makes it an unwise place for the uninitiated to search for information; a few good places to start include @notreallyobsessive, on London's council housing, and the self-explanatory @birminghammodernist, @liverpoolmodernist, @sheffieldmodernist, @leedsmodernist and @modernistswansea, most of them by the local chapters of the Manchester Modernist Society. Alternatively, there are those websites that document particular areas, which I've found particularly useful while composing this book. These are *Something Concrete + Modern* and *Real Tyne*, on the North-East; *Mainstream Modern* and *Modern Mooch*, on the North-West; *The Joy of Concrete*, on Clydeside; and, on everywhere, Edinburgh University's invaluable *Tower Block Archive*. That online estate agent which does modernist houses is a guilty pleasure, if you like that sort of thing.

AUTHOR'S ACKNOWLEDGEMENTS

Thank you first of all to those I've talked to online or off about bits of this book, who've suggested entries online or off, and who have come along on walks – Fatema Ahmed, Joel Anderson, Ben Austwick, Marcus Barnett, Barnabas Calder, Valeria Costa Kostritsky, Gillian Darley, Robert Doyle, Colin Ferguson, Merlin Fulcher, Pippa Goldfinger, Laura Grace Ford, David Grandorge, Lynsey Hanley, Phineas Harper, Charles Holland, Juliet Jacques, Verity-Jane Keefe, Ruth Lang, Patrick Lynch, Jonathan Meades, Douglas Murphy, Alex Niven, Stefi Orazi, Hannah Proctor, Agata Pyzik, Catherine Slessor, Otto Saumarez Smith, Daniel Trilling, Matthew Whitfield, Will Wiles, Tom Wilkinson, Ellis Woodman, Christopher Woodward and Sadie Young. And a big thank you to anyone who has ever invited me to a place over the years.

This book was written by a pedestrian, and the overwhelming majority of it was compiled via Europe's most expensive and fragmented railway network (I hope you're grateful). However, many people stepped in to drive me to places, so an especially heartfelt thank you to intrepid drivers Rob Annable, Graham Chalmers, Fiona Jardine, Adrian Jones, Richard King, Simon Manton Milne, Jonathan Salmond, Ben Thompson, Jon and Karen Topping, Oak Wells, and especially Maggie Fricker and Carol Whalen.

Thank you to Tom Penn, whose idea this book was, and who patiently accepted its many, many delays since I began it in 2015; to Richard Atkinson, for his enthusiasm, his superb and exacting editing, his always useful suggestions and for bicycle couriering from Clapham; to Richard Duguid, Sam Fulton and Imogen Scott for production; to Mark Handsley for his excellent and patient copy-editing; to Peter Dawson for his superb design and highly appropriate use of Calvert; and to Chris Matthews, for agreeing to the trying task of taking the photographs for this volume and for understanding so well what I wanted from these.

With love to Carla Whalen, my chosen companion on this island.

PHOTOGRAPHER'S ACKNOWLEDGEMENTS

The photographs within this book would not have been possible without the participation of various people and organizations. This commission was really thanks to Owen Hatherley, whose vision and thoroughness gave the project a solid foundation, and to Richard Atkinson at Penguin, who instilled a clear creative direction. The architectural photographer Gareth Gardner gave expert tuition and technical advice – without his insights the pictures would not have the same quality. Gareth also put me in touch with Ed Tyler, who was kind enough to let us use his photographs of the Glasgow School of Art building. This commission was principally based on my previous work with Adrian Jones, aka Jones the Planner. Adrian and Jean Jones also kindly provided accommodation in Yorkshire. Similarly, in North Devon, generous hospitality was given by Jenny and Julian Wilczek, who also helped with childcare. Closer to home, Julie and Paul Matthews were on hand for childcare and regular nourishment.

Access to buildings and help with general enquiries were given by the following:

James Bennett, St Catherine's College, Oxford; Roger Boden, Keble College, Oxford; Sophie Clapp, Boots, Nottingham; the Reverend Canon Kathryn Fitzsimons, Church of the Epiphany, Gipton, Leeds; Asha Eade-Green, Coventry Cathedral; Catherine Gledhill, Dartington Hall Trust, Devon; the Reverend Rachel Heskins, St John the Baptist Church, Lincoln; the Reverend Caroline Hewitt, Northenden Church and William Temple Church, Manchester; Niall Hammond, Keele; Liz Jansson, 78 Derngate, Northampton; Marcus Luporini, Kardomah Café, Swansea; Nick Milne, Robinson College, Cambridge; Mark Needham, Midland Hotel, Morecambe; Huw Moseley and Ken Williams, Kingfisher Centre, Redditch; David Rowe, Eden Project; Christopher Walker, Flax Bourton.

The Twentieth Century Society was very helpful in obtaining contacts for my Oxbridge visits, and here thanks go to Peter Ruback, Claire Price, Otto Saumarez Smith, Barnabas Calder and Geraint Franklin. Finally, I would like to thank Emily Wilczek and Ida Matthews for their immeasurable love and kindness throughout.

INDEX OF BUILDINGS

References in *italics* are to illustrations within the text; those in **bold** are to the colour plate sections.

A167(M) Pedestrian Bridges, Newcastle, 483
A9 Bridge, Helmsdale, Sutherland, 542, 554
Abbey Walk Multistorey Car Park, Grimsby, 463
Abbotsford Visitor Centre, 495, *495*
Aberystwyth, University of, 303–4, *303*
Accordia Estate, Cambridge, 174, 204, 211
Ackroydon Estate, Wimbledon, 29, 110
Adelaide House, City of London, 47–8
Adelphi Hotel, Strand, 49
AEG factory, Berlin, 26
Aga Khan Centre, King's Cross, 154, 155–6
Alban Gate (London Wall), 36, 62
Alexandra Road, Swiss Cottage, 63, 147, 148–9, 150, 151, 159, 241, 294, 504; **B.4**
Alexandra Square, Lancaster University, 452–3
All Saints Church, Clifton, Bristol, 271
Allerton Library, Liverpool, 428
Alpha Tower, Birmingham, 316, *316*
Alton Estate, Roehampton, 29, 89, 94, 110, 111, 112–13, *113*, 143, 309, 312; **A.13**
Amsterdam Stock Exchange, 47
Anderston Centre, Glasgow, 526
Andrew Melville Hall, University of St Andrews, 510–11, *510*; **B.7**
Anniesland Court, Glasgow, 525, 531
Apex Drive, Frimley, 70, 217–18, *217*; **B.9**
Apollo Bingo, Rhyl, 300
Apollo Pavilion, Peterlee, 458, 472–3, *473*, 475
Appleton Tower, University of Edinburgh, 499
Aquatics Centre, Stratford, 42
Aqueduct Village, Telford, 336
ArcelorMittal Orbit, Olympic Park, London, 155
Arden House, Hoxton, 129–30

The Ark, Hammersmith, 169
Arlington House, Margate, 234, *234*
Armada Way, Plymouth, 273, 459
Arndale Centre, Luton, 192
Arndale Centre, Manchester, 32, *33*
Arndale Centre, Poole, 259
Arnold Estate, Bermondsey, 81, *82*
Arnos Grove Underground Station, 46, 102, 137–8, 158, 436; **D.1**
Arnos Pool, Enfield, 141
34 Arthur Road, Edgbaston, 312
Artist-Constructor Houses, Flax Bourton, 254, 260–61, *261*
Arts & Social Studies Library, University of Cardiff, 296–7
Arts Building, University Centre Somerset, Taunton, 262, *262*
Arts Centre, University of Aberystwyth, 284, 303–4, *303*
Arts Faculty Buildings, 'Sidgwick Site', Cambridge, 207
Arts Tower, University of Sheffield, 40, 47, 63, 366, 369, *369*, 403–4, 502; **A.11**
Ashington House, Bethnal Green, 128
Ashley Building, University of Birmingham, 308, 312, *313*
Assembly Rooms, Derby, 260, 362
Athena Cinema, Leicester, 347; **C.3**
Attenborough Arts Centre, University of Sussex, *238*, 239
Attenborough Building, University of Leicester, 348, *349*, 350
Aub Drawing Studio, Bournemouth, 264–5, *265*
Auditorium Building, Chicago, 424

Balfron Tower, Brownfield Estate, Poplar, 127, *127*, 128, 166, 168; **B.2**
Balham Underground Station, 108
Ballance Street Council Houses, Bath, 257
Baltic Centre for Contemporary Art, Gateshead, 37, 103, 322, 458, 474, 477, 478, 496–7, 532
Bangor University, 301–2, 304–5
Bank of England, Leeds, 350, 382, *382*
Bank of England, Liverpool, *18*
Baptist Church, Bilston, 320
Barber Institute, University of Birmingham, 309

Barbican Arts Centre, London, 67–8
Barbican Estate, City of London, 30, 56, 62, 66–8, *67*, 93, 128, 144, 148, 159, 163, 205, 482; **D.12**
Barclays Bank, Lincoln, 361–2
Barclays House, Poole, 259
Barker's Pool, Sheffield, 371, 374
Barking Town Hall, 120, 286
Barking Underground Station, 126
Barnsley Indoor Market, 191, 378–9
Barton House, Bristol, 269–70
Basing View Business Park, Basingstoke, 220
Bata Estate, East Tilbury, 176–8, *177*
Bata Factory, East Tilbury, 176–8, *177*
Bata Hotel, East Tilbury, 176–8
Bata Village Hall, East Tilbury, 176–8
Bath, University of, 259, 360
Bath Technical College, 257
Battersea Power Station, 25, 53, 102, 108–9, 203, 434
Bayard House, Blackfriars, 61
BBC Scotland, Glasgow, 532
'Beach Hut in the Style of Nicholas Hawksmoor', Folkestone, 241
Beacon Arts Centre, Greenock, 539
Bear Brook Office Park, Aylesbury, 220–21, *221*
Bedford Mansions, Northampton, 347
Bedwell Suburb, Stevenage, 182–3
Bedzed, Beddington, 117–18
The Beehives, St John's College, Oxford, 227, *227*
Beetham Tower, Manchester, 38, 409, 410–11, *410*
Beeversleigh Flats, Rotherham, 217, 366, 378, *378*; **B.11**
Belgrade Theatre, Coventry, 90, 241, 325, *325*
Bell Tower, University of Aberystwyth, 303–4
Bellenden School, Peckham, 105–6, *106*
Beresford Hotel, Glasgow, 519–20
Bermondsey Station, Jubilee Line, 101–2
Bernat Klein Studio, Selkirk, 493–4, *494*; **B.19**
Berwick Workspace, Berwick-on-Tweed, 478
Bevin Court, Finsbury, 54–5, *54*, 123, 126, 162; **C.5 & C.6**

BFI Southbank (formerly Museum of the Moving Image), 84
Bilbao Metro, 133, 529
Bill Douglas Centre, University of Exeter, 257, 258
Bilston Health Centre, 320–21
Birkbeck College School of Arts, cinema, Bloomsbury, 75
Birmingham, University of, 309, 312–14, *313*, 360, 453
Birmingham Central Library (demolished), 310, 314, 315, 335, 418, 468
Birmingham New Street Signal Box, 166, 188, 314, 373
Birmingham Repertory Theatre, 314–15
135 Bishopsgate, City of London, 71
22 Bishopsgate, City of London, 78
Black Friar Pub, London, 19
Blackbird Leys, Oxford, 209
Blackburn Meadows Biomass Plant, Sheffield, 372
10 Blackheath Park, Blackheath, 96
Blackpool Tower, 448
Blackwall Tunnel, London, 35
Blaenau Gwent Civic Centre, Ebbw Vale, 289
Blavatnik School of Government, Oxford, *232*, 233
The Bluecoat, Liverpool, 432, 433
BOAC Headquarters, former, Heathrow Airport, 162, 169, 426
Bolton Town Hall, 417
Bonar Hall, University of Dundee, 542, 543
Boots D10 ('Wets'), Beeston, 161, 344, 356–7, *356*
Boots D6 ('Drys'), Beeston, 161, 344, 356–7
Boots D90, Beeston, 161, 268, 344, 360
Boscombe Pier, Bournemouth, 258
Boston City Hall, USA, 382
Boston Manor Underground Station, 157
Bourdon Building, Glasgow School of Art, 528
Bowes Road Library, Enfield, 143
Boyd Orr Building, University of Glasgow, 524, 525
Bradford, University of, 388
Bradford and Bingley headquarters, Bingley (demolished), 366, 389
Branch Hill Estate, Hampstead, 63, 147, 151–2, *152*, 223, 503
Brandon Estate, Camberwell, 89–90
Brecon County Library, 284, 292

Brindleyplace Café, Birmingham, 317
Bristol, University of, 269
Bristol & West House, Bournemouth, 258
Bristol Hotel, Bristol, 268
British Home Stores, Edinburgh, 501–2
British Library, 46, 137, 143–4, 154, 209, 242, 280, 453, 504, 530; **D.7 & D.8**
British Museum, 16, 264
British Overseas Airways Corporation (BOAC), Glasgow, 527, *527*
British Rail Maintenance Unit, Paddington, 166
Britoil Building, Glasgow, 530–31
Brixton Recreation Centre, 115
Broadcasting Place, Leeds Beckett University, 383
Broadgate House, Coventry, 324
The Broadwalk, Crawley, 216
55 Broadway, Westminster, 65
Brooke House, Basildon, 186–7, *187*
Brownfield Estate, Poplar, 127–8, *127*, 166, 168; **B.2**
Broxbourne Station, 126, 188
Brucciani's Café, Morecambe, 450
Brunel Centre, Swindon, 262–3
Brunel University, Lecture Theatre, 165
Brunswick Centre, Bloomsbury, 63, 98, 144; **B.6**
Brunswick Park Primary School Dining & Assembly Hall, Camberwell, 92
Brynmawr Rubber Factory, South Wales, 227, 284
Brynmor Jones Library, University of Hull, 463
BT Tower, Birmingham, 314, 389
Buckinghamshire County Hall, Aylesbury, 216
Bull Ring, Birmingham, 314, 317, 429
Bull Yard & City Arcade, Coventry, 308, 329
Burdock Way, Halifax, 391; **B.1**
Burrell Collection, Glasgow, 529–30, *530*
Bus Shelters, Brighton, 237, 248
Bus Station, Exeter, 256, 257
Bus Station, former, Milton Keynes, 225
Buxton House, Huddersfield, 386–7
Byker Estate, Newcastle, 102, 169, 223, 458, 476, 481, 484–5, 500; **C.10**

and Erskine's Clare Hall, 208
as last great heroic housing scheme, 35, 485, 488
Southwyck House compared to, 115
Byker Viaduct, Newcastle, 486, *487*, 488
Byron Court, Harrogate, 393–4

'Ca' d'Oro', Glasgow, 13, *14*
Cables Wynd House, Leith, 492, 500–501, *501*
Café Bar, Earl Street, Coventry, 331
Café d'Jaconelli, Glasgow, 518, 521
Café Indie, Scunthorpe, 461
Café Oto, Dalston, 136
Cala Drive, Edgbaston, 308, 312, 336
Calthorpe Estate, Edgbaston, 312
Cambridge Barracks Estate, Woolwich, 11, *11*
Cambridge Gardens, Norbiton, 110
Cambridge University Library, 25
Camden Mews, Camden, 149
Camp Grove Estate, Norwich, 199–200
Campus West, Welwyn Garden City, 192
8 Canada Square, Canary Wharf, 131
Canada Water Estate, Rotherhithe, 90–91
Canada Water Station & Bus Station, 101–2
Canary Wharf Docklands Light Railway Station, 131
Canary Wharf Underground Station, 101–2, 133, *133*; **A.15**
Candle House, Leeds, 376, 382
30 Cannon Street, City of London, 65
80 Cannon Street, City of London, 64
Canongate Redevelopment, Edinburgh, 492, 500, 501, 508
Capital Tower, Cardiff, 297
Carbrain Estate, Cumbernauld, 535
Cardiff, University of, 296–7
Cardiff Bay, 284, 298–9
Cardiff Central Station Concourse, 295
Cardiff City Hall, 295, 296
Cardiff Empire Pool, 284
Carlisle Civic Centre, 422, 451
Carlsberg Brewery, Northampton, 350
Cascades flats, London's Docklands, 42, 131–2, 133, 136

Castle House, Southampton, 245, 247

'Castle Keep', Sheffield (demolished), 372

Castle Market, Sheffield (demolished), 168, 366, 369, 372, 390, 394

Castrol House, Marylebone, 63

Catford Centre, London, 32–3, 98, 117

Cathays Park, Cardiff, 295, 296–7

Cathedral Church of St Michael & All Angels, Coventry, 308, 326, 327, 501; **C.24**

Cavendish Campus, University of Westminster, 58; **B.5**

5 Caversham Road, Kentish Town, 146, 152, 162

Cement Works, Rugby, 337

Cemex Construction Aggregate Works, Angerstein Wharf, Charlton, 100, 102, 123

Central Area Housing, Middlesbrough, 469

Central Café, Saltmarket, Glasgow, 518

Central Hill Estate, Gipsy Hill, 94–5, 95, 113, 114, 309

Central Library, Bristol, 21

Central Library, Exeter, 256

Central Library, Swinton, 413

Central Mosque, Glasgow, 530

Central Parade, Walthamstow, 122–3

Central Police Station, Cardiff, 296

Central Precinct, Coventry, 308

Central St Martin's Art School, King's Cross, 154, 155

Central Station, Merseyrail, Liverpool, 431

Centre for Mathematical Sciences, Cambridge, 211

Centre North-East, Middlesbrough, 468

Centre Point, Holborn, 60, 439

Centre Pompidou, Paris, 105

Chalkwell House, Stepney, 128

Chamberlain Gardens, Birmingham, 309–10, 312

Chandlers Ford Library, Eastleigh, 250–51

Chandos Hall, Manchester (demolished), 407

Channel 4 Building, Westminster, 71–2, 71

The Chantry, Harlow, 180–81

Chaplaincy, Lancaster University, 452, 453; **D.14**

Chapter House, Truro Cathedral, 277

Charing Cross Hotel, London, 49

Charing Cross Station, London, 36, 49

Charles Street Car Park, Sheffield, 376

Charles Wilson Building, University of Leicester, 348–50, 349

Charlotte Turner Gardens, Deptford, 98

Chartist Bridge, Blackwood, 294

Chatham Dockyard, 13, 240

Cheese Lane Shot Tower, Bristol, 267, 269

Chelmsford Indoor Retail Market, 191

Chesterfield Library, 200, 362

Chetham's School of Music, Manchester, 398, 411; **D.25**

Chichester Festival Theatre, 239

Chiswick Business Park, 170, 170

Chiswick Flyover, 163, 164

Chiswick Park Underground Station, 157, 158, 158; **A.7**

Chrisp Street Market, Poplar, 122

Christ the King, Cockfosters, 141

Christchurch House, Streatham Hill, 109–10

Church of the English Martyrs, Wallasey, 437

Church of the Epiphany, Gipton, Leeds, 367, 380, 399

Church of the Sacred Heart, Hillsborough, Sheffield, 367

Churchill College, Cambridge, 204–5, 209, 211, 246

Churchill Gardens, Pimlico, 53, 57, 521

Churchill Plaza, Basingstoke, 220

CIS Tower, Manchester, 399, 403–4, 404, 437, 502

Citigroup Tower, Canary Wharf, 131

Citrus Hotel, Cardiff, 296

City Campus, City of Glasgow College, 534

City Lit, Holborn, 74–5, 376

City of Glasgow College, 534

Civic Centre Extension & Computer Centre, Swinton, 412

Civic Centre, Mold, 284

Civic Centre, Oldham, 418–19

Civic Offices, Portsmouth, 250

Clapham South Underground Station, 108

Clare Hall, Cambridge, 208, 208, 209

Clarence Pier, South Sea, 245

15 Clerkenwell Close, Clerkenwell, 77–8, 77

Clickimin Centre, Lerwick, 557

Cliff Lift, Shanklin, 244

Cliff Road Studios, Camden, 146, 152, 163

Clifton Cathedral, Bristol, 252–3, 254, 270–71, 428; **B.30**

Clock Chambers, Wolverhampton, 321

Coal Drops Yard, King's Cross, 156

Coal Exchange, Leeds, 155

Coastguard Station, Tynemouth, 476–7

Cockaigne Housing Group, The Ryde, Hatfield, 189–90, 216

Cockfosters Underground Station, 121, 137, 138, 138, 158

Cohen House, Chelsea, 160, 171

Coleg Harlech, 284, 302–3, 302

College Bank Flats, Rochdale, 396–7, 398, 415

Colliers Wood Underground Station, 108

Combined Physics Building, University of Loughborough, 359–60

Commercial Union Tower, City of London, 62–3

Comyn Ching Triangle, Covent Garden, 36, 36

Concourse, University of Sheffield, 374

Conference Centre, Harrogate, 393

Congress House, Bloomsbury, 55, 334

Congress Theatre, Eastbourne, 241

Contact Theatre, Manchester, 73, 410

16 Cook Street, Liverpool, 13, 423

Co-operative Bank Headquarters, former, Stockport, 419

Co-operative Department Store, Coventry, 324

Co-operative Department Store, Doncaster, 377, 377

Co-operative Department Store Extension, Ipswich, 198, 377

Co-operative Department Store, Huddersfield, 120, 384–5, 384, 400, 435

Co-operative Department Store, Newcastle, 385, 435, 479–80, 480; **C.12**

Co-operative Department Store, Southport, 400, 435

Co-operative Emporium, Bradford (Sunwin House), 120, 384–5, 400, 435

Co-operative Society, Woolwich, 83, 377, 435

Co-operative Wholesale Society, Manchester, 399–400

Corn Exchange, Exeter, 256–7
Corner Fielde, Streatham Hill, 109–10
Corporation House, Middlesbrough, 469
Corpus Christi College, Leckhampton, Cambridge, 206
Corringham, Bayswater, 162–3
Cotton Gardens, Kennington, 95
Coty Cosmetics Factory, 'Brentford Golden Mile', 159
County College, Lancaster University, 452, 453
County Hall, London, 96
County Hall, Truro, 254, 276–7, 276, 278, 418; **B.18**
County Library, Morecambe, 455
Courthouse, Chesterfield, 361
Coventry, University of, 329, 330–31
Coventry Point, Coventry, 330
Coventry Railway Station, 101, 328, 334
Cowan Court, Churchill College, Cambridge, 205, 211
Cowgate Housing Towers, Edinburgh, 506, 506
Cranbrook Estate, Globe Town, 126, 162; **C.15**
Crawford's High Holborn, 49
Crawley Museum, 216
Creek Vean, Cornwall, 275
Cressingham Gardens, Tulse Hill, 95, 113–14, 209
Crestwood School, Eastleigh, 219, 250–51
Crittall Window Factory, Silver End, 175
Crystal Palace, National Sports Centre, 93
The Cube, Birmingham, 310, 318
Cumbernauld Technical College, 536
Cumbernauld Town Centre, 536
Currys Factory, 'Brentford Golden Mile', 159
Curve Theatre, Leicester, 347
Custom House, Woolwich, 11
Czech & Slovak Embassies, Notting Hill Gate, 164, 165, 166

Daily Express Building, Fleet Street, 50, 50, 161, 357, 400
Daily Express Building, Glasgow, 50, 161, 357, 400, 518–19, 519
Daily Express Building, Manchester, 50, 161, 357, 398, 400, 400; **A.14**
Daily News Building, New York City, 49

Daily Telegraph Building, Fleet Street, 50
4 Dale Street, Liverpool, 424, 429–30, 429
Daneshill House, Stevenage, 185
Darlington Town Hall, 468
Dartington Hall, Totnes, 255–6, 255; **A.6**
David Mellor Cutlery Factory, Hathersage, 363, 363
David Murray John Tower, Swindon, 262–3
Dawson Heights, East Dulwich, 6–7, 42, 93–4, 114, 168, 558; **B.13**
Dawson House, Billingham, 468–9
DC Thomson Headquarters, Dundee, 544
De Breyne Building, Keble College, Oxford, 231
De La Warr Pavilion, Bexhill-on-Sea, 178, 212–13, 214, 234–5, 235, 237, 243; **A.5**
De Montfort University, Leicester, 73, 351
Dean Clough Mills, Halifax, 388, 391
Dee of Trongate, Glasgow, 526
The Deep, Hull, 465
Defences & Shelters, Hastings & St Leonards, 235–6
78 Derngate, Northampton, 344, 345–7, 346
Design Museum, Bermondsey, 100
Devon House, Exeter, 256, 257
Devonshire Dock Hall, Barrow-in-Furness, 450, 455
Dickinson Robinson Building (1 Redcliffe), Bristol, 267–8, 267, 270
Dingles Department Store, Plymouth, 273
Dirty House, Shoreditch, 391
District Asylum Boiler House, Melrose, 494
Divinity Faculty, 'Sidgwick Site', Cambridge, 207
Dollan Baths, East Kilbride, 538, 539
Dollis Hill Synagogue, 161
Dominion Cinema, Edinburgh, 499
Donnybrook Quarter, Bow, 38, 134–5, 135, 147; **D.21**
Dorset Estate, Shoreditch, 123–4, 124, 126, 162, 524
Dove Street Flats, Stokes Croft, 268, 270
Dreamland Cinema, Margate, 234; **C.2**
Duddeston Four Estate, Birmingham, 309–10
Dudley Zoo, 308, 319–20, 319

Duffryn Estate, Newport, 294
Dumbarton Court, Streatham Hill, 109–10
Dundasvale Court, Glasgow, 522, 524, 525–6, 531
Dundee, University of, 542, 543, 543
Dundee Contemporary Arts, 542, 544, 544
Dundee Repertory Theatre, 543
Dunelm House, University of Durham, 456–7, 458, 470–71
Durham, University of, 374, 456–7, 458, 470–71, 555

E. Pellicci, Bethnal Green, 121, 288
Eaglestone, Milton Keynes, 223, 294
East Anglia, University of, 34, 174, 190, 198, 198, 338, 360
bucolic-futurist environment of, 198, 369, 394, 452, 453, 508
concrete pyramids/ziggurats at, 198, 207, 508
Sainsbury Centre at, 169, 174, 202, 202
East Finchley Underground Station, 143
East Square, Basildon, 183, 186–7, 187
East Tilbury, Essex, 141, 174, 175, 176–8, 177, 256
Eastrop Park, Basingstoke, 220
Echo Building, Loughborough, 357
Economist Plaza, St James's, London, 47, 58–9, 58, 69, 196; **A.3 & A.4**
Eden Court Theatre, Inverness, 542, 554–5, 554
Eden Project, Cornwall, 254, 280–81, 281, 304, 351
Edinburgh, University of, 297, 499, 499, 501
Edith Morley Building, University of Reading, 219
Edward Everard Printworks, Bristol, 266
Einstein Tower, Potsdam, 234
Elbephilharmonie, Hamburg, 103
Elephant and Castle Shopping Centre, Walworth, 91, 416
Elgar House, Kidderminster, 332–3
Ellenbray Toys & Stationery, Frome, 260
Elliott School, Putney, 112
Elmdon Building, Birmingham Airport, 309, 426
Elsfield, Kentish Town, 146, 147
Embankment Place, London, 49
Embassy Court, Brighton, 236, 236

Emley Moor Telecommunications Tower, 350, 389, *389*, 429
Empire Memorial Sailors' Hostel, Limehouse, 120
Endavoe & Undirhoul, Scalloway, Shetland, 542, 558
Engineering & Allied Employers' Federation, Birmingham, 310–11, *311*
Engineering Building, University of Leicester, 58, 169, 207, 230, *342–3*, 348–50, 381–2, 510–11, *606–7*
Engineering Research Station, Killingworth, 475, *476*; **A.20**
Epic Development, Sheffield, 373–4
Epping Walk Bridge, Hulme, Manchester, 409
Eros House, Catford, 69, 90, 94, 98, 117
Essex, University of, Colchester, 34, 190–91, *190*, 329, 338, 360, 369, 394, 470, 508; **A.18**
Estria Road, Edgbaston, 312
Euston Tower, London, 60
Everyman Theatre, Liverpool, 433, *433*
Exchange House, Broadgate, City of London, 71, 268
Exchange Theatre, Manchester, 398
Exeter, University of, 257–8
Express Lift Test Tower, Northampton, 350, *351*, 429
The Eye, Bristol, 267, 271

FACT arts centre, Liverpool, 432
Faculty of English, 'Sidgwick Site', Cambridge, 207
Fairfield Halls, Croydon, 90, 116
Fairwater Shopping Precinct, Cwmbran, 291
Faraday House, Queen Victoria Street, City of London, 72
Farnum House, Basingstoke, 220
Fawley Oil Refinery, 244, 246, 247
Fawley Power Station, 244
Fawood Children's Centre, Harlesden, 171
Feilden & Mawson office, Norwich, 200
Felixstowe, St Andrew's Church, 195
20 Fenchurch Street ('Walkie-Talkie'), City of London, 347
Ferndale Avenue Nursery, Wallsend, 475, 482
Finland Station, Leningrad, 273
Finlandia Hall, Helsinki, 335
Finnish Church, Rotherhithe, 89
Finsbury Health Centre, London, 52, 96, 160, 524

FirstSite gallery, Colchester, 347
Fitzgerald House, Poplar, 122
Fitzhugh Estate, Wandsworth, 110
Flaxman Building & Film Theatre, Staffordshire University, Stoke-on-Trent, 340
Fleet Road, Camden, 63, 114, 134, 147–8, *148*, 149, 223
Florey Building, Oxford, 230–31; **B.17**
The Folly, Barking, 135
Forth Rail Bridge, 15, 285, 437
Forton Services, M6, 453–4
Forum, Billingham, 467, 468
The Forum, University of Exeter, 258
Friary Court, Glasgow, 531
66 Frognal, Hampstead, 140, 156
Frognal Close, Hampstead, 140
Fulwell Cross Library & Leisure Centre, Ilford, 126
Fylingdales Solid State Phased Array Radar, Raytheon, 393

6–10 Gaisford Street, Kentish Town, 34, 146, 152, 162
Gala Fairydean Stadium, Galashiels, *490–91*, 492, 493
Gants Hill Underground Station, 46, 121–2
Garden Quadrangle, St John's College, Oxford, 233
Gardners' Warehouse, Glasgow, 13
Garton House, Hornsey, 152–3
Gateshead Station, Tyne and Wear Metro, 477; **A.9**
Gateway (now Mountbatten) House, Basingstoke, 71, 220, 530
Gateway House, Manchester, 407, *407*
Gemeentemuseum, The Hague, 504
85–91 Genesta Road, Plumstead, *82*, 83
Geography & Planning Building, University of Sheffield, 374
40 George Square, University of Edinburgh, 499
George's Dock Building, Liverpool, *24*
Gibson Street Flats, Newcastle, 480–81
Gillette Factory, Brentford, 159
Gipton, Church of the Epiphany, 80; **D.2 & D.3**
Glascarnoch Dam, 542, 550
Glasgow, University of, 380, 524–5
Glasgow College of Building & Printing, 522–3, *523*
Glasgow Film Theatre, 520, *520*

Glasgow School of Art, 20–21, 345, 514, 515–16, *516*, 528, 533–4; **A.1**
Glasgow Science Centre, 532
Glasgow Subway, 529
Gleadless Valley, Sheffield, 31, 309, 366, 367–8, *368*, 378
Golden Lane Estate, Clerkenwell, 55–6, *56*, 93, 128, 130, 369; **A.12**
Golden Mile Amusements, Blackpool, 451, 454
Goldings House & Goldings Crescent, Hatfield, 191
Goldsmiths Centre for Contemporary Art, New Cross, 106–7, *107*
Gosport Town Hall, 246
Govan Lyceum, Glasgow, 520
Govan Station, Glasgow, 529
Grafton & Estella, Portsmouth, 249
Graham Sutherland Building, Coventry University School of Art & Design, 329
Grahame Park, Colindale, 146–7
Granada Cinema, Woolwich, 83
Granary Square, King's Cross, 155
Granary Wharf, Leeds, 382
Grand Union Walk, Camden, 153, *153*, 304
Graphical House, Glasgow, 524
Gravelly Hill Interchange, Birmingham ('Spaghetti Junction'), 315
Great Hall, University of Aberystwyth, 303–4
Great Northern Tower, Manchester, 411
Green Bridge, Mile End, 134
Green Dragon Lane Estate, Brentford, 163, 164
Greenock Central Library, 538–9; **D.13**
Greenwich Town Hall, 84, 120, 195
Greig Hall, Bergen, 350
Grimsby Borough Architects, 462–3
Grimsby Central Library, 461, 462–3, *462*
Grosvenor Estate, Pimlico, 48
Grosvenor House, Birmingham, 310
Guild Hall, Preston, 445, *445*
Guildhall, Portsmouth, 250
Gulbenkian Centre, University of Hull, 463

H10 Hotel, Lambeth, 104–5
Hackney Free School, 136
Hackney Town Hall, 120
Hadrian Bridge, Newcastle, 483

Hadrian Trunk Switching Centre, Newcastle, 480–81
Haggerston School, Hackney, 129, *129*
54 Hagley Road, Birmingham, 316–17
Halifax Borough Architects Dept, 386
Halifax Headquarters, 350, 366, 382, 386, 388–9, *388*, 391, 503; **B.23**
Halifax Swimming Pool, 386
Hallfield Estate, Paddington, 162
The Hallgate Estate, Blackheath, 87–8, 93, 215, 247
Hamilton House, Bristol, 270
Hamilton Square Station, Merseyrail, Birkenhead, 431, 434
Hammersmith & West London College, 169
Hammonds of Hull, 459, 461
Harbour Lights Cinema, Southampton, 251
Harlow, St Paul's Church, 186
Harlow Market Square, 183
Harlow Town Station, 126, 166, 188
Harris Museum, Preston, 444, 445
Harvey Court, 'Sidgwick Site', Cambridge, 207, 209
Hastings Contemporary (formerly Jerwood Gallery), 235, 242
Hatfield Market Place & The Town Inn, 183, 188–9
Haus der Kulturen der Welt, Berlin, 403
Haymarket Theatre, Leicester, 350
Hayward Building, Keble College, Oxford, 231; **B.16**
Hayward Gallery, South Bank, 85
Heather Ridge Arcade, Camberley, 218
Heathgate Estate, Norwich, 199
Heathrow Hilton, 169
Hedell's Park Estate, Lerwick, Shetland, 550–51, *551*
Hemel Hempstead, Marlowes Car Park, 189
Hepworth Gallery, Wakefield, 392, *392*
Herbert Art Gallery & Museum, Coventry, 308, 331
Herbert Manzoni Building, University of Loughborough, 359–60
Hermit's Castle, Achmelvich, 542, 551–2, *552*
Heron Tower, City of London, 74
Herschel Building, University of Newcastle, 481, *481*
Hide Tower, Pimlico, 57

High and Over House, Amersham, 215, 347
High Cross House, Dartington Hall, Totnes, 255–6, *255*; **A.6**
High Kingsdown, Bristol, 254, 270
High Level Bridge, Newcastle, 15
High Point, Bradford, 390, *390*
High School, Newport, 284
63 High Street, Nairn, 550
High Sunderland, Selkirk, 493
Highfield Bus Interchange, Southampton, 245
Highgate New Town, 63, 150, *150*; **B.3**
Highland House, Salford, 413–14, *413*
Highpoint, Highgate, 27, 52, 83, 110, 139
Highpoint 2, Highgate, 27, 123, 139
Hilda Besse Building, St Anthony's College, Oxford, 229–30, 233
Hillhead Public Library, Glasgow, 528
Hillhead Station, Glasgow, 529
Hillingdon Civic Centre, Uxbridge, 168, 394
Hillman House, Coventry, 330
Hilversum Town Hall, 25, *25*, 195, 334
History Faculty, 'Sidgwick Site', Cambridge, 207, 230, 510; **B.29**
Hockley Circus, Birmingham, 314, *315*, 335, 412; **B.21**
Holburne Museum Extension, Bath, 264
Holland House, City of London, 46; **A.2**
Hollings Building ('Toast Rack'), Manchester, 398, 401–2, *401*, 405
Homes for Change, Manchester, 398, 409
Hoover Factory, Merthyr Tydfil, 288
Hoover Factory, Perivale, 159, 269, 288, 356
The Horn, Errol, near Perth, 553
Horniman Museum, Forest Hill, 79, 119
Hornsey Library, 139
Hornsey Town Hall, 25, 139, 143, 195, 225, 235
Hounslow West Underground Station, 157–8
A House for Essex, Wrabness, 193–4, *194*
House of Fraser, Cardiff, 295
Hove Town Hall, 240
Hoylake Station, 436

Huddersfield Library & Art Gallery, 385, 507
Hull, University of, 463
Hull College, 459
Hull Co-operative, 416, 461–2, *461*
Hull Railway Station, 444
Hull Truck Theatre, 465
Hulme Arch, Manchester, 409
Humber Bridge, 290, 437, 458, 463–4, *464*, 465
Hunterian Art Gallery, University of Glasgow, 524, 525
Hutchesontown, Glasgow, 531
Hutchesontown B, Glasgow, 514, 522, 526, 531
Hutchesontown C, Glasgow, 522, 531
Hyde Park Barracks, Knightsbridge, 65, 165–6
Hyde Park, Sheffield, 371–2
'Hydro' Concert Hall, Glasgow, 532

Ibex House, City of London, 51
Ibis Hotel, Nottingham, 355
Ibis Hotel, Portsmouth, 250
IBM Building, London, 548
IBM Cosham, Portsmouth, 248, 412
Ideal House, Soho, 48, 49
IG-Metall Trade Union Headquarters, Berlin, 235
iMAX cinema, Waterloo, 85
Imperial Chemical Industries, Wilton, 469
Imperial Docks Grain Elevator, Leith, 496–7, *497*
Imperial War Museum North, Trafford, 37, 42, 414, 474, 497; **B.31**
Impington Village College, Cambridgeshire, 27, 203–4, *204*
Inland Revenue HQ, Nottingham, 363
Institut Français, South Kensington, 53
Institute of Education, Bloomsbury, 64, *64*; **B.22**
International Rectifier, Newport, 294
International Wool Secretariat, Ilkley, 387–8, *387*
Isokon Building, Belsize Park, 27, 40, 110, 139–40, *140*, 236, 329
'Italian Chapel', Lamb Holm, Orkney, 542, *549*, 550

James Knott Memorial Flats, Tynemouth, 474
James Street Multistorey Car Park, Ebbw Vale, 292
James Street Station, Merseyrail, Liverpool, 431

Jesmond Library, 475, 482
Jesmond Station, Tyne and Wear
        Metro, 486, 488, *488*
John Lewis, Aberdeen, 547–8
John Lewis, Sheffield, 371
John Player Factory, Nottingham
        (demolished), 354
Jubilee Campus, University of
        Nottingham, 344, 354–5, *354*
Jubilee Library, Brighton, 241
Jubilee Line extension, London
        Underground, 37–8, 101–2,
        133
Judge Institute, Cambridge, 42, 205,
        210, *210*
'JW3' Jewish Community Centre,
        Hampstead, 156

Kardomah Café, Swansea, 288–9,
        289; **C.4**
Keble College, Oxford, *18*, 231, *231*
Keele University Chapel, Newcastle-
        under-Lyme, 308, 338, *339*;
        D.4 & D.5
Keeling House, Bethnal Green, 94,
        124–5, 348, 370
The Keep Estate, Blackheath, 87–8
Kendal's Department Store,
        Manchester, 398, 400–401, *401*
Kenmore Park School, Harrow, 141,
        143
Kensal House, Kensal Green, 160
Kensington Town Hall, 471
Kent, University of, 394
1–6 Kerry Avenue, Stanmore, 141
Kettle's Yard, Cambridge, 208–9
Kibble Palace, Glasgow, *13*, *14*
Kidz About, Swindon, 263; **B.25**
King Edward School, Birmingham,
        309
Kingfisher Centre, Redditch, 68, 335,
        336–7, *377*
'King's Cross Central', 42, 104–5,
        154–6, 211, 531
King's Cross Station, London, 15,
        154, 155
King's Gate, Victoria, 76–7
Kingsgate Bridge, University of
        Durham, 374, *456–7*, 458, 470,
        555
Kingsland Estate (Cossack Green),
        Southampton, 243–4, *243*
Kingsmead Flats, Bath, 256
Kingston Bridge, Glasgow, 526–7
Kingston Centre, Kingston-
        upon-Thames, 117
Kingsway Tunnel Ventilation Tower,
        Liverpool, 430–31, *430*
Kirkgate Centre, Bradford, 391

Knowle West Media Centre, Bristol,
        271
Kodak House, Holborn, 21, 47, 48,
        497
Kylesku Bridge, *540–41*, 542, 555

La Tourette monastery, 30, 303
Laban Centre, Deptford, 104
The Labworth, Canvey Island, 178,
        229
Lace Market, Nottingham, 355
Ladbrooke Place, Norwich, 199,
        200; **C.7**
Lakeshore Drive Apartments,
        Chicago, 30, 268–9
Lakeshore Estate, Killingworth, 475,
        476
Lambeth Towers, 94
Lanark County Buildings, Hamilton,
        276, 502, *512–13*, 514, 537;
        A.10
Lancaster, University of, 394, 452–3,
        452
Lancaster Institute for the
        Contemporary Arts, Lancaster
        University, 452, 453
Lancastrian Hall, Swinton, 413
Lanchester Library, University of
        Coventry, 73, 330–31, *331*; **C.21**
The Lane Estate, Blackheath, 87–8
Lanes Centre, Carlisle, 451
Langham House Close, Ham, 111–12
Langlee Estate, Galashiels, 367, 493
Lansbury Estate, Poplar, 29, 122,
        394
Lantern, Blackburn Cathedral, 442
Larkhall Estate, Clapham, 108
The Laurieston Pub, Glasgow, 531
Laver Building, University of Exeter,
        257, 258; **C.18**
Law Faculty, 'Sidgwick Site',
        Cambridge, 207
The Lawn, Harlow, 180; **C.14**
Leadenhall Building
        ('Cheesegrater'),
        City of London, 73–4
The Leas, Folkestone, 240–41
Lee House, Manchester, 399
Lee Longlands, Derby, 358, 435
Leeds, University of, South Campus,
        93, 205, 366, 381–2, *381*; **B.32**
Leeds Beckett University, 383
Leeds City Station Concourse, 380
Leeds Inner Ring Road, Woodhouse
        Lane Section, 380–81, 406, 527
Leeds Town Hall, 417
Leicester, University of, 58, 169,
        207, 230, *342–3*, 344, 348–50,
        381–2, 510–11, *606–7*

Leigham Court Road Sheltered
        Housing, Streatham, 114
Lenton Flats, Nottingham
        (demolished), *32*
Lever House, New York, 404
Lewisham Park, 92
Leyland Motor Company, Glasgow,
        518
Liberty's department store,
        Regent Street, 49
Library, University of Edinburgh,
        297, 499, 501
Library, University of Portsmouth,
        250
Lijnbaan, Rotterdam, 324
LILAC housing co-operative, Leeds,
        39, 189, 271, 383
Lillington Gardens Estate, Pimlico,
        34, 57, 76, 169, 209, 249, 360,
        469; **C.16**
Lime Street Station, Merseyrail,
        Liverpool, 431
Lincoln, University of, 358
Lincolnshire Motor Company
        Showrooms, Lincoln, 358
Lion Chambers, Glasgow, 517–18
Little Bispham Tram Station,
        Blackpool, 448
Liverpool, University of, 428–9
Liverpool Anglican cathedral, 426,
        428
Liverpool Medical Institution, 433
Liverpool Playhouse Extension,
        429
Lloyd's of London, 37, 41, 46, 68,
        69–71, *69*, 72, 144, 218, 244,
        263; **B.28**
Llwyn Isaf Park, Wrexham, 301
London School of Economics, 75–6
London Zoo, Aviary, 145
London Zoo, Elephant House,
        145, 525
London Zoo, Penguin Pool, 138–9,
        145, 320
Loughborough, University of,
        359–60
Loughborough Junction Estate,
        Brixton, 115
Loughton Underground Station,
        179, *179*
Lower Precinct Mural, Coventry,
        325; **C.17**
Lowry Arts Centre, Salford Quays,
        414
Ludham & Waxham, Gospel Oak,
        147
Luma Lightbulb Factory, Glasgow,
        520
Luton Airport, EasyJet Hangars, 192

M8, Glasgow, 406, 526–7

Maggie's Dundee, Ninewells Hospital, 542, 545, 555

Maggie's Fife, Victoria Hospital, Kirkcaldy, 37, 511, 556

Maggie's Glasgow, Gartnavel General Hospital, 511, 514, 532–3, *533*, 555

Maggie's Highlands, Raigmore Hospital, Inverness, 555–6

Magistrates' Court, Blackpool, 454–5

Magistrates' Court, Chorley, 443–4

Magistrates' Court, Northampton, 348

Magistrates' Court, Sheffield, 374

Magna Science Adventure Centre, Rotherham, 379

Maiden Lane Estate, Camden, 114, 134, 151, 156, 355, 503

Maidenhead Library, 219, *219*, 250

The Mailbox, Birmingham, 318

Maisons Jaoul Houses, outside Paris, 30, 112, 165, 239

The Malings, Newcastle, 458, 489

Manchester, University of, 401–2, 405, 408
  UMIST, 406–7

Mancunian Way Flyover, Manchester, 406

Manor House Underground Station, 137

Manors Car Park, Newcastle, 483

Marconi factory, Chelmsford, 26

Mareel Arts Centre, Lerwick, 557

Margate Railway Station, 22, *22*, 23

Margery Fry Building, Somerville College, Oxford, 228–9

Marine Court, St Leonards, 236–7

Maritime Academy, Warsash, 246–7

Mark Hall, Harlow, 180–81; **C.8**

Mark Hall North, Harlow, 180, 183

Market & Clock Tower, Shipley, 385–6, *386*

Markham Moor Service Station, 41, 301, 344, 358, 359

The Matchworks, Liverpool, 424

Mathematics Building, University of Southampton, 245

Maths & Social Sciences Building, UMIST, 406–7

Matrix House, Basingstoke, 220

Mea House, Newcastle, 483

Meakin Estate, Bermondsey, 81

Meeting House, University of Sussex, 239

Melbourne Court, Newcastle, 480–81

Memorial Garden & St Matthew's Close, Walsall, 181, 321

Merrion Centre, Leeds, 378

Mersey Tunnel Entrance, Liverpool, 424, 425

Mersey Tunnel structures, Liverpool/Birkenhead, 422, 424–5, 426, 430–31, *430*, 434, *435*

Mersey Tunnel Ventilating Station, Liverpool, 424–5

Merseyrail, Liverpool, 431, 488

Merseyrail Stations, Liverpool, 431

Merseyway Centre, Stockport, 415–16, *416*

Metallurgy & Minerals Building, University of Birmingham, 313, 360

Metro Central Heights, Walworth (former Alexander Fleming House), 91–2, 129, 186

Metropolitan Cathedral, Liverpool, 79, 183, 270, 426, 427–8; **C.27 & C.28**

Metropolitan Centre, Barnsley, 379, *379*

Metropolitan House, Birmingham, 316–17

MI6 Headquarters, Vauxhall, 36

Michael Faraday Memorial, Walworth, 91

Middle East Centre, St Anthony's College, Oxford, 230, *232*, 233

Middlesbrough Institute of Modern Art, 468

Middlesex Street Estate, Whitechapel, 128

Midland Hotel, Morecambe, 422, 447, *447*

Milford Towers, Catford, 98

Millennium Bridge, Gateshead, 37, 414, 458, 465, 477, 478, 532

Millennium Bridge, London, 102

Millennium Centre, Cardiff, 284, 298–9; **C.24**

Millennium Dome, North Greenwich, *37*, 155

Millennium Galleries, Sheffield, 375

Millennium Mills, Royal Victoria Dock, 119–20, 123, 474

Millennium Stadium, Cardiff, 298

Millennium Village Phase 1, Greenwich, 102

Milton Keynes, Art Gallery & Theatre, 226

Milton Keynes, Shopping Building, 100, 214, 440

Milton Keynes Railway Station, 214, 224–5, *225*; **A.19**

Milton Keynes Station Square, 224–5

Ministry of Defence, London, 28

Monte Carlo Café, Halifax, 386

Moore Street Electricity Substation, Sheffield, 373, *373*, 494

Moorfields Station, Merseyrail, Liverpool, 431

Moorfoot, Sheffield, 374–5

Moray Mews, Finsbury Park, 38; **D.22**

Morden Underground Station, 108

Morris Walk Estate, Charlton, *10*

Moscow Planetarium, 348

Moss Heights, Glasgow, 514, 520–21, 531

Mostyn Gallery (Oriel Mostyn), Llandudno, 304, *304*

The Mount, Campden Hill, 163

Mountbatten (formerly Gateway) House, Basingstoke, 71, 220, 530

Muirhead Tower, University of Birmingham, 313–14; **B.12**

Multistorey Car Park, Truro, 277–8

Murray Edwards College, Cambridge, 205, 209

Murray Mews, Camden, 116, 140, 149

Murray's Mills, Ancoats, Manchester, *13*

Museum of London, 62

Museum of Scotland, Edinburgh, 355, 503–4, *503*

Museum of the Moving Image (now BFI Southbank), 84

National Film Theatre, Southbank, 84

National Library of Scotland Causewayside Building, Edinburgh, 492, 503

National Maritime Museum, Falmouth, 280

National Provincial Bank, St Andrew's Cross, Plymouth, 273

National Space Centre, Leicester, 351

National Theatre, Southbank, 44–5, 46, 84, 144; **B.24**

NatWest Tower, Birmingham, 310

NatWest Tower, City of London, 61, 66, 73, 439

Neckinger Estate, Bermondsey, 81

Nelson Barracks Estate, Norwich, 199

Netherfield, Milton Keynes, 223, 233, 294, 441

Netherthorpe, Sheffield, 367, 372

The Never Turn Back Pub, Caister-on-Sea, 197, *197*

New Art Gallery, Walsall, 118, 264, 304, 308, 321, 322–3, *323*, 355, 556

New Ash Green Estate, near Dartford, 87, 240, 247

New Century House, Manchester, 403, 404

New Civic Buildings, Paisley, 537

The New Club, Edinburgh, 501–2

New Court, Christ's College, Cambridge, 206–7, *206*

New Hall Place, Liverpool, 431

New Tyne Bridge, 437, 458, 466, 477, 479, *479*, 483; **C.11**

New Ways, Northampton, 175, 215, 300, 344, 345, 347

New York Times Building, Manhattan, 105

Newbury Park Underground Station Bus Shelter, 121, 122

Newcastle, University of, 481

Newcastle City Centre Walkway System, 62, 310, 382, 431, 483–4

Newcastle Civic Centre, 276, 471, 482; **C.13**

Newcastle Railway Station, 101

Newport Civic Centre, 286–7

Newport Street Gallery, Vauxhall, 118

Newton Building, Nottingham Trent University, 352; **D.10 & D.11**

Ninewells Hospital, Dundee, 545

NLA Tower, Croydon, 116, *116*

Non-Academic Staff Building, University of Bath, 259, 260

Norrish Library, Portsmouth, 214, 249–50, *249*; **B.15**

North Euston Hotel, Fleetwood, 451

North Lincolnshire Civic Centre, Scunthorpe, 460, *460*

North Woodside Estate, Glasgow, 528

Northam Estate, Southampton, 244–5

Northcote House, University of Exeter, 257

Northgate House, Darlington, 469

Northumbria, University of, Newcastle, 483

Norwich City Hall, 195–6, *196*, 286

Norwich House, Liverpool, 423, 424

Notarianni's Milk Bar & Restaurant, Eastbourne, 237

Nottingham Contemporary, 118, 344, 355; **D.15 & D.16**

Nottingham Playhouse, 352, *353*, 395

Nottingham Trent University, 352

Nottingham University, 354–5

Nuclear Physics Laboratory, Oxford, 230, *231*

Nuffield College, Oxford, 227

Nuffield Theatre, Southampton University, 245

Number 1 Poultry, City of London, 72

Oakwood Underground Station, 137, 138

Oasis Leisure Centre, Swindon, 263

Ocean Court, Stonehouse, Plymouth, 274

Odeon Cinema, Hanley, 338

Odeon Cinema, Harrogate, *364–5*, 393

Odeon Cinema, Loughborough, 357

Odeon Cinema, Newport, 287, *287*

Odeon Cinema, Woolwich, 83

Odhams Walk, Covent Garden, 34

66 Old Church Street, Chelsea, 160

Old Fishmarket Close Housing, Edinburgh, 506

Old Library, Lerwick, Shetland, 553

Old Library, University of Exeter, 257, 258

Old Vic Annex, Lambeth, 89

Oldbury Wells School, Bridgnorth, 162, 333

Oldham Art Gallery & Library, 419

Olympic Stadium, Helsinki, 448

One Arthouse Square, Liverpool, 432

One Canada Square, Canary Wharf, 71, 131, 133

One Pancras Square, King's Cross, 154, *155*

One Smithfield, Hanley, 340

Oriel Chambers, Liverpool, 13, 229, 418, 422, 423–4, *423*, 430

Oriel Mostyn (Mostyn Gallery), Llandudno, 304, *304*

Ormskirk Street United Reformed Church, St Helens, 440

Orozco Garden, Camberwell, 88–9

Oslo City Hall, 482

Ossulston Estate, Somers Town, 41, 81, 108, 137, 546

Osterley Underground Station, 46, 157

Ostrava Town Hall, 507

Otoprojects, Dalston, 135–6

Our Lady & St Francis School, Glasgow, 523–4

Our Lady of Fatima, Harlow, *180*, 181

Our Lady's High School, Cumbernauld, 536; **A.17**

Ouseburn Farm, Newcastle, 489

Owens Park, Fallowfield, Manchester, 405

Oxford Road Station, Manchester, 403, *403*

219 Oxford Street, London, 55

Paddington Station, London, 13, 15

Palace of Art, Glasgow, 519–20

Palestra, Southwark, 104

Pallant House Gallery, Chichester, 209, 242, 280

Palm House at Kew Gardens, 13

Palmer Building, University of Reading, 219

Pannier Market, Plymouth, 254, *272*, 273–4

The Parade, University of Bath, 259

Park Hill housing estate, Sheffield, 31, 354, 366, 368, 370–71, *370*, 467

neglect/defacing of, 303, 332, 370–71, 402

in steeply falling landscape, 94, 277, 371

and 'streets in the sky', 10, 131, 199, 247, 370, 381

and Urban Splash, 269, 370–71, 402, 484

Park Royal Underground Station, 157–8; **A.8**

Parkleys Estate, Ham, 87, 111–12, *111*, 218, 247, 441; **C.9**

Parkside, Finsbury Park, 154

'Parson's Polygon' ventilation shaft, Newcastle, 486, 488

pathways and landscaping, Cumbernauld, 535; **C.19 & C.20**

Paton Watson Quadrate, Plymouth, 274

Pavilion Café, Avenham Park, Preston, 446

Pearl Assurance House, Plymouth, 273

Peckham Library, 42, 103, 104, 134

Pedways, City of London, 60–62, *61*, 66–7, 382, 431, 483

Pegasus Court, Grahame Park, Colindale, 38, 146–7

Penrhys, Rhondda, 291–2

Peppers Ltd, Hanley, 338

Percy Circus, Finsbury, 54

47A Percy Gardens, Tynemouth, 477

Perivale Underground Station, 157

Persistence Works, Sheffield, 376

Peter Jones Department Store, Chelsea, 160, *161*

Philharmonic Hall, Liverpool, 422, 426, 437

Physics Tower, University of Exeter, 257–8, *258*

111 Piccadilly, Manchester, 405–6

Piccadilly Centre, Manchester, 32

Piccadilly Circus Underground Station, London, 48, 121

Piccadilly Plaza, Manchester, 340, 406, 407

Pier Arts Centre, Stromness, Orkney, 556, *556*, 557; **D.20**

Pier 6 Connector, Gatwick Airport, 221

Pilkington Headquarters, St Helens, 422, 437–8; **A.16**

Pilkington Library, University of Loughborough, 359–60

Pimlico Ventilation Shaft, 68, 337

Pioneer Health Centre, Peckham, 81, 520

Pirelli Tower, Milan, 316

Pitt Rivers Museum, Oxford, 16

Plastic Classroom, Preston, 409, 422, 445–6, *446*, 451

Plaza Cinema, Port Talbot, 288

Pleasure Beach Casino, Blackpool, 448–50, *449*

Plimsoll Swing Bridge, Bristol, 267

Plymouth Civic Centre, 273

Plymouth Guildhall, 273

The Pods, Scunthorpe, 460–61

The Point, Milton Keynes, 225–6, *226*

Point Royal, Bracknell, 216–17

Police Headquarters, Blackpool, 454–5, *454*

Police Headquarters, Wrexham, 300–301, 303

Police Station, Chorley, 443–4

Police Station, Northampton, 348

Polish Cultural & Social Association (POSK), Hammersmith, 166

Polygon Road, King's Cross, 150–51

Pont Transbordeur, Marseille, 285

Pontio, Bangor, 304–5

Poplar Town Hall, 120–21

Port Talbot Steelworks, 288

Portcullis House, Westminster, 65, 71, 72, 363

Portes cochères, Milton Keynes, 222, *224*, 225

Porthill Court, Aberdeen, 546–7

Portsdown Park, Portsmouth (demolished), 32

Portsmouth, University of, 250

Post Office, Kirkwall, Orkney, 552–3, *553*

Post Office, Scunthorpe, 459

Post Office Tower, Fitzrovia, 59, *59*, 66, 429

Potteries Museum & Art Gallery, Hanley, 308, 340, 341, *341*

Prague Pensions Institute, 96

The Precinct, Coventry, 324

Precinct Centre, University of Manchester, 408

Prefabs, Wythenshawe, 401

Preston Bus Station, 42, 193, 350, 382, *420–21*, 422, 444

Prince Street Car Park, Bristol, 268

Prince's Tower, Rotherhithe, 100

Princessshay, Exeter, 256, 257

The Priory Estate, Blackheath, 87–8

The Public, West Bromwich, 103, 505

Public Baths, Northampton, 345, 348

Public Toilets, Hay-on-Wye, 288

Public Toilets, Westbourne Grove, 170, 317

Pullman Court, Streatham Hill, 109–10, *109*

Purcell Room, South Bank, 85

Pyrene Factory, 'Brentford Golden Mile', 159

Quarry Hill flats, Leeds (demolished), 366, 380

Queen Anne's Gate, Westminster, 65, 165

Queen Elizabeth Hall, Oldham, 418–19

Queen Elizabeth Hall, South Bank, 85, 419

Queen Elizabeth II Law Courts, Liverpool, 431–2

Queen Elizabeth Square, Glasgow, 531

Queen Margaret Union, University of Glasgow, 524, 525

Queen Mary College, London, 75

Queen Square, Crawley, 216

60 Queen Victoria Street, City of London, 66, 72; **D.26**

Queen's Building, De Montfort University, Leicester, 73, 351; **C.22**

Queens Café, Govanhill, Glasgow, 518, 521

Queen's Gardens, Hull, 459

Queen's House, Greenwich, 123

Queensgate Market, Huddersfield, 366, 390–91; **B.20**

Queensway, Crawley, 216

Queensway, Stevenage, 183, 184–5, *185*

Queensway Towers, Southend, 191

R7, King's Cross, 154, 155

Radar Station, Fleetwood, 450–51, *450*

Radisson Hotel, Glasgow, 532

Radomes, RAF Menwith Hill, Radio Corporation of America, 393, 455

Raigmore Hospital, Inverness, 555–6

Ramsden House, Huddersfield, 386–7

Rankine Building, University of Glasgow, 524, 525

Ratcliffe-on-Soar Power Station, 361, *361*, 372

Ravenscourt Park Hospital, Hammersmith, 158, 497

Reading, University of, 218–19

Red House, Chelsea, 170–71

Red House, south-east London, 17

Redbridge Underground Station, 121–2

1 Redcliffe (Dickinson Robinson Building), Bristol, 267–8, 270

Redcliffe Flats, Bristol, 254, 266–7, *266*, 268

Redditch Central Library, 335

Reflection Court, St Helens, 437

Regent Court, Hillsborough, Sheffield, 367

Regent's Park Mosque, London, 126, 530

Regent's Park Villas, London, *35*

Regional Seat of Government, Accordia Estate, 204, 211

Registry Office, Preston, 443

Reid Building, Glasgow School of Art, 528, 533–4

Retail Market, Coventry, 325–6

Retaining Wall, Inner Ring Road, Kidderminster, 332–3, 335–6

Ritz Hotel, London, 424

Riverside Campus, City of Glasgow College, 534

Roath Lock Studios, Cardiff, *282–3*, 299

Robin Hood Gardens, Poplar, 56, 128, 130–31, 147, 293

Robinson College, Cambridge, *172–3*, 209–10, 536, 538

Rochdale Town Hall, 415

Roche Chemicals, Welwyn Garden City, 178

Rockefeller Center, New York City, 49

Rogano's, Glasgow, 518, 521

Roger Stevens Building, University of Leeds, 381–2, *381*; **B.32**

Rogers House, Wimbledon, 115–16

Ronchamp chapel, 443, 551

Rosebery Mansions, King's Cross, 154, 155
Rosemount Square, Aberdeen, 108, 137, 542, 546, *546*
Rothschild's, City of London, 42, 76
The Rotunda, Birmingham, 314, 429
The Round House, Barrow-in-Furness, 455
Royal Albert Memorial Museum Extension, Exeter, 256, 257
Royal Arcade, Norwich, 19, *20*, 195
Royal College of Physicians, Regent's Park, 144, *145*
Royal Commonwealth Pool, Edinburgh, 492, 502, *502*
Royal Conservatoire, Glasgow, 528
Royal Corinthian Yacht Club, Burnham-on-Crouch, 27, 176, 448
Royal Exchange Theatre, Manchester, 408–9, *408*
Royal Festival Hall, London, 29, 41, 55, 84, 90, 325
Royal Liver Building, Liverpool, 47, 424
Royal Opera House, 223
Royal Spa Centre, Leamington Spa, 335
Royal William Victualling Yard, Plymouth, 274
Runcorn Shopping City, 439–40
Rush Common Council Flats, Brixton Hill, 109
Ruskin Library, Lancaster University, 452, 453
Ruskin Park House, Camberwell, 80
Russell Court, Cambridge, 209

Sackler Restaurant, Hyde Park, London, 233
Sage Music Centre, Gateshead, 37, 477–8, 532
Said Business School, Oxford, 233
Sainsbury Centre, University of East Anglia, Norwich, 169, 174, 202, *202*
Sainsbury's, Camden, 153, 304
St Andrew & St George Parish Church, Stevenage, 184; **C.26**
St Andrew's Court, Gravesend, 238
St Andrew's Gardens, Liverpool ('Bull Ring'), 108, 137, 422, 425–6, *425*, 546
St Andrew's House, Edinburgh, 492, 497–8, *498*
St Andrews, University of, 510–11, *510*
St Anthony's College, Oxford, 229–30, *232*, 233

St Austell Library, 275, 276
St Bernard's Houses, Croydon, 116–17, *117*, 178
St Bride's Church, East Kilbride, 514, 537–8; **D.6**
St Catherine's College, Oxford, 63, 209, 214, 228, *228*, 350; **D.24**
St Charles Borromeo, Kelvinside, Glasgow, 521–2
St Cross Church, Glasgow, 20
St Cross Libraries, Oxford, 200, 228, *229*
St Cuthbert's Co-operative, Edinburgh, 497
St David's Hall, Cardiff, 297–8
St David's Hotel, Harlech, 303
St Dunstan's College Dining Hall, Catford, 92
St Enoch Centre, Glasgow, 531
St Enoch Station, Glasgow, 529
St Fagans National Museum of History, Cardiff, 284, 297
St Gabriel's Church, Blackburn, 437, 442
23 St George's Street, Canterbury, 237–8
St James' Barton, Bristol, 269–70
St James Park Stadium, Newcastle, 486
St James the Less, Pimlico, 57
St James's Station, Tyne and Wear Metro, 486
St John the Baptist, Lincoln, 344, 358–9, *359*; **C.25**
St John's Beacon, Liverpool, 246
St John's Beacon, Liverpool (Radio City Tower), 389, 429
St John's Centre, Liverpool, 429
St John's Church, Barrow-in-Furness, 448
St John's College, Oxford, 227, 231, 233
St John's Estate, Bermondsey, 81
St Leonards Place, Norwich, 199, 200
30 St Mary Axe ('Gherkin'), City of London, 38, 47, 73–4, 460
St Mary's Church, Leyland, 442–3, *443*
St Mary's Church, Woolwich, 8
St Michael & All Angels Church, Wythenshawe, 80, 398, 399; **D.28**
St Monica's Church, Bootle, 435–6, *436*, 437, 442
St Nicholas Centre, Aberdeen, 547, *548*
St Nicholas's Church, Gipton, Leeds, 380

St Olaf House, Southwark, 81, 237
St Olave's Estate, Bermondsey, 81
St Pancras Station, London, 13, 15, 16, 101, 154
St Paul's Church, Bow Common, 125
St Paul's Tower, Sheffield, 375, 376
St Peter's Arcade, Liverpool, 257, 432–3
St Peter's Church, Wolverhampton, 322
St Peter's Seminary, Cardross, 514
St Saviour's Church, Eltham, 80, *80*, 399, 436
St Saviour's Church, Paddington, 168
St Stephen Walbrook Church, City of London, 76
St Thomas' Hospital, Lambeth, 96, 440
St Thomas White Building, St John's College, Oxford, 231; **D.23**
St Vincent Street Chambers ('Hat Rack'), Glasgow, 517–18
St Wilfrid's Church, Brighton, 237
Salford, University of, 412
Salford Civic Centre, 25, 195, 412
Salford MediaCity, 414
Salford Technical College, former, University of Salford, 412
Salmon Leap Flats, Chester, 441, *441*
Saltash Library, 275–6, *275*
Salters Hall (London Wall), 62
Salvation Army Hostel, Newcastle, 486
Sassoon House, Peckham, 81
Saut Girnal Wynd & The Towers, Dysart, 493, 500, 508, 550–51
Savoy Centre, Glasgow, 527–8
Savoy Hotel, Strand, 49
Saw See Hock Student Centre, London School of Economics, 75–6
Saxon Court, King's Cross, 154, 155
Scale Lane Swing Bridge, Hull, 465
Scalloway Museum, 558
Scapa Flow Fortifications, Orkney, 542, 549–50
Sceaux Gardens, Camberwell, 88, 309
School of Architecture & Engineering, University of Bath, 259–60
School of Art & Design, Wolverhampton, 321
School of Biological Sciences, Brambell Building, Bangor University, 301–2

School of Construction Management & Engineering, Reading, 218–19

School of Oriental & African Studies Library, Bloomsbury, 64

School of Slavonic & East European Studies, Bloomsbury, 73

Schröder House, Utrecht, 504

Scotland Street School, Glasgow, 20–21, 516, 517, *517*

Scottish Ambulance Service, Glasgow, 524

Scottish Parliament, Edinburgh, 492, 504–5, *505*

Scottish Widows, Edinburgh, 502–3

Scunthorpe Central Library, 464

SeaCity, Southampton, 379

Seamount Court, Aberdeen, 542, 546–7; **A.22**

Segedunum Roman Fort Visitor Centre, Wallsend, 478

Selfridges, Birmingham, 317

Senate House, London, 40, 51, 138, 295; **D.9**

Senedd, Cardiff, 284, 298–9, *298*

Severn Bridge/Pont Hafren, 276, 290, *291*, 437, 463

Severn Crossing, Second (1996), 290

Shakespeare Centre, Stratford-upon-Avon, 333–4

Shakespeare Memorial Theatre, Stratford-upon-Avon, 332

The Shard, Borough, 78, 105

Sheep Street Shops, Stratford-upon-Avon, 333

Sheffield, University of, 369, 374, 376

Shell Centre, South Bank, 87

Shell UK Exploration & Production Ltd, Aberdeen, 530, 548

Shell-Haus, Berlin, 51

Shell-Mex House, Embankment, 49

Shetland Museum & Archives, Hay's Dock Café, Lerwick, 557

Shirehall, Shrewsbury, 334–5

Shopping Building, Milton Keynes, 223–4

Shredded Wheat Factory, Welwyn Garden City, 175, 178, 424

Shrewsbury Market Hall, 308, 334, *334*

'Sidgwick Site', Cambridge, 207, 209, 362; **D.27**

Sidney Street Ventilation Tower, Birkenhead, 434

Siedlung Halen, Bern, Switzerland, 116

Silver End, Essex, 174, 175, 215, 347

Silver Jubilee Bridge, Runcorn, 437

Simmonds Aerocessories Factory, 'Brentford Golden Mile', 159

Simpson's, Piccadilly, 51

Sky Tower, Rhyl, 300

Smallbrook, Queensway, Birmingham, 311

Smithdon School, Hunstanton, 30, 174, 196–7, 228, 428

Snamprogetti House, Basingstoke, 220

Solar Campus, Wallasey, 41, 438–9

Solarhus, Lerwick, 557

Somerset Estate, Battersea, 90–91

Somerville College, Oxford, 228–9

Somerville Square & Coltburndale, Burntisland, 367, 493, 500, 507–8, 550–51

Sound House, University of Sheffield, 376

Sound Mirror, Redcar, 393, 466

South Bank Centre, London, *2–3*, 30, 84, 85, *86*, 87, 324

South Bank Coke Oven Tower, Middlesbrough, 466, *467*

80–90 South Hill Park, Hampstead, 143

South London Gallery, Camberwell, 88–9

14 South Parade, Bedford Park, 157

South Wimbledon Underground Station, 108

South Yorkshire Police Headquarters, Sheffield, 374

Southampton, University of, 245, 359, 481

Southampton Benches, 243, 244

Southampton Civic Centre, 286

Southampton Way Estate, Camberwell, 89

Southgate housing scheme, Runcorn (demolished), 440

Southgate Underground Station, 137, 138

Southside Garage, Edinburgh, 496, *496*

Southwark Station, 101–2

Southwyck House, Brixton, 115

Spa Green, Finsbury, 46, 52, *53*, 139, 162

Space House, Holborn, 47, 59, 75

Speke Aerodrome, Liverpool, 309, 422, 426–7; **D.17**

Spinnaker Tower, Portsmouth, 246

Sports Centre, University of Liverpool, 428–9

Sports Centre Extension, Coventry, *306–7*, 308, 330

Stafford Railway Station, 334

Staffordshire, University of, 340

Stansted Airport, 41, 174, 192–3, 202, 221, 281, 426

Star and Shadow Cinema, Newcastle, 305, 458, 489

State Cinema, Grays, 179

Station Hall, Middlesbrough, 467

Stephen Lawrence Centre, Deptford, 104

Stevenage Station, 126, 188

Stirling, University of, 257, 338, 492, 508–9, *509*, 545, 555; **A.21**

Stockholm Central Library, 137–8

Stockholm City Hall, 25, 195–6, 334

Stockport Town Hall, 418

Stopford House, Stockport, 416, 418, 455

The Stow, Harlow, 181

Strathcona Building, University of Birmingham, 312, *313*

Sudbury Town Underground Station, 157–8

Sugden's Mill Silos, Brighouse, 385

Sun Centre, Rhyl, 284

Sun House, Hampstead, 22–3, *23*, 30, 139, 140

Sun Houses, Amersham, 215

Sunderland Civic Centre, 322, 471–2, *471*

Sunderland Museum & Library, 470

Sunny Blunts, Peterlee, 472–3, 475

Sunnymead Flats, Crawley, 215

Susan Lawrence School, Poplar, 122

Sussex, University of, 165, 190, 238–9, *239*, 245, 338, 360, 369, 394, 452, 453, 482, 501

Swan House, Newcastle, 483; **B.10**

Swansea Civic Centre, 293, *293*, 303; **B.14**

Swansea Guildhall, 195, 284, 286, *286*; **D.18**

Swansea Indoor Market, 289

Sydney Harbour Bridge, 479

Sydney Hotel, Bath, 264

Tamar Suspension Bridge, 275, 276

Target House, St James's, London, 69

Tate & Lyle Sugar Refinery, Silvertown, 123

Tate & Lyle Sugar Silo, Liverpool, 427, *427*, 430

Tate Britain, Pimlico, 118, 278

Tate Liverpool, 278

Tate Modern, Southwark, 76, 102–3, 203, 278, 434, 474

Tate St Ives, 209, 278–9, *279*, 504, 556

Taylor Street Ventilation Tower, Birkenhead, 434

Tees Transporter Bridge, Middlesbrough, 15, 458, 466
Telephone Exchange, Hanley, 340
Temple of Peace and Health, Cardiff, 295, 296
1 Temple Way, Bristol, 270
Templewood School, Welwyn Garden City, 182
Tennis & Bowls Pavilion, Wythenshawe, 402
Thames Barrier, Charlton, 99, *99*
Thames Barrier Park, Silvertown, 123, 132
'Thames Gateway' flats and houses, 178
Thamesmead Estate, 96–8, *97*
Theatre Royal Extension, Glasgow, 534
Theatre Royal Extension, York, 395, *395*
Theatre Royal, Plymouth, 274, 352
Theological College, Chichester (now old people's home), 239
Thomas Linacre Centre, Wigan, 415
Tidal Surge Barrier, Hull, 465
Tinsley Viaduct, Sheffield, 372
Tooting Bec Underground Station, 108, 157
Tooting Broadway Underground Station, 108
Torness Nuclear Power Station, Dunbar, 495
Tottenham Court Road Underground Station, 68, 337
Tower Building, University of Cardiff, 296–7
Tower Building, University of Dundee, 543, *543*
The Towers, University of Loughborough, 359–60
Town Centre, Cumbernauld, 514
Town Centre Gardens, Stevenage, 182–3, *183*, 184
Town House, Kirkcaldy, 507
Town Square, Stevenage, 181, 183, 184–5, 186
Towner Gallery, Eastbourne, 241
Toynbee Hall, Whitechapel, 119
Transport Museum, Glasgow, 532
Transportable Accommodation Module, Bristol, 271
Transporter Bridge, Newport, 15, 285, *285*, 434, 466; **B.26**
Transporter Bridge, Warrington, 434
Tredegar Library, 284, 292–3
Trellick Tower, 46, 128, 164, 166–8, *167*, 186, 350
Tremlett Grove Estate, Upper Holloway, 147

Triad Building, Bootle, 439
Tricentre, Swindon, 263–4
Tricorn Centre, Portsmouth (demolished), 69, 249
Trinity Green, Gosport, 246, 386
Trinity Hall, Aberdeen, 547
Trinity Square ('Get Carter') car park, Gateshead (demolished), 69, 477
Truro Courts of Justice, 278
Turner Contemporary, Margate, 242
Turnpike Centre, Leigh, 398, 417–18, *417*
Turnpike Lane Underground Station, 137
TV-am Building, Camden, 36
The Twitten, Crawley, 215–16
Ty Pawb, Wrexham, 305
Tyne and Wear Metro, 431, 458, 486–9
Tyne Tunnel Ventilation Shaft, Jarrow, 475

Underpasses and portes cochères, Milton Keynes, 60, 222, *222*
Unicentre & Guild Centre, Preston, 445
Unilever Detergent Powder Plant, Warrington, 434
Unité d'Habitation, Marseille, 30, *31*, 113, 443, 523
Unity Towers, Liverpool, 432
University Café, Hillhead, Glasgow, 518, 521
University Library, Cambridge, 79, 203
University Library, Nottingham, 354
University of East London, North Woolwich, 132
Universum Cinema, Berlin, 25
Upperthorpe, Sheffield, 372
US Embassy, Grosvenor Square, 49
Usk Street Cluster Blocks, Globe Town, 124–5
Uxbridge Underground Station, 121, 138, 157, 158

Vale House, Jesmond, 485–6, *485*
2, 4, 6, 8, 10 Valencia Road, Stanmore, 141
Vanbrugh Park Estate, Blackheath, 93
Vaughan Building. Somerville College, Oxford, 228–9
Victoria & Albert Museum, Dundee, 542, 545
Victoria Centre, Nottingham, 32, 352–4, *353*
Victoria Centre, Southend, 191

Victoria Square, Bolton, 416–17
Viewpoint, Basingstoke, 220
Villa Cook, outside Paris, 30
Villa Marina, Llandudno, 284, 300; **C.1**
Vittorio Emanuele Civic Circus, Bolton, 417

Wakefield Market, 391
Walmgate Bar Housing, York, 394
Walsall Borough Architects Dept, 322
Walsall Civic Centre, 322
Walsall Town Hall, 322
Walter's Way & Segal Close, Honor Oak Park, 79, 100–101
Waltham Forest Town Hall & Assembly Halls, Walthamstow, 120
Wanstead Underground Station, 121–2
Warwick, University of, 328–9, *328*, 394, 452
Warwick Crest, Edgbaston, 312
Waste-to-Energy Dome, Marchwood, 251
Water Gardens, Cwmbran, 289–90
Water Gardens, Harlow, 180, 186, 187–8, 290
Water Gardens, Hemel Hempstead, 181
Water Gardens, Marylebone, 163
14 Watergate Street, The Rows, Chester, 439
Waterloo International Terminal, 101
Waterloo Station, 85, 101
Watermeads Estate, Mitcham, 114, 294
Waterworld, Wrexham, 300–301
Watford, Hille House, 185–6
Watney Market, Stepney, 130
Wavertree Court, Streatham Hill, 109–10
Weissenhof Estate, Stuttgart, 263
Well Hall Estate, Eltham, 19
Welsh Back Granary, Bristol, 15, *15*
Wembley Arena, 161
Wembley Stadium, 162
West Riverside, Salford, 413–14
Westbourne Grove, Public Toilets, 134
Westbury Estate, Clapham, 90–91
Western Bank Library, University of Sheffield, 40, 366, 369; **A.11**
Westminster, University of, 58
Westminster City Hall, 76–7
Westminster Underground Station, 63, 72–3, 101–2, 133; **B.27**

Weston Shore, Southampton, 245, 248

Westside, Ealing, 171

Westway, North Kensington, 163–4, 166, 406

The Wheatsheaf pub, Camberley, 218

Wheeleys Road, Edgbaston, 312

'White City' Housing Estate, Berlin, 178

Whitechapel Gallery, 79, 119

Whitechapel Idea Store, 119, 134

Whitworth Art Gallery Extension, Manchester, 411

Wigan Civic Centre, 417

William Booth Training College, Camberwell, 79–80, 203

William Stone Building, Peterhouse, Cambridge, 205, *205*

William Temple Memorial Church, Wythenshawe, 404, *405*

Willis Building, Ipswich, 174, 200–201, *201*, 263

1–3 Willow Road, Hampstead, 142, *142*, 185, 256

Willow Tea Rooms, Glasgow, 345, 347, 516–17

Wills Memorial Building, University of Bristol, 269

Wilton Power Station, Middlesbrough, 466

Winchester Law Courts, 247

Winchester School of Art, 247

Winter Gardens, Sheffield, 375, *376*

Winter Gardens, Sunderland, 470

Winter Gardens, Ventnor, 243

Wolfson Building. Somerville College, Oxford, 228–9

Wolverhampton Civic Centre, 322

Wolverhampton Civic Halls, 320

88 Wood Street, City of London, 67, 72

Wood Street Police Station, City of London, 57, 72, 352

Woodside Ventilation Tower, Birkenhead, 434; **D.19**

Woolwich Royal Arsenal, 8, 11

Worland Gardens, Stratford, London, 38, 134, 136

World's End Estate, Chelsea, 168, 247

Wrexham Guildhall, 300–301

Wyncote Sports Pavilion, Liverpool, 428

Wyndham Court, Southampton, 214, 245, 248; **B.8**

Wyndham Estate, Camberwell, 90–91

Wythenshawe Estate, Manchester, 23, 398, 399, 401, 402, 404

Wyvern Theatre, Swindon, 260

YMCA, Nottingham, 352

York, University of, 34, 190, 338, 359–60, 366, 369, 394, 452, 462

York Station, 101

Zig Zag Building, Victoria, 41, 76–7

INDEX OF ARCHITECTS

3DReid, 399
6A Architects, 88–9, 211, 226, 280

A. H. Roberts, Kinnear & Gordon, 496
Aalto, Alvar, 11, 34, 94, 335
Abbott, Laurie, 70, 218–19
Abercrombie, Patrick, 60, 273, 274
Aberdeen, David Du Roi, 55, 334
Aberdeen Burgh Architects Dept, 546–7
Ackroyd, S. W., 83
Adam, Robert (neoclassical architect), 70–71
Adam, Robert (Postmodern classicist), 34
Adams, Jonathan, 298–9
Adjaye, David, 84
Adjaye Associates, 84, 104, 134, 391
AHMM architects, 135, 432
AHR Architects, 529
Ahrends Burton & Koralek (ABK), 219, 231, 239, 250
Alex Gordon & Partners, 296
Alex Robertson & Partners, 291–2
Alison Brooks Architects, 38, 211
Alison Hutchinson & Partners, 500–501
Allen, S., 361
Allies & Morrison, 74–5, 79, 207, 256, 257, 376
Alsop, Will, 42, 103, 104, 107, 171, 378–9, 505
Alsop & Störmer, 103, 171
Anderson, W. J., 520
Ando, Tadao, 414
Andresen, Brit, 529–30
Andrew, E. P., 461
Andrew Merrylees Associates, 503
Andrew Wright Associates, 460–61
Andrzej Blonski Architects, 226
Ansell, H. Benson, 247
Anthony Hunt Associates, 202, 280
APEC Architects, 440
Archigram architects, 70, 85, 87, 145, 264–5
Architects Co-Partnership, 190–91, 227, 470–71
Architype, 79
Armour, Cornelius, 520
Arnodin, Ferdinand, 285
Arthur Swift & Partners, 330, 352

Arup, Ove, 10, 22, 178, 229, 294, 320, 354, 458, 470
 see also Arup Associates; Ove Arup & Partners
Arup Associates, 71, 216–17, 248, 268, 344, 359–60, 374
 Byker Viaduct, Newcastle, 486, 488
 Philip Dowson at, 206, 216–17, 228–9, 230, 231, 313–14, 348, 350
 Peter Foggo at, 64, 220, 229
 and Oxbridge colleges, 206, 209, 228–9, 230, 231
 Derek Sugden at, 216–17
Ash Sakula, 489
Ashburner, E. H., 385
Aslin, C. H., 182
Assael, John, 411
Assemble architects, 106–7, 135–6
Associated Architects, 318
Atelier 5 architects, 116–17
Atkinson, Robert, 50, 309
Austin-Smith:Lord, 432
Avanti architects, 320
Avery, Brian, 84, 85
Avery Associates, 84

Babtie Shaw & Morton, 554
Bailey, Douglas, 123, 162
Bailey, Sidney, 358
Baker, Herbert, 23
Bannerman, David Gordon, 537
Barber, Peter, 38–9, 134–5, 136, 146–7
Barry, Charles, 388
Basil Spence & Partners, 326, 481, 500
Basil Spence, Bonnington & Collins, 60, 65, 165–6, 238–9, 245, 257–8
Basil Spence, John Bonnington & Partners, 471–2
Basildon Corporation, 186–7
Baynes & Co, 331
BDP, 225–6, 372, 394–5, 451, 511, 532, 557
 see also Building Design Partnership
Beaton, Douglas, 325–6
Beaumont, J. A., 400–401
Becher, Bernd, 107, 280, 466
Becher, Hilda, 107, 280, 466
Bedford, Eric, 59
Beech, Gerard, 428

Behrens, Peter, 21, 175, 215, 344, 345, 347
Belcher, John, 23
Bennett, T. P., 453–4, 459
Bennetts Associates, 241, 332
Benoy, 317
Benson, Gordon, 151–2, 355, 503–4
Benson & Forsyth, 355, 503–4
Berger, Leon, 243, 244–5
Berlage, Hendrik Petrus, 21, 47, 504
Bermondsey Metropolitan Borough Architects Dept, 81
Bernard Engle & Partners, 386–7, 415–16
Bicknell & Hamilton, 166, 188, 314
Bioregional, 117
biq, 432, 433
Birmingham City Council Architects Dept, 309–10
Biscoe & Stanton, 168
Blackpool Corporation, 448
Blomfield, Reginald, 23, 27, 264
Blonski, Andrzej, 226
Bloomfield, E. H., 426–7
Bočan, Jan, 164
Böhm, Dominikus, 436
Boissevain & Osmond, 91
Bonnet, Patrice, 53
Bonnington, John, 471–2
Booth, Roger, 422, 443, 445–6, 450–51, 452, 453, 454, 455
Borowiecka, Magda, 115
Bosschaerts, Constantine, 141
Bottomley, Philip, 90–91
Bournemouth Borough Engineers Dept, 258
Bradbury, Ronald, 428, 520–21
Braddock & Martin-Smith, 367, 368
Bradshaw, D. T., 483
Bradshaw Gass & Hope, 417
Bradshaw Rowse & Harker, 429–31
Breconshire County Architects Dept, 292
Breuer, Marcel, 21–2, 28, 43
Brighton Council Borough Surveyors Dept, 237
Bristol City Architects Dept, 266–7, 268
British Rail architecture, 126, 166, 188, 314, 328, 334, 403
Bronstein, Pablo, 241
Broome, Jon, 100, 101
Brown, David, 380
Brown, John, 347

Brown, Neave, 115, 147–9, 241, 504
Brown, Patricia, 380
Brunel, Isambard Kingdom, 13
Brunton, John, 389, 390, 391
Buckinghamshire County Council
    Architects Dept, 216
Building Design Partnership, 58,
    350, 361, 382, 388–9, 405, 422,
    444, 445, 469, 522
    see also BDP
Bullivant, Robert, 300, 347
Bunshaft, Gordon, 60, 268, 404
Burchett, H. W., 141, 143
Burnet, John James, 20, 21, 22, 47–8
    see also Burnet Tait & Lorne; Sir
    John Burnet & Partners; Sir John
    Burnet, Tait, Wilson & Partners
Burnet & Tait, 47–8
Burnet Tait & Lorne, 158, 175, 273,
    497–8
Burrell Foley Fischer, 251
Burridge, P. F., 191
Burton, John, 258
Butterfield, William, 17–18, 70, 231

Cachemaille-Day, Nugent Francis,
    80, 367, 380, 398, 399, 404, 436
Cachemaille-Day Welch & Lander,
    80
Cadbury-Brown, H. T., 168
CADW, 292, 301
Calatrava, Santiago, 42, 290, 414,
    463–4
Camberwell Borough Architects
    Department, 88
Cambridge City Council Architects
    Dept, 209
Camden Council Architects Dept,
    146, 147–9, 150–52, 241
Capon, Kenneth, 190
Cappocci, Achille, 121
Cardiff City Architects Dept, 296
Carey Jones, 376
Carr, David, 507
Caruso St John Architects, 38, 42,
    118, 308, 321, 322–3, 344, 355,
    556
Cassidy & Ashton, 452
Casson, Hugh, 207
Casson Conder & Partners, 145,
    207, 260, 362
Castle Park Dean & Hook, 463
Cecil Howitt & Partners, 418–19
Cemex, 337
Cesar Pelli & Associates, 131
Chalk, Warren, 85
Chamberlin Powell & Bon, 55–6, 58,
    60, 66, 93, 205, 240–41, 366,
    381–2

Chancellor, Frederick, 179
Chapman Taylor, 256, 257
Charles B. Pearson & Partners, 451,
    460
Charles Holloway James, 195–6
Chatham Borough Council
    Architects Dept, 240
Cheeseman, Kenneth, 437
Cheesman, Wendy, 149
Chell, Rex, 329
Chermayeff, Serge, 160, 214, 234–5
Chesterfield Borough Architects
    Dept, 361
Chipperfield, David, 38, 42, 154,
    155, 242, 392, 532
City of Stoke-on-Trent Environmental
    Services Dept, 341
Clare, A. D., 243
Cleeve-Barr, A., 182
Clendinning, Max, 403
Coates, Wells, 21, 27, 40, 139–40,
    236
Cockerell, Charles Robert, 17–18
Cogswell, A. E., 245
Coleman Ballantine, 530
Coles, George, 83
Collective Architecture, 537
Collick, Richard, 387–8
Collins, E. V., 415
Colquhoun, Alan, 15, 152, 153, 162,
    333
    see also Colquhoun & Miller
Colquhoun & Miller, 119, 146, 152–3,
    162, 333
Colwyn Foulkes & Partners, 302–3
Conder, Neville, 207
Connell, Amyas, 21, 215
Connell Ward & Lucas, 140, 215
Conran & Partners, 375, 376
Conran Roche, 100
Cook, Peter, 264–5
Cook, Sidney, 94
Cooper, Edwin, 23
Copcutt, Geoffrey, 536
Cornwall County Architects Dept,
    254, 275–7
Corporation of Bath, 256
Corporation of London Architects
    Dept, 60, 128
Cotton Ballard & Blow, 310
Cottrell & Vermeulen, 105–6
Covell Matthews & Partners, 406
Covell Matthews Architects, 547–8
Coventry City Council Architects
    Dept, 324, 325–6, 329, 330, 331
Cox, Oliver, 29
CRAB, 264–5
Crabtree, William, 160
    see also Johnson & Crabtree

Crawford, Ian, 325–6
Crawley Development Corporation,
    215, 216
Cropper, J. W., 384–5, 399–400, 435
Crouch & Coupland, 109
Crowe, Ralph, 334–5
Crowe, Sylvia, 239, 502
Cruikshank & Seward, 406–7, 412
Cubitt Atkinson & Partners, 178
Cullinan, Edward, 149, 267
Culpin, Clifford, 84, 120–21
Cumbernauld Development
    Corporation Architects Dept,
    535–6
Curtis, W. T., 141, 143
Cwmbran Development Corporation
    Architects Dept, 281, 289–90
CZWG, 42, 131–2, 134, 154, 170,
    317, 531

Dakin, Maurice, 378
Dalgleish, Kenneth, 236–7
Daniel, Thomas Brammall, 120
Danish Embassy, Belgravia, 63
Darbourne & Darke, 57, 76
Darlington, S., 341
Darlington Borough Architects Dept,
    468
David Chipperfield Architects, 38,
    42, 154, 155, 242, 392, 532
Davies, Anthony B., 186–7
Denby, Elizabeth, 160
Denis Clarke Hall, Scorer & Bright,
    358–9, 361–2
Denys Lasdun & Partners, 64, 84,
    85–7, 144, 198, 206–7, 348,
    428–9
    see also Drake & Lasdun;
    Lasdun, Denys
Derbyshire, Andrew, 168, 394
Derrick Humphrys & Hurst, 186
Deutscher Werkbund, 21, 345
Diamond Redfern & Partners, 321
Dixon, Jeremy, 223, 233
    see also Dixon Jones
Dixon del Pozzo, 469
Dixon Jones, 233, 432–3
Dobson, John, 480, 483
Dorward Matheson Gleave
    & Partners, 524
Dossor, John, 467
Douglas Stephen & Partners, 162–3,
    262–3, 405–6
Doulton & Co, 266
Dowson, Philip, 206, 216–17, 228–9,
    230, 231, 313–14, 348, 350
Drake, Lindsay, 162
Drake & Lasdun, 162
Drew, Jane, 180–81, 189, 437–8

Dryburgh, John, 296
Dudok, Wilhelm Marinus, 84, 120, 139, 158, 195
Duggan Morris, 154, 155
Dunlop, Alan, 532
Dunster, Bill, 117
Durnin, Leo, 546

E. N. Underwood & Partners, 269
Ealing Borough Council Architects Dept, 171
Eames, Charles, 34
Eames, Ray, 34
Easton, John Murray, 179
Easton & Robertson, 219
Ecclestone, A. W., 197
Edmund Kirkby & Sons, 423, 424
Edward Cullinan Architects, 132, 207, 211
Edwards, David, 237
Egeraat, Erick van, 468
Eisenman, Peter, 42
Ekins, L. G., 479–80
Elder & Cannon Architects, 531
Elder Lester & Partners, 467, 468–9
Ellis, Peter, 13, 423–4
Ellis & Clarke, 50
Ellis Williams Architects, 304, 474
Emberton, Joseph, 51, 176, 448–50
Engelback, Norman, 85
EPR Architects, 220
Eric Parry Architects, 264
Erith, Raymond, 28, 195
Erskine, Ralph, 35, 36, 102, 115, 169, 208, 209, 223, 475, 476, 484–5
Esso Engineers, 244
Etchells, Frederick, 49
Evans, Eldred, 278–9
Evans & Shalev, 278–9, 504
Exeter City Architects Dept, 256–7

F. D. Williamson & Associates, 300–301
Faczynski, Jerzy, 442–3
Fairhurst, Harry S., 399
Fairhurst, William, 526–7
Farmer & Dark, 220, 244, 431–2
Farrell, Terry, 35–6, 49, 62, 278, 465
FAT Architecture, 193–4, 299
Faulkner-Brown Hendy Stonor, 359–60
Faulkner-Brown Hendy Watkinson Stonor, 296–7, 486, 488
    see also Faulkner-Brown Hendy Stonor; Williamson Faulkner-Brown & Partners
Featherstone Young, 305
Feilden & Mawson, 200, 362

Feilden Clegg, 376
Feilden Clegg Bradley, 211, 245, 256, 267, 362, 383
Ferguson Mann, 269
Fidler, Alwyn Sheppard, 215, 216, 309–10
Finch, George, 94, 95, 115, 251
Fletcher, Banister, 159
Fobert, Jamie, 209, 278, 279
Foggo, Peter, 64, 66, 72, 220, 229
Foggo Associates, 64, 72
Forrest, Bill, 146
Forrest, G. Topham, 137
Forsyth, Alan, 151–2, 355, 503–4
Foster, Norman, 41, 102, 149, 412, 414, 532
    the 'Gherkin', 38, 47, 73–4
    Great Court at the British Museum, 264
    houses in Milton Keynes, 223
    Jubilee Line extension, 37–8, 101–2
    Sage Music Centre, Gateshead, 37
    Sainsbury Centre, 169, 174, 202
    Stansted Airport, 192–3
    Wembley Stadium, 162
    works in East Anglia, 169, 174
    see also Foster & Partners; Foster Associates
Foster & Partners, 73–4, 131, 133, 477–8
Foster Associates, 160, 192–3, 200–201, 202, 207, 248, 263
Frampton, Kenneth, 162–3, 389
Fraser, Alan, 465
Fraser, Richard, 247
Frederick Gibberd Partnership, 122, 126, 180, 183, 257, 333, 335, 401, 427–8, 459
Frederick MacManus & Partners, 147
Freeman Fox & Partners, 290, 372, 463–4
French, Alec, 273
Freud, Ernst, 22, 140
Frost, Peter, 209
Fry, Maxwell, 22–3, 24, 81, 140
    and Jane Drew, 180–81, 189, 437–8
    and Walter Gropius, 160, 203–4
Fuller, Buckminster, 34, 193, 280, 393
Fuller Hall & Foulsham, 51
Future Systems, 317

G. Maunsell & Partners, 406
Gahura, František Lýdie, 176–8
Gardham, Edgar, 367
Gareth Hoskins Architects, 557

Gasson, Barry, 529–30
Gaudí, Antoni, 19
Gavin Paterson & Sons, 527–8
GEC–Mowlem, 131
Gehry, Frank, 42, 542, 545
Gelder & Kitchen and Mouchel, 474
Gibberd, Frederick, 29, 109, 110, 126, 162, 180, 183, 187–8, 530
Gibson, Donald, 324, 325, 331
Gibson, Richard, 149
Giles, Bob, 169
Gillespie Kidd & Coia (GKC), 42, 209–10, 514, 521–2, 523–4, 527, 536, 537–8, 543
Gilling Dod & Partners, 441
Gillinson Barnett & Partners, 378
Glasgow City Council Architects Dept, 520–21, 525–6, 528
Glenn Howells Architects, 271
gm+ad architects, 532
Goalen, Gerard, 180, 181
Goldfinger, Ernő, 21–2, 91–2, 127–8, 129, 142, 166–8, 185–6, 195, 238
Gollins Melvin Ward, 62, 63, 73–4, 220–21, 359–60, 369, 531
Goodhart-Rendel, H. S., 81, 237
Goodman Short & Knowles, 329
Gordon, Rodney, 69, 90, 91, 98, 218
Gough, Piers, 170
Gowan, James, 58, 112, 150–51, 348
    see also Stirling & Gowan
Gracie, Vernon, 484–5
Graham, Bruce, 268
Graham Winteringham, 314–15
Granger, W. F., 234
Gravesend Borough Council Architects Dept, 238
Greater London Council Architects Dept, 84, 85, 96–8, 99, 128, 130, 146, 169
Grenfell-Baines, George, 123
Grey, T. Lindsay, 544
Griesmann, Inette, 216
Grimshaw, 62, 101, 280–81, 304–5, 351
Grimshaw, Nicholas, 41
    see also Grimshaw; Nicholas Grimshaw & Partners
Gropius, Walter, 15, 22, 28, 43, 175, 223, 255, 403
    and Maxwell Fry, 160, 203–4
    grain silos as major inspiration, 385
    Impington Village College, 27, 203–4
    Model Factory in Cologne (1914), 143, 517
    66 Old Church Street, Chelsea, 160

Group Architects DRG, 267–8
Groupe Signes, 132
Groupwork, 77–8
Grzesik, M. F., 166
Gwynne, Patrick, 96, 395

H & D Barclay, 539
Hadfield, C. M. E., 367
Hadid, Zaha, 37, 42, 230, 233, 265, 299, 504, 511, 532
Hall O'Donohue & Wilson, 429
Halliday Meecham Architects, 412
Hamilton, David, 486
Hamlyn, William Henry, 380, 436
Hampshire County Council Architects Dept, 219, 250–51
Happold, Buro, 101–2
Harrington, Frank, 109
Harris, E. Vincent, 23, 28, 262
Haswell, John, 459
HAT Projects, 242
Hatfield Development Corporation Architects Dept, 188–9
Hawkins/Brown, 332
Haworth Tompkins, 42, 87, 331, 433
Hay, G. S., 324, 403–4
Headley, W. R., 328, 334, 403
Heaps, Stanley, 157
Heatherwick, Thomas, 156
Henley Halebrown, 136
Henson, A. E., 347
Hepworth, Philip Dalton, 120
Herron, Ron, 85
Hertfordshire County Council Architects Dept, 182
Herzog & de Meuron, 102–3, 104, 233, 474
Hicklin, F. K., 275, 276–7
Hill, G. E., 238
Hill, Oliver, 121, 122, 447
Hill, William, 417
Hind Woodhouse Partnership, 439
Hirst, Peter, 262
Hodgkinson, Patrick, 63, 207
Hoffmann, Josef, 21
HOK Sport, 298
Holden, Charles
    55 Broadway, Westminster, 65
    James Knott Memorial Flats, Tynemouth, 474
    modernist Tube stations of, 46, 48, 51, 102, 108, 121, 137–8, 143, 157–8, 179, 436
    move to modernism of, 21
    post-war austerity Tube stations, 121–2
    post-war work for London University, 51, 64–5

Senate House, London, 40, 51, 138, 295
Holford, William, 60, 61, 257, 258, 394
Holl, Steven, 528, 533–4
Hollamby, Ted, 89, 94
Holland, Charles, 194
Holliday, Clifford, 184–5
Honeyman & Keppie, 20, 516, 528
Hood, Raymond, 49
Hopkins, Michael, 38, 41, 65, 71, 72–3, 101–2, 363
Hopkins, Patricia, 41, 65, 71, 72–3, 101–2, 363
Hopkins Architects, 65, 71, 72–3, 267, 268, 344, 352, 354–5, 363
Horta, Victor, 19
Housden, Brian, 143
Howard, William, 507
Howell & Amis, 143
    see also Howell Killick Partridge & Amis
Howell Killick Partridge & Amis, 218–19, 229–30, 233, 312, 329
Howitt, L. C., 398, 401–2
Howitt, T. C., 286–7, 352
Hoyles, F. H., 386
Hudspith, Walter, 470
Hugh Martin & Partners, 530–31
Hughes, John, 425–6
Humphreys, G. E., 304
Hunt, Anthony, 202, 280
Hunter, William Henry, 434
Hurd, Robert, 500
Hutchinson, Maxwell, 419
Hutchison Locke & Monk Architects, 537
Hyde-Harrison, Ann, 149
Hyde-Harrison, David, 149

Ian Simpson Architects, 410–11
IBI Group architects, 378, 379
ICI, 466, 467
Ingham, Keith, 42, 444
Irredale, Ralph, 325–6

J. Holmes & Partners, 525
J. M. Austin-Smith & Partners, 215–16
Jackson, Peter, 367, 368
Jacobsen, Arne, 63, 214, 228
James A. Roberts Associates, 429
James Williamson & Partners, 550
Jamie Fobert Architects, 278, 279
Jeeves, Gordon, 49
Jefferson Sheard & Partners, 373–4, 376
Jellicoe, Geoffrey, 181, 189, 273, 321
Jencks, Charles, 132, 428, 545, 555, 556

Jiricna, Eva, 101–2
John Brunton & Partners, 390, 391
John Madin Design Group, 316–17, 330, 335
John McAslan & Partners, 154, 155
Johnson, W. A., 384–5, 399–400, 435
Johnson & Crabtree, 243–4
Jones, Carey, 382–3
Jones, Edward, 47, 66, 223, 233
    see also Dixon Jones
Jones, Inigo, 123
Joseph's Architects, 49
JT Group, 270

Kahn, Louis, 206, 218, 313, 348, 405–6
Kaplický, Jan, 317
Karakusevic Carson Architects, 38
Karfík, Vladimír, 176–8
Kaufmann, Eugene, 182
Kay, Tom, 149
Kaye, Sidney, 60
Keenlyside, Roy, 361
Kenyon, George, 482
Keppie Henderson & Partners, 524, 528
King, Laurence, 442
Kininmonth & Spence, 496
Klerk, Michel de, 21
Kohn Pedersen Fox, 74
Koolhaas, Rem, 42, 163
Korn, Arthur, 22
Kuma, Kengo, 542, 545

Lacoste, Gerald, 141
Laings, 525–6
Laird, Michael, 534
Lambeth Borough Architects Dept, 94–6, 113–14, 115
Lanarkshire County Architects Dept, 537
Lancashire County Council Architects Dept, 443–4, 445–6, 450–51, 452, 453, 454, 455
Lasdun, Denys, 162, 200, 238, 344, 428–9, 548
    as designer of towers/ziggurats, 87, 144, 198, 202, 207, 348
    National Theatre, Southbank, 84, 85–7
    New Court, Christ's College, Cambridge, 206–7
    Royal College of Physicians, Regent's Park, 144
    SOAS and IoE, Bloomsbury, 64–5
    University of East Anglia, 198, 202
    Usk Street and Keeling House for LCC, 124–5, 348, 370
Lautner, John, 394

Lavender & Twentyman, 321
Law & Dunbar-Nasmith Architects, 554–5
LDN Architects, 495, 539
Le Corbusier, 24, 26, 27, 30, 112, 175, 239, 303, 424, 443, 522–3
  and Brutalism, 30–31
  'Five Points of Modern Architecture', 9, 29
  grain silos as major inspiration, 385
  paintings by, 463
Leach Rhodes & Walker, 413–14
Leathart, Julian Rudolph, 234
Leeds City Architects Dept, 382–3
Leonard, Gavin, 171
Leonard Manasseh & Partners, 129–30
Lescaze, William, 255–6
Leslie Jones & Partners, 259
Levete, Amanda, 317
Levitt Bernstein, 408–9, 556
Lewis, Brian, 157
Lewis, Eric Langford, 300–301
Lewisham Borough Architects Dept, 92, 98–9
Libeskind, Daniel, 37, 42, 414
Lifschutz Davidson Sandilands, 156
Ling, Arthur, 325, 330
Lissitzky, El, 74, 192, 245, 393, 444
Little, Sidney, 235–6
Liverpool City Council Architects Dept, 425–7, 428
London County Council Architects Dept, 29, 84, 85, 89–90, 91, 92, 93, 98–9, 112–13, 137, 143, 147
Long, M. J., 143, 144, 242
Long & Kentish, 143, 280
Loos, Adolf, 21, 157, 171
Louis de Soissons Partnership, 257
Lubetkin, Berthold, 22, 96, 118, 472, 486, 524
  Bevin Court, Finsbury, 54–5, 126, 162
  Communist Party affiliations of, 29, 54
  Constructivist-baroque staircases of, 54–5, 123–4
  Cranbrook Estate, Globe Town, 126–7
  Dorset Estate, Shoreditch, 123–4, 524
  Dudley Zoo, 308, 319–20
  Finsbury Health Centre, London, 52, 524
  Highpoint/Highpoint 2, 27, 52, 83, 139
  influence on social architecture of fifties London, 112, 162

Penguin Pool of London Zoo, 138–9
  retires to become pig farmer, 123, 139, 524
  Spa Green, Finsbury, 52, 139, 162
  and Tecton Collective, 52, 54, 138–9, 308, 319–20
Lubetkin & Pilchowski, 83
Lubetkin and Tecton, 52, 54, 138–9
Lucas, Colin, 140, 215
Luder, Owen, 32–3, 70, 117, 218, 249, 477
Lutyens, Edwin, 23, 48, 427, 459
Lynch, Patrick, 38, 41, 76, 129–30
Lynch Architects, 76–7, 129–30
Lynn, Jack, 131, 370, 371–2
Lyons, Eric, 87–8, 111–12, 168, 215, 240, 247, 336
Lyons Israel Ellis, 58, 89, 248, 320–21, 333, 522

MacCormac, Richard, 38, 102, 294, 452, 453
MacCormac Jamieson Prichard, 101–2, 233, 452, 453
  see also MacCormac, Richard
Maccreanor Lavington, 38, 104–5, 154, 155, 211
Macintosh, Kate, 42, 93–4, 114, 251
Mackie Ramsey & Taylor, 547
Mackintosh, Charles Rennie, 20–21, 22, 47, 157, 344, 345–7, 514, 515–17, 525
MacMillan, Andy, 42, 209–10, 521–2, 523–4, 527, 536, 537–8, 543
Madin, John, 308, 310–11, 318, 320, 330, 336, 418
  see also John Madin Design Group
Maguire, Robert, 125
Make Architects, 60, 62, 310, 318, 355
Maki, Fumihiko, 154, 155–6
Maki & Associates, 154, 155–6
Malcolm Fraser Architects, 478
Manchester City Council Architects Dept, 401–2
March, Lionel, 114
Mardall, Cyril, 22
Marsh, George, 59, 60, 316
Marshman Warren Taylor, 274
Martin, Leslie, 29, 85, 114, 205, 207, 208–9, 228, 463, 528
Marwick, T. Waller, 498
Mason, Hilda, 195
Massey, Cecil, 83
masterplan, 531
Mather, Rick, 241
Matthew, Robert, 85

Maufe, Edward, 23
Mauger, Paul, 182
MawsonKerr, 489
Maxwell Hutchinson & Partners, 419
Mazaud, Jean-Robert, 251
McAlpine, 455
McAslan, John, 160, 345
McAslan, Troughton, 100
McChesney, Ian, 446
McDowall Bendetti, 465
McInnes Gardner & Partners, 548
McKissack, James, 520
McLaughlin, Niall, 235
McMorran & Whitby, 33, 57
McNair & Elder, 520
McRobbie, J. A., 292
Mecanoo, 315, 411
Melnikov, Konstantin, 24, 348, 381–2
Mendelsohn, Erich, 22, 25, 28, 100, 120, 160, 214, 234–5, 300, 377, 384–5, 435
Mercer, W. H. G., 415
Metzstein, Isi, 42, 209–10, 521–2, 523–4, 527, 536, 537–8, 543
Meunier, John, 529–30
Mewes & Davis, 424
MICA Architects, 90
Michael Manser Associates, 169
Michael Wilford & Partners, 414
Middlesbrough Borough Architects Dept, 469
Middlesex County Council Architects Dept, 141, 143
Mies van der Rohe, 30, 40, 62–3, 88, 89, 196, 268–9, 369, 404
Miller, James, 518
Miller, John, 333
Mills Beaumont Leavey Channon, 409
Milner, J. M., 462–3
Milton Keynes Development Corporation Architects Dept, 222–5
Ministry of Building & Works, 340, 476–7, 480–81, 552–3
Miralles, Enric, 504–5
Moffett, Alina, 128
Moffett, Noel, 128
Moira & Moira, 550–51
Morgan, Emslie A., 438–9
Moro, Peter, 85, 274, 352, 395, 463
Mosscrop, Stuart, 100, 222, 223–5
Mott Hay & Anderson, 275, 276, 290, 437, 479
muf architects, 135
MUMA, 411
Munby, A. E., 415
Munk, Knud, 350
Murphy, Richard, 331, 506, 544

Murray, Gordon, 532
Murray, Keith, 125
MWT Architects, 277–8

Napper Architects, 470
National Nuclear Corporation, 495
Neatby, William, 266
Neutra, Richard, 367
Newby, Frank, 145
Newcastle City Architects Dept,
    480–81
Newcastle City Engineers and
    Planning Dept, 483
Newton Architects, 489
Nicholas Grimshaw & Partners,
    153–4
Nicoll Russell Studios, 543
Niemeyer, Oscar, 60, 235
Noble, Harry, 330
Norman & Dawbarn, 10, 309
Norrish, Ken, 249–50
Norwich City Architects, 199–200

O'Donnell & Tuomey, 75–6
Office of Works, 459
OMA (Office for Metropolitan
    Architecture), 42, 76, 511,
    514, 532–3
Organ, Bob, 260–61
Organ, Tim, 260–61
Orozco, Gabriel, 88, 89
Oud, J. J. P., 30
Outram, John, 42, 205, 210, 278
Ove Arup & Partners, 389, 470, 555
Owen, Dale, 296–7, 303
Owen Luder Partnership, 32–3, 70,
    90, 91, 98, 117

Pace, George Gaze, 338, 404
Page/Park Architects, 531, 534, 554,
    555–6
Panter Hudspith, 256, 257
Paoletti, Roland, 101–2
Paolozzi, Eduardo, 68, 336, 337
Parkes, Derek, 464
Parnacott, Horace W., 120
Parry, Eric, 38
Patel Taylor architects, 99, 132
Patterson, Gordon, 182–3
Paxton, Joseph, 93
Pearson, J. L., 277
Pelli, Cesar, 131, 133
Pelli Clarke Pelli, 76
Penoyre & Prasad, 250
Percival, David, 199–200
Percy Emerson Culverhouse, 295
Percy Thomas Partnership, 270–71,
    284, 286, 289, 295, 296–7,
    298–9, 301–2, 412

Perret, Auguste, 21, 127, 185, 195
Peter Barber Architects, 38–9,
    134–5, 136, 146–7
Peter Moro & Partners, 352
Peterlee Development Corporation
    Architects, 472–3
Phippen Randall & Parkes (PRP),
    189–90, 216
Piano, Renzo, 105
Pick, Frank, 48, 108, 121–2, 137
Pierre-Yves Cochin, 250
Pite, Beresford, 23
PLP Architecture, 78
Plymouth City Council Architects
    Dept, 273, 274
Ponti, Gio, 316
Pooley, Fred, 216
Porphyrios, Demetri, 155, 156, 317
Portsmouth City Council Architects
    Dept, 249–50
Potter, Robert, 271
Powell Alport & Partners, 292
Powell & Moya, 53, 60, 62, 239
PreFab Design, 478
Prestwich, Ernest, 412
Prestwich, J. C., 348, 417–18
Price, Cedric, 70, 145
Pringle Richards Sharratt, 331, 375,
    419
Property Services Agency, 374–5
Pullen, Roger K., 236–7
Purcell Architects, 297, 442

Quick, C. W., 293

R. Seifert & Partners, 59, 60, 66, 116,
    316, 407, 526
Rafael Viñoly Architects, 347
Rainiers, Peter, 188
Rank, J. S., 418
Raynish, R. Lewis, 245
Redfern, Gordon, 289–90, 291
Reiach & Hall, 499, 501–2, 531, 534,
    556
Reid, John, 218
Reid, Sylvia, 218
Rendel Palmer & Tritton (engineers),
    99
Renzo Piano Building Workshop,
    105
RHWL Architects, 340
Richard Gibson Architects, 557, 558
Richard Murphy Architects, 544
Richard Rogers Partnership, 37, 67,
    69–72, 170, 217–18, 294, 298–9
Riches, Mikhail, 371
Rick Mather Architects, 241
Rietveld, Gerrit, 504
Ritchie, Ian, 101–2

RMJM (Robert Matthew Johnson-
    Marshall), 58, 168, 259, 394,
    445, 483, 499, 501–2, 504–5,
    508–9, 522, 543, 545
Robbrecht en Daem, 119
Robert Atkinson & Partners, 90
Robert Paine & Partners, 237–8
Roberts, James A., 429
Robinson, Fitzroy, 65
Robinson, John Charles, 448
Roche, Fred, 100, 222, 223–5,
    439–40
Roger Stephenson Studio, 411
Rogers, Richard, 37, 41, 69–72,
    73–4, 115–16, 144, 275
    see also Richard Rogers
    Partnership; Rogers Stirk
    Harbour
Rogers, Su, 149, 275
Rogers Stirk Harbour, 73–4, 103,
    170
Rogerson & Spence, 524, 528
Ronald Ward & Partners, 55
Rosenberg, Eugene, 22, 96
Rowe, H. B., 256–7
Rowse, Herbert J., 424–5, 426,
    430–31, 434, 437
Royal Engineers, 466
Russell Diplock Associates, 234
Rutherford, Derek, 262
Ryder & Yates, 55, 248, 475, 483,
    486
Ryder Architecture, 483
Rylander, Sven, 424

Saarinen, Eero, 49
Salmon, James, 20, 517–18
Salvisberg, Otto, 178
Samuely, Felix, 22
Scarpa, Carlo, 331, 341, 544
Schreiber, Gaby, 216
Schumacher, Patrik, 37
Scorer, Sam, 41, 344, 358–9, 361
Scott, Adrian Gilbert, 122
Scott, David, 551–2
Scott, Elizabeth, 332
Scott, George Gilbert, 524
Scott, Giles Gilbert, 25, 40–41,
    79–80, 84, 102–3, 108–9, 203,
    352, 367
Scunthorpe Borough Architects
    Dept, 464
Seely & Paget, 184, 448
Segal, Walter, 35, 36, 42, 100–101
Seifert, Richard, 47, 59, 66, 75, 407
Sergison Bates, 154, 280
Sert, Josep Lluís, 499
Seymour Harris Partnership, 297–8
Shalev, David, 278–9

Shankland, Graeme, 416–17
Shankland Cox, 416–17, 465
Sharp, Thomas, 256
Shaw, Norman, 157
Shedkm, 424
Sheffield City Council Architects
    Dept, 367–8, 370–72, 374
Sheffield City Council Urban Design
    Team, 371
Shekhtel, Fyodor, 19
Shepheard Epstein, 452
Sheppard, Richard, 165, 204–5
Sheppard Robson, 165, 204–5,
    246–7, 359–60, 452
Sherren, B. C., 273
Short, Alan, 73, 330–31, 351
Short Associates, 73, 330–31, 351,
    410
Shorten, Derrick, 328
Shropshire County Architects Dept,
    334–5
Shuttleworth, Ken, 73
Simon Carves Otto, 466
Simpson, Ian, 38, 410–11
Simpson, John, 34
Sir John Burnet & Partners, 297
Sir John Burnet, Tait, Wilson
    & Partners, 403–4
Skidmore Owings & Merrill (SOM),
    71, 74, 268–9, 360
Skinner, Francis, 29, 123, 162, 524
Skinner Bailey & Lubetkin, 54–5,
    123–4, 126–7, 162, 524
Skipper, George, 195
Sloman, Albert, 190
SMC Alsop, 104
Smith, Ivor, 131, 370, 371–2
Smith, John, 329
Smithson, Alison and Peter, 30, 47,
    58–9, 128, 259–60, 326, 369
    Robin Hood Gardens, Poplar, 56,
    128, 130–31
    Smithdon School, Hunstanton,
    196–7, 428
    'streets in the sky' concept, 11,
    48, 56, 130–31
Snøhetta, 242
Soissons, Louis de, 108, 175, 247
Somerset County Architects Dept,
    262
Southampton City Council
    Architects Dept, 243, 244–5, 248
Southgate, F. G., 122–3
Space & Place, 460–61
Spence, Basil, 34, 42, 62, 65, 165–6,
    186–7, 238–9, 245, 297, 492
    Coventry Cathedral, 326, 501
    early work, 496
    in Edinburgh, 496, 500, 501

Hutchesontown C in Glasgow,
    522, 531
see also Basil Spence & Partners;
    Basil Spence, Bonnington
    & Collins; Basil Spence, John
    Bonnington & Partners; Spence
    Glover & Ferguson
Spence Glover & Ferguson, 501,
    502–3
SPT Architects, 529
Stansfield-Smith, Colin, 250–51
Stanton Williams, 154, 155, 318
Steel Company of Wales, 288
Stephen Rowland Pierce, 195–6
Stevenage Corporation Architects
    Dept, 182–3, 184–5
Stillman & Eastwick-Field, 57
Stirling, H. J. W., 273, 274
Stirling, James, 72, 207, 230–31, 278,
    344, 348, 362, 440, 510–11
see also Stirling & Gowan
Stirling & Gowan, 58, 92, 111–12,
    348
Stjernstedt, Rosemary, 94–5, 309
Stockport Council Borough Council
    Architects Dept, 418
Street, G. E., 57, 271
Stubbings, Rex, 189
Sugden, Derek, 216–17
Sullivan, Louis, 19, 47–8, 424
Summers, Royston, 275–6
Sunderland City Architects Dept,
    470
Surface Architects, 75
Sydney Clough, Son & Partners, 110

T. Bowhill, Gibson & Laing, 499
T. H. Johnson & Son, 377
Tabori, Peter, 115, 150–51
Tagliabue, Benedetta, 504–5
Taha, Amin, 77–8
Tait, Thomas, 47–8, 273, 347, 497–8,
    519–20
see also Burnet Tait & Lorne; Sir
    John Burnet & Partners; Sir John
    Burnet, Tait, Wilson & Partners
Tate & Lyle Engineering Dept, 427
Taut, Bruno, 26
Tayler & Green, 34, 199, 200
Taylor, John, 367–8
Team 4 (Richard and Su Rogers/
    Norman Foster with Wendy
    Cheesman), 115–16, 149
Tecton Collective, 52, 54, 83, 138–9,
    162, 308, 319–20
Teggin & Taylor, 250
Terry, Quinlan, 28, 34
Terry Farrell & Partners, 49, 60, 465
Thomas, Alfred Brumwell, 418

Thomas, J. L., 289
Thomas, Percy, 412
Thomas, Walter Aubrey, 424
Thorp, John, 382–3
Tom Mellor & Partners, 454–5
Toms & Partners, 109
Tony Fretton Architects, 170–71
Tornbohm, E. A., 468
Townsend, Charles Harrison, 79,
    119
Trehearne & Norman, 163
Trevett, G. A., 112
Tripe & Wakeham Partnership, 192,
    431
Tripos, 69
Tyrrell, J. E., 246

Uren, Reginald, 83, 139
Utzon, Jørn, 43

Vallis, Bill, 260
Velarde, Francis Xavier, 422, 435–6,
    437, 442
Verner Rees Laurence & Mitchell, 92
Vincent, Leonard, 184–5
Voysey, C. F. A., 157

W. Campbell & Son, 439
W. H. Saunders & Son, 246
Wakeford Jeram & Harris, 268
Walker, Derek, 223
Wallis, Thomas, 159, 288
Wallis Gilbert & Partners, 159, 288
Walls & Pearn, 273–4
Walter Underwood & Partners,
    524
Walters, Roger, 146–7
Walton, George Henry, 302–3
Walton, Maurice, 350
War Office, 549–50
Ward, Basil, 21, 215
Ward, John, 126
Ward, Roland, 245
Warren, B., 374
Watson, James, 538–9
Webb, Aston, 309
Webb, Philip, 17
Weddell Inglis & Taylor, 519–20
Weedon, Harry, 25, 179, 284, 287,
    300, 338, 357, 393
Weeks, Ronald, 270
Weightman & Bullen, 442–3
Welch & Lander, 80, 157, 158
Wells-Thorpe, John, 240
West Glamorgan Architects Dept,
    293
Wheeler & Sproson, 34, 367, 493,
    500, 507–8, 550–51
Whicheloe Macfarlane, 269–70

Whinney, Son & Austen Hall, 65
White Design, 271, 383
White, M. C., 496
Whitfield, William, 374, 524, 525
Wigan Borough Architects Dept, 417, 418–19
Wigglesworth, Gordon, 146–7
Wigglesworth, Sarah, 131
Wilford, Michael, 414
Wilkinson Eyre, 221, 258, 290, 379, 409, 414, 532
WilkinsonEyre, 37
William Arnot & Co., 466
William Holford & Partners, 257, 258
Williams, Laurence, 333–4
Williams, Owen, 50, 81, 161–2, 315, 344, 356–7, 400, 518–19
Williamson Faulkner-Brown & Partners, 354, 468, 475, 477, 482

see also Faulkner-Brown Hendy Stonor; Faulkner-Brown Hendy Watkinson Stonor
Wilson, Colin St John, 143, 144, 205, 242, 280
Wilson, Hugh, 408, 409
Wilson Mason & Partners, 259
Winter, John, 256
Wirral Corporation, 438–9
Witheford Watson Mann, 119
Wolton, Georgie, 146, 152, 163
Wolverhampton City Architects Dept, 322
Womersley, J. L., 367–8, 408, 409
Womersley, Peter, 492, 493–4
Wood, Douglas, 141
Wood, Renton Howard, 329
Woodhouse, George, 417
Woodroffe Buchanan & Coulter, 191
Woodward, Christopher, 47, 66, 88, 222, 223–5

Wornum, George Grey, 108
Wren, Christopher, 76
Wright, Frank Lloyd, 268
Wright & Wright Architects, 465
Wyatt, Matthew Digby, 13
Wylie Shanks & Underwood, 522–3

Yates, Peter, 55, 486
Yeadon, Derek, 225
York City Council Architects Dept, 394
Yorke Rosenberg & Mardall (YRM), 58, 89, 96, 122, 192, 221, 263–4, 328–9, 371, 374, 440, 522
Youngman, G. P., 438, 535

Zaha Hadid Architects, 233, 511
Zetland County Council, 553
Zogolovitch, Roger, 170

GENERAL INDEX

References in *italics* are
to illustrations.

Aachen, Germany, 333
Abercrombie Plan, 60, 273, 274
Aberdeen, 108, 137, 530, 542, 546–8
Aberystwyth, 284, 303–4
abstract art, 15, 20, 22, 279, 387
  in churches, 184, 186, 359, 399,
    442
  William Mitchell, 290, 314, *315*,
    329, 332, 335–6, 387–8, 412,
    417–18, 428
  mosaics, 79, 139, 178, 184, 186,
    187, 216, 236, 237, 246, 273,
    274, 288, 289, 326, 337, 385,
    387
  murals, 189, 198, 305, 325, 415
  Victor Pasmore, 472, 482
  reliefs, 55, 59, 164, 289, 300, 311,
    314, 387–8, 462, 485–6, 528
  sculpture, 91, 290, 335–6, 412,
    481, 488
  tapestries, 53, 463
  the Vorticists, 21, 49, 81
Achmelvich, 542, 551–2
AEG, 26
Aird, Lucy, 525
Amersham, 215, 347
Anderson, Charles, 538, 539
Another Green World (Brian Eno
    album), 164
Anti-Ugly Action, 28
Architectural Association, 149, 223,
    264, 441, 482
Arndale company, 32
art deco, 8–9, 24–5, 35, 42, 49, 50,
    83, 159, 450
Art Nouveau, 13–15, 19, 20, 21,
    79, 119, 157, 195, 266, 345–7,
    515–18, 525
'Artist-Constructor Ltd' (Bob and
    Tim Organ), 260–61
Arts and Crafts movement, 81, 110,
    136, 194, 309, 312, *331*, 345,
    405, 538
  extreme hostility to industrial
    modernity, 16–17
  interwar pebbledash version, 27
  LCC fire stations, 19
  and Charles Rennie Mackintosh,
    20–21, 157, 345–7, 515–17
  route to modern architecture
    from, 19–21, 157

shift from labour to society, 18–19
  and Alan Short, 73, 351, 410
  and Stockholm City Hall, 25,
    195–6, 334
Ascherson, Neal, *Stone Voices*, 504
Ashmole, Bernard, 215
Attlee, Clement, 122
Aumonier, Eric, 143
Austin-Smith, John Michael, 215–16
'avant-garde', 214, *226*, 241, 330,
    355
  Artist-Constructor Houses,
    Flax Bourton, 254, *261*
  Arts and Crafts movement
    anticipates, 16–17
  and Dartington Hall, Totnes, 255
  and Deconstructivism, 37
  Dutch, 139
  London Transport instead of, 137
  London's art scene, 119
  and Postmodernists, 35
  in Sheffield, 371–2, *373*

Baijo, G., 184–5
Baltic Exchange, IRA bombing of, 73
Bangor, 301–2, 304–5
Banham, Reyner, 31, 196, 357, 438
Barclay, Jim, 538
'barcode facade' craze, 126, 155,
    211, 264, 398, 407, 411, 432
Barden, Kenneth, 246, 386
Barking Central, 135
Barnsley, 191, 378–9, 388
Barrow-in-Furness, 422, 448, 450,
    455
Basildon, 183, 186–7
Basingstoke, 71, 220, 530
Bassett-Lowke, Wenman Joseph,
    345–7
Bata (Czechoslovakian shoe
    manufacturer), 176–8
Bat'a, Tomáš, 176
Bath, 181, 254, 256, 257, 259–60,
    264, 360
Bauhaus, 15, 28, 51, 137, 203, 255,
    347, 356, 424
Bayley, Stephen, 130
Beckett, Andy, *When the Lights
    Went Out*, 557
Belfast, 43
Belsky, Franta, 184
Berlin, 25, 26, 51, 178, 235, 256, 403
Berwick-on-Tweed, 478
Betjeman, John, 87

Bevan, Aneurin, 52, *53*, 290, 292
Beveridge, William, 51
Bevin, Ernest, 55
Bexhill-on-Sea, 178, *212–13*, 214,
    234–5, 237, 243
'Bilbao Effect' idea, 545
Billingham, 467, 468–9, 472
Birkenhead, 431, 434
Birmingham, 27, 31, 33, 166, 308,
    309–18, 373, 389, 412, 426, 429
  Central Library (demolished), 310,
    314, 315, 335, 418, 468
  Edgbaston, 308, 310–11, 312
  University of, 309, 312–14, 360,
    453
Black Lives Matter protests, 499
Blackburn, 33, 422, 442
Blackheath, 87–8, 93, 96, 215, 247
Blackpool, 422, 448–50, 451, 454–5
Bletchley Park, 439
Bolton, 416–17
Bonham, John, 335
Bootle, 437, 439
Bossányi, Ervin, 158
Bournemouth, 258, 264–5
Boyson, Alan, 415, 461–2
Bracknell, 216–17
Bradford, 32, 366, 384–5, 387–8,
    390, 391
Brandt, Bill, 391
Brazil, 60
Brentford 'Golden Mile', 159, 164
Brett, Lionel, Lord Esher, 191, 324
bridges
  A9 Bridge, Helmsdale, Sutherland,
    554
  at the Barbican, 67
  Calatrava's bridge over the Irwell,
    414
  Chartist Bridge, Blackwood, 294
  Forth Rail Bridge, 15, 285
  Green Bridge, Mile End, 134
  Hadrian Bridge, Newcastle, 483
  High Level Bridge across the
    Tyne, 15, 477, 479
  in Hulme, Manchester, 409
  Humber Bridge, 463–4, 465
  Kingsgate Bridge, University of
    Durham, *456–7*, 458, 470–71
  Kingston Bridge, Glasgow, 526–7,
    555
  Kylesku Bridge, *540–41*, 555
  Millennium Bridge, Gateshead, 37,
    458, 477, 478

Millennium Bridge, London, 102
New Tyne Bridge, 458, 466, 477,
   479, 483
Plimsoll Swing Bridge, Bristol, 267
at railway stations, 188, *225*
Scale Lane Swing Bridge, Hull,
   465
Severn Bridge/Pont Hafren, 290,
   291
Silver Jubilee Bridge, Runcorn,
   437
Tamar Suspension Bridge, 276
at Thamesmead Estate, 97–8
Transporter Bridges, 15, 285, 434,
   466
Waterloo Bridge, 84
Wilkinson Eyre's in Salford, 414
Bridgnorth, 308, 333
Brighouse, 385
Brighton, 236, 237, 241, 248
Bristol, 15, 21, *252–3*, 254, 266–71,
   428
British Empire, 16, 17, 28, 93, 119
   late-imperial style architecture,
      23–4, 27, 28, 47, 48, 76, 399,
      418, 424, 459, 539
British Rail, 33, 126, 166, 188, 314,
   328, 334, 403
Brown, Derek, 461
Brown, Ralph, 183
Brownfield, Alice, 136
Bruntwood (developers), 405–6,
   413–14
Brutalism
   Laurie Abbott as link to
      High-Tech, 217–18
   Alton Estate and architectural
      history, 112–13
   Barbican as great achievement of,
      66–8
   and Baroque images of power, 65
   in Birmingham, 310, 311, 312–14,
      315, 316–17
   in Bloomsbury, 63, 64–5
   in Bristol, 267, 268, 269–71
   and British Library, 144
   and British Rail, 126, 166, 188,
      314, 334
   in Cambridge, 204–7, 209–10
   and Camden Council, 46, 63,
      94, 114–15, 134, 146, 147–9,
      150–52, 223, 241, 333, 504
   in Cardiff, 296–8
   cathedral buildings, 270–71, 277
   in Central London housing, 55–6,
      57, 63
   Central Mosque, Glasgow, 530
   churches, 125, 168, 404, *405*, 440,
      442–3, 521–2, 537–8

Coleg Harlech, 302–3
in Cornwall, 276–8
County/Town Halls/Civic Centres,
   216, 240, 276–7, 293, 322, 412,
   417, 468, 471–2, 537
in Coventry, 329–30
Czech & Slovak Embassies,
   Notting Hill Gate, 164, *165*
Dawson Heights, East Dulwich,
   93–4
demolition of housing blocks,
   10–11
at Durham University, 470–71
earliest buildings in London, 89
in east London housing, 124–5,
   127–31
in East Midlands, 348–51, 352–4,
   359–60, 361, 362
in Edinburgh & east Scotland,
   492, 493–4, 500–501, 507–8,
   510–11
and egalitarian values, 28, 113,
   115, 124–5
emergence of in Britain, 30, 41
as enduringly controversial, 28,
   30, 31, 33, 41, 66–8, 148–9,
   166–8
engagement with history, 34, 144,
   227, 231, 247, 248
flyovers of west London, 163–4
and 'functional tradition', 12
in Glasgow, 521–2, 523–5, 526–8,
   530
and Goldfinger, 91–2, 127–8, 129,
   166–8, 185–6
Rodney Gordon on, 98
in Greater Glasgow, 521–2, 523–5,
   526–8, 530, 536, 537–9
in Greater Manchester, 398,
   404, 406–7, 408, 409, 412–14,
   415–18
at Heathrow Airport, 162
in Highlands & Islands, 551–2,
   554–5
and ideal plans of the
   Renaissance, 92
individuality within collective
   structure, 34, 94, 128
Lancaster University, 452–3
Lasdun's great public buildings,
   64–5, 84–7, 144–5, *145*, 198,
   348, 428–9
and Le Corbusier, 30–31
in Leeds, 380–82
'Lego building' at Reading, 218–19
libraries, 64–5, 191, 205, 228,
   249–50, 275, 292–3, 297, 301,
   335, 354, 360, 362, 413, 428,
   453, 463, 464, 501, 528, 538–9

in Liverpool, 427, 428–9, 430–32
Luder's approach to, 32–3, 90, 98,
   117
Manchester University, 408
in Metropolitan Yorkshire, 370–73,
   374–5, 376, 378–9, 380–82, 385,
   386–91, 392
National Sports Centre,
   Crystal Palace, 93
New Brutalism, 10, 103, 111–12,
   204, 376, 412
in Newcastle, 480–81, 483–4,
   486–9
in north-east, 458, 463, 464–5,
   466, 468, 469, 470–73, 476–7,
   480–81, 483–4, 486–9
in north London housing, 146,
   147–9, 150–52
in north-west, 422, 427, 428–9,
   430–32, 439, 440, 442–5, 452–5
in northern Scotland, 542, 543,
   545, 547–8
in Norwich City Centre, 199–200
in Nottingham, 352–4
in Oxford, 227–31
in Pimlico, 57
in Plymouth, 274
and Postmodernists, 34, 35, 525
and post-WW2 carve-up of city
   centres, 31
principles/tenets of, 30
private houses, 149, 216–17, 236,
   240–41
railway stations, 188, 334
and Royal College of Art, 28
school buildings, 92, 129, 169,
   196–7, 523–4, 536
seen from City of London
   Pedways, 61, 62, 66–7
in Sheffield, 370–72
Richard Sheppard variety, 204–5
and shift in post-WW2 housing
   policy, 31
shifting meanings in 1955–70
   period, 143
shopping centres/markets, 32–3,
   63, 98, 130, 191, 192, 291,
   352–4, 390–91, 415–16
and the Smithsons, 30, 47, 58–9,
   130–31, 174, 196–7, 259–60
'softs' and 'hards' at LCC, 112–13
and South Bank buildings, 84–7
on south coast, 234, 236, 238–41
in south-east London housing,
   90–91, 93–9
in south-west, 254, 259–62
in south-west London housing,
   111, 112–15
at Southampton University, 245

Brutalism (*cont.*)
  Southampton-Portsmouth
    conurbation, 214, 244, 246–7,
    248, 249–50
  and Span estates, 88
  and Basil Spence, 62, 65, 165,
    238–9, 245, 492, 500
  Stirling & Gowan, 111–12
  Thames Barrier, 99
  Thamesmead Estate, 96–8
  today's wave of nostalgia towards,
    33, 373
  topographic and regional
    specificity, 34, 57
  Trellick Tower, 166–8
  in twenty-first century, 136, 304,
    392, 394–5, 465, 537
  university buildings in London,
    58, 64–5
  University of Essex, 190–91
  at University of Leicester, 348–50
  at University of St Andrews,
    510–11
  in Wales, 284, 289–90, 291, 292–3,
    300–304
  in west London housing, 164,
    166–8
  in West Midlands, 321–2, 333–4,
    335–6, 337, 338, 340–41
  at York University, 394–5
Buffalo, New York, 48
building industry
  CLASP system, 462
  corruption scandals of 1960s/70s,
    33
  deregulated market, 35
  'Design and Build' construction,
    147
  deskilling/alienation of workers,
    18
  pre-WW2 corruption in, 28
  system-building, *10*, 31, *32*, 110,
    246, 412, 415, 462, 476, 485,
    522, 546–7
  see also developers
Burntisland, 493, 500, 507–8,
    550–51
Burton, Decimus, 451
Butler, Simon, 488

Caister lifeboat disaster (1901),
    197
Calder, Barnabas, 66, 85, 529, 551
Calvert, Margaret, 488
Camberley, 218
Cambridge, 25, 39, 42, 79, *172–3*,
    181, 203–11, 246, 536, 538
  Accordia Housing Estate, 174,
    204, 211

rationalist 'school' of architecture
    at, 38, 174, 207, 209, 211
  'Sidgwick Site', 207, 209, 230,
    362, 510
Camden, London Borough of, 31, 46,
    63, 94, 114–15, 134–5, 146–52,
    153–4, 223, 241, 333, 441, 504
Canary Wharf, London Docklands,
    101–2, 116, 131, 170
Canterbury, 237–8
Cardiff, *282–3*, 284, 295–9
Carlisle, 422, 451
cathedral architecture, 79, 183,
    270–71, 277, 326, *327*, 426,
    427–8, 442
Chadwick, Lynn, 360
Chandra, Avinash, 438
Channel Islands, 43
Charles, Prince of Wales, 73, 87,
    143, 268
Chatham, 240
Chelmsford, 191
Chernikhov, Iakov, 70
Chester, 439, 441
Chesterfield, 200, 361, 362
Chicago, 26, 34, 48, 424
  Illinois Institute of Technology, 30,
    196, 369
  Lakeshore Drive Apartments, 30,
    268–9
Chicago School, 30, 40, 47, 399,
    479–80, 497, 544
  and Louis Sullivan, 19, 47–8, 424,
    544
Chichester, 214, 239, 242
Chorley, 422, 443–4
Christfaith Tabernacle, 83
Church Commissioners, 8–9
Churchill, Winston, 87
cinemas, 128, 225, 251, 288, 300,
    320, 335, 347, 499, 520, 555
  Bill Douglas Cinema Museum,
    258
  cinema at Birkbeck's School of
    Arts, 75
  Expressionist architecture, 179,
    234, 300
  generic Odeon style, 25, 179, 234,
    300, 520
  IMAX at Waterloo, 85
  Odeon Cinemas, 25, 41, 83, 179,
    234, 287, 300, 338, 357, *364–5*,
    393
  Star and Shadow Cinema,
    Newcastle, 305, 458, 489
  in Woolwich, 83
cladding, flammable, 164, 412, 525
Clarke, Geoffrey, *327*, 481
CLASP system, 462

Classical Modernism
  art galleries on south coast, 241,
    242
  British Library, 143–4
  in Cambridge, 207, 211
  in Central London, 76–7
  characteristics of, 41
  in east London, 119, 134–5, 136
  and Exeter's reconstruction,
    256–7
  Museum of Scotland, Edinburgh,
    503–4
  New Art Gallery, Walsall, 118,
    264, 304, 308, 321, 322–3, 355,
    556
  in north London, 143–4, 146–7,
    152–3, 154
  Peter Barber's social housing
    schemes, 38–9, 134–5, 136,
    146–7
  Salmon Leap Flats, Chester, 441
  in Scotland, 503–4, 506, 531, 534,
    556
  in south-east London, 79, 100
  in south-west London, 114–15
  Tate St Ives, 278–9
  in twenty-first century, 264, 355,
    382–3, 392, 411, 506
  in west London, 170–71
  Whitechapel Gallery, 119
classical tradition, 41, 51, 76–7, 79,
    119, 384
  and Postmodernists, 34–5
  Ruskin's moral view of, 17
  in Scotland, 17
  see also Classical Modernism;
    Modern Classicism;
    neoclassical architecture
Cliff, Clarice, 340
climate change, 39
A Clockwork Orange (Stanley
    Kubrick film), 96–7, 165
Clydeside, 30, 209, 514, 521, 536,
    537, 538, 550
Coalbrookdale, 336
Coin Street Community Builders
    scheme, Lambeth, 36
Colchester, 347
  University of Essex, 34, 190–91,
    329, 338, 360, 369, 394, 470,
    508
Concrete Society, 406
Congrès International
    d'Architecture Moderne (CIAM),
    27
conservation areas, 77–8
Conservative Party, 35, 36, 48
  Cameron's slashing of arts
    budgets, 489

Gove's libertarian, low-budget
schools programme, 136
Nicholas Ridley's 'Enterprise
Zones', 170
Thatcherite redevelopment
of London, 131
Constructivism, 15, 81, *82*, 137, 176,
225, 298, 309, 337, 381, 443
and asymmetry, 63, 236, 287, 400,
437
Boots in Beeston, 356–7
building's circulation on its
outside, 69–70, 140, 153–4, 263,
294
Channel 4 Building, Westminster,
71–2
characteristics of, 40, 140, 171
Wells Coates' buildings, 27, 40,
139–40, 236
Dutch dilution of, 426
Functional Method, 171
and Lloyd's of London, 69–70
Lubetkin and Tecton's work, 52,
54–5, 83, 123–4, 126, 138–9,
162, 319–20
Lubetkin's staircases, 54–5,
123–4, 524
Melnikov pioneers, 24, 161
neo-Constructivists, 386
and Postmodernists, 35
in Scotland, 502, 503, 509, 520,
524, 525
sculpture, 54–5, 319, 350, 388,
509
theatre sets of Vsevolod
Meyerhold, 100
unbuilt Soviet projects, 34, 69–70,
71, 140, 192, 355
Cook, Jonquil, 447
Co-operative movement buildings,
41, 234, 366
in Bradford, 120, 384–5
in Coventry, 324
in Doncaster, 377
in Edinburgh, 498
in Huddersfield, 120, 384–5
in Hull, 458, 461–2
in Ipswich, 198
in Manchester, 399–400
in Newcastle, 385, 435, 479–80
in Southport, 435
in Woolwich, 83
Cornwall, 254, 275–81
Corporation of London, 66, 78
Costello, Elvis, 159
Coventry, 29, 73, 90, 101, 184, 216,
241, *306–7*, 308, 324–31, 334,
501
Coventry, F. H., 273

Crawley, 215–16
'Critical Regionalism' of Frampton,
38
Crosland, Tony, 463
Croydon, 90, 166–7, 178
the Crystal Palace, 17, 93
Cullen, Gordon, 78, 325
Cumbernauld, 31, 438, 514, 535–6
Cummins, Kevin, 409
Cunliffe, Mitzi, 405
The Cure (rock band), 216
Curtis, Ian, 401
Cwmbran New Town, 289–90, 291
Czechoslovakia, 26, 27, 40, 120, 164,
176–8, 507
Czech Cubist movement, 73, 357

Dada, 35
Darlington, 468, 469
Debord, Guy, 189
Deconstructivism (Parametricism),
37, 39, 42, 75, 233, 465, 511,
545
decorum, 15–16
Delaunay, Sonia, 53
Derby, 260, 344, 358, 362, 435
Derbyshire, Matthew, 135
'desire lines', 9
Dessau, 203, 255, 356
'Kornhaus' riverside café, 178
Torten estate in, 223
Deutsch, Oscar, 287, 338
developers
and Benoy, 317
and Brunswick Centre,
Bloomsbury, 63
Bruntwood, 405–6, 413–14
carving-up of city centres for, 31,
32
and Coventry City Centre, 326
and Cumbernauld Town Centre,
536
deregulated market from 1980s,
35, 61
gaming of planning system, 60
Richard Grainger, 480, 483
Harry Hyams, 59, 60
Lakeshore, Bristol, 268–9
and listing system, 224
in Milton Keynes, 224
naming of towers by, 73, 74
Olympia and York, 131
'planning gain' process, 68
power over local authorities, 38,
130
'regeneration' of Park Hill by,
370–71, 484
and Robin Hood Gardens, Poplar,
130, 131

and Southend-on-Sea, 191
Span, 87–8, 168, 240, 247, 312
Urban Splash, 268–9, 314,
370–71, 424, 447
vacuous designation of 'iconic',
76
Dobson, Frank, 81
Doctor Who, 299
Doncaster, 366, 377
Dorn, Marion, 447
Dundee, 542, 543–5
Durham, 374, *456–7*, 458, 470–71,
555
Dutch Expressionism, 351, 426
Dysart, 493, 500, 508, 550–51

East Kilbride, 29, 188, 514, 535,
537–8, *539*
Eastbourne, 237, 241
Eastleigh, 250–51
Ebbw Vale, 289, 292
Ecomodernism
and Will Alsop, 171
BedZed, Beddington, 117–18
in Cambridge, 207, 211
in Cardiff, 298–9
characteristics of, 41–2
in Coventry, 330–31
David Mellor Factory, Hathersage,
363
and Hampshire County Council,
250–51
Jubilee Campus, Nottingham,
354–5
LILAC housing co-operative,
Leeds, 39, 189, 271, 383
in Manchester, 403, 409
National Maritime Museum,
Falmouth, 280
in north-east England, 460–61,
478, 489
Otoprojects, Dalston, 135–6
Pavilion Café, Avenham Park,
Preston, 446
in Scotland, 495, 555–6, 557–8
Segal's self-building system,
100–101
in Sheffield, 367–8, 375
Solar Campus, Wallasey, 438–9
in south-east London, 79, 100–101
Southampton University Bus
Interchange, 245
'sustainable architecture', 42,
118
University of East London, north
Woolwich, 132
White Design architects, 271, 383
Ede, H. S. ('Jim'), 208, 209
Ede, Helen, 208, 209

Edgbaston, Birmingham, 308, 310–11, 312
Edinburgh, 34, 39, 411, 448, 492, 496–506, 508
  Richard Murphy's schemes in, 506
  Princes Street redevelopment, 501–2
Eliot, T. S., 369
Elmhirst, Dorothy, 255
Elmhirst, Leonard, 255
Emett, Rowland, 189
An Englishman Abroad (play and film), 521
Epstein, Jacob, 55, 326
Esher, Lionel, 191, 324
'ethical fallacy' concept, 17
Exeter, 254, 256–8
Expressionism
  in 1930s Manchester, 399–401
  'Amsterdam School', 47, 84
  and art deco, 53
  Battersea Power Station, 25, 102, 108–9
  in Central London, 47, 53, 65, 75–6
  characteristics of, 40–41
  churches/chapels, 80, 141, 195, 338, 367, 380, 399, 435–6, 437, 442
  cinemas, 179, 234, 300
  in east London, 120, 122
  in east of England, 179, 186, 188, 195
  Fidler in Birmingham, 309–10
  and H. S. Goodhart-Rendel, 81, 237
  in Greater Manchester, 415
  Greenwich Town Hall, 84
  London Underground stations, 137, 157–8
  and Middlesex schools, 141
  and Modernist Eclectic, 42
  railway stations, 188
  and Giles Gilbert Scott, 25, 79–80, 102–3, 108–9, 203
  Shakespeare Memorial Theatre, Stratford-upon-Avon, 332
  in south-east London, 79–81, 84, 102–3, 104–5
  in south-west London, 108–9
  Theatre Royal Extension, York, 395
  in west London, 157–8, *159*, 161–2
  and Owen Williams, 161–2
  YMCA, Nottingham, 352

Fabian Society, 19
Factory Records, Manchester, 407

Falmouth, 280
Fascism, 21–2
Feibusch, Hans, 287
Festival of Britain (1951), 55, 85, 87, 93, 121, 324, 402
Fife, 34, 492, 507–8, 511
Filler, Martin, 414
financial crisis (2008), 38
Finland, 11, 30, 89, 94, 291, 335, 448, 542, 558
fire stations, 8, 19, 357
First World War, aftermath of, 28
Flax Bourton, Somerset, 254, 260–61
Fleetwood, 450–51
Fleming, Ian, 142
Fletcher, Richard, 387
Folkestone, 240–41
football stadiums, 486, *490–91*, 492, 493
Forsyth, Bruce, 386
Foucault, Michel, 16
Franklin, Geraint, 147
Freedom (Anarchist bookshop/publisher), 119
Frink, Elisabeth, 127
Frome, 254, 260
Fulcher, Raf, 488
'Functional Tradition' of English architecture, 12, 70, 242, 391

Gabo, Naum, 96, 235, 278, 556
Galashiels, *490–91*, 492, 493
Gallacher, Willie, 507
Games, Abram, 28
Garden Cities, 19, 21, 23, 174, 175, 180–81, 192
garden suburbs, 19, 27, 28
Gardiner, Margaret, 556
Garman, Kathleen, 322
Gateshead, 31, 33, 37, 98, 458, 474, 477–8, 532
Gaudier-Brzeska, Henri, 208, 209
Geddes, Patrick, 500
General Strike (1926), 28
Georgian tradition, 58, *59*, 111, 216, 238
  and 1–3 Willow Road, Hampstead, 142
  in Blackheath, 88
  in Bridgnorth, 333
  in Bristol, 270
  and Giles Gilbert Scott, 25
  in Durham, 470
  in Edinburgh, 501
  in Gordon Square, Bloomsbury, 75
  in Hatfield, 188–9
  in Lincoln, 361–2
  in Liverpool, 426, 429

  in Margate, 234
  in Northampton, 345, *346*
  Thatcher gives new lease of life to, 200
  see also neo-Georgian architecture
Germany
  art museum in Aachen, 333
  Berlin, 25, 26, 51, 178, 235, 256, 403
  early modernism in, 26, 27
  Expressionist movement, 25, 40, 75, 234, 287, 436, 442
  interwar housing programmes, 26–7
  Weimar Republic, 30, 53, 109, 137, *161*, 166, 234, 358, 377, 384–5
  Weimar *Zeilenbau* ('line-building'), 53
  see also Dessau
Gibraltar, 43
Gill, Eric, 447
Glasgow, 13, *14*, 27, 506, 514–24, 525–34
  Daily Express Building, 50, 161, 357, 400, 518–19
  Gartnavel General Hospital, 511, 514, 532–3, 555
  huge post-WW2 high-rise estates, 514, 520–21, 522, 525–6
  Imperial Exhibition (1938), 519–20
  motorways through, 406, 518, 526–7
  move towards modernism in, 20–21, 515
  new towns planned around, 29, 31, 188, 514, 535–6, 537–8
  post-war Scottish-Italian style, 519, 521
  post-WW1 industrial unrest, 28
  School of Art, 20–21, 345, 514, 515–16, 528, 533–4
  and system-building, 31, 522, 546
  topography of, 516, 518
  University of, 380, 524–5
Glendinning, Miles, 415
Golden Syrup, 123
Googie style, 41, 92, 358–9, 368, 403, 450–51, 453–4, 455, 467, 521, 553
Google Streetview, 43
Gosney, Harold, 463
Gosport, 246, 386
Gothic architecture
  in Bangor, 305
  and Expressionism, 40, 122
  Hanseatic, 57
  medieval, 17
  northern-Italian, 15, 17

old Coventry Cathedral, 324
in Taunton, 262
see also neo-Gothic architecture
Govan, Glasgow, 520, 529, 532
Gove, Michael, 136
Grainger, Richard, 480, 483
Gravesend, 238
Gray, Alasdair, 529
Great Exhibition (London, 1851),
17, 93
Greater London Council (GLC), 85,
96–8, 146, 169
Greenfields (greasy spoon in Luton),
192
Greenock, 538–9
Greenwich, 38, 84, 102, 120, 123,
195
Grenfell Tower fire (2017), 164, 415,
471
Grimsby, 461, 462–3
Grindrod, John, *Concretopia*, 116,
522
Guilty Men (collectively written
book), 28

Halifax, 350, 366, 382, 386, 388–90,
391, 503
Halter, Roman, 150
Hamilton, 276, 502, *512–13*, 514, 537
Hampstead, 22–3, 27, 30, 139, 140,
143, 156
Branch Hill Estate, 63, 147, 151–2,
223, 503
1–3 Willow Road, 142, 185, 256
Hampstead Garden Suburb, 19
Harlow, 29, 31, 126, 166, 183, 186,
187–8, 290
Harrogate, *364–5*, 393–4
Harwood, Elain, 460
Hastings, 235–6, 242
Hatfield, 183, 188–90, 191, 216
Helmsdale, Sutherland, 542, 554
Hemel Hempstead, 181, 189
Hepworth, Barbara, 245, 275, 278,
279, 337, 361, 392, 556
Heron, Patrick, 279
High-Tech architecture
Laurie Abbott as link to Brutalism,
217–18
by BDP, 225–6
22 Bishopsgate, City of London,
78
Barnabas Calder on, 529
in Cambridge, 207, 211
in Camden, 149, 153–4
Channel 4 Building, Westminster,
71–2
the 'Cheesegrater', 73–4
Chiswick Business Park, 170

4 Dale Street, Liverpool, 429–30
David Mellor Factory, Hathersage,
363
Devonshire Dock Hall, Barrow-in-
Furness, 455
early examples, 64, 115–16, 160,
174, 200–201, 248
in East Midlands, 351, 354–5
Eden Project, 280–81
emergence of in 1970s, 34
Terry Farrell tries, 35–6
fusion of retro with, 72
the 'Gherkin', 38, 47, 73–4
Glasgow Subway Stations, 529
in Greater Manchester, 404,
408–9, 419
Heathrow Hilton, 169
Heron Tower, City of London, 74
Lloyd's of London, 37, 41, 46, 68,
69–71, 263
at London Zoo, 145
Maidenhead Library, 219
Matrix House, Basingstoke, 220
Meccano cited as scource for, 263
and the military, 248
as modernist, 36–7
in the north-east, 465, 470, 474,
477–8
in Oxford, 230–31
principles/tenets of, 34, 41, 64
Sainsbury Centre, 169, 174, 202
The Shard, Borough, 78, 105
Solar Campus, Wallasey, 438–9
in South Wales, 285, 294, 298–9
Stansted Airport, 41, 174, 192–3
James Stirling's 'Red Trilogy',
230–31
in Swindon, 262–3
Thames Barrier, 99
Tube Stations, 68, 72–3, 101, 133
in twenty-first century, 221, 251,
432, 470
Waterloo International Terminal,
101
in West Midlands, 317, 332, 337
Willis Building, Ipswich, 174,
200–201, 263
in Yorkshire, 379, 393
Hillier, Bevis, 24
Hilton, Roger, 275
Hirst, Damien, 118
The History Man (book and
television drama), 453
Hitchcock, Henry-Russell, 176
Hjaltland Housing Association, 558
Hodgkin, Howard, 85
homelessness, 38, 60, 68, 85, 222
adjacent to luxury flats, 406
Hoskins, John, 468

housing
Accordia Estate, Cambridge, 211
Arts and Crafts movement, 19,
27
Case Study Houses, 140
15 Clerkenwell Close, Clerkenwell,
77–8
comprehensive redevelopment
programme in Glasgow, 514,
520–21, 522, 525–6
co-operative schemes, 39,
189–90, 271, 383
Corporation of London, 66–7
crisis in London today, 38
'cross-subsidy' projects, 136
high-modernist terraced houses,
83
Homes for Change, Manchester,
409
Isokon Building, Belsize Park,
139–40
The Lawn, Harlow, 180
'Low-Rise, High-Density', 31, 38,
41, 81, 98–9, 108, 114–17, 137,
147–52, 209, 294
New Labour-style 'mixed
communities', 102, 117–18
post-war dominance of
modernism, 28–32, 34
post-war political numbers game,
31
Regent Court, Sheffield, 367
Salmon Leap Flats, Chester, 441
Segal's self-building system,
100–101
slums in pre-WW2 Glasgow, 514
Span estates, 87–8, 168, 240, 247,
312
speculative housing of New
Labour era, 37, 38
Streatham Hill, 1930s, 109–10
in suburbs for middle-class
professionals, 111–12, 218
Thatcher's impact on, 205
housing, local authority/social
in 1960s/70s Glasgow, 525–6, 528
in 1970s Milton Keynes, 223
in 1980s, 35, 152–3
in Aberdeen, 542, 546–7
build quality, 10, 11, 30, 31–2
built by Church Commissioners,
8–9
Byker Estate, Newcastle, 484–5
Camberwell Borough Architects
Department, 88
Camden Council schemes, 134–5,
223, 241
Camden Council style of 1970s,
147–52

housing (*cont.*)
  in Central London, 48, 52, 53,
    55–6, 57, 63
  conversion to luxury housing,
    370–71
  in Coventry, 330
  in Cumbernauld, 535–6
  demolition of Brutalist blocks,
    10–11, 31–2
  direct-labour organizations, 9, 10,
    200
  early LCC estates, 19
  in Edinburgh, 492
  Erskine's Lakeshore estate, 475,
    476
  in Fife, 492, 507–8
  Garden Cities/garden suburbs,
    19, 21, 23, 27, 28, 174, 175, 178,
    180–81, 182, 184, 192
  Gleadless Valley, Sheffield, 31,
    309, 366, 367–8
  'Homes for the Future' (late 1990s
    Glasgow), 523–4
  interwar housing programmes,
    23–4, 26–7, 46, 48, 81–3, 98–9,
    108, 137
  interwar influence of Red Vienna,
    41
  interwar LCC estates, 38, 41, 81,
    98–9, 108, 137
  James Knott Memorial Flats,
    Tynemouth, 474
  LCC post-war housing, 29, 31,
    41, 89–91, 110, 112–13, 124–5,
    127–8
  and Lutyens, 48
  and need for regular
    maintenance, 30, 32, 88, 95, 98,
    160
  neo-Victorian suburban houses,
    11
  in Newcastle, 481, 484–5
  in Norwich City Centre, 199–200
  in Nottingham, 352–4
  Park Hill scandal, Sheffield,
    370–71, 402
  and post-1980 Brutalism, 35
  in post-1990 Glasgow, 523–4, 531
  post-war dominance of Brutalism,
    30–32, 34
  post-war dominance of
    modernism, 28–32, 34
  post-WW2 building programmes,
    28–32, 34, 244–5, 246, 247, 248,
    266–7, 268, 309–10, 401, 469
  post-WW2 building programmes
    in London, 46, 52–7, 63, 88–99,
    110, 112–15, 123–31, 147–52,
    162, 166–8, 171

  in post-WW2 Glasgow, 520–21
  rehabilitation in 1990s Bath, 256
  St Mary's Comprehensive
    Redevelopment Area,
    Woolwich, 8, 9–12
  in Scottish borders, 493
  seductive promises of system-
    building, 31–2
  in Shetland, 542, 550–51, 558
  on south coast, 234, 240
  in south-east London, 81–3
  Southampton-Portsmouth
    conurbation, 247, 248, 249
  in twenty-first century, 38, 134–5,
    136, 146–7, 154, 155
Huddersfield, 366, 384–5, 386–7,
  390–91, 507
Hughes, Robert, 472
Hull, 29, 324, 416, 444, 458, 459,
  461–2, 465
Hungary, 26
Hyams, Harry, 59, 60

Ibis hotels, 250, 355
Illinois Institute of Technology, 30,
  196, 369
Industrial architecture
  Defences & Shelters, Hastings
    & St Leonards, 235–6
  Fawley Oil Refinery, 244
  at Heathrow Airport, 162
  Imperial Docks Grain Elevator,
    Leith, 496–7
  Midwestern 'Daylight Factory'
    genre, 424
  in north-east England, 466, 474
  Port Talbot Steelworks, 288
  Regional Seat of Government,
    Accordia Estate, 204
  Scapa Flow Fortifications, 549–50
  Shredded Wheat Factory, Welwyn
    Garden City, 175
  Silver Jubilee Bridge, Runcorn,
    437
  on the Thames, 100, 119–20, 123
  Torness Nuclear Power Station,
    Dunbar, 495
  Transporter Bridges, 15, 285, 434,
    466
  in Warrington, 434
industrial revolution, 12–16, 39
  and Arts and Crafts movement,
    16–17, 18–19
inequality, 39, 43, 62, 68, 520
International Style
  in Birmingham, 309–10, 312,
    314–15, 316–17
  blueprint for council estates
    of 1950s/60s, 53

  in Bristol, 266–9, 271
  British variant, 22–3, 25, 27, 29,
    33–4, 203–4
  in Cambridge, 203–4, 207, 208–9
  in Camden, 114–15, 146–7, 153,
    223, 241
  at Canary Wharf, 131
  in Central London, 49, 50, 51,
    52, 53, 55–6, 57, 58–63, 66, 71,
    78
  development of (1918–28), 22–3,
    24, 96
  early examples in Britain, 46, 49,
    215, 347
  in East Anglia, 196–7, 200
  in east London, 120–21, 131
  in East Midlands, 345, 347, 352,
    358, 360, 361–2
  at East Tilbury, 176–8
  in Edinburgh & east Scotland,
    496, 498, 499, 501–3, 508–9
  in Glasgow, 518–19, 520–21,
    522–3, 525–6, 532–3
  glass towers and curtain walls,
    33, 34, 36, 40, 63
  in Greater Manchester, 412, 415,
    418–19
  Holden and Pick's tube stations,
    137, 143, 157–8
  homogeneous architecture of,
    29–30
  and Arne Jacobsen, 63, 228
  Lanark County Buildings,
    Hamilton, 537
  in Liverpool, 428, 429, 431
  in London commuter belt north,
    175–8, 185, 189–90, 191
  in London commuter belt south,
    215, 220–21
  loss of faith in, 29–30, 52
  in Manchester, 400, 403–4, 405–6,
    407, 410–11
  in Metropolitan Yorkshire, 366,
    369, 371, 373–4, 378–9, 386–7,
    393–4
  and Mies van der Rohe, 30, 40,
    62–3, 88, 369
  in Milton Keynes, 222–5, 226
  Moderne as preferred in UK, 41
  MOMA's epochal exhibition (1932),
    27, 176
  in Newcastle, 480–81, 482–3,
    485–8
  Niemeyer's warping of, 60
  in north-east England, 460, 461,
    462–4, 467, 468–9, 475, 477
  in north London, 137, 139–40,
    142–3, 146–7, 153, 155–6
  in north Wales, 304–5

in north-west England, 422,
437–8, 439–40, 443, 448–50, 451
in northern Scotland, 543, 546–7
in Oxford, 63, 228
and Paris World Expo (1925), 24
pedestrian walkways, 60–62
Peter Jones Department Store,
Chelsea, 160, *161*
railway stations, 224–5, 431, 467,
477, 486–8
Severn Bridge/Pont Hafren, 290,
291
in Sheffield, 369, 371, 373–4
in Shetland, 553
and the Smithsons, 58–9, 196–7,
428
in Solent area, 243–5, 248, 250
and South Bank buildings, 84–7
in south-east England, 214, 215,
222–5, 226, 228, 234–5, 237,
241, 243–5, 247, 248, 250
in south-east London, 81, *82*, 83,
84–90, 91, 91–2, 96
in South Wales, 289, 290, 292,
295–6, 297
in south-west England, 275
in south-west London, 109–10,
116
Span estates, 87–8, 312
'towers in a park' genre, 92
Town Halls/Civic Centres, 120–21,
289, 418–19, 451, 460
in twenty-first century, 304–5,
410–11, 532–3
two distinct modes of, 40
UK buildings of Gropius, 160,
203–4
in West Country, 255–6, 257,
263–4, 266–9, 271
in west London, 157–8, 160, *161*,
162–3
in West Midlands, 309–10, 312,
314–15, 316–17, 320–21, 328–9,
334–5, 340
and Owen Williams, 50, 400,
518–19
1–3 Willow Road, Hampstead,
142, 185, 256
Inverness, 542, 554–6
Ipswich, 198, 377
Iraq Museum, Baghdad, 516
Ironbridge, 336
Isle of Man, 43
Isle of Wight, 43, 243, 244
Italy
Classical Modernism in interwar
period, 30, 41
'Italian Chapel', Lamb Holm,
Orkney, 542, *549*, 550

Italian Futurism, 63, 179, 518,
528
'Italian hill town' trope, 34, 190,
378–9, 388, 493
Italian Rationalism, 163, 268, 493
Italian Renaissance, 17, 67, 68,
92, 126, 127, 136, 153, 211, 259,
279
post-war Scottish-Italian style,
519, 521

Jacobs, Jane, 11, 300–301
Japan, 30
Jarrow, 475
Jenkins, Simon, 201
Jennings, Humphrey, 28
Jesmond, 475, 482, 485–6, 488
Johnson, Philip, 176
Johnston, Tom, 550
Jones, Arian, 415
Jorn, Asger, 189
Joy Division, 401, 408, 409, 418

Kapoor, Anish, 466
Kehoe, Louise, 123
Kidderminster, 308, 332–3, 335–6
Kidder-Smith, G. E., 112–13
Killingworth, 468, 472, 475–6
King, Scott, 135
Kingsway, Holborn, 47, 49, 59
Kirkcaldy, 37, 507, 511
Klein, Bernat, 493–4
Knol, Annette, 489
Knowles, Justin, 245
Kolíbal, Stanislav, 164
Komisarjevsky, Theodore, 83
Kossowski, Adam, 443

Labour Party, 8, 28
footbridges of New Labour era,
477
New Labour and culture, 134,
135, 264, 322
New Labour higher education
policy, 132
urban planning in New Labour
era, 37–8, 102, 117–18, 322,
371, 376, 378–9, 407, 432,
460–61, 477
Lacons (brewers), 197
Lambert, Maurice, 186
Lambeth, London Borough of, 31,
34, 36, 46, 94–6, 113–14, 115
Lansbury, George, 122
Larkin, Philip, 328, 463
Latin America, 30
Leamington Spa, 335
Leeds, 350, 366, 376, 378, 380–83,
410, 417

Inner Ring Road, Woodhouse
Lane Section, 380–81, 406, 527
LILAC housing co-operative, 39,
189, 271, 383
University of, 93, 205, 366, 381–2
left-wing politics
in 1930s Leeds, 380
Adshead Plan in Southampton
(1943), 243–4
Brixton Recreation Centre, 115
and the Byker Estate, 484
Communist politics, 10
Corbyn's 'For the many not
the few', 385–6
Crosland's *The Future of
Socialism*, 463
'cultural Bolshevism', 140
and Festival of Britain (1951), 87
and Finsbury Health Centre, 29,
160
Kensal House, Kensal Green, 160
and Liverpool, 425–6
Marxist thought, 18, 162
and Merthyr Tydfil, 288
Militant Tendency, 36, 425
and modern architecture, 26, 27,
28, 29, 36, 96
political rejection of under
Thatcher, 35
in Poplar, 120–21, 122
in post-WW2 period, 28–9
and post-WW2 Walsall, 321
'Red Vienna', 38, 41, 81, *82*, 98–9,
108, 110, 136, 137, 425–6, 474,
542, 546
and rise of Postmodernism, 34
Graeme Shankland, 416–17
Socialist Realism, 29, 55, 121, 287,
324, 387, 462
Tecton Collective, 52, 54–5, 83,
123–4, 126, 138–9, 162
and use of North Sea oil revenues,
557
see also Labour Party
Leicester, 73, 344, 347, 350, 351
University of, 58, 169, 207, 230,
342–3, 344, 348–50, 381–2,
510–11, *606–7*
Leigh, 398, 417–18
Leith, 492, 496–7, 500–501
Lenin, 54
Lerwick, 547, 550–51, 553, 557
Letchworth Garden City, 19, 174,
175
Lewisham, London Borough of, 35,
92, 100–101
Leyland, 442–3
Life on Mars (television drama
series), 418

Lincoln, 344, 358–9, 361–2
listing system
    abrupt listings to avert
        demolition, 389, 391
    as blunt instrument, 361
    and British Library, 144
    cladding of listed buildings, 467
    and Coventry, 324, 326, 329
    demolition of listed buildings, 227,
        284
    demolition of unlisted areas of
        listed sites, 113, 187–8, 269
    and developers, 224
    different rules for modernist
        buildings, 186–7, 467
    extensions/interventions on
        listed buildings, 217, 332, 530,
        538
    and fame of architects, 160
    Grade 1 listing for Lloyds
        Building, 70
    listed artworks on unlisted
        buildings, 388
    listed-building consent for
        demolition, 497
    and local authorities, 114, 472
    and John Madin, 310
    Penguin Pool of London Zoo, 139
    Shakespeare Centre, Stratford-
        upon-Avon, 333–4
    and the Smithsons, 130
    successes of, 369, 460
    in Wales, 292, 301, 303
Liverpool, 18, 23, 24, 27, 47, 107,
    108, 389, 422, 423–33
    Liverpool One, 432–3
    Merseyrail, 431, 488
    Metropolitan Cathedral, 79, 183,
        270, 426, 427–8
    Oriel Chambers, 13, 229, 418, 422,
        423–4, 430
    Tate Liverpool, 278
    Viennese style in, 108, 137,
        425–6, 546
Living Architecture (charity), 193
Llandudno, 284, 300, 304
local authority housing, interwar
    council suburbs, 28
Loddon District Council, Norfolk,
    200
London
    candidates for 'first modernist
        building in', 49
    current boom in, 39
    dominance of within UK, 43
    intelligentsia as MARS group's
        lab rats, 27
    interwar government and bank
        buildings, 23, 28

    as late starter in modern
        architecture, 46
    new towns planned around, 29,
        31, 174, 180–90, 191, 214, 215,
        216–17
    strict height limits (1890s), 47
    today's housing crisis in, 38
London County Council (LCC), 10,
    46, 79, 80, 143
    Architects Department, 29, 84, 85,
        89–90, 91, 92, 93, 98–9, 112–13,
        137, 143, 147
    and Arts and Crafts movement,
        18–19
    interwar neo-Georgian/Red
        Viennese housing, 38, 41, 81,
        82, 98–9, 108, 110, 137
    Kingsway slum clearance project,
        47
    Motorway Box plan, 163–4
    National Sports Centre, Crystal
        Palace, 93
    Ossulston Estate, Somers Town,
        41, 81, 108, 137, 546
    post-war housing, 29, 31, 41,
        89–91, 110, 112–13, 115, 124–5,
        127–8, 147
    and Scandinavian aesthetic, 29,
        112
    schools division, 92, 112
    'softs' and 'hards' at, 112–13
    and South Bank buildings, 84–7
    standard types for towers, 90–91
London Underground, 37–8, 46, 48,
    63, 72–3, 101–2, 143
    Central Line, 121–2, 157–8, 179
    District Line, 157–8
    Jubilee Line extension, 133
    Northern Line, 108
    Piccadilly line, 51, 121, 137, 157–8
    Victoria Line, 121–2, 488
London Zoo, 85, 138–9, 145, 320,
    525
Loughborough, 357, 359–60
Luton, 192
Luxemburg, Rut Blees, 76–7
luxury flats/villas
    Accordia Estate, Cambridge, 211
    adjacent to homelessness, 406
    in Amersham, 215
    in Bristol, 268–9
    buildings transformed into, 120
    Byron Court, Harrogate, 393–4
    canalside in Camden, 153–4
    conversion of council houses to,
        370–71
    'cross-subsidy' deals, 136
    Embassy Court, Brighton, 236
    in Hampstead, 22, 23, 27, 139, 156

    Lakeshore, Bristol, 268–9
    in Liverpool, 432
    in London's Docklands, 100, 131–2
    Mies van der Rohe's in USA, 88,
        268–9
    'New London Vernacular', 154
    in Newcastle, 483
    pre-war building of, 109–10
    in Putney, 112
    St Paul's Tower, Sheffield, 376
    Salmon Leap Flats, Chester, 441
    in Stanmore, 141
    in west London, 162, 163

Major, John, 73
Malevich, Kasimir, 355
Malkovich, John, 296
Manchester, 38, 39, 73, 398,
    399–411, 414, 432
    Arndale Centre, 32, 33
    CIS Tower, 399, 403–4, 437, 502
    Daily Express Building, 50, 161,
        357, 398, 400
    Metrolink, 448, 486
    mills/warehouses of industrial
        revolution, 12, 13, 15, 23, 399
    new interwar council suburbs, 23,
        27, 398, 399, 401, 402, 404
Mandela, Nelson, 115
Manic Street Preachers, 294
Manzoni, Herbert, 310
Margate, 22, 23, 214, 234, 242
Marr, Johnny, 407
Martin, Mary, 337, 509, 555
A Matter of Life and Death (Powell
    and Pressburger film), 143
McCombie, Grace, 480
Meades, Jonathan, 262–3, 432
Meadows, Bernard, 55
Meccano, 263
Meek, James, 126
Melrose, 494
Merthyr Tydfil, 288
Merton, London Borough of, 114–15
Metabolist movement, Japan, 536
Meyerhold, Vsevolod, 100
Middlesbrough, 15, 458, 466–7,
    468, 469
Middlesex County Council, 46, 141,
    143
Millbank, 19
Milton Keynes, 31, 34, 35, 60, 100,
    214, 216, 222–6, 294, 336, 440
Mitchell, William, 187, 290, 314, 315,
    329, 332, 335–6, 340, 387–8,
    412, 417–18, 428, 459
Mock Tudor architecture, 49
Modern Architecture Research
    Group (MARS), 27, 33, 36, 37

Modern Classicism
  in Cambridge, 211
  in Central London, 48, 49, 51–2,
    57
  characteristics of, 40
  Chicago School, 30, 40, 47, 399,
    479–80, 497, 544
  in east London, 120, 121–2
  in Huddersfield, 385
  'King's Cross Central', 154–6
  late free-classical buildings, 57,
    352
  in Liverpool One, 432–3
  London Underground stations,
    46, 48, 51, 108, 121–2, 137–8,
    157–8, 436
  and Lutyens, 48
  Newport Street Gallery, Vauxhall,
    118
  Pallant House Gallery, Chichester,
    242
  and Plymouth's reconstruction,
    273
  St John's Church, Barrow-in-
    Furness, 448
  in Scotland, 507
  and South Bank buildings, 84–7
  in south-east London, 79–80,
    104–5
  in South Wales, 286–7, 295
  in south-west London, 108
  Town/City Halls/Civic Centres,
    120, 139, 195–6, 286–7
  at University of Birmingham,
    309
  at University of Exeter, 257–8
  in west London, 157–8, 159
Moderne style
  in Central London, 49, 50, 51, 53
  cinemas, 25, 41, 83, 179, 287, 300,
    338, 357, 364–5, 393, 499, 520
  Co-ops, 41, 83, 435
  in east London, 120–22
  in East Midlands, 347, 348, 357
  in east of England, 175, 178, 179,
    197, 198
  in Greater Manchester, 399, 400,
    412, 415
  jazz modern, 24
  in Liverpool, 424–5, 426–7
  in Metropolitan Yorkshire, 367,
    377, 380, 384–5, 391, 393
  Modernistic category (1930s), 24
  in north-east England, 459, 474,
    477, 479–81, 488
  in north London, 141, 143
  in north-west England, 435,
    436–7, 447, 448, 450
  prevalence of in UK, 41

  in Scotland, 496, 497–8, 499, 518,
    519–20, 521, 544, 550
  in south-east England, 215, 234,
    235–7
  in south-east London, 80, 83
  in south-west England, 256, 258,
    273, 280
  in south-west London, 109–10
  streamline moderne, 24, 197, 234,
    236–7, 338, 477, 544
  in Wales, 287–8, 295, 300
  in west London, 158, 159
  in West Midlands, 309, 321,
    332–3, 338
modernism
  aggressive counter-reaction, 29,
    33, 50, 151
  arrives in Britain as an innovation,
    21–2, 24, 26, 47
  buildings laid out towards the
    sun, 9, 10
  and climate change, 39
  different rules applied to listed
    buildings, 467
  domination in 1945–79 period,
    28–34
  early development of European
    Movement, 21–2, 24, 26, 47
  and exiles from Europe, 21–2, 46
  form following function notion,
    465
  and interwar German, 26, 27
  Le Corbusier's 'Five Points', 9, 29
  London intelligentsia as MARS
    group's lab rats, 27
  luxury flats and villas in
    Hampstead, 22, 23, 27
  'machine aesthetic', 15, 47, 60, 63,
    68, 72, 176, 188, 234, 412, 443,
    519, 543
  'machine-Gothic', 49, 69, 120, 133,
    206, 229, 348, 390
  and Charles Rennie Mackintosh,
    20–21, 345–7, 515–17
  need for regular maintenance, 30,
    32, 88, 95, 98, 160
  and new conception of space, 9,
    10, 15, 20, 24, 27, 38, 56, 88
  new trends from 1970s, 34
  and Penguin Pool at London Zoo,
    138–9, 320
  reactionary and racist attacks on,
    27
  rejection of continuity, 11–12, 15,
    203, 418
  route to from Arts and Crafts,
    19–21, 157
  route to modern architecture
    from, 157

  structural integrity notion, 465
  three categories of in UK, 33–4
  today, 38–9
  today's wave of nostalgia towards,
    33, 373
  and Victorian modernity, 12–15,
    16
  viewed as dangerously left-wing,
    26, 27
  see also Scandomodernism and
    entries for the architectural
    styles listed in the glossary
    (pp. 40–42)
The Modernist (magazine), 406, 407
Modernist Eclectic, 42, 74–5, 76,
    77–8, 105–7, 241, 242, 251, 433,
    544, 545, 557
Moholy-Nagy, László, 28
Moore, Henry, 89, 122
Morecambe, 422, 447, 450, 455
Morris, William, 17, 18, 19
Moscow, 26, 348, 381–2
  Metro, 108, 121
motor manufacturers, 26
Murphy, Douglas, 128, 150, 221,
    265, 529
Museum of Modern Art, New York,
    27, 40, 176

Nairn, 550
Nairn, Ian, 20, 78, 84, 108–9, 112,
    125, 188, 215, 216, 254, 369,
    508
National Health Service (NHS), 29,
    52, 89, 96
National Lottery, 37
Natural History museums, 16
Nazi Party, 27
neo-Baroque architecture, 101, 239,
    274, 314, 352, 384, 443, 470
  architecture of late-imperial
    Britain, 22–4, 27, 28, 35, 47
  and the Barbican, 67, 68
  and Brutalist images of power, 65
  Edwardian Baroque, 22–4, 27, 28,
    35, 47, 250, 295, 296, 384, 418
  Lubetkin's staircases, 54–5,
    123–4, 525
  in Manchester, 15–16
  old County Hall, London, 96
  Town Halls in north-west England,
    417, 418
neoclassical architecture, 17–18, 28,
    40, 48, 49, 54, 57, 77, 113, 222,
    223, 371
  in 1910s/20s Glasgow, 517
  Adam room at Lloyds, 70–71
  built after the war, 33, 64–5, 227,
    352, 354

neoclassical architecture (*cont.*)
  in Cardiff, 295, 296
  Harris Museum, Preston, 445
  Holden's post-war work in
    Bloomsbury, 51, 64–5
  and interwar town planning, 184,
    295
  in Liverpool, *433*
  Shell Centre, South Bank, 87
  Tube Stations, 108
neo-Georgian architecture, 29, 40,
  72, 88, 174, 216, 351, 361, 412,
  459, 520
  and Hornsey Town Hall, 139
  interwar LCC housing, 38, 81,
    98–9, 108
  in Liverpool, 426
  in Newcastle, 481
  Thatcher gives new lease of life
    to, 200
  in Welwyn Garden City, 175, 182
neo-Gothic architecture, 21, 35, 195,
  231, 257, 351, 384, 411
  Barrow-in-Furness Town Hall, 455
  in Blackburn, 442
  Cardiff Castle, 296
  and Giles Gilbert Scott, 79, 102,
    108, 203
  in Coventry, 326, 330, 501
  Liverpool Cathedral, 426, 428
  'machine-Gothic', 49, 69, 120, 133,
    206, 229, 348, 390
  in north-east England, 467, 468,
    469
  Palace of Westminster, 96
  in Pimlico, 34
  Pitt Rivers Museum, Oxford, 16
  planning of the Gothic Revival, 70
  Rochdale Town Hall, 415
  Ruskin's favoured Italian Gothic,
    17–18
  Truro Cathedral, 277
  in Winchester, 247
neoliberalism, 37
neo-Tudor architecture, 216
Netherlands, 27, 40, 42, 104, 137,
  139, 141, 155, 504
  'Amsterdam School', 47
  Scando-Dutch campaniles, 334
New Brutalism, 10, 103, 111–12,
  204, 376, 412
New Delhi, 23, 48
New Earswick (garden suburb), 19
New Empiricism, 29, 41
New Towns, 29, 31, 174, 180–90,
  191, 214, 215, 216–17, 335,
  336, 458
  in the north-east, 123, 336, 458,
    472–3, 475–6

  Runcorn in 1960s, 439–40
  in Scotland, 29, 31, 188, 514,
    535–6, 537–8
  in South Wales, 289–90, 291
  in West Midlands, 308, 336–7
New York City, 34, 49, 51, 60, 105,
  131, 404
Newcastle, 15, 33, 55, 101, 310, 422,
  458, 475, 479–89
  Byker Estate, 35, 102, 115, 169,
    208, 223, 458, 469, 476, 481,
    484–5, 488, 500
  City Centre Walkway System, 62,
    382, 431, 483–4
  Civic Centre, 276, 471, 482
  Co-operative Department Store,
    385, 435, 479–80
  Star and Shadow Cinema, 305,
    458, 489
Newham, London Borough of, 31,
  32, 136
Newman, John, 295
Newport, 15, 284, 285, 286–7, 294,
  434, 466
Newton Aycliffe, 472
nineteenth-century architecture,
  12–15
  extreme separation between
    architecture and engineering,
    15–16
  facades, 15–16
  maintenance of *decorum*, 15–16
Niven, Alex, 227
Norfolk, 30, 34, 195, 200, 228
Norris Green, Liverpool, 23
North of Scotland Hydro-Electric
  Board, 550
Northampton, 344, 345–7, 348,
  350–51
Northern Ireland, 43
Norway, 89, 482, 542, 549, 557, 558
Norwich, 19, *20*, 31, 195–6, 199–200
Nottingham, 32, 118, 161, 344,
  352–5, 363, 395

'Objective One' EU money, 294
Odeon Cinemas, 25, 41, 83, 179,
  234, 287, 300, 338, 357, *364–5*,
  393
The Offence (Sidney Lumet film),
  217
oil-boom architecture, 530–31
Oldham, 398, 417, 419
Olivier, Lawrence, 239
Olympia and York (developers), 131
Olympics, London (2012), 136
'organic' architecture, 34
Orkney, 43, 542, 549–50, 552–3, 556
Owen, Robert, 404

Oxford, 16, 39, 209
  University of, *18*, 63, 209, 214,
    227–33, 350

Paisley, 537
Parametricism (Deconstructivism),
  37, 38, 42, 75, 233, 465, 511,
  545
Paris Exhibition of Decorative Arts
  (1925), 24
Parr, Martin, *Boring Postcards*, 416
Pasmore, Victor, 337, 387, 472–3,
  482
Peace, David, *Red Riding* trilogy,
  418
Pearman, Hugh, 13
'People's detailing' (New
  Empiricism/Festival Style)
  Byker Estate, Newcastle, 484–5
  in Cambridge, 208, 209
  in Central London, 52, 54, 55
  Coventry Cathedral, 326, *327*
  in East Anglia, 197–8
  in east London, 121, 122–4, 126
  in East Midlands, 361
  in Greater Manchester, 401–2,
    416–17
  Liverpool Metropolitan Cathedral,
    427–8
  in London commuter belt north,
    180–83, 184–5, 186–9, 191
  in London commuter belt south,
    215–16, 218
  in Metropolitan Yorkshire, 367–8,
    385–6, 394
  and National Theatre, 84–7
  in north-east England, 459, 461–2,
    470, 475, 482, 484–5
  in north London, 139, 149
  in north-west England, 438–9, 442
  origins of term, 10, 41
  and Scandomodernism, 29, 41
  in Scotland, 500, 507–8, 524,
    535–6, 550–51, 552–3
  the Smithsons oppose, 30
  in south-east England, 223, 237–8,
    240, 245–6
  in south-east London, 87–8, 90,
    94–5, 98–9, 102
  in south-west England, 256–7,
    258, 270, 273–4
  in south-west London, 110–11,
    112–13
  Span estates, 87–8, 240
  in Wales, 288–9, 291–2, 300–301
  in west London, 162, 169
  in West Midlands, 310–11, 321,
    324–7, 331, 333, 334
Perry, Grayson, 193–4

Perth, Scotland, 553
Peterlee, 123, 336, 458, 472–3, 475
Pevsner, Nikolaus, 19, 21, 29, 159,
    200, 203, 435
Picturesque tradition, 29
Piper, John, 186, 198, 428
Plymouth, 29, 254, 256, *272*, 273–4,
    324, 352, 459
Poland, 26, 442–3
Poole, A. J., 186
Poole, Dorset, 259
Portsmouth, 31, 32, 33, 69, 98, 214,
    246, 248–50, 412
Postmodernism
    in Bath, 256
    Brutalist, 525
    Byker Estate, Newcastle, 484–5
    in Cambridge, 209–10
    at Canary Wharf, 131
    in Central London, 49, 52, 61, 62,
        68, 71, 72, 73
    characteristics of, 34–5, 38, 42,
        100, 153, 200, 278, 465, 529
    'Collage City'/'Townscape'
        version, 529–30
    in Cornwall, 277, 278–9
    in east London, 126, 131–2, 134,
        135–6
    in East Midlands, 348, 351, 362
    and Engineering Building at
        Leicester, 348
    and Terry Farrell, 35–6, 278, 465
    FAT Architecture, 193–4, 299
    in Greater Manchester, 410, 415,
        416, 418, 419
    historical reference in, 34–5, 42,
        165, 168, 348, 351, 465, 529
    luxury flats in London's
        Docklands, 100, 131–2
    and Richard MacCormac, 102,
        233, 294, 453
    New Labour era, 251, 336–7, 371
    in north-east England, 464, 465,
        469, 484–5
    in north-west England, 442, 450,
        451, 452
    in Norwich City Centre, 199–200
    and oil boom architecture,
        530–31
    in Oxford, 233
    Pevsner coins term, 200
    and Richard Rogers, 37
    in Scotland, 503–5, 510, 525,
        529–31, 547
    Scott-Brown and Venturi as
        theorists of, 299, 358
    Scottish Parliament, 504–5
    Alan Short's buildings, 73,
        330–31, 351, 410

in south-east England, 220–21,
    223, 233
in south-east London, 98, 100,
    102
Ty Pawb, Wrexham, 305
in west London, 168, 169, 170
in West Midlands, 317, 318,
    330–31, 336–7, 341
Poulson, John, 64
Powers, Alan, *Modern: The Modern
    Movement in Britain*, 260
Preston, 33, 409, 420–21, 422, 443,
    444–6
Private Finance Initiative (PFI), 37,
    92, 105, 114, 241, 262, 296, 419,
    504, 532, 545
promenade architecturale, 49, 151,
    210, 241, 242, 279, 438, 472,
    531, 557
Pseudomodernism, 134, 298–9, 317,
    318, 414, 432, 532
    and Will Alsop, 103, 104
    characteristics of, 42
    and Terry Farrell, 465

Quinn, Lulu, 557

Radio On (Chris Petit film), 163
Rationalism, 152–3, 155, 163, 174,
    268
Ravilious, Eric, 241, 447
RCA (Radio Corporation
    of America), 393
Reading, 218–19
Redcar, 393, 466
Redditch, 68, 308, 335, 336–7
Rees, Peter, 78
Regent Street, London, 27
Reilly, Charles, 423
Reklamarchitektur (advertising
    architecture), 159
Renaissance architecture, 17, 68,
    92, 126, 127, 136, 153, 211,
    259, 279
Repulsion (Roman Polanski film), 53
Reyntiens, Patrick, 428
Rhyl, 300
Richards, J. M., 12
Ridley, Nicholas, 170
Ritchie, Walter, 331
road systems
    approach roads for Blackwall
        Tunnel, 128, 130
    in Birmingham, 311
    Burdock Way, Halifax, 391
    in Carlisle, 451
    in Derby, 362
    Great West Road, London, 159,
        164

Kidderminster ring-road, 332–3
LCC Motorway Box plan, 32
in Leeds, 380–81, 406
M8 Motorway in Glasgow, 406,
    518, 526–7
in Manchester, 406
Mersey Tunnel, 424–5, 426,
    430–31, 434, *435*
and New Towns, 182, 336
St Helens ring-road, 437
Tinsley Viaduct, 372
Truro ring-road system, 277–8
Tyne Tunnel, 475
the Westway, London, 163–4, 166,
    406
Rochdale, *396–7*, 398, 415
Romanticism, 476
Ronan Point tower collapse
    (May 1968), 32
roofs
    flat, 27
    pitched, 9, 27, 29
Rotha, Paul, 28
Rotherham, 366, 378, 379
Roubíček, René, 164
Royal College of Art, 28
Rugby, 337
Rumsfeld, Donald, 516
Runcorn, 437, 439–40
Ruskin, John, 17, 19
Ryan, Sally, 322
Ryanair, 192, 202

St Agnes, Cornwall, 277
St Helens, 437–8, 440
St Ives, Cornwall, 275, 278–9
St Louis, Missouri, 48
St Mary's Comprehensive
    Redevelopment Area,
    Woolwich, 8, 9–12
Saler, Michael, 137
Salford, 25, 38, 195, 398, 412–14
Sant'Elia, Antonio, 63
*Saturday Night and Sunday
    Morning* (book and film),
    354–5
Scalloway, Shetland, 542, 558
Scandomodernism
    Aalto's Finnish rural modernism,
        94–5, 291
    Carlsberg Brewery, Northampton,
        350
    churches around Surrey Docks,
        89
    in Coventry, 324
    and Ralph Erskine, 208, 484–5
    and Frederick Gibberd, 290
    and Hampshire County Council,
        214

Scandomodernism (*cont.*)
   influence on UK civic buildings, 25
   and New Town architecture, 182, 184, 186, 215
   Newcastle Civic Centre, 482
   and 'People's detailing' term, 29, 41
   in post-1980 period, 34, 169
   and Reading University, 219
   Scando-Dutch campaniles, 89, 257, 334
   in Scotland, 507, 536, 557
   'softs' and 'hards' at LCC, 112–13
   in South Wales, 291, 292
   spire at All Saints, Clifton, 271
   and Rosemary Stjernstedt, 309
   Stockholm City Hall, 25, 195–6, 334
   Trinity Green, Gosport, 246
   at University of Exeter, 257
   at University of York, 395
   Wrexham Guildhall, 301
school buildings, 92, 112, 129, 141, 169, 196–7, 523–4, 536
Scotland, 19–20, 43, 492, 493–5, 507–11, 514, 535–9
   classical tradition in, 17
   Highlands & Islands, *512–13*, 514, 549–58
   see also Aberdeen; Dundee; Edinburgh; Glasgow
Scott, Geoffrey, 17
Scott, Ridley, 469
Scott, Walter, 495
Scott-Brown, Denise, 299, 358, 451
Scottish Baronial style, 20, 515, 516
Scottish Nationalist Party (SNP), 557
Scunthorpe, 459, 460–61, 464
Second World War, 28, 52, 85, 285, 326
   bomb damage, 8, 32, 54, 88, 122, 243–4, 254, 271, 273–4, 286, 326, 459, 467, 470, 539
'Secured by Design' police policies, 522, 526
Selkirk, 493–4
Serra, Richard, 71
Sharples, Joseph, 429–30
Sheffield, 30, 363, 366, 367–76, 454
   Arts Tower, 40, 47, 63, 366, 369, 403–4, 502
   Castle Market (demolished), 168, 366, 369, 372, 390, 394
   Gleadless Valley, 31, 309, 366, 367–8, 378
   housing/urban planning policy, 31, 34, 116, 168, 199, 367–8, 370–76, 380, 475

Park Hill housing estate, 10–11, 31, 94, 130, 131, 199, 247, 249, 267, 269, 277, 303, 332, 354, 366, 368, 370–71, 381, 402, 467, 484
   Supertram, 448, 486
Shetland, 43, 542, 550–51, 553, 557–8
Shipley, 385–6
Shoreditch, 19
Shrewsbury, 308, 334–5
Siemens, 8, 26
Silkin, Lewis, 184
Situationist International, 120
Skelton, John, 324
slums
   clearance/replacement, 8–9, 47, 122, 127, 246, 292, 484, 492, 500, 514, 529, 551
   of industrial revolution, 12, 33, 368, 484, 492
Smith, Otto Saumarez, *Boom Cities*, 416–17
Smith, T. Dan, 481, 485
Socialist Realism, 29, 55, 121, 287, 324, 387, 462
Southampton, 31, 243–5, 247, 248, 251, 324, 379
Southend-on-Sea, 191
Southport, 400, 435
Southsea, 245
Southwark, London Borough of, 88, 105–6
Soviet Union, 26, 40, 54
   Finland Station, Leningrad, 273
   as international patron of modernist architecture, 27
   Russian Constructivism, 137, 140, 171, 176
   see also Moscow
Spain, 42
Span (property developer), 87–8, 168, 240, 247, 312
staircase designers, 54–5, 103, 118, 123–4, *124*, 290, 447
Stamp, Gavin, 28
steel and glass style, 13, *20*
   and Chicago School, 30, 47, 48
   and High-Tech, 41
   steel frames, 47, 48, 51
Steller, Fritz, 391
Stephenson, George (muralist), 415
Stephenson, Joan, 415
Stevenage, 31, 126, 181, 182–3, 184–5, 186, 188
De Stijl, 112, 137, 347, 355, 426, 517
Stockholm, 25, 26, 137–8, 195–6
Stockport, 398, 415–16, 417, 418, 419, 455

Stockton-on-Tees, 458
Stoke-on-Trent, 308, 338, 340–41
Stratford-upon-Avon, 332, 333–4
Sunderland, 31, 322, 458, 470, 471–2
Supermodernism (Pseudomodernism)
   and Will Alsop, 103, 104, 171
   in Birmingham, 317
   in Cardiff, 298–9
   characteristics of, 42
   Peter Cook in Bournemouth, 264–5
   Curve Theatre, Leicester, 347
   in east London, 134
   in Glasgow, 533–4
   in Greater Manchester, 414
   Herzog & de Meuron's buildings, 104, *232*, 233
   at Leeds Beckett University, 383
   One Smithfield, Hanley, 340
   Persistence Works, Sheffield, 376
   in south-east London, 103–4
   Wakefield Market, 391
Sutherland, Graham, 326
Swansea, 195, 284, 286, 288–9, 293, 303, 324
Sweden, 25, 29, 41, 89, 169, 246, 271, 291, 362, 401, 485, 542, 558
Swindon, 260, 262–4
Swinton, 412, 413, 417
Swiss modern architecture, 116–17, 178

Tafuri, Manfredo, 16
Tait, Margaret, 556
Taunton, 254, 262
Taylor, Nicholas, 99, 101
Tel Aviv, 23
Telford, 308, 336
Telford, Thomas, 554
Tew, Patricia, 182
Thatcher, Margaret, 35, 200, 455
   Archive at Churchill College, 205
Thompson, D'Arcy, *On Growth and Form*, 288
Thompson, E. P., 328
Throbbing Gristle (music and arts group), 235
Todd, Peter, 462–3
Tooting, 19, 108, 157
Totnes, 255–6
Tottenham, 19
Tower Hamlets, London Borough of, 130
Townscape, term, 78
trade unions and labour movement, 8, 26, 28, 377

Congress House, Bloomsbury, 55
Tolpuddle Martyrs, 123
Tranmere Rovers FC, 439
Trespa, 155, 276, 305, 310, 465, 477, 557
Tressell, Robert, *Ragged Trousered Philanthropists*, 28
Trowbridge, John, 324
Truro, 254, 276–8, 418
Tynemouth, 474, 476–7
Tyneside, 38

United States, 28, 40, 41, 47–8
American architects' work in UK, 49
Midwestern 'Daylight Factory' genre, 424
US Embassy, Grosvenor Square, 49
see also Chicago; Chicago School; New York City
Urban Splash (developers), 268–9, 314, 370–71, 424, 447
urban-planning policy
in 1980s London, 71
Abercrombie Plan, 60, 273, 274
and Arts and Crafts movement, 16–17, 18–19
baleful influence of Oxford/ Cambridge/Bath, 181, 183
carve-up of city centres, 31, 32
comprehensive redevelopment schemes, 8–12, 31, 32, 90, 191, 353, 373–4, 416–17, 445, 522
conservation areas, 77–8, 187
corruption scandals of 1960s/70s, 33
'Critical Regionalism' of Frampton, 162
'cross-subsidy' deals, 136
deregulated market, 35
the developers' era (1976–97), 35
dominance of modernism in 1945–79 period, 28–34
dual carriageways/ring roads, 32
emergence of Brutalism, 30–31
failings of listing system, 187–8
failures of 1980s/90s, 36
Garden Cities, 19, 21, 23, 174, 175, 180–81, 192

garden suburbs, 19, 27, 28
Glasgow of Mackintosh era, 20–21
ideas of 'Red Vienna', 38, 41, 81, *82*, 98–9, 108, 110, 136, 137, 380, 425–6, 474, 542, 546
and the International Style, 22–3
and late-imperial style, 23–4, 27, 28, 47, 48, 76, 399, 418, 424, 459, 539
low-rise, high-density schemes, 31, 63, 94–5, 114–17, 134–5, 147–9, 151, 199–200, 207, 209, 294, 367, 370, 506
'mixed-use schemes', 76, 94, 257, 317, 370
New Labour era, 37–8, 102, 117–18, 322, 371, 376, 378–9, 407, 432, 460–61, 477
New Towns, 29, 31, 123, 174
'planning gain' process, 68
Public–Private 'planning gain', 362
shape of City's skyscrapers, 78
slum clearance/replacement, 8–9, 47, 122, 127, 246, 292, 484, 492, 500, 514, 529, 551
in twenty-first-century London, 154–6
urban regeneration era, 38, 146, 186–7, 250, 280, 322, 340, 370–71, 392, 398, 460–61, 465, 466, 467, 468, 523, 532, 545
Victorian modernity's *decorum*, 15–16
Uxbridge, 121, 138, 157, 158, 168, 394

Vatican II reforms, 270, 428, 442–3
Venturi, Robert, 299, 358, 451
'vernacular', 11, 34, 335, 374–5, 554, 555
'New London Vernacular', 134, 154, 155, 171, 209, 531
A Very Peculiar Practice (TV series), 313
Vienna, 26, 41
Viennese style, 41, 81–2, 98–9, 108, 110, 136, 137, 425–6, 474, 546
Vorticists, 21, 49, 81

Wakefield, 389, 391–2
Wales, 43, 284
North Wales, 300–305
South Wales, *282–3*, 285–99
Wallasey, 437, 438–9
Wallsend, 475, 478, 482
Walsall, 181, 321, 322–3, 355
New Art Gallery, 118, 264, 304, 308, 321, 322–3, 355, 356
Warp Films, 371
Warp Records, 379
Warrington, 434
Warsaw School of Economics, 73
Wates (volume housebuilders), 116–17
Weimar Germany, architecture of, 30, 53, 109, 137, *161*, 166, 234, 358, 377, 384–5
Weiner, Martin, *English Culture and the Decline of the Industrial Spirit*, 394
Welwyn Garden City, 174, 175, 178, 182, 184, 192
West African Evangelical churches, 83
West Bromwich, 103, 505
Westminster, Duke of, 48
Whiteread, Rachel, 119
Wigan, 398, 415, 417
Wiggins Teape paper merchants, 220
Wiles, Will, 68
Wills Tobacco (later Imperial Tobacco), 269
Winchester, 247
Wittkower, Rudolf, 92, 279
Wolverhampton, 320, 321–2
Woodford, James, 385
Woolwich, 8–12, 83, 377
Workers' Educational Association, 302
Wrexham, 300–301, 303, 305
Wynne, David, 482

Yencesse, Hubert, 181
York, 34, 101, 190, 338, 359–60, 366, 369, 394–5, 452, 462
Yugoslavia, 325

Engineering Building, Leicester (p. 348)

PARTICULAR BOOKS

UK | USA | Canada | Ireland | Australia
India | New Zealand | South Africa

Particular Books is part of the Penguin Random House group of companies
whose addresses can be found at global.penguinrandomhouse.com

Penguin
Random House
UK

First published in Particular Books 2021
001

All photographs by Chris Matthews, except: Owen Hatherley **A.21**, **B.25**, **D.20**, 31, 74,
106, 107, 109, 116, 117, 124, 129, 155, 170, 179, 194, 197, 205, 206, 208, 221, 227, 232
(above), 232 (below), 262, 265, 279, 304, 328, 363, 379, 427, 443, 460, 481, 495, 506,
509, 530, 539, 540–41, 549, 551, 552, 553, 556. Ed Tyler **A.1**, 515 (left), 515 (right).
Gareth Gardner 26, 97, 185. Richard Atkinson 2, 153, 559

Book design and layout: Peter Dawson, www.gradedesign.com

Typesetting: Cheshire Typesetting Ltd, Cuddington, Cheshire

The main reading text of this book is set in Calvert, a geometric slab serif, designed
by Margaret Calvert in 1980. Calvert is renowned for having created most of the
British road and traffic-warning signs with Jock Kinneir in the 1950s and 1960s,
and the typeface Transport used on road signs throughout Britain. The sans serif
used is Akkurat Pro, designed by the Swiss type designer Laurenz Brunner in 2004.

Printed and bound in Italy by L.E.G.O. S.p.A.

The authorized representative in the EEA is Penguin Random House Ireland,
Morrison Chambers, 32 Nassau Street, Dublin D02 YH68

A CIP catalogue record for this book is available from the British Library

ISBN: 978–0–241–53463–2

www.greenpenguin.co.uk

MIX
Paper from
responsible sources
FSC® C018179
www.fsc.org

Penguin Random House is committed to a
sustainable future for our business, our readers
and our planet. This book is made from Forest
Stewardship Council® certified paper.

Congress House, Bloomsbury, 55
Tolpuddle Martyrs, 123
Tranmere Rovers FC, 439
Trespa, 155, 276, 305, 310, 465, 477, 557
Tressell, Robert, *Ragged Trousered Philanthropists*, 28
Trowbridge, John, 324
Truro, 254, 276–8, 418
Tynemouth, 474, 476–7
Tyneside, 38

United States, 28, 40, 41, 47–8
American architects' work in UK, 49
Midwestern 'Daylight Factory' genre, 424
US Embassy, Grosvenor Square, 49
see also Chicago; Chicago School; New York City
Urban Splash (developers), 268–9, 314, 370–71, 424, 447
urban-planning policy
in 1980s London, 71
Abercrombie Plan, 60, 273, 274
and Arts and Crafts movement, 16–17, 18–19
baleful influence of Oxford/ Cambridge/Bath, 181, 183
carve-up of city centres, 31, 32
comprehensive redevelopment schemes, 8–12, 31, 32, 90, 191, 353, 373–4, 416–17, 445, 522
conservation areas, 77–8, 187
corruption scandals of 1960s/70s, 33
'Critical Regionalism' of Frampton, 162
'cross-subsidy' deals, 136
deregulated market, 35
the developers' era (1976–97), 35
dominance of modernism in 1945–79 period, 28–34
dual carriageways/ring roads, 32
emergence of Brutalism, 30–31
failings of listing system, 187–8
failures of 1980s/90s, 36
Garden Cities, 19, 21, 23, 174, 175, 180–81, 192

garden suburbs, 19, 27, 28
Glasgow of Mackintosh era, 20–21
ideas of 'Red Vienna', 38, 41, 81, *82*, 98–9, 108, 110, 136, 137, 380, 425–6, 474, 542, 546
and the International Style, 22–3
and late-imperial style, 23–4, 27, 28, 47, 48, 76, 399, 418, 424, 459, 539
low-rise, high-density schemes, 31, 63, 94–5, 114–17, 134–5, 147–9, 151, 199–200, 207, 209, 294, 367, 370, 506
'mixed-use schemes', 76, 94, 257, 317, 370
New Labour era, 37–8, 102, 117–18, 322, 371, 376, 378–9, 407, 432, 460–61, 477
New Towns, 29, 31, 123, 174
'planning gain' process, 68
Public–Private 'planning gain', 362
shape of City's skyscrapers, 78
slum clearance/replacement, 8–9, 47, 122, 127, 246, 292, 484, 492, 500, 514, 529, 551
in twenty-first-century London, 154–6
urban regeneration era, 38, 146, 186–7, 250, 280, 322, 340, 370–71, 392, 398, 460–61, 465, 466, 467, 468, 523, 532, 545
Victorian modernity's *decorum*, 15–16
Uxbridge, 121, 138, 157, 158, 168, 394

Vatican II reforms, 270, 428, 442–3
Venturi, Robert, 299, 358, 451
'vernacular', 11, 34, 335, 374–5, 554, 555
'New London Vernacular', 134, 154, 155, 171, 209, 531
A Very Peculiar Practice (TV series), 313
Vienna, 26, 41
Viennese style, 41, 81–2, 98–9, 108, 110, 136, 137, 425–6, 474, 546
Vorticists, 21, 49, 81

Wakefield, 389, 391–2
Wales, 43, 284
North Wales, 300–305
South Wales, *282–3*, 285–99
Wallasey, 437, 438–9
Wallsend, 475, 478, 482
Walsall, 181, 321, 322–3, 355
New Art Gallery, 118, 264, 304, 308, 321, 322–3, 355, 356
Warp Films, 371
Warp Records, 379
Warrington, 434
Warsaw School of Economics, 73
Wates (volume housebuilders), 116–17
Weimar Germany, architecture of, 30, 53, 109, 137, *161*, 166, 234, 358, 377, 384–5
Weiner, Martin, *English Culture and the Decline of the Industrial Spirit*, 394
Welwyn Garden City, 174, 175, 178, 182, 184, 192
West African Evangelical churches, 83
West Bromwich, 103, 505
Westminster, Duke of, 48
Whiteread, Rachel, 119
Wigan, 398, 415, 417
Wiggins Teape paper merchants, 220
Wiles, Will, 68
Wills Tobacco (later Imperial Tobacco), 269
Winchester, 247
Wittkower, Rudolf, 92, 279
Wolverhampton, 320, 321–2
Woodford, James, 385
Woolwich, 8–12, 83, 377
Workers' Educational Association, 302
Wrexham, 300–301, 303, 305
Wynne, David, 482

Yencesse, Hubert, 181
York, 34, 101, 190, 338, 359–60, 366, 369, 394–5, 452, 462
Yugoslavia, 325